What They Said
in 1987

What They Said In 1987

The Yearbook Of World Opinion

Compiled and Edited by

ALAN F. PATER

and

JASON R. PATER

MONITOR BOOK COMPANY

NINETEENTH ANNUAL EDITION

Printed in the United States of America

Library of Congress catalogue card number: 74-111080

ISBN number: 0-917734-17-3

WHAT THEY SAID is published annually by Monitor Book Company,
Beverly Hills, California. The title, "WHAT THEY SAID," is a trademark owned exclusively by Monitor Book Company and has been duly
registered with the United States Patent Office. Any unauthorized use is
prohibited.

To

The Newsmakers of the World . . .

May they never be at a loss for words

Preface to the First Edition (1969)

Words can be powerful or subtle, humorous or maddening. They can be vigorous or feeble, lucid or obscure, inspiring or despairing, wise or foolish, hopeful or pessimistic . . . they can be fearful or confident, timid or articulate, persuasive or perverse, honest or deceitful. As tools at a speaker's command, words can be used to reason, argue, discuss, cajole, plead, debate, declaim, threaten, infuriate, or appease; they can harangue, flourish, recite, preach, discourse, stab to the quick, or gently sermonize.

When casually spoken by a stage or film star, words can go beyond the press-agentry and make-up facade and reveal the inner man or woman. When purposefully uttered in the considered phrasing of a head of state, words can determine the destiny of millions of people, resolve peace or war, or chart the course of a nation on whose direction the fate of the entire world may depend.

Until now, the *copia verborum* of well-known and renowned public figures—the doctors and diplomats, the governors and generals, the potentates and presidents, the entertainers and educators, the bishops and baseball players, the jurists and journalists, the authors and attorneys, the congressmen and chairmen-of-the-board—whether enunciated in speeches, lectures, interviews, radio and television addresses, news conferences, forums, symposiums, town meetings, committee hearings, random remarks to the press, or delivered on the floors of the United States Senate and House of Representatives or in the parliaments and palaces of the world—have been dutifully reported in the media, then filed away and, for the most part, forgotten.

The editors of *WHAT THEY SAID* believe that consigning such a wealth of thoughts, ideas, doctrines, opinions and philosophies to interment in the morgues and archives of the Fourth Estate is lamentable and unnecessary. Yet the media, in all their forms, are constantly engulfing us in a profusion of endless and increasingly voluminous news reports. One is easily disposed to disregard or forget the stimulating discussion of critical issues embodied in so many of the utterances of those who make the news and, in their respective fields, shape the events throughout the world. The conclusion is therefore a natural and compelling one: the educator, the public official, the business executive, the statesman, the philosopher—everyone who has a stake in the complex, often confusing trends of our times—should have material of this kind readily available.

These, then, are the circumstances under which *WHAT THEY SAID* was conceived. It is the culmination of a year of listening to the people in the public eye; a year of scrutinizing, monitoring, reviewing, judging, deciding—a year during which the editors resurrected from almost certain oblivion those quintessential elements of the year's *spoken* opinion which, in their judgment, demanded preservation in book form.

WHAT THEY SAID is a pioneer in its field. Its *raison d'etre* is the firm conviction that presenting, each year, the highlights of vital and interesting views from the lips of prominent people on virtually every aspect of contemporary civilization fulfills the need to give the *spoken* word the permanence and lasting value of the *written* word. For, if it is true that a picture is worth 10,000 words, it is equally true that a verbal conclusion, an apt quote or a candid comment by a person of fame or influence can have more significance and can provide more understanding than an entire page of summary in a standard work of reference.

The editors of *WHAT THEY SAID* did not, however, design their book for researchers and

PREFACE TO THE FIRST EDITION (1969)

scholars alone. One of the failings of the conventional reference work is that it is blandly written and referred to primarily for facts and figures, lacking inherent "interest value." *WHAT THEY SAID*, on the other hand, was planned for sheer enjoyment and pleasure, for searching glimpses into the lives and thoughts of the world's celebrities, as well as for serious study, intellectual reflection and the philosophical contemplation of our multifaceted life and mores. Furthermore, those pressed for time, yet anxious to know what the newsmakers have been saying, will welcome the short excerpts which will make for quick, intermittent reading—and rereading. And, of course, the topical classifications, the speakers' index, the subject index, the place and date information—documented and authenticated and easily located—will supply a rich fund of hitherto not readily obtainable reference and statistical material.

Finally, the reader will find that the editors have eschewed trite comments and cliches, tedious and boring. The selected quotations, each standing on its own, are pertinent, significant, stimulating—above all, relevant to today's world, expressed in the speakers' own words. And they will, the editors feel, be even more relevant tomorrow. They will be re-examined and reflected upon in the future by men and women eager to learn from the past. The prophecies, the promises, the "golden dreams," the boastings and rantings, the bluster, the bravado, the pleadings and representations of those whose voices echo in these pages (and in those to come) should provide a rare and unique history lesson. The positions held by these luminaries, in their respective callings, are such that what they say today may profoundly affect the future as well as the present, and so will be of lasting importance and meaning.

ALAN F. PATER
JASON R. PATER

Beverly Hills, California

Table of Contents

PART THREE: GENERAL

Editorial Treatment

ORGANIZATION OF MATERIAL

Special attention has been given to the arrangement of the book—from the major divisions down to the individual categories and speakers—the objective being a logical progression of related material, as follows:

(A) The categories are arranged alphabetically within each of three major sections:

> Part One: "National Affairs"
>
> Part Two: "International Affairs"
>
> Part Three: "General"

In this manner, the reader can quickly locate quotations pertaining to particular fields of interest (see also *Indexing*). It should be noted that some quotations contain a number of thoughts or ideas— sometimes on different subjects—while some are vague as to exact subject matter and thus do not fit clearly into a specific topic classification. In such cases, the judgment of the Editors has determined the most appropriate category.

(B) Within each category the speakers are in alphabetical order by surname, following alphabetization practices used in the speaker's country of origin.

(C) Where there are two or more quotations by one speaker within the same category, they appear chronologically by date spoken or date of source.

SPEAKER IDENTIFICATION

(A) The occupation, profession, rank, position or title of the speaker is given as it was *at the time the statement was made* (except when the speaker's relevant identification is in the past, in which case he is shown as "former"). Thus, due to possible changes in status during the year, a speaker may be shown with different identifications in various parts of the book, or even within the same category.

(B) In the case of a speaker who holds more than one position simultaneously, the judgment of the Editors has determined the most appropriate identification to use with a specific quotation.

(C) The nationality of a speaker is given when it will help in identifying the speaker or when it is relevant to the quotation.

(D) SPECIAL NOTE: Candidates for their parties' 1988 U.S. Presidential nominations may be shown as such even before they made their "official announcements." This occurred when it was obvious that they were going to be candidates, and the Editors of *WHAT THEY SAID* considered it important to so indicate. (An exception was Vice President George Bush, who was not identified as a candidate until his official announcement.)

THE QUOTATIONS

The quoted material selected for inclusion in this book is shown as it appeared in the source, except as follows:

(A) *Ellipses* have been inserted wherever the Editors have deleted extraneous words or overly long passages within the quoted material used. In no way has the meaning or intention of the quotations been altered. *Ellipses* are also used where they appeared in the source.

(B) *Punctuation and spelling* have been altered by the Editors where they were obviously incorrect in the source, or to make the quotations more intelligible, or to conform to the general style used throughout this book. Again, meaning and intention of the quotations have not been changed.

(C) *Brackets* ([]) indicate material inserted by the Editors or by the source to either correct obvious errors or to explain or clarify what the speaker is saying. In some instances, bracketed material may replace quoted material for the sake of clarity.

(D) *Italics* either appeared in the original source or were added by the Editors where emphasis is clearly desirable.

Except for the above instances, the quoted material used has been printed verbatim, as reported by the source (even if the speaker made factual errors or was awkward in his choice of words).

Special care has been exercised to make certain that each quotation stands on its own and is not taken "out of context." The Editors, however, cannot be responsible for errors made by the original source, i.e., incorrect reporting, mis-quotations, or errors in interpretation.

DOCUMENTATION AND SOURCES

Documentation (circumstance, place, date) of each quotation is provided as fully as could be obtained, and the sources are furnished for all quotations. In some instances, no documentation details were available; in those cases, only the source is given. Following are the sequence and style used for this information:

Circumstance of quotation, place, date/Name of source, date:section (if applicable), page number.

Example: *Before the Senate, Washington, Dec. 4/The Washington Post, 12-5:(A)13.*

The above example indicates that the quotation was delivered before the Senate in Washington on December 4. It was taken for *WHAT THEY SAID* from *The Washington Post*, issue of December 5, section A, page 13. (When a newspaper publishes more than one edition on the same date, it should be noted that page numbers may vary from edition to edition.)

(A) When the source is a television or radio broadcast, the name of the network or local station is indicated, along with the date of the broadcast (obviously, page and section information does not apply).

(B) An asterisk (*) before the (/) in the documentation indicates that the quoted material was written rather than spoken. Although the basic policy of *WHAT THEY SAID* is to use only *spoken* statements, there are occasions when written statements are considered by the Editors to be important enough to be included. These occasions are rare and usually involve Presidential messages and statements released to the press and other such documents attributed to persons in high government office.

INDEXING

(A) The *Index to Speakers* is keyed to the page number. (For alphabetization practices, see *Organization of Material*, paragraph B.)

(B) The *Index to Subjects* is keyed to both the page number and the quotation number on the page (thus, 210:3 indicates quotation number 3 on page 210); the quotation number appears at the right corner of each quotation.

(C) To locate quotations on a particular subject, regardless of the speaker, turn to the appropriate category (see *Table of Contents*) or use the detailed *Index to Subjects*.

(D) To locate all quotations by a particular speaker, regardless of subject, use the *Index to Speakers*.

(E) To locate quotations by a particular speaker on a particular subject, turn to the appropriate category and then to that person's quotations within the category.

(F) The reader will find that the basic categorization format of *WHAT THEY SAID* is itself a useful subject index, inasmuch as related quotations are grouped together by their respective categories. All aspects of journalism, for example, are relevant to each other; thus, the section *Journalism* embraces all phases of the news media. Similarly, quotations pertaining to the U.S. President, Congress, etc., are in the section *Government*.

MISCELLANEOUS

(A) Except where otherwise indicated or obviously to the contrary, all universities, organizations and business firms mentioned in this book are in the United States; similarly, references made to "national," "Federal," "this country," "the nation," etc., refer to the United States.

(B) In most cases, organizations whose names end with "of the United States" are Federal government agencies.

SELECTION OF CATEGORIES

The selected categories reflect, in the Editors' opinion, the most widely discussed public-interest subjects, those which readily fall into the over-all sphere of "current events." They represent topics continuously covered by the mass media because of their inherent importance to the changing world scene. Most of the categories are permanent; they appear in each annual edition of *WHAT THEY SAID*. However, because of the transient character of some subjects, there may be categories which appear one year and may not be repeated the next.

SELECTION OF SPEAKERS

The following persons are always considered eligible for inclusion in *WHAT THEY SAID*: top-level officials of all branches of national, state and local governments (both U.S. and foreign), including all United States Senators and Representatives; top-echelon military officers; college and university presidents, chancellors and professors; chairmen and presidents of major corporations; heads of national public-oriented organizations and associations; national and internationally known diplomats; recognized celebrities from the entertainment and literary spheres and the arts generally; sports figures of national stature; commentators on the world scene who are recognized as such and who command the attention of the mass media.

The determination of what and who are "major" and "recognized" must, necessarily, be made by the Editors of *WHAT THEY SAID* based on objective personal judgment.

Also, some persons, while not generally recognized as prominent or newsworthy, may have nevertheless attracted an unusual amount of attention in connection with an important issue or event. These people, too, are considered for inclusion, depending upon the specific circumstance.

SELECTION OF QUOTATIONS

The quotations selected for inclusion in *WHAT THEY SAID* obviously represent a decided minority of the seemingly endless volume of quoted material appearing in the media each year. The process of selecting is scrupulously objective insofar as the partisan views of the Editors are concerned (see *About Fairness*, below). However, it is clear that the Editors must decide which quotations *per se* are suitable for inclusion, and in doing so look for comments that are aptly stated, offer insight into the subject being discussed, or into the speaker, and provide—for today as well as for future reference—a thought which readers will find useful for understanding the issues and the personalities that make up a year on this planet.

ABOUT FAIRNESS

The Editors of *WHAT THEY SAID* understand the necessity of being impartial when compiling a book of this kind. As a result, there has been no bias in the selection of the quotations, the choice of speakers or the manner of editing. Relevance of the statements and the status of the speakers are the exclusive criteria for inclusion, without any regard whatsoever to the personal beliefs and views of the Editors. Furthermore, every effort has been made to include a multiplicity of opinions and ideas from a wide cross-section of speakers on each topic. Nevertheless, should there appear to be, on some controversial issues, a majority of material favoring one point of view over another, it is simply the result of there having been more of those views expressed during the year, reported by the media and objectively considered suitable by the Editors of *WHAT THEY SAID* (see *Selection of Quotations*, above). Also, since persons in politics and government account for a large percentage of the speakers in *WHAT THEY SAID*, there may exist a heavier weight of opinion favoring the philosophy of those in office at the time, whether in the United States Congress, the Administration, or in foreign capitals. This is natural and to be expected and should not be construed as a reflection of agreement or disagreement with that philosophy on the part of the Editors of *WHAT THEY SAID*.

Abbreviations

The following are abbreviations used by the speakers in this volume. Rather than defining them each time they appear in the quotations, this list will facilitate reading and avoid unnecessary repetition.

ABC:	American Broadcasting Companies
ABM:	anti-ballistic missile
AFL-CIO:	American Federation of Labor-Congress of Industrial Organizations
AIDS:	acquired immune deficiency syndrome
ANC:	African National Congress
ASEAN:	Association of South-East Asian Nations
CBS:	Columbia Broadcasting System (CBS, Inc.)
CEO:	chief executive officer
CIA:	Central Intelligence Agency
COLA:	cost of living adjustment
CPB:	Corporation for Public Broadcasting
D.C.:	District of Columbia
DOT:	Department of Transportation
EEC:	European Economic Community
ERA:	equal rights amendment
FAA:	Federal Aviation Administration
FCC:	Federal Communications Commission
F.D.R.:	Franklin Delano Roosevelt
GAO:	General Accounting Office
GNP:	gross national product
IBM:	International Business Machines Corporation
INF:	intermediate-range nuclear forces
IRS:	Internal Revenue Service
IV:	intravenous
KGB:	Soviet secret police
MBA:	master of business administration
MGM:	Metro-Goldwyn-Mayer
MIT:	Massachusetts Institute of Technology
NAACP:	National Association for the Advancement of Colored People
NASA:	National Aeronautics and Space Administration

NATO:	North Atlantic Treaty Organization
NBA:	National Basketball Association
NBC:	National Broadcasting Company
NCAA:	National Collegiate Athletic Association
NEA:	National Education Association
NFL:	National Football League
NHL:	National Hockey League
NSC:	National Security Council
PAC:	political action committee
PBS:	Public Broadcasting Service
PLO:	Palestine Liberation Organization
PR:	public relations
PTL:	Praise the Lord Ministry (religious group)
RCA:	Radio Corporation of America (RCA Corp.)
RDA:	recommended daily allowances
R&R:	rest and relaxation
RSC:	Royal Shakespeare Company
SDI:	strategic defense initiative
SPD:	Social Democratic Party (West Germany)
TV:	television
UCLA:	University of California-Los Angeles
U.K.:	United Kingdom
UN:	United Nations
UNESCO:	United Nations Educational, Scientific and Cultural Organization
UNO:	Unified Nicaraguan Opposition
U.S.:	United States
U.S.A.:	United States of America
USGA:	United States Golf Association
U.S.S.R.:	Union of Soviet Socialist Republics

The Quote of the Year

Fed by a steadily advancing system of instantaneous global communication, world public opinion is rapidly emerging as a force capable of decisive influence over the policies and conduct of government—no matter how popular or how dictatorial . . . Today, in Beirut, Seoul or Chernobyl, in Johannesburg, Geneva or Managua, millions of people—separated by geography, but united through the modern miracle of telecommunications—are swept into the rite of participation. As in a Greek drama—and often guided by the loudest chorus—a moral sense envelops the participants, crying out for action and eventual resolution. And, increasingly, those in responsible positions are compelled to respond. It is this modern drama that we must understand. We must understand the choruses, the actors and those who move them.

—CHARLES Z. WICK
Director, U.S. Information Agency.
Before U.S. Advisory Commission on
Public Diplomacy, Sept. 16.

The State of the Union Address

Delivered by Ronald Reagan, President of the United States, at the Capitol, Washington, January 27, 1987.

May I congratulate all of you who are members of this historic 100th Congress of the United States of America. In this 200th anniversary year of our Constitution, you and I stand on the shoulders of giants, men whose words and deeds put wind in the sails of freedom.

However, we must always remember that our Constitution is to be celebrated not for being old, but for being young, young with the same energy, spirit and promise that filled each eventful day in Philadelphia's State House. We will be guided tonight by their acts; we will be guided forever by their words.

Now, forgive me, but I can't resist sharing a story from those historic days. Philadelphia was bursting with civic pride in the spring of 1787, and its newspapers began embellishing the arrival of the Convention delegates with elaborate social classifications.

Governors of States were called "Excellency." Justices and Chancellors had reserved for them "Honorable" with a capital "H." All others were referred to as "the following respectable characters."

Well, for this 100th Congress, I invoke special executive powers to declare that each of you must never be titled less than Honorable with a capital "H."

New House Speaker

Now, there's a new face at this place of honor tonight. Please join me in warm congratulations to Speaker of the House Jim Wright. Mr. Speaker, you might recall a similar situation in your very first session of Congress 32 years ago. Then, as now, the Speakership had changed hands, and another great son of Texas,

Sam Rayburn—"Mr. Sam"—sat in your chair. I cannot find better words than those used by President Eisenhower that evening: "We shall have much to do together; I am sure that we shall get it done, and that we shall do it in harmony and goodwill."

Tonight, I renew that pledge. To you, Mr. Speaker, and to Senate majority leader Bob Byrd who brings 34 years of distinguished service to the Congress, may I say: Though there are changes in this Congress, America's interests remain the same. I am confident that, along with Republican leaders Bob Michel and Bob Dole, this Congress can make history.

Economic Accomplishments

Six years ago, I was here to ask the Congress to join me in America's new beginning.

The results are something of which we can all be proud. Our inflation rate is now the lowest in a quarter of a century. The prime interest rate has fallen from the 21½ percent the month before we took office to 7½ percent today and those rates have triggered the most housing starts in eight years.

The unemployment rate, still too high, is the lowest in nearly seven years and our people have created nearly 13 million new jobs. Over 61 percent of everyone over the age of 16, male and female, is employed, the highest percentage on record.

Let's roll up our sleeves, go to work and put America's economic engine at full throttle.

Iran Scandal

We can also be heartened by our progress across the world. Most important, America is at peace tonight and freedom is on the march. We have done much these past years to restore our defenses, our alliances and our leadership in the world. Our sons and daughters in the services once again wear their uniforms with pride.

But though we have made much progress, I have one major regret. I took a risk with regard to our action in Iran. It did not work, and for that I assume full responsibility.

The goals were worthy. I do not believe it was wrong to try to establish contacts with a country of strategic importance or to try to save lives. And certainly it was not wrong to try to secure freedom for our citizens held in barbaric captivity. But we did not achieve what we wished and serious mistakes were made in trying to do so. We will get to the bottom of this and I will take whatever action is called for.

But in debating the past, we must not deny ourselves the successes of the future. Let it never be said of this generation of Americans that we became so obsessed with failure that we refused to take risks that could further the cause of peace and freedom in the world.

Much is at stake here, and the nation and the world are watching to see if we go forward together in the national interest, or if we let partisanship weaken us.

And let there be no mistake about American policy: We will not sit idly by if our interests or our friends in the Middle East are threatened, nor will we yield to terrorist blackmail.

Now, ladies and gentlemen of the Congress, why don't we get to work?

I am pleased to report that because of our efforts to rebuild the strength of America, the world is a safer place. Earlier this month, I submitted a budget to defend America and maintain our momentum to make up for neglect in the last decade. I ask you to vote out a defense and foreign affairs budget that says "yes" to protecting our country.

While the world is safer, it is not safe.

Soviet Military and Foreign Ventures

Since 1970, the Soviets have invested $500 billion more on their military forces than we have. Even today, though nearly 1 in 3 Soviet families is without running hot water, and the average family spends two hours a day shopping

for the basic necessities of life, their Government still found the resources to transfer $75 billion in weapons to client states in the past five years, clients like Syria, Vietnam, Cuba, Libya, Angola, Ethiopia, Afghanistan and Nicaragua.

With 120,000 Soviet combat and military personnel and 15,000 military advisers in Asia, Africa and Latin America, can anyone still doubt their single-minded determination to expand their power? Despite this, the Congress cut my request for critical U.S. security assistance to free nations by 21 percent this year, and cut defense requests by $85 billion in the last three years.

These assistance programs serve our national interests as well as mutual interests, and when the programs are devastated, American interests are harmed. My friends, it is my duty as President to say to you again tonight that there is no surer way to lose freedom than to lose our resolve.

Today, the brave people of Afghanistan are showing that resolve. The Soviet Union says it wants a peaceful settlement in Afghanistan, yet it continues a brutal war and props up a regime whose days are clearly numbered. We are ready to support a political solution that guarantees the rapid withdrawal of all Soviet troops and genuine self-determination for the Afghan people.

Latin America

In Central America, too, the cause of freedom is being tested. And our resolve is being tested there as well. Here, especially, the world is watching to see how this nation responds.

Today, over 90 percent of the people of Latin America live in democracy. Democracy is on the march in Central and South America. Communist Nicaragua is the odd man out, suppressing the church, the press and democratic dissent and promoting subversion in the region. We support diplomatic efforts, but these efforts can never succeed if the Sandinistas win their war against the Nicaraguan people.

Our commitment to a Western Hemisphere safe from aggression did not occur by spontaneous generation on the days we took office. It began with the Monroe Doctrine in 1823 and continues our historic bipartisan American policy. Franklin Roosevelt said we " . . . are determined to do everything possible to maintain peace on this hemisphere." President Truman was very blunt: "International communism . . . seeks to crush and undermine and . . . destroy the independence of the Americans . . . we can't let that happen here."

And John F. Kennedy made clear that " . . . Communist domination in this hemisphere can never be negotiated."

Some in this Congress may choose to depart from this historic commitment, but I will not.

This year, we celebrate the second century of our Constitution. The Sandinistas just signed theirs two weeks ago, and then suspended it. We won't know how my words tonight will be reported there, for one simple reason: there is no free press in Nicaragua.

Nicaraguan freedom fighters have never asked us to wage their battle, but I will fight any effort to shut off their lifeblood and consign them to death, defeat or a life without freedom. There must be no Soviet beachhead in Central America.

We Americans have always preferred dialogue to conflict and so we always remain open to more constructive relations with the Soviet Union. But more responsible Soviet conduct around the world is a key element of the U.S.-Soviet agenda. Progress is also required on the other items of our agenda as well, real respect for human rights and more open contacts between our societies, and, of course, arms reduction.

Arms Control and SDI

In Iceland last October, we had one moment of opportunity that the Soviets dashed because they sought to cripple our Strategic Defense Initiative, S.D.I. I wouldn't let them do it then. I won't let them do it now or in the future. This is the most positive and promising defense program we have undertaken. It's the path, for both sides, to a safer future; a system that de-

fends human life instead of threatening it. S.D.I. will go forward.

The United States has made serious, fair and far-reaching proposals to the Soviet Union and this is a moment of rare opportunity for arms reduction. But I will need, and American negotiators in Geneva will need, Congress's support. Enacting the Soviet negotiating position into American law would not be the way to win a good agreement. So I must tell this Congress I will veto any effort that undercuts our national security and our negotiating leverage.

Trade

Today, we also find ourselves engaged in expanding peaceful commerce across the world. We will work to expand our opportunities in international markets through the Uruguay round of trade negotiations and to complete an historic free trade arrangement between the world's two largest trading partners, Canada and the United States.

Our basic trade policy remains the same: we remain opposed as ever to protectionism because America's growth and future depend on trade. But we will insist on trade that is fair and free. We are always willing to be trade partners but never trade patsies.

Now from foreign borders, let us return to our own because America in the world is only as strong as America at home.

This 100th Congress has high responsibilities. I begin with a gentle reminder that many of these are simply the incomplete obligations of the past. The American people deserve to be impatient because we do not yet have the public house in order.

We've had great success in restoring our economic integrity, and we've rescued our nation from the worst economic mess since the Depression.

Budget Deficiency

But there's more to do. For starters, the Federal deficit is outrageous. For years I've asked that we stop pushing onto our children the excesses of our Government. What the Congress finally needs to do is pass a constitutional amendment that mandates a balanced budget and forces Government to live within its means. States, cities and the families of America balance their budgets. Why can't we?

Next, the budget process is a sorry spectacle. The missing of deadlines and the nightmare of monstrous continuing resolutions packing hundreds of billions of dollars of spending into one bill must be stopped.

We ask the Congress, once again: Give us the same tool that 43 Governors have, a line-item veto so we can carve out the boondoggles and pork that would never survive on their own. I will send the Congress broad recommendations on the budget, but first I'd like to see yours. Let's go to work and get this done together.

Now, let's talk about this year's budget. Even though I have submitted it within the Gramm-Rudman-Hollings deficit reduction target, I've seen suggestions that we might postpone that timetable. Well, I think the American people are tired of hearing the same old excuses. Together, we made a commitment to balance the budget; now, let's keep it.

As for those suggestions that the answer is higher taxes, the American people have repeatedly rejected that shopworn advice. They know that we don't have deficits because people are taxed too little; we have deficits because big government spends too much.

Next month, I will place two additional reforms before the Congress.

Welfare

We've created a welfare monster that is a shocking indictment of our sense of priorities. Our national welfare system consists of some 59 major programs and over 6,000 pages of Federal laws and regulations on which more than $132 billion was spent in 1985.

I will propose a new national welfare strategy, a program of welfare reform through state-sponsored, community-based demonstration projects. This is the time to reform this outmoded social dinosaur and finally break the poverty trap. We will never abandon those who,

through no fault of their own, must have our help. But let us work to see how many can be freed from the dependency of welfare and made self-supporting.

Next, let us remove a financial specter facing our older Americans, the fear of an illness so expensive that it can result in having to make an intolerable choice between bankruptcy and death. I will submit legislation shortly to help free the elderly from the fear of catastrophic illness.

Now, let's turn to the future.

Competitiveness

It is widely said that America is losing her competitive edge. Well, that won't happen if we act now. How well prepared are we to enter the 21st century? In my lifetime, America set the standard for the world. It is now time to determine that we should enter the next century having achieved a level of excellence unsurpassed in history.

We will achieve this: first, by guaranteeing that Government does everything possible to promote America's ability to compete. Second, we must act as individuals in a quest for excellence that will not be measured by new proposals or billions in new funding. Rather, it involves an expenditure of American spirit and just plain American grit.

The Congress will soon receive my comprehensive proposals to enhance our competitiveness, including new science and technology centers and strong new funding for basic research.

The bill will include legal and regulatory reforms and weapons to fight unfair trade practices. Competitiveness also means giving our farmers a shot at participating fairly and fully in a changing world market.

Education, Drugs, School Prayer

Preparing for the future must begin, as always, with our children.

We need to set for them new and more rigorous goals. We must demand more of ourselves and our children by raising literacy levels dramatically by the year 2,000. Our children should master the basic concepts of math and science, and let's insist that students not leave high school until they have studied and understood the basic documents of our national heritage.

There's one more thing we can't let up on. Let's redouble our personal efforts to provide for every child a safe and drug-free learning environment. If the crusade against drugs succeeds with our children, we will defeat that scourge all over our country.

Finally, let's stop suppressing the spiritual core of our national being. Our nation could not have been conceived without divine help. Why is it that we can build a nation with our prayers but we can't use a schoolroom for voluntary prayer? The 100th Congress of the United States should be remembered as the one that ended the expulsion of God from America's classrooms.

Excellence in America

The quest for excellence into the 21st century begins in the schoolroom but must go, next, to the workplace. More than 20 million new jobs will be created before the new century unfolds, and, by then, our economy should be able to provide a job for everyone who wants to work.

We must also enable our workers to adapt to the rapidly changing nature of the workplace and I will propose substantial new Federal commitments keyed to retraining and job mobility.

Over the next few weeks, I will be sending the Congress a complete series of these special messages, on budget reform, welfare reform, catastrophic illness, competitiveness, including education, trade, worker training and assistance, agriculture and other subjects.

The Congress can give us these tools, but to make these tools work, it really comes down to just being our best. That is the core of American greatness.

The responsibility of freedom presses us towards higher knowledge and, I believe, moral and spiritual greatness. Through lower taxes and smaller government, government has its

ways of freeing people's spirits. But only we, each of us, can let the spirit soar against our own individual standards.

Excellence is what makes freedom ring. And isn't that what we do best?

We're entering our third century now, but it's wrong to judge our nation by its years. The calendar can't measure America because we were meant to be an endless experiment in freedom, with no limit to our reaches, no boundaries to what we can do, no end point to our hopes.

The Constitution

The United States Constitution is the impassioned and inspired vehicle by which we travel through history. It grew out of the most fundamental inspiration of our existence: that we are here to serve Him by living free, that living free releases in us the noblest of impulses and the best of our abilities. That we would use these gifts for good and generous purposes and would secure them not just for ourselves, and for our children, but for all mankind.

Over the years, nothing has been so heartwarming to me as speaking to America's young. And the little ones especially, so fresh-faced and so eager to know; well, from time to time, they'll ask about our Constitution.

I hope you Members of Congress will not deem this a breach of protocol if you'll permit me to share these thoughts again with the young people who might be listening or watching this evening.

I have read the constitutions of a number of countries, including the Soviet Union's. Some people are surprised to hear they have a constitution, and it even supposedly grants a number of freedoms to its people. Many countries have written into their constitutions provisions for freedom of speech and freedom of assembly. If this is true, why is the Constitution of the United States so exceptional?

The difference is so small, it almost escapes you, but it's so great it tells you the whole story in just three words: We the People.

In those other constitutions, the Government tells the people what they are allowed to do. In our Constitution, we the people tell the Govern-

7

ment what it can do and that it can do only those things listed in that document and no others.

Virtually every other revolution in history just exchanged one set of rulers for another. Our revolution is the first to say the people are the masters and government is their servant.

The People of America

Don't ever forget that. Someday, you could be in this room, but wherever you are, America is depending on you to reach your highest and be your best, because here, in America, we the people are in charge.

Just these words.

We the people. Those are the kids on Christmas Day looking out from a frozen sentry post on the 38th Parallel or aboard an aircraft carrier in the Mediterranean. A million miles from home. But doing their duty.

We the people. Those are the warm-hearted whose numbers we can't begin to count who'll begin the day with a little prayer for hostages they will never know and M.I.A. families they will never meet. Why? Because that's the way we are, this unique breed we call Americans.

We the people. They're farmers on tough times, but who never stop feeding a hungry world. They're the volunteers at the hospital choking back their tears for the hundredth time caring for a baby struggling for life because of a mother who used drugs. And you'll forgive me a special memory, it's a million mothers like Nellie Reagan who never knew a stranger or turned a hungry person away from her kitchen.

We the people. They refute last week's television commentary downgrading our optimism and idealism. They are the entrepreneurs, the builders, the pioneers, and a lot of regular folks, the true heroes of our land who make up the most uncommon nation of doers in history. You know they're Americans because their spirit is as big as the universe, and their hearts are bigger than their spirit.

We the people. Starting the third century of a dream and standing up to some cynic who's trying to tell us we're not going to get any better.

Are we at the end? Or are we at the beginning? Well, I can't tell it any better than the real thing, a story recorded by James Madison from the final moments of the Constitutional Convention, September 17, 1787. As the last few members signed the document, Benjamin Franklin—the oldest delegate at 81 years, and in frail health—looked over towards the chair where George Washington daily presided. At the back of the chair was painted the picture of a sun on the horizon. Turning to those sitting next to him, Franklin observed that artists found it difficult in their painting to distinguish between a rising and setting sun.

I know if we were there, we could see those delegates sitting around Franklin, leaning in to listen more closely to him. Then Dr. Franklin began to share his deepest hopes and fears about the outcome of their efforts, and this is what he said:

"I have often . . . looked at that behind the President without being able to tell whether it was rising or setting: But now at length I have the happiness to know that it is a rising and not a setting sun."

You can bet it's rising because, my fellow citizens, America isn't finished; her best days have just begun.

PART ONE

National Affairs

The American Scene

Bruce Babbitt
Former Governor
of Arizona (D); Candidate
for the 1988 Democratic
Presidential nomination

1

It's almost as if the leadership of our country is saying: "Making a million bucks speculating is what America is all about." That's wrong, because what America is all about is people working with their hands producing things. And we're going to recapture our greatness when the leadership of this country will recognize that difference, and take action against the speculators and say to the people who are producing with their hands: "You are what America is all about. And we are going to begin to use government to make sure that you are getting a fair shake."

TV campaign spot/
The Christian Science Monitor,
5-14:6.

Howard H. Baker, Jr.
Chief of Staff
to President of the
United States Ronald Reagan

2

I'm disturbed by the lack of patriotism [in the U.S.] . . . The President [Reagan] talks about value-free education. We've grown so laid-back, urbane, sophisticated, too many people think patriotism and values are beneath them. I think that's corrosive and dangerous . . . What concerns me is that we're becoming a bland society, valueless. [Happiness] is dynamic. People are neither happy nor unhappy; they are passive, comfortable. Materialism is a palliative. People now are not fiercely pro or against anything.

Interview, Washington/
The New York Times,
5-12:12.

Joseph R. Biden, Jr.
United States Senator, D-Delaware;
Candidate for the 1988 Democratic
Presidential nomination

3

For too long in this society, we have celebrated unrestrained individualism over common community. For too long as a nation, we have been lulled by the anthem of self-interest. For a decade, led by [President] Ronald Reagan, self-aggrandizement has been the full-throated cry of this society: "I've got mine, so why don't you get yours?" and "What's in it for me?" We must rekindle the fire of idealism in our society, for nothing suffocates the promise of America more than unbounded cynicism and indifference.

Announcing his candidacy for President,
Wilmington, Del., June 9/
The New York Times, 6-10:10.

James H. Billington
Director,
Woodrow Wilson International
Center for Scholars;
Librarian of Congress-designate
of the United States

4

I think the American people as a whole are much stronger, more resilient and capable of fresh creative effort than the leadership they're getting. And by that I don't mean just political leadership: I mean opinion-forming, value-setting leadership. I mean all our elites. Americans are a very ingenious people. If you go to places where ingenuity can be measured, there's as much activity as there ever was. What's more, this nation has the values that everyone else wants. Our kind of functioning democracy, our ability to deal with ethnic, religious, ideological plurality—if you read the cultural signals from a lot of countries, this is what they are all groping for. This is what they would like to achieve. It's our market that

11

WHAT THEY SAID IN 1987

(JAMES H. BILLINGTON)

everybody wants into. But we're not being led very well.

At dialogue at Woodrow Wilson Center,
Washington, June/
Los Angeles Times, 7-26:(V)5.

Daniel J. Boorstin
Former Librarian of Congress
of the United States

1

One thing I like about America is this fuzziness of social classes and attitudes toward everything. We don't make a distinction in this country between high and low culture. Almost everybody in America expects his children to go to college. This creates problems, too: We have made colleges easy enough for anybody. But that fluidity, the creative chaos of democracy, is something that I value.

Interview/Los Angeles Times, 9-17:(V)30.

George Bush
Vice President of the United States

2

We are not, and cannot be, a pure democracy. Ours is a representative government which requires an expression of views to impart its very special magic. If by intolerance or ignorance we fail to encourage and consider a broad range of views on public matters, we disadvantage only ourselves. If we fail to vote, if we fail to speak out, we are not participating fully in the American experience.

At celebration of U.S. Constitution's
200th anniversary, Philadelphia, May 25/
The New York Times, 5-26:11.

Liz Carpenter
Journalist

3

Fifty years ago, we had a terrible Depression. Who would have thought it would be the aristocratic country squire from Hyde Park [Franklin Roosevelt] to give us a social conscience and put government and the country to work? We survived a massive war, and who would have imagined it would be the cocky high-school graduate/haberdasher from Independence [Harry Truman] wise enough to lift Europe out of the ashes of that war? And in the aftermath, that it would be the military man [Dwight Eisenhower] who would check the excesses of the Pentagon's military-industrial complex? The wealthy, swashbuckling Boston Lancelot [John Kennedy] rallied us to ask what we could do for our country and ennobled public service as a career. No Harvard or Stanford graduate gave us our agenda for education. It came from the Johnson City graduate of a small state teachers college [Lyndon Johnson]—the same Texan who put civil rights into law and action. It was the Commie hunter from California [Richard Nixon] who made us recognize Red China. The Michigan football center [Gerald Ford] who opened up access lines to government. The Christian Southern Baptist [Jimmy Carter] who brought the Jews and Arabs to the altar of the peace table. Maybe, just maybe, it will be the jingoistic hawk [Ronald Reagan] who will bring us into an arms-control treaty and lay down the swift sword.

At National Press Club, Washington/
USA Today, 7-7:(A)9.

Walter Cronkite
Former anchorman, CBS News

4

America's potential for leadership is in her political, social and economic strength, not her military power. Our national image has been tarnished in recent years, and continues to serve as a kind of universal whipping boy. Still, it is the American image that attracts, like a great transglobal magnet, the most ambitious as well as the most oppressed and hopeless among the earth's peoples.

At Brandeis University commencement,
May 17/The New York Times, 5-18:17.

Mihaly Csikszentmihalyi
Professor of behavioral science,
University of Chicago

1

If there is such a thing as "America," with its peculiar dreams, its unique political and economic patterns, its values and habits of life-style, it is because generation after generation of fathers and mothers have passed on to their sons and daughters some distinctive information. If this information were no longer transmitted successfully, America as we know it would no longer exist.

The Christian Science Monitor,
1-30:(B)12.

Mario M. Cuomo
Governor of New York (D)

2

Surely there have been times in our history when some have doubted the [American] dream, when leaders have succeeded by telling people that we were trying to do too much, aspiring too grandly, that indeed there was not room for everyone, that the price for the success of most of us was that some of us should be left behind. We have been told that recently. It has been argued that this nation's destiny is fulfilled when we've leveled life's playing field only enough to allow to prosper those who begin by being the strongest competitors. And as for the rest, those who never even made it to the playing field? We are told there's just no room.

At gathering of Center
for Law in the Public Interest,
Los Angeles, Feb. 11/
The New York Times, 2-12:18.

Richard G. Darman
Deputy Secretary of the Treasury
of the United States

3

I'm kind of an almost syrupy believer in the specialness of the American ideal, which to my mind means this land of near-limitless potential, this land that welcomes the down-

trodden, disadvantaged, troubled from all over the world, this land of enormous opportunity, market-oriented to some extent, missionary in a non-imperialist sort of way. I have this idealized conception of America which, I think, it's important for us all to try to serve.

Interview/
The Washington Post, 4-7:(A)15.

Robert J. Dole
United States Senator, R-Kansas;
Candidate for the 1988
Republican Presidential nomination

4

We are an insular people by historical predisposition and natural inclination. Somewhere in the pantheon of instructive American slogans must be an honored place for the one that says: "You mind your business, and I'll mind mine." We like to think of minding our own business as a virtue. Like other virtues, it isn't practiced much, but it's there in the grain anyway.

Interview/
The Washington Post, 6-13:(A)13.

Don Edwards
United States Representative,
D-California

5

Every day an American wakes up, he or she is less free as far as private information [about them] is concerned.

USA Today, 10-16:(A)8.

Amitai Etzioni
Sociologist; Director,
Center for Policy Research,
George Washington University

6

People are all gung ho on defense. But when it comes to the notion of serving their country, there's a very thin support. There is no wide sense that the average middle-class American—especially white, especially male—has to serve his or her country.

Interview, Aspen, Colo./
The Christian Science Monitor, 4-3:16.

WHAT THEY SAID IN 1987

Richard A. Gephardt
United States Representative,
D-Missouri; Candidate for the 1988
Democratic Presidential nomination

1

. . . our society has yet to address and conquer the problems of illiteracy, high-school drop-outs, disease, teen-age pregnancy, malnutrition, drug dependency, alcohol abuse, family violence and most of the things that kill the dignity and hope of human beings.

At United States Conference of Mayors,
Nashville, Tenn./The Washington Post, 6-18:(A)14.

2

My folks worked hard and saved so my brother and I could get the education they never had. I remember it well—sitting with them on our front porch, a little brick bungalow on Reber Place—on those warm summer nights. They talked with us about working hard, being honest, doing good, aiming high. The air was hot and muggy, but it was full of dreams. America was on the move.

Announcing his candidacy for President,
Feb. 23/Los Angeles Times, 6-22:(I)16.

3

There is a sense [in the U.S.] that something is missing. There's been this worshiping of doing well individually, but it is not allowing us to do well individually or as a nation. What we missed in all this, and what the country is beginning to understand, is that human issues, a sense of community, treating everybody decently, is vital to our success.

The New York Times, 6-22:11.

Allen Ginsberg
Poet

4

In this society, the velocity of money speeds up the mind so there's hardly any space to observe thought and the texture of mind. The speed of everything is symbolized by the favorite businessman's drug, cocaine. Mind has gotten so solidified with aggressive hyperactivity, chasing material goods—condominiums and cocaine and designer noses—that people don't allow themselves the space to observe the quality of their lives. And they are generally pretty unhappy.

Interview/U.S. News & World Report, 2-16:74.

Barry M. Goldwater
Former United States Senator, R-Arizona

5

I am always optimistic about my country. I'm an optimist because of the young people and their attitude. If I looked only at the elected officials and the Congress, the war is over. But I think the American people are beginning to realize what awful shape we are in.

Interview, Scottsdale, Ariz./
The Christian Science Monitor, 8-25:6.

Gary Hart
Former United States Senator,
D-Colorado; Candidate for the 1988
Democratic Presidential nomination

6

The test of our dedication to our country—to our most basic sense of patriotism—is not our willingness to sacrifice our lives, though if necessary we will do so in defense of our nation. The test of genuine patriotism today is our willingness to invest our personal and national treasure in the skills and talents of our young people.

At Duke University, Jan. 27/
The Washington Post, 1-27:(A)9.

Charles J. Haulk
Vice president and senior economist,
Mellon Bank, Pittsburgh

7

One of the questions is, "Is there a general malaise in the United States?" We have researchers and entrepreneurs out there, but is the intensity level as high as it is among the Germans or Japanese or Taiwanese? The difference is in intensity of effort. Once people get to a certain standard of living, it's hard to get them to push harder. People have said for centuries that capitalism sows the seeds of its own destruction because, as people get more money, they care more about leisure. So is there something about the Japanese or the Germans that pushes them beyond where we are?

The Washington Post, 4-17:(A)18.

14

Daniel K. Inouye
United States Senator, D-Hawaii

1

. . . unlike Communism, in a democracy such as ours, we are not afraid to wash our dirty linen in public. We're not afraid to let the world know that we have failures and we do have shortcomings . . . We don't, after the fact, let the world know only of our successes. And I think we should recall that we did not prohibit any member of the world press to film and record one of the bloodiest chapters of our domestic history, the demonstrations and riots in the civil-rights period . . . I've always felt that as long as we daily reaffirm our belief in and support of our Constitution and the great principles of freedom that was long ago enunciated by our Founding Fathers, we'll continue to prevail and flourish.

At Iran-contra hearings, Washington,
July 14/Los Angeles Times, 7-15:(I)10.

Jesse L. Jackson
Civil-rights leader;
Candidate for the 1988
Democratic Presidential nomination

2

I know that if America can turn its back on the family farmer, it's open season on everybody. The farmers defy all stereotypes. You can't call them black or brown, lazy, don't want to work, patriotism questionable. Also, when the middle-American white family farmer identifies with the progressive movement, it suggests there are profound changes possible. I walked down the streets of Cudahy, Wisconsin, with 6,000 workers. On some porches there were American flags, Confederate flags, and Jesse Jackson pictures.

Interview/Mother Jones, October:32.

John Paul II
Pope

3

Among the many admirable values of this nation [the U.S.] there is one that stands out in particular. It is freedom. The concept of freedom is part of the very fabric of this nation as a political community of free people. Freedom is a great gift, a great blessing of God . . . This is the freedom that America is called to live and guard and to transmit. She is called to exercise it in such a way that it will also benefit the cause of freedom in other nations and among other peoples.

To U.S. President Reagan, Miami,
Sept. 10/Los Angeles Times, 9-11:(I)16.

P. X. Kelley
General and Commandant,
United States Marine Corps

4

We are approaching in this country the fundamental problem with the moral fiber of the future youth of America. I've made a recommendation that [since] we've got an institute for everything else—we've got an institute for AIDS and all these things—why not have an institute for patriotic values?

To reporters, Washington, June 25/
The Washington Post, 6-26:(A)3.

George J. Mitchell
United States Senator, D-Maine

5

In America, disagreement with the policies of the government is not evidence of lack of patriotism. I want to repeat that: In America, disagreement with the policies of the government is not evidence of lack of patriotism. Indeed, it's the very fact that Americans can criticize their government, openly and without fear of reprisal, that is the essence of our freedom and that will keep us free.

At Iran-contra hearings, Washington,
July 13/The New York Times, 7-14:8.

6

Most nations derive from a single tribe, a single race. They practice a single religion. Common racial, ethnic, religious heritages are the glue of nationhood for many. The United States is different. We have all races, all religions. We have a limited common heritage. The

WHAT THEY SAID IN 1987

(GEORGE J. MITCHELL)

glue of nationhood for us is the American ideal of individual liberty and equal justice. The rule of law is critical in our society. It's the great equalizer, because in America everyone is equal before the law.

At Iran-contra hearings, Washington/
The Washington Post, 7-15:(A)2.

V. S. Naipaul
Trinidadian author

1

Americans are really very nice, very humane people. What a humane civilization and culture to have been created from a big melting pot!

Interview/
The Wall Street Journal, 11-2:28.

C. V. Devan Nair
Former President of Singapore

2

After having been in this country [the U.S.] for little more than a year, I have come to appreciate that one of the advantages the average educated Asian has over the average educated American is that he knows more about you [Americans] than you do about him. I speak your language. You don't speak mine. I have read your great books, which I have come to love as if they were my own.

At Indiana University/
The Wall Street Journal, 5-29:22.

Ronald Reagan
President of the United States

3

You can go to another country to live. You can go to France, but you can't become a Frenchman. You can go to Japan, and you can't become Japanese. But people from every corner of the world can come to America and become Americans.

Interview, Washington/
USA Today, 9-11:(A)11.

Pat Robertson
Evangelist;
Candidate for
the 1988 Republican
Presidential nomination

4

[At current birth rates of 1.8 live births per thousand population,] by the year 2020 we [the U.S.] are not going to have enough money to take care of all the retirees, there won't be enough money for government, there won't be enough people to expand the markets. And our share of the world population—I'm talking about the total West—will have come in 100 years from 33 per cent of all the people in the world to 7½ per cent. That not only means that we will no longer have any dominance in the world, but our culture and our values will at that point be squeezed out by many other conflicting ideologies, by other national interests. This means what we'll be as a nation, extremely vulnerable as well as our allies in Europe. This is a very, very serious matter long-range, for our children, grandchildren, everything else.

To Crisis Pregnancy
anti-abortion group,
White River Junction, Vt., Oct. 22/
The New York Times, 10-24:9.

Patricia Schroeder
United States Representative,
D-Colorado

5

The next President is going to be sworn in in 1989. That's just 11 years from the 21st century. All of the things that we have done in the 20th century that we're not proud of haven't been solved. We will turn over to the next century an incredible nuclear arsenal, which this country brought to the planet. There's the environment, ozone, the trade area. Politically, we haven't dealt with the American family in a realistic way. We've dealt with it in a Norman Rockwell-painting way.

Des Moines, Iowa, June 12/
Los Angeles Times, 6-13:(I)22.

Donald Shriver
President,
Union Theological Seminary,
New York

1

[With President Reagan, you have a] massive reassertion of the rights of the individual, with little correlative attention to the obligations of the individual to the rest of the country . . . We need more leaders who will help us to tend to our national needs, rather than telling us to tend to our own knitting.

The Christian Science Monitor, 12-1:6.

Margaret Thatcher
Prime Minister
of the United Kingdom

2

[Telling the American media to be more positive on the U.S. instead of concentrating too much on such matters as the Iran-contra scandal]: I beg of you, you should have as much faith in America as I have. Cheer up, cheer up. Be more upbeat. America is a strong country, with a great President, a great people and a great future.

Broadcast interview/
"Face the Nation," CBS-TV, 7-19.

Ben Wattenberg
Demographics analyst,
American Enterprise Institute

3

[On the lower birthrate in the 1960s, '70s and '80s that will produce a smaller number of adults]: Business is going to be discombobulated. I see the housing industry tearing its hair out. I see problems in the military. I see enormous problems headed this way with Social Security and retirement.

Time, 2-23:28.

Arnold R. Weber
President, Northwestern University

4

What does [present-day immigration to the U.S.] mean in terms of schools? What does it mean in terms of the workplace? What does it mean in terms of the way we live? . . . Are we going to end up with 42 holidays? . . . [The ultimate question is] how to permit the richness and degree of diversity associated with ethnic cultures, while at the same time trying to understand those elements that hold us all together as a people.

Interview, Northwestern University/
The Christian Science Monitor, 9-21:21.

Civil Rights • Women's Rights

Floyd Abrams
Lawyer

1

[Arguing against proposed prohibition of cigarette advertising in newspapers, magazines and on billboards]: Censorship is contagious and habit-forming. [The First Amendment protects] even speech we disapprove of or disdain. In this country, we don't strike out at speech to deal with social problems. We try to persuade people . . . with more speech.

At American Bar Association convention,
New Orleans/Los Angeles Times, 2-17:(I)15.

Bella Abzug
Former United States Representative,
D-New York

2

Is America less of a nation than Iceland? Is America less of a nation than Denmark? Is America less of a nation than England? If those countries are man enough to elect a woman [head of government], I think America can do so as well.

At National Women's Political Caucus convention, Port-
land, Ore., Aug. 21/The New York Times, 8-22:6.

3

It's not that women are better [than men], but we haven't had the chance to be corrupted by power.

At National Women's Political Caucus convention,
Portland, Ore./USA Today, 8-24:(A)6.

Michael J. Barnes
Assistant professor of psychology,
Hofstra University

4

Black children can learn racial pride and self-respect if the models and reinforcements are strong enough. But during the 1960s we were naive in thinking it was just enough to say "Black is Beautiful." In our society, black and Latino children are bombarded with images—in movies, toys, books—that tell them theirs is not the preferred race. Most heroes, like Rambo and He-Man, and most authority figures, like police and teachers, are white. The message is that authority, beauty, goodness and power most often have a white face.

At American Psychological Association meeting,
New York, Aug. 30/The New York Times, 8-31:13.

Kevin Berrill
Director, anti-violence project,
National Gay and Lesbian Task Force

5

We're hearing story after story of bitter harassment of gays on college campuses across the country. We're accustomed to thinking of colleges as islands of tolerance. And in some ways, they are. For gays on campus, these are the best of times and the worst of times. There are more gay-rights organizations and programs than ever. At the same time, we're seeing an unprecedented report of incidents directed against gays.

The New York Times, 4-24:8.

Mary Frances Berry
Member, United States Commission
on Civil Rights

6

Basically, I'm an optimist [about women's rights]. I honestly believe—and I'm sorry, I know this sounds boring—that in the end, truth and justice will prevail. All the women who are getting into state legislatures means that the ERA goal will be accomplished. Not this year, not next year—it'll take time, though not as long as women's suffrage. My mother used to tell me, "Remember, sometimes when it seems like you're losing, you're winning. It all comes out in the wash."

Interview/"Ms.," January:95.

Stephen Bokat
Vice president and general counsel,
Chamber of Commerce of the United States

1

[Supporting the Supreme Court's ruling upholding companies' affirmative-action programs]: This decision is very positive for businesses, since it gives them the freedom to do their own thing, to voluntarily implement their own affirmative-action plans, without fear of a reverse-discrimination suit. There had started to be a real rash of reverse-discrimination suits, and I think a lot of employers were nervous about being caught between a rock and a hard place.

March 26/The New York Times, 3-27:10.

Erma Bombeck
Newspaper columnist

2

I guess I've always resented that we [housewives] were treated as a subhuman culture— only capable of slushing, waxing, dusting. We were much more than that. I had a great deal of pride in what I did. I also had a degree in English and I had a brain. I've always felt like no one really knew us. I've always been on the side of the housewife and homemaker, and when she went out to the labor force, I was her Number 1 cheerleader, because this is where she should have been. There's a running theme in my work. That is: "If you think this job is great, try it sometimes." I'm proud of the fact that we can balance all this stuff. I'd like to see a businessman taking a Barbie doll bra out of a sweeper bag.

Interview/USA Today, 9-29:(D)5.

Julian Bond
Former Georgia State Legislator (D)

3

I hear this argument constantly, particularly from some of the blacks in the Reagan Administration. They claim that affirmative action creates in the minds of all whites the idea that all blacks who've come into new positions over the last several years did so solely because of affirmative action, and are therefore unqualified. I suspect that many, many white people feel this way, even about the guy who has laboriously worked his way up the ladder, step by step. It's a false notion that seriously impacts on black people, but I think it's a *white* problem. It's nothing that blacks ought to spend a lot of time worrying about.

Panel discussion, Cooper Union,
New York/Harper's, February:38.

Robert H. Bork
Judge, United States Court of Appeals
for the District of Columbia; Nominee
for Associate Justice,
Supreme Court of the Unites States

4

[Defending himself against criticism that he is against women's rights]: On my Court of Appeals record . . . I have voted more often than not for the female party in the case. There is no . . . ground in my record anywhere to suspect that I would not protect women as fully as men.

At Senate Judiciary Committee hearing
on his confirmation, Washington,
Sept. 16/USA Today, 9-17:(A)8.

5

My objection to the Equal Rights Amendment [for women] was that legislatures would have nothing to say about these complex cultural matters and had no chance to . . . express a judgment. People would go straight, you know, straight to court and challenge any distinction and the [Supreme] Court would have to write the complete body of what's allowable, discrimination or whatever it is. A reasonable-basis test allows a little more play in the joints, I think, for the Court to listen to the legislatures and look at the society and bring evidence in, and so forth. If you want to say that the Equal Rights Amendment really would enact the same thing as the reasonable-basis test, then my objection to the Equal Rights Amendment drops out . . . there is no reasonable basis to segregate the races by toilet facilities. There *is* a reasonable basis to segregate the genders by

(ROBERT H. BORK)

those facilities. And when I said to you that you can't treat gender exactly the same as you do race, all I meant was some distinctions are reasonable as to gender, such as the one we mentioned . . . The same one would not be reasonable as to race.

At Senate Judiciary Committee hearing on his confirmation, Washington, Sept. 16/The New York Times, 9-17:12.

1

I've always been against laws that discriminate. In the '60s, in my libertarian phase, I opposed what I considered government interference with individual liberty. I changed my mind on that and said so publicly in 1971. My thinking as a voter ever since is, does the law do more good than harm? Civil-rights laws meet that test.

Interview/Time, 9-21:18.

William J. Brennan, Jr.
Associate Justice,
Supreme Court of the United States

2

Certainly, we as lawyers know the difference between formal and real equality, and therefore we must lead the fight to close the gap between the two. Legislation to date has had little more than formal value because, quite frankly, it has cost us, the establishment, almost nothing. Real equality will cost us something. For example, are we willing to pay the substantially higher taxes necessary to make up for past legal deprivations and create a truly just and equitable society? Are we willing to permit public housing rent subsidy in our neighborhoods? Are we willing to let our sons bear the same risk in time of war as the sons of the poor and the deprived? If not, all our good works in legal-assistance programs, public-defender offices and the like are meaningless tinkerings which do little more than salve our own consciences.

At Ohio State University College of Law commencement, May 17/The New York Times, 5-18:17.

William E. Brock
Secretary of Labor of the United States

3

[Supporting affirmative action]: I don't believe in reverse discrimination. I don't think anybody does. There's a difference between having reverse discrimination and a quota system, which this country does not support, and having in place a program to affirmatively take special steps to help those people who have been disadvantaged by discrimination in the past. Obviously, I'm presenting that program under the Executive order of the President [Reagan]. So, as far as I'm concerned, this Administration is of one mind on the subject.

Interview/USA Today, 9-3:(A)9.

Gro Harlem Brundtland
Prime Minister of Norway

4

Because you're a woman, they try to say she should be "more feminine," which means that she should have less deliberate and well-thought-through meanings and she shouldn't express them as well. It becomes a kind of turning argument, you know. But they're really saying, when you come to the bottom line: A woman should not lead because she shouldn't be like a leader in what she says or does . . . Women have other experiences in life, and that does make some differences. But of course the difference between individuals is greater than the difference between the sexes, so it never overrides that human experience that we all have to contribute . . .

Interview, Oslo, Norway/The New York Times, 1-6:4.

Clarence H. Burns
Mayor of Baltimore

5

[On his being Baltimore's first black Mayor]: What has happened to me is a miracle that could only happen in America. I am at the peak of a personal mountain-top, and the altitude is just fine . . . There are those who hold the opinion that my beginnings are too humble to

(CLARENCE H. BURNS)

be Mayor. There are those who believe that my academic credentials are inadequate. There are those who believe that I'm not eloquent enough to speak as Mayor. They are entitled to their opinions; this is America. But you know what I think.

Inaugural address, Baltimore,
Jan. 26/The New York Times, 1-27:11.

George Bush
Vice President of the United States

1

In our open and pluralistic democracy, we've got to remember to give each other a little breathing room. Racial diversity is not a problem in America—but intolerance sometimes is.

At Dillard University, May 18/
The New York Times, 5-19:12.

2

I oppose abortion. I oppose Federal funding for abortion. I want to see the *Roe vs. Wade* [Supreme Court decision legalizing abortions] changed so that it won't legalize abortion. You know, this is a tough subject for people. It's [a] very difficult subject for a lot of people even to discuss. A few years ago you couldn't even talk about it openly. A million and a half abortions a year, a million and a half! That's not right. Err on the side of life. Err on the side of human life.

To high-school students, Waterloo, Iowa,
Oct. 6/The New York Times, 10-7:13.

Nabers Cabaniss
Deputy Assistant Secretary
for Population Affairs,
Department of Health and
Human Services of the United States

3

I have strong pro-life [anti-abortion] convictions. That is the motivating factor in the work I do . . . In my earlier days, I opposed abortion, but I thought the wrongness in abortion was the infliction of pain upon innocent life.

But if pain is the issue, you could justify euthanasia, or even infanticide, as long as you anesthetize the child. I could not go along with the logical consequences of my own beliefs when I framed the argument that way. As soon as society starts deciding what life is meaningful and judging by arbitrary standards such as pain, we put ourselves into a morally reprehensible position. So I rejected the pain argument, the idea that you could justify the destruction of human life so long as no pain is involved.

Interview, Washington/
The New York Times, 9-16:18.

Jimmy Carter
Former President of the United States

4

There is still an element of racism that is inherent in perhaps all of us. I try not to be a racist and wouldn't call myself a racist, but I have feelings that border on it and that are embarrassing to me sometimes. [I recall] when the television screens were filled with little Ethiopian and Sudanese children walking along with distended bellies and dying in the arms of their mothers . . . It's hard for me to believe that one of those children, in the eyes of God, is as important as [my daughter] Amy. How many of those little black kids does it take to equal one Amy? Fifteen? Twenty? Ten? Five? I think the answer is one. But it's hard for me to believe this. I think all of us to some degree are guilty of an insensitivity to the needs and ideas of others.

Before Rice Institute for Political Analysis,
Houston, Feb. 16/The Washington Post, 2-18:(C)1.

John E. Chubb
Senior fellow, Brookings Institution

5

The feminist agenda as a political viewpoint has not taken the country by storm in the past few years. Drawing attention to one's feminism is not likely to be a winning strategy . . . [Feminists] might be better served in finding [political] candidates sympathetic to their concerns

21

(JOHN E. CHUBB)

without the label which the public is resisting right now.

The Christian Science Monitor, 10-21:5.

Martha Layne Collins
Governor of Kentucky (D)

1

I don't always agree with [women's-rights groups]. And I don't always do what they expect of a woman. I'm not the marching type. I have tried to show every way I know that I'm for equal rights, that I am trying to promote women and help them. I tell them that they should be involved, but they have to study the issues. We talk about women's issues; I think all issues are women's issues.

Interview/USA Today, 4-6:(A)11.

Roxanne Conlin
*President, Legal Defense
and Education Fund,
National Organization for Women*

2

There are two types of sexual harassment that are forbidden. Unwanted sexual contact is the key, and the word is "unwanted." This sexual harassment is not hugging; that's acceptable. It's not any kind of interchange that is inoffensive to either party. It is unwanted sexual contact that's made a term or condition of employment. And that means the boss who suggests to one of his employees that, in order to get a good assignment, or raise, or in order to retain her job, that she has to sleep with him, or at least go out with him, or engage in some kind of sexual activity. That is classical sexual harassment. The other kind that's been recognized by courts around the country is an atmosphere so rife with sexual content that it destroys the morale and the ability of women to work there.

Interview/USA Today, 4-22:(A)11.

Pierre S. du Pont IV
*Former Governor of Delaware (R);
Candidate for the 1988
Republican Presidential nomination*

3

I don't believe anybody in America is really in favor of [hiring] quotas [for minorities]. No one believes that there should be a system by which the next person to be hired by a company must be of a certain race or religion or belief. Affirmative action is a tool I used as Governor to increase the pool of applicants for jobs and to increase the pool of applicants for promotion. I think that's appropriate.

Interview/USA Today, 12-29:(A)9.

Jean Bethke Elshtain
*Professor of political science,
University of Massachusetts*

4

The change in feminism can be seen as an analogy for progressiveness as a whole. For instance, the anti-reaction to the Equal-Rights Amendment pushed feminists to recognize that "family" was here to stay.

The New York Times, 8-20:12.

Mervin Field
Public-opinion analyst

5

When anyone [such as a feminist] is perceived as running on behalf of some special interest, it doesn't help. Some of the most successful women candidates—[U.S. Senator] Barb [Mikulski] and [San Francisco Mayor] Dianne Feinstein among them—were successful because they showed themselves as competent politicians, not feminists.

The Christian Science Monitor, 10-21:5.

John Hope Franklin
*Professor of legal history,
Duke University*

6

[Opposing the nomination of Robert Bork for the Supreme Court]: Perhaps the greatest

(JOHN HOPE FRANKLIN)

concern is that the remarkable and historic strides that this country has made during the past 35 years, and at least mitigating some of the cruder aspects of its problem of race, could become the victim of one [Bork] who has rarely shown judicial restraint in this area. There is no indication in his writings, his teachings or his rulings that this nominee has any deeply held commitment to the eradication of the problem of race, or even of its mitigation. One searches his record in vain to find a civil-rights advance that he supported from its inception. The landmark cases I cited earlier have done much to make this a tolerable, tolerant land, on which persons of African descent can live. I shudder to think how Judge Bork would have ruled in any of them had he served on the Court at the time that they were decided. We cannot afford the risk of having a person on the United States Supreme Court whose views make it clear to me that his decisions in this area would be inimical to the best interests of this nation and the world.

At Senate Judiciary Committee
hearing on Bork's nomination,
Washington, Sept. 23/
The New York Times, 9-24:12.

Edith Gilson
Author; Senior vice president,
J. Walter Thompson Company

1

. . . we [today's women] must be more in tune with the generation behind us. They are not as willing to make sacrifices [for women's rights]. If we don't make it easier for these women, we will lose them. I have much hope for the younger generation. But women like me have to set the stage to make it happen . . . We go from one extreme to the next. First, there was the perfect housewife. Nobody could do that. Now it is the perfect success [which is equally unrealistic]. There must be a middle territory. If we can be ourselves and not go to extremes—either the sex symbol or the Amazon—and accomplish professional satisfac-

tion and personal success, that will give us a sense of pride.

Interview, New York/
The Christian Science Monitor, 3-31:28.

W. Wilson Goode
Mayor of Philadelphia

2

Supreme Court Justice Thurgood Marshall has said it has taken several [Constitutional] amendments, a Civil War and momentous social transformation to change the system of government and its respect for the individual freedoms and human rights we hold as fundamental today. It is critical to remember these words and realize that this document [the U.S. Constitution] did not originally mean all the people. At the [Constitutional] Convention the states ratified the Constitution, including a clause termed the Great Compromise. This compromise counted the more than 700,000 black slaves in our nation not as individuals but only as three-fifths of a man. Such a compromise points to the reality that the Constitution was not a perfect document. But today our refined Constitution can be viewed as a framework to be applied to diverse elements of our society as we lay claim to being a nation of we, the people. It is noteworthy that I stand here today as the great-grandson of a slave presiding over the fifth-largest city in this country. It points out how far we have come in this country and how far our Constitution has indeed evolved.

At ceremony celebrating the Constitution's
200th anniversary, Philadelphia, May 25/
The New York Times, 5-26:11.

Mikhail S. Gorbachev
General Secretary,
Communist Party of the Soviet Union

3

Women [in the Soviet Union] are working in all sectors of the economy, and they dominate such spheres as public health, education and culture . . . An active and equal participation of women in social production, in political, scientific and cultural activities, has boosted wom-

WHAT THEY SAID IN 1987

en's authority, their self-respect, sense of dignity and independence from men. But this has not always been accompanied by changes making any easier the performance of their inherent functions as housewife and mother. Certain problems have become more acute because of shortcomings in the consumer-services sector and retail trade. Thus, the social load on women has increased.

At World Congress of Women, Moscow,
June 23/Los Angeles Times, 6-24:(I)5.

Morton Halperin
Director, Washington office,
American Civil Liberties Union

1

The only prediction I think one can make comfortably is that we can't rely on the government to protect our civil liberties no matter who the government is, and no matter how much more affirmatively they look at civil rights [than the Reagan Administration. It was Franklin] Roosevelt who locked up the Japanese, [Harry] Truman who started the loyalty security program, and Jimmy Carter who said that there should be no demonstrations in the United States while the Iran hostage crisis was on. [Beyond that,] if you look around the country, threats to civil rights go on every day: closing down school newspapers, depriving people of rights in criminal cases, banning textbooks. The Supreme Court has steadily been eroding the rights of defendants in criminal trials and the rights of all of us to be free of police surveillance.

At ACLU conference, Philadelphia/
The New York Times, 6-22:8.

A. Leon Higginbotham, Jr.
Judge, United States Court of Appeals
for the Third Circuit; Former Commissioner,
Federal Trade Commission

2

We should . . . celebrate during this bicentennial [of the U.S. Constitution] the historic moments when our nation's consciousness moved forward—as when President Dwight D. Eisenhower, though not in sympathy with Brown vs. Board of Education, nevertheless insisted that the decree of the district court in Little Rock be enforced so that 11 black children would be admitted to the high school, even if it required calling out Federal troops. We should celebrate the perspective and actions of President John F. Kennedy, who rejected Governor George C. Wallace's efforts to stop two fully qualified black students from going to the University of Alabama, and then told the nation: "The heart of the question is whether all Americans are to be afforded equal rights and equal opportunities, whether we are going to treat our fellow Americans as we want to be treated." We should further celebrate the broad view of President Lyndon B. Johnson, who asserted: "You do not take a person who, for years, has been hobbled by [racial] chains and liberate him, bring him up to the starting line of a race and then say, 'You are free to compete with all the others,' and still justly believe that you have been completely fair." Thus it is not enough just to open the gates of opportunity. All our citizens must have the ability to walk through those gates, and this challenge is the next and the more profound stage of the battle for civil rights.

Before National Association of Black Journalists,
Miami, Aug. 21/Los Angeles Times, 9-15:(II)5.

Benjamin L. Hooks
Executive director, National Association
for the Advancement of Colored People

3

Today, black Americans enjoy over $200-billion in gross national income. Today, blacks occupy meaningful and influential positions in the corporate community. There are hundreds of black millionaires [and] hundreds of thousands of black professionals who are quietly living a middle-class existence in integrated suburban areas around the nation. We have black astronauts, black engineers, architects, construction managers, black models, black actors. The morning television news program [the

(BENJAMIN L. HOOKS)

Today show] is dominated by a black man, Bryant Gumbel. Another black man, Bill Cosby, is king of prime-time TV. Oprah Winfrey dominates the morning talk-show circuit . . . The National Association for the Advancement of Colored People, more than any other group, can claim—and rightfully so—the credit for many of these victories . . . [But] the NAACP is neither blind to the plight of our less-fortunate brothers and sisters, nor deaf to their cries. Our long-range planning document, which is intended to point the Association's direction into the 21st century, addresses the troubling concerns of crime and violence in the black community, of drug and substance abuse, of teen-age pregnancy, of school dropouts and youth unemployment. We are working to enhance and implement our back-to-school/stay-in-school program; to stimulate the work ethic . . . We know that black America must do much of this work itself, for it is our future we must save. If we are not prepared to work for our salvation, our race will be doomed.

At NAACP conference,
New York, July 6/
The Wall Street Journal, 7-9:28.

Roy Innis
President,
Congress of Racial Equality

1

We [blacks] don't need any more civil-rights laws. We need to clear our neighborhoods of drugs and crime. Our stores close early; that means fewer jobs for us. Prices are high in our community; so we shop elsewhere, and our community fades away. People tell us to fight "slavery" and "racism" in America. I say don't let American liberals deceive us with these two words. Our mission should be for each of us to become qualified for the job he or she wants.

Interview, Brooklyn, N.Y./
The Christian Science Monitor, 3-20:6.

Jesse L. Jackson
Civil-rights leader;
Candidate for the 1988
Democratic Presidential nomination

2

. . . people have gotten more used to me. The result of all this is that there's less of a debate about a black for President and more of a discussion about Jackson himself. [Now] I can be scrutinized like the others [running for the nomination]. I can be required to take and pass the character test. In my mind, I, at least, am finally where [the late civil-rights leader Martin Luther King] wanted us to be, at the place where I can be judged for the content of my character rather than the color of my skin.

U.S. News & World Report, 11-16:37.

Reggie Jackson
Baseball player,
Oakland "Athletics"

3

There are only three major changes I've undergone in my life. Between the ages of zero and 14, I was colored. Between the ages of 14 and 30, I was Negro. And between the ages of 30 and the present, I'm black.

Los Angeles Times, 5-4:(III)2.

Anthony M. Kennedy
Judge, United States Court
of Appeals for the Ninth Circuit;
Nominee for Associate
Justice, Supreme Court
of the United States

4

Discrimination arises from several sources. Sometimes it's active hostility and sometimes it's just insensitivity and indifference. Over the years, I have tried to become more sensitive to the establishment of visible barriers to the advancement of women and minorities in society.

At Senate Judiciary Committee hearing
on his confirmation, Washington, Dec. 14/
Los Angeles Times, 12-15:(I)24.

WHAT THEY SAID IN 1987

Donald Kennedy
President, Stanford University

1

Blacks and, to a somewhat lesser extent, Hispanics, have had a string of very discouraging messages, which affect each group's sense of how well it is doing in society. Black students I talk to are often quick to say, "The experience of being black in America in 1987 is worse everywhere, in our perception, than it was half a dozen years ago." Now, that's said by some people at age 20 who may or may not have a real sense of what things were like at 14. But if that's the perception, it's important to understanding how people feel.

*At symposium sponsored by
"U.S. News & World Report"/
U.S. News & World Report, 4-20:67.*

Edward M. Kennedy
United States Senator, D-Massachusetts

2

Housing discrimination is American apartheid. It is one of the most virulent forms of bias. The [recent racial] violence of Howard Beach and Forsyth County is the bitter fruit of the racism that is fostered by segregated housing.

*Before the Senate, Washington, Feb. 19/
The New York Times, 2-20:13.*

Alan L. Keyes
*Assistant Secretary
for International Organizations,
Department of State
of the United States*

3

I'm obsessed with the question of justice because a certain kind of injustice was obviously a very important part of what I am, like all black people in America, and there was a strong emotional reaction to that. But really, the question raised by injustice is not an emotional question only. The question raised by injustice is, "What is justice?"

*Interview, Washington, Sept. 17/
The Washington Post, 9-18:(D)8.*

Edward I. Koch
Mayor of New York

4

[On a U.S. Supreme Court decision upholding a California county's hiring of a woman instead of a man for a public-works job]: Was he the victim of reverse discrimination? I don't think so. In fact, Santa Clara [County's] policy reminds me of our civil-service system. The three top scorers on a test are referred to an agency to decide who of the three best merits its needs. There's no rule that the number-one finisher be hired first. Such a system doesn't discard merit in favor of artificial hiring criteria . . . The pool from which a person is hired consists only of those well-qualified for the job to be filled. Applicants must meet common standards while agencies can meet their specific needs. Some people say the Court's majority opinion . . . is a historic breakthrough for women's rights. Others side with the blistering dissent of [Supreme Court] Justice [Antonin] Scalia who fears it will transform civil-rights laws into "an engine for discrimination." To me, the decision was neither historic nor disastrous. It's just common sense.

The Wall Street Journal, 4-30:26.

Cyndi Lauper
Singer

5

Sometimes people try to make you feel you can never attain what you want [because you're a woman] and you should just accept your position. I'd never accept that. When I was 10, I was told somebody's got to clean the fish. Well, my idea of feminism is that everyone cleans the fish.

Interview/Cosmopolitan, April:103.

Jeffrey Levi
*Executive director,
National Gay and Lesbian Task Force*

6

We [in the gay community] are no longer seeking *just* a right to privacy and a right to protection from wrong. We also have a right—

(JEFFREY LEVI)

as heterosexual Americans have already—to see government and society affirm our lives. Now, that is a statement that may make some of our liberal friends queasy. But the truth is, until our relationships are recognized in the law—through domestic-partner legislation or the definition of beneficiary, for example—until we are provided the same financial incentives in tax law and government programs to encourage *our* family relationships, then we will not have achieved equality in American society.

Before National Press Club, Washington,
Oct. 9/The Washington Post, 10-13:(A)18.

Kate Rand Lloyd
Editor, "Working Woman" magazine

1

[On whether Superwoman, the woman who "has it all," is a myth]: People don't want to hear about Superwoman at all. The odd thing is . . . they're *being* Superwomen, but they've relaxed a little. They really don't care if there are dust mice rolling around under the bed. They've noticed that nobody ever died of yellow waxy buildup, and they don't care, because they are doing it all, if "all" means they have a career, they have a husband, they have a family. I'm sometimes bewildered by the enormous amount of media attention given to how difficult it is to have it all. If you went out there and counted on your fingers, you would find hundreds of thousands, probably a million or more, women are doing just that.

Interview/The Christian Science Monitor, 2-9:23.

Glenn C. Loury
Professor of political economy,
Kennedy School of Government,
Harvard University

2

When blacks come into an organization through an aggressive affirmative-action program, they don't have the track record that will make it possible for them to succeed in the corporate environment. White people invariably

say: "These people wouldn't be here if it weren't for affirmative action. They'll never really be leaders." Blacks who succeed in the world of business know something the rest of us are reluctant to talk about: It *matters* if the white man doesn't respect us. We don't like to talk about it because for so long, when we [blacks] were objectively good, we didn't get what we had coming. So now we don't even want to credit the idea that the opinions of our white peers, however misguided, might actually be relevant to our ultimate success. But if we want to see blacks as CEOs of major corporations, at some point we're going to have to defer to the freely conveyed judgments of the whites in these environments with respect to the abilities of the blacks who wish to enter them. That's where affirmative action gets in the way.

Panel discussion, Cooper Union,
New York/Harper's, February:38.

Glenn C. Loury
Under Secretary of Education
of the United States

3

I've said to black leaders that the civil-rights movement is over. The problem today is not opportunity but the ability to take advantage of it. We have to shift the agenda. This isn't 1955 any more.

Interview, Cambridge, Mass./
The Christian Science Monitor, 3-27:21.

Thurgood Marshall
Associate Justice,
Supreme Court of the United States

4

[Saying that, in celebrating the Constitution's bicentennial, it should be remembered that the original document sanctioned slavery and denied the vote to women]: [The Constitution was] defective from the start, requiring several amendments, a civil war, and momentous social transformation to attain the system of Constitutional government and its respect for the individual freedoms and human rights we hold as fundamental today . . . [The Founding

27

WHAT THEY SAID IN 1987

(THURGOOD MARSHALL)

Fathers] could not have imagined, nor would they have accepted, that the document they were drafting would one day be construed by a Supreme Court to which has been appointed a woman and the descendent of an African slave.

*Before San Francisco Patent
and Trademark Association, Maui, Hawaii,
May 6/The Washington Post, 5-7:(A)1,18.*

1

The biggest thing we brag about in this country on the ethical side is that it's a great melting pot. As I sit and look at it now at this late date, I have come to the definite conclusion that if the United States is indeed the great melting pot, the Negro either didn't get in the pot or he didn't get melted down.

Interview/USA Today, 9-9:(A)7.

Edwin Meese III
Attorney General of the United States

2

I consider myself one of the foremost defenders of civil rights in the United States.

U.S. News & World Report, 2-16:11.

Howard M. Metzenbaum
United States Senator, D-Ohio

3

[Addressing Supreme Court nominee Robert Bork]: I cannot tell you strongly enough that the women of this country are terribly, terribly apprehensive about your appointment. I have traveled throughout Ohio, I have traveled throughout the country, and it's unbelievable to me the kinds of people that come up to me—a clerk, a woman who was from an economically strong social group; you get on an elevator, you walk past somebody in a hallway. And the women's groups, frankly, are afraid. They're afraid of you. Yesterday you said women and blacks who know your record on the court need not fear you. But the fact is, Judge Bork, they do fear you. They're concerned; they're frightened . . . Women of America, in my opinion,

have much to be worried about in connection with your appointment. Blacks as well. And it's only fair to say that you've made it quite clear in your appearance before this panel that you're not a frightening man, but you are a man with frightening views.

*At Senate Judiciary Committee hearing
on Bork's nomination, Washington, Sept. 18/
The New York Times, 9-19:9.*

Kate Michelman
*Head, National
Abortion Rights Action League*

4

[The Pope's] anti-abortion, anti-contraception policy stems less from concern for the sanctity of human life and more from ancient and powerful anti-woman dogma. He doesn't speak in this area for women and men who value the right of planning a family. We're missing the center of this debate. The center is really about the value of women's lives.

USA Today, 9-15:(A)8.

Melba Moore
Actress

5

I never can forget that I'm a black person. When I don't have my chauffeur or my bodyguard, and I'm out on the street trying to get transportation, I'm reminded very bluntly that I'm black, when the cab driver passes me by to pick up a blonde-haired, blue-eyed young lady who gets the cab, and I don't.

Interview/USA Today, 9-17:(A)11.

Toni Morrison
Author

6

Racism is still alive, in the sense that we still believe in inferior and superior people. It's an intellectual idea that surfaced at the same time another intellectual idea surfaced—the rights of man. And it has always been a scholarly pursuit. It has been called religion, history, eugenics, biology—anything. But it was racism.

Interview/U.S. News & World Report, 10-19:75.

Irene Natividad
Executive director,
National Women's Political Caucus

1

I think it's interesting that, during what I call the seven-year reign of the Reagan Administration, women have been able to hold onto their rights given the concerted effort that this Administration has made to overturn them, erode them. I think part of the reason is testimony to the efforts that the women's organizations have made to maintain those rights, but also because there is strong public support there for our issues. What they're saying is that the issues that women care about are not just women's issues, but are community issues.

Interview/USA Today, 8-26:(A)9.

Charles Pasqua
Minister of the Interior of France

2

[On his decision to ban several sexually oriented magazines]: Liberty is not license, and it is essential to protect the young. When it's a question of inciting the young to debauchery, I do not intend to be tolerant.

Paris, March 20/The New York Times, 3-21:2.

Malcolm Post
Former president,
University Club of California

3

[Saying private clubs that admit only men should be permitted by law and not prohibited because of alleged violation of women's civil rights]: Men like a night out with the boys, without children or wives, where they talk about fly fishing, the *49ers* football team, tell dirty jokes and smoke smelly cigars.

USA Today, 12-8:(A)10.

Maureen Reagan
Co-chairman,
Republican National Committee

4

I don't think there's anybody more in favor of affirmative action than I am. Most affirmative-action provisions have been even more helpful to women than to blacks or Hispanics, because we were really left out of a great many things that boys, regardless of race or religion, were included in.

Interview/USA Today, 2-25:(A)11.

Ronald Reagan
President of the United States

5

I would challenge all of you to pledge yourselves to building an America where incidents of racial hatred do not happen because racism has been banned not just from the law books, but from the hearts of the people. You should accept nothing less than making yours a generation free of bigotry, intolerance and discrimination.

Broadcast address to the nation, Washington,
Jan. 15/Los Angeles Times, 1-16:(I)15.

6

[On the late civil-rights leader Martin Luther King, Jr.]: Even those who had disagreements with Dr. King now recognize that the changes he helped bring about were right and, in the long run, made our country stronger. But the cleansing process is not easy. We needed such an individual to mobilize our people and organize a movement that would touch the conscience of our nation.

Broadcast address to the nation, Washington,
Jan. 15/The Washington Post, 1-16:(A)3.

7

In the 1950s and the 1960s, great strides [in civil rights] were made through political action. The legal sanctions of bigotry and discrimination were torn away. Laws protecting the civil rights of all Americans were put in place, and racism was, in effect, outlawed. These great achievements did not come easy . . . The civil-rights movement earned the respect and gratitude of all good and decent Americans, even some who may at first have had reservations about what was happening. Yet changes in the law, and the political struggle itself, brought social progress that enormously strengthened the moral foundation of the United States. The po-

WHAT THEY SAID IN 1987

litical and legal battle is obviously not over. We must remain vigilant, inside and outside of government.

At Tuskegee University, May 10/
The New York Times, 5-11:9.

Carl Rowan
Political columnist and commentator

1

I've looked at several polls lately, and they show blacks far less inclined to celebrate the [U.S.] Constitution than are white Americans. And it is for the simple reason that they believe the one area in which this Constitution has been defective is in the delivery of absolute and equal justice.

Interview/USA Today, 9-9:(A)7.

Phyllis Schlafly
President, Eagle Forum

2

I don't agree [with feminists] that the elected bodies of this land don't reflect adequately the concerns of the general populace on the wide range of issues affecting women and the home. And even if that were true, the answer is not electing feminists.

The Christian Science Monitor, 10-21:5.

Harold T. Shapiro
President, University of Michigan

3

While it's true that we in higher education cannot solve society's racial problem by ourselves, I don't think we've made an adequate contribution in this area—in part because we don't talk about it honestly, because it's very difficult to do so. It's also partly because we think relatively simple things like standard affirmative-action procedures really deal with an issue that is very much more complex and challenging than we had thought 20 years ago . . . Black students attending predominantly white colleges in 1987 come from quite a different environment than the black students at-

tending predominantly white colleges in 1967. They come from a situation where they're a majority and are coming to their first demanding experience as a minority. But our thinking hasn't changed in 20 years.

At symposium sponsored
by "U.S. News & World Report"/
U.S. News & World Report, 4-20:67.

Martin M. Shapiro
Professor of law
and political science,
University of California,
Berkeley

4

Desegregation is not integration. Federal judges have become tin gods and little dictators. They have turned "Thou shalt not segregate" into "The law requires you to integrate," [even though] most Americans opposed [school] busing [for racial balance].

The Christian Science Monitor, 2-11:19.

Eleanor Smeal
Former president,
National Organization for Women

5

[Calling for the election of more feminists to government offices]: It's obvious to me that for a movement that is fighting for equality in job opportunity and public decision-making, one of the first steps is equality of representation . . . But even if all the feminists that ran in the average election won, we would still be a small proportion of the office-holders . . . In state legislature after state legislature, abortion rights, women's rights, civil rights and workers' rights are under attack. While major corporate interests are over-represented, the needs of ordinary people are under-represented. If we are ever to turn around these disastrous trends, we must inspire more feminists to seek public office.

Interview, Los Angeles/
The Christian Science Monitor, 10-21:5.

Anne Mollegen Smith
Editor-in-chief,
"Working Woman" magazine

1

I believe that you [a woman] can have it all, and you can even enjoy it all. But if you're trying to be the perfect mother, the perfect boss, the perfect volunteer worker, the perfect wife, the perfect daughter, there's going to be a good deal of stress. If you have a good relationship with your husband and your parents, if you have the satisfaction of being around a growing child, if you have accomplishments in work, if you feel you're part of a larger community, you have so many sources of satisfaction and personal support, and so many chances to be happy. I feel there's great strength in multiple roles. To lock yourself into one role only is . . . putting all your eggs into one basket.

Interview/The Christian Science Monitor, 2-9:23.

Margaret Chase Smith
Former United States Senator, R-Maine

2

I am proud of what I did as a woman. But I didn't do it as a feminist. In fact, I moved over to the Senate in 1949 and, to be honest with you, I never was a "woman" candidate. And when I was elected in the Senate, I was one of two U.S. Senators from Maine. I wasn't a "woman" Senator . . . I think of women differently than most people do. I think of women as being people. I hope that what I have done will do for future women what the pioneer women did for me.

Interview/USA Today, 5-29:(A)11.

Elisabeth Soderstrom
Opera singer

3

When I see women fighting for Women's Lib, I find that rather ridiculous. Because women have always been ruling the men, haven't they? Many things men do to women are a sort of revenge.

Interview/Opera News, 2-14:10.

Niara Sudarkasa
President, Lincoln University

4

[On the racial pressure on black students at mostly white universities and recent incidents against them]: There's no question that black students in many of these institutions have become dispirited. In some cases, they have become alienated because they haven't felt the institutions have reached out and tried to reflect the total student body, tried to incorporate some of their experience, their culture, into the mainstream curriculum, so that everybody would feel that this is a pluralistic environment in which to study. Blacks too often feel as if they are marching into a foreign camp when they're at some institutions.

Interview/USA Today, 10-12:(A)13.

Charles E. Tate
President, Booker T. Washington Foundation

5

The enterprise process has to involve more than just the entrepreneur. It must also include investors, backers and a lot of other folk. The government's minority-business approach doesn't leave room for that. Its emphasis is on the individual entrepreneur and—again, the distributional mode—on delivering a "fair share" of government contracts to minorities. But it does not solve our problem to allow a few cronies of public officials to make half a million dollars, or even a million. Think of all the cities that are being rebuilt. How much of that redevelopment includes blacks in an equity position, as opposed to just getting a few small contracts? That's not economic development; that's only getting a little bit of the action after the deals have already been shaped by white people.

Interview/The Washington Post, 11-2:(A)15.

Benjamin Ward
Commissioner of Police of New York City

6

[On the possibility of civil-rights street demonstrations this summer]: I think that there are some groups, perhaps more and more actively

(BENJAMIN WARD)

involved than in past years, that have an agenda for this summer, in which I think we may see more taking to the streets and more demonstrations, more active role on the street. I think it's coming out of frustration. I think we've gone through six years of a government at the Federal level that has sent out the kind of signals that will frustrate, infuriate people, minority groups particularly, and particularly blacks.

Interview, New York, March 1/
The New York Times, 3-5:17.

Finis Welch
Economist, Unicon Research Corporation

1

We need to rethink a lot of [school] desegregation strategies in favor of less stringent or less mandatory programs. As a society, we have spent far too many resources trying to see that our children attend similar schools, or some racial balance is attained. But what has it all meant in terms of skill acquisition?

The New York Times, 5-20:16.

Charles Vert Willie
Sociologist,
Harvard University

2

[The U.S. is a] defective, racist, sexist, classist nation. [As we understand that] these labels are unworthy of a great democracy . . . [we] can rid ourselves of them.

Interview, Boston/
The Christian Science Monitor,
6-10:1.

Commerce • Industry • Finance

James Abdnor
Former United States Senator,
R-South Dakota

1

If we fail agriculture, we will have a rural America without purpose and an America without its heritage.

USA Today, 2-18:(A)14.

Frank Annunzio
United States Representative,
D-Illinois

2

[Calling for credit-card interest rates to be limited to no more than eight points above one-year Treasury securities yields]: In today's market, where the average credit-card interest rate is more than 18 per cent, that would mean an interest rate of no more than 15.5 per cent. If banks can't make money at 15.5 per cent interest rates, then they should get the hell out of the banking business.

Los Angeles Times, 10-29:(I)33.

Roger Anteweldt
Deputy Assistant Attorney General,
Antitrust Division, Department of
Justice of the United States

3

[On criticism of the Reagan Administration's permissive attitude toward corporate mergers]: In international markets you want to be as efficient as you can and there have been a lot of mergers related to that. There is perhaps a concern about a perceived increase in concentration in the American economy, and concentration bothers some people from a social setting. But to the extent that there are concerns about that, the antitrust laws aren't the appropriate way to get at it.

The Christian Science Monitor,
7-3:11.

Rand V. Araskog
Chairman, ITT Corporation

4

The Japanese know that, to grow and succeed, they have to export. So they buy their own products to keep their companies strong. In the United States, if I asked half the people in this building what kind of car they wanted to buy, they'd probably say BMW or a Japanese car. Japanese don't think that way. If they opened every floodgate in Japan, they'd have to order people at gunpoint to buy U.S. goods because of that island mentality.

Interview/USA Today, 4-7:(A)11.

Bruce Babbitt
Former Governor of Arizona (D);
Candidate for the 1988
Democratic Presidential nomination

5

American [corporate] executives reward themselves with huge bonuses during the good times, but console themselves with layoffs [of employees] as soon as times turn bad.

Time, 3-30:33.

6

Balanced trade simply means that the international system is only going to work when countries export on the average about as much as they import, and when countries are required by international agreement to balance their multilateral trading accounts. Balanced trade cannot be legislated by demagogues in the United States Congress. But it can be negotiated with our trading partners in the international arena. We did it at Bretton Woods in 1945. But now the world has changed and the rules haven't.

The Washington Post, 7-4:(A)6.

James A. Baker III
Secretary of the Treasury
of the United States

7

Many governments, including the United States, contributed to a deeper and longer

(JAMES A. BAKER III)

world-wide depression in the 1930s by adopting isolationist economic policies. In an effort to stimulate domestic demand and employment, governments erected high tariffs and other barriers to protect their domestic producers from imports. They also undermined currency arrangements in an attempt to promote exports and generate jobs. These autarchic actions choked off international trade and capital flows.

Before Congressional committee, Washington/
The New York Times, 3-20:34.

1

[Commercial banks must develop options] from which all banks with debt exposure can choose in providing continuing support for debtor reforms. Governments cannot develop such a menu for the banks—they must do it themselves. But governments can encourage them to think creatively, and to provide a range of financing alternatives which will help keep the banks' doors open to international finance.

At International Monetary Fund conference,
Washington, April 9/
The Washington Post, 4-10:(A)16.

Malcolm Baldrige
Secretary of Commerce of the United States

2

Free trade is absolutely necessary to the future economic well-being of the world. It's also true that occasionally we have to *insist* on fair trade because, literally, our fair-trade laws are the bedrock on which free trade stands.

Interview, Washington/
The New York Times, 5-19:10.

Terry Barr
Vice president,
National Council of Farmer Cooperatives

3

[On reductions in Federal subsidies to big farmers]: You push those subsidies down one place, and they just pop up somewhere else. If you want to find the holes in a program, just

toss them out to farmers. No one is more innovative in finding ways to use them.

The New York Times, 6-15:1.

Joseph R. Biden, Jr.
United States Senator, D-Delaware;
Candidate for the 1988
Democratic Presidential nomination

4

. . . no protectionist trade law can solve our economic problems when their [U.S. trading partners'] workers work harder than ours, their managers manage better than ours, and their goods and services are of a higher quality than ours. It is a bitter truth but one that must be told . . . I would tell our people that we must demand better of our nation, better of ourselves, and better of our political society.

Announcing his candidacy for President,
Wilmington, Del., June 9/
The Washington Post, 6-10:(A)4.

James H. Billington
Director, Woodrow Wilson International
Center for Scholars; Librarian of
Congress-designate of the United States

5

Look at our corporate leaders. I believe they're paid much higher than their German or Japanese counterparts. They're way over-paid, even though they under-produce. This reflects a kind of moral decision that goes very deep in the way we choose to allocate rewards in our society. No wonder we don't look to the long term.

At dialogue at Woodrow Wilson Center,
Washington, June/Los Angeles Times, 7-26:(V)5.

John Bolsover
Chief executive, Baring International
Investment Management Ltd. (Britain)

6

[On the recent stock-market crash]: What we're looking for is a dramatic change in the United States attitude toward government spending. It's tragic how Washington has missed the

(JOHN BOLSOVER)

opportunities to reduce the [Federal budget] deficit during a period of economic strength in recent years. Now, we're finally seeing the consequences.

The New York Times, 10-23:38.

John C. Burton
Dean, Business School,
Columbia University

1

There's a spectrum in why students are here [in business school]. Students are here for a variety of reasons and few of them are purely academic. Our feeling is that the study of business is used by the students to get into positions that have the greatest impact on society. That's where the action is and that's the objective of our best students. But they are also not blind to the economic benefits.

New York, Oct. 13/
The New York Times, 10-14:16.

George Bush
Vice President of the United States;
Candidate for the 1988
Republican Presidential nomination

2

Today, we're [the U.S.] in a global economic battle with Japan, Europe and the emerging nations. Our future depends on our ability to compete. To do that, we need new technologies, new businesses and new jobs. It is savings and investment that finance new businesses and it is new businesses that provide new jobs and create economic growth. To get the savings and investment that we need, I would cut the capital-gains tax to 15 per cent on investments that are held for at least a year.

At economic forum, Atlanta, Oct. 14/
The New York Times, 10-15:1.

John Clemens
Professor of management, Hartwick College

3

[Business] management is one of the humanities. It's about people getting along with people.

Classic stories, whether they're ancient Greek or Roman or Renaissance or 19th-century tales or Hemingway novels, focus on major people-problems. The problems raised in the stories are unforgettable archetypes of the problems that managers face every day [in business].

Interview/U.S. News & World Report, 6-8:BC5.

Clark M. Clifford
Former Secretary of Defense
of the United States

4

[On the recent stock-market crash]: The similarities to 1929 make me very uneasy. We have not felt the shock of Black Monday yet. In one week's time over $1-trillion was lost by the listed securities, and that is an enormous setback. It will take a while for the fallout to work itself to the surface, but we are in for a very, very difficult time.

The Christian Science Monitor, 11-5:36.

Mario M. Cuomo
Governor of New York (D)

5

[On insider stock trading]: It's particularly distressing to see people who make hundreds of millions of dollars, who park their Porsches next to their Maseratis next to their Jaguars and don't know where to put their Jacuzzis, have to rip you off more.

USA Today, 3-13:(A)4.

John A. Czepiel
Associate professor of marketing,
School of Business, New York University

6

[On the proliferation of advertising in all areas of society]: Any time there is a gathering of people that an advertiser wants to reach, it will find a way of reaching them. We may not like it. And we may find it intrusive. But I can guarantee you one thing: This is not something that is going to go away.

Los Angeles Times, 4-24:(I)27.

John C. Danforth
United States Senator, R-Missouri

1

[On U.S. problems with Japan over that country's trade barriers to American products]: Nothing really works [in negotiating with Japan]. We negotiate, we harangue, we demand, we cry, we sob, we plead—and nothing happens. The problem with Japan is we negotiate down one barrier, and you find five more have cropped up to take its place.
At Senate Finance Committee hearing, Washington, Feb. 19/The Washington Post, 2-20:(A)12.

2

Terrible is the only word for the July [U.S.] trade deficit. The real message of July's report is that it will make absolute the determination of Congress to send the President a major trade bill.
Sept. 11/Los Angeles Times, 9-12:(I)15.

Robert J. Dole
United States Senator, R-Kansas;
Candidate for the 1988
Republican Presidential nomination

3

Do we want to build a [trade] wall around America? And tell everyone else, "Keep out; don't send us your products, even when they're competitive"? I don't think so . . . If some other country is making something that is competitive, they ought to be able to get it into this country . . . If we're not competitive, we shouldn't blame someone else. But if we are competitive, then we ought to have the right to get into those markets.
Interview/The Washington Post, 6-13:(A)13.

4

We all take pride in the stereotype of the can-do, enterprising American who has a good idea and turns that idea into a successful business. If we want to rekindle that entrepreneurial spirit, making us once again the economic model for other countries, we will have to rely on the small-business community—just as we have in the past . . . The best incentive we can

provide is to protect small business from unnecessary governmental mandates and restrictions.
Interview/U.S. News & World Report, 9-28:(A)16.

Pete V. Domenici
United States Senator, R-New Mexico

5

The United States of America can continue to talk about unfair [trade] policies [of foreign governments]. But the truth is, the competition that is defeating us is not unfair. It is just superior.
Before House Committee on Science, Space and Technology, Washington, June 10/ The Washington Post, 6-11:(A)17.

Peter F. Drucker
Professor of social science and management, Claremont (Calif.) Graduate School

6

There are some exceedingly well-managed Japanese firms, but the proportion is no greater than here [in the U.S.]. Most Japanese companies are managed differently—not better, differently. There are many things we can learn from them. But every Japanese management practice is of American origin, not Japanese. Only they practice it, and we just preach it. A real difference in the Japanese is that they work. Also, the Japanese do not go in for the unconscionable executive salaries we pay.
Interview/U.S. News & World Report, 2-2:23.

7

If you work in an organization that doesn't want innovation, let alone that penalizes anybody who rocks the boat, don't innovate. Your rewards are probably not even in heaven— they're certainly not here on earth. I'm not saying it's bound to be unsuccessful, but that it's bound to be frustrating. But that's not what people are hearing now. They hear, "Young man—or woman—go to work and reform the bureaucracy from within." Well, I'm not saying it can't be done, but that life is too short, and

(PETER F. DRUCKER)

the chances are not terribly good in an organization that refuses to innovate. All that will happen is that you'll get beaten up. But in this country, thank goodness, you're perfectly free to go to work elsewhere.

Interview/Newsweek, 10-5:(S)7.

John F. Fisher
Senior vice president,
Banc One Corporation

1

Banks don't put money into where things are going; they only put money into where they are.

The Wall Street Journal, 6-12:(D)5.

Peter Furniss
Managing director,
Smith Barney, Harris Upham

2

[On the current high-riding bull stock market]: It's like a college frat party. The music is loud, and everybody is having a wild time. But, sooner or later, the cops are coming to bust up the party.

Time, 8-24:36.

Richard A. Gephardt
United States Representative, D-Missouri;
Candidate for the 1988
Democratic Presidential nomination

3

[On the take-over and insider stock-trading scandals on Wall Street]: Corporations have become chips in a casino game, played for high stakes by people who produce nothing, invent nothing, grow nothing and service nothing. The [stock] market is now a game itself . . . Corporations are now forced to watch the market more closely than they watch their customers.

At Security Industry Institute,
Wharton School of Business/
The Washington Post, 3-18:(A)2.

Harvey Goldschmid
Professor of business law,
Columbia University Law School

4

[On the increasing use of bankruptcy by large corporations for a variety of reasons]: On certain levels, one is uncomfortable with a process that brings the Judicial Branch so heavily into running our major corporations and to making decisions as to how they ought to be reorganized. Given the new use of bankruptcy laws by major companies, Congress should revisit the laws.

The Christian Science Monitor, 4-14:4.

Nicholas Goodison
Chairman, London Stock Exchange

5

[On the recent stock-market crash]: Action on the political level is needed to stabilize confidence. I would particularly like to see action on the United States budget deficit. That would in time have a big effect on the United States trade deficit and would be seen as a corrective action.

The New York Times, 10-23:38.

Richard A. Grasso
Vice president for capital markets,
New York Stock Exchange

6

The technical evolution that has occurred in this [securities] business since the early 1980s has advanced to the point where globalization of equity trading is a reality. There are many issues—call them world-class issues if you will—that today have a literal 24-hour market the same as gold—the Exxons, the Royal Dutches, the IBMs—those types of companies which have a 24-hour supply and demand on a round-the-globe basis. Technology is really critical to any formalization of this 24-hour process, particularly the advent of electronic delivery networks, the growth of the personal computer, and the ability to develop sophis-

37

(RICHARD A. GRASSO)

ticated softwear to monitor risk and security prices.

Interview/
Sky (Delta in-flight magazine),
October:14.

Alan Greenspan
Former Chairman, Council of
Economic Advisers to the President
of the United States (Gerald R. Ford)

1

All [corporate] takeovers are, of necessity, voluntary in the sense that investors induce shareholders to sell their shares. Therefore, any alteration in the law or its associated regulations must be based on the presumption that the voluntary agreement between the two consenting parties currently violates the rights of third parties. So-called "green mail" is a third-party rights violation. It is essentially an agreement between management and one or more shareholders to buy back their stock at a price not available to the remaining shareholders. Since it is the other shareholders' resources which are being employed to buy back a single shareholder's stock, there is a clear violation of third-party—i.e., other shareholders'—rights.

Before Senate Banking Committee,
Washington, Jan. 27/
The Wall Street Journal, 2-27:10.

Alan Greenspan
Chairman, Federal Reserve Bank

2

It is essential that Congress come to grips with the difficult decisions that must be made to update our [banking] laws to the new circumstances of technology and competition. All of these developments have amounted to a very much more competitive environment for banking, while at the same time banking has been frozen within a regulatory structure fashioned some 50 years ago.

Before House Energy
and Commerce Subcommittee,
Washington, Oct. 5/
Los Angeles Times, 10-6:(IV)2.

Pehr Gyllenhammar
Chairman, Volvo A.B. (Sweden)

3

Over the last 24 months we have had to live with currency fluctuations that are unheard of in modern history. It's very dangerous for industrial growth. Business today is already encouraged to look too much to the short term. What's happening in the foreign-exchange markets doesn't help. It distorts perspective, creates an added interest in short-term dealings in financial markets and distracts industry.

Interview, New York/The New York Times, 2-3:28.

Neil E. Harl
Professor of economics, Iowa State University

4

Farmers are on an unrelenting course to cut the costs of production, more than I've ever seen. They are learning to deal with adversity, setting cash aside, maneuvering to a point where they don't have to go to the bank for loans, paying closer attention to soil tests and fertilizer use. We're seeing very little new debt. Farmers are scared, trying to scramble back from the edge . . . People are just not wanting to take on risk. The crunch of the last four or five years has had an impact. It will take two generations before we return to the old ways, but we will. I'm sure of that.

Interview/The Washington Post, 4-11:(A)12.

5

I don't think you will see government completely out of agriculture in our lifetimes. After all, food is too important to be left entirely at the mercy of the marketplace.

USA Today, 9-9:(A)6.

John Heinz
United States Senator, R-Pennsylvania

6

We're not going to remain the world's greatest economic power by being the best corporate raiders. Our executives would do much better to tend to the real businesses they're supposed

(JOHN HEINZ)

to be in. You can't compete with the Japanese if you're fighting a guerrilla war on Wall Street.
At Senate Banking Committee hearing,
Washington, March 4/
The New York Times, 3-5:10.

Soichiro Honda
Founder,
Honda Motor Company (Japan)

1

[On managing a company]: Generally speaking, people [employees] work harder and are more innovative if working voluntarily, compared to a case when people are being told to do something . . . You have to act as if everyone around you is a guest, a customer—and that will affect the product. People talk about innovation, but it doesn't just happen. If you think people are very important and you want to improve their lives, that's when innovation occurs . . . The worst kind of [company] president is a person who eats in fancy restaurants, smoking a fat cigar and thinking well of himself, while employees work in a dirty factory, with their hands dirty. If you're like a god, people will respect you, but they won't come close. So employees should feel that the president has made some mistakes.
Interview, Tokyo/
The New York Times, 1-12:34.

Jesse L. Jackson
Civil-rights leader;
Candidate for the 1988
Democratic Presidential nomination

2

Small business deserves as much assistance, if not more, through our tax structure, Federal policy, legislation and regulation, than big business. President Reagan tilted toward big business. I would tilt toward the development of small business.
Interview/
U.S. News & World Report, 9-28:(A)18.

Adnan Khashoggi
Entrepreneur, Industrialist

3

When I am trying to broker a deal, in diplomacy or business, I don't tell the truth to both sides all the time. You should let both sides let off steam and feel vindicated. Then it's time to encourage both to be generous in victory. You can usually have a deal if each has something the other wants, as long as you can defuse the psychological land mines . . . I am a trader. If I can make a decent profit, I prefer to take it and get out. There are others who hang on to an investment in the hope of realizing profits several times the money invested. They are welcome to their method. I prefer mine.
Time, 1-19:31,32.

Michael Kinsley
Editor, "The New Republic"

4

Felix Rohatyn, writing in *The New York Review of Books*, warns that "a cancer has been spreading . . . called greed" in the financial community. Of course, not all of us are blessed with Rohatyn's ability to make millions of dollars every year without being greedy.
Newsweek, 3-16:17.

Lane Kirkland
President, American Federation
of Labor-Congress
of Industrial Organizations

5

It is a troubling time for the Western corporation. But those troubles cannot be laid at the door of the trade-union movement . . . It was not the unions that created the staggering trade deficit that threatens the American economy . . . It was not the unions that created the international debt crisis . . . So it will not do to blame the unions for the problems besetting the corporation, although this continues to be a popular sport in many Western democracies. Nor can these problems be attributed to increasing intervention by the state. In this decade, the political trend in the United States and Western Europe

(LANE KIRKLAND)

has been toward less state intervention, not more. No, today the corporation is under siege from within, its vulnerabilities exposed by the gyrations on Wall Street, the indictments for insider [stock] trading, [and] the continuing merger mania.

At St. Gallen School
of Business Administration, Switzerland/
The Washington Post, 6-24:(A)24.

Tadashi Kume
President,
Honda Motor Company (Japan)

1

[On his company's encouragement of employees to disagree with management and offer their own ideas]: If you don't make a daily effort, people tend to agree with executives, because they have a big influence. So I tell people that if the president says a crow is white, you have to argue back that a crow is really black.

Interview, Tokyo/The New York Times, 6-15:28.

Tadashi Kuranari
Foreign Minister of Japan

2

Despite economic frictions, the United States and Japan are becoming increasingly interdependent. The United States is Japan's largest trading partner, and Japan is the United States' second largest . . . These strong bonds of trade and investment, I think, give the lie to people who look only at the trade imbalance and superficially conclude that Japan is somehow a closed market, indulges in unfair trade practices or maintains an array of invisible trade barriers. The relationship is much deeper and broader—and much better—than the trade figures alone would indicate. It is, I assure you, not all friction. I hope that there will be continued balanced expansion in trade and determined efforts to stop protectionism.

Interview/Nation's Business, January:56.

Richard L. Lesher
President, Chamber of Commerce
of the United States

3

You can boil business down to revenue and expenses, and there are always a lot of government expenses or government-imposed expenses that affect business. If we were to meet 75 years from now to consider the business issues, you could count on certain things being repeated, like trade and global competition. Economics and the marketplace are not pure science. You don't produce a single correct solution. It's a continuing process of compromise as conditions change.

Nation's Business, May:76.

Robert Lessin
Managing director, Morgan Stanley & Company

4

[On foreign acquisitions of U.S. companies due to the falling value of the dollar and other factors]: The perception by foreign companies is that there's a window open to them now. They've got a lot of capital over there and we will see a number of very high quality strategic acquisitions by major participants in 1988 . . . The Japanese have a strategic imperative to acquire. There is a compelling case for them to come into the American markets in a major way. There are cost-of-capital advantages, strategic advantages and a fear of [U.S.] protectionism. It's not clear when it will happen but, when it does, it will happen in a wave.

The New York Times, 11-27:29,32.

Donald B. Marron
Chairman, Paine Webber Group;
Former governor,
New York Stock Exchange

5

[Saying there should be changes in the rules covering corporate take-overs in order to reduce the incidence of insider stock trading]: I reluctantly conclude that Wall Street cannot solve this problem alone. The stakes are too high. The impact is too broad. It will require the

(DONALD B. MARRON)

joint efforts of Wall Street and Washington. There are relatively infrequent periods when there are legislative windows, where people are all of the view that legislation is appropriate and the time has come for it. I think there is a unique opportunity for the Congress.

Before Senate Securities Subcommittee,
Washington, Feb. 24/
The Washington Post, 2-25:(F)2.

1

[On the recent stock-market crash]: You learn how inter-related we [in the world's securities markets] are and how small we are. Nowhere is that exemplified more than people staying up all night to watch the Japanese markets to get a feeling for what might happen in the next session of the New York market. The next thing we learn is you can't let computers do all your thinking for you. Part of the decline was triggered or exacerbated by computer-directed trading strategies, and they clearly aren't designed to work in markets of this scale and this volatility.

The New York Times, 10-22:37.

Forrest McDonald
Professor of history,
University of Alabama

2

[In the 19th century,] we imported far more than we exported. We would buy mainly from Britain, and so we'd send them cotton and they'd send us manufactured goods. And we'd rack up deficit after deficit after deficit. How was the balance of payments recitified? They get pieces of paper—in the form of United States government debt, corporate debt, private debt, shares in corporations . . . Now, what's happening in the 1980s? The Japanese are exporting to us a lot more than they're importing from us. We're not in trouble: The *Japanese* are in trouble, because they're accumulating pieces of paper in precisely the same way the British accumulated pieces of paper in the 19th century . . . And all of a sudden the capacity of

American business to generate capital is multiplied greatly by the fact of the Japanese pieces of paper. And now we're laying the foundation for a tremendous expansion of American business . . . Corporations don't pay off their debts any more than governments pay off their debts: You refinance them when they get mature.

Interview, Washington/
The Christian Science Monitor, 5-12:6,7.

Mark L. Melcher
Director of Washington research,
Prudential Bache Securities

3

Generally speaking, Washington views Wall Street as a giant casino, and it views losses and gains there accordingly. Protests about the financial markets being central to our capitalistic economy are not universally understood or believed.

The New York Times, 10-29:14.

Howard M. Metzenbaum
United States Senator, D-Ohio

4

[Criticizing the scale of corporate mergers and takeovers]: In my view, the record is clear. The Reagan Administration has created the most permissive merger climate of the last 70 years. It claims to be for free competition. Yet it has turned its back on the antitrust laws— laws that are essential to making the free-enterprise system work.

The Christian Science Monitor, 7-3:11.

Edward H. Meyer
Chairman, Grey Advertising

5

[Let's produce TV] advertising that absolutely demands attention. Advertising you can't take your eyes off. Advertising that's so interesting, so intriguing, so handsome, so exciting that the viewer's brain is sucked into it and really gets involved.

At Association of National Advertisers meeting,
San Diego, Oct. 21/The New York Times, 10-22:51.

James C. Miller III
Director, Federal Office of
Management and Budget

1

The next time you hear someone refer to a "hostile take-over" [of a company], ask them two questions: One, "would you view someone's making you a great offer on, say, your house, as a hostile act?" Two, "who owns companies—managers or shareholders?" If they think an offer to buy is a hostile act, they've got emotional problems. If they think managers own firms, they haven't been to high school. If they answer both questions correctly, ask them not to embarrass themselves in the future by referring to "hostile take-overs."

Before United Shareholders Association,
June 15/The Wall Street Journal, 10-26:22.

Kiichi Miyazawa
Minister of Finance of Japan

2

[Japan] cannot remain constantly the defendant in the dock, listening to allegations that we damage the markets of our export countries. It is time for us to adjust our goals. We must reduce our exports to the U.S. so that we cease to supply occasion for the reproach that we hurt their markets. This will check American protectionism . . . Many of our critics on these matters have an antiquated idea of how open our markets are. We have been open to foreign goods for years. Foreign businessmen living in Japan know this.

Interview/ World Press Review, January:51.

Mike Moore
Minister of Overseas Trade
of New Zealand

3

[Criticizing farm subsidies]: There's an obscene misallocation of resources in Japan, the EEC and the U.S., which is imposing an ever-increasing burden on taxpayers and consumers. The solutions are simple. It's only vested interests that complicate them. Feed the hungry, break the Third World debt cycle and reform the economies of Europe, the U.S. and Japan by transferring the agricultural subsidies to viable new areas of commerce, dictated by the market.

At Agra-Europe symposium, London/
Los Angeles Times, 2-15:(I)5.

Daniel Oliver
Chairman, Federal Trade Commission

4

Two years ago, we saw a proposal to ban alcohol advertising. Last year came a proposal to ban tobacco advertising. Again this year, we see bills to ban tobacco ads. The justification given for depriving citizens of information is that they are better off without it. Other justifications have been given for advertising bans in the past. I oppose these attempts to deprive citizens of information necessary to make their own decisions. Informed choice is the essence of our economic as well as political system, and advertising is a fundamental part of the process by which consumers become informed.

Before House subcommittee, Washington,
April 3/The Washington Post, 4-10:(A)26.

John O'Toole
Executive producer,
"Modern Maturity," PBS-TV

5

[Advertisers] love it when we [consumers] get confused. Because advertising is essentially getting people to buy things they don't need—for the wrong reasons.

The Washington Post, 5-26:(A)20.

David Packard
Co-founder, Hewlett-Packard Company;
Former Deputy Secretary of Defense
of the United States

6

[On U.S. concern about Soviet appropriation of Western technology]: I think we've gone overboard in putting restrictions on technology transfer. For us to maintain strength, individual companies have to have a market for their products. There have to be some restrictions, but

(DAVID PACKARD)

the Soviet Union doesn't have much trouble acquiring the technology it needs. In 1981, the Soviets gave Caterpillar Tractor a very large order for pipe-laying machinery. The [U.S.] Administration blocked the sale, and Moscow bought the equipment from Kamatsu in Japan. Today, Kamatsu dominates the tractor market, and Caterpillar is in trouble. Now, that's a case where you just shot yourself in the foot over concern about technology transfer.

Interview/Los Angeles Times Magazine, 2-22:25.

Scott Pardee
Vice chairman, Yamaichi International (America); Former Senior Vice President, Federal Reserve Bank of New York

1

[On the declining value of the dollar in world markets]: There is something to worry about. The lower dollar raises the costs of imports and raises prices in this country. It is an actual and a potential factor for inflation. We already have inflation in the U.S., and the further decline of the dollar can exacerbate it. Second, Americans have worked very hard to build companies and produce the assets we have. As the dollar goes down, it depreciates those assets, making them cheap in world markets. Depreciating manufactured goods so they will sell better is one thing, but to depreciate assets that we already have is another. In effect, we're giving assets away to foreign investors . . . Then there is the fact that bank capital in the U.S. is measured in dollars. This leaves American banks in a less competitive capital position vis-a-vis their foreign counterparts.

Interview/U.S. News & World Report, 11-16:60.

H. Ross Perot
Industrialist

2

For my company to succeed, I've got to have something that you want to buy, right? It's got to be better than all your other choices. And I can't force you to buy my things through protectionism, trade barriers and what have you. I need you to buy my products because they are better. Now, anything that's less than that, and I am in deep trouble.

Interview/USA Today, 3-3:(A)9.

John J. Phelan, Jr.
Chairman, New York Stock Exchange

3

Hostile [corporate] take-overs were inevitable because the assets of corporations were certainly way below what they were obviously worth in the marketplace. And when the [industrialist] T. Boone Pickenses of this world began to buy oil companies, they realized it was cheaper to buy reserves than to build them. Then others came in and, in non-resource industries, saw the parts were worth more than the whole. All of which had probably a very good impact on corporations.

Interview/USA Today, 9-29:(A)11.

4

Our public image didn't become tarnished because of [the] insider trading [scandal]. Everybody thought there would be a great loss of confidence in the markets, but more and more people are in the market than ever before. What it did focus on was not the market and not the institutions, but—perhaps unfairly—young individuals.

Interview/USA Today, 9-29:(A)11.

T. Boone Pickens
Industrialist

5

[On the many recent corporate takeovers]: The reason you've seen so many deals [in the past few years] is that managements have done such a poor job. Consequently, the assets of a company can be purchased very cheaply in the stock market.

Interview/
The Christian Science Monitor, 3-31:19.

43

WHAT THEY SAID IN 1987

William Proxmire
United States Senator, D-Wisconsin

1

[On the rise of insider stock trading]: Right now, it is far too easy for market manipulators to make a quick killing by putting a company into play and cashing in on the rise of the price of its stock. When all the dust is settled, I will push for a comprehensive overhaul of our laws regulating insider trading and corporate takeovers.

Feb. 13/Los Angeles Times, 2-14:(I)1.

A. Barry Rand
Corporate vice president,
Xerox Corporation

2

We have got to develop an obsession with satisfying customers. We've got to do everything we can to make sure that we get the affirmative vote of our customers . . . We may drive for [internal] efficiency, but the customer doesn't necessarily care how lean we are. He cares about us meeting his needs.

Interview, Rochester, N.Y./
The New York Times, 5-22:25.

Ronald Reagan
President of the United States

3

We have protected the freedom of expression of the author, as we should. But what of the freedom of expression of the entrepreneur, whose pen and paper are capital and profits and whose literature is the heroic epic of free enterprise?

Before Canadian Parliament, Ottawa,
April 6/USA Today, 4-7:(A)4.

4

The final answer to the trade problems between America and Japan is not more hemming and hawing, not more trade sanctions, not more voluntary restraint agreements—though these may be needed as steps along the way—and certainly not more unfulfilled agreements. The answer is genuinely fair and open markets on both sides of the Pacific. And the sooner, the better.

Before Chamber of Commerce
of the United States, Washington,
April 27/The Washington Post, 4-28:(A)4.

5

[Arguing against an amendment by Rep. Richard Gephardt that would provide for U.S. trade retaliation against countries which restrict U.S. imports and thus create a favorable trade balance for themselves]: The Gephardt amendment moves in precisely the wrong direction by closing our markets, rather than opening foreign markets. It would brand us as clear violators of international agreements, thus undermining our ability to negotiate new trade agreements, to broaden, rather than restrict, world trade. And it would subject the United States to counter-retaliations which would curtail rather than expand U.S. exports.

To Republican Congressmen/
Los Angeles Times, 4-30:(I)15.

6

[On U.S. differences with Japan over trade]: Even the closest of friends have differences. Ours is the challenge of keeping trade and commerce, the lifeblood of prosperity, flowing equitably between our peoples. To do that, we must address the current unsustainable trade balance [favoring Japan]. It has spawned calls for protectionism [in the U.S.] that would undo the shining economic accomplishments we've achieved together. Progress will not happen on its own. Tangible actions must be taken by us both. We would like to see Japan, for example, open its markets more fully to trade and commerce.

At welcome ceremony for visiting Japanese
Prime Minister Yasuhiro Nakasone, Washington,
April 30/Los Angeles Times, 5-1:(I)1.

7

Some countries, which have taken full advantage of America's openness [of markets], must realize that times have changed. Today, any country selling heavily in the United States, whose markets are not substantially open to

(RONALD REAGAN)

American goods, risks a backlash from the American people. No country that closes its own markets, or unfairly subsidizes its exports, can expect the markets of its trading partners to remain open.

Speech on 40th anniversary
of Marshall Plan, Washington, June 1/
The Washington Post, 6-2:(A)11.

1

[Governments must] move to dismantle trade-distorting subsidies and labor laws that promote unemployment. Agricultural subsidies, for instance, have been some of the worst culprits behind our growing trade frictions [by giving some nations unfair advantage in world markets]. Let's jointly defuse this expensive "farms race" by setting a goal of a subsidy-free world for the year 2000.

Broadcast address, Venice, Italy,
June 5/Los Angeles Times, 6-6:(I)20.

2

There has been a chorus of American politicians playing to the fears of working people, singing the song of [trade] protectionism and charging that, as a result of the trade deficit, [U.S.] jobs will go overseas, unemployment will rise, and the United States will be deindustrialized. It sounds good as part of a political campaign speech, but as an old Virginia lawyer once told his hometown jury, "tain't so." Unemployment has declined in the United States by 40 per cent since late 1982, even as our trade deficit has grown. In Japan and Germany, countries with large trade surpluses, unemployment has gone up. And a long-term analysis shows us holding our own in manufacturing jobs.

Before meetings of World Bank and
International Monetary Fund, Washington,
Sept. 29/The New York Times, 9-30:33.

3

[On the recent stock-market crash]: We've seen in the last week . . . that there is real concern on Wall Street. The recent turbulence in the stock market suggests that those who are investing in the future of our economy are worried that something—some roadblock—may be put in the way of that future. The disruption in our markets is sending a signal loud and clear to get our economic house in order. The markets are reacting more to the actions—and inactions—of government than to the [Federal budget] deficit itself, which has been shrinking—down nearly 30 per cent since the last fiscal year.

At Labor Department, Washington, Oct. 23/
Los Angeles Times, 10-24:(I)22.

John Reed
Chairman,
Citicorp (Citibank, New York)

4

[On his bank's decision to accept large losses on its Third World loans]: We are totally dependent on the global banking system functioning, and we would not do anything that we felt was destructive to that. The judgment was that it made sense to do it and that it would not have a negative impact on the banking system, and that it might indeed break the logjam in terms of flexibility . . . We will definitely lend new money. We have said consistently and constantly we will lend money any time it makes sense. And making sense means there has to be some reasonable prospect that the money is going to get paid back.

Interview/Los Angeles Times, 6-12:(I)24.

Donald T. Regan
Former Chief of Staff to President
of the United States Ronald Reagan

5

[On the insider-stock-trading scandals]: . . . I condemn these recent practices on Wall Street. My antidote for that, incidentally, is a little Draconian. But it goes along with my whole temperament . . . If those people actually went to jail for two or three years, it would be the greatest antidote and it would stop others from the same practice.

At business conference sponsored by
Loyola Marymount University, Los Angeles,
April 16/Los Angeles Times, 4-17:(I)3.

Felix G. Rohatyn
Senior partner,
Lazard Freres & Company

1

I am an investment banker. For the last two years, many of the best and brightest in my business have been pleading guilty to illegal acts [in the securities business] and marching off to jail. Successful, wealthy, intelligent men turned out to be greedy, arrogant and corrupt. Why? Because, as much as anything else, this situation underlines one of the realities of the so-called service society. Whereas making things, and the activities related to products, were the main preoccupation of prior generations, making money, and the activities related to money, are the driving forces of our society today. To be wealthy is not sinful; nor is poverty a virtue. But the pursuit of wealth and power is so pervasive today as to create something that may be entirely new—namely, a money culture. When such a culture grows cheek-by-jowl with extreme poverty, it is potentially dangerous.

At Long Island University commencement/
The New York Times, 6-3:27.

Patricia Schroeder
United States Representative,
D-Colorado

2

I'm for free trade, but not if everyone else but us gets it free. What I mean is that the amount we spend to protect our allies is about the same amount by which our imports exceed our exports. We need a more fair sharing of the cost of the common defense. In addition, we have to knock down barriers to our products in countries that have free access to our markets.

Interview/
U.S. News & World Report, 9-28:(A)18.

John Sculley
Chief executive officer,
Apple Computer, Inc.

3

In the industrial age, the CEO sat at the top of a hierarchy and didn't really have to listen to anybody. He made all of the decisions. In the information age, you have to listen to ideas of people regardless of where they are in the organization, because we are looking at a network as a metaphor, not a hierarchy.

Broadcast interview/
Nation's Business, December:14.

John S. R. Shad
Chairman, Securities and Exchange
Commission of the United States

4

Insider [stock] trading is difficult to detect and even more difficult to prosecute. Unlike an investigation of a crime such as bank robbery, where enforcement authorities generally know at the outset that an illegal act has been committed, insider-trading investigations typically are commenced to examine suspicious trades or trading patterns that may indicate a violation of the law, but may also reflect legitimate trading.

Before Senate subcommittee, Washington,
May 13/The Christian Science Monitor, 5-15:12.

5

We have not eradicated insider [stock] trading, but we certainly have inhibited it. And as a consequence, the multimillions of dollars of profits that had been siphoned off the market by insider traders . . . now are flowing through to the investing public. I came here in May, 1981, and in 1981 I was reading articles in leading publications that said insider trading was so pervasive nothing could be done about it. A lot of people took those articles as a license to engage in the activity. I made the comment that we were going to come down on that activity with hobnail boots.

Interview/Los Angeles Times, 6-16:(IV)8.

6

On insider [stock] trading, the marketplace is incredibly sensitive in responding to these adverse headlines. And what concerns me is that the adverse headlines will be used as excuses for all kinds of other legislation. I think any legislative responses to insider trading should be considered on their own merits, and

(JOHN S. R. SHAD)

that tender-offer, merger and acquisitions problems should be considered on their merits, and not lumped together. Insider trading is not the driving force behind tender offers. It's a parasitical activity.

Interview, Washington/
The New York Times, 6-24:29.

George P. Shultz
Secretary of State of the United States

1

People refer to protectionist pressures in the United States. There is a difference between pressures for protection and protection itself. We in the United States [Reagan Administration] resist such pressures . . . [But] it is not possible for every country in the world to be a net exporter at the same time. So something will have to give here [in Asia], and it will be, possibly, a traumatic experience.

At ASEAN meeting, Singapore, June 18/
Los Angeles Times, 6-19:(I)8.

Andrew C. Sigler
Chairman, Champion
International Corporation

2

The unfettered buying and selling of U.S. corporations solely for the purpose of financial speculation and profit is one of the most destructive phenomena of the 20th century. We are seeing the destruction of wealth-creating enterprises that were built over many generations.

Before Senate Banking Committee, Washington,
March 4/The New York Times, 3-5:10.

Lawrence G. Smith
Executive vice president,
New York branch, National Commercial
Bank of Saudi Arabia

3

Americans have always had ambiguous feelings about business people. People consider banking a high-status job, for example, but they generally hate their bankers.

The New York Times, 1-29:31.

Donald Stone
Vice chairman, New York Stock Exchange

4

[On the recent stock-market crash]: I was in combat during World War II, and the feeling you had in your stomach was the same as when you were under fire, except here [in the stock market] you didn't risk your life—just all your assets.

Interview/The New York Times, 10-22:36.

Robert S. Strauss
Former Special Trade Representative
for the President
of the United States (Jimmy Carter)

5

[On the U.S.-Japan trade crisis]: There's no question that Japan must change many of their practices. Japan simply has a terrible "buy Japan" procurement policy, for one. The Kansai airport [where the U.S. is blocked from bidding on an $8-billion project] is a perfect example. The way they [the Japanese] have behaved by not buying foreign telecommunications equipment is another example . . . I think the only way to get them to change is by being very blunt and very tough and very firm, but it can't be done by ministers nibbling around the edges of these problems. I don't think you settle it by resolving six disputes over citrus imports, nor do I think you settle it with kind of a cockamamie [micro-] chip agreement that any person could read, and know it wasn't going to work.

Interview/U.S. News & World Report, 4-13:46.

Donald Trump
Industrialist; Real-estate developer

6

I've always been a believer in the fact that if a man is capable in terms of a business sense at one business, it's very likely he is going to be capable in another. I think that, to a large ex-

(DONALD TRUMP)

tent, knowledge can be instinct. Oftentimes you'll see someone doing well in one industry and also able to do well in others. While you'll very rarely see somebody who was a failure in one industry who is successful in another.

Interview, New York/
The New York Times, 3-5:30.

John Van de Kamp
Attorney General of California

1

In recent years, the lack of firm, consistent Federal antitrust enforcement has created a confusing and dangerous situation. As large and small firms merge at an alarming rate, too often the result is less competition, higher prices and higher unemployment.

March 10/Los Angeles Times, 3-11:(I)15.

Paul A. Volcker
Chairman, Federal Reserve Board

2

A declining dollar at some point has high costs and risks. It generates inflationary pressures. Uncertainties about the future direction of currency values could dampen the willingness of others to place or maintain funds in the United States—funds upon which, for the time being, we are utterly dependent.

Before Joint Congressional Economic Committee,
Washington, Feb. 2/The New York Times, 2-3:28.

3

The simple facts are that we [the U.S.] are spending more than we produce and that we are unable to finance at home both our investment needs and the Federal deficit. Those are not conditions that are sustainable for long—not when, as at present, the influx of capital from abroad cannot be traced to a surge in productive investment . . . The richest country in the world ought to be exporting capital, not importing capital.

Before Senate Banking Committee, Washington,
Feb. 19/The New York Times, 2-20:30.

4

. . . we plainly do want and need improvement in our trade balance. There are some encouraging signs in that respect. But there are also practical limits as to how fast the necessary massive shift in resources can be accomplished if the momentum of world expansion is to be maintained. Undercutting investment and growth abroad at a time when growth prospects are already relatively weak is neither in their interest nor ours. Undercutting our own prospects for price and financial stability by a weak dollar is equally unattractive. What we need now, instead of more depreciation, is action here and abroad to carry through on those other measures needed to support growth and adjustment—specifically, action to reduce the budget deficit here, and to provide stimulus abroad. We need time for those actions, and the earlier depreciation, to work their effects. And we need the patience to see it through, without embarking on self-destructive protectionist policies.

Before Senate Banking subcommittee,
Washington, April 7/
The Washington Post, 4-8:(F)1.

5

Japanese banks, by our standards, operate on very low profit margins, and there is a feeling that this permits them to price services more aggressively. It is an example of an area where some international consistency might be helpful to the health of international banking.

Before House Financial
Institutions Subcommittee, Washington,
July 30/The New York Times, 7-31:21.

Robert M. White
President,
National Academy of Engineering

6

We [the U.S.] are in danger of losing the competitiveness battle on the manufacturing floor. One of the things that the Japanese have done very well, and we have done poorly, is to understand the concept of design for manufacturability . . . Design [a product] so that you

(ROBERT M. WHITE)

can produce it at low cost and [with] high quality. That's where we have been deficient.

Interview, Washington/
The Christian Science Monitor, 3-26:5.

Pete Wilson
United States Senator, R-California

1

[On just-announced U.S. tariffs of 100 per cent placed on certain Japanese imports as a sanction against Japanese restrictions on U.S. imports]: I hope that today's announcement is just one part of a new get-tough policy against unfair trade practices. It is long overdue that we put aside diplomatic niceties and strike directly to defend our international economic interests. We have finally fired back in what has long been a trade war with the Japanese. The problem was that Japan was the only one waging it.

Washington, March 27/
Los Angeles Times, 3-28:(I)23.

Abner W. Womack
Agricultural economist

2

I don't think there's been any time in history that you could find farmers more dependent on the government for their income than under the current situation . . . Free-market agriculture [without government influence on prices] looks like $20-billion to $25-billion agriculture annually . . . and yes, it will carry more people out of production . . . The ones who will be left will be fairly strong farmers.

Los Angeles Times, 10-12:(I)15.

Walter B. Wriston
Former chairman,
Citicorp (Citibank, New York)

3

[On the recent stock-market crash]: We learned what we always knew—that is, when

markets reach an all-time high, there's always a correction. This correction was sharper and deeper than had been anticipated, but it was not the end of the world. There is nothing fundamentally the matter with our economy. All you have to do is look at corporate profits, unemployment, any measures you want. The second thing we've learned is that markets are stronger than anybody. Here was a market that took the worst hit in the history of our country and it functioned, and that in itself is a tremendous lesson.

The New York Times, 10-22:25.

Clayton K. Yeutter
Special Trade Representative
for President of the United States
Ronald Reagan

4

[On just-announced U.S. tariffs of 100 per cent placed on certain Japanese imports as a sanction against Japanese restrictions on U.S. imports]: Japan is a great friend, and we take this action out of sorrow, not because we want to demonstrate American machismo. We're doing it because we believe that it's the appropriate time and place for action of this nature . . . And I'm convinced that the government of Japan will now do its very best to reverse this situation . . .

Washington, March 27/
Los Angeles Times, 3-28:(I)23.

5

[On the July record U.S. trade deficit]: Today's figures should not be an excuse for special-interest protectionism. Despite our disappointment, we must keep these figures in perspective. The U.S. economy would not be able to absorb such a high level of imports if it were not expanding at a healthy pace.

Sept. 11/Los Angeles Times,
9-12:(I)15.

Crime • Law Enforcement

Gary Bauer
Assistant to President
of the United States
Ronald Reagan for Domestic Policy

1

All Americans worry about crime. Conservatives should talk about it and it shouldn't sound like we're only trying to protect suburbia. We've allowed our concern about crime to be portrayed as racist, as if we were speaking in some sort of code. The Americans for whom day-in, day-out crime is a fact of life are those in inner-city urban neighborhoods. Our inability to control crime is thwarting efforts to revive inner-city neighborhoods.

Interview, Washington, Feb. 13/
The Washington Post, 2-14:(A)3.

G. Robert Blakey
Professor of law,
University of Notre Dame

2

[On the 1970 Racketeer Influenced and Corrupt Organizations statute of which he was the architect]: It is now the prosecutive tool of choice in sophisticated organized-crime, white-collar crime, political-corruption and terrorist cases. It's sort of a statute for all seasons.

The Washington Post, 6-13:(A)6.

Robert H. Bork
Judge, United States Court of Appeals
for the District of Columbia;
Nominee for Associate Justice,
Supreme Court of the United States

3

[On the exclusionary rule]: Where no deterrence of un-Constitutional police behavior is possible, a decision to exclude probative evidence with the result that a criminal goes free to prey upon the public should shock the judicial conscience even more than admitting the evidence.

Interview/USA Today, 7-2:(A)2.

William J. Brennan, Jr.
Associate Justice,
Supreme Court of the United States

4

We cannot focus public attention on the lawlessness in the streets and not on its causes—poverty and injustice. Those who dwell in urban tenements and rural shacks, as well as their sympathizers, seeing no tangible results, ask what good are laws and court decisions [and might be tempted by] apostles of violence and revolution.

At Ohio State University College
of Law commencement, May 17/
The New York Times, 5-18:17.

Charles M. Carberry
Lawyer; Former Chief,
Securities and Commodities Fraud Unit,
U.S. Attorney's office

5

I really do enjoy fraud [cases]. I like putting puzzles together, and I like, in an abstract way, seeing how people create various artifices. I mean, there are some *great* schemes out there. The thing about fraud is that there are no limits to innovation. It's almost like reading a new novel every day.

Esquire, December:97.

Julius Chambers
Counsel, National Association
for the Advancement of Colored People's
Legal Defense Fund

6

The fact is that race and other illegitimate factors enter every day in cases involving capital punishment. We are committed to carrying on the fight against a system that allows such injustice.

April 22/Los Angeles Times, 4-23:(I)23.

Alan Dershowitz
Professor of law, Harvard University

1

[Criticizing the acquittal of Bernhard Goetz, who shot a group of men he claimed threatened him on a New York subway]: The jury decided that no man is reasonable when he's surrounded by four thugs. It's hard to pay attention to lines drawn by academics in a classroom.

The New York Times, 6-19:11.

Bill Domm
Member of Canadian Parliament

2

[On his support for capital punishment]: The measure of the sanctity of life is how you deal with the person who [first] violated that sanctity. Society shows the sanctity it has for life by how it punishes those who violate the sanctity of human life.

Interview, Ottawa, Canada/
Los Angeles Times, 4-13:(I)6.

Andrew L. Frey
Deputy Solicitor General
of the United States

3

I think [the] Miranda [rule] was wrong, but if I were the Attorney General I wouldn't even ask the Supreme Court to overrule it. I think a majority of the Court probably thinks it was wrong as a matter of abstract Constitutional doctrine, but I don't think they would vote to overrule it because I think most of them feel it would send the wrong message to the American public. Miranda, I think, to a lot of people is a symbol that we respect people's rights, some would say too elaborately; but to the man in the street it's an ingrained part of their view of the American system of justice. You think cops and robbers, you think Miranda warnings.

The New York Times, 2-13:12.

Rudolph W. Giuliani
United States Attorney
for the Southern District of New York

4

I do not believe that the Mafia, or La Cosa Nostra, will be an organization that means any-

thing to any of us a decade from now, or maybe even five years. If we continue to do what we do [vigorously prosecuting Mafia members], I think that in four years, five years, six years, seven years, it is something that will be part of our history rather than a part of contemporary America.

At conference on crime in America,
Providence, R.I., March 1/
The New York Times, 3-3:14.

5

This has been the Mafia's worst year. We keep making gains and they keep getting moved backward. If we take back the labor unions, the legitimate businesses, eventually they [the Mafia] become just another street gang. Spiritually, psychologically, they've always been just a street gang.

The New York Times, 3-11:19.

6

Criminal behavior is not a function of economics in the United States; it is a function of a lack of values . . . We have to think of alternative ways . . . of teaching values. [It can be too late to teach values in college.] They can reinforce things you learned earlier . . . But if the base isn't there, they can't instill it.

Interview, New York/
The Christian Science Monitor, 3-31:4.

Ira Glasser
Executive director,
American Civil Liberties Union

7

If you don't have criminal evidence as the standard for searches, searches will be done based on politics.

Broadcast interview/"Moyers: In Search
of the Constitution," PBS-TV, 6-18.

Joseph Graves
Professor of criminal justice,
University of Texas, El Paso

8

If I were in charge of a prison and there was [a] pending announcement that was going to up-

(JOSEPH GRAVES)

set the inmates, I would try to get together those viewed as [inmate] leaders and converse with them and see how they would react. In any prison, jail—or anywhere you detain people—the administration has to be able to perceive and predict when an uprising might occur. They need to have an antenna, an eye out, to have a feel for what the prisoners are doing, thinking or planning to do.

USA Today, 11-24:(A)3.

Charles Henry
Chairman,
Amnesty International U.S.A.

1

The death penalty, as practiced in the United States, is an international human-rights issue. We fail to recognize that the death penalty never has been and never can be administered fairly.

At seminar, Atlanta,
June 29/USA Today, 6-30:(A)3.

Lois Haight Herrington
Director, White House Conference
for a Drug-Free America, Department
of Justice of the United States

2

We used to think that people on drugs were sleepy types who went through life without harming anybody. But we are seeing, study after study, that show that the relationship to drugs and crime is very large.

At drug conference, Cincinnati/
USA Today, 11-17:(A)2.

John J. Hill
Deputy Chief of Police
of New York City

3

[To new Police Academy graduates]: We can teach you to shoot. We can teach you the law. We can teach you the rules and regulations. But there is one thing that we cannot teach you and

that is about people. The bottom line is to treat people as people, and you'll get by.

New York, July 8/
The New York Times, 7-9:15.

Roy Innis
President,
Congress of Racial Equality

4

[Approving the acquittal of Bernhard Goetz, who shot a group of black men he claimed threatened him on a New York subway]: I couldn't believe the good people of this city would convict that man for doing what was natural and what was necessary and what anybody else would have done. I think the verdict was fantastic. Justice prevailed.

USA Today, 6-18:(A)8.

Jesse L. Jackson
Civil-rights leader;
Candidate for the 1988
Democratic Presidential nomination

5

A four-year scholarship to any state university in America will cost less than $25,000. A four-year scholarship to any state prison in America will cost between $80,000 and $140,000. Schools at their worst are better than jails at their best.

At Senate hearing, Washington/
USA Today, 2-18:(A)4.

Lane Kirkland
President, American Federation
of Labor-Congress
of Industrial Organizations

6

[On suggestions that the Teamsters Union may be infiltrated by organized crime]: I do not believe that 1.6 million teamsters are corrupt. In fact, I know very well and I have strong feelings to the contrary. If there are individuals in the teamsters, as in any other institutions, including the press, who violate that trust or

(LANE KIRKLAND)

break the law, then they should be prosecuted and the case should be proven.

The New York Times, 12-1:28.

Edward I. Koch
Mayor of New York

1

[On the acquittal of Bernhard Goetz, who shot a group of men he claimed threatened him on a New York subway]: There may be some who misperceive the case and will think, somehow or other, vigilantism is acceptable; and we're saying now to those who are concerned: we will never permit that. And we're saying to those who might seek to engage in it that we'll come down on you as hard as we possibly can.

Nashville, Tenn., June 16/
Los Angeles Times, 6-17:(I)23.

2

[To new Police Academy graduates]: Do your best and we will stand by you. And if we see you doing something maliciously wrong, we will not stand by you; we will kick you out.

New York, July 8/
The New York Times, 7-9:15.

3

I believe the [New York construction] industry is not doing what it could to oppose organized crime. They are not criminals themselves, but the difference between bribery and extortion is very difficult. If you are being extorted and accept it and don't go to the cops, then you are contributing to the strength of organized crime.

Interview, New York, Sept. 9/
The New York Times, 9-10:17.

Thurgood Marshall
Associate Justice,
Supreme Court of the United States

4

[Arguing against capital punishment]: I'm not going to be swayed by this emotional business. I think that it's cruel and inhuman to kill somebody. They say, "Well, we had the death penalty when the Constitution . . ." and that's true. You also put people in jail for debt. You did a lot of other things then that you don't do now. The difficulty is if you make a mistake, you can correct it. If you put a man in jail wrongfully, you can let him out. But death is rather permanent. And what do you do if you convict a man illegally and un-Constitutionally and find it out later? What do you say? "Oops"?

Interview/USA Today, 9-9:(A)7.

Joseph McNamara
Chief of Police of San Jose, Calif.

5

[On the acquittal of Bernhard Goetz, who shot a group of black youths he claimed were threatening him on a New York subway]: The racial polarization and the level and fear of crime in our country are at an all-time high. The fact that Goetz was immediately dubbed "hero vigilante" should tell us several things . . . That feelings between blacks and whites have worsened, and there is a legitimate fear of kids like that in a subway or on a city street. The real problem is that there are hundreds of thousands of kids like that, who have no real family life, who have dropped out of school, do not know how to read, have never worked, are on a cycle of welfare, and who will never work. They've got no chance to participate in the American system, they're bitter, they're committing a lot of crime, and they're very, very dangerous.

Interview/USA Today, 6-3:(A)13.

Brian Mulroney
Prime Minister of Canada

6

I am not persuaded the death penalty works as a deterrent. Nor am I persuaded it is appropriate as a punishment. On the contrary, I believe it is repugnant, and I believe it is profoundly unacceptable.

Before Canadian House of Commons,
Ottawa/The Washington Post, 7-1:(A)26.

WHAT THEY SAID IN 1987

Burt Neuborne
Professor,
New York University Law School

1

[On the acquittal of Bernhard Goetz, who shot a group of men he claimed threatened him on a New York subway]: The jurors had so little faith in the criminal-justice system, both to protect us and to bring the guilty to justice, that they were willing to tolerate a degree of vigilante behavior that I think rationally cannot be justified.

The New York Times, 6-19:11.

Ian Percival
Member of British Parliament

2

Of course there is no need for a death penalty in a civilized society—but first get your civilized society.

Before British Parliament, London/
U.S. News & World Report, 4-13:11.

John Powell
Legal director,
American Civil Liberties Union

3

[Criticizing a Supreme Court decision permitting the holding without bail of criminal defendants believed to be dangerous]: [The decision is] completely at odds with our historic tradition that everyone is innocent until proven guilty. This ruling permits the government to jail first and try later.

May 26/Los Angeles Times, 5-27:(I)1.

Nancy Reagan
Wife of President
of the United States Ronald Reagan

4

[I have] a message for the drug dealers and producers and pushers, and the message is this: The parents and young people of the world are going to drive you out of business. We're the ones who are going to be the pushers from now on. We're going to push you out of our schools, out of our communities, out of our countries and out of existence.

At forum sponsored by Swedish Lions Club,
Stockholm, June 9/Los Angeles Times, 6-10:(I)13.

William S. Sessions
Director,
Federal Bureau of Investigation

5

I am stunned that the American people have apparently decided to collectively sit back and let the drug menace overtake us. We have not, as families or a society, made the determination that we will not use drugs . . . I think we ought to have absolute outrage and do what it takes to wipe this scourge off the face of the earth.

At Commonwealth Club, San Francisco,
Dec. 21/Los Angeles Times, 12-22:(I)33.

Stephen J. Solarz
United States Representative,
D-New York

6

[Introducing a bill limiting immunity from prosecution given foreign diplomats who commit serious crimes in the U.S.]: It is in no nation's interests to be represented by rapists, rogues or drug peddlers.

USA Today, 6-26:(A)5.

James E. Starrs
Professor of law and forensic science,
George Washington University

7

[On the increasing use of laboratory analysis in criminal investigations]: There is a gathering momentum, almost a tidal wave of concern, over the general question of professional training, ethics, conflict of interest—that whole ball of wax. Most often what you find is that forensic testimony is much too new and incomprehensible for the legal community. The courts will rubber-stamp what the experts say.

The New York Times, 12-22:8.

James K. Stewart
Director, National Institute of Justice

1

Individuals who commit crimes commit between six and eight times the amount of crimes when they're using drugs. The use of drugs is the accelerator to criminal activity.

The New York Times, 2-19:16.

Victor Streib
Professor,
Cleveland-Marshall College of Law

2

There are about 20,000 intentional homicides every year in the United States, and there are only about 300 death sentences a year. So what we have been doing throughout most of our history is saying that only about 2 per cent of all people who commit such homicides are going to get the death penalty . . . The rest of them get long-term imprisonment. Where juveniles are involved, the argument is that they should not be within that 2 per cent who get the death penalty. They should be within the 98 per cent who get long-term sentences, often life imprisonment, but not death. . . . The law has made clear over the centuries that someone has to get old enough before we think they are acting with an adult maturity and sensitivity to what's happening. How can you deny him adult rights and privileges based upon age, but not to give protection against adult punishment based upon age is inconsistent.

Interview/USA Today, 11-9:(A)13.

Wilbert Tatum
Editor-in-chief and chairman,
"The New York Amsterdam News"

3

[Criticizing the acquittal of Bernhard Goetz, who shot a group of men he claimed threatened him on a New York subway]: [The verdict is] a tragic miscarriage of justice, not so much in terms of the young men [who were shot], but in terms of the fear it has engendered in all of us. There is no question that there is now license

for an open season, and those who would not be criminals will begin to take advantage of it.

The New York Times, 6-18:18.

Anthony P. Travisono
Executive director,
American Correctional Association

4

[Criticizing plans to increase sentences and end parole for many Federal crimes]: They're creating a welfare system by taking men's responsibility away from them. We give them a bed and three squares, and their women and children go on welfare. The state says, "Welcome, we're going to take care of you for the next three or four years." It costs $16,000 a year to keep a man in prison. Prison space should be reserved for the heinous, violent predator. Other people should be dealt with some other way.

The Christian Science Monitor, 4-8:7.

Peter V. Ueberroth
Commissioner of Baseball

5

Each sgement of society has to stand up and say: Illegal drugs are a menace. We don't want them in our whatever—our union, business, school. We don't want anyone around who uses drugs. We think they're vile, vicious, un-American. They cause crimes on our sisters and our brothers. Let's get rid of them. Companies have policies on the most mundane things. You get policies on chiropractors, on dress codes, Christmas giving, all kinds of policies. Here's an item that's ripping the country apart, and business looks the other way. If they find somebody, they quietly fire him and try to avoid a lawsuit. Stick him with somebody else. That's what baseball used to do. If a guy had a problem, teams had a great solution—they'd trade him.

Interview/Esquire, February:78.

John Van de Kamp
Attorney General of California

6

The traditional organizations of the Mafia, or La Cosa Nostra, control a relatively small

(JOHN VAN DE KAMP)

and unimportant part of criminal activity here [in California]. The biggest and fastest-growing threats to public safety in California come from newer forms of organized crime—[Asian gangs that] prey almost exclusively on California's millions of law-abiding Asian citizens and, even more frequently, on the hundreds of thousands of new immigrants who have settled here . . . Unless we send word across the Pacific that this is a dangerous and inhospitable place for gangs to do business, the stage could be set for [a] disaster in California.

San Francisco, July 8/
The New York Times, 7-9:11.

Alexander V. Vlasov
Minister of Internal Affairs
of the Soviet Union

1

The struggle against drug addiction, and the criminal activities that go with it, has moved up to become one of the top priority tasks of the internal forces [in the Soviet Union] . . . No, [we are not punishing] an illness, but those guilty of making themselves ill and of becoming a danger to society by their life-style and behavior, by their illegal activities with narcotics, and by the real threat to their own health and the health of those around them.

Interview/The Washington Post, 1-7:(A)15.

William F. Weld
Assistant Attorney General,
Criminal Division, Department of
Justice of the United States

2

[Saying there is a vast array of safeguards against erroneous executions in capital-

punishment cases]: It is not brutal or unfeeling to conclude that the remote chance of error inherent in any punishment scheme must be weighed against the substantial benefits in terms of protection of society, and innocent lives that reinstitution of the death penalty would bring about.

Feb. 17/
The New York Times, 2-18:13.

William Wilkins
Federal appeals court judge;
Chairman,
Sentencing Commission
of the United States

3

[Calling for mandatory and increased prison sentences for many Federal crimes]: We want to take the two extremities of our justice system, the hanging judge and the Babe Ruth judge, and pull them in together. [Because of] unwarranted disparity [in sentencing], fairness is sometimes lacking.

News conference,
Washington, April 13/
Los Angeles Times, 4-14:(I)18.

Roy L. Williams
Former president,
International Brotherhood
of Teamsters

4

I think that organized crime was filtered into the Teamsters Union a long time before I came there, and it'll be there a long time after I'm gone.

Testimony at racketeering trial, June 1/
The New York Times, 6-2:1.

Defense • The Military

David Abshire
Former United States Ambassador
to the North Atlantic Treaty Organization

1

A war is not likely to start at the nuclear level. As in 1914 and 1939, it would probably start with conventional forces, no doubt with miscalculation and misperception. With Moscow's northern fleet possibly able to dominate the Norwegian Sea, and the Soviet Army's Operational Maneuver Groups with tactics reminiscent of Guderian's in the May 1940 breakthrough with France, there is a military threat of a surprise attack and quick, if limited, victory. Such a threat cannot be deterred with the threat of nuclear weapons when we are significantly less than equal [with the Soviets] at lower nuclear levels. Meeting this new task of deterrence—deterrence at the conventional level—should be at the top of NATO's agenda for the 1990s.

At School of Foreign Service,
Georgetown University, April/
The Wall Street Journal, 6-3:30.

Kenneth L. Adelman
Director, Arms Control and Disarmament
Agency of the United States

2

The Soviets seem far more anxious for an [arms-control] agreement with [U.S. President] Ronald Reagan before he leaves office than I had thought . . . Arms control, by and large, serves Soviet interests far more than it serves our interests, and they have a real stake in having arms control be the centerpiece of U.S.-Soviet relations . . . There will be a tendency [among Western populations] to see the Soviets as a lesser threat because of this arms control. There will be a rush for economic detente to give [Moscow] loans and technology transfer, and all that. In terms of European public opinion, the Europeans now see [Soviet leader Mik-hail] Gorbachev as more eager for peace and arms control than Reagan, which is harmful.

Interview, Washington, Sept. 9/
Los Angeles Times, 9-10:(I)6.

3

If there are a lot of crazy countries in the world that have chemical weapons and have not agreed to ban them, it makes no sense for the United States to give up a deterrent chemical-weapons force . . . The big problem is that this stuff is spreading like wildfire. When the talks [to eliminate chemical weapons] began, there were something like five chemical-weapon states. Now there are 15 to 20 chemical-weapon states.

The New York Times, 11-16:4.

Sergei F. Akhromeyev
Chief, Armed Forces General Staff
of the Soviet Union

4

[On the proposed U.S. space defense system]: . . . we are deeply convinced that creating a space-based ABM defense to cover the territory of the United States would radically step up the military threat toward the Soviet Union. In that case, the United States would have the strategic defense of its territory which, according to the opinion of the U.S. Administration, is intended to defend only the United States from an attack on the part of the Soviet Union. At the same time, the United States would have in its hands the strategic forces capable of delivering a strike against Soviet territory. That is, the United States would have a nuclear sword and a space-based nuclear shield. That means the Soviet Union would also have to equip itself with a nuclear shield, which means an eternal, never-ending arms race. In which case there can be no talk whatsoever about increasing security for both sides.

Interview, Moscow, Oct. 27/
The New York Times, 10-30:4.

57

Georgi A. Arbatov
Director, Soviet Institute
of U.S.A. and Canadian Affairs

1

The whole meaning of [military] force changes now. You can have a lot of military force and you cannot use it. The only size of war where you can be successful is a Grenada-size war; anything bigger creates great problems. All of the intricate military strategies are built on a foundation of illusions, if you really analyze the fundamentals. How can the weapons be used, where does the present trend lead and what is your interest to have a war?

Interview, Moscow/
Los Angeles Times, 5-14:(I)28.

Norman Augustine
Chairman, Defense Science Board

2

It may well be that one can build a financial system based on a service economy, but I feel certain it's not possible to fight a war with a service economy.

Before Senate Defense Industry and Technology
Subcommittee, Washington, March 16/
The Christian Science Monitor, 3-18:20.

Howard H. Baker Jr.
Chief of Staff to President
of the United States Ronald Reagan

3

[On current U.S.-Soviet arms-control talks]: As far as I know, this is the first time they're [the Soviets] willing to talk publicly about short-range [missiles], where they have a huge advantage, because we don't have any. So that's real progress. I really look forward to the pursuit of that branch of arms negotiations. The ultimate objective of the President of the United States is to see the world rid of nuclear weapons, and I therefore welcome this suggestion by the Soviet Union that they're willing to discuss not only strategic weapons, which directly affect us, and intermediate-range weapons, which were thought to be the principal subject of the discussions, and now they're talking about theatre [short-range] weapons . . . This whole thing spells major forward movement between the United States and the Soviet Union that is the basis for optimism that we may be able to have historic progress in this field in the next several months.

To reporters, April 15/
Los Angeles Times, 4-16:(I)15.

4

[President Reagan] would love to have an arms-control agreement [with the Soviets], but he's not afraid to fail. An agreement in his term [of office] is not important. A *good* agreement is important . . . [But] he's not put off by those [in the U.S.] who are apprehensive [about signing an agreement with the Soviets]. He's spent more time rearming America than any President since F.D.R., and he's the most conservative President since Coolidge. And if you can't trust Ronald Reagan on arms control, who can you trust?

Interview, Washington/
The New York Times, 5-12:12.

5

[On the U.S.-Soviet INF arms-control treaty which will come up for a vote by the U.S. Senate]: [The treaty] will be very attractive and very appealing to the vast majority of Senators, [although some conservatives] are very concerned about this treaty or any treaty with the Soviet Union, and many of them are especially concerned about verification [of compliance by the Soviets]. I don't know what particular techniques will be employed to try to remove the concerns of individual Senators, but I remain convinced that, on balance, the value of this treaty and the nature of verification [procedures] make it attractive enough so that it will be ratified by the U.S. Senate.

To reporters, Santa Barbara, Calif., Nov. 25/
The Washington Post, 11-26:(A)51.

Geli Batenin
Spokesman, Ministry of Defense
of the Soviet Union

6

[Criticizing the U.S. for not going along with an 18-month Soviet nuclear-test ban]: A

(GELI BATENIN)

historic chance for ending nuclear tests once and for all has been missed at this stage. It is a matter of deep regret that the United States Administration considered it possible to continue its own nuclear-test program and stage two explosions already this year, totally ignoring the wishes of the world public. Washington's irresponsible policy has placed before us the need to terminate the unilateral moratorium.

News conference, Moscow, Feb. 26/
The New York Times, 2-27:3.

Perrin Beatty
Minister of Defense of Canada

1

The strategic threat in the north is continuing to grow. The Soviets are producing submarines at the rate of one, say, every five weeks . . . many of them nuclear. They have the largest nuclear fleet in the world. They've demonstrated their ability to go under ice. This year we expect them to deploy both subsonic and supersonic versions of submarine-launched cruise missiles with an operational range of about 2,500 miles. Now, by penetrating deeply into our north, certainly all of Canada and a significant portion of the strategic spots in the United States could be brought within range.

Interview, Ottawa/
The Christian Science Monitor, 3-23:9.

Joseph R. Biden, Jr.
United States Senator, D-Delaware;
Candidate for the 1988
Democratic Presidential nomination

2

[Criticizing the proposed U.S. space defense system]: We cannot succumb to [those] who would pull a "Star Wars" cover over our heads—a modern Maginot Line—ravaging our economic capital, nuclearizing the heavens and yielding the fate of our children's world to the malfunction of a computer.

Announcing his candidacy for President,
Wilmington, Del., June 9/
Los Angeles Times, 6-10:(I)16.

Zbigniew Brzezinski
Professor of government,
Columbia University; Former Assistant
to the President of the United States
(Jimmy Carter) for National Security Affairs

3

. . . the SDI [the proposed U.S. space defense system] has been an important negotiating leverage [in arms-control talks between the U.S. and the Soviet Union]. This point is now conceded, even by some of the critics of the SDI. The Soviets have learned that it simply does not pay to attack the SDI head on, and therefore they're trying to create a context in which the domestic opposition to the SDI [in the U.S.] will attempt to scuttle the program on the ground that arms-control progress makes new strategic programs less necessary. In general, I think it is useful to recall that in the last several years the Soviets have on several occasions aborted negotiations, and then they came back once convinced of U.S. firmness. It is a good lesson to remember.

Los Angeles Times, 3-10:(II)5.

4

The Soviets over the years have made hay by proposing a nuclear-free zone in Europe, which is part of the effort to denuclearize Europe. I think we could score political points and emphasize the linkage between battlefield nuclear weapons and conventional forces by proposing that any reduction in battlefield nuclear weapons be tied immediately to a large and symmetrical reduction in tank forces of both sides, because it is the massed tank formations that pose the greatest threat of a sudden conventional attack.

To reporters/
The Christian Science Monitor, 6-25:5.

5

I think the Soviet Union would like a breathing spell, and part of that breathing spell is to reach arms-control agreements with us. However, the Soviets are essentially in favor of limited agreements, which are portrayed by the mass media in the West as comprehensive agreements, thereby resulting in a widespread

(ZBIGNIEW BRZEZINSKI)

impression that the Cold War is over. This is why I favor a policy by the United States which is designed to smoke [Soviet leader Mikhail] Gorbachev out. . . . Offer him comprehensive accommodation. Couple the INF agreement with proposals regarding significant conventional [forces] reduction in Europe . . . We should propose openly the neutralization of Afghanistan . . . If Gorbachev were to buy such a wider package, it would be an indication that he was interested in more than a breathing spell.

Interview/USA Today, 11-3:(A)11.

Dale Bumpers
United States Senator, D-Arkansas;
Candidate for the 1988
Democratic Presidential nomination

1

If we insist on spurring our technological horses still faster toward an ever-receding mirage of strategic security, we will ultimately find ourselves with a thin glitzy exterior shielding a hollow interior of economic chaos.

At Columbia University, March 2/
The Washington Post, 3-5:(A)26.

George Bush
Vice President of the United States

2

[Supporting the proposed U.S. space defense system]: Maybe not in the short term, but in the long term, SDI will be, in my view, an effective deterrent. Isn't it better, as we move forward in the nuclear age, to put weapons at risk, not people?

At U.S. Naval Academy commencement,
May 20/Los Angeles Times, 5-21:(I)13.

George Bush
Vice President of the United States;
Candidate for the 1988
Republican Presidential nomination

3

Today we are on the verge of an historic arms agreement with the Soviets. It didn't come cheap, and it didn't come easy. If this treaty is finalized, we will, for the first time in the nuclear age, actually reduce—not just limit, but reduce—the number of nuclear weapons in the world. It is a new beginning—and it was born of the stability and strength we [the U.S.] have shown for nearly seven years.

At Linn-Mar High School, Cedar Rapids, Iowa,
Oct. 13/The New York Times, 10-14:16.

4

[On the proposed U.S.-Soviet arms-control treaty that would eliminate all land-based intermediate-range nuclear missiles in Europe]: This is the first time in the nuclear age that we are getting rid of an entire generation of nuclear weapons, and that's good for my grandchildren and good for the rest of the world. I'm for it, the President's [Reagan] for it, the Joint Chiefs are for it, and I don't see why you can't say, hey, if it's verifiable, it's a good idea to get rid of 1,600 warheads from the Soviet Union for 400 of ours, and then go on to do what I said, work on conventional forces, work on chemical weapons.

Broadcast debate among Republican
Presidential candidates, Houston/
"Firing Line," PBS-TV, 10-28.

Robert C. Byrd
United States Senator,
D-West Virginia

5

[On the proposed U.S.-Soviet arms-control treaty that will come up for U.S. Senate ratification]: I encourage the [Reagan] Administration not to rush to conclusion of the negotiations, but to close all possible loopholes, to secure the very best arrangements possible and not to be rushed by the impending summit schedule [when Soviet leader Mikhail Gorbachev visits Washington]. Summits can come and go, but we will have to live with a treaty far beyond the time when the memories of the Reagan-Gorbachev summit, or even of the Reagan Presidency, have faded . . . The country is likely to get a razzle-dazzle selling job from this unlikely political duet, but we should keep in mind that it is not the song that matters, but the

(ROBERT C. BYRD)

black-and-white text of the document to which these leaders put their signatures.

Before the Senate, Washington, Dec. 2/
Los Angeles Times, 12-3:(I)1,12.

Frank C. Carlucci
Secretary of Defense-designate
of the United States

1

Without having had a chance to study it thoroughly, obviously I think we may well be talking about a smaller military force. I would rather have a smaller force that is effective, and that has the necessary equipment, the necessary ammunition, the necessary personnel, than to have a larger structure that is not effective.

At Senate Armed Services Committee hearing
on his confirmation, Washington, Nov. 12/
The New York Times 11-13:11.

Lawton Chiles
United States Senator, D-Florida

2

If the Congress and the President [Reagan] want more defense spending, we will have to raise the money to get it. If the revenues don't go up to pay for the extra defense spending, the level of defense spending doesn't go up, either. I think this is a fair way to get things done.

Washington, May 5/
Los Angeles Times, 5-6:(I)29.

Jacques Chirac
Premier of France

3

These [Soviet-U.S.] negotiations, in which we [French] have not taken part . . . will, it seems, permit a reduction in the number of intermediate-range missiles in Europe. So much the better. But I do not want us to move toward the illusion that an important step has been taken in security matters. What is important is

to reduce the large central arsenals that threaten the world.

Bordeaux, France, Sept. 18/
Los Angeles Times, 9-19:(I)11.

William E. Colby
Board member, Committee
for National Security; Former Director
of Central Intelligence of the United States

4

[On verification of Soviet adherence to proposed arms treaties]: I think it important to have a clear understanding of the purpose of verification. It is not to give us evidence to use in a court of law against the Soviets, but rather to protect our country against surprise . . . With respect to verification, it is important to understand how much is necessary . . . Our challenge is to ensure verification adequate to protect our national security without demanding so much that we shoot ourselves in the foot. As the President [Reagan] himself has admitted, there will never be any such thing as "absolute" verification—and there need not be.

Before Senate Foreign Relations Committee,
Washington, Jan. 15/
The Washington Post, 1-21:(A)20.

Alan Cranston
United States Senator, D-California

5

The [War Powers] Act has been a failure. It has not prevented Presidents from pursuing risky military adventures before enlisting Congressional support. It has not facilitated unity between the Legislative and Executive branches.

Los Angeles Times, 10-26:(I)10.

Mario M. Cuomo
Governor of New York (D)

6

[On the U.S.-Soviet INF arms-control treaty recently agreed to by President Reagan and Soviet leader Mikhail Gorbachev]: Now is the time to hold INF in some kind of escrow until we can get agreements that really matter:

(MARIO M. CUOMO)

START, which goes to cutting missiles aimed at us directly, and conventional forces, where the imbalance is great. I'd agree with Gorbachev on INF, shake his hand and sign the deal—but I wouldn't submit it to the Senate for ratification until we're pretty sure we've got the other agreements in hand. I know how popular it would be to make this deal and destroy that first missile on TV, but that's not leadership. And I suspect Reagan is making the deal now for his legacy, and that if he had another term, he'd hang back just as I'm suggesting. This is the point at which I'd play hardball.

Interview, Albany, N.Y./
U.S. News & World Report, 12-14:20.

George Deukmejian
Governor of California (R)

1

Ultimately, the freedom of the United States depends on our ability to defend ourselves and our allies. A strong defense requires personnel, equipment, determination—and money. Waste must be eliminated, but strength must not.

Before Heritage Foundation, Washington,
Nov.17/Los Angeles Times, 11-18:(I)27.

John D. Dingell
United States Representative,
D-Michigan

2

One must inquire . . . whether the Pentagon is more interested in procuring new systems than having ones that work. This says to me that [the Pentagon] can't seem to control the procurement system either as to price or performance. They can't seem to correct abuses even when they are pointed out to them. They are extraordinarily secretive about failures to meet deadlines and contract dates . . . They are more interested in looking out for the contractor than they are in the performance of the weapons system.

The Washington Post, 9-25:(A)10.

Robert J. Dole
United States Senator, R-Kansas;
Candidate for the 1988
Republican Presidential nomination

3

[On the proposed U.S. space defense system]: . . . SDI is not a stumbling block to arms control. And it should be more evident, to the thoughtful, that the continued vigorous pursuit of SDI is vital—vital to the prospects for a good strategic-arms-control agreement, vital to the security of America in the 1990s and beyond . . . We can't just give it away, or bargain it away, or legislate it away . . . There is no higher priority than preserving the promise, and the prospect, of SDI.

Interview/The Washington Post, 6-13:(A)13.

4

[On critics of President Reagan, on both the left and right, regarding his arms-control policies, and the new U.S.-Soviet INF agreement which some conservatives do not want]: Ronald Reagan deserves every ounce of credit he is getting. He deserves an apology, too, from his liberal critics, who have been castigating him for seven years for being "anti-arms control." Ronald Reagan deserves a personal apology from a few gadflies on the right fringe—who owe what little political profile they have to this President and who ought to be profoundly ashamed of themselves for their attacks on a great President.

At Gannett-USA Today meeting, Washington,
Dec. 7/Los Angeles Times, 12-8:(I)27.

Allen Drury
Author; Former journalist

5

I think that, inevitably, our military machine has become very important, not only to us but to many other nations around the world. Either because they're for it, or depend upon it, or are opposed to it. And that's why I think that, gradually, there's come this increase in power, plus the fact that the Pentagon has become very important to Congress. Every time the Pentagon has a project, it has to be in somebody's dis-

(ALLEN DRURY)

trict, somebody's state, employing somebody's constituents, giving them some benefit politically, so that means that this very incestuous relationship has developed over the years.

Interview/USA Today, 1-7:(A)9.

Yuri V. Dubinin
Soviet Ambassador to the United States

1

[On the "zero-zero" option for nuclear missiles in Europe]: There are all kinds of conditions that turn these zeros into spiked zeros . . . For example, the question of nuclear warheads for West German missiles. Well, what is the right of West Germans to demand nuclear warheads? They are American, and how [can you] leave these American nuclear warheads in Europe and speak about zero?

Interview, Washington, June 16/
Los Angeles Times, 6-17:(I)10.

Michael S. Dukakis
Governor of Massachusetts (D);
Candidate for the 1988
Democratic Presidential nomination

2

We need a strong nuclear deterrent. We have a strong nuclear deterrent. But we also need strong conventional forces if we are serious about reducing the chance of nuclear war, because conventional weakness invites conventional war, because conflict anywhere is potentially conflict everywhere, and because conventional war can escalate into nuclear war.

Before Dallas Democratic Forum, Nov. 13/
The Washington Post, 11-14:(A)3.

3

Between us and the Soviet Union there are 50,000 nuclear warheads or weapons out there. In the last six-and-a-half years, a greater and greater percentage of the defense budget has gone to nuclear warfare in a time when most people agree that if we have to use military force in the future it's much more likely that it

will be conventional, not nuclear . . . Taking out those [nuclear] weapons systems will be required to stabilize the defense budget.

Interview/Mother Jones, December:50.

Edwin B. Firmage
Professor of law, University of Utah

4

Both the Americans and the Soviets fear chemical weapons. Chemical weapons present a danger because they're cheap and easy to produce—they can be a poor man's monster weapon.

The New York Times, 11-20:4.

Gerald R. Ford
Former President of the United States

5

[President Reagan] certainly has taken some steps in diplomacy that could lead to a constructive negotiation between the United States and the Soviet Union on nuclear weapons . . . I only hope the momentum we see will not result in a bad agreement. Sometimes momentum gets people to make concessions that, in retrospect, they wish they hadn't made. But I trust that President Reagan and his advisers will be firm in what is essential, primarily in the verification area.

Interview/
U.S. News & World Report, 12-7:33.

J. William Fulbright
Former United States Senator,
D-Arkansas

6

[Saying the U.S.-Soviet ABM Treaty strictly prohibits testing and development of such defensive systems as President Reagan's proposed space defense system]: Neither the President [at the time of the signing of the treaty in 1972], the Secretary of State, nor any of the President's arms-control advisers suggested that the treaty would permit development, testing and deployment of antiballistic missiles in space or under any technology not then exist-

(J. WILLIAM FULBRIGHT)

ing. The treaty was understood to represent a commitment—a permanent commitment—to security based on the strategic principle of mutual deterrence.

At joint hearing of Senate Judiciary and Foreign Relations Committees, Washington, March 11/The Christian Science Monitor, 3-12:3.

John R. Galvin
General, United States Army;
Commander-in-Chief, Southern Command;
Supreme Allied Commander/
Europe-designate

1

The United States has to have the capability to project power. We've always had a secure Western Hemisphere, which has allowed us to not worry about our borders and to simply project power, either east or west, in critical situations, like World War I and World War II. If we have an unstable southern border, it will inhibit our ability to do that, and thus it'll inhibit our ability to defend ourselves.

Interview/USA Today, 3-31:(A)9.

Richard A. Gephardt
United States Representative, D-Missouri;
Candidate for the 1988
Democratic Presidential nomination

2

In pursuit of arms, the [Reagan Administration] has busted the budget of the United States. They have broken the back of American agriculture and many a basic industry . . . Is there an ounce more of security in a nation of rusting plants that once produced tons of rubber and steel? Is there security in a nation whose green fields are turning to dust?

Speech, Iowa, April 24/
The Washington Post, 4-25:(A)6.

3

The Democratic [Presidential] nominee cannot be against every new [U.S.] weapons sys-

tem and earn the trust of the American people. If that is our posture, we don't deserve to win the Presidency.

At American University, Washington, Sept. 25/ The New York Times, 9-26:10.

Albert Gore, Jr.
United States Senator, D-Tennessee;
Candidate for the 1988
Democratic Presidential nomination

4

We have never known anything but a nuclear arms race. When we were born, it was at the beginning of the nuclear age. We have watched as that arms race has gone from a handful of weapons to more than 30,000 weapons. We've moved from a world with one nuclear power to 10 or 12 nuclear powers, with the prospect of many more. We have watched as the nation's outlook on the future has changed from extreme optimism at the end of World War II to a quality of pessimism now that is different from anything that came previously in American history.

To reporters/
The Christian Science Monitor, 5-18:32.

Mikhail S. Gorbachev
General Secretary,
Communist Party of the Soviet Union

5

If an [East-West] agreement were reached on medium-range missiles [in Europe]—and I am confident that it is possible—this would be of tremendous political significance. Until now, only the process of armament was under way, but in this case disarmament would start. It would create an atmosphere of greater trust . . . We would like an agreement on medium-range missiles to stimulate talks on strategic-arms reduction linked with non-withdrawal from the anti-ballistic-missile treaty, to prompt the opening of talks on conventional armaments and armed forces, to speed progress in the elimination of chemical weapons. It would also im-

(MIKHAIL S. GORBACHEV)

prove psychologically the prospect of settling regional conflicts.

At meeting with Iceland's Prime Minister
Steingrimur Hermannsson, Moscow,
March 2/Los Angeles Times, 3-3:(I)6.

1

Our principle is simple: All weapons must be limited and reduced, and those of wholesale annihilation eventually scrapped. Should we have any balance to redress, we must redress it, not by letting the one short of some elements build them up, but by having the one with more of them scale them down. The historic goal before us, that of a demilitarized world, will have to be achieved stage by stage, of course. In each phase there must definitely be respect for mutual interests and a balance of reasonable sufficiency constantly declining. Everybody must realize and agree: Parity in the potential to destroy one another several times over is madness and absurdity.

At "For a Nuclear-Free World,
For the Survival of Humanity" forum, Moscow,
Feb. 16/The Christian Science Monitor, 3-18:14.

2

[On those in the West who are calling for change in the Soviet system as well as arms reduction]: We propose dismantling the entire system of weapons of mass annihilation and reducing other weapons to the level of sensible sufficiency. In response, we are being offered a dismantling of a social system—our system. The absurdity of this "dilemma" does not even deserve refutation.

At luncheon for Indian
Prime Minister Rajiv Gandhi, Moscow,
July 3/Los Angeles Times, 7-4:(I)3.

3

Some time back, the sides [the U.S. and the Soviet Union] had several scores of atomic bombs apiece. Then each came to possess hundreds of nuclear missiles and, finally, the arsenals grew to include several thousands of nuclear warheads. Not so long ago, Soviet and

American scientists . . . arrived at the unanimous conclusion that 95 per cent of all nuclear arms of the U.S.A. and the U.S.S.R. can be eliminated without stability being disrupted. This is a killing argument against the "nuclear deterrence" strategy.

Sept. 16/Los Angeles Times, 9-17:(I)14.*

4

As long as there is a danger of war and as long as the drive for social revanchism forms the core of Western strategies and militarist programs, we shall continue to do everything necessary to maintain our defense capability at a level ruling out imperialism's military superiority over socialism.

Speech, Moscow, Nov. 2/
The Washington Post, 11-3:(A)26.

5

[On the proposed U.S. development of a space defense system]: Practically, the Soviet Union is doing all the United States is doing, and I guess we are engaged in research, basic research, which relates to these aspects which are covered by the SDI of the United States. But we will not build an SDI, we will not deploy SDI, and we call upon the United States to act likewise.

American broadcast interview,
Moscow, Nov. 28/NBC-TV, 11-30.

6

Yesterday, the President of your country [U.S. President Reagan] and I signed a treaty eliminating a whole class—to be more precise, two classes—of nuclear arms. As a result, the world will be rid of a total of some 2,000 deadly warheads. The number is not all that big, but the treaty's significance goes far beyond its specific content. We regard it as a start in implementing the program of building a nuclear-free world, which I proposed on behalf of the Soviet leadership and the Soviet people almost two years ago, on January 15, 1986. Since then, I have been asked many times whether I continue to believe in the feasibility

(MIKHAIL S. GORBACHEV)

of that program. My answer is yes, I most certainly do.

*At U.S. State Department luncheon
in his honor, Washington, Dec. 9/
The Washington Post, 12-10:(A)32.*

Giovanni Goria
Prime Minister of Italy

1

The peace of the world has been maintained for the last 30 years through preserving a [strategic military balance between East and West]. To break such a balance—or, more importantly, to lead one side or the other to fear that this might be about to happen—would almost inevitably be a step backward in the effort to keep the peace and pursue disarmament. So we must keep balance as our central goal. It is, of course, essential that the United States and its allies be absolutely determined to do everything necessary to assure their defense. But at the same time we must keep balance as a central goal.

*Interview, Washington, Dec. 15/
The New York Times, 12-16:3.*

Alfred M. Gray, Jr.
*General and Commandant,
United States Marine Corps*

2

I believe the nation expects us [the Marines] to be the premier force in readiness and preparedness. They expect us to be warriors. I think the nation loves our Marine Corps, and I think they pray for us and they support us. But they also place some very special demands on us, and one is that we be the premier military organization in the world. I'm not sure if we're that good, but that's exactly where we're going to go if we aren't.

*To reporters, Washington, Aug. 12/
Los Angeles Times, 8-13:(I)33.*

3

I don't think [Marine] boot camp is tough enough. [The Marine of the future is] going to

be a tough guy. He's going to be what his idea of a Marine was in the first place . . . what he joined to be . . . This nation desperately needs at least one outfit that can call themselves truly military professionals.

USA Today, 11-27:(A)2.

Andrei A. Gromyko
President of the Soviet Union

4

The aim of the Soviet proposals in this field [arms control] is for nuclear arms never to be used, and this requires that nuclear arms be destroyed. In reply, all sorts of maneuvers are being undertaken [by the U.S.] with the aim of sidestepping the solution of burning issues. All this shows that at present the American [Reagan] Administration apparently does not have serious intentions to search for accords.

*To U.S. Ambassador to the Soviet Union
Jack Matlock, Moscow, April 6/
The Washington Post, 4-7:(A)13.*

Alexander M. Haig, Jr.
*Former Secretary of State
of the United States; Candidate for the 1988
Republican Presidential nomination*

5

[Saying the pending U.S.-Soviet INF arms-control treaty weakens deterrence]: For the United States and its allies to deter Soviet aggression, we need the forces, nuclear and conventional, here and in Europe, to convince the Kremlin that a challenge can be met across the spectrum of force.

*Before World Affairs Council, Washington,
Nov. 16/The Washington Post, 11-17:(A)4.*

Gary Hart
*Former United States Senator, D-Colorado;
Candidate for the 1988
Democratic Presidential nomination*

6

The American people, in this day and age—given the Soviet Union, the Warsaw Pact, given challenges around the world—are not going to

(GARY HART)

vote into office a bunch of people that they think will not defend the country. [Former Senator George McGovern's] hatred of the Vietnam war led him to use language that led other people to believe that he didn't care about defending the country. So it began to evolve in my own mind during that period, and after I came here, that as you advocated reduction in reliance on nuclear weapons, you had to advocate something in the area of conventional forces.

The Washington Post, 1-20:(A)6.

Gary Hart
Former United States Senator, D-Colorado;
Former candidate for the 1988
Democratic Presidential nomination

1

[Saying the U.S. spends too much on the military and not enough on the economy]: What if America awakens one day with a larger nuclear stockpile [than the Soviets], but the Soviet Union has better laboratories, steel mills, machine-tool factories, schools and research centers, agriculture production, biomedical innovation, superconductor technology and public services for its citizens? Consider, if you will, that the U.S. might continue blindly on its present course of excessive nuclear armament, travelling alone and pointlessly down a blind alley of history, and ending up militarily muscle-bound, uncompetitive in industry, agriculture or technology, irrelevant to the world of the 21st century—and broke.

Before Philadelphia World Affairs Council,
Sept. 10/Los Angeles Times, 9-11:(I)30.

Denis Healey
Foreign-affairs spokesman,
Labor Party of Britain

2

[Supporting a Soviet arms-control offer to remove medium-and short-range missiles from Europe]: We stand at an historic turning point. The striking thing is that the Soviet Union is offering to give up [military] strength that the

West doesn't have . . . Compared to the alternative, the Soviet offer is the best . . . [For the West] to turn it down . . . seems perverse in the extreme.

News conference, Moscow, May 12/
Los Angeles Times, 5-13:(I)8.

Jesse Helms
United States Senator,
R-North Carolina

3

The Senate needs to wake up and smell the coffee—America is in gravest mortal danger and we should abrogate the ABM treaty [because it is] impeding our ability to defend our supreme national interests. [As for SDI,] deployment is the name of the game, and it is absolutely essential to American national security.

Before the Senate, Washington/
The Washington Post, 4-13:(A)8.

4

The rapid deployment of this [SDI space defense] system is the best hope for our country to deter Soviet nuclear blackmail in the near term. While the Soviets are violating the key provisions of the ABM Treaty, the [U.S.] Congress is *de facto* binding the President [Reagan] to an excessively restrictive interpretation of the treaty. This decision is unilateral disarmament in which international law is being misinterpreted and used as a red flag fig leaf for appeasement of Russia.

Los Angeles Times, 11-20:(I)15.

Geoffrey Howe
Foreign Secretary of the United Kingdom

5

The harsh facts of life—geography and Soviet advantages in conventional and chemical forces—make nuclear deterrence indispensable for the forseeable future to the security of the West, and of Western Europe in particular.

Brussels, April 16/
The Christian Science Monitor, 4-17:9.

67

Fred C. Ikle
Under Secretary for Policy,
Department of Defense
of the United States

1

Nearly every war in this century . . . was preceded by years of a growing crisis or, at least, was not decided in the first campaign. Hence, industrial mobilization—if launched soon enough—could make a big difference. Early in the first Reagan Administration, Secretary [of Defense Caspar] Weinberger therefore decided that the Defense Department had to improve its preparations for a production surge. We have since worked this issue quietly and tested our progress in several exercises.

Before Society of Manufacturing Engineers,
Nov. 9/The Washington Post, 11-11:(A)22.

J. Bennett Johnson
United States Senator, D-Louisiana

2

[On Defense Secretary Caspar Weinberger]: To try and get information out of Weinberger at a hearing is one of the great challenges of being in Washington.

USA Today, 1-16:(A)4.

Victor Karpov
Chief Soviet negotiator
at arms-control talks in Geneva

3

There are more and more signs that the United States does not actually want the elimination of medium-range missiles in Europe. [Their so-called] "zero option" was a bluff from the very start . . . An agreement on the elimination of Euromissiles can be prepared in the course of three, four or five to six months at most. But this takes the wish and good-will from both sides. We are prepared to eliminate all of our medium-range missiles in Europe, to scrap all the SS-20s, whose number is 243, together with their launching pads . . . [The Soviet Union has] a stake in the agreement becoming a real contribution to European security. But, if instead of that, they wish to palm

off on us a scrap of paper as a cover for the preservation of the U.S. nuclear potential in Europe, we will not agree to that.

Interview/The Washington Post, 3-23:(A)1,14.

Jack Kemp
United States Representative,
R-New York; Candidate for the 1988
Republican Presidential nomination

4

The Soviets approach arms control much the same way [pop artist] Andy Warhol approached art: anything you can get away with.

Newsweek, 3-16:17.

5

Too many in this [Reagan] Administration have taken the easy way out, of over-selling arms control [with the Soviets] and fostering false hopes about the eventual abolition of nuclear weapons. And Europeans have indulged in pro-arms-control rhetoric to appease peace movements . . . If [Soviet leader Mikhail] Gorbachev truly were sincere about reducing international tensions . . . then we should see this change reflected in Soviet foreign policy. Instead, Soviet aggression continues. Soviet espionage has become more brazen and Soviet terrorism and subversion more widespread . . . If we sign a new INF treaty, we will be issuing a warrant of respectability for Gorbachev. We will be helping the Soviets hide behind arms control while they are embarked on aggression throughout the world.

Before Heritage Foundation, Washington,
May 22/Los Angeles Times, 5-23:(I)26.

Edward M. Kennedy
United States Senator,
D-Massachusetts

6

The question is not whether it would be nice to have two more [aircraft] carriers. The question is where do we hurt the most as a nation. We're probably hurting more in our land forces.

The Washington Post, 3-16:(A)6.

John Kerry
United States Senator,
D-Massachusetts

1

Whether or not people were for or against [U.S. involvement in the Vietnam war], I'm sure we have very similar views about how America ought to make judgements about putting soldiers into places of risk. I think a universal theme for all of us would be: Don't ever put soldiers in that position again, asking them to make those sacrifices without guaranteeing that you're going to follow through and give them the capacity to win.

The New York Times, 5-28:12.

Henry A. Kissinger
Former Secretary of State
of the United States

2

[On the progress toward a European INF arms-control agreement between the U.S. and the Soviet Union]: I think this agreement will be seen as the beginning of a disassociation between Europe and the United States. It does not reduce the danger to Europe; it does not improve the military situation.

U.S. News & World Report, 9-7:31.

Helmut Kohl
Chancellor of West Germany

3

I am prepared to say today that when all Soviet and American missiles [in Europe] are finally scrapped, then the [West German] *Pershing* 1A missiles will not be modernized, but rather destroyed.

Aug. 26/USA Today, 8-27:(A)4.

John F. Lehman, Jr.
Secretary of the Navy
of the United States

4

Running an operation like this [Navy contracting] is just like flying a helicopter. You can't put it on autopilot. If you do, it is going to

go into a crash. Management has to be day-to-day, not micromanagement, but a steady firm hand by the senior executive. And if you start neglecting it, or take a holiday, or turn it over to the Office of the Secretary of Defense, or something like that, we can slip back into the problems of the past.

Interview, Washington/
The New York Times, 3-11:28.

John F. Lehman, Jr.
Former Secretary of the Navy
of the United States

5

[On criticism of aircraft carriers]: The critics argue that "if you buy a carrier, you've got to buy all these frigates and cruisers to protect it." Actually, the truth is what the Falklands War illustrated—that it is genuinely the reverse: You buy the carriers to protect everything else. You have to have frigates, destroyers and cruisers to do naval tasks—hunting submarines, convoying, and the like. But you need the carrier for a dome of air superiority over the whole surface fleet.

Interview/U.S. News & World Report, 6-15:28.

Ronald F. Lehman
United States arms-control negotiator;
Former Deputy Assistant Secretary
of Defense of the United States

6

On the nuclear testing issue, we have made it absolutely clear for many years to the Soviet Union that the conditions for a comprehensive test-ban treaty are not at hand. Instead of responding with acceptance of that situation, the Soviets responded by proposing a [nuclear-test] moratorium which they knew we would not accept. They were trying to influence public opinion, because it's a complex issue that's not easy to explain to the public.

Interview/USA Today, 3-12:(A)9.

James A. McClure
United States Senator, R-Idaho

7

[Expressing reservations about President Reagan's INF arms-control treaty negotiated

WHAT THEY SAID IN 1987

(JAMES A. McCLURE)

with the Soviet Union]: We still have a lot of faith in Reagan but there is a lot of distrust of the negotiating process, a feeling that it leads to concessions that are unwise . . . a problem that is almost endemic to any Presidency. It's not so much INF . . . but what's next.

The Washington Post, 11-25:(A)15.

John Moore
Captain, British Navy (Ret.);
Editor, "Jane's" (naval reference book)

1

The Soviet Navy has introduced four classes of nuclear attack submarines [since 1976], all with higher speeds than the [U.S.] Los Angeles [class], at least three with an increased diving depth, all with a far higher power density and a much superior armament. There has been little basic change in American attack submarine affairs during the last 15 years. Because of conformism, conservatism and complacency, the U.S. Navy will not have a radically new design of submarine at sea until 1994 . . . It is willful self-deception to ignore the possibility that there is today at sea a [Soviet] submarine of tremendous power, of considerable silence, and propelled not by a propeller but by skate-like ripple of water.

Los Angeles Times, 8-20:(I)5.

Edward C. Myers
General (ret.) and former Chief of Staff,
United States Army

2

As you go into a budget freeze or a budget decrease, the [military] services immediately start feeding on each other like a pack of piranhas. What you need is, one, a Secretary of Defense who is willing to put his foot down and prioritize and get the most out of the resources we have; and, two, a Secretary who is willing to work with Congress and not stonewall consistently as [retiring Defense Secretary Caspar Weinberger] did.

Interview/The New York Times, 11-6:10.

Sam Nunn
United States Senator, D-Georgia

3

[Criticizing the Reagan Administration's quantitative method of comparing U.S. and Soviet military strength, saying that method exaggerates the Soviets' relative power]: These superficial net assessments continue to be presented in isolation from the myriad of other factors that must be considered when assessing our relative capabilities . . . By portraying tanks against tanks and artillery tubes against artillery tubes, these assessments suggest that our strategy is to pit strength against strength on a quantitative basis.

At Senate Armed Services Committee hearing,
Washington, Jan. 12/
Los Angeles Times, 1-13:(I)7.

4

We've got too many weapons systems being produced, and we're not producing any of . . . them at efficient rates. When you take all the coffee-pot [overcharge] scandals and all the hammers [that were overcharged for] and all those things we read about, and multiply them by 10,000, you don't have the kind of waste in dollars that you do when you stretch too many weapons systems . . . That's where the real waste and fat is.

Los Angeles Times, 1-19:(II)5.

Joseph S. Nye, Jr.
Professor of international affairs,
Harvard University

5

One of the troubles in assessing the threat of nuclear proliferation is deciding just what it is that you're talking about—capabilities, intentions, legal determinations or political situations. The non-proliferation treaty itself approaches things in an all-or-nothing way that's almost like virginity: once lost, it's lost forever. In reality, there are many steps, even after a country has conducted a nuclear explosion, that affect the ultimate questions of whether there's a likeli-

(JOSEPH S. NYE, JR.)

hood of a nuclear arms race or a likelihood of weapons being used.

Interview/
U.S. News & World Report, 3-23:35.

Phyllis Oakley
Spokeswoman for the Department
of State of the United States

1

[On the U.S. refusal to go along with an 18-month Soviet nuclear-test ban]: As we have said before, when the Soviets choose to resume nuclear testing is their decision. The U.S. position on nuclear testing is clear. As long as we depend on nuclear weapons for our security, we must insure that those weapons are safe, secure, reliable and effective. This demands some level of underground nuclear testing, as permitted by existing treaties.

Washington, Feb. 26/
The New York Times, 2-27:3.

David Packard
Co-founder, Hewlett-Packard Company;
Former Deputy Secretary of Defense
of the United States

2

[Supporting development of the U.S. space defense system]: The policy of "mutual assured destruction" is not a very attractive way to live, and I think there's every reason to try to find a better approach. The reason there is opposition to "Star Wars" is that many people think we're spending too much on defense, and they think if we make a commitment to "Star Wars," it's going to cost some damn billion dollars more on top of everything else. The whole "Star Wars" concept, I think, is not very thoroughly understood. We're getting to the point where nuclear blackmail is a real possibility. There may be a real justification for a defense against that situation. I think it would be a big mistake to worry about a few billion dollars and cut back "Star Wars."

Interview/
Los Angeles Times Magazine, 2-22:24.

Richard N. Perle
Assistant Secretary for International
Security Policy, Department
of Defense of the United States

3

The verification of an agreement [with the Soviets] to abolish all nuclear weapons is not difficult, or very difficult: It is impossible. What Western leader would turn in his country's last remaining nuclear weapon on the strength of assurances—mere words—that the Soviets had done the same?

At meeting of NATO representatives,
Munich, West Germany/
The Washington Post, 2-5:(A)23.

4

Arms control so easily becomes an incantation rather than policy. To get good agreements, you have to be prepared to resist bad ones because it's easier to get bad arms-control agreements. It is easy to mistake insistence on a good agreement for opposition to any agreement. It is much too easy to equate arms-control agreements with peace, and the fervor with which one desires them with the desire for peace itself. We have underestimated our capacity to bring the Russians into a more stabilized regime because [U.S.] Administrations in the past have been so keen to get any agreement.

Interview/The New York Times, 3-13:12.

Ronald Reagan
President of the United States

5

I have become convinced that the only way we can bring our adversaries to the bargaining table for arms reduction is to give them a reason to negotiate while at the same time fulfilling our responsibility to our citizens and allies to provide an environment safe and secure from aggression. We have built our defense capabilities back toward levels more in accord with today's requirements for security. Modest and sustained growth in defense funding will be required to consolidate the real gains we have made.

Budget message to Congress, Washington,
Jan.5*/The New York Times, 1-6:10.

WHAT THEY SAID IN 1987

(RONALD REAGAN)

1

[On his proposed space defense system]: SDI truly serves the purposes of offensive-weapons reduction. SDI can help us move toward a safer world. I have repeatedly pledged that SDI capabilities will never be used for offensive purposes. Like an effectively verifiable arms-reduction agreement with which all parties comply, SDI can reduce the risk of war and the threat of ballistic missiles to mankind. It can reduce the danger of accidental warfare and give us the kind of insurance policy we need against violations of a future arms-reduction treaty. And it has been a singularly effective instrument for bringing the Soviets to the bargaining table.

Washington, March 23*/
The Washington Post, 3-24:(A)26.

2

It is the fact that NATO was willing to deploy its own . . . missiles while simultaneously seeking a balanced and verifiable arms-reduction agreement that brought the Soviets back to the negotiating table in 1985 and gave us the opportunity to achieve—for the first time in history—deep reductions in, and possibly the elimination of, an entire class of nuclear weapons.

Venice, Italy, June 4*/
Los Angeles Times, 6-5:(I)14.

3

I hesitate to make optimistic statements. Always have. But at the same time I can't deny that I believe there is an increased opportunity for a [U.S.-Soviet] summit conference, and an increased opportunity for actual reductions of armaments, particularly of the nuclear kind . . . [Soviet leader Mikhail Gorbachev] is the first Soviet leader in my memory that has ever advocated actually eliminating weapons already built and in place.

News Conference, Venice, Italy,
June 11/Los Angeles Times, 6-12:(I)16.

4

We [the U.S. and Soviet Union] can wrap up an [arms-control] agreement on intermediate-range nuclear missiles promptly. We ask ourselves: Are we entering a truly new phase in East-West relations? Is far-reaching, enduring change in the post-war standoff now possible? Surely, these are our hopes.

Speech, Los Angeles/Time, 9-7:12.

5

Any [U.S.-Soviet arms-control] treaty I agree to must provide for effective verification, including on-site inspection of facilities before and during reductions, and short-notice inspections afterward. All in all, the verification regime we have put forward is the most stringent in the history of arms-control negotiations. I will not settle for anything less.

At U.S. Military Academy, West Point, N.Y.,
Oct. 28/The New York Times, 10-29:8.

6

From the Krasnoyarsk radar facility [in Soviet Central Asia], whose very construction violated the 1972 ABM Treaty that the Soviets so vocally claim they want to preserve, to their modernized deployments around Moscow of the world's only ABM system, the Soviet Union's own SDI [space defense] projects have become big news throughout the world in recent months. We know this. They know that we know. We know that they know that we know. It's time for them to stop the charade and admit their own deep involvement in the strategic defense work.

Before American Council
on Life Insurance, Washington, Nov. 16/
Los Angeles Times, 11-17:(I)9.

7

[On retiring Defense Secretary Caspar Weinberger]: When Cap came to this job more than six years ago, the Navy had been permitted to dwindle from more than 1,000 ships to less than 500. There were planes that couldn't fly for lack of spare parts. And our men and women in uniform were seeing their pay in real terms shrink, while pay in the private sector rose. With Caspar Weinberger at the helm, we

(RONALD REAGAN)

turned that around, and today we have a military that is once again ready, able and willing.

At Weinberger's farewell ceremony,
Washington, Nov. 17/
Los Angeles Times, 11-18:(I)15.

1

I cherish no illusions about the Soviets . . . For them, past arms-control treaties were like diets: The second day was always the best, for that's when they broke them.

Before American Council of Life Insurance,
Nov. 18/The Washington Post, 11-23:(A)2.

2

[On criticism of the INF arms-control treaty he has worked out with the Soviet Union]: The objections that we are hearing—and, yes, from some of our own, you might say, [political] allies and own forces [in the Republican Party and the conservative movement]—they are based on a lack of knowledge as to what this treaty contains, and particularly are they ignorant of the advances that have been made in verification [of compliance with the treaty]. I think that some of the people who are objecting the most and just refusing even to accede to the idea of ever getting any understanding—whether they realize it or not, those people, basically down in their deepest thoughts, have accepted that war is inevitable and that there must come to be a war between the two superpowers . . . I haven't changed from the time I made a speech about [the Soviet Union being] an evil empire, and I think I could sum up my own position on this with the recitation of a very brief Russian proverb: "Doveryai no proveryai." It means "trust but verify." And there would be no way that I could sign a treaty just to be signing a treaty, and with my fingers crossed that everything was all right. This is why it is hinged on arriving at solid verification measures and [Soviet] agreement to them.

Interview, Washington, Dec. 3/
Los Angeles Times, 12-5:(I)12;
The New York Times, 12-4:10.

Charles E. Redman
Spokesman for the Department
of State of the United States

3

We view the growing number of proposals for regional nuclear-free zones as having the potential to undermine the policy of deterrence which has been the cornerstone of Western security since World War II. A proliferation of such zones in the Free World, unmatched by disarmament in the Soviet Bloc, is clearly detrimental to Western security.

Washington, Feb. 5/
Los Angeles Times, 2-6:(I)5.

Rozanne Ridgway
Assistant Secretary for European and
Canadian Affairs, Department of State
of the United States

4

There is one assumption I don't challenge. And that is that the United States has a national-security interest in defending itself, and that we live in a nuclear world that may, in fact, for a long time require nuclear weapons.

The Washington Post, 9-16:(D)16.

Bernard W. Rogers
General, United States Army;
Supreme Allied Commander/Europe

5

[Saying he is concerned about the rush to a Soviet-West Europe arms-control agreement]: I wish somebody would run out there and say "Time out!" We are moving . . . fast on something that is critical to this [Western] alliance. You know, if we are not careful, [Soviet leader Mikhail] Gorbachev will continue to grease that slope [to a denuclearized Europe] and we'll slide down it to the point where we make Western Europe safe for conventional war. We're concerned for political and economic reasons, and we're intimidated—and that's [the Soviet Union's] objective. And if she can get rid of all the nuclear weapons, if she can break the coupling between the strategic nuclear forces of the United States and its umbrella over Western Eu-

WHAT THEY SAID IN 1987

(BERNARD W. ROGERS)

rope, she's achieved what she wants, because there is no way, there is no way that nations in Western Europe can find the resources for sufficient conventional forces [to offset Soviet conventional superiority]. The resources aren't there. And so, as a consequence, it's that nuclear umbrella tied to the U.S. that is the basis of our deterrent.

Interview, Mons, Belgium, April 22/
The Christian Science Monitor, 4-23:32.

1

The first-use option [of nuclear weapons] is a vital factor in there, because the Soviet Union has to continue to be faced with the prospect that if she aggresses against us that we will use nuclear weapons as we believe necessary and appropriate, which could very well escalate to a strategic nuclear exchange. I happen to believe it would, and I happen to believe it would do so quite quickly. And that's the one thing she fears.

Interview, Mons, Belgium, April 22/
The Christian Science Monitor, 4-23:32.

2

[Saying the U.S. Reagan Administration is rushing too fast into a European arms agreement with the Soviet Union]: When the future of Western Europe is at stake, I don't know why it is so necessary to make decisions in the aftermath of meetings in Moscow, to rush into this, other than the fact that certain Administrations are going out of existence by certain time frames. Is it more important to have these things accomplished on certain people's watch, or is it more important in the long term to ensure what we are doing is right to the future of Western Europe? I happen to believe that the latter is more important. But then, I am only a dumb infantryman trying to make a living as a commander in Europe, and with only 10 days to go [to retirement].

Interview, Mons, Belgium, June 17/
The Washington Post, 6-18:(A)33.

Bernard W. Rogers
General (ret.), United States Army;
Former Supreme Allied Commander/Europe

3

[Criticizing the proposed U.S.-Soviet arms-reduction agreement covering nuclear weapons in Europe]: What bothers me is that this agreement violates the two cardinal principles for arms-control negotiations. One is, accept no proposal that impacts adversely on the credibility of the deterrence of NATO. This one does. And secondly, arms-control accords are not an end in themselves. They're a means to an end—greater security at less cost . . . We give up the *Pershing 2* missile, the weapons system that the Soviets fear the most because it could bring them immediate pain within 13 minutes. On their soil. Secondly, it reduces our options. Those together reduce the credibility of NATO's deterrence in the eyes of the Soviets. I'm concerned because it puts us on the slippery slope of denuclearization in Western Europe, and I think that is dangerous . . . NATO has never had sufficient conventional forces.

Interview/USA Today, 10-30:(A)11.

Edward L. Rowny
U.S. arms-control negotiator

4

If you make the world safe for conventional warfare [by reducing nuclear weaponry], you haven't helped things, because we've been relatively stable since World War II. The Soviets have not moved against Western Europe, but they have this huge conventional imbalance. We've kept the peace largely because we're ready [with nuclear retaliation] if they move with a conventional war. But if you have reductions in the strategic [nuclear] arms and don't have equal reductions redressing the balance on the conventional, then you haven't helped the situation. You may have exacerbated it with the Europeans being quite alarmed, because the Europeans do not want to pay the large cost for being equal to the Soviets.

Interview/USA Today, 2-3:(A)9.

(EDWARD L. ROWNY)

1

Verification [of Soviet adherence to arms-control agreements] is the Achilles heel to a lot of these agreements. About 77 per cent of the people in the United States want an arms-control agreement. [But] exactly the same percentage in this poll don't trust the Russians . . . The people don't trust them for good reason. The Soviets look at treaties as something to mind if its suits their interest. By talking about verification, they create the illusion that they are in favor of on-site inspection. But it's another thing to try to pin them down. You can't; you don't. They slip off the hook every time.

Interview/USA Today, 2-3:(A)9.

Roald Sagdeyev
Director,
Soviet Space Research Institute

2

[On the proposed U.S. space defense system]: We need some kind of insurance policy on SDI; otherwise what is advertised innocently as a testing program [by the U.S.] could lead to rapid deployment of a full-scale system. Unrestrained SDI testing would confront our military planners with the requirement of more offensive systems, not less. It's that simple.

Interview/Time, 9-21:29.

Andrei D. Sakharov
Dissident Soviet physicist

3

My attitude on [U.S.] President Reagan's Strategic Defense Initiative [space defense system]—which I wrote about even before he proclaimed the program—is that it cannot be implemented effectively in a military-strategic sense. I think that a potential enemy with highly developed technology always can find a means to overcome space defenses. It is much easier and cheaper to overcome space defenses than to create them. If the SDI is created, the U.S.S.R. will find ways to make it ineffective at every stage.

Interview, Moscow/
U.S. News & World Report, 1-12:31.

4

[Soviet leader Mikhail] Gorbachev says he will agree to any mutual system for verification against cheating [on an East-West arms-control agreement]. But there's very tight security on these issues in the Soviet Union. Would you have experts in verification traveling to areas where there is no foreigner and few Soviets have ever been? I can't believe this is the way it will happen.

Interview, Moscow/
U.S. News & World Report, 4-20:31.

Patricia Schroeder
United States Representative,
D-Colorado

5

[Criticizing U.S. nuclear-weapons testing while the Soviet Union has a moratorium on such tests]: I think the President's [Reagan] pushing the test two days ahead of schedule when the American people didn't want to test, when Congress didn't want to test, when the world didn't want to test, was the most arrogant exercise of power I've seen in a long time.

Mercury, Nev., Feb. 5/
The New York Times, 2-6:5.

Charles E. Schumer
United States Representative,
D-New York

6

I think [the Defense Department] is awash in extra money. The Pentagon is like a squirrel's lair—there's lots of little acorns hidden away.

The Washington Post, 10-5:(A)4.

Eduard A. Shevardnadze
Foreign Minister of the Soviet Union

7

[Calling for the removal of U.S. nuclear warheads from West German *Pershing* missiles as part of an East-West arms-control deal]: Seventy-two U.S. nuclear warheads now stand between us and an agreement on intermediate- and shorter-range missiles. We have done all in

(EDUARD A. SHEVARDNADZE)

our power. We have removed everything that could stand in the way of an agreement. Our partners have found the snags. The main one is the *Pershing* 1-A missile.

At United Nations Disarmament Conference,
Geneva, Aug. 6/The New York Times, 8-7:1.

1

[Criticizing the proposed U.S. "Star Wars" space defense system]: No organization, no set of rules, no code of behavior can save the world in the few minutes between the launching of a missile and a nuclear holocaust. If and when the implementation of the "Star Wars" program begins, the "shagreen leather" of that time interval will shrink much further.

At United Nations, New York, Sept. 23/
The New York Times, 9-24:6.

2

Nuclear weapons and security are not synonymous. Security becomes stronger when those weapons disappear.

At United Nations, New York,
Sept. 23/Los Angeles Times, 9-24:(I)11.

George P. Shultz
Secretary of State
of the United States

3

[Criticizing those who argue against a proposed nuclear-arms reduction pact for Europe between the U.S. and the Soviet Union]: Europe will be more safe, definitely [with the arms-control agreement] . . . How can you say that we become militarily worse off when they [the Soviets] eliminate around 2,000 warheads, [and] we eliminate around 350? . . . It boggles my mind that anybody could think that . . . They don't do arithmetic.

Broadcast interview/"This Week
With David Brinkley," ABC-TV, 9-20.

4

[On the recently agreed U.S.-Soviet INF treaty]: The reality is that, if the peace movement had had its way, there would be no INF treaty. It was only by doing what the peace movement didn't want [installing U.S. nuclear missiles in Europe] that we got the result the peace movement apparently wanted. We did it [deployment] over the objection of the peace movement. But that is what led to the situation that made possible negotiation of this agreement. I would hope that the people in the movement would take a second look and admit that they were wrong. In order to have peace, you have to show some strength.

News conference, Oslo, Norway,
Dec. 14/The Washington Post, 12-15:(A)25.

Margaret Thatcher
Prime Minister
of the United Kingdom

5

Conventional weapons have never been enough to deter a war. Two world wars showed us that. A world without nuclear weapons may be a dream, but you cannot base a sure defense on dreams.

Moscow, March 30/
The Washington Post, 3-31:(A)28.

6

The nuclear deterrent is the most powerful deterrent against war the world has ever known. It must remain.

Before International Democratic Union,
West Berlin, Sept. 25/
Los Angeles Times, 9-26:(I)8.

Leo Tindemans
Foreign Minister of Belgium

7

If decisions are made in [nuclear] arms control that are not intelligent, we will go back to having only conventional forces. Having only conventional forces is a condition in which world wars take place.

To reporters, Washington, Feb. 6/
The Washington Post, 2-7:(A)17.

Huang Tingwei
Specialist in disarmament,
International Relations Institute
(China)

1

[On U.S.-Soviet arms-control talks]: Even if the INF and short-range missiles are eliminated, the United States and Soviet Union can use strategic weapons to achieve their military aims. [Moreover,] with increasingly lethal weapons, the numbers [of missiles scrapped] aren't so significant. From a pure military standpoint, this [INF arms-control] agreement could have been reached long ago.

The Christian Science Monitor,
10-2:10.

Jurgen Todenhofer
Former spokesman,
disarmament committee,
Christian Democratic Party
of West Germany

2

[On the U.S.-Soviet INF arms-control agreement affecting missiles in Europe]: I am personally very disturbed by this treaty. Nuclear weapons were brought in in the first place in the 1950s to act as a shield against a conventional war of swords, as a deterrent. Now we are laying down the shield without blunting the sword. NATO hopes that the Warsaw Pact will voluntarily reduce its conventional superiority. But what will we do in two years if [Soviet leader Mikhail] Gorbachev stops smiling?

The New York Times, 12-10:10.

Carlisle A. H. Trost
Admiral and Chief of Operations,
United States Navy

3

If we are going to make sea power work in the 21st century, we are going to have to maintain our advantage. When you consider what the Germans were able to achieve in two world wars . . . you have to respect the potential of the Soviet Navy.

U.S. News & World Report, 6-15:38.

Lowell P. Weicker, Jr.
United States Senator, R-Connecticut

4

[Saying Congress should exert more control over the President's power to deploy U.S. forces in world hot spots]: We [in Congress] will vote for the hardware of war, but we will not participate in any decision about the employment of that hardware. Missing in action— the Constitution of the United States and the War Powers Act of 1973—[these are] unreported casualties.

Oct. 2/Los Angeles Times, 10-3:(I)10.

Caspar W. Weinberger
Secretary of Defense
of the United States

5

[On the proposed U.S. space defense system]: We are now seeing opportunities for earlier deployment of the first phase of strategic defense than we previously thought possible. We may be nearing the day when decisions about deployment of the first phase can be made . . . There is no doubt the SDI research effort is achieving dramatic results. We are rapidly validating a number of technologies and technical concepts which provide sufficient evidence of the feasibility of a strategic defense system.

Before National Space Foundation,
Colorado Springs, Colo., Jan. 22/
The Washington Post, 1-23:(A)17.

6

. . . It would be exceedingly unwise to withdraw any significant number of U.S. troops from Europe, as some in my country advocate. Such a move would send the worst kind of signal to allies and adversaries alike. And to maintain America's current level of security, such a withdrawal of U.S. forces actually would cost us *more*, not less, in dollar expenditures—but it would cost us all vastly more in a weakened NATO that could encourage the Soviets to believe they could make a successful attack. So I can tell you that [U.S.] President Reagan and I will continue to fight any moves to reduce

WHAT THEY SAID IN 1987

(CASPAR W. WEINBERGER)

America's contribution to NATO. Indeed, it is our firm belief that, in view of the constantly growing Soviet offensive military power, we all, including the U.S., need to do more.

> *At Propeller Club,*
> *Istanbul, Turkey, March 19/*
> *The New York Times, 4-23:36.*

1

Regardless of who is General Secretary of the Soviet Union and how young he is or how healthy he is or how well he dresses, their policy remains exactly the same. [The Soviet objective is] to acquire an increasing amount of enormous military strength each year, without any restraints imposed by public opinion and public debate.

> *Before House Armed Services Committee,*
> *Washington, March 24/*
> *The New York Times, 3-25:8.*

2

That decade of [U.S. military] neglect [the 1970s] was fed, really, by a most insidious idea—that somehow American power was immoral. We began by doubting the war in Vietnam, and we ended by doubting ourselves.

> *Farewell address,*
> *Washington, Nov. 17/*
> *The New York Times, 11-18:11.*

Pete Wilson
United States Senator, R-California

3

[On the proposed U.S. space defense system]: You are not talking about a perfect, leak-proof defense. That is not required in order for SDI to become a tremendously effective defense, so effective as to make almost irrational a Soviet first strike. What we have now is no defense. We depend entirely on a deterrent, one that is not tremendously convincing.

> *Interview, Los Angeles, June 22/*
> *Los Angeles Times, 6-23:(I)3.*

Jim Wright
United States Representative,
D-Texas

4

The United States is spending this year some $300-billion on the unproductive implements of warfare, and the Soviet Union is spending a like amount . . . Each week we add 35 more nuclear bombs to our stockpile—while many Americans go hungry and some go homeless, the illiterate are not taught, and hundreds of thousands are unable to get the financial assistance they need to go to college.

> *At University of Texas*
> *at Austin commencement, May 23/*
> *The New York Times, 5-25:9.*

Alexander Yakovlev
Member, Politburo,
Communist Party of the Soviet Union

5

As for the [forthcoming U.S.-Soviet] summit, I expect what I think both sides expect. Just the fact that we will sign an agreement on medium- and short-range nuclear missiles would be of great psychological importance. We do not feel this now; it hasn't sunk in. But later, we will have a different perception of the world around us. For 30 or 40 years, we have said, "No, no, no," like woodpeckers pecking away at a tree; and all of a sudden we said, "Yes." Now we can see that we can live without missiles. The psychological consequences could be profound.

> *Interview/*
> *U.S. News & World Report, 11-16:52.*

Paul Yost, Jr.
Admiral and Commandant,
United States Coast Guard

6

Almost any major port in the United States could be closed for long periods of time by saboteurs. The amount of support a battle group needs at sea, or that Europe would require in a full-time war situation, is mind boggling. It

(PAUL YOST, JR.)

would take a steady stream of ships out of our ports with oil, food, ammunition, machinery, every possible thing; and if you bottled up several ports, it would make it very difficult to move that stuff out.

Interview/USA Today, 10-21:(A)9.

Zhao Ziyang
Premier of China

1

. . . the international arms market is very complicated. If a country has the money and is ready to pay a high price, it will have no trouble in finding ways to acquire weapons.

Interview, September/Los Angeles Times, 10-24:(I)4.

The Economy • Labor

F. Gerard Adams
Professor of economics,
University of Pennsylvania

1

Our calculations suggest that estimates of large job losses and dire consequences to the economy as a result of raising the minimum wage do not stand up to scrutiny. The costs of minimum-wage increase to the economy as a whole will be small in the aggregate and imperceptible to the individual. The gain will be a return to the standards of wage equity which originally inspired minimum-wage legislation 50 years ago.

Congressional testimony/
The Washington Post, 8-18:(A)15.

Bruce Babbitt
Former Governor of Arizona (D);
Candidate for the 1988
Democratic Presidential nomination

2

[The] Gramm-Rudman [Federal budget-balancing law] is everything that is wrong and rotten in Washington. Gramm-Rudman is a statement that nothing really matters—there are no choices. Presidential libraries have the same priority as sick children. The homeless are indistinguishable from a military band. Medical research means no more than junk mail out of Congress . . . The ability to govern means the ability to make choices. And if you can't make choices and you can't justify them, then you have no business being in government and you should get out.

The Washington Post, 7-4:(A)6.

James A. Baker III
Secretary of the Treasury
of the United States

3

For all the talk about America's lack of competitiveness [in the world economy], Japan's economy has actually grown no faster than America's since 1982. And if you consider simply the growth of domestic demand, leaving out exports, America has grown at a rate more than 50 per cent faster than Japan. America has created millions of new jobs, while Japan has created very few.

Before Japan Society, New York,
April 15/The New York Times, 4-16:26.

Sam Beard
Chairman, National Committee
on Jobs and Small Business

4

We need a whole new view of education. The way things used to work, a student would get a diploma, get a job, and keep it the rest of his life. [Today,] with the world being small, there is tremendous turnover in our jobs. To remain competitive, we need ongoing education and retraining. We need better links with our institutions of higher learning, business leadership and our financial leadership.

Interview/USA Today, 2-5:(A)9.

Joseph R. Biden, Jr.
United States Senator, D-Delaware;
Candidate for the 1988
Democratic Presidential nomination

5

[Saying that labor unions are having war declared against them by business interests during the Reagan Administration]: The chambers of commerce understand what is at stake. They are about the business of seeing to it that your [unions'] say and your share in the economic bounty and prosperity of America are fundamentally changed. If you [unions] don't understand that, you're in the wrong business.

At AFL-CIO Maritime Trades
Department conference, Bal Harbour, Fla.,
Feb. 13/ Los Angeles Times, 2-14: (I)18.

1

The Japanese, the Europeans, the Koreans—they don't want to compete [with the U.S.]; they want to beat our brains out [economically] . . . I don't want [the U.S.] to compete; I want to win, flat-out win.

To AFL-CIO leaders/
The Washington Post, 4-16:(A)14.

2

For too long in this society, we have celebrated individualism over community. For a decade led by [President] Ronald Reagan, self-aggrandizement has been the full-throated cry of our society—"Got mine, get yours, what's in it for me?" In the final analysis, our government can be no more than a catalyst . . . Only a wholesale commitment by our entire society—our managers, our workers, our consumers—to revitalize and reconstruct our economy will suffice.

Speech/The Washington Post, 5-1:(A)18.

3

Control over our economic destiny has been endangered. The risk is that we will no longer lead the world; that we will no longer control American jobs and American assets; that our economy will be held hostage to the wishes and whims of foreign corporations and foreign powers . . . [This is] what a President should do today: Call the captains of industry and the chieftains of labor into his office . . . and say to them, "Here's what successful businesses here and abroad are doing . . . Why don't you go out and get the job done, too?"

At Wharton School of Economics,
University of Pennsylvania, May 14/
Los Angeles Times, 5-15:(I)4.

William E. Brock
Secretary of Labor
of the United States

4

There has to be a greater spirit of cooperation between government, business and labor. Business and labor have spent too much time kick-

ing each other in the shins and not realizing that the threat comes from outside this country. They've got to work together, and they realize that. That's very healthy. I see more labor-management cooperation now than a few years ago . . . On the part of labor unions, you have a great deal of interest in improving productivity, in reducing absenteeism. You see management much more interested in the well-being of workers and the involvement of workers, and improving the quality of life in the plant. There is a clear pattern of improved relationships between workers and management in this country that bodes well for the future.

Interview/USA Today, 9-3:(A)9.

George Bush
Vice President of the United States;
Candidate for the 1988
Republican Presidential nomination

5

I hope this doesn't sound too confrontational, but the Congress appropriates every single dime and spends every single dime. And when the going gets great and the market's going up, fine, everything's great. And then when something goes wrong, they point the finger at the President of the United States. I don't think it's fair. We have sent budget after budget to [Capitol] Hill that would bring [the budget deficit] down, not by raising taxes, but by restraining spending.

Campaign speech before
Chamber of Commerce, Laconia, N.H.,
Nov. 10/The Washington Post, 11-11:(A)4.

Don Butler
President, California Merchants
and Manufacturer's Association

6

[On the controversy over paid maternity leave for female employees]: If I'm an employer and I've weighed all the candidates, I'm going to hire either a male or an older woman. And that is discrimination we don't want; but it will happen because business people are practical.

Newsweek, 1-26:24.

WHAT THEY SAID IN 1987

Robert C. Byrd
United States Senator,
D-West Virginia
1

[On the large Federal budget deficits]: It's like having a big banquet and getting out of town before the waiter brings the ticket.

USA Today. 6-17:(A)4.

Lawton Chiles
United States Senator, D-Florida
2

Everyone believes we need to reduce this terrible debt we have, now over $1-trillion; but somehow, when it comes to specifics, there are always some programs we find sacrosanct . . . Other programs we're willing to cut, but they turn out to be someone else's children. It's easier to shoot a budget resolution than to make one.

Before the Senate, Washington,
April 27/ Los Angeles Times, 4-28:(I)13.

Bill Clinton
Governor of Arkansas (D)
3

About 1973, America began to fall from its complacent perch atop the world's economy into a cauldron of competition for which we were ill prepared. From 1979 to 1985, the great American job machine created 9.3 million new jobs. It had to, in order to accommodate the last of the baby-boomers and the huge influx of women workers. The bad news is that 44 per cent of those jobs were poverty-level jobs, twice the percentage of the 12 million jobs created in the previous six-year period, 1973-1979, and the 20 million jobs created in the decade before that, 1963-1973. From 1981 to 1986, 40 per cent of the American people experienced a *real decline* in income. Twenty per cent held their own, 40 per cent had an increase.

Before National Press Club, Washington,
Feb. 17/ The Washington Post, 2-19:(A)26.

4

The budget straitjacket we've gotten ourselves into and the economic uncertainties of the years ahead make it impossible for a responsible person to commit [specific amounts of money] as President for certain programs . . . That is one of the legacies of the last seven years [of the Reagan Administration].

At United States Conference of Mayors,
Nashville, Tenn./
The Washington Post, 6-18:(A)14.

Charles Craypo
Chairman, department of economics,
University of Notre Dame
5

Employers still generally have the momentum [in negotiations with labor]. They're going for the third and fourth straight rounds of concessions [from labor], using the threat that otherwise they'll shut down. Workers and unions are resisting concessions now because their experience leads them to believe it won't save their jobs. It's those two forces that are colliding.

The New York Times, 3-12:11.

Oliver H. Delchamps
Chairman, United States
Chamber of Commerce
6

Business must stand united in opposition to the current slippery, back-door effort to raise taxes. If we wait until later to fight, when tax hikes are larger and a more visible threat to economic growth, it may be too late. Now is the time to innoculate our society against this virus, to state clearly to our elected representatives that they simply must bring their spending addiction under control. There is no other solution to the [Federal budget] deficit problem.

Nation's Business, October:80.

Robert J. Dole
United States Senator, R-Kansas;
Candidate for the 1988
Republican Presidential nomination
7

If you're not a farmer, keep in mind you have the best food bargain in the world. Less

(ROBERT J. DOLE)

than 10 per cent of your disposable income goes for food, and that's down from 17 per cent a decade ago. That's because of the farmer's productivity. And, oh yes, [we have] a costly farm program. And the farmer gets a check; it's called a subsidy by some. But indirectly, the American consumer gets a subsidy because of these very low prices.

Interview/
The Washington Post, 6-13:(A)13.

1

[On the national debt]: We do not expand opportunity when we burden our children with debt from our own self-indulgence. We will either sacrifice for our children, or we will continue to make our children sacrifice for us. We have the privilege of choosing. Our children do not.

Campaign address, Russell, Kan./
The Washington Post, 11-11: (A)3.

2

[On the current stock-market crash]: Whether the drop in the market today was because of a lack of confidence, I do not know—a lack of confidence in the White House, a lack of confidence in the Congress, a combination of each . . . I hope this drop is only temporary. We have just finished our 60th month of economic growth. That is five years. That is a great record. But I do believe that the [Federal budget] deficit is public enemy Number 1. Unless we address it, it is going to be right out there causing us problems down the road.

Before the Senate, Nov. 30/
The Washington Post, 12-2:(A)24.

Thomas R. Donahue
Secretary-treasurer,
American Federation of Labor-Congress
of Industrial Organizations

3

This is a land of high and chronic unemployment, in which, at this time of relative prosperity, 12 million Americans are wholly or partially unemployed. Year after year . . . good, useful, well-paying jobs, which generations of skilled workers have used to build self-reliant families, are being wiped out by attrition or by sudden-death plant closings.

At National Conference on Work
and Family Life, March 30/
The Washington Post, 4-8:(A)20.

Donald Doyle
President,
Kentucky Fried Chicken-USA

4

People are finding they're still productive—and, in fact, more productive—as they get older and more experienced; so the trend that saw lowering of retirement age several years ago is now reversing. The legal aspects of mandatory retirement also have changed. More people have decided they want to stay in the work force longer; they want to be active, and they want to have a good source of income.

Interview/USA Today, 7-23:(A)11.

Peter F. Drucker
Professor of social science
and management, Claremont (Calif.)
Graduate School

5

The U.S. has been undergoing an enormous industrial restructuring. We have moved several million people out of smokestack industries, and we are still operating at the lowest unemployment rate in the Western world. At less than 6 per cent for adult men, U.S. unemployment is probably even lower than Japan's. For in Japan, the bulk of the unemployment is concealed; Japanese companies keep people on the payroll even if there is no work for them at all. And don't forget, we have made the biggest demographic change any country has ever made in terms of labor-force participation of women. It's an incredible achievement. What did we do right? I don't know. I don't understand it.

Interview/
U.S. News & World Report, 2-2:23.

1

Lifetime employment expresses the most profound conviction of modern Japan, that the large enterprise is run primarily for its employees, at least as long as it does not get into severe financial trouble.

USA Today, 7-30:(A)8.

Michael S. Dukakis
Governor of Massachusetts (D);
Candidate for the 1988
Democratic Presidential nomination

2

I am a full-employment Democrat. Make no mistake about it. Economists sit around and debate what we mean by full employment, but I'll tell you what full employment is: It's an economy in which every citizen who is able to work has a decent job at a decent wage.

At Hispanic Presidential Forum,
Los Angeles, Aug. 24/
Los Angeles Times, 8-26:(I)12.

Pierre S. du Pont IV
Former Governor of Delaware (R);
Candidate for the 1988
Republican Presidential nomination

3

There are two kinds of political leaders in America: the pie slicers and the pie breakers. And the pie slicers are always arguing about how the pie should be divided up. [New York Governor] Mario Cuomo is an excellent pie slicer. And so was [1984 Democratic Presidential nominee] Walter Mondale. I'm on the other side. I would put my energies into making the pie bigger, so that everyone's slice is a little bit bigger, rather than arguing over the angle of the knife that's slicing the pie.

Interview, Wilmington, Del./
The Christian Science Monitor, 3-11:6.

4

How could the trade deficit and the debtor-nation status of America be so depressing while . . . we have created 13 million net new

jobs? That's 20 times as many as the Japanese and three-to-four times as many as the Germans. Our unemployment rate is dropping, our inflation rate has gone through the floor.

To reporters/
The Christian Science Monitor, 8-3:5.

5

The President [Reagan] should "just say no" to new taxes. In my years as Governor, I discovered that when you give the legislature the eye of a needle, they drive an 18-wheeler through it.

The Washington Post, 10-26:(A)3.

6

I think there are two things in the economics of the United States that are much more important than balancing the budget. One is to run a low-inflation economy, because inflation destroys everybody. The second is to run a high-employment economy. We're doing well. If we don't impose taxes or pass protectionist trade bills, we'll continue to do so.

Interview/USA Today, 12-29:(A)9.

Amitai Etzioni
Sociologist; Director,
Center for Policy Research,
George Washington University

7

From 1820 to 1920, we [the U.S.] plowed a lot back into the economy. [But after the Depression and World War II,] we had one generation that basically spent more than we produced—running down what three generations saved. So then we went to everybody else in the world, especially the Japanese, and they loaned us several hundred billions so we could go on with this Coke commercial, with this party, with this hedonism, without tightening our belt. We're very close to the end of it, because people just won't loan us that much more. We've run down our inheritance. We've borrowed from everybody all we can borrow. Who's going to give us the next 200 billion?

Interview, Aspen, Colo./
The Christian Science Monitor, 4-3:16.

1

[On the recent stock-market crash]: We need to tighten our belts, and that can be done through super-inflation or through courageous leadership. But who will tell the people this? The President's pulpit has lost its power, even if he [President Reagan] had the right message.

The Christian Science Monitor, 11-5:36.

J. James Exon
United States Senator, D-Nebraska

2

The entire Gramm-Rudman [Federal budget-balancing] process actually delays serious action on the deficit . . . Rather than force action, the Gramm-Rudman process fakes action. After two years of operation, by and large, Gramm-Rudman has not worked. The new version of the law does not bring with it a new promise of deficit reduction. If anything, it pushes difficult decisions away from this Congress and President Reagan onto the next Congress and the next President. It is a way for Congress to congratulate itself for having fiscal courage without making a single decision on the spending and revenue issues which produce the debt and deficit.

The Washington Post, 10-27:(A)19.

Charles Forte
Chairman,
Trust House Forte Ltd. (Britain)

3

We believe that when staff consider they need a trade-union representation, then we have failed in our jobs of being good managers. I believe that very often a minority in a trade union can subvert the communications between management and staff. We could not tolerate a situation, which occurs in some industries, where management is not allowed to manage . . . [But] anyone who works for us is free to join a trade union if he wishes to do so. I am a great believer in personal freedom, not only for myself but for others. Indeed, within our organization, many trade unions are represented. But

I firmly believe that a person also has the right not to join a union if he does not want to. I am totally opposed to bullying, blackmail and restrictive practices [by unions].

Forte magazine, Winter:16.

Wyche Fowler, Jr.
United States Senator, D-Georgia

4

You walk around the White House grounds and mention "supply-side economics" today, and they will shoot you.

USA Today, 8-7:(A)4.

John Kenneth Galbraith
Professor emeritus of economics,
Harvard University

5

[On the recent stock-market crash]: The debacle marks the last chapter of Reaganomics. It is the product of supply-side economics—the irresponsible tax reduction, the high interest rates that bid up the dollar and subsidized imports, and the trade deficit that put a lot of unstable money in foreign hands . . . The prospect of the current [Reagan] Administration doing anything is hampered by the fact that it believes that God is a Republican and will handle things.

Interview/Newsweek, 11-2:49.

Richard A. Gephardt
United States Representative, D-Missouri;
Candidate for the 1988
Democratic Presidential nomination

6

I know this position will not be popular with everyone. But people sitting in cushy offices, in secure jobs, have no right to tell workers on assembly lines that their hopes and livelihood have to be sacrificed on the altar of a false and rigid free-trade ideology.

Announcing his candidacy for President,
Feb. 23/Los Angeles Times, 6-22:(I)16.

1

I want to recall our attention to what our economy is really all about: not money, but people. The original Greek word "economy" meant "the management of a household or family" . . . We must let the Greeks remind us that the fundamental purpose of our complicated and technical economy is the well-being of our families.

At Securities Industry Institute,
Wharton School of Business/
The Washington Post, 3-18:(A)2.

2

What's at the root of [today's stock-market] plunge, as well as many of our other economic problems, is the current [Reagan] Administration's fiscal policy. We've been relying on paper profits and the good-will of our allies to finance our two [budget and trade] deficits. We've got to stop borrowing growth from the future.

Oct. 19/Los Angeles Times,10-20:(I)15.

Robert M. Giordano
Chief economist,
Goldman, Sachs & Company

3

[On Alan Greenspan taking over from Paul Volcker as Chairman of the Federal Reserve Board]: Mr. Greenspan is a good man, but he does not have Mr. Volcker's record and he will not be given the benefit of the doubt. In the eyes of the financial markets, he is guilty until proven innocent. Mr. Volcker had enough experience and credibility that he could receive the benefit of the doubt. He could buy a lot of time with words like "the dollar has gone down enough," or "interest rates are too high."

The New York Times, 6-3:29.

Albert Gore, Jr.
United States Senator, D-Tennessee;
Candidate for the 1988
Democratic Presidential nomination

4

The voodoo chickens of Reaganomics have come to roost. [Today's] severe decline in stock-market prices reflects a deep loss of confidence, here and abroad, in the Reagan Administration's economic policies.

Oct. 19/Los Angeles Times, 10-20:(I)15.

Phil Gramm
United States Senator, R-Texas

5

Balancing the [Federal] budget is like going to heaven: Everybody wants to balance the budget, but nobody wants to do what you have to do to balance the budget.

U.S. News & World Report, 7-13:13.

William H. Gray III
United States Representative,
D-Pennsylvania

6

[On "user fees"]: It walks like a duck, it smells like a duck, it quacks like a duck—it's a tax.

USA Today, 4-27:(A)5.

Jack Grayson
Author; Chairman,
American Productivity Center

7

The American dream is coming to an end. It isn't there yet, but if we don't change, that dream and the extensions of it are not going to happen for our children, grandchildren and for some of you . . . Most people do not realize what's happened to incomes in this nation. Household income is now 8 per cent *less* than 1973 [in] real dollars. Real compensation per hour is equal to that of 1969. And real weekly earnings are *less* than they were in 1962.

At conference of managers, Oak Brook, Ill./
The Christian Science Monitor, 7-3:5.

Alan Greenspan
Former Chairman, Council
of Economic Advisers to the President
of the United States (Gerald R. Ford)

8

[On the growth of U.S. debt]: At some point, some economic accident would likely

(ALAN GREENSPAN)

happen . . . and we could be in the worst economic straits for any period since the 1930s . . . If America does not increase its capital-investment rates, which means increase its basic savings, we are going to fade from the scene as a huge superpower eventually.

Broadcast interview taped April 8/
"Face the Nation", CBS-TV, 6-7.

Alan Greenspan
Chairman, Federal Reserve Board

1

Perhaps I should thank in advance the creators of all those events that will make the next four years easygoing—inflation which always stays put, a stock market which is always a bull, a dollar which is always stable, interest rates which stay low and employment which stays high. But most assuredly, I would be thankful to those who have the capability of repealing the laws of arithmetic which would make all the foregoing possible.

Upon his swearing-in as Chairman/
Los Angeles Times, 8-31:(I)13.

Pehr Gyllenhammar
Chairman, Volvo A.B. (Sweden)

2

In the U.S., you can still fire people if you don't need them. In Europe, you can't reduce your work force through dismissals unless a business is hopeless, so the dialogue will be more complicated. However, well-managed European firms have learned more about working with their employees because you can't dispose of them. Understanding employees is one of the keys to organizing work differently.

Interview, New York/
The New York Times, 2-3:28.

David Halberstam
Author, Journalist

3

For the first time, there is a real awareness that we are in a major [economic] crisis, that

an era has ended. You certainly see it among [state] Governors, who are acutely aware that the number of truly middle-class jobs, particularly for non-college graduates, are diminishing, and that they are being replaced by jobs with nowhere near the economic and social leverage.

Interview/USA Today, 2-11:(A)11.

David Hale
Economist,
Kemper Financial Services

4

[On the aftermath of the recent stock-market crash]: We've already had the first stage, where the President [Reagan] makes statements that are useless. The second stage involves coming up with a policy package that the markets judge to be inadequate. That triggers the third stage, which involves an even worse financial crisis.

U.S. News & World Report, 11-9:25.

Jesse Helms
United States Senator,
R-North Carolina

5

If you want to stop economic growth and destroy jobs and drive up prices that consumers pay for everything they buy, just increase taxes, especially excise taxes. [President] Ronald Reagan is absolutely right in promising to veto any tax increase, excise taxes included. We must cut Federal spending and Federal taxes and unshackle the free-enterprise system.

TV spot/The New York Times, 8-20:12.

Jesse L. Jackson
Civil-rights leader;
Candidate for the 1988
Democratic Presidential nomination

6

There is something very wrong with an economy where Wall Street profits soar while working people scramble . . . When the stock market hits new records but manufacturing jobs hit new lows, when corporate profits keep

WHAT THEY SAID IN 1987

(JESSE L. JACKSON)

climbing, yet job salaries are plunging, when it is safer and more profitable in this country to sell Mercedes-Benz sedans than John Deere tractors—then it is time to get America Inc. back on the track.

Speech, Greenfield, Iowa, March 19/
The New York Times, 3-20:10.

1

While I strongly support the goal of lowering our [Federal] budget deficit, I do not believe in setting rigid, fixed targets far in advance. Meeting the challenge of changing domestic and international financial conditions requires more flexibility . . . I do not believe the most important decisions of government—our budget priorities—should be put on automatic pilot.

Answer to questionnaire sponsored by
Roosevelt Center for American Policy Studies/
The Washington Post, 9-17:(A)25.

2

[On the recent stock-market crash]: We are all in the economic trenches now, even if, on Wall Street, the trenches are mahogany-lined. Layoffs, farm foreclosures, bank failures, rising debt and falling wealth are our common ground. Wall Street and [Chicago's] LaSalle Street cannot escape Main Street and Rural Route 3. We are one.

At forum sponsored by New York State
Democratic Committee, New York, Oct. 30/
The New York Times, 10-31:9.

John Paul II
Pope

3

The value of work does not end with the individual. The full meaning of work can only be understood in relation to the family and society as well. Work supports and gives stability to the family. In each community and in the nation as a whole, work has a fundamental social meaning. It can, moreover, either join people in the solidarity of a shared commitment or set them at odds through exaggerated competition, exploitation and social conflict. Work is a key to the whole social question, when that "question" is understood to be concerned with making life more human.

Homily, Monterey, Calif., Sept. 17/
Los Angeles Times, 9-18:(I)4.

Manuel H. Johnson
Vice Chairman,
Federal Reserve Board

4

The U.S. economic expansion is now extending into its fifth year and is already among the longest in peacetime history. While the over-all rate of economic growth has been rather modest since mid-1984, averaging about 2 1/2 per cent a year, that growth has been sufficient to create about 7 million new jobs during this period. At the same time, inflation has continued to moderate as further progress has been made toward the objective of over-all price stability. Running counter to past cyclical patterns, labor cost pressures have also remained subdued . . . As we all know, however, the current economic setting is not problem-free. There are important risks facing a continued stable expansion. Important trade imbalances exist with many of our principal industrial trading partners. These imbalances are due in part from relatively more rapid growth in the U.S. economy combined with more attractive investment opportunities here. This combination produced capital inflows, dollar appreciation and, consequently, a large trade deficit. While such trade imbalances are not likely to be indefinitely sustainable, "quick fix" solutions to the problem, such as fostering excessive dollar depreciation or protectionist trade legislation, seem particularly inappropriate. What is important is that we attempt to maintain healthy returns to capital and adopt policies encouraging genuine economic growth. This approach fosters the wherewithal to finance the trade deficit and allows for its gradual resolution over time.

Speech, Washington, March 5/
The Washington Post, 3-20:(A)16.

Jerry Jordan
Chief economist,
First Interstate Bancorp; Former Member,
Council of Economic Advisers
to President of the United States
Ronald Reagan

1

[On Alan Greenspan being named to replace Paul Volcker as Federal Reserve Chairman]: [At one time] the view was that no one, but no one, could replace [then Fed Chairman] William McChesney Martin. Then the view was that no one, but no one, could replace Arthur Burns [as Fed Chairman]. Now we've had Volcker—and the same view has been built up. In eight years, I suspect, there'll be the same attitude about Alan Greenspan.

Interview/
Los Angeles Times, 6-4:(I)22.

Henry Kaufman
Chief economist,
Salomon Brothers, Inc.

2

The [Federal Reserve Board's] dilemma is that dollar weakness is undermining its domestic objectives, with the result that monetary policy cannot anticipate economic weakness—and can at best react to it belatedly.

The New York Times, 3-30:21.

Edward W. Kelley, Jr.
Member,
Federal Reserve Board

3

I think everybody is in the pro-growth camp. The question is growth at what expense. I'm very, very optimistic about the long-term potential of this economy. We are somewhere around midstream in a very fundamental transition of the old smokestack-oriented economy to the new post-industrial, information-based economy. The kind of change, the order of magnitude, is one that I don't think any economy has ever successfully achieved before without having re-

ally massive problems. And we're doing it very successfully.

Interview, Washington/
The New York Times, 6-18:12.

Irwin L. Kellner
Chief economist, Manufacturers
Hanover Bank, New York

4

Even if you assume that domestic businesses and consumers are tapped out and no longer buying, the fact that the trade deficit has now fallen in real terms for two quarters, and is likely to continue to fall, means that the output side of the economy will continue to grow. And even if exports don't keep increasing so rapidly, it means that more of what people buy domestically will be made domestically rather than abroad; enough to lift output and keep us out of recession.

Los Angeles Times, 6-18:(I)18.

5

They used to say that all roads lead to Rome, but now I think all roads are leading to higher interest rates. With economic growth improving, higher inflation and oil prices, and the need for [new Federal Reserve Board Chairman Alan] Greenspan to establish himself as an inflation fighter, I don't see how higher rates are avoidable.

Los Angeles Times, 7-1:(I)16.

6

[On the recent stock-market crash]: The consumption part of the economy is going to look very different in the fourth quarter [of 1987] and 1988 because of what happened. Some large retailers were already reporting a consumer slowdown last week. They must be very nervous because, with the approaching holiday season, some of them have already ordered goods and some have already paid for them. If the consumer stays home from the annual Christmas party, then there is going to be a huge surplus of inventory and a slowdown in production for months after that. A recession could start as early as the turn of the year.

Oct. 23/Los Angeles Times, 10-24:(I)20.

Jack Kemp
United States Representative, R-New York;
Candidate for the 1988
Republican Presidential nomination

1

Under [the late President] Herbert Hoover, three mistakes turned the [stock-market] crash of '29 into the Great Depression: tight money, protectionism and a tax increase. We must avoid all three [following the recent market crash]. Recent history shows that Congress uses every penny of a tax increase for higher spending.

The Washington Post, 10-26:(A)3.

Edward M. Kennedy
United States Senator,
D-Massachusetts

2

The minimum wage is not a living wage, and it is not a decent society in which a full-time job means a lifetime in poverty.

At Senate Labor Committee hearing,
Washington, Jan. 13/
Los Angeles Times, 1-14:(I)11.

3

[Calling for legislation requiring 60 days' notice of plant closings to employees]: The days of the feudal barons are over. Are we going to treat people like people, or like chattels in corporate America?

U.S. News & World Report, 7-20:13.

Lane Kirkland
President, American Federation
of Labor-Congress
of Industrial Organizations

4

[Criticizing a Federal proposal to put the Teamsters Union, suspected of being involved with organized crime, under government supervision]: A government-supervised trade union, like an employer-supervised union, is a contradiction in terms. If the Justice Department brings suit seeking supervision over an international union, the AFL-CIO will do whatever is useful and productive in the legal circumstances to prevent such supervision.

At AFL-CIO convention, Miami Beach,
Oct. 26/Los Angeles Times, 10-27:10.

Lawrence B. Krause
Professor of international relations,
University of California, San Diego

5

There's nothing that says that America has to be richer than other countries. National power comes from hard work, savings, investment and good policy. If we don't work hard, if we don't save, if we don't have good policy, we won't reverse this [growing national debt].

Los Angeles Times, 11-6:(I)26.

Robert Lekachman
Professor of economics,
Lehman College,
City University of New York

6

As a result of [President] Reagan's blatant appeal to the greed of his constituency, the most affluent 10 to 20 per cent of the population, we got not the promised surge of new investment but a binge of wasteful consumption, profiteering in real-estate development and stock-market manipulation, none of which has improved the situation of the United States in world markets.

The New York Times, 10-22:35.

Sar Levitan
Director, Center of Social Policy
Studies, George Washington University

7

[Supporting an increase in the minimum wage]: I think the recognition is quite widespread that if they [Congress] don't raise the earnings of the working poor, then it puts a very strong disincentive for welfare people to move on to economic self-sufficiency. There's a good chance that Congress will move now [to raise the minimum wage] because this is one important goal that can be achieved without exacerbating the deficit problem.

The New York Times, 1-7:28.

Dieter Mertens
West German economist

1

Inflation is regarded by most [West] Germans as on a par with Communist domination, and morally equivalent to the work of the devil.

Time, 11-16:56.

James C. Miller III
Director, Federal Office
of Management and Budget

2

Last year our budget quenched the fire-breathing part of the deficit dragon. This year we are going to throw a net over it and get it under control . . . I'm kind of tired of hearing statements [from Congressional opposition] that the budget is "dead on arrival." The budget can be dead on arrival only if somebody on Capitol Hill kills it. It was sure alive when it left my office.

To columnists, Washington, Jan. 5/
The Washington Post, 1-6:(A)8.

3

[Warning the Federal Reserve not to raise interest rates]: Our greatest danger is over-reaction [to the dropping dollar and trade problems]. I'm concerned about the Fed's over-reaction. I'm concerned about what I see in recent data showing a substantial fall in the money supply, I am concerned that over-reaction today on inflation numbers may portend a substantial slowdown a year from now. I need not tell you that has political consequences. My fear is that if we get into a recession we are in deep soup, and there is no question about it.

To reporters,
Washington, April 16/
The New York Times, 4-17:1.

4

[Saying the government is cracking down on those who have long-delinquent tax and loan debts]: A message to every American who owes the Federal government money: Hands up, we've got you covered.

U.S. News & World Report, 8-3:5.

Larry Mishel
Economist, industrial union department,
American Federation of Labor-Congress
of Industrial Organizations

5

[The U.S. is] losing good, high-paying jobs. Our wage structure is deteriorating . . . We are unlikely to be able to sustain our standard of living if things continue. That's the bottom line—how are people going to be able to live? We're faltering. We will continue to . . . We're undergoing a large structural change. it means we have to make choices as to what type of economy we want to have. I see us shifting to a lower standard of living with low productivity growth and a deterioration of job opportunities.

Los Angeles Times, 8-23:(I)2.

Daniel P. Moynihan
United States Senator, D-New York

6

[On cuts in Federal spending he says are the result of the Gramm-Rudman budget-balancing law]: If you voted for Gramm-Rudman, you voted for these cuts. Nothing the President has done [in cutting back spending] should surprise anybody. Why do people express surprise that the President is doing what the law clearly mandates? The law is wrong. The sponsors knew what it was going to do. What do you do with the hypocrisy of people who voted for Gramm-Rudman, and scream and shout when the cuts . . . come about?

The New York Times, 2-9:10.

Manfred Neumann
Director, Institutes
for Stabilization and Structural Policy,
Bonn University (West Germany)

7

The [U.S.] budget deficit is coming down this year, but this reduction is a one-time affair. This means that the structural deficit will not be reduced until the 1990s. Reaganomics was not what we expected. We expected it to be supply-side: deregulation, tax incentives for real in-

(MANFRED NEUMANN)

vestment. But it turned out to be a big machine to increase demand [through deficits].

The Washington Post, 10-22:(A)25.

William Niskanen
Former Member, Council
of Economic Advisers to President
of the United States Ronald Reagan

1

The Fed[-eral Reserve] cannot serve two masters. It can pursue exchange-rate stability with tight money or it can stabilize the domestic economy with easier money. It cannot do both. And it would be a disaster for the U.S. economy and the world if the Fed hadn't turned on a dime after the [recent] stock crash and started looking after the U.S. economic expansion. The foreign-exchange markets understand this, even if the finance ministers do not.

Newsweek, 11-9:33.

Robert D. Orr
Governor of Indiana

2

We are a nation under economic attack and unprepared for the rigors of international competition. If we do not do something now to become competitive, the next generation will become the first in 15 generations of Americans to inherit a standard of living lower than that of their parents . . . Government alone cannot repair the nation's economy . . . But government—and especially state government—has a vital role.

Before Indiana Legislature, January/
The Washington Post, 2-25:(A)23.

Bob Packwood
United States Senator, R-Oregon

3

[On the recent stock-market crash]: As a barometer at home there has not been great turmoil among the people outside the market. It has not created great aggravation and worry in

the public, and to the extent that there is no urgency in the grass roots, maybe we're reflecting that [by still not reaching a fiscal compromise between the White House and Congress].

The New York Times, 11-5:1.

H. Ross Perot
Industrialist

4

You cannot give bonuses to the people at the top when you've had a bad year, and you tell the people who are doing the work that they're going to have to tighten their belt. In a war, you feed the troops first, and then you feed the officers. The troops actually have to go do the fighting. And it's a whole lot easier to plan than it is to fight. You've got to take care of the working people first.

Interview/USA Today, 3-3:(A)9.

5

[On the recent stock-market crash]: Hopefully, this is God tapping us on the shoulder, saying, "While you're still strong, stop abusing yourself." It's a warning that we need to clean up our debt and get our act together before we get the big shock . . . We are on a non-stop binge, punishing our economy. It's outrageous that our elected officials say the fundamentals of the economy are sound; *none* of the fundamentals are sound.

Interview/Newsweek, 11-2:49.

Jackie Presser
President,
American Brotherhood of Teamsters

6

[On his union's re-joining the AFL-CIO after 30 years]: Today, without question, is a historic event. I believe the future will hold that the Teamsters Union being back in the AFL, joining forces together . . . are going to create the greatest political giant that this country has ever seen.

At AFL-CIO convention, Miami Beach, Fla.,
Oct. 29/Los Angeles Times, 10-30:(I)14.

Ronald Reagan
President of the United States

1

The current economic expansion, now in its 50th month, is already one of the longest of the post-war era and shows promise of continuing to record length. This has not been due simply to chance; it is the result of successful policies adopted during the past six years. Disposable personal income is at an all-time high and is still rising; total production and living standards are both increasing; employment gains have been excellent. Inflation, which raged at double-digit rates in 1980, has been reduced dramatically . . . And insupportable growth in tax burdens and Federal regulations has been halted, an intolerably complex and inequitable income-tax structure has been radically reformed, and the largest management-improvement program ever attempted is in full swing in all major Federal agencies. It has been a good six years. Now in its fifth year, the current expansion already has exceeded five of the seven previous post-war expansions in duration, and leading economic indicators point to continued growth ahead. Our policies have worked.

Budget message to Congress, Washington,
Jan. 5/The New York Times, 1-6:10.*

2

The American people worked long and hard to cut tax rates and win tax reform. And my pledge to veto any tax-rate increase remains rock solid. It's time Congress cut the Federal budget and let the family budget alone. We would not have to fight this battle all year, every year, if the Congressional budget process were not so desperately in need of reform. The budget process at the Federal level is unworkable, and this yearly deficit-feeding process must stop.

News conference, Washington, March 19/
The New York Times, 3-20:6.

3

Congress needs to change the way it does business on the budget. They need ways of ensuring that they will stick to budget decisions once they're made—no back-door spending, no

missed targets, no swearing off the bottle of spending only to take a nip the next morning.

Before United States Chamber of Commerce,
Washington, April 27/
Los Angeles Times, 4-28:(I)13.

4

I'm sure you remember that back in 1981, the year I attended my first summit, our own economy as well as the global economy was then in grave danger. We had inflation running at 10 per cent or more in industrialized countries; not to mention high interest rates, excessive tax burdens, and too much government regulation and interference. Worse than all of this, there was virtually no agreement among world leaders on how to deal with this looming crisis. Well, in the intervening years, we have made progress. With the American economy leading the way, we started an international movement toward more economic growth and greater individual opportunity by lowering taxes and cutting government regulation. We brought down interest rates, cut inflation, reduced unemployment and confounded the experts by showing that economic growth could be sustained not just for one or two years but steadily— for more than four years.

Broadcast address to the nation after
returning from Venice economic summit meeting,
Washington, June 15/The New York Times, 6-16:6.

5

Using taxes to cure deficits is like using leeches to cure anemia. We're not going to counter one evil with another. We're going to eliminate them both. Deficits are going to [go] the way of high taxes. They're both being mowed down to make way for a new era of growth and opportunity.

To Republican Senators, Washington,
June 16/The New York Times, 6-17:13.

6

Some in the Congress are reverting to their old habits of tax and tax, spend and spend. They're squandering your hard-earned money on politically motivated spending projects and special-interest payoffs. Well, I say no way. No

(RONALD REAGAN)

way are the American people going to be made to foot the bill for the tax-and-spend crew on Capitol Hill. I'm keeping [my] pencil at the ready in my desk. And believe me, any tax-hike bill that makes it into the Oval Office won't make it out alive.

To Dictaphone Corp. employees, Melbourne, Fla.,
June 22/Los Angeles Times, 6-23:(I)13.

1

[On his continued push for a balanced-budget amendment and a line-item veto]: Some said that I was singing golden oldies, nothing new. Well, the line-item veto and the balanced-budget amendment may be oldies, but they're goodies. And those who think they don't stand a chance on the charts had better keep their dial tuned to this station. It's rock-and-roll time again at the White House.

Before National Federation
of Independent Business, Washington,
June 23/The New York Times, 6-24:9.

2

The working people of this country need to know their jobs; take-home pay, homes and pensions are not vulnerable to the threat ot a grandiose, inefficient and overbearing government, something Jefferson warned us about 200 years ago. It is time to finish the job Jefferson began and to protect our people and their livelihoods with restrictions on government that will ensure the fundamental economic freedom of the people, the equivalent of an Economic Bill of Rights.

Independence Day address, Washington,
July 3/Los Angeles Times, 7-4:(I)2.

3

Once we got the Federal government out of their way, the American people launched an economic expansion that is in its 56th month and still setting records. The people created more than 13 million jobs, 60 per cent of which are in managerial, professional, technical or other high-paying occupations. Unemployment is the lowest since December, 1979. The per-centage of our working-age population at work is near record levels. We are going into our fifth consecutive year of inflation below 5 per cent. Adjusted for inflation, disposable personal income has reached new highs over the past four years. And when the stock market broke through the 2500 level, it was almost three times its level of September, 1981.

Interview, Washington/
Nation's Business, September:74.

4

To those who say we must weaken America's defense [by spending less on it], they're nuts. To those who say we must raise the tax burden on the American people, they, too, are nuts.

Signing a deficit-reduction bill,
Washington, Sept. 30/
The Washington Post, 10-5:(A)4.

5

The American economy is sound and strong . . . If corrections or fluctuations do occur [such as the recent stock-market crash], as long as consumers do not over-react by losing confidence, our expansion will continue. Let's also remember a critical reason for this expansion was our decision to reduce taxes in 1981 . . . I'm proud that since 1913 my [Republican] Party had reduced taxes 10 times and increased them only once.

Oct. 24/The Washington Post, 10-28:(A)14.

Donald T. Regan
Former Chief of Staff to President
of the United States Ronald Reagan

6

In [British] Parliament, when the budget is written, the chief finance minister takes [it] in and it's there for perhaps a period of a month. And there are hearings on it for one month only. And then it's an up-or-down vote. It's not like [the U.S.] Congress where they pull it all apart. And various members can shove in their pet projects "here" or they can add or subtract "there." [In Britain,] the Prime Minister has the right to set that budget up. And in one

(DONALD T. REGAN)

month it's up or down. And it's always exciting because, if it's down, then the party in power falls and there is a new election. So they pass that budget, and they go on to other things. [But in the U.S.,] this President has to spend an enormous amount of time on a budget that is never passed.

At business conference sponsored by Loyola Marymount University, Los Angeles, April 16/Los Angeles Times, 4-17:(I)25.

Alice M. Rivlin
Director of economic studies, Brookings Institution; Former Director, Congressional Budget Office

1

The deficit is not one of our most difficult problems. Conceptually, we know what to do: raise taxes or cut spending. Everybody has agreed we have to do some of each.

USA Today, 6-23:(A)10.

Charles S. Robb
Former Governor of Virginia (D); Chairman, Democratic Leadership Council

2

For labor, adaptability is the key. Rigid work rules and job classifications, resistance to new technologies that transform the work place, wage demands devorced from long-term company performance, a relentlessly adversarial stance toward employers—all these today are anachronisms that ultimately work to the disadvantage of working men and women.

Before Economic Club of Detroit/ The New York Times, 3-12:10.

Paul Craig Roberts
Economist

3

In a sluggish world economy, there are good reasons why the Federal Reserve should not tighten monetary policy to prevent depreciation of the dollar. The Federal Reserve can either stabilize the exchange rate or it can stabilize the economy. If the Fed puts the dollar first and the economy second, it is in effect adopting a yen standard and transforming the Fed into a de facto branch of the Bank of Japan. This is inconsistent with the normal Congressional emphasis, reflected in the Humphrey-Hawkins Act, that the Fed stabilize the U.S. economy. Moreover, adoption of a yen standard is a good way to elevate Japanese financial interests and move the yen into the dollar's role as the reserve currency.

Before House Domestic Monetary Policy Subcommittee, Washington, June 4/ The Wall Street Journal, 6-12:10.

Felix G. Rohatyn
Senior partner, Lazard Freres & Company

4

Today, conservatives and liberals alike have participated in the greatest borrowing binge in this country's history, and both camps wrongly pretend that freedom can only be maintained by an ever-escalating arms race, on Earth and in space. Freedom consists of more than freedom from domination. It consists of freedom from dependency on foreign capital and in the ability of all our citizens to fulfill their destiny. That is not the case in America today. As a country, we are no longer independent economically. As individuals, too many Americans are condemned from birth to being economic wards of the state and are under-equipped educationally to compete.

At Long Island University commencement/ The New York Times, 6-3:27.

Dan Rostenkowski
United States Representative, D-Illinois

5

This President [Reagan] is the biggest deficit spender in our history. The President's anti-tax rhetoric is no less astounding than his anti-deficit speeches. He has signed the three largest tax increases in our history . . . I'm tired of

WHAT THEY SAID IN 1987

(DAN ROSTENKOWSKI)

this game of smoke and mirrors. I'm tired of his bashing the Congress on the deficit.

Before the House, Washington, June 23/
The Washington Post, 6-24:(A)6.

Robert Schmermund
Press secretary,
Republican National Committee

1

There are still [economic] problems out there that need to be solved, but let's remember where we were [before the Reagan Administration took office], let's remember our starting point . . . There is no comparison when you are talking about double-digit inflation and interest rates of 21.5 per cent [before Reagan]. I think the young people of today . . . are realizing that there are different ways to solve problems, and that one of the best ways to help everyone across the board is having a strong economy.

The Christian Science Monitor, 5-12:4.

Helmut Schmidt
Former Chancellor of West Germany

2

The [economic] circumstances [of the recent stock-market crash] are [molded] by the economic behavior of three major countries. First of all, the United States has lived beyond its means. There were budget deficits of almost $200-billion a year, and American capital formation was not big enough to cover them. Second, the [West] Germans have conducted a relatively deflationary monetary and budgetary policy. The Germans are living below their means, while the Americans are living beyond their means. Third, the same can be said for Japan as for Germany—with the difference that Japan's mistake is twice as big.

Interview/Newsweek, 11-2:49.

William Schneider
Fellow, American Enterprise Institute

3

If we are heading for a serious recession, it's very hard to see how the Democrats can lose in

1988 . . . No way can the Reagan Administration escape blame for this one. [And] one thing people still like about Democrats is they stand for protecting Americans from economic adversity—that holds the whole damn Party together.

Oct. 19/Los Angeles Times, 10-20:(I)15.

Patricia Schroeder
United States Representative,
D-Colorado

4

Employers have generally failed to adapt their family and medical-leave policies to the needs of workers. A minimum Federal standard is needed if families are to continue playing their traditional role.

Newsweek, 1-26:22.

George P. Shultz
Secretary of State of the United States

5

Given the importance of exports, particularly exports in manufactures, to all of your countries, you are going to have to work hard to diversify your markets. While you may be able to maintain your current market share in the United States, you clearly will not be able to look to the U.S. to take major increases in your exports. [The reason is] not necessarily because of U.S. protectionism, but simply because of the adjustments the U.S. economy will have made in order to service our large growing external debt . . . Your flexibility and pragmatism will be challenged perhaps as never before over the next few years, as the world economic system adjusts to the inevitable, and in my view, possibly rapid decline, in the U.S. trade deficit.

To foreign ministers of members of Association
of Southeast Asian Nations, Singapore,
June 19/The New York Times, 6-20:17.

Paul Simon
United States Senator, D-Illinois;
Candidate for the 1988
Democratic Presidential nomination

6

You have two trends in this country. One is that the demand for unskilled labor is going

96

(PAUL SIMON)

down. And that isn't going to change. The second is that the pool of unskilled labor is going up. That can change, but it will not change dramatically or quickly. That means that this very sizable pool of unemployed that we have in our country is going to continue to exist, and we're not going to let them starve. So we face the choice of paying people for doing nothing, or paying them for doing something. It makes infinitely more sense to pay people for doing something.

Interview/USA Today, 3-16:(A)13.

1

Some people say if you have an economic agenda that requires balancing the [Federal] budget, you can't have a social agenda. I would argue precisely the opposite—that those who say we can continue to indefinitely borrow from our children and grandchildren and generations to come in fact are eroding our ability to do what we ought to do in education, in health care, and in other things. Some people say, when I talk about this combination, that they are in conflict. I'm going to have to gradually persuade my opponents and my friends in the media that they are not in conflict.

*Campaign rally, Indianola, Iowa/
Los Angeles Times, 11-27:(I)1.*

Allen Sinai
*Chief economist,
Shearson Lehman Brothers*

2

The [latest] unemployment report was really a super report on the labor market. The incredible job-creating machine in the United States is now creating jobs in services and goods alike, suggesting the economy has a much stronger underpinning than might have been suspected. The report is a very positive sign for continued growth in income, consumer spending and a very solid rise in real GNP for the second half.

Aug. 7/The Washington Post, 8-8:(A)1.

Sharon Spigelmyer
*Director of loss prevention,
National Association of Manufacturers*

3

It's my impression that [company] concern for [employee] safety has never been higher, not only because of a concern for the workers, but because workers' compensation costs [that] companies have to pay when employees are injured have never been higher. There is no question that companies are trying to improve productivity, but that's not diminishing their efforts to improve safety. In fact, every company I deal with now ties a plant manager's performance rating to plant safety. That would give managers an incentive not to go for higher productivity at the sake of safety.

Los Angeles Times, 3-2:(I)12.

Herbert Stein
*Scholar, American Enterprise Institute;
Former Chairman, Council of Economic
Advisers to the President
of the United States (Richard Nixon)*

4

[On international economic summit meetings among heads of state]: I don't think discussion at this level is routinely, regularly necessary. [Former President] Nixon could get himself well-informed on economic matters when they got serious enough with briefings at Camp David. He didn't have to go to Venice [site of the current economic summit] for that.

The New York Times, 6-8:8.

Graciela Testa-Ortiz
*Director, forecasting section,
United States Chamber of Commerce*

5

[Saying high minimum wages add to inflation and unemployment]: The evidence is incontrovertible. Nevertheless, the myths persist, and every few years legislators propose yet another increase in the minimum wage. In the process, they congratulate themselves for such a clear expression of their superior morality and compassion. Yet, this exercise in easy eth-

(GRACIELA TESTA-ORTIZ)

ics only leads to greater hardship for all Americans . . . To young, inexperienced workers, minimum-wage jobs are an extension of schooling, since those jobs offer them the training and the work experience to move on to higher-paying jobs. The [higher] minimum wage deprives the youth of America not only of the opportunity to get a job, but also of needed experience and on-the-job training, while it does nothing to alleviate poverty.

Nation's Business/June:38.

James R. Thompson
Governor of Illinois (R)

1

Keeping taxes low is great—unless your tax system doesn't produce enough revenue to give you a first-class state. And as I try to tell audiences around the state who are against the philosophy of tax and spend, tax and spend, there are worse things than tax and spend. Borrow and spend is worse; that's why Washington's in trouble. Spend and spend without knowing where the money is coming from, which is what the [Illinois] Legislature likes to do, is worse. And the failure to spend for things that are needed, whether it's education or transportation, is worse.

Interview/USA Today, 3-23:(A)13.

Lester C. Thurow
Professor of economics,
Massachusetts Institute of Technology

2

When the United States was overtaking Great Britain as the world's economic leader between 1860 and 1900, America had the best-educated, most skilled labor force in the world. Mass high-quality compulsory education was an American invention, and America rode it to economic success. Where America once had the best-educated labor force, it now has a labor force that does not stand comparison with most of the industrial world.

The Christian Science Monitor, 7-22:17.

3

The [recent] stock-market crash may even help the economy. It will do so because it scared the Federal Reserve Board into changing its policies. Lower interest rates may well in the end stimulate the economy more than the stock-market crash depressed it.

Los Angeles Times, 11-1:(I)32.

Leo Troy
Professor of labor economics,
Rutgers University

4

The [labor] unions feel they've come to the end of the line on givebacks and concessions. They want back what they gave up and they're a little more restive. On the other hand, economic conditions are still working against them, particularly in manufacturing—just look at the trade balance with Japan—and employers are not willing to give in.

The New York Times, 3-12:11.

William Vander Zalm
Premier of British Columbia, Canada

5

Most governments don't ever want to touch labor law. They are much afraid of it. [But] we [his party] emphasized the rights of individuals. We believe unions will become far more effective and stronger when the individual has a total say in the union. We have removed any opportunity for people to coerce or use threats against others in the work place or otherwise.

Interview, Richmond, B.C./
The Christian Science Monitor, 12-22:11.

Paul A. Volcker
Chairman, Federal Reserve Board

6

A self-generating, cumulative process of currency depreciation and inflation serves no one's interest. Economic history is littered with examples of countries that acted as if currency depreciation alone could substitute for other

(PAUL A. VOLCKER)

action to restore balance and competitiveness to their economies.

Before Congressional Joint Economic Committee, Washington, Feb. 2/ The Washington Post, 2-3:(C)2.

Charles Wolf, Jr.
Director of internatioal economic policy research, Rand Corporation

1

It is no more accurate to think of the United States as dependent on foreign financing as it is to think of the Japanese and Germans as dependent on the United States as a place to invest their extra savings. Foreign investors—governments and people—are looking for places to put their dough that will be safe and remunerative—and the United States is attractive to these governments and people.

Los Angeles Times, 11-6:(I)26.

Jim Wright
United States Representative, D-Texas

2

[President Reagan] isn't opposed to taxes; he's just opposed to taxes on rich people. I'd rather postpone a tax cut for the people making more than $150,000 than cut back on the fight against drugs, or Medicare and Medicaid benefits, or help for kids going to college.

To reporters, Washington, Jan. 9/ The Washington Post, 2-10:(A)5.

3

The President [Reagan] sometimes likes to criticize Congress for what he calls "big spending." [But thanks to Congressional cuts in Reagan-proposed defense spending,] the plain truth is that for the six years of this Administration, Congress actually has appropriated less in total spending than Mr. Reagan has asked us to appropriate. The basic disagreement is not over how much to spend. It's where to spend it, what we get for it and who pays the bill, ourselves or our children.

Broadcast address to the nation, Washington, Jan. 27/Los Angeles Times, 1-28:(I)15.

4

What you face and what Congress faces . . . is a mentality in the White House which believes two fantasies: first, that giving tax cuts to wealthy people does not add to the deficit; second, that spending more and more money on military equipment does not add to the deficit. Until we can overcome that state of mind, there isn't any money for the things we really want to do.

To college presidents, Washington, Feb. 6/Los Angeles Times, 2-7:(I)21.

5

At a time when we need serious and constructive attention to budget deficits, the President [Reagan] subjects himself to ridicule by shouting old slogans and preposterous claims that sound more like a sideshow barker than a President.

June 23/Los Angeles Times, 6-24:(I)14.

Education

Mortimer Adler
Educator; Director, Institute
for Philosophical Research

1

What facts a student should know is the least important part about a child's education. A student can cram in information, but unless he really understands it, it's easily forgotten.

U.S. News & World Report, 9-28:93.

Robert Armstrong
Executive director,
Henry Luce Foundation

2

It is still true—though perhaps unconsciously—that when senior appointments [in academia] are to be made, the chairman of the search committee is very likely to be in touch with his colleagues at other universities, and the names put forward are likely to be self-replicating, and male. Unless there is a woman who has achieved particular eminence, her name is not likely to occur. Being overlooked by the old-boy network appears to work against women of all ages. In the entry-to-mid-level academic ranks, there have been significant changes for the better. It is in the upper ranks that the real problem still exists.

The Christian Science Monitor, 10-23:19.

Charles E. Ballinger
Executive secretary,
National Association
for Year-Round Education

3

[Calling for a 12-month school year]: Those of us in year-round education believe educators simply cannot justify that long, three-month summer vacation any more. The nine-month schedule was never designed for education in the first place. It's a 19th-century agricultural-economic schedule.

The New York Times, 10-14:1.

Terrel H. Bell
Former Secretary of Education
of the United States

4

Thirty per cent of our ninth-graders drop out without graduating from high school. That's a nation-wide figure. That's 30 per cent of our rising generation that we're losing each year. In addition, there are millions of families in America where no member has ever earned a college degree. We have youth unemployment that's three times higher for minorities than for the majority population. We simply need to solve this problem of so many drop-outs, and so many failures of students to attain enough education so they can be independent and productive members of our society.

Interview/USA Today, 10-27:(A)13.

William J. Bennett
Secretary of Education
of the United States

5

There are some things to be said for rote and memorization and getting the facts and getting the answer right. We Americans, being a pragmatic people, would therefore be well advised to learn what we can from Japanese education—if only because of its manifest success.

Newsweek, 1-12:61.

6

Total national spending for education has climbed steadily . . . Although education is primarily a state and local responsibility, this [Reagan] Administration has been at the forefront of the reform movement . . . American education has improved on this Administration's watch.

Before Senate Labor and
Human Resources Committee,
Washington, Jan. 14/
The New York Times, 1-15:11.

(WILLIAM J. BENNETT)

1

States and local [school] jurisdictions have constructed a system of textbook adoption that responds to the demands of almost every constituency: teachers, parents, publishers, elected officials and interest groups. Every possible constituency, that is, but one—the most important one: the readers, our students . . . States and local jurisdictions have established regulations governing the content of schoolbooks, and they have appointed committees to judge available texts against their guidelines. These committees are not always chosen for their expertise. Membership is often based on politics, geography or role . . . [There] is a lack of confidence in the ability of our students to learn from demanding, well-written, good textbooks. Book-adoption committees have relied on "readability formulae" to assign a level of difficulty to given texts. These formulae involve counting the numbers of syllables in words and of words in sentences. Writing that is "too complex" may be disqualified for use of a certain grade level. The result? Books with short, choppy sentences, limited vocabulary, homogenized tone and monotonous, unnatural prose style.

Before school division,
Association of American Publishers,
Washington, Jan. 20/
The New York Times, 2-4:8.

2

Washington seems to be the only place where education is measured by input rather than output.

USA Today, 2-4:(A)8.

3

The Blob is continuing to grow. By the Blob I mean the educational bureaucracy, that part of the educational system which does not consist of students, does not consist of teachers, does not consist of principals; it consists of others, many doing a very fine job. But do we need them all? . . . [If] the number of students in a school district or in a state declines, the Blob

still grows. The administrative bureaucracy gets bigger and bigger. And, I can tell you as someone who's in charge of [an] administrative bureaucracy, when it gets bigger and bigger, it gets harder and harder to run, and accountability tends to get lost.

News conference, Feb. 10/
The Wall Street Journal, 6-19:20.

4

I've criticized the quality of higher education from the very beginning, and now the Number 1 best-seller in the country—*The Closing of the American Mind*—makes exactly that point. I've complained about the cost of higher education, and that is no longer idiosyncratic. I've talked about more choice at the elementary and secondary level. Now there are magnet schools all over the country.

Interview, June 10/
The New York Times, 6-11:14.

5

[Saying the National Education Association relies too much on requests for more funds to make education better]: Give me a break! And give the American people a break. Once again, the NEA reveals its cash-register mentality. While continuing to resist every promising and significant education reform in the states, the NEA returns to its favorite obsession—money. [The U.S. spends] more on education than ever before and more than any other country in the world . . . Important reforms are being made. When will the largest and most intransigent of the nation's education associations figure it out?

Los Angeles Times, 6-28:(I)5.

6

There are greater, more certain and more immediate penalties in this country for serving up a single rotten hamburger than for furnishing a thousand schoolchildren with a rotten education. This must change.

At symposium sponsored by
University of North Carolina,
Chapel Hill, Sept. 11/
The Christian Science Monitor, 9-14:7.

WHAT THEY SAID IN 1987

Joseph R. Biden, Jr.
United States Senator, D-Delaware;
Candidate for the 1988
Democratic Presidential nomination

1

Our students must go to school longer; they should go to school more than 180 days a year. We must demand more of our teachers . . . If you're saying it costs money, you're damn right it costs money.

Speech/The Washington Post, 5-1:(A)18.

James H. Billington
Director, Woodrow Wilson
International Center for Scholars;
Librarian of Congress-designate
of the United States

2

There has been an erosion of values within our opinion-making, norm-setting culture. Just take the leading universities. Nobody from these institutions serves in the armed forces any more. Nobody from these universities physically works in the productive side of the economy, actually making things.

At dialogue at Woodrow Wilson Center,
Washington, June/
Los Angeles Times, 7-26:(V)5.

James Blanchard
Governor of Michigan (D)

3

[On his state's unique funding plan for college tuitions]: Somebody puts down $3,500 now, or the equivalent in payroll deductions. And we guarantee, when the child reaches 18, there will be four years free of tuition at any one of our public colleges or universities. They get to pick the college at the time, assuming they can get admitted. If they decide not to go to school, the purchaser gets the money back with interest . . . Every state's going to end up doing it. Each state's a little different, and they'll have to tailor it to their own needs. If a child is told his name is on a certificate that says if you study hard and work hard, your college is paid for, they're much more likely to

work hard and study hard. I see the tuition-guarantee program as a great motivator.

Interview/USA Today, 3-30:(A)13.

Allan Bloom
Author; Professor,
University of Chicago

4

Today's "select" students are so much slacker intellectually that they make their predecessors look like prodigies of culture.

U.S. News & World Report, 9-28:86.

Julian Bond
Former Georgia State Legislator (D)

5

My little girl brought a note home from school that said, "Julia be late too often." What kind of teacher wrote that note? Is he teaching *my* daughter how to read and write? I'm talking about a public school in Atlanta. If that teacher's main concern is wages and hours and whether or not he has to sit in a study hall and does he get a rest period, then some other force is going to have to move in. The parents are going to have to say: "It's my education that helped put me where I am today. So I want my children to get the best possible education they can."

Panel discussion, Cooper Union,
New York/Harper's, February:46.

William G. Bowen
President, Princeton University

6

My worry is less that we will unthinkingly charge too much [tuition] than that we will unthinkingly charge too little, and make too small a provision for [student] financial aid. It is sometimes necessary to pay for what is really valuable.

The Wall Street Journal, 3-2:20.

7

One of the reasons why people look to universities for guidance and have such affection for them is that, in a splintering, fragmenting

(WILLIAM G. BOWEN)

world, they somehow stand for the proposition that ultimately things do hang together or should—that there is a wholeness there that people need desperately. Part of what we're discussing is how to give reality to that longing while at the same time respecting greater depth of knowledge in a number of areas.

At symposium sponsored by "U.S. News & World Report"/ U.S. News & World Report, 4-20:67.

William E. Brock
Secretary of Labor
of the United States

1

It's an insane tragedy that 700,000 people get a diploma each year and can't read the damned diploma.

Newsweek, 1-26:19.

2

Public education has been a failure for the last 20 or 25 years. We've got 23 million illiterates—people who can't read at the fourth-grade level. Another 40 million are marginally illiterate; they read between the fourth-and ninth-grade levels. Yet the overwhelming majority of new jobs created in the U.S. will require post-secondary education.

Nation's Business, September:56.

Edmund G. Brown, Jr.
Former Governor of California (D)

3

More science, more math, more language, tougher requirements all the way down the line . . . Whatever the costs and whatever the problems in terms of public funding, America has to make a much greater commitment in education, in working, retraining and in our level of public and private research.

Interview, Tokyo, Jan. 19/ Los Angeles Times, 1-20:(I)15.

George Bush
Vice President of the United States

4

In higher education, as in the lower grades, we should demand more—more real learning and less basket-weaving. But in higher education today, the question is just as much access as it is quality—economic access. Many middle-class families are panicked by the high costs of four years of college—the specter of $100,000 per child. Such figures may be exaggerated by projections of inflation. But as parents plan for the future, image is just as important as reality, if fears of economic hardship deter bright and able students.

At National Conference of State Legislators, Indianapolis, July 28/The New York Times, 7-29:11.

Bruce M. Carnes
Deputy Under Secretary of Education
of the United States

5

[Approving of cutbacks in Federal grants for students, in favor of students *borrowing* from the government to cover college costs and later having to pay back the loans]: Who should pay the bill—the student or the cab driver who didn't even go to college? Nobody's holding a gun to these people's head and saying, "You will take this loan, and you will go to this expensive school."

The New York Times, 1-29:7.

Jeanne Chall
Professor of education,
Harvard University

6

It's at fourth grade and above that we have a reading slump. That's where children begin to use reading as a tool for learning. They need the vocabulary and knowledge of the world to read well and to gain in comprehension. And that's where the schools need improvement . . . To understand the materials read at fourth grade and above requires knowledge of complicated literary language and knowledge of the

WHAT THEY SAID IN 1987

world. The students need more context and more content. Illiteracy is the wrong label for their problem.

The Washington Post, 8-17:(A)8.

Lynne V. Cheney
Chairman, National Endowment
for the Humanities
of the United States

1

The humanities have fallen on hard times. Between 1975 and 1985, a decade in which the total number of bachelors degrees was increasing, the number of degrees in philosophy was down by almost 40 per cent, in history down by about 50 per cent, in literature down by 60 per cent. One recent study that comes out of UCLA shows that over the past 20 years the number of people saying they were going to major in history was down by 80 per cent. At the same time, what you see is that the approach to life these students are taking has changed drastically. It used to be that if you asked them what purpose their college education was, it would be to "find out more about myself, to develop a philosophy of life." Now, if you ask them, they say, "It's to make a lot of money."

Interview, Los Angeles/
Los Angeles Times, 6-3:(V)2.

2

[School textbooks teaching about democracy] seem to be more oriented in teaching how to think and not in giving substantive things to think about . . . Charts and graphs are important, but most important I think is whether a textbook can captivate a child's imagination, whether it can unfold events in a way to show their significance.

July 29/The New York Times, 7-30:15.

Marva Collins
Educator

3

[On the "Marva Collins way" of teaching]: First of all, not just to be a teacher. I teach peo-

ple to be free. They're not bounded by thinking that their answers must be mine . . . We make them feel that together we can do things. The average teacher tells children, "Get in your seat, sit down, shut up" . . . It's not class sizes, it's not things. It's just an attitude.

Interview, Chicago/USA Today, 1-14:(D)5.

William Cunningham
President, University of Texas, Austin

4

We [in higher education] can talk about morals. We can talk about values. We can work at teaching those things. But the truth is, if students don't have a strong set of values and morals when they come to campus, we're not going to teach them at the university. For any of us to think that we are, is just teasing ourselves and society. We're not going to correct all the ills of parents who have not done a good job.

At symposium sponsored by
"U.S. News & World Report"/
U.S. News & World Report, 4-20:68.

Mario M. Cuomo
Governor of New York (D)

5

[We in U.S.] now have 23 million illiterates, and [we're] behind much of the world in education. [We're] uneducated and under-educated— and still [we're] powerful. Imagine where [we] would be if [we] got rid of the 23 million illiterates and had only 5 million!

Interview, Albany, N.Y./
The Washington Post, 11-19:(A)23.

Peter Diamandopoulos
President, Adelphi University

6

[On colleges conferring honorary degrees on people who may have unpopular political beliefs]: My position is that I don't believe that individuals of distinction and quality ought to be innocent of political beliefs. A very distinguished physicist may hold abhorrent political beliefs. Do we therefore eliminate him from

(PETER DIAMANDOPOULOS)

consideration because his political beliefs are unattractive? If so, we must throw aside the question of merit.

The New York Times, 5-18:17.

Albert J. DiUlio
President,
Xavier University, Cincinnati

1

Undergraduate education in America has never been better and is improving rapidly. The problem lies in the expectations, which are, like so many other things in American life, increasing at a faster pace than any institution or groups of institutions can satisfy.

U.S. News & World Report, 10-26:51.

Michael S. Dukakis
Governor of Massachusetts (D);
Candidate for the 1988
Democratic Presidential nomination

2

[We must take] a hard look at our national accounts and never again allow one generation of Americans to steal from a future generation. We must ask ourselves why it is that at a time when the nation is piling up the biggest deficits in its history, a Republican Administration is unable or unwilling to collect $110-billion a year in taxes owed that aren't being paid. That doesn't make any fiscal sense, and it's just not fair.

Speech/The Washington Post, 5-1:(A)18.

Henry Falk
Director of public relations,
Pace University

3

[On those chosen to speak at college commencements]: I've been in public relations for 20 years, and as long as I can remember, the popular commencement speakers have been Senators, Congressmen, show-business types, to attract the media and add a little extra glitter to commencement exercises.

Interview/The New York Times, 6-8:15.

James L. Fisher
President emeritus,
Council for Advancement and
Support of Higher Education

4

A dispassionate look at today's political and educational landscape suggests that nobody . . . is going to do much to help students pay for college. Indeed, the situation calls for fundamental changes to the American psyche, both in the general public and within the educational community. This reorientation is not helped by distortions from higher education and Federal and state governments, as they at once blame one another for rising college costs and lament increasing student indebtedness. If borrowing substantial sums for college is not accepted, the time may come when, faced with a choice—college or no?—the student may say no, and countless worthy institutions may be forced to merge, cut back or close. Then the very future of our society will be at stake, but it will be too late to turn back.

Los Angeles Times, 12-13:(I)3.

Ronald Frank
Dean,
Clarence School of Management,
Purdue University

5

Universities are going to find that they don't have a monopoly on education. We're obviously getting sharply increased needs for educational skills from people in business, but if universities are unwilling to change their academic calendar, their hours, and where the training is being done, then corporations are going to do it themselves. And it's not just delivery [of education]. We have to design courses that are useful for businesses.

The Christian Science Monitor, 7-23:17.

WHAT THEY SAID IN 1987

Richard A. Gephardt
United States Representative,
D-Missouri;
Candidate for the 1988
Democratic Presidential nomination

1

I was always very supportive of public education, worked [as a St. Louis alderman] for bond issues and elections, and have felt from the earliest moment I can remember that education was the key to our country. And I feel that especially now because of the very strong challenges we face, both economically and militarily . . . Education, training [and] skills are the most important thing to securing the kind of future we want. And if I'm elected [President], I will make education and training and research the most important goals of my Administration.

Interview, Washington/
The Christian Science Monitor, 4-14:7.

2

Americans know we're falling behind [in education]. Our kids aren't getting sufficient education to make our economy work. If we're going to make our economy first again, we've got to start in the first grade.

At symposium sponsored by
University of North Carolina,
Chapel Hill, Sept. 11/
The Christian Science Monitor, 9-14:7.

A. Bartlett Giamatti
Former president, Yale University

3

Being the president of a university is a great privilege, and it's fascinating in many ways. But intellectually stimulating it's not.

Interview/
The Christian Science Monitor, 7-16:36.

Joan Girgus
Dean, Princeton University.

4

[Saying today's college students are serious about their education]: This is a group of students that takes the world to be a serious place

and takes their own lives as lives that have the potential for happiness and pleasure—but not without cost and not without work. And they don't believe that it will come through luck.

The New York Times, 5-12:14.

Hanna Holborn Gray
President, University of Chicago

5

. . . liberal education is in itself oriented toward the teaching of a very profound set of values which has nothing to do with ethics. It has to do with trying to teach the values and habits of intellectual integrity. If that in itself is not a profound moral value and the basis for thinking through a set of ethical issues, I don't know what is. Intellectual integrity, after all, has something to do with respect for evidence and different points of view, plus an attempt to understand the moral issues that are attached to the pursuit of knowledge—and those embedded in much knowledge. There's a tendency to feel liberal education is one thing and teaching values is another. I think the attempt to make intellectual integrity an internal habit of graduates is the most important thing about teaching values.

At symposium sponsored by
"U.S. News & World Report"/
U.S. News & World Report, 4-20:68.

Harvey Grotrian
Director of financial aid,
University of Michigan

6

[On the rise in college tuition costs]: We're seeing more in the way of sticker shock lately. Parents are wondering where you go after you've gone through your resources, sold your stock, taken out a second mortgage and are still thousands of dollars short.

The New York Times, 1-29:7.

F. Sheldon Hackney
President, University of Pennsylvania

7

One of the peculiarities of education is that our customer is also our product. That confuses

(F. SHELDON HACKNEY)

most analogies between universities and profit-making enterprises.

Time, 4-20:70.

David Harman
Professor, Teacher's College,
Columbia University

1

We ought to emphasize literacy as a national objective. But it's an escape from dealing with the real, very complicated problems of disadvantage to say we can teach people reading, and unemployment and family problems will be reduced . . . There's a value to reading in people's lives that transcends putting a widget in a wadget. Literacy is a value, not a mechanical skill.

The Washington Post, 8-17:(A)7.

Gary Hart
Former United States Senator,
D-Colorado; Candidate for the 1988
Democratic Presidential nomination

2

Not all educational reforms require money. We have 25 million adult Americans who are illiterate, and millions more children who are not reading up to the level they need to. You can help solve that problem. I would like to know how many of you [students] would like to give a few hours a week or month to help children read better? We also have adults who can't read the writing on a medicine bottle or even road signs. How many of you would be willing to donate your time to help those adult Americans, particularly if you got a student loan or some educational opportunity in exchange for that?

To students at
George Washington High School,
Los Angeles, Jan. 29/
Los Angeles Times, 1-30:(I)26.

Jesse Helms
United States Senator,
R-North Carolina

3

I am convinced that the problems of education in America can be traced to the time that the Federal government began to intrude in what previously had been purely a function and responsibility of state and local government. I am further convinced that the more our schools rely on so-called Federal aid, the worse the problems will become.

Interview/The Washington Post, 12-8:(A)25.

Robert Hess
President, Brooklyn (N.Y.) College

4

When I asked students what they were majoring in, it used to be that everyone said accounting, business, health, science and so forth. All pre-meds were majoring in biology and chemistry. But now they seem to be majoring in classics and history. The number of English majors is very large and enrollment in history has steadily increased.

The New York Times, 5-12:14.

E. D. Hirsch, Jr.
Professor of English,
University of Virginia

5

For young kids, facts are more important than learning to think for themselves. Kids first need a basis for thought. Walk into language-arts classes across the U.S., as I've been doing, and you find kids staring at the walls. They're bored, disconnected, confused—even though they can pronounce the words.

Interview, San Francisco/
The Christian Science Monitor, 4-13:23.

John P. Holdren
Professor of energy and resources,
University of California, Berkeley

6

We are now facing the prospect that defense research in general and "Star Wars" [the proposed U.S. space defense system] in particular, will be the largest source of Federal funds likely to be available [to universities] for at least a decade to come. Since universities do the bulk of the country's basic research . . .

WHAT THEY SAID IN 1987

(JOHN P. HOLDREN)

and train the majority of American scientists . . . we have to ask what that will mean for our universities and the country as a whole.

Los Angeles Times, 4-13:(I)18.

Bill Honig
California State Superintendent
of Public Instruction

1

. . . there seems to be an understanding among the profession that we need to improve the quality of teachers coming in. Either we deliver the goods, or we're going to lose public education. We have to transform teaching into a true profession.

The Washington Post, 5-16:(A)6.

2

[On the teaching of history]: The biggest complaint we've gotten from kids is that history is fragmented, history is not interesting. But these topics—like the American Revolution, the framing of the Constitution, the fall of the South—ought to be the most interesting topics around. Instead, kids are just running through a bunch of facts, and they're not getting a feel for real events, for the ideas people fought for, and they're not getting the connections [between past and present]. They are losing a democratic understanding of life.

Los Angeles Times, 6-15:(I)3.

Gerard Indelicato
President, Bridgewater
(Mass.) State College

3

Students and parents are beginning to understand just what a "liberal education" is and how that translates economically to jobs and careers. Narrow technical training, once thought of as a key to success, is more and more seen as a long-term risk, as in, "Will the job I'm training for still exist in the year 2000?"

U.S. News & World Report, 10-26:51.

David T. Kearns
Chairman, Xerox Corporation

4

American business will have to hire more than a million new service and production workers a year who can't read, write or count. Teaching them how and absorbing the lost productivity while they are learning will cost industry $25-billion a year for as long as it takes.

U.S. News & World Report, 5-18:67.

5

Business and education have largely failed in their partnerships to improve the schools. Business let education frame the problem and set the agenda. They hurt more than they help, because they keep shoring up a system that needs deep structural changes. Public education has put this country at terrible competitive disadvantage. The American work force is running out of qualified people.

Open letter to Presidential candidates,
Oct. 26/The New York Times, 10-27:12.*

Eamon M. Kelly
President, Tulane University

6

Our [tuition] policy is total Robin Hood. We put our tuition up as high as possible and then put most of the extra money into financial aid [for students who cannot afford to pay].

The New York Times, 5-14:13.

Donald Kennedy
President, Stanford University

7

We don't have policy control over any income item except tuition. The only place we can go for improvement is our private patrons because our public patrons are pulling away. You can tighten your belt and reduce expenditures, but in the end the only place you can turn to make things balance is tuition.

News conference/
U.S. News & World Report, 3-9:54.

William Kristol
Chief of Staff,
Department of Education
of the United States

1

[On the failure of students to repay college loans]: It really is a disgrace—schools with 50, 60, 70 per cent default rates. Back in the late '70s, people were appalled at default rates of 10 to 12 per cent. If half the kids [with loans at an educational institution] are in default, something's gone terribly wrong.

The Washington Post, 10-20:(A)19.

William J. Lawrence
Professor of economics,
Graduate School of Business,
Pace University

2

I sure hope there is a trend back to the liberal arts. I can do much more with students who have a good basic knowledge of English literature and history. Students who have no sense of history or literature are missing so much. Those who do can be more creative and objective.

The New York Times, 1-6:47.

Li Peng
Vice Premier of China; Chairman,
State Education Commission

3

A school should not be judged just by how many of its students enter colleges and how many post-graduates it trains. The basic criterion is whether the graduates are useful citizens who can contribute to the . . . development of the country.

The Christian Science Monitor, 5-5:9.

Forrest McDonald
Professor of history,
University of Alabama

4

I don't think I would ever have prophesied that I would ever say this. But I think the answer is in education. I really do believe that if discipline and dedication could somehow be restored to the teaching profession down at the beginning levels, the transformation of the American character could be just astonishing.

Interview, Washington/
The Christian Science Monitor, 5-12:7.

Edwin Meese III
Attorney General
of the United States

5

[Saying teachers should be tested for drug use]: We in the Department of Justice view freedom from drugs as a valid condition of employment for school teachers. [Schools have a duty to] take a leadership role in the over-all struggle against drugs . . . This duty falls most obviously to our public schools; yet it can be shared as well by the private and religious schools that have made such superb contributions to the education of American citizens throughout our history. To a kid hesitating over drugs, and perhaps under some nefarious peer pressure to experiment with them, the example of a drug-using teacher might be just the thing to put him over the barrier and into the squalid, self-destructive, dead-end world of drug use.

At University of Mississippi, March 19/
The Washington Post, 3-20:(A)15.

Steven Muller
President,
Johns Hopkins University

6

I personally am very concerned about students' respect for the ideas of others. As I go around my institution, the people who are really committed to freedom of expression are in the minority. Everybody values freedom of expression for himself or herself, but for a whole variety of reasons, they're not in favor of the freedom of people to express a view they regard as profoundly obnoxious. The intolerance, the lack of civility, which I think is partly built into

WHAT THEY SAID IN 1987

our whole society now, is also evident on the campuses.

At symposium sponsored by
"U.S. News & World Report"/
U.S. News & World Report, 4-20:67.

Frank Newman
President,
Education Commission of the States

1

[On the Los Angeles Board of Education's vote for a 12-month school year]: I think the Los Angeles decision is a very good thing. I'm glad someone big is trying it. And everybody, especially hard-pressed communities with overcrowded schools, will be watching very closely. But there will be a lot of opposition simply because it's change. It's a deep-seated American tradition that kids don't go to school in the summer and teachers don't teach.

The New York Times, 10-14:17.

Donna Oliver
Biology instructor, Cummings
Senior High School, Burlington, N.C.;
National Teacher of the Year

2

What [students] learn in school determines their decisions, and how they make those decisions will eventually affect the country. If you want to make a lasting impression on society, or make an imprint on the world, there is no better place than the classroom.

Ebony, November:151.

Vito Perone
Educator, Carnegie Foundation
for the Advancement of Teaching

3

Teachers obviously stand for something. I don't think there's anything neutral about a school . . . Rules of civility, how one exchanges ideas, respect for persons and for their property—these are all issues I think people in

a classroom have to deal with. A classroom is a community of a kind. It has operating principles, issues that one normally associates with values.

The Christian Science Monitor, 1-30:(B)6.

Diane Ravitch
Adjunct professor
of history and education,
Teachers College, Columbia University

4

There is a need to squeeze out some of the junk from the curriculum. History, literature, math, science and the arts should be taught throughout 13 years of schooling—all are the basic foundation of a life-long education.

U.S. News & World Report, 9-28:94.

Ronald Reagan
President of the United States

5

The secret to educational quality is not in the pocketbook, but in the heart. It's in the simple dedication of teachers, administrators, parents and students to the same basic, fundamental values that have always been the wellspring of success, both in education and life in our country.

At Hickman High School,
Columbia, Mo., March 26/
Los Angeles Times, 3-27:(I)34.

6

To teach what we're teaching in schools today without any attention to morality or the right and wrong of things, this is absolutely wrong . . . [For example,] how do you teach—start talking about sex to children and to young people without the moral side of that question being brought up? Just treat it like a physical thing such as eating a ham sandwich? And too much of this is going on.

Interview, Washington, April 28/
Los Angeles Times, 4-29:(I)17.

(RONALD REAGAN)

1

[On schools that have succeeded in educating poor children]: They don't use poverty as an excuse for failure and they don't wait around for new Federal programs before they start to do their jobs. [Their message to children is,] no matter who you are, or where you're from, you can learn . . . They know there are no such things as black values and white values, or poor values and rich values. They know there are only basic American values. They know that lower standards are double standards, and double standards are wrong.

Speech, Washington, May 20/
The New York Times, 5-21:13.

2

I am for morality. In fact, I wish there was some more of it taught in our schools. The desperation to make sure that we separate church and state in our places of education has led to value-free education, which means that teachers don't teach with any idea of saying what is morally right or wrong. Well, I think that kids want adults to tell them what's morally right or wrong.

To reporters, Washington/
U.S. News & World Report, 5-25:25.

Frank Rhodes
President,
Cornell University; President,
American Council on Education

3

We can cultivate the spirit of liberal learning only through the selection and nurture of faculty who regard teaching as a moral activity. But that brings up a caution: The nurture of the intellectual development of others involves a fragile relationship and an awesome responsibility. The role of the faculty is not proselytizing. Moral development ought to be the by-product rather than the purpose of our teaching. Yet, without acknowledgment of the moral dimensions of our world, we risk creating informed cynics and critics who know the price everything and the value of nothing.

At Harvard University/
The Christian Science Monitor, 1-30:(B)9.

Felix G. Rohatyn
Senior partner,
Lazard Freres & Company

4

A recent article indicated that business schools were going to encourage the study of ethics as part of the curriculum. If graduate schools have to discover ethics, then we are truly in serious trouble. I no more believe that ethics can be taught past the age of 10 than I believe in the teaching of so-called creative writing. There are some things that you are born with, or they are taught by your parents, your priest or your grade-school teacher. But not in college or in graduate school. I believe that businesses should go back to basics in recruiting, should forget about the business schools and recruit the best young liberal-arts students we can find.

At Long Island University commencement/
The New York Times, 6-3:27.

Neil Rudenstine
Provost, Princeton University

5

[On the increasing costs of higher education]: We can't be compared to General Motors. We don't have a fixed product, like a car, that we continually make cheaper. We are part of the knowledge explosion that has become very powerful and sophisticated. Work in microbiology, exploring the cosmos—that's costly. We're talking about the central mission of the college—expansive learning. That's important for individuals, and society. We aren't just training people for jobs.

The Christian Science Monitor, 3-13:23.

Albert Shanker
President,
American Federation of Teachers

6

[Calling for reform in school textbooks that teach about democracy]: We are not talking about cheerleading. We are talking about thinking about understanding our ideals, about knowing our past—the unfortunate and evil as

111

WHAT THEY SAID IN 1987

well as the good. That is not indoctrination; that is education in the best sense of the word.

July 29/The New York Times, 7-30:15.

Lee Shulman
Professor of education,
Stanford University

1

We have created an organizational division in the universities, and given to one end of that division—the arts and sciences department—the responsibility for teaching content, and given to the departments of education the responsibility of teaching how to teach, and neither worries much about the other. It is a false distinction. It's impossible to know how to teach *in general.* The teacher of the American Revolution has to know both a great deal about the American Revolution and a variety of ways of communicating the essence of the American Revolution to a wide variety of students, in a pedagogically interesting way.

National Public Radio interview/
The Washington Post, 9-7:(A)19.

Christina Hoff Sommers
Professor of philosophy,
Clark University

2

Students come to college today as moral stutterers. They haven't been taught much respect for what I call "plain moral facts"—the need for honesty, integrity, responsibility. It doesn't take a blue-ribbon commission to see this. Students don't reason morally. They don't know what that means.

The Christian Science Monitor, 1-30:(B)1.

Anne Sturtevant
Financial-aid director,
Emory University

3

[On the rise in college tuition costs]: A lot of families are wondering whether college is

worth the sacrifice. Do we really want to go into debt and sacrifice family vacations for 10 years so Johnny can get a liberal-arts degree with unknown rewards?

The New York Times, 1-29:7.

Lee Roy Sullivan
Principal, Countryside High School,
Clearwater, Fla.

4

Parents stop here [at school] at seven o'clock in the morning and leave their child and expect us to take care of any problems during the day. Now schools are getting blamed for a lot of problems students have, the dropout rate being just one. Somewhere there has to be a cutoff on accepting all the social aspects of raising a child. Somewhere it's got to stop—the public assumption that schools will raise their son or daughter.

The Christian Science Monitor, 2-9:34.

Kenneth Travers
Professor of education,
University of Illinois

5

The demands of a high-tech society require that we upgrade the quality of mathematical education our children are getting. Maybe we could get by with a mediocre performance in math 20 and 30 years ago, but I'm not sure we can afford this any longer.

Time, 1-26:65.

Ling-chi Wang
Associate professor of
Asian-American studies,
University of California, Berkeley

6

As soon as [U.S. college] admissions of [Asian-American] students began reaching 10 or 12 per cent, suddenly a red light went on. [Since 1983,] at Berkeley, Stanford, MIT, Yale, in fact all the Ivy League schools, admission of Asian-Americans has either stabilized or gone down. I don't want to say it was conspiracy, but

(LING-CHI WANG)

I think all of the elite universities in America suddenly realized they had what used to be called a "Jewish problem" before World War II, and they began to look for ways of slowing down the admissions of Asians.

The New York Times, 1-19:8.

Clifton R. Wharton, Jr.
Chancellor,
State University of New York

1

My life as an educator has always been at-risk. As a college administrator, I teetered between two poles—my personal goal to set high standards for education and to make the concerns of students top priority, and the taxpayers' desire for tight budgets and influential directors and key politicians, to downgrade the concerns of students, our most important product.

Interview, Albany, N.Y./
The Christian Science Monitor, 2-2:23.

Clifton R. Wharton, Jr.
Former chancellor,
State University of New York

2

[U.S. Secretary of Education William Bennett] has been attacking colleges and universities for raising tuition, then doing his best to bring about the kind of funding cuts that make tuition hikes inevitable.

At Colgate University commencement,
May 24/The New York Times, 5-25:9.

Merry White
Director of international education,
Graduate School of Education,
Harvard University

3

Our expectation is that Japanese children are all sitting in rows [in elementary school], quiet, hands folded in laps. But there's a big surprise when you walk into a Japanese elementary-school classroom. You think: "Oh, my God,

who's in charge here? This is terrible." It's very, very noisy. Kids are jumping all around and calling out answers to questions. American teachers would be appalled; they seem to be afraid of kids. But Japanese teachers are relaxed and stand off to one side, not trying to control the classroom. When you really listen to what the kids are shouting, they're not teasing each other or planning recess games. They're engaged in the work and are shouting out answers in friendly competition. They're so involved that the teacher often says that the noise level is the measure of her ability to motivate the kids.

Interview/
U.S. News & World Report, 1-19:65.

Robert M. White
President,
National Academy of Engineering

4

A person who goes to school and is trained, unless he keeps up with his field, will become obsolete very quickly . . . [There are] within the United States today, many many different modes for acquiring continuing education. But what you actually find, in contrast to what is available, is that [while] many individuals will take advantage of continuing education—keep themselves up to snuff . . . many are not motivated. We have an enormous investment in these people . . . [Their] career-long education is essential.

Interview, Washington/
The Christian Science Monitor, 3-26:5.

Laval S. Wilson
Superintendent of Schools of Boston

5

Nearly 20 per cent of our first-graders are failing. This is because many children have no pre-school training. So we are requiring two years of kindergarten before first grade. Then our elementary schools will offer after-school day-care centers. This will permit working parents to have their children under supervision throughout the school day. These children will

WHAT THEY SAID IN 1987

(LAVAL S. WILSON)

have a good start toward education, too . . . Every high school and every middle school needs after-school projects that broaden the students' interests. I'm not talking about varsity spectator sports. I'm thinking of school bands, both concert and marching; school choruses; and student interest groups such as engineering club, French club, science club, honor societies, debating teams . . . Sure, we want to close the intellectual gaps among our students. But our children have so many other talents and interests beyond book knowledge. We can develop the whole child.

The Christian Science Monitor, 5-27:5.

The Environment • Energy

John Ahearne
Former Chairman,
Nuclear Regulatory Commission
of the United States

1

Nuclear power is extraordinarily controversial in this country; essentially, the U.S. public doesn't like it. So the agency charged with regulating it will be under constant scrutiny.

The Christian Science Monitor, 5-28:1.

Bruce Babbitt
Former Governor of Arizona (D);
Candidate for the 1988
Democratic Presidential nomination

2

I am one of those people who deeply resents not having been born in the 19th century, when there were still open places to explore.

Los Angeles Times, 3-11:(I)18.

Richard E. Benedick
Deputy Assistant Secretary for
the Environment, Health and
Natural Resources, Department
of State of the United States

3

[On the just-signed 24-nation pact to reduce the release of chemicals that can harm the earth's ozone shield]: This is perhaps the most historically significant international environmental agreement. For the first time, the international community has initiated controls on production of an economically valuable commodity before there was tangible evidence of danger.

Montreal, Sept. 16/
The New York Times, 9-17:1.

Hans Blix
Director General,
International Atomic Energy Agency

4

Nuclear power will survive today and expand tomorrow . . . The nuclear industry is geared to

living by the demand that no accident must occur, can occur [or] will be allowed to occur with any significant radioactive releases.

Interview, Vienna, Sept. 18/
Los Angeles Times, 9-19:(I)5.

Gordon M. Boyd
Executive director, New York
State Legislative Commission
on Solid Waste Management

5

[Saying the country is running out of space in garbage landfills]: This is a crisis. And it will get much worse before it gets better. Nationally, we are running out of space, and at an accelerating rate. It's happening on a logarithmic curve.

The New York Times, 2-12:12.

Robert C. Byrd
United States Senator,
D-West Virginia

6

The drop in oil prices, while certainly a major factor, is not the sole culprit of our growing dependence on imported oil. Believing that the best energy policy is no energy policy, the Reagan Administration took a meat ax to America's domestic energy programs.

The Washington Post, 8-26:(A)3.

Steve Cowper
Governor of Alaska (D)

7

I identify with the kind of environmental movement that says, "Clean up your mess, do it right, don't poison anybody." The part that rushes out and says development is dirty— they're not my people. The wildlife-protection people, however, are. Look, I've run for office four times in my life. The oil companies have opposed me every time. Whatever I do, I sure

WHAT THEY SAID IN 1987

(STEVE COWPER)

as hell don't pack water for the oil industry. But they're right. Production in [Alaska's Arctic National Wildlife Refuge] can be done in an environmentally safe way and in a way that protects the wildlife.

Interview/USA Today, 11-25:(A)13.

Harold Denton
Director, Office of
Nuclear Reactor Regulation,
Nuclear Regulatory Commission
of the United States

1

[On the accident at the nuclear power plant in Chernobyl, U.S.S.R., last year]: People think there is no clear-cut nexus between the specific occurrence of this accident and our [U.S.] plants. [Yet, while] that particular accident can't happen [in the U.S.], it does not say that we cannot have severe accidents . . . This is basically a hazardous technology if not properly operated. This means you have to have discipline in the control room, detailed procedures and a knowledgeable staff that doesn't go bypassing safety systems in the dark of the night to run a test . . . We need to focus on these operating details, the training of operators, and make sure we don't have anything that comes close [to Chernobyl]. You can't have very many of these events before the public says, "This technology isn't mature enough. Let's go back to coal."

Los Angeles Times, 4-27:(I)1,9.

Lawrence Downing
President, Sierra Club

2

We think the [Reagan] Administration is speaking out of both sides of their mouth. On one hand, [they say,] "Sure, let's have a 65 mile-an-hour speed limit," and on the other hand, "We've got an energy crisis; we've got to conserve, so we need more gas and oil." They've cut out all the alternate-energy funds. There's no solar program any more : . . Now

the Administration would not have us think conservation because they want to help out the oil and gas industry.

Interview, Boston/
The Christian Science Monitor, 8-3:3.

James Marston Fitch
Director of historic preservation,
Beyer Blinder Belle, architects

3

[On the architectural preservation movement in the U.S.]: Actually, in view of what was happening to the built world in America, the movement appeared at the last possible moment, the fifty-ninth minute. In that sense, it's remarkable what's been accomplished in such a short time. The average person is so dismayed, offended and outraged by the dominance and misuse of technology, running all the way from TV commercials up to nuclear war, that he is beginning to think, "Well, hadn't we better re-evaluate what we're giving up before we plunge any further?" Preservation is one reflection of that thinking.

Interview/American Heritage, April:89

James C. Fletcher
Administrator, National Aeronautics
and Space Administration
of the United States

4

Earth is a spacecraft in a deadly vacuum, with a life-support system as precious as is an astronaut's backpack.

The Christian Science Monitor, 3-31:16.

George T. Frampton, Jr.
President, Wilderness Society

5

[Criticizing the Reagan Administration's plans for opening Alaska's Arctic National Wildlife Refuge for oil and gas exploration]: In its rush to be chief advocate for the oil companies, the Reagan Administration has lost all credibility when it comes to the Arctic Refuge. Its agenda

(GEORGE T. FRAMPTON, JR.)

is clear: oil at any cost. But the American public will not stand for it.

April 20/The New York Times, 4-21:12.

Robert P. Gale
Professor, University of California, Los Angeles; Coordinator of treatment for victims of Chernobyl nuclear-plant accident in the Soviet Union

1

Nuclear energy is not inherently good or inherently bad. It's how civilization uses it. In the long term, we have to develop reactors which are inherently safe and which do not depend on human beings for their safety . . . [But] the likelihood of another major accident somewhere in the world in the next 10 years is not less than 25 per cent. Or that in the United States the probability of a core meltdown within the next 20 years is about 50 per cent . . . A nuclear accident anywhere in the world is everywhere in the world. Nuclear energy is an international event. We can't afford to have national interests dictate technologies which are by definition international.

News conference, Bonn, West Germany, June 26/Los Angeles Times, 6-27:(I)3.

Mikhail S. Gorbachev
General Secretary, Communist Party of the Soviet Union

2

No country is likely to radically solve the energy problem on its own, any more than develop the riches of the world's oceans. Only joint action can weaken and remove the global danger of an ecological seizure.

To foreign political parties and workers' organizations, Moscow, Nov. 4/Los Angeles Times, 11-5:(I)12.

Mahbubul Haq
Minister of Planning and Development of Pakistan

3

Tropical forests are disappearing at the rate of 11 million hectares a year, an area the size of Belgium or Austria. More than a billion people already are suffering from the loss. Developing countries that once exported forest products now have to spend $10-billion a year to import them. Add to that the widespread loss of unique ecosystems and extinction of plant and animal genetic resources—it's the stuff of screaming headlines.

At Strategy Meeting on Tropical Forests, Bellagio, Italy, July 3/ Los Angeles Times, 7-4:(I)4.

Larry D. Harris
Professor of forest wildlife ecology, University of Florida

4

Stewardship of land should be based on the principle that resources are not given to us by our parents, but are loaned to us by our children.

Los Angeles Times, 6-22:(I)15.

John S. Herrington
Secretary of Energy of the United States

5

. . . initiatives must be taken to strengthen the U.S. oil and gas industry and to reduce our growing dependence on insecure imported oil. Even with continued conservation and efficiency and substantial contributions from other energy resources . . . our economic and energy security is inextricably tied to the fates and fortunes of our domestic petroleum industry through this century.

The Christian Science Monitor, 3-18:4.

6

[On U.S. plans to boycott Iranian oil]: The American people would rather walk than buy Iranian oil. We do not want to support the Iranian war effort [against Iraq]. We are using too much imported oil. If we are going to cut back, we should start with Iranian oil. The boycott is a good idea, and it makes a good statement.

To Kuwaiti journalists, Kuwait, Oct. 6/The New York Times, 10-7:8.

117

WHAT THEY SAID IN 1987

(JOHN S. HERRINGTON)

1

The nuclear-waste issue is probably the toughest issue we deal with in the Department of Energy. I feel we will get to a permanent waste repository for both defense and commercial waste. It won't be during the time that I'm in office, but I think the program will move forward, and the solution will be deep geologic storage for nuclear waste. The experts have looked at this for years. Deep geologic burial of nuclear waste is the right way to go. Japan is doing it; Sweden is doing it; France is doing it. And we ought to do it.

Interview/USA Today, 10-29:(A)7.

2

[Saying the U.S. today can withstand a cut-off of foreign oil supplies better than during the 1973 Arab oil embargo]: We can put between three and four million barrels a day into the refining capacity of the United States alone. In the United States alone we have 120 days of supplies, which protect us against any dislocation—three times greater than anything we have seen in 1973 and 1979 . . . As long as [the 540 million barrels in the emergency Strategic Petroleum Reserve] exist, we are readily able to handle any dislocation and rein in any panic that may ensue.

Interview/
The New York Times, 11-28:17,18.

Donald Hodel
Secretary of the Interior
of the United States

3

[Advocating opening Alaska's Arctic National Wildlife Refuge for oil and gas exploration]: Our nation has proven that we need not choose between exploring for and developing the energy necessary for survival and growth on one hand, and protecting the environment on the other. We can have both.

News conference,
Washington, April 20/
The Christian Science Monitor, 4-21:5.

John Paul II
Pope

4

The earth will not continue to offer its harvest, except with faithful stewardship. We cannot say we love the land and then take steps to destroy it for use by future generations. I urge you to be sensitive to the many issues affecting the land and the whole environment, and to unite with each other to seek the best solutions to these pressing problems.

Homily, Monterey, Calif., Sept. 17/
Los Angeles Times, 9-18:(I)4.

Robert Kasten
United States Senator, R-Wisconsin

5

Every day of delay in upgrading international environmental protection means that more scarce tropical forest is lost forever. We are losing an entire species, causing excessive soil erosion, polluting the world's waterways and impoverishing the people of less-developed nations who must depend on basic natural resources.

The Christian Science Monitor, 3-30:7.

Thomas H. Kean
Governor of New Jersey (R)

6

The same fear and uncertainty that moved [environmentalist] Rachel Carson 25 years ago today has been translated into an irrational attitude that cares not for the health of the planet as a whole, but only for the part of the planet that is located in our backyards.

The New York Times, 6-25:17.

Stanley L. Krugman
Director of
Timber Management Research,
United States Forest Service

7

[The commercial lumber industry] didn't discover forestry, and practice tending forests and regrowing them, until after World War II.

(STANLEY L. KRUGMAN)

Companies only *harvested* prior to that . . . We've made most of the mistakes. But the United States is large enough and has such a variety of forests and relatively low population pressures, that when we screwed up the East, the Great Lakes states and the South, we had the West to move to. With exceptions, such as the Tennessee Valley, we didn't denude cutover lands. We didn't eliminate the natural cover and degrade the soil. We harvested our interest, but we didn't bankrupt our principal.

Los Angeles Times, 6-22:(I)14.

Richard K. Lester
Associate professor of
nuclear engineering, Massachusetts
Institute of Technology

1

The climate is not particularly hospitable for major new initiatives in the nuclear [power] area. But there is an argument to be made for pursuing nuclear research at a politically feasible level. We shouldn't assume that the current public view is immutable.

The Christian Science Monitor, 4-28:18.

Roger J. Mahony
Roman Catholic Archbishop
of Los Angeles

2

I think the whole question of air pollution, acid rain—we have created that. God, in His wisdom, created a balance in creation that we as human beings shortsightedly have upset very often. I think we've realized that you simply cannot tamper with nature and natural law without eventually realizing that doesn't work.

Interview/USA Today, 5-13:(A)11.

Jesus Marden dos Santos
President, Post Graduate Council,
Institute for Space Research (Brazil)

3

People complained and pricked the consciences of others, the government acted, and,

finally, companies themselves have learned it is better not to pollute . . . Today, no one is willing to propose a major industrial construction project in Brazil without including the costs of an environmental-impact study. Anyone who ignored it would be shunned by the others.

World Press Review, April:54.

Thomas McMillan
Minister of the Environment
of Canada

4

[On an agreement between the U.S. and Canada to clean up pollution in the Niagara River, near the famous falls]: The Niagara is more than a river—it is a lesson in what happens when neighbors dump garbage on one another's front lawn.

U.S. News & World Report, 2-16:9.

5

We are a global village. Everything one country does has an effect on another. Unless that message seeps in, we are going to have more than chaos; we are going to have annihilation, given population growth and greater and greater and greater demands on scarce resources . . . The Third World is destroying itself with desertification and drought and . . . other things because of the immediate exigencies of their economic needs. They are cutting down forests to have heat on the hearth and destroying other things to put food on the table . . . There have to be fundamental changes in the way the world exercises stewardship over the resources. No longer can these decisions be made on a nation-state basis. Many of the threats are trans-boundary. Pollution doesn't carry a passport.

Ottawa, Canada/
The Christian Science Monitor, 7-10:12.

Sally K. Ride
American astronaut

6

[On the environmental uses of low-altitude satellites]: There are a range of things [to

119

(SALLY K. RIDE)

study]. One is the buildup of greenhouse gases in the atmosphere—we need to know how fast the concentration of the gases is increasing. Two, we need to study the buildup of methane in the atmosphere. Third is the potential depletion of the ozone layer. And there are others. We need to know more about the effect of El Nino [the warm ocean current], not only on ocean temperature and currents, but also on the global weather pattern. Then there's acid rain. And another example is deforestation in the Amazon—as we eliminate the trees there, what are we doing to the atmosphere? . . . We're discovering that there's a lot of interaction between things that occur in the ocean and the atmosphere, between things that occur on a continent and the atmosphere.

Interview/
"Ms.," July-Aug.:181.

Bud Shuster
United States Representative,
R-Pennsylvania

1

Clean water is not an expenditure of Federal funds; clean water is an investment in the future of our country.

The Washington Post, 1-9:(A)8.

Randall Snodgrass
Alaska program director,
Wilderness Society.

2

[Criticizing Interior Secretary Donald Hodel for recommending opening Alaska's Arctic National Wildlife Refuge for oil and gas exploration]: This is a step backwards into the dark ages of [former Interior Secretary] James Watt. Except that this time it's Donald Hodel taking the executioner's ax to one of this nation's great national treasures.

April 20/
The Christian Science Monitor, 4-21:5.

Thomas Speis
Director of United States
Nuclear Regulatory Commission's
study group on the Chernobyl nuclear
power-plant accident in the U.S.S.R.

3

[The accident] reminds us of the continuing importance of safe design in both concept and implementation of operational controls, of competence and motivation of plant management and operating staff to operate in strict compliance with controls, and of back-up features of defense in depth against potential accidents. Although a large nuclear power-plant accident somewhere in the United States is unlikely because of design and operational features, we cannot relax the care and vigilance that have made it so.

Washington, Feb. 6/
The New York Times, 2-7:9.

Robert T. Stafford
United States Senator, R-Vermont

4

We know asbestos causes cancer, and we know it is out there in surprisingly large amounts in Federal buildings, in stores and office buildings, restaurants, banks, gyms, theatres, day-care centers, and other buildings open to the public.

The New York Times, 6-11:10.

Donald E. Starsinic
Chief, Population Estimates Branch,
Bureau of the Census
of the United States

5

[Fertility] seems relatively stable now at a low level. The baby boom is over and . . . there is no particular reason to expect, in the near future, a turn-up. People are concerned with the quality of life, and if they have to choose between having more children and maintaining the life they have experienced, I expect they will go toward quality of life.

Washington, June 9/
Los Angeles Times, 6-10:(I)4.

John Varley
Research administrator,
Yellowstone National Park

1

[On whether park administration should include active intervention into natural processes, such as helping preserve species on the edge of extinction]: Most of the parks were set apart at a time in our nation's history when we hadn't even invented the word ecosystem. The park philosophy, as articulated in legislation and in policy, strives to create a situation where natural processes are left alone. You run into a situation in which you're going against the very tenets for which the parks were created, and yet, on the other hand, you can have species slipping away. It's an issue we're ill-prepared to grapple with.

The New York Times,
2-3:17.

S. P. Zalygin
Soviet author

2

The problem is that we set economic tasks and then go about accomplishing them at any price. As a result, we're incurring a mountain of debt to nature—a debt that will eventually have to be repaid, whether we like it or not. Man is a part of nature, and in struggling against nature we're fighting ourselves. In ancient times, people sensed not just their attitude toward, say, a forest or a herd of animals, but also the attitude of that forest or herd toward them. Now all we know is what we need from nature. We've lost the psychological connection that would let us know the natural world's attitude toward us. Maybe we're not as smart as we think we are when we laugh at the pagans who drew no distinction between animate and inanimate objects.

Panel discussion of Soviet writers and
scientists/Los Angeles Times, 6-22:(I)15.

Foreign Affairs

Kenneth L. Adelman
Director, Arms Control and
Disarmament Agency
of the United States

1

[There was] a joke that was told a few years ago by one of the Soviet [arms-control] negotiators by the name of Yuli Kvitsinsky to our negotiators in Geneva. The story goes this way: A man visits the city of Leningrad and goes to the zoo, where he sees a marvelous sight. There in the lion's cage is the lion sitting side-by-side with a lamb. Well, this fellow is just astonished, and he hurries on his way, feeling happy and uplifted. The next day he sees the same thing, so he decides to ask the zookeeper: "You know, that display in the lion's cage is the most marvelous thing I have ever seen. How do you ever train the lion to do it?" The zookeeper answers, "We don't train him—we just give him a different lamb every day." Now, that's a peculiar story, but it's not a bad way of approaching . . . arms control and human freedom. The moral of this story is clear: When it comes to assessing what is really going on in the Soviet system, things are not often exactly what they seem.

Before Chicago Bar Association, January/
The Wall Street Journal, 2-23:22.

Richard Allen
Former Assistant to President
of the United States Ronald Reagan
for National Security Affairs

2

[On the National Security Council's role in the current Iran-contra scandal]: Something did go fundamentally wrong with the National Security Council, and in my view it was when the NSC was taken operational after I left [in 1981]. When this Administration came into office in 1980, I took the NSC back down to the basement. And you guys [in the press] wrote that the NSC had been defanged and demoted to

the basement. The idea wasn't to reduce its stature; the object was to make the NSC more of a coordinating body and less of a body that would drive foreign policy.

Interview, Washington/
The Christian Science Monitor, 6-16:17.

Oscar Arias
President of Costa Rica

3

We do not judge, much less condemn, any other nation's political or ideological system, freely chosen and never exported. We cannot require sovereign states to conform to patterns of government not of their own choosing. But we can and do insist that every government respect those universal rights of man that have meaning beyond national boundaries and ideological labels.

Accepting the 1987
Nobel Peace Prize, Oslo, Dec. 10/
The Washington Post, 12-11:(A)22.

Les Aspin
United States Representative,
D-Wisconsin

4

The [political] right thinks the only evil in the world is the Soviet Union. The left focuses on nuclear war and tends to forget about the Soviet Union. We have to focus on both evils, and Democrats have to realize that you can be for arms and arms control at the same time.

The Christian Science Monitor, 3-24:36.

Chester G. Atkins
United States Representative, D-Massachusetts

5

America has proudly been a place of sanctuary for those in danger [in their own countries]. The Reagan Administration has perverted this principle, turned it on its head [by picking and

122

(CHESTER G. ATKINS)

choosing from which countries refugees will be accepted]. You run because your life is in danger. Whether the fear is from the left or the right should make no difference. Our asylum policy should be ideologically neutral.

The Washington Post, 7-29: (A)4.

Bruce Babbitt
Former Governor of Arizona (D);
Candidate for the 1988
Democratic Presidential nomination

1

We must never again trade anything of value for [an American held hostage somewhere in the world]. And if we take that pledge seriously, then some of the hostages may not be coming home.

Announcing his candidacy for President,
Manchester, N.H., March 10/
The Washington Post, 3-11: (A)6.

2

We must never forget that public diplomacy counts. [Soviet leader] Mikhail Gorbachev is a more popular figure in Europe than [U.S. President] Ronald Reagan—at least in part because he works at it. It is long past time to start matching him [Gorbachev], speech for speech and proposal for proposal. Through the words and deeds of our leaders, we are conducting what amounts to a debate, America and Russia, between one way of life and another.

At Center for Strategic and
International Studies, Washington,
Sept. 29/The Washington Post, 10-1: (A)20.

3

We must face the fact in this country that a successful foreign policy cannot be bought on the cheap. Foreign aid amounts to just one-fifth of 1 per cent of America's national wealth, which puts us at the very bottom of the list of industrial nations. It may not be popular and it may be hard to explain, but sending money abroad is a powerful and effective investment in our own security.

At Center for Strategic and
International Studies, Washington,
Sept. 29/The Washington Post, 10-1: (A)20.

4

[U.S. President] Reagan is still in 1949 asking "Who lost China?" The answer is, the Soviets did. In the post-war competition, the U.S. has won and the Soviet Union has lost. Marxism is dead; the Chinese know it and the Soviets know it. The driving political and economic forces in the world today are those for which we stand.

At Tufts University, Sept. 30/
The Christian Science Monitor, 10-2:5.

5

We are on the threshold of some pretty extraordinary changes in this world. American values are winning all over the world. Over the last 30 or 40 years, we have created a world of unparalleled opportunity. Japan is an American victory. The Chinese are telling us that Marxism is dead, that they are looking to the West . . . Marxism is on the wane.

Interview, Oak Creek Canyon, Ariz./
The Christian Science Monitor, 10-16:6.

Howard H. Baker, Jr.
Chief of Staff to President
of the United States Ronald Reagan

6

[On revelations of Soviet women agents seducing U.S. Marine guards at the American Embassy in Moscow in order to obtain secret information]: I don't think the United States would do what the Soviets have done. The scope and extent of it really represents an invasion of our sovereign rights. That's what an Embassy compound is: a piece of sovereignty in another land.

To reporters aboard Air Force One,
April 9/The Washington Post, 4-10: (A)18.

WHAT THEY SAID IN 1987

James David Barber
Historian, Duke University

1

[On the U.S. Iran-contra scandal]: This has destroyed [U.S. President] Reagan's credibility in world politics. There is no informed chief of state of any other nation who will be able to rely on a major public policy statement by this President.

The New York Times, 7-17:5.

Michael R. Beschloss
Adjunct historian of
American politics and diplomacy,
National Museum of
American History, Washington

2

We are one of the two superpowers, and you've got this enormous, fragmented, conflict-ridden foreign policy and national security system which depends ultimately on the ability and eagerness of a President to resolve these conflicts, to take these musicians and make them into a symphony. That is why it is important we elect a President who has, if not foreign-policy experience, at least enough knowledge of this problem so that he is not overcome by these forces but is in control of them from the first day he walks into the White House.

Interview, Washington/
The New York Times, 1-28:12.

Joseph R. Biden, Jr.
United States Senator, D-Delaware;
Candidate for the 1988
Democratic Presidential nomination

3

I take issue with the unbridled ambition of [the late President] John Kennedy's foreign policy of the early 1960s, because that policy did not always lead us into making the most prudent commitments . . . I would amend Kennedy's words. While we cannot pay any price and bear any burden, we must pay the right price and bear the right burden.

At Kennedy School of Government,
Harvard University, May 28/
Los Angeles Times, 5-29:(I)18.

Don Bonker
United States Representative,
D-Washington

4

Sanctions [against foreign countries] are not a partisan issue, although political liberals favor trade restrictions on right-wing governments, like South Africa and Chile, and conservatives like them on Marxist countries. Both [political] parties readily support sanctions on terrorist countries. Sometimes it is about all you have available short of war if you feel you have to "do" something.

Los Angeles Times, 2-7:(I)22.

David L. Boren
United States Senator,
D-Oklahoma

5

If you are going to be involved effectively in various areas of the world in supporting insurgencies, you have to hold to a minimum the number of involvements you have. It's like being on a family budget: You have only so much money to spend, and you better spend it effectively. If you spread yourself too thin by being involved in too many places, it won't work.

Los Angeles Times, 3-31:(I)7.

6

[Addressing retired Major General Richard Secord on his involvement in the U.S. Iran-contra scandal]: Did you not wake up some morning and think, "How did I, as a private individual, start exercising all this responsibility to make foreign policy for the United States of America, in lieu of Congress, the Secretary of State, the President of the United States, members of the National Security Council?" Did you not have even a moment of humiliation about your judgment in substituting yourself for the Constitutional processes of this country?

At Iran-contra hearings,
Washington, May 7/
Los Angeles Times, 5-8:(I)1.

Bill Bradley
United States Senator,
D-New Jersey

1

[On surveys showing American students do not know enough about world geography]: This news is not only shocking, it is frightening. We depend on a well-informed populace to maintain the democratic ideals which have made our country great. When 95 per cent of some of our brightest college students cannot locate Vietnam on a world map, we must sound the alarm. We cannot expect to be a world leader if our populace doesn't even know who the rest of the world is!

The Washington Post, 4-21:(A)19.

2

A society governed by a centralized, one-party state that insists on dictatorial control is inherently unstable. History teaches that instability and great military power are a dangerous combination. That is why Soviet power has been such a problem for the rest of the world, especially for Eastern Europe.

At town-hall meeting between
Soviet and American citizens,
Chautauqua, N.Y./
The New York Times, 10-27:23.

Jack Brooks
United States Representative,
D-Texas

3

[On the U.S. Iran-contra scandal]: The story of the Iran-contra affair as it has unfolded in the past six months is the story of a group of people who, in their zeal to accomplish their personal goals, turned their backs on our system of government. When they couldn't justify their policies publicly, they simply hid their activities from the American people, from the Congress, and even from key officials of their own Administration.

At Iran-contra hearings,
Washington, May 5/
The Christian Science Monitor, 5-6:40.

Edmund G. Brown, Jr.
Former Governor of California (D)

4

As I see it, the challenge from our friends who are economic competitors is almost as great, if not as great, as the challenge from our historic adversary, the Soviet Union; and we are draining away our scientific and governmental resources, focusing on the narrow challenge of Soviet-American relations, while we are paralyzed in face of the trade deficit and the severe competition coming from throughout the rest of the world.

Interview, Tokyo/
Los Angeles Times, 1-20:(I)15.

Lester Brown
Founder, Worldwatch Institute

5

For a generation now, world leaders have been preoccupied with this East-West conflict, the arms race, while the Japanese have quietly begun redefining geopolitics in economic rather than military terms. So Japan has emerged as a power that economically is so strong that it has, in many situations, far greater influence than the U.S., which is losing its economic power in the world. The U.S. is focusing so much of its budget and its manpower on the arms race, has concentrated so much on the military definition of power, that we've lost sight of the fact that real influence in the world derives not so much from the number of tanks but from the productivity of one's factories. The Japanese have left us in the dust.

Interview, Washington/
Los Angeles Times, 2-19:(V)14.

Gro Harlem Brundtland
Prime Minister of Norway

6

To secure our common future we need a new international ethic that looks beyond narrow and short-sighted national ambitions. It is the only way we can pursue our own self-interests on a small and closely knit planet.

April 27/Los Angeles Times, 4-28:(I)6.

WHAT THEY SAID IN 1987

Zbigniew Brzezinski
Professor of government,
Columbia University; Former
Assistant to the President of
the United States (Jimmy Carter)
for National Security Affairs

1

I think [U.S.-Soviet summit meetings] can be mildly useful in advancing understanding and ratifying some agreements. They can be counter-productive in generating excessive expectations, which then produce a letdown, such as the Nixon-Brezhnev summit meetings of the early 1970s, with the phrases about a generation of peace that came out of them. They can be damaging if they generate profound misconceptions on both sides, as seems to have been the case with the Kennedy-Khrushchev meetings in 1961 . . . I don't view summits as the source of salvation for a relationship that is essentially competitive, but I don't see them as acts of one-sided American capitulation either, which is what the doomsayers always proclaim.

Interview/The New York Times, 12-3:8.

Maurizio Bucci
Italian Ambassador
to the United Nations

2

Americans are disappointed in the UN. They do not accept the fact that the leading body in the UN is no longer the Security Council but the General Assembly, where no veto is possible. The UN membership has grown from 45-to-50 members in the 1940s to 159 today, thanks to decolonization. The Americans do not accept the consequences of decolonization. They say, "We pay too much and we are rewarded so badly." But this is the body, and you have to accept this body.

Interview/TWA Ambassador, April:42.

Dale Bumpers
United States Senator, D-Arkansas;
Candidate for the 1988
Democratic Presidential nomination

3

[On Soviet leader Mikhail Gorbachev's program for openness and reform in the Soviet Union]: For 70 years [the U.S.] has waited for the old Bolsheviks to die off and a new Soviet leader to emerge. Now that one has, one who has already taken major steps to deal with socialist oppressions as well as socialist inertia, his ability to continue reforms that we believe fundamental to a new and realistic arrangement between us depends in no small way on our responses . . . If the Soviets should take the unprecedented steps of allowing some uncensored press, permitting honest trials by citizens' peers, providing choices of more than one candidate in elections, allowing freer emigration and getting out of Afghanistan, with still no favorable U.S. response, then we may find some of our staunchest allies of the past cosying up to the Soviets for such advantages, principally trade, as may benefit them.

At Columbia University, March 2/
The Washington Post, 3-5:(A)26.

George Bush
Vice President of
the United States

4

[On criticism that the U.S. went against its policy of not negotiating with terrorists when it covertly sold arms to Iran, after which American hostages were released in Lebanon]: When we intercepted the hijackers of the [cruise ship] *Achille Lauro* and helped bring them to justice, we took tremendous risks on behalf of [an anti-terrorism] policy that was born of great conviction. When we flew our bombers for hours through the night to attack Libya's [terrorist] training camps, we again put our policy on the line. It is, therefore, with a profound sense of loss that I view this existing perception that we have abandoned our policy of not negotiating with terrorists. There is a very thin and delicate line between talking with terrorists and negotiating with terrorists . . . We do not make concessions to terrorists. We do not pay ransoms. We do not release prisoners. We do not encourage other countries to give in to terrorists. And we do not agree to other acts that might encourage future terrorism.

Speech, Jan. 20/USA Today, 2-12:(A)10.

(GEORGE BUSH)

1

Over the last 20 years we have witnessed a departure from the way we have conducted foreign policy for nearly two centuries. Congress has asserted an increasingly influential role in the micro-management of foreign policy— foreign operations, if you will—and at the same time, Congress, through the use of laws . . . ushered courts and lawyers into an uncomfortable but very visible role in the development of our foreign policy. I don't believe that the founders intended that our foreign policy should be conducted and reviewed by grand juries . . . I don't think the founders anticipated or intended judicial intervention into foreign policy . . . The envisioned role for Congress was political, not regulatory. My own feeling is we must simplify—deregulate, if you will—the conduct of foreign policy generally and covert actions particularly.

To conservative lawyers' group,
Washington, Jan. 30/
The Washington Post, 1-31:(A)16.

2

We face an adversary [the Soviet Union] that considers our decency and democratic values as weakness. To them, struggle, violence and power over others is vital to success. The modern Soviet regime has been ideologically driven to expand its global reach, not shrinking from the use of threat or force.

At U.S. Naval Academy commencement,
May 20/Los Angeles Times, 5-21:(I)13.

3

I ran the Central Intelligence Agency [in 1976-77]. People say that's a liability [in running for the Presidency in 1988]. They say, "You ought to tiptoe away from that a little bit." But I led something at a very difficult time. I went in there when it had been demoralized by the attacks of a bunch of little untutored squirts from Capitol Hill, going out there, looking at these confidential documents without one simple iota of concern for the legitimate national-security interests of this country. And I stood up for the CIA then, and I stand up for it now.

And defend it. So let the liberals wring their hands and consider it a liability [in running for the Presidency]. I consider it a strength.

At Republican fund-raising dinner,
Los Angeles, June 3/
The New York Times, 6-8:13.

4

In foreign policy and intelligence, the relationship between Congress and the President should be a partnership, based on honest dealings and mutual respect, not on rigid legislative restrictions that reflect a frozen moment of political consensus. But with legislation ranging from the War Powers Resolution to the Boland Amendment, Congress has tied the President's hands tighter and tighter in the conduct of foreign policy over the last 15 years . . . [Recently, 100 legislators] went to court alleging that the deployment of U.S. forces in the Persian Gulf constitutes a violation of the War Powers Act. What kind of wacky world is this where the President is taken to court every time he moves our troops around?

At American Legion convention,
San Antonio, Aug. 25/
The New York Times, 8-26:11.

5

[On U.S. Marine Lt. Col. Oliver North's public popularity during his Senate testimony about his involvement in the U.S. Iran-contra scandal]: Ollie stood up there, took the heat, and the American people in every bar in Chicago and every bowling alley in Texas and every little home said: "Hey, this guy believes in something, and I can identify with it" . . . He believed passionately in something. He believed passionately that every American life is precious. He who is held hostage is precious. We've got to do something about it. He believed it. He came through.

Broadcast interview, Dec. 6/
Los Angeles Times, 12-5:(I)1,24.

6

[On Soviet leader Mikhail Gorbachev]: I'll trust him more when 30,000 or 200,000 Jews are out of the Soviet Union. I'll trust him more

(GEORGE BUSH)

when 106,000 Soviet troops are out of Afghanistan. I'll trust him more when 30,000 Cuban troops are out of Angola and when the Soviet Union is no longer spending $1-billion in Central America.

At Republican fund-raising luncheon,
New York, Dec. 14/
The New York Times, 12-15:13.

Robert C. Byrd
United States Senator,
D-West Virginia

1

[Suggesting a new site for the Soviet Embassy in Washington, following revelations of Soviet bugging and spying at the U.S. Embassy in Moscow]: We should put the Soviets in a swamp somewhere. Let's see if we can't find a good one that's got some alligators in it.

U.S. News & World Report, 4-20:13.

2

[On the U.S. Iran-contra scandal]: The White House became a haven for a conspiracy of silence and cover-up fundamentally at odds with our Constitutional system of openness and checks and balances. The rule of law was flagrantly disregarded, and habits of power inherently undemocratic were fostered and encouraged. A culture of lying, a willingness to deceive even the Secretary of State, followed by an epidemic of amnesia, led to the wholesale diminishment and corruption of the public estate. Yet . . . a denial of democracy in so-called defense of democracy is no virtue.

Before the Senate, Washington, July 30/
The Washington Post, 7-31:(A)7.

3

This [Reagan] Administration thinks it's omnipotent, omniscient and omnipresent [in foreign policy]. It knows everything. It can do anything. It doesn't have to answer to anybody . . . We [the Congress] continue to get the back of the hand from the Administration. [The Reagan Administration frequently] gets a bit in

its teeth and is determined to go hog wild [on foreign policy].

Sept. 30/Los Angeles Times, 10-1:(I)6.

4

[On Soviet leader Mikhail Gorbachev]: I cannot overstate the need for realism in evaluating a Soviet "great communicator." The television tube can be a beguiling, entrancing hypnotist. An impressive and pleasing style is commendable, but when the security of our society and that of our allies is at stake, results are all that count.

Before the Senate, Washington, Dec. 2/
Los Angeles Times, 12-3:(I)12.

Jimmy Carter
Former President
of the United States

5

President Reagan has not been inclined to use negotiation and diplomacy as a means to achieve our nation's goals nearly so much as have his Democratic and Republican predecessors. He's more inclined to exert America's military strength, either the actual use of it or the threat of it. When I was in office, I was constantly involved in negotiations. This was the case with my Republican predecessors. This has not been the case in the last six years. There's been more of an inclination to form a contra [rebel] army [in Nicaragua] and overthrow the Sandinistas, or to inject the Marines into Lebanon and to use American battleships to shell the villages around Beirut, and so forth. This is just a different basic philosophy.

Before American Chamber of Commerce,
Cairo, March 19/
The New York Times, 3-20:4.

Dan Casey
Executive director,
American Conservative Union

6

[On Soviet leader Mikhail Gorbachev's summit visit to Washington and the seemingly good impression he made on Americans]: There's not

(DAN CASEY)

a PR firm in America that could have accomplished what Gorbachev has so far been able to accomplish—sometimes with [U.S. President Reagan] as his unwitting accomplice . . . [Gorbachev launched] a PR coup in order to lull the [U.S.] Congress and the American people into providing more primarily economic benefits to the Soviet Union. I'll give you dollars to donuts we're going to have a rush of companies investing in the Soviet Union; we're going to have our Secretary of Commerce lifting restrictions on trade.

USA Today, 12-11:(A)2.

Dick Cheney
United States Representative,
R-Wyoming

1

[On the U.S. Iran-contra scandal]: Once the President [Reagan] decided he was going to trade arms for hostages, once he decided he was going to undertake a covert action and not notify the Congress, once somebody in the White House decided that some of those funds would be diverted to support the contras [Nicaraguan rebels]—once those things occurred, it seems that it was almost guaranteed that there would indeed be a Congressional inquiry.

To reporters, Washington, June 22/
The Christian Science Monitor, 6-25:32.

2

[On the U.S. Iran-contra scandal hearings]: [It's] important to point out what these hearings did not show. There is no evidence that the President [Reagan] had any knowledge of the diversion of profits from the [Iran] arms sale to the [contra rebels of Nicaragua] . . . There is also no evidence of any effort by the President or his senior advisers to cover up these events . . . Evidence clearly shows that the President and the Attorney General were the ones primarily responsible for bringing these events and matters to the attention of the nation

. . . These hearings have demonstrated conclusively, in my opinion, that the President has indeed been telling the truth.

At Iran-contra hearings,
Washington, Aug. 3/
The Washington Post, 8-4:(A)6.

Clark M. Clifford
Former Secretary of Defense
of the United States

3

[On the Congressional Iran-contra hearings]: For someone to suggest that this kind of inquiry now weakens our system just does not understand our system. If the feeling gets around that any person can violate our laws or procedures with impunity, others will follow that course, instead of the legal path. It is absolutely necessary to go through [the hearings] to protect our system.

The Christian Science Monitor, 5-8:3.

William S. Cohen
United States Senator,
R-Maine

4

[On the U.S. Iran-contra scandal]: What's going to come out of this [investigation of the scandal] is not so much whether or not crimes were committed, but what are the policy implications of the "privatization" of the formulation of foreign policy. You have individuals as high as Cabinet officials undertaking solicitations of private individuals and other governments to find a policy that this country has either refused to do or was unable to do.

The New York Times, 1-20:6.

5

[On U.S. foreign covert operations]: You end up having a covert program which is deniable only to the American people. The people who receive the [covert] money know it. You want the enemy to know it. You want the Soviet Union to know it. You want the Cubans to know

(WILLIAM S. COHEN)

it. But we take the position that we can't tell the American people, and that gives us deniability.

Los Angeles Times, 3-31:(I)7.

1

[On revelations of U.S. Marine guards at the Embassy in Moscow being seduced by Soviet women as a way for the Soviets to spy on the Embassy]: Why should we use such men, some of whom are lacking in maturity, for what essentially is not a military role . . . Having them serve for a year or more in a foreign environment may be too long, at least it is too long without enough R&R breaks. We should either have shorter terms or rotate them more. We need to find ways to help them cope with the stress of living in a hostile environment and give them tight supervision.

Interview, April 1/
Los Angeles Times, 4-2:(I)30.

2

[Addressing former Presidential National Security Adviser John Poindexter on his testimony at the U.S. Iran-contra hearings]: I find it troubling when you say that "I withheld information from Congress, but I did not mislead it" or that "the [Reagan] Administration support for the [Nicaraguan contra rebels] was secret activity, but not covert action" or that "the United States acquiesced in the initial shipment of TOW weapons, but did not authorize it" or that "the transfers of funds for the sale of weapons was a technical implementation, not a substantive decision" and that "we did not trade arms for hostages, even though Mr. [Albert] Hakim and [retired Air Force Major General Richard] Secord arrived at the formula of 1½ hostages for 500 TOWs" . . . And I would respectfully suggest that if the Administration would like to regain the strong support of the American people, and I hope that it will, that it has to . . . [stop] insulting their intelligence and tell them the direct, unvarnished truth.

At Iran-contra hearings, Washington,
July 20/The Washington Post, 7-21:(A)7.

William E. Colby
Former Director of
Central Intelligence of
the United States

3

The intelligence process is often like a jigsaw puzzle. That is, the picture becomes clear long before the last piece is put in.

Before Senate Foreign Relations
Committee, Washington, Jan. 15/
The Washington Post, 1-21:(A)20.

Charles Colson
Former Special Counsel to the
President of the United States
(Richard Nixon)

4

[On Lt. Col. Oliver North's involvement in the U.S. Iran-contra scandal]: My first reaction to Ollie North was, "Go get 'em, boys." But the more I reflected on it, the more nervous I got. In the Nixon White House, you couldn't make any foreign-policy decision, I don't care how insignificant, without the President. The fact [in the Iran-contra scandal] that foreign policy could be conducted out of the basement of the White House without the President [Reagan] knowing about it—I slept less well that night [after learning about it from the Iran-contra hearings].

Interview/Newsweek, 10-19:10.

Thomas E. Cronin
Constitutional scholar

5

We have to recognize that we have set up a system of government that is neither tidy nor efficient . . . and that, if a President cannot persuade the other branch of government [Congress] of the validity, legitimacy and desirability of a given public policy—such as trading with a terrorist nation or giving military aid to the contra rebels in Nicaragua—that the framers of the Constitution believed that *inaction*, meaning no policy, no activity, was preferable to action. Now, in the late 20th century, when we have a President [Lyndon] Johnson or a [Rich-

(THOMAS E. CRONIN)

3

ard] Nixon or a [Jimmy] Carter or a [Ronald] Reagan saying, "This Congress isn't allowing me to do things I want to do, therefore I'm going to do them through covert operations," or, "I'm going to do it through undeclared foreign policy with White House aides, CIA agents and others engaged in things"—but not letting the Congress know and not winning their consent or asking for their advice—I think the framers would say that was wrong.

Interview, Boston/
The Christian Science Monitor, 4-13:36.

Mario M. Cuomo
Governor of New York (D)

1

[On the U.S. Iran-contra scandal hearings]: I think, frankly, it is that yearning for inspiration, for edification, that produced the phenomenon we witnessed during the [Iran-contra] hearings. So badly did we want a true believer, a hero, in the early days of the hearings, many of us were fooled into overlooking the fact that the men we chose to hoist onto our shoulders [those involved in the Iran-contra scandal] were in the process of destroying one of our most important values of all—the rule of law.

At Democratic fund-raising dinner,
Indianapolis, July 28/
The New York Times, 7-29:11.

2

[On U.S.-Soviet relations]: We can begin by insisting on the common sense of things with a new realism, a new realism that sees the stupidity in the dehumanizing of one another, a new realism that recognizes the obvious—that while we are two strong people with different histories, different ideologies, who will be competitive for many years to come, there is a living world of difference between vigorous competition and violent hostility.

At Chautauqua Institution conference,
Aug. 23/The New York Times, 8-24:9.

We haven't begun to consider the possibility of China—we're doing nothing with them. We're doing nothing with the Soviet Union. We have a lot of conservatives who say, "God forbid you should ever do business with them; that's what they're waiting for, to make you weak!" Maybe we have to be smart enough to do business with them without getting raped. What's the matter? Must you assume that the United States of America is a dummy, that we're not smart enough to make a deal without making ourselves vulnerable?

Interview, Albany, N.Y./
The Washington Post, 11-19:(A)23.

4

I think it would be a mistake to be fooled by [Soviet leader Mikhail] Gorbachev's talent, his charm and his candor. No matter how well he dresses it up, and he is a charming man, [the Soviets'] philosophy hasn't changed.

USA Today, 12-14:(A)4.

John C. Danforth
United States Senator, R-Missouri

5

. . . perhaps the time has come for some sort of review to take place . . . on what the role of the U.S. Senate should be in foreign policy. Clearly, we have some role. I mean, we do have the role of confirming Ambassadors and giving advice and consent to treaties. But does the role of the U.S. Senate in foreign policy extend to constantly tinkering with everything, fine-tuning everything? We had this big debate—it still rages—on the War Powers Act, [and] the son of the War Powers Act . . . We [in Congress] are going to be not only 535 secretaries of state, we are going to be 535 commanders-in-chief. Talk about lack of clear signals, lack of clarity from the position of the United States of America in foreign policy; we are a cacophony of confusion. I would submit that no reasonable person anywhere in the world can predict how the United States stands on any foreign-policy issue.

Before the Senate, Oct. 6/
The Washington Post, 10-22:(A)23.

WHAT THEY SAID IN 1987

Miguel d'Escoto
Foreign Minister of Nicaragua

1

[The] Soviet Union has become the personi-fication of ethical and moral norms in interna-tional relations . . . a great torch which emits hope for the preservation of peace on our planet.

Accepting the Lenin Peace Prize, Moscow/
U.S. News & World Report, 12-21:40.

Robert J. Dole
United States Senator, R-Kansas;
Candidate for the 1988
Republican Presidential nomination

2

[Soviet leader Mikhail] Gorbachev is a phenomenon—the first truly modern Soviet leader. We cannot underestimate him or his im-pact. In the long run, he is more dangerous and threatening to our country and our ideals than all the brashness and bluster of a [Nikita] Khrushchev, all the stolid determination of a [Leonid] Brezhnev. We have to understand, and to convince the world that, at bottom, he is sell-ing the same worn-out solutions.

Interview/The Washington Post, 6-13:(A)13.

3

In the past 25 years, most—not all, but most—of our difficulties have come from those foreign entanglements President [George] Wash-ington warned us against. Yet we could not find a more dangerous time than the present to kneel to the temptations of isolationism. Nothing could be more irresponsible than to feed the false hope that we can lock our doors and close our minds to the world.

Interview/The Washington Post, 6-13:(A)13.

4

The Soviet threat is a lot different in nature than the Iran-Libya threat. But the basic goal is the same: to get Uncle Sam out of the way. Be-cause once you get rid of Uncle Sam, you've

got a clear path to spread whatever brand of ag-gression and oppression you happen to espouse.

At American Legion convention,
San Antonio, Aug. 25/
The New York Times, 8-26:11.

5

[On the War Powers Resolution]: My own view, as one who took part in the 1973 debate and voted for the Resolution, is that it was not crafted to handle the kind of situation we [now] have in the [Persian] Gulf [where U.S. forces are protecting oil tankers from Iranian attack]. It was intended to do one main thing: to keep what started out as one-shot, in-and-out inter-ventions in shooting wars from turning into permanent commitments—permanent American involvement in those wars.

Before the Senate, Washington, Oct. 9/
The Washington Post, 10-10:(I)9.

Michael S. Dukakis
Governor of Massachusetts (D);
Candidate for the 1988
Democratic Presidential nomination

6

[On the U.S. Iran-contra scandal]: I don't know what our foreign policy reflects now. There are no principles; there are no values. That bunch of conservatives in the White House wouldn't know the rule of law if it hit them in the face.

Before Democratic Party leaders,
Cleveland, July 17/
The New York Times, 7-18:8.

7

Where those military dictatorships systemati-cally deny human rights to their people, we can't just sit there doing nothing. I didn't spend 16 months of my life in Korea so a bunch of Korean generals can deny human rights to peo-ple in [South] Korea . . . I think the next Presi-dent of the United States is going to have to confront the issue of whether or not we are go-

(MICHAEL S. DUKAKIS)

ing to continue to support military dictatorships. The reason this is so important is because when we do so, we sow the seeds for radical revolution.

At Democratic Presidential
candidates' debate, Des Moines, Iowa,
Sept. 27/Los Angeles Times, 9-28:(I)12.

1

I hope we're [the U.S.] learning some lessons from history—that cozying up to [Cuba's late dictator] Batista or to [Nicaragua's late dictator] Somoza or to [Chile's dictator] Pinochet, or to anyone else like them is a bad idea . . . We always should be working to insure that people have no doubt about where the United States stands when it comes to human rights and democracy in these nations. Do we have the right to intervene and overthrow a government we don't happen to agree with? No, we don't. It's illegal. We ought to understand that.

Interview/Mother Jones, December:26.

Pierre S. du Pont IV
Former Governor of Delaware (R);
Candidate for the 1988
Republican Presidential nomination

2

An anti-terrorist policy in this country ought to have a number of elements to it. First is not to glorify the hostage-takers. Second, we should not trade things for hostages—arms, medical supplies, grain. Third, the United States, when it can demonstrate who is responsible for a hostage-taking, ought to retaliate in an appropriate way. Fourth, the President should never say exactly what he's going to do. And finally, anyone who can be demonstrated to have been involved in a hostage-taking ought to be flagged for the rest of his life in all the civilized parts of the world, and that person ought to be brought to justice, even if it's 20 years from now.

Interview/USA Today, 12-29:(A)9.

Daniel J. Evans
United States Senator,
R-Washington

3

[Criticizing the Senate's interference in running foreign policy]: I fear we are perilously close to trivializing our whole process. It is easy to bash foreign operations, and it is fun to go after the Department of State. But I can tell you that foreign governments do not understand what we are doing. We intermittently dash to the floor [of the Senate] and produce our ideas of foreign policy and dash off to the next item on the agenda. We constantly harp on the old faithfuls. I believe it is time for some restraint. This plea may fall on deaf ears, but if we continue on our course, this body will become as irrelevant as the House of Lords.

The New York Times, 10-12:10.

Paul Freedenberg
Assistant Secretary for
Trade Administration,
Department of Commerce
of the United States

4

[On why the U.S. uses trade sanctions against foreign countries more than other nations do]: First, we are the leaders of the free world and must set an example; second, we have the strongest economic system with the most leverage; and third, we don't have the traditions of world trade that others have . . . Our allies don't see trade relevant to foreign-policy questions.

Los Angeles Times, 2-7:(I)23.

Richard N. Gardner
Professor, department of law,
Columbia University;
Former United States
Ambassador to Italy

5

The [U.S.] Reagan Doctrine is regarded as inconsistent with U.S. treaty commitments by virtually all legal scholars and by all U.S. allies in NATO and Latin America. Our right to defend Central American countries against Nic-

WHAT THEY SAID IN 1987

(RICHARD N. GARDNER)

araguan aggression or to aid the Afghan insurgents who are fighting against an invading Soviet army is, of course, beyond question. But by asserting the right to organize military insurgencies to topple regimes we regard as undemocratic we are espousing a dangerous doctrine that we would never accept if claimed by our adversaries against undemocratic regimes like Chile, [South] Korea or South Africa. And let us not forget that Israel's enemies in the United Nations continue to assert the right to go to war against it on the spurious claim that Israel is a "racist" regime.

Speech, New York, May 13/
The Washington Post, 5-22:(A)26.

John Glenn
United States Senator, D-Ohio

1

The [U.S.] Iran-contra [scandal] mess is proof . . . that we cannot be content with [CIA] internal reviews alone. It is simply a fact that self-audit is justifiably subject to suspicion and distrust. To expedite such independent reviews, Congress established the GAO.

The Washington Post, 7-1:(A)17.

Roy Godson
Director, National Strategy
Information Center

2

[On revelations of Soviet spying at the U.S. Embassy in Moscow]: I don't know why everyone's so surprised . . . The Soviets have been doing this for years. I interviewed several KGB agents who told me that the main job of their section was breaking into Embassies. That's what they did for a living.

USA Today, 4-10:(A)8.

Mikhail S. Gorbachev
General Secretary,
Communist Party of the Soviet Union

3

In America—and this cannot be denied—there are forces to which hostility is profitable, which need the U.S.S.R. to have "the enemy image" and which use high-powered information media to sow hatred toward the Soviet people . . . [But] there is no alternative to coexistence. This is not the question of whether we like each other or not. This is something outside politics. America will be such as is liked by the Americans. But the Soviet Union, too, will not build its society by following recipes from the outside.

Before former U.S. government officials,
Moscow, Feb. 4/The Washington Post, 2-5:(A)25.

4

It is often said—we still hear it—that there is some threat stemming from the Soviet Union, a Soviet threat to peace and freedom. We want to be understood, and we hope that the world community will at least acknowledge, that our desire to make our own country better will hurt no one, with the world only gaining from this.

Moscow, Feb. 16/
The Christian Science Monitor, 2-20:1.

5

I believe the situation in the world is such that it differs fundamentally from what it used to be. The empires are all gone. All of those nations want not only independence and autonomy, but they want to live a better life. And now, just try and imagine 2.5 billion people in Asia and in Latin America, disposed of vast natural resources, vast manpower resources, and yet they are in debt. It calls out for a solution. However strong we might be, we cannot dictate our values or impose our way of life upon others. That means . . . the need to respect the choice of every nation.

American broadcast interview,
Moscow, Nov. 28/NBC-TV, 11-30.

6

[On U.S. criticism of human rights in the Soviet Union]: We believe our human rights are better than your human rights. Our standard of living may be lower than yours, but we believe in the right to a decent standard of living of every human being, of every individual's right to security. You [the U.S.] have some different views. You seem to view human rights as

(MIKHAIL S. GORBACHEV)

wholly a matter of emigration [from the Soviet Union] . . . Examine your own record. You won't let everyone into your country who leaves some other country, or wishes to. You seem to accept everyone who wishes to leave the Soviet Union. Yet you do not accept everyone who wishes to leave Mexico for your country. Take a look at your own record on human rights while you criticize ours.

At meeting with members of
U.S. Congress, Washington, Dec. 9/
Los Angeles Times, 12-10:(I)29.

Albert Gore, Jr.
United States Senator, D-Tennessee;
Candidate for the 1988
Democratic Presidential nomination

1

There is a neo-isolationist impulse that has come out of the Vietnam [war] experience that has not been put in perspective in the [Democratic] Party. The nominating process [for President] has served to push the candidates to the left and make each of them scared they will be outflanked on the left by someone who plays to this neo-isolationist impulse. Therefore, the mainstream Democratic voter listening to the dialogue feels disillusioned and confused about where the traditional Democratic consensus has gone.

To reporters, Washington, Oct. 21/
The Washington Post, 10-22:(A)6.

Allan Gotlieb
Canadian Ambassador
to the United States

2

Americans know that their role in the world is pivotal; that their country is powerful, not just influential; that, judged by a number of standards, theirs is the most powerful country on earth. Americans know there are *Minuteman III* missiles in silos in Kansas and elsewhere, and *Trident* submarines concealed beneath the seas. Americans comprehend, if anyone can

comprehend, their awesome capacity for destruction. They know that it is their responsibility to control those weapons. They realize that one day, God forbid, it may be their duty to defend themselves and the alliance by using them. They may wish it were otherwise, but they accept this power and the responsibility of custodianship it entails. No Canadian has ever borne such responsibility. Few Canadians can, therefore, comprehend the impact this has on the American character and on their world outlook. Not that most Americans welcome the responsibility. And, to their credit, and to our benefit, I believe, they are not comfortable with the idea of empire. Most would prefer to be left alone.

Toronto, April 9/
The Washington Post, 4-17:(A)22.

Lee H. Hamilton
United States Representative,
D-Indiana

3

As long as I've been in the Congress, the President, every President, calls for bipartisanship in foreign policy, and we all want bipartisanship in foreign policy. But bipartisanship requires Congress' informed consent. It cannot merely be a call to support the President's policy.

At Iran-contra hearings, Washington,
May 14/Los Angeles Times, 5-15:(I)23.

4

Under the Constitution, the Executive and the Congress both play a key role in making American foreign policy. And the members of this committee, of both parties, of all persuasions, have a deeply felt desire to show that our government's system of shared powers works. And I do not see how that can be done, unless those of us who are charged with that responsibility speak to one another the truth.

At Iran-contra hearings,
Washington, June 3/
The New York Times, 6-4:6.

WHAT THEY SAID IN 1987

(LEE H. HAMILTON)

1

[On the U.S. Iran-contra scandal]: An elaborate private network was set up to carry out the foreign policy of the United States. Private citizens, many with divided loyalties and profit motives, sold arms and negotiated for the release of American hostages. Private citizens were given top-secret codes and encryption devices and had access to Swiss bank accounts, used for United States covert actions and operations. The President [Reagan] was involved in private and third-country fund-raising for the contras [Nicaraguan rebels]. Wealthy private contributors were courted at the White House, solicited in coordination with government officials and given what they were told was secret information. American policy became dependent on the contributions of private individuals and third countries . . . Privatization of foreign policy is a prescription for confusion and failure. The advancement of American national interests depends on the full use of the many resources of the United States government. We are ill-served when it is otherwise. The use of private parties to carry out high purposes of government make us the subject of puzzlement and ridicule.

At Iran-contra hearings, Washington,
June 9/The New York Times, 6-10:8.

2

Covert action should always be used to supplement, not to contradict, our foreign policy. It should be consistent with our public policies. It should not be used to impose a foreign policy on the American people which they do not support . . . A few [people in government] do not know what is better for Americans than Americans know themselves. If I understand our government correctly, no small group of people, no matter how important, no matter how well-intentioned they may be, should be trusted to determine policy [in secret]. As President [James] Madison said: "Trust should be placed not in a few, but in a number of hands."

At Iran-contra hearings, Washington,
July 14/Los Angeles Times, 7-15:(I)10.

3

[Addressing former Presidential National Security Advisor John Poindexter about his testimony on the Iran-contra scandal]: You began your testimony by saying that the function of a National Security Adviser is to present options and to advise the President. Yet you told the committees "the buck stops here with me." That is not where the buck is supposed to stop. You wanted to deflect blame from the President [Reagan] but that is another way of saying you wanted to deflect responsibility from the President. And that should not be done in our system of government.

At Iran-contra hearings, Washington,
July 21/The New York Times, 7-22:6.

Garrett Hardin
Ecologist

4

Since Ethiopia has far too many people for its resources, if you give food and save lives and thus increase the number of people, you increase suffering and ultimately increase the loss of life . . . When you propose doing something, ask if it will help not just for the moment, but for the future. Most [foreign] aid does more harm than good.

Interview/The New York Times, 6-30:25.

Gary Hart
Former United States Senator,
D-Colorado;
Former candidate for the 1988
Democratic Presidential nomination

5

For the first time in many years, the pre-eminent Soviet leader [Mikhail Gorbachev] is younger than the American President [Reagan]. More importantly, while the current American President seeks to recapture a mythical time in America's past—whether the 1920s or the 1950s—the new Soviet leader is clearly anticipating the 21st century.

Before Philadelphia
World Affairs Council, Sept. 10/
Los Angeles Times, 9-11:(I)30.

Arthur A. Hartman
Former United States Ambassador
to the Soviet Union

1

[On revelations of Soviet espionage at the U.S. Embassy in Moscow, which included the seducing of U.S. Marine Corps guards by Soviet women agents]: Professionals, those who are authorized to have contacts [with Soviets] and do the kinds of jobs we can only do in Moscow, know how to handle themselves. The others, I'm afraid, are going to have to be very carefully supervised. And there are not many Americans who want to come over and be very carefully supervised in a place like Moscow, that offers so little in the way of distraction and entertainment.

Interview, Washington/
Los Angeles Times, 5-2:(I)31.

Orrin G. Hatch
United States Senator, R-Utah

2

[On the U.S. Iran-contra hearings]: As we near the end of these hearings . . . I'm struck more and more how terribly overblown this whole affair has been. We [at the hearings] have elevated the art of beating a dead horse to new heights.

The Washington Post, 7-22:(A)2.

Howell Heflin
United States Senator, D-Alabama

3

[On the U.S. Iran-contra scandal]: As the truth is found and told, we may well conclude, sadly, that in the course of pursuing democratic principles in foreign lands, we may have subverted them at home. These hearings are about affirmation. Yes, they're about rogue elephants, Persian rug merchants, loose cannons, soldiers of fortune, privateers, profiteers, believers, hostages, contras. But they are also about separation of powers, national security, Fifth Amendment rights, allegations of misconduct, charges of cover-up, the right to know, and importantly, they're about the rule of law. Passion for the

rule of law. Yes, these hearings are about the elevation of respect for the rule of law and Constitutional principles above ideology and power.

At Iran-contra hearings, Washington,
May 5/Los Angeles Times, 5-6:(I)17.

Pat Holt
Former Chief of Staff,
U.S. Senate
Foreign Relations Committee

4

The big problem in recent years is the exaggeration of Presidential power [in foreign policy]. Congress has the wherewithal to use [power]. They like the prestige of being consulted. But they're usually willing for the buck to stop on the President's desk.

The Christian Science Monitor, 2-3:21.

Arnold Horelick
Director, Rand-UCLA
Center for the Study of
Soviet International Behavior

5

[Soviet leader Mikhail] Gorbachev has said they will publish their military budget in two or three years, but who knows what that means? In the meantime, without enough data, we [in the U.S.] have a tendency to make worst-case estimates. It's hard for Americans to know how to influence an adversary's foreign policy if all the decisions are made in a black box.

The Washington Post, 12-2:(A)30.

Jerry Hough
Professor of political science,
Duke University

6

This period in history, this decade, will go as the end of the post-World War II era. It will go down as the period in which the United States lost its obsession with the Soviet Union as the purpose of all evil.

USA Today, 12-4:(A)6.

Duncan Hunter
United States Representative,
R-California

1

[The Soviets] play for the long run. Their game plan is going to span many American Administrations. You have to sustain, sustain, sustain. And the problem with democracies is, it's very difficult to build an endurance in difficult foreign policies.

The New York Times, 5-28:12.

Samuel P. Huntington
Director,
Center for International Affairs,
Harvard University

2

There is this group of foreign-policy and defense specialists, people who spend their time commuting between New York and Boston and Washington, who know each other, who are in these groups advising the [1988 Presidential] candidates. That doesn't mean there's consensus or agreement, although I suppose there's more agreement now on foreign-policy issues than there has been over the last 10 or 15 years. The bitter division over Vietnam has tended to disappear, and I don't see people taking extreme positions in the same way that people often took 10 years ago. There's simply less polarization now.

Interview/The New York Times, 6-4:10.

Henry J. Hyde
United States Representative,
R-Illinois

3

[On the Boland Amendment—which banned many types of U.S. aid to the contras, rebels fighting the Sandinista government of Nicaragua—and its application in the Iran-contra scandal]: If the Boland Amendment wanted to foreclose all government funds, why didn't it simply say so? Can the Congress use its power of the purse to cut off, restrict or amend the President's Constitutional powers to be the supreme spokes-

man for America in foreign policy, the sole operator? . . . I don't think so.

At Iran-contra hearings, Washington,
June 8/Los Angeles Times, 6-9:(I)17.

4

You have to have [Administration] people who understand that you can't run a foreign policy against Congress. If Congress won't agree with you, you have to try to change Congress. You don't run a policy out of the back door.

The New York Times, 8-7:5.

Bobby R. Inman
Former Deputy Director
of Central Intelligence
of the United States

5

. . . the role of intelligence agencies [is] making judgments, not just writing history. When you do that, you're never 100 per cent right. But your value is greater.

Los Angeles Times, 2-3:(I)14.

6

[On security problems at U.S. Embassies around the world, especially in light of recent incidents of Soviet espionage at the U.S. Embassy in Moscow]: What the incident in Moscow should awaken us to is that the problems and vulnerabilities are widespread. While the Soviets most skillfully exploit them, they are not the only ones trying, and vulnerabilities are at least as large, if not larger, in other places where the guard is not so high.

The New York Times, 4-22:8.

Daniel K. Inouye
United States Senator,
D-Hawaii

7

[On the U.S. Iran-contra scandal]: The story is one not of covert activity alone but of covert foreign policy. Not secret diplomacy, which Congress has always accepted, but secret policy-making, which the Constitution has al-

(DANIEL K. INOUYE)

ways rejected. It is a tale of working outside the system and of utilizing irregular channels and private parties, accountable to no one, on matters of national security, while ignoring the Congress and even the traditional agencies of Executive foreign-policy making. The story is both sad and sordid. It is filled with inconsistencies and often unexplainable conduct. None of the participants emerges unblemished. People of great character and ability, holding positions of trust and authority in our government, were drawn into a web of deception and despair.

At Iran-contra hearings, Washington,
May 5/The New York Times, 5-6:8.

1

[On the Congressional hearings into the U.S. Iran-contra scandal]: By eliciting and examining the entire story, we believe our nation will emerge stronger, for we also believe that sunlight is the best disinfectant.

USA Today, 5-7:(A)10.

2

[Addressing former Presidential National Security Adviser John Poindexter on his role in the Iran-contra scandal]: When we sit here and listen to your testimony in which you tell us that you have either withheld information from or misled or misinformed the Congress of the United States, that you have withheld information from the President [Reagan], that you have either withheld information from or misled or misinformed the highest-ranking Cabinet members of the United States, that you have withheld information from your most trusted deputy, Colonel [Oliver] North—I don't think it is improper for any member of this panel to characterize that testimony as being incredible, mind-boggling, chilling.

At Iran-contra hearings, Washington,
July 17/The New York Times, 7-18:1.

3

[On the U.S. Iran-contra scandal hearings]: I believe we have largely succeeded in piecing together the incredible chapters of this chilling

story and presenting to our fellow citizens a chronology of events as they occurred. However, we may never know with precision and truth why it ever happened . . . In describing their motive for riding roughshod over the Constitutional restraints built into our form of government, Admiral [John] Poindexter and Lieutenant Colonel [Oliver] North used almost the identical words. "This is a dangerous world," they said. That, my fellow citizens, is an excuse for autocracy, not for policy, because no times were more dangerous than when our country was born, when revolution was our midwife . . . Out of this experience may we all better understand and appreciate our Constitution, strive harder to preserve it and make a fresh start at restoring the trust between the branches of government. For in America, as 200 years ago, the people still rule.

At Iran-contra hearings, Washington,
Aug. 3/The Washington Post, 8-4:(A)6.

Jesse L. Jackson
Civil-rights leader;
Candidate for the 1988
Democratic Presidential nomination

4

[The U.S.] brand of foreign policy is contemptuous of the Third World and foreign people. Our foreign policy is an extension of our domestic policy and attitudes. Just as we cannot relate to black, Hispanic or Asian people in this country, we do an even worse job of relating to people who live north and south. We must overcome that infirmity if we are to maintain our stature as a respected world power.

Interview/Mother Jones, October:33.

Brian Jenkins
Director,
research program on subnational
conflict and political violence,
Rand Corporation

5

Clearly, the bombing of Libya [by the U.S. in 1986 in retaliation for Libyan terrorism] changed the equation. It suggested to nations that use

WHAT THEY SAID IN 1987

(BRIAN JENKINS)

terrorism as an instrument of policy that they risk retaliation. They may choose to dismiss that risk or to accept it, but they're going to have to take it into account.

Los Angeles Times, 10-11:(I)19.

Jack Kemp
United States Representative,
R-New York; Candidate for the 1988
Republican Presidential nomination

1

Diplomacy without any threat of force or any use of force is diplomacy which becomes emasculated when dealing with the central trauma of the 20th century, the struggle between democracy and totalitarianism.

At Rivier College, Aug. 27/
Los Angeles Times, 8-28:(I)36.

Edward M. Kennedy
United States Senator,
D-Massachusetts

2

Again and again and again, in South Africa, in Chile, and now in South Korea, the [U.S.] Reagan Administration has shown its contempt for the struggle for democracy in other lands. We have learned to our regret in Congress that quiet diplomacy in this Administration means no diplomacy.

The Christian Science Monitor, 6-22:5.

Ali Khameini
President of Iran

3

The dominant thinking in the political world today believes that without reliance on one of the power blocs, no movement may survive . . . Our [Iranian] revolution proved that imperial-minded powers may be ignored, and that black-mailing may not be effective provided there is belief in a power more powerful, belief in God Almighty.

At United Nations, New York,
Sept. 22/The New York Times, 9-23:6.

Stanley Kutler
Historian,
University of Wisconsin, Madison

4

One of the worst cliches of modern Constitutional history is the notion that the President was given absolute control over foreign policy . . . There is nothing in the literature of the Constitution that sustains that proposition.

Los Angeles Times, 9-17:(I)1.

Gerald Lamberty
President,
American Foreign Service Association

5

From long years of practical experience, we've learned that when you're dealing with hostages you can't let the kidnapper believe he's gotten something valuable out of it. If you do, you're only asking for more . . . If you are going to get into ransoming, then you either have to close up Embassies or live within an armed compound and not be able to act very effectively as the eyes and ears of the American government overseas.

Interview/
The Christian Science Monitor, 1-23:1,32.

Paul Laxalt
Former United States Senator,
R-Nevada

6

[On Marine Lt. Col. Oliver North's Congressional testimony about his role in the U.S. Iran-contra scandal]: The praise he is receiving is more than deserved. But what has really come through, aside from the merit or demerit of the [Iran-contra] plan and all that, is the fact—and this is reassuring to me—is that basic values like honesty, patriotism, subscribing to principle are not passe. The vast majority of American citizens consider that to be a vital element of American society today. And that's what Ollie North has been about this last week.

At Young Republican National
Federation convention, Seattle/
Los Angeles Times, 7-12:(I)15.

Patrick J. Leahy
United States Senator,
D-Vermont
1

The Soviets are allowed to play by entirely different rules than we do. Our Embassy over there [in Moscow], the new Embassy that's being built, is in a swamp surrounded by buildings controlled by the KGB. Their Embassy is sitting up on Mount Alto, here in Washington, with antennas that can go into the Pentagon, the White House, Treasury, CIA, everything else.
Broadcast interview/
"Face the Nation," 4-5.

John Lofton
Conservative
political writer-analyst
2

If there is a policy that's dumber, more quixotic and historically more bankrupt than trying to get Communists to give up in negotiations what they have gained on the battlefield, I don't know [what it is]. The fatal flaw is the presupposition that whatever is agreed to during such a negotiation would be worth . . . the paper any agreement would be printed on . . . Lenin said treaties were like pie crusts—made to be broken.
U.S. News & World Report, 6-1:39.

Charles William Maynes
Editor,
"Foreign Affairs" magazine
3

You have to distinguish between what the politicians say and what the historians will write. History's judgment will be that the U.S. had little to do with the success of the opposition in [South Korea]. But politically, it will be a tremendous boost for [U.S. President] Reagan's fortunes. You claim credit for successes that take place on your watch. Fairly or unfairly, you assume blame for the failures.
The Christian Science Monitor, 7-2:5.

Robert C. McFarlane
Former Assistant to President
of the United States Ronald Reagan
for National Security Affairs
4

[Saying the U.S. use of covert activity to aid the contra rebels in Nicaragua, which is part of the Iran-contra scandal, was wrong]: There are two basic reasons for this. The first is that you can never achieve a sufficient level of resources through a covert policy to cope with a determined effort backed by the Soviet Union . . . The other reason for not making covert action the core of policy is that you cannot get public and Congressional support for such a policy. If you decide to engage in conflict with a Soviet client in whom the Russians are prepared to make a substantial investment, you must have the American people and the U.S. Congress solidly behind you. Yet it is virtually impossible, almost as a matter of definition, to rally public support behind a policy that you can't even talk about.
At Iran-contra hearings, Washington,
May 11/The New York Times, 5-12:6.

5

In the six months since the [U.S.] Iran-contra controversy erupted, many people have come to believe there is something wrong with the way this country makes foreign policy. They probably don't know how wrong. True, the nation's foreign-policy apparatus does produce its share of success. Failures, like those in the Iran-contra affair, do not happen every day. But on any policy issue where party or ideological interests diverge substantially, the system is becoming increasingly subject to incoherence or paralysis.
At Iran-contra hearings, Washington,
May 11/Los Angeles Times, 5-12:(I)15.

6

The perhaps central and most important quality of a great power, as seen by allies and enemies, is constancy: being able to count on commitments once made, whether you're an ally or an enemy.
At Iran-contra hearings, Washington,
May 13/The New York Times, 5-14:6.

(ROBERT C. McFARLANE)

1

. . . I want the record to be clear regarding my beliefs about how our government should function in the sensitive area of covert action under our Constitution . . . Simply put, we aren't in a competition with a democratic opponent [the Soviet Union]. For the other side, unrestrained covert actions are a way of life; and just as they support Leninist political parties in developing countries, we had better be able to use a range of means to support people who aspire to freedom, or they will perish, and our own freedom, as we know it, will be in jeopardy. I also believe there is a consensus around that both the funding level and the intended scope of covert activity should be relatively modest. Any foreign-policy issue that will take significant funding for a long period of time, had better have the understanding and support of the American people going in. That support is engendered by vigorous public debate—something that is impossible in the case of covert actions, which must remain private.

At Iran-contra hearings,
Washington, July 14/
The New York Times, 7-15:6.

Matthew F. McHugh
United States Representative,
D-New York

2

This [Reagan] Administration, in the eyes of Congress, cannot be fully trusted. And therefore Congress, to protect its legitimate role, has to try to impose limits, to tighten reporting requirements, things which wouldn't be necessary if the Administration were perceived as being sensitive to Congressional rights and responsibilities . . . There will always be a groping for the proper balance in the foreign-policy area between Congress and the Executive Branch. That's something built in when you have dual responsibility. The imprecision always creates some tension.

The New York Times, 6-2:14.

Edwin Meese III
Attorney General of the United States

3

Terrorists cannot be granted immunity simply because they threaten the loss of innocent life. We have a moral obligation to other potential hostages . . . not to capitulate to hostagetakers. To do so would only encourage many more incidents and many more threats to human life.

At terrorism conference, Washington/
The Christian Science Monitor, 1-22:32.

John Melcher
United States Senator,
D-Montana

4

[On the Iran-contra scandal in the U.S.]: There has been a three-year principal preoccupation of the National Security Council in dealing arms to foreign brokers, a [Iranian Ayatollah] Khomeini sting operation with elaborate Middle Eastern intrigues. This is not America's finest hour. None should confuse the Iran-contra shameful transgressions as examples of clean government. Free enterprise and fair trade take on a new concept. Got an arms deal? Cut me in. Deposit my loot in my Swiss bank account. When the law is stretched or fractured, shred the records . . . The truth is, the National Security Council has been lacerated, is as naked as a plucked chicken, eviscerated and ready for the frying pan. What went on here? It went on right here, not somewhere else, and it is not a novel or screenplay—it went on right here in the nation's capital.

Before the Senate, Washington,
June 5/The Washington Post, 6-16:(A)14.

Allan H. Meltzer
Professor of economics
and public policy,
Graduate School
of Industrial Administration,
Carnegie-Mellon University

5

For the past 40 years, the United States has had the relative wealth and power to maintain

(ALLAN H. MELTZER)

or impose a degree of political, economic and trade stability on much of the world. We have not always succeeded; we have made mistakes; but we have avoided the return to the disorder that characterized the inter-war period, particularly the 1930s. If we solve our problems of trade and debt by reducing our relative wealth, we move to a position of co-equal in a multi-centered world. New arrangements must develop for sharing responsibility for defense, finance, trade and the maintenance of such order as can be provided. We have done little to develop arrangements commensurate with the reduced role that our relative wealth and power will bring. If we fail to increase productivity, such planning is essential to avoid a return to the uncertainties of the inter-war period.

Before Senate Banking Committee,
Washington/The Wall Steet Journal, 3-9:22.

Adam Michnik
Polish historian

1

The only real measure of [positive] change [in the Soviet Union] is improvement in human rights. If [Soviet leader Mikhail] Gorbachev really wants to show that he rejects militarism and imperialism, then he must allow people to live freely in their own societies.

Interview, Warsaw, Poland/
The Washington Post, 5-22:(A)1.

Terry Miller
United States observer
to United Nations Educational,
Scientific and Cultural Organization
(UNESCO)

2

We see the election of a new Director General [of UNESCO] as a first step in a long process of revitalization that will be needed before the U.S. returns [to UNESCO] . . . We haven't really seen a constituency in the U.S. that seemed concerned about UNESCO. People who might have defended UNESCO before are too

busy trying to defend the United Nations in New York. A return would mean obtaining an allocation of $40-million a year from a tight-fisted [U.S.] Congress. To do that, UNESCO would have to show that it was worth more than other competing international organizations.

To reporters, Paris/
The Christian Science Monitor, 10-19:13.

George J. Mitchell
United States Senator,
D-Maine

3

[On U.S. government officials involved in the Iran-contra scandal]: [It is clear that people] thought that their patriotism and their commitment to the cause was more important than obeying the law . . . It is clear there is an effort underway to create the impression that patriotism, commitment to a cause, sincerity of belief, lack of venal motive somehow combined to justify evading the law.

Washington, June 10/
The Washington Post, 6-11:(A)20.

4

The [U.S.] Iran-contra scandal is about the rule of law. It reminds us of how much democracy asks of us, how quickly its demands can become frustrating to those who, even though acting with patriotic motives, are convinced that they alone possess the truth, that they alone know what's best.

Broadcast address to the nation,
Washington, Aug. 12/
The New York Times, 8-13:6.

Walter F. Mondale
Former Vice President
of the United States;
1984 Democratic Presidential nominee

5

[On the U.S. Iran-contra scandal]: Look, I don't want to get into an "I told you so" posture. It was a theme in my last campaign, but who listened? I said the President [Reagan] is out of touch, out of control, uninformed, un-

WHAT THEY SAID IN 1987

willing to accept responsibilities for mistakes and burdened by some ideological Rambo-like concepts bound to get us in trouble. Who listened? . . . It was all so knowable. These people in the White House had no sense of history. Did they really think they could get away with it—violate the law and nobody would care? Fool around with these [Iranian] Khomeini crazies without getting burned? They were so full of hubris, so full of their own ideology. They were so ignorant of what they were involved with and so contemptuous of fundamental rules of law and truth.

> *Interview, Washington/*
> *The New York Times, 3-4:24.*

John Norton Moore
Professor of law,
University of Virginia

1

When the Congress tries to limit the Executive's power in foreign policy, it has to do it clearly. Any ambiguity will be determined in favor of the President.

> *The Washington Post, 5-18:(A)8.*

Daniel P. Moynihan
United States Senator,
D-New York

2

There is a great deal of concern, and among some people it edges over toward alarm, that we have no foreign-policy decision-making system. The possibility of awful mistakes looms on every horizon . . . [For example,] there is a feeling that [the Reagan Administration is] going to rush to a summit [with the Soviets] and sign an agreement. You hear that among conservative Republicans. From liberal Democrats you hear they're going to rush to war. There are very few points in the spectrum where there is not great anxiety.

> *The New York Times, 6-13:2.*

Oliver L. North
Lieutenant Colonel,
United States Marine Corps

3

[On his involvement in the U.S. Iran-contra scandal]: I can tell you this: Everything that I did was done in the best interests of the United States of America. This Marine is never going to plead guilty to anything, ever.

> *TV Interview, Virginia/*
> *The New York Times, 5-29:8.*

4

[On his involvement in the U.S. Iran-contra scandal]: Throughout the conduct of my entire tenure at the National Security Council, I assumed that the President [Reagan] was aware of what I was doing and had, through my superiors, approved it. I sought approval of my superiors for every one of my actions and it is well-documented. I assumed when I had approval to proceed from either Judge [William] Clark, Bud McFarlane or Admiral [John] Poindexter [all former Presidential National Security Advisers], that they had indeed solicited and obtained the approval of the President. To my recollection, Admiral Poindexter never told me that he met with the President on the issue of using residuals from the Iranian [arms] sales to support the Nicaraguan [contra] resistance, or that he discussed the residuals or profits for use by the contras with the President, or that he got the President's specific approval. But again, I wish to reiterate that, throughout, I believed that the President had indeed authorized such activity.

> *At Iran-contra hearings, Washington,*
> *July 7/Los Angeles Times, 7-8:(I)9.*

5

I think it is very important for the American people to understand that this is a dangerous world . . . and they ought not to be led to believe . . . that this nation cannot or should not conduct covert operations. By their very nature, covert operations, or special activities, are a lie. There is great deceit, deception practiced in the conduct of covert operations. They are at essence a lie. We make every effort to deceive the

(OLIVER L. NORTH)

4

enemy as to our intent, our conduct, and to deny the association of the United States with those activities.

At Iran-contra hearings, Washington,
July 7/Los Angeles Times, 7-8:(I)9.

1

[On questions about his shredding documents that might have been relevant to the investigation of the U.S. Iran-contra scandal]: The reason for shredding documents and the reason the government of the United States gave me a shredder—I mean, I didn't buy it myself—was to destroy documents that were no longer relevant, that did not apply or that should not be divulged . . . That's why the government buys shredders by the tens and dozens and gives them to people running covert operations, not so that they can have convenient memories [when testifying before committees].

At Iran-contra hearings, Washington,
July 7/The Washington Post, 7-8:(A)15.

2

[On his involvement in the U.S. Iran-contra scandal]: Lying does not come easy to me . . . But I think we all had to weigh in the balance the difference between lives and lies.

At Iran-contra hearings, Washington/
Los Angeles Times, 8-5:(I)16.

Sam Nunn
United States Senator,
D-Georgia

3

History has clearly demonstrated that an effective foreign policy strategy must be based on a calculated relationship between ends and means. A nation whose publicly declared goals far exceed its capabilities is in a high-risk posture.

At Senate Armed Services
Committee hearing, Washington,
Jan. 12/Los Angeles Times,
1-13:(I)7.

[Criticizing U.S. agencies for frequently ignoring and mishandling those who defect to the U.S. from Soviet-bloc countries]: We must better learn how to assist and utilize the genuine defector, who usually arrives at our doorstep in his flight for freedom with nothing more than the shirt on his back. If we as a society ignore [the defector], we may be turning our backs on the very important contributions he can make, contributions which can be extremely valuable keys [to] a society which is otherwise shielded from us by a huge police and intelligence apparatus.

The Christian Science Monitor, 10-9:6.

5

[On U.S.-Soviet relations]: We ought to shake hands and talk to them, but I think we ought to count our fingers when we get through shaking hands.

USA Today, 10-26:(A)5.

6

Leaders of great powers must anticipate the effect tomorrow of the decisions they make today. Threats to stability are not always apparent as they develop. The gloss of detente in the early 1970s has now faded, for example, because it obscured Soviet military expansion. A corollary is that arms-control agreements can contribute to stability—providing both sides play by the rules and perceive the deal, over time, as even-handed.

Interview/
U.S. News & World Report, 12-14:32.

David O'Brien
Constitutional scholar,
University of Virginia

7

The Founding Fathers set up shared powers in foreign policy. A lot of action in foreign affairs was handed to the President, but Congress has the right to limit his action. Congress ultimately makes the law and appropriates money,

WHAT THEY SAID IN 1987

and it's disingenuous for the [Reagan] Administration to claim otherwise now.

The Christian Science Monitor, 5-21:36.

William L. O'Neill
Professor of history,
Rutgers University

1

America was at the peak of its power and affluence between 1945 and 1960. We were the only nation that prospered. Former competitors like Germany and future competitors like Japan were completely knocked out by World War II. It's hard to imagine when we will again have such an overwhelming economic advantage. And there will never be a time when we have so much security in our own hemisphere, unless arms control becomes much more effective than we have any reason to expect.

Interview/

U.S. News & World Report, 3-23:74.

Howard Phillips
Chairman, Conservative Caucus

2

[Criticizing President Reagan for being more conciliatory toward the Soviet Union, and for the U.S.-Soviet arms-control treaty he has agreed to]: [President Reagan has become] a useful idiot for Soviet propaganda [and] a weak man with a strong wife and a strong staff . . . [He] is little more than the speech reader-in-chief for the pro-appeasement triumvirate of [White House Chief of Staff] Howard Baker, [Secretary of State] George Shultz and [new Defense Secretary] Frank Carlucci.

News conference, Dec. 4/
Los Angeles Times, 12-5:(I)12.

3

It is foolish to look to [President] Reagan for effective anti-Communist leadership. I have always regarded him as a man who simply read his cue cards, and now he has the wrong people writing them.

U.S. News & World Report, 12-21:41.

Richard Pipes
Former Director,
Soviet and East European Affairs,
National Security Council
of the United States

4

[On U.S.-Soviet summit meetings]: There are a tremendous number of people who believe that our trouble with the Soviet Union is due to misunderstandings and that, if the two leaders could simply get to know each other, they can clear up the problems in the relationship. But this is not the case. What happens is, of course, for a variety of reasons, the problems don't get solved, and then the Russians say, "We came full of hope and we were willing to make agreements, but the United States was not sincere." Then there is a sort of letdown that leads to pressure building up on the Presidency or even to a worsening of relations.

Interview/The New York Times, 12-3:8.

John M. Poindexter
Former Assistant to President
of the United States Ronald Reagan
for National Security Affairs

5

[On his involvement in the U.S. Iran-contra scandal]: I have always lived by the honor concept. I still live that way today. One of the things you also learn at the Naval Academy is the ability to exercise independent judgments that are in the best interests of the United States. My whole time as National Security Advisor, I worked very hard to do the best that I could to protect the national security of the United States . . . I don't have any regrets for anything that I did. I think the actions that I took were in the long-term interests of the country . . . And I'm not going to be apologetic about it.

At Iran-contra hearings, Washington,
July 20/The New York Times, 7-21:5.

6

[On his involvement in diversion of funds in the U.S. Iran-contra scandal]: Although I was convinced that we could properly do it and that

(JOHN M. POINDEXTER)

the President [Reagan] would approve it, if asked, I made a very deliberate decision not to ask the President, so that I could insulate him from the decision and provide some future deniability for the President if it ever leaked out.

At Iran-contra hearings,
Washington/Los Angeles Times, 8-5:(I)16.

Yevgeny Primakov
Director,
Soviet Institute of World Economics
and International Relations

1

[On a recent speech by U.S. President Reagan]: I waited for constructive proposals—there weren't any. I waited for a constructive tone—there wasn't any. But I did find a bright side. He said we [the Soviet Union] are far from American standards of democracy. I say, "Thank God."

Chautauqua, N.Y., Aug. 26/
The New York Times, 8-27:4.

Jean-Bernard Raimond
Foreign Minister of France

2

[On Soviet leader Mikhail Gorbachev's program for reform in the Soviet Union]: We [in the West] must exercise a double vigilance. On the one hand, we must be watchful for everything that is new and not assume that nothing is going to change in the Soviet Union. On the other hand, we must make sure that we do not succumb to illusions or make concessions costly to the interests of the West.

Time, 3-2:24.

Ronald Reagan
President of the United States

3

[Addressing the National Security Council staff on that agency's operations in the wake of the U.S. Iran-contra scandal]: Views must be fully aired. Agency participation should not be short-cut. I want the range of options developed for my consideration. Legal issues must be addressed head-on and the rule of law respected. And, of course, the recommendations and decisions must be properly documented. Sound management of the NSC process ultimately depends upon the skills and integrity of each of you here.

Washington/Los Angeles Times, 3-4:(I)17.

4

[On the U.S. Iran-contra scandal]: . . . I take full responsibility for my own actions and for those of my Administration. As angry as I may be about activities undertaken without my knowledge, I am still accountable for those activities. As disappointed as I may be in some who served me, I am still the one who must answer to the American people for this behavior. And as personally distasteful as I find secret bank accounts and diverted funds—as the navy would say, this happened on my watch.

Broadcast address to the nation,
Washington, March 4/
The New York Times, 3-5:12.

5

[On the recent high-seas rescue of Soviet sailors by U.S. Coast Guard helicopters]: I hope and pray that no matter how stormy [are] international affairs, the leaders of the world can look at what happened between these fliers and sailors and be duly inspired. After all, this good planet whirling through space isn't so very different from a ship upon the sea. We must reach out to each other in good will, for we have no other alternative.

Washington, March 17/
Los Angeles Times, 3-18:(I)4.

6

[On the criticism of his Administration over the U.S. Iran-contra scandal]: Remember the flap [some time ago] when I said, "We begin bombing [the Soviets] in five minutes"? Remember [the flap] when I fell asleep during my audience with the Pope? Remember [the flap

WHAT THEY SAID IN 1987

(RONALD REAGAN)

about my visit to the Nazi cemetery at] Bitburg? Boy, those were the good old days!
Before Gridiron Club/
Newsweek, 4-13:19.

1

Establishing an environment where tensions are lessened demands realism and a willingness to stand by our values and commitments in the face of threats, walkouts and woeful predictions. We need to remember, too, that voices of panic or accommodation disrupt the careful pursuit of peace when in their rush to sign an agreement or initial a treaty, they lose sight of justice and world freedom as goals of American foreign policy.
Before Los Angeles World Affairs Council,
April 10/Los Angeles Times, 4-11:(I)6.

2

It has become fashionable in some quarters to act as if the Central Intelligence Agency were somehow not completely a part of our own government—as if it were not constantly working against hostile powers who threaten the security of the American people. So long as I am President, I will never consent to see our intelligence capability undermined.
At swearing in of William Webster
as Director of Central Intelligence,
Langley, Va., May 26/
Los Angeles Times, 5-27:(I)4.

3

[In the old days, Congress] had a committee that would investigate even one of their own members if it was believed that that person had Communist involvement or Communist leanings. [Now] they've done away with those committees. That shows the success of what the Soviets were able to do in this country . . . Some years ago—I happen to know, because I've been a student of the Communist movement for a long time, having been a victim of it some years ago in Hollywood—the Communist Party was to call upon their "willing idiots"—their term—not just liberals who weren't Com-

munists, [to spread their doctrine] . . . They were to engage in a campaign that would make anti-Communism unfashionable [in the U.S.]. And they have succeeded . . . [Now] even among people that are anti-Communist, there is a tendency to say, "Oh, you know, enough of that, hey, don't, this is old-fashioned McCarthyism," and so forth. [Soviet sympathizers] are taking advantage of this now.
Interview, Washington, Sept. 28/
Los Angeles Times, 10-1:(I)4.

4

[On U.S.-Soviet summit meetings]: Let me repeat what I have said before: Summits can be useful for leaders and for nations—occasions for frank talk and a bridge to better relations. It would be good for [Soviet leader Mikhail] Gorbachev to see this country for himself. I am ready to continue and intensify our negotiations, but a summit is not a pre-condition for progress on the agenda at hand. When the General Secretary [Gorbachev] is ready to visit the United States, I and the American people will welcome him.
At U.S. Military Academy,
West Point, N.Y., Oct. 28/
The New York Times 10-29:8.

5

Even as their economy flags at home, the Soviets spend billions to maintain or impose Communist rule abroad—from Eastern Europe to Cuba, Cambodia, South Yemen, Angola, Ethiopia, Nicaragua and Afghanistan. [In Afghanistan,] it's time for them to pull out and go home. [In Angola,] this fall's Communist offensive, the biggest ever in Angola, ended in a rout for the Soviets and their proteges. [Around the world,] the Soviets truly are beginning to feel the sting of free people fighting back. When I meet with [Soviet leader Mikhail] Gorbachev [next week in Washington], I'm going to ask him: "Isn't it time that the Soviet Union put an end to these destructive, wasteful conflicts around the world?"
At Heritage Foundation,
Washington, Nov. 30/
The New York Times, 12-1:7.

(RONALD REAGAN)

1

[On Soviet leader Mikhail Gorbachev]: No other Russian leader has ever agreed to eliminate weapons they already have [such as in the pending U.S.-Soviet arms agreement]. He is also the first Russian leader who has never reiterated before the great national Communist congress that the Soviets are pledged to world expansion—a one-world Communist state. That has been the stated goal of previous leaders. He has said no such thing.

To high-school students,
Jacksonville, Fla., Dec. 1/
Los Angeles Times, 12-2:(I)6.

2

We are not trying to impose our system on others. But we cannot ignore clear historical lessons. From countries which respect the rights and freedoms of their own citizens, one can expect with more confidence respect for the rights and freedoms of other countries.

Interview/Los Angeles Times, 12-5:(I)13.

Elliot L. Richardson
Former Attorney General
of the United States

3

[On the popularity among the public of Marine Lt. Col. Oliver North who testified to a Congressional committee about his involvement in the U.S. Iran-contra scandal]: [It is] not hard to understand . . . the appeal of Ollie North to people who would otherwise be watching [TV] soaps. It is easy to picture Gary Cooper or Jimmy Stewart playing North, or North playing Gary Cooper or Jimmy Stewart. [But North] stands convicted out of his own mouth of conspiring to deceive and to evade accountability to the duly constituted authorities of the Executive Branch and the Congress, as well as the American people. He admits lying as a means to an end whose priority over legislative constraints he presumed to judge for himself. The fact that the NSC staff members could assume such a role is frightening in itself. That it should be condoned and, indeed, extolled by

leading officials of the Republican Party is deeply dismaying.

Letter to U.S. Rep. Guy Vander Jagt/
The Washington Post, 8-27:(A)2.

Eugene V. Rostow
Former Director,
Arms Control and Disarmament Agency
of the United States

4

Thus far, the Reagan Doctrine has been explained in terms of ideology rather than the geo-politics of the national interest. The first few tentative American and allied moves in the direction of a more active defense—in Lebanon, in Libya and in Nicaragua—have been poorly planned and badly executed. But in democracies, the first few steps toward a new policy usually have that character. If we learn from our mistakes, the Reagan Doctrine could become an indispensable supplement to the policy of containment, which has been the cornerstone of Western foreign policy since 1947. The West cannot remain mesmerized forever within the limits of its 1947 posture, waiting for Soviet posture to mellow . . . I can imagine no better antidote for the frustration and irritability which now characterize allied relationships than allied cooperation in mounting successful applications of counterforce at outposts of the Soviet empire and shifting geographical points around its periphery. The Soviet empire is extremely vulnerable to such a peninsular strategy.

At National War College, June 16/
The Washington Post, 6-30:(A)18.

Donald H. Rumsfeld
Former Secretary of Defense
of the United States

5

[On the U.S. Iran-contra scandal Congressional investigations]: We'll know more than we ever wanted, and probably more than ever happened. We've got those press people looking for Pulitzers, Congress looking to re-election, and lawyers with their meters running.

USA Today, 1-21:(A)4.

Andrei D. Sakharov
Dissident Soviet physicist

1

An economically healthy Soviet Union would in some ways represent a more direct challenge to the Western economic system. But far worse would be a poor and struggling Soviet Union, more likely to see itself threatened by the West's economic might, and therefore potentially more explosive in international affairs.

Interview/
U.S. News & World Report, 4-13:27.

John D. Scanlan
United States Ambassador
to Yugoslavia

2

Ideally, an Ambassador should be both a manager and an expert. But if I had to choose between the two qualities, I'd pick the one with substantive knowledge and leave the management to a good [Deputy Chief of Mission]. I wouldn't want a superb manager who doesn't know much about the country. In the countries I've served in—particularly in Eastern Europe— an Ambassador like that wouldn't be of much use.

The Washington Post, 4-27:(A)6.

James R. Schlesinger
Former Secretary of Defense
of the United States

3

Soviet security services have extensively permeated our new chancery building [at the U.S. Embassy] in Moscow with a full array of intelligence devices for which we do not yet understand either the technology or the underlying strategy. As a nation, we failed to allow for the boldness, thoroughness and extent of the penetration. Our task now is to take whatever steps are necessary to render the building secure and operationally effective . . . We should bear in mind one central consideration: A reasonably secure and effective Embassy in Moscow is more productive to our interests than its Soviet counterpart in Washington is to theirs. Mani-

festly, a window on a closed society is more valuable than yet another window on an open society.

Before Senate Budget Committee,
Washington, June 29/
The New York Times, 6-30:1;
Los Angeles Times, 6-30:(I)13.

4

[On revelations of Soviet penetration of security at the U.S. Embassy in Moscow]: In past years, the Soviets were sufficiently behind us that we were able to detect penetrations, and neutralize them. That was the assumption in building this facility [in Moscow]. We now face a rising curve in Soviet technology, with no gap between what the Soviets can do and what we can do; indeed, in some areas they have been ahead of us . . . With respect to both Embassy construction and operations, we have a lot to learn from the Soviets . . . The Soviets have thought long and hard about how to design Embassies for security, and they have thought long and hard about the construction process, under the watchful eye of the Soviet security services. It would not be embarrassing for the United States to learn from the Soviets, who have thought long and hard in this area. The solution to our problems will be neither easy nor cheap. It will require major changes at the Embassy complex; some might say radical changes.

Before Senate Budget Committee,
Washington, June 29/
The Washington Post, 7-1:(A)18.

Robert D. Schultzinger
Professor of diplomatic history,
University of Colorado

5

[On George Shultz's five years as Secretary of State]: It's been a stylistic success. With Shultz, there's a sense that things are in control. When you remember what things were like with [President Reagan's first Secretary of State, Alexander] Haig, that's quite an accomplishment . . . [Shultz is] not an innovator. He doesn't have a grand design the way [former Secretary of State] Henry Kissinger did—or for

(ROBERT D. SCHULTZINGER)

that matter the kind of apocalyptic vision that the Reagan Administration had at the beginning. He's more of a consolidator.

The Christian Science Monitor, 5-4:6.

Brent Scowcroft
Member,
Tower Commission investigation
of National Security Council

1

The National Security Council exists for only one purpose, to advise the President in his awesome task of directing the national-security policy of the country. It does not make decisions. As the manager of this system, the National Security Adviser must insure, at a minimum, that matters which come before the NSC cover the full range of issues on which a review is required, that a full range of options is considered together with their opportunities and their risks, that all relevant intelligence and other information is available to all participants, especially the President, and that Presidential decisions are fully understood and are implemented in the manner in which the President intended . . . The NSC staff, which serves the National Security Adviser and the President, should be small, highly competent and experienced in policy-making. It should be able neither to substitute for nor not to duplicate the work of the agencies. It should not undertake operational functions except in the rarest of circumstances. Even then, that should be done only at the express direction of the President, following a judgment [that] there are no feasible alternative ways to accomplish the task.

News conference, Washington,
Feb. 26/The New York Times, 2-27:6.

Richard V. Secord
Major General,
United States Air Force (Ret.)

2

[On the U.S. Iran-contra scandal]: Given the political circumstances that exist in our country today, I understand the necessity for the President to notify Congress [of covert operations]. With respect to Iran, hindsight is wonderful, but it seems to me that there was a big political error on the part of the President [Reagan] not to at least notify the [Congressional leadership] . . . What I have a problem with is the continual assumption in this country that covert operations are wrong. I mean, this is a dangerous world we live in today, and sometimes the President, who has the responsibility for the security of this nation, largely in my opinion, has to have this tool available . . . In my opinion, the whole world is laughing at us [because of the Iran-contra scandal hearings]. We've heard a lot of talk about the cleansing effect of these kinds of hearings. I don't share that belief at all . . . What I think it does is open up our guts to the rest of the world. They not only don't trust us like they used to, they also laugh at us.

At Iran-contra hearings, Washington,
May 8/Los Angeles Times, 5-9:(I)26.

George P. Shultz
Secretary of State
of the United States

3

The more you make out of hostages, the more value is placed on them by the hostage-takers. If there is such a thing as a silver lining in the Iran-contra affair, it is an understanding of why it is wrong to trade for hostages in this terrorist kind of environment. I think people understand that more deeply. And the amount of political capital to be made out of clobbering the President [Reagan] because he hasn't instantly gotten somebody released perhaps will lessen somewhat. If we say things and do things that suggest that there's nothing in this world we wouldn't do to get these hostages out, that's a bad line to take.

Interview/
U.S. News & World Report, 2-9:29.

4

[On revelations of Soviet spying at the U.S. Embassy in Moscow]: We didn't break into

(GEORGE P. SHULTZ)

their Embassy. They broke into our Embassy. They invaded our sovereign territory, and we're damned upset about it. We're upset at them and we're also upset at ourselves . . . It is quite obvious to everybody that you operate in Moscow in a very hostile environment, as they're constantly trying to compromise your facilities . . . That is no news to anyone . . . [But] however much you may realize that they are constantly trying to compromise us, the reality of it is a shock. Expected though their efforts may be, it certainly distresses me and distresses us all.

News conference, Washington,
April 8/Los Angeles Times, 4-9:(I)32.

1

Foreign affairs is not always a zero-sum game. We do not necessarily advance our own vital interests at another nation's cost.

USA Today, 6-15:(A)10.

2

This problem of managing transitions in countries from one kind of government to a more democratic government is extremely tricky. We have seen it all around the world and we have been involved in it all around the world. Each thing is different. We try to be there and to give counsel, to use our influence to see that these transitions take place in a peaceful and orderly way, and in a way that is as consistent as possible with democratic principles. We've had a few cases where it didn't work. It didn't work in Nicaragua; it didn't work in Iran. We pay a heavy penalty when it doesn't work. So we have a big stake in seeing this movement to democracy succeed.

To reporters, enroute to Singapore,
June 17/Los Angeles Times, 6-18:(I)12.

Paul Simon
United States Senator, D-Illinois;
Candidate for the 1988
Democratic Presidential nomination

3

[Criticizing U.S. Lt. Col. Oliver North's involvement in the Iran-contra scandal]: Colonel North is not a hero. Our heroes are not those who lie and cheat and destroy evidence and subvert the laws that they are sworn to uphold and to implement.

Before Democratic Party leaders,
Cleveland, July 17/
The New York Times, 7-18:8.

Ronald I. Spiers
Under Secretary for Management,
Department of State
of the United States

4

. . . I'm told that [former Secretary of State] Henry Kissinger said he could run foreign policy in the United States with 25 people. Well, he could maybe take care of two or three major issues . . . but he couldn't do what we're required to do in terms of commercial work, the consular system, the world-wide communications network, security, building Embassies, transporting people, paying them and all of this, which is beyond the ken of some people. I hope I'm not in this job indefinitely.

Interview/
The Washington Post, 4-13:(A)13.

5

[Criticizing budget restrictions affecting the U.S. State Department]: It's a tragedy. We will be losing some of our most skilled and experienced people, our institutional memory, which will reduce our level of effectiveness. I've been in the State Department for 32 years, and I've never seen things this bad.

The New York Times, 12-12:10.

Monteagle Sterns
Former United States Ambassador
to Greece

6

Embassies are too big today for Ambassadors to be able to ignore their management responsibilities and busy themselves with being scholars of the local culture. Still, the one thing an Ambassador can supply to the U.S. government that no one else can is a sense of the for-

(MONTEAGLE STERNS)

eign environment in which U.S. policy initiatives must function. That requires a very high degree of sensitivity to the country and a profound knowledge of the country in all its aspects.

The Washington Post, 4-27:(A)6.

Robert S. Strauss
Former chairman,
Democratic National Committee

1

[On whether being a lame duck will adversely affect President Reagan's ability to influence U.S. foreign policy]: In foreign policy, he can be influential till the last hour that he's in office, till he turns the key, walks out and turns off the lights.

U.S. News & World Report, 11-30:18.

Lewis Tambs
Former United States Ambassador
to Colombia and to Costa Rica

2

[On the controversy about responsibility in carrying out foreign-policy initiatives, as a result of the U.S. Iran-contra scandal]: . . . you can't really expect people in the field to be Constitutional lawyers, because I think you can see what the implications would be. That if any officer in the field, be he in the Foreign Service or . . . the CIA—whatever—if he, in effect, is obliged to check with his own personal lawyer before he carries out an order given to him by a legitimate superior, that the entire government is going to come to immobilization and paralysis . . . The people in the field who are trying to do a job are going . . . to assume that orders from Washington are legal and legitimate. And I certainly do not want to see the United States government brought to paralysis while people are getting private legal counsel before they carry out orders from their legitimate superiors.

At Iran-contra hearings, Washington,
May 28/The Washington Post, 5-29:(A)17.

Margaret Thatcher
Prime Minister
of the United Kingdom

3

If America does not take the leadership role . . . she injures the interests of the free world. America is the flagship of freedom . . . She must sail into the sunrise and not look back at things that may or may not have happened.

Broadcast interview, Washington/
Los Angeles Times, 7-18:(I)18.

Eugene C. Thomas
President,
American Bar Association

4

[On the U.S. Iran-contra hearings]: I would have thought that the proper thing to do was to limit the public Congressional hearings to matters that would not compromise our national security abroad and would not have risked impeding the proper protection of the innocent and the prosecution of the guilty at home. The public has been entertained, but now the public doesn't realize that that show may have cost them the real system that belongs to all of us, and that's justice. And it isn't enough to protect people. We've got to be a country that upholds our laws. And it was being addressed like a Lucille Ball show, like a sideshow and a carnival.

Interview/USA Today, 8-11:(A)11.

John Tower
Former United States Senator,
R-Texas; Chairman,
Tower Commission investigation
of National Security Council

5

The President is the ultimate decision-maker in national security. No one can or should pretend otherwise. We could not long endure exercise of Executive power by committee. A strong Executive with the flexibility to conduct foreign and diplomatic affairs is an essential feature of our form of government. Those who serve as Presidential advisers on national-security issues have a special responsibility. This is true for this

(JOHN TOWER)

[Reagan] or any other Administration. The advisers must assure that the President gets the best counsel possible. A President may not follow their advice, but the advisers have a clear responsibility to continue to bring to his attention matters that are pertinent even after the decision is made.

News conference,
Washington, Feb. 26/
The New York Times, 2-27:6.

Paul S. Trible, Jr.
United States Senator,
R-Virginia

1

[On the U.S. Iran-contra scandal]: I believe the President [Reagan] when he says he didn't know about the transfer of the diversion monies [to the Nicaraguan contra rebels] . . . and I will continue to believe him until proven otherwise . . . But nevertheless, it's hard to justify the sweep of these activities from Iran to Central America. The contras were not well served. Our anti-terrorism strategy is a shambles, and the ability of Ronald Reagan to be a strong and decisive and successful President has been diminished by all of this.

The Washington Post,
6-9:(A)17.

2

[On those involved in the U.S. Iran-contra scandal who have testified before the investigation committee]: One of the most troubling aspects, I think, of the testimony thus far has been the kind of unapologetic embrace of untruth. We've seen the withholding of information, evasion, false and misleading statements, made to virtually everyone: to the President, to key members of the Administration, to Congress, to the American people. Now, in a free society, that doesn't work.

At Iran-contra hearings,
Washington, July 20/
Los Angeles Times, 7-21:(I)14.

Stansfield Turner
Former Director
of Central Intelligence
of the United States

3

The CIA is three-headed: the technical side, the analysts and the spooks. Nobody [at the head of the CIA] is going to be perfectly tuned to all three.

Newsweek, 10-12:26.

Cyrus R. Vance
Former Secretary of State
of the United States

4

[On the scandal involving the covert sale by the U.S. of arms to Iran]: The Iranian arms sale was naive, wrong and severely damaging to our national interests and credibility. This great nation—if it is to remain worthy of global leadership—cannot again manage its foreign relations as an amateur.

Before Senate Foreign Relations Committee,
Washington, Jan. 14/USA Today, 1-15:(A)4.

Richard von Weizsacker
President of West Germany

5

At present, the Soviet Union is making great efforts to gain ground. Its program is designed to bring about fundamental changes in domestic structures and mentalities. To this end, it seeks to widen cooperation with other countries. Of course, the U.S.S.R. wants to serve its own purposes and not to do us [in the West] a favor. At the same time, Moscow may very well have a genuine interest in finding new ways of communication with us. Is this a disadvantage for us? The U.S.S.R. is neither a mere public-relations system founded exclusively on ideology nor a blindly obsessed world revolutionary. At the top of the East-West agenda is not the final apocalyptic struggle between good and evil, but a growing number of problems which neither East nor West can solve on its own.

At Harvard University commencement/
The Christian Science Monitor, 6-17:13.

Thomas Walker
Professor of political science,
Ohio University

1

[The U.S. has] got to learn to live with the natural process of change [in the world]. Even if change doesn't immediately appear to be in our interest, we can find ways of dealing with it. We've learned in Iran and Nicaragua that when we try to thwart change we're only inviting trouble.

The Christian Science Monitor, 3-24:19.

Vernon A. Walters
United States Ambassador/
Permanent Representative
to the United Nations

2

The United Nations is essential for the world, not so much for what it has done but for what it must do to make the world a place of peace and justice . . . It is a meeting place for all nations, great and small. Many nations, very small ones, who have only a few ambassadors, can deal with other nations. It is a place where nations who have no relations can establish them. Last year, I was charged with negotiating the establishment of diplomatic relations between the U.S. and Outer Mongolia. The UN has made aggression a shameful thing. People fear condemnation there even though it might not yet have teeth, but it still has a long way to go and it is our duty to help it.

At Boston College commencement/
The Christian Science Monitor, 6-15:23.

3

[Saying the U.S. should restore its full UN contributions in light of reforms undertaken by the United Nations]: If the United States does not demonstrate support for those reforms by moving to restore those reductions, the full implementation of the [UN] budgetary and administrative reforms may be compromised . . . When you're not paying your dues, it's hard to pound on the table and say you've got to do this, you've got to do that. If we met our as-

sessed contributions, we could speak with an even louder voice.

Interview, Washington/
The Christian Science Monitor, 6-17:3.

William H. Webster
Director of Central Intelligence
of the United States

4

[On Americans who sell secrets to the Soviets in return for money]: We are confronted with a new breed—a breed of volunteer spies who are motivated primarily by their own greed . . . [The Soviets] have adapted their [U.S. spy] recruitment techniques to appeal to the worst in human nature. They call it the "typical American attitude toward money"—an attitude that says that it's okay to sell anything [to the Soviets] if the price is right.

At his swearing-in as CIA Director,
Washington, May 26/USA Today, 5-27:(A)2.

5

You can build your [intelligence] capability in the sky—and it's awesome what we're doing and what we need to do in the future—but it will not really faithfully tell you *why* people are doing things, what their intentions are and what their capabilities are. Sometimes you get their intentions out of technical coverage, sometimes you can measure their capabilities based on imagery and how much you think they've produced, and so on. But trying to understand the "why" of it still is very much a human intelligence-gathering function.

Interview, Washington, Oct. 5/
Los Angeles Times, 10-6:(I)10.

6

We [the CIA] have no right to have a policy of our own, and we're not going to have one. What we do has to support not a secret agenda but the public foreign policy of this country, and it has to be done in a way that reflects the President's desire to do it.

To reporters, Washington, Oct. 7/
The New York Times, 10-8:6.

WHAT THEY SAID IN 1987

(WILLIAM H. WEBSTER)

1

I believe very strongly in maintaining a covert-action capability within this Agency. But I also believe that it does not drive the wagon. You have an established foreign policy in which secret activities are necessary because of relations with other countries that do not want that relationship made public. [Covert action] is not necessarily a last resort, but it tends to become a last resort. I think we always have to ask ourselves whether there are alternatives. Would the alternative always be preferable? Perhaps I can answer that indirectly by saying that covert actions represent less than 3 per cent of our resources.

Interview/Newsweek, 10-12:29.

Caspar W. Weinberger
Secretary of Defense
of the United States

2

[On the U.S. Iran-contra scandal]: I think we should all be concerned that over-reaction to the Iran controversy could lead to another dangerous period of American withdrawal, isolationism and confusion about its proper role in the world . . . We cannot afford to become a one-issue country. International events will not wait for the outcome of internal studies and Congressional investigations, no matter how important or necesary they are . . . Were the Congress to react to the Iran affair with additional restrictions on Presidential discretion, the consequences would be extraordinarily dangerous to the future of American foreign policy.

Before National Press Club, Washington,
Jan. 15/Los Angeles Times, 1-16:(I)26.

3

[On Soviet leader Mikhail Gorbachev's warm welcome during his recent summit visit to Washington]: I don't think just because he wears Gucci shoes and smiles occasionally and acknowledges that he's got a wife before his funeral means that the Soviet Union has changed its basic doctrines. It seems all new just because his predecessors were all very dour-

looking chaps that wore overcoats that brushed the ground and growled at everybody and didn't give a damn about world opinion. They conveyed the general impression that they were a bunch of tough beasts . . . I think Gorbachev's attempt to court world opinion is succeeding now because it's a novelty . . . I think it's awfully early to conclude that this is a warm, caring, trusting man who's not going to do anything wrong. He's got claws, and every once in a while those claws come out.

Interview, Washington/
The New York Times, 12-12:1,7.

John C. Whitehead
Deputy Secretary of State
of the United States

4

We [the U.S.] support the United Nations. We are in favor of it. We were the leading country in founding it. But we'd like to see it work to our interest, which it hasn't always done. We have been particularly concerned about its administration and budgeting process, and we believe strongly that these should be reformed because the staffs are too large and the budgets run-away. The [U.S. Reagan] Administration has tried for 6 1/2 years to follow a track of support on the one hand and, on the other, pressing for reforms and changes to improve [the UN's] administration and reduce its budget.

Interview/
The Washington Post, 11-14:(A)8.

Charles Z. Wick
Director,
United States Information Agency

5

. . . fed by a steadily advancing system of instantaneous global communication, world public opinion is rapidly emerging as a force capable of decisive influence over the policies and conduct of governments—no matter how popular or how dictatorial . . . Today, in Beirut, Seoul or Chernobyl, in Johannesburg, Geneva

(CHARLES Z. WICK)

or Managua, millions of people—separated by geography, but united through the modern miracle of telecommunications—are swept into the rite of participation. As in a Greek drama—and often guided by the loudest chorus—a moral sense envelops the participants, crying out for action and eventual resolution. And, increasingly, those in responsible positions are compelled to respond. It is this modern drama that we must understand. We must understand the choruses, the actors and those who move them.

Before U.S. Advisory Commission
on Public Diplomacy, Sept. 16/
The Washington Post, 9-23:(A)20.

Paul Wilkinson
Authority on terrorism

1

[When terrorists and their sponsors see that] the going is good—when they know they are going to get massive publicity, when they can see that they've made gains in terms of shipments of arms, [and] when they feel that they can gain more of these tactical objectives—then it seems to me quite unrealistic to assume that by humanitarian plea, or by trying to appeal to reason, you will make inroads into the ideas of the group and get them to curb their propensity for taking Westerners [hostage].

Interview, Aberdeen, Scotland/
The Christian Science Monitor, 2-2:23.

Jim Wright
United States Representative,
D-Texas

2

[On the Reagan Administration's covert Iran-contra scandal]: Human nature being what it is, the Congress would be far more inclined to forgive human error on the part of the Administration—an error of judgment—if we had been brought in on the judgment initially, if we had been given an opportunity to say, "Hey, for crying out loud, don't do it!" If they want us with them on the crash landing, they're going to have to take us with them on the take-off. This is a government of law, not a government of men. And quite apart from the enormously significant Constitutional relationship which has been breached [by not consulting Congress], exists the human relationships which are an inseparable part of the equation.

To reporters, Washington, Jan. 9/
The New York Times, 1-10:6.

3

[On President Reagan's criticism of Wright for meeting with Nicaraguan President Daniel Ortega without first obtaining State Department clearance]: I don't have to get permission and I think it would be demeaning in a sense to have to get permission . . . I regard the relationship between the Executive and the Legislative Branch as a co-equal relationship. One does not extend one's wrist for slapping.

To reporters, Washington, Nov. 16/
Los Angeles Times, 11-17:(I)1.

Government

Allan Adler
Legislative counsel,
Washington office,
American Civil Liberties Union

1

[The Reagan Administration] wants to curtail the Freedom of Information Act. They're limiting press access to public officials. Government employees are threatened with prosecution under various provisions of the espionage laws if they leak information. The Administration has an obsession with technology transfers to the Soviet bloc. They try to limit the dissemination of unclassified information by scientists, and censor what can be presented at scientific meetings. They use a national-security rationale to cover just about everything.

Los Angeles Times, 8-30:(III)4.

Les Aspin
United States Representative,
D-Wisconsin

2

The House doesn't want to go on one tack for too long. If it hits a couple of votes going left, the boys are then looking to tack back and go to the right. The rhythm of the place is important. You want to structure a debate so you catch the wave. It's like surfing.

The New York Times, 5-13:12.

Bruce Babbitt
Former Governor of Arizona (D);
Candidate for the 1988
Democratic Presidential nomination

3

My basic case against the Federal government is that it is into everything, and in the process is destroying the vitality and independence of state and local governments, while neglecting the things it ought to be doing.

Los Angeles Times, 3-11:(I)18.

4

[I understand that] a lot of people are turned off by politics—that they don't believe the politicians are telling them the truth. I used to believe that. I didn't have any confidence at all in politicians. But we must ask for the best. The answer to inadequate leadership is not lower expectations, but higher expectations.

Campaign TV spot/
The Washington Post, 5-16:(A)3.

Howard H. Baker, Jr.
Chief of Staff to President
of the United States Ronald Reagan

5

[Comparing his job as Chief of Staff to when he was Senate majority leader]: Everybody doesn't love me. That's a popular myth. I was never a quiet, compromising person. As majority leader, I was knocking heads together, asking people to do unpopular things. There was blood and entrails all over the floor . . . Now [as Chief of Staff to the President] I just paddle down the corridor to the Oval Office, and somebody else makes the decisions.

Interview/
U.S. News & World Report, 4-13:21,22.

6

One of the most remarkable things about the [U.S.] Constitution is its relevance to the 20th century. There is simply no way that our bright young Founding Fathers could have anticipated that document could serve so well and fit neatly into the 20th and 21st centuries, but it does . . . The framers created a system that has the ability to resonate to the electoral point of view and preference, but it has a stability in a three-part system that is unique. It is difficult to believe that they could have known what a marvelous instrument they devised. It has done extremely well. It is resilient and adaptable, and will continue to be resilient and adaptable and relevant for a long time.

Interview/USA Today, 9-16:(A)15.

GOVERNMENT

James A. Baker III
Secretary of the Treasury
of the United States

1

Government is just too big. The President is beset with too many, often conflicting, opinions, and he spends an inordinate time resolving differences among his advisers and stroking advisers who are there because their existence has been legislated.

The Christian Science Monitor, 2-5:21.

Ross K. Baker
Professor of political science,
Rutgers University

2

In a world in which toy parliaments and sham legislatures are the rule, ours is a representative system that really *does* represent. It is remarkably open, astonishingly accessible, and a more accurate reflection than most would imagine of the American people themselves.

The Christian Science Monitor, 2-6:18.

3

The era of the amateur in public life is over. We preserve the image of the New England town meeting as the ideal, when in fact it's a quaint relic.

The Christian Science Monitor, 5-15:19.

Marion Barry
Mayor of Washington

4

I believe government should be the protector of last resort for the young, the elderly, the poor, the powerless and the dispossessed. But ultimately it is the people themselves who must seize the opportunities that government provides . . . Let us acknowledge that government can give every businessman a chance for success: through urban revitalization programs, aggressive minority set-asides and economic development. But it is up to the individual to make a difference.

Inaugural address, Washington,
Jan. 2/The Washington Post, 1-3:(A)16.

5

Government can't do everything by itself. It has to have the matching cooperation of the citizens . . . And what I'm trying to do is preach, teach, explain, cajole, ask, urge, push, pull and everything I can to get this cooperative relationship where it's a two-way street.

News conference, Washington,
April 15/The Washington Post, 4-17:(A)9.

William J. Bennett
Secretary of Education
of the United States

6

There's a hell of a lot more to leadership than standing up and saying let's spend other people's money.

USA Today, 6-10:(A)4.

7

[On whether smoking marijuana in one's youth should bar people from high public office in adulthood]: Youthful indiscretions are allowed. Youthful indiscretions should not be a bar to public office and public trust . . . It would be crazy to say that anybody who ever smoked marijuana is therefore disqualified. [As mentioned in the classic Greek drama *Oedipus at Colonus*]: "Take a man in the totality of his acts." Youthful indiscretions are allowed. Doesn't the Bible say we all sin? St. Paul, seven times a day? We're sinners.

Interview, Nov. 9/
Los Angeles Times, 11-10:(I)15.

Michael R. Beschloss
Adjunct historian of
American politics and diplomacy,
National Museum of
American History, Washington

8

What you often find in the higher levels of government today are bureaucratic game players. There is a discernible group of people whose ambition is to achieve a high position in the Executive Branch and to shape their careers in that way. Nowadays, if someone wants to be

159

(MICHAEL R. BESCHLOSS)

in government it is necessary they be rather good combatants. The result is that a lot of people who are thoughtful and have expertise who would be useful in government tend to be shunted aside because they don't have those combative political skills.

Interview, Washington/
The New York Times, 1-28:12.

Daniel J. Boorstin
Librarian of Congress
of the United States

1

In the university, it is possible for a person to take a position and write vigorous polemical articles on either side of an issue and affirm that position against all comers. He doesn't have to compromise with his colleagues; he is sharpening his tongue and his metaphors. But in Washington, there is what I call the therapy of action. In the Congress, you have to be civil to each other. You may vote against me on this bill, but I may need you next week on another vote.

Interview, Washington/
The New York Times, 1-31:8.

Daniel J. Boorstin
Former Librarian of Congress
of the United States

2

We are a society that glories in giving people access [to government, its buildings and archives], and access creates risk. When you let the general public participate in government, it is risky; when people from off the street walk into a building, it is risky; when you let everyone learn about everything—the dogmas and the doctrines of governments that stand for evil and slavery—it is risky. But that is what democracy is all about. The only place that is risk-free is the tomb.

The New York Times, 10-13:12.

David L. Boren
United States Senator,
D-Oklahoma

3

[On White House Chief of Staff Donald Regan]: The most fundamental problem is that Regan seems to want to filter all of the views [on issues] himself. He seems to view his job as resolving all conflicts before they are submitted to the President. But this President [Reagan] really needs conflict presented; he needs to hear all points of view.

The New York Times, 2-19:14.

Dale Bumpers
United States Senator, D-Arkansas;
Candidate for the 1988
Democratic Presidential nomination

4

In Washington, every time some politicians wake up with a headache, they want to amend the Constitution. I belong to the "wait just a minute" club.

Campaigning for nomination,
Iowa/USA Today, 3-16:(A)4.

Quentin N. Burdick
United States Senator,
D-North Dakota

5

[Criticizing the televising of Senate sessions]: Longer speeches [and] grandstanding were reasons why I voted against Senate TV [last year]. It seems my fears were well-founded.

The Christian Science Monitor, 6-3:4.

Warren E. Burger
Chairman, commission on the
bicentennial of the U.S. Constitution;
Former Chief Justice
of the United States

6

[Disagreeing with those who advocate a new Constitutional convention to consider new amendments]: It would be a grand waste of time. If you have a tire go flat on your car, you

(WARREN E. BURGER)

don't throw the car away. If your carburetor isn't working, if it's too lean, you don't throw the car away. You fix it . . . For 200 years this car [the Constitution] has not been just "pretty good." It is not perfect, as Franklin said, but the best thing of its kind that was ever put together. Here these extraordinary guys took and did the impossible, and it has worked.

Interview, Washington/
The New York Times, 4-16:10.

1

[On those who criticize the U.S. Constitution]: Every document, except perhaps the Ten Commandments, has its flaws, and maybe if you worked at it you could find flaws in that, too.

U.S. News & World Report, 5-25:15.

George Bush
Vice President of the United States

2

Was the [U.S.] Constitution a document of its time? Yes. Was it a document of compromise? Yes, again. Did it have its imperfections? Of course it did. In fact, the Framers recognized the Constitution's imperfections, and they created a system of government that's managed to channel the wisdom and decency of our citizens toward repairing imperfections . . . Our Constitution provides both bedrock and vantage point. Adherence to plain language and precedent lend stability. Amendments and judicial interpretation permit responsible progress. Our American heritage is grounded in a living Constitution.

At celebration of Constitution's 200th
anniversary, Philadelphia, May 25/
The New York Times, 5-26:11.

3

When I became Vice President I said I would sublimate my own passions, to a certain degree, and support this President [Reagan], and I've taken some flak for it. But that doesn't bother me. As I [have said], "In the Bush

family we don't consider loyalty a character flaw; we consider it a strength."

At Republican fund-raising dinner,
Los Angeles, June 3/
Los Angeles Times, 6-5:(I)33.

Robert C. Byrd
United States Senator,
D-West Virginia

4

[Criticizing the practice of many Senators to leave early on Fridays while there are still votes to be taken, and saying he will take steps to ensure more attendance]: This Senator is not going to stand supinely by in silence and quaking with fear and let others say, "Well, I'm going home; let's not have any votes" . . . I don't expect to get kudos from everybody, maybe anybody. I understand I'm not very well liked around here anyhow. But I didn't get elected to be liked here. I got elected because I thought I could do a job. This is a challenge . . . Let it be a lesson to those who nonchalantly walk off at 1 o'clock on Friday afternoon and think, "Well, school's out; we don't have any more votes."

Washington, May 29/
The Washington Post, 5-30:(A)8.

5

We are continually amazed by the failings of those in power who, in defense of democracy, ignore its most basic and fundamental tenets. It is clear that a policy without checks and balances is a policy that too often loses its way.

At ceremony commemorating
the Great Compromise, Philadelphia,
July 16/The Washington Post, 7-17:(A)4.

6

It is my belief that 1987 was a year of Constitutional challenge and struggle regarding the separation of powers . . . The Congress and the [Reagan] Administration were engaged in a vigorous and most serious debate over how the power of this government, derived from the people, should be exercised.

Los Angeles Times, 12-23:(I)4.

WHAT THEY SAID IN 1987

Jimmy Carter
Former President
of the United States

1

I think [President Reagan has] overlooked a valuable resource in his [failure to consult] with his predecessors, not just me but the others. When I was President, I was constantly calling upon [former] Presidents Ford and Nixon to help me with important issues, keeping them thoroughly briefed on a continuing basis. President Reagan has not used that at all. It's a choice he has a right to make.

Interview/
USA Today, 6-9:(A)11.

2

I think there are certain standards of morality and ethics that never do change, whether you're growing peanuts or in the White House. And they don't change even in a fast-changing technological world. The American people kind of want a royal family in the White House. They like the pomp and ceremony a lot more than I liked it . . . I think the arrogance of power comes when a President thinks that because he's been elected, he's above the law and Constitution and can act unilaterally, even sometimes illegally—as though he was a sovereign ruler. And this was the case obviously with Watergate. I think it's the case with the so-called Iran-contra affair.

Interview, Washington/
The Christian Science Monitor,
7-9:21.

Robert P. Casey
Governor of Pennsylvania (D)

3

The genius of the [U.S.] Constitution is that it has room for 50 different state constitutions and 150 million different versions of life, liberty and the pursuit of happiness.

At celebration of Constitution's
200th anniversary,
Philadelphia, May 25/
The New York Times, 5-26:10.

William P. Clements, Jr.
Governor of Texas (R)

4

[Saying businessmen should run for public office]: I'd be the first to acknowledge that, historically, our national selection in either party has not been in the business community. I'm a little prejudiced, but that would be a good idea. Business backgrounds and business abilities lend themselves to government.

Interview/USA Today, 4-20:(A)13.

William S. Cohen
United States Senator,
R-Maine

5

We need people who can conduct action and take action and cut through the bureaucracy. But the fact is that speed of action was never the absolute goal of democracy, because a king is faster than a Congressman on any given day. They [the Founding Fathers] decided that the future of a democracy should be debate, deliberation, discussion and even dissent, so that the leaders might at least have the opportunity to act wisely rather than quickly or passionately.

At Iran-contra hearings,
Washington, July 24/
The Washington Post, 7-25:(A)9.

Edwin L. Crawford
Executive director,
New York State
Association of Counties

6

[On the growing role of counties in dispensing services]: What has happened in New York over the last 30 years is that counties have become the delivery system for almost every human service program. For example, the Medicaid budget 20 years ago was $200-million across the state. It is now $8-billion. And it is administered by the counties with approximately 20 per cent of the cost [being] paid by the counties.

The New York Times, 6-10:10.

Mario M. Cuomo
Governor of New York (D)

1

We often campaign in poetry, but then we're always required to govern in prose. In the end, much of campaign rhetoric proves to be an impediment to appropriate policy-making.

At Johns Hopkins University School
of Advanced International
Studies commencement, May 28/
The Washington Post, 5-29:(A)4.

2

We Democrats believe in a single fundamental idea that describes better than any speech can what a proper government should be—the idea of family, mutuality, the sharing of benefits and burdens for the good of all, feeling one another's pain, sharing one another's blessings.

At Democratic fund-raising dinner,
Indianapolis, July 28/
The New York Times, 7-29:11.

3

We [the U.S.] need strong leadership, leadership which knows the course charted by the Constitution and can guide the nation through the turbulent political currents of this time; leadership which can inspire an attitude that reflects our political pluralism, but is capable of rising beyond ideology, campaign poetry and narrow partisanship; leadership which ties together our disparate elements: Congress, political factions, the public and private sectors, the regions, all in pursuit of our principal national goals; leadership strong enough to live by the rule of law. Common sense and our history teach that such leadership will have to be supplied by our President.

Before Council on Foreign Relations,
Washington, Oct. 13/
The New York Times, 10-15:14.

John C. Danforth
United States Senator,
R-Missouri

4

[On his loss of the Chairmanship of the Commerce Committee due to the Democrats'

becoming the majority party in the Senate]: All things considered, I'd rather be in the majority. But I don't think that I have been reduced to a lump . . . The job of Chairman is a mixed blessing. It gives you control of an agenda so that you can mark up bills and focus on matters that are of specific interest to you. But the job also consists of presiding over long hearings and making sure that a lot of miscellaneous legislation gets enacted that you have no particular interest in.

Interview, Washington/
The New York Times, 2-9:10.

5

Our tendency in the Senate is to focus on today's issue, today's news. Every tendency here is to put off the big questions and deal with what is at hand . . . We know, for example, as politicians, how easy it is to get locked into positions. You take a vote today, and then a month later you arrive on the floor of the Senate and walk up to the desk in the well and you are told how you voted on the issue a month before. Inertia sets in.

Before the Senate, Washington,
June 2/The New York Times, 6-8:12.

Richard G. Darman
Deputy Secretary of the Treasury
of the United States

6

I think if we're speaking of "running the government," there's a somewhat simpleminded conception of how power works in the American political system that presumes that Presidents have great power, and if they're not exercising it, that their aides or their delegates have great power. In my opinion, none of the above have great power. Power is highly fragmented, much more than in just the civics text version of separation of powers. Power is dispersed, and the effective people are people who can build coalitions where the coalitions represent a critical mass that can move the system. But single individuals, whether Presidents or anybody else in the system—staff or whatever—simply do not have anything remotely like

163

(RICHARD G. DARMAN)

the power that is presumed to reside in their offices.

Interview/The Washington Post, 4-7:(A)15.

George Deukmejian
Governor of California (R)

1

Some equate a visionary Administration with the number of massive and expensive programs that are proposed. [But] we embrace the vision of our nation's founders that only limited government is compatible with liberty and democracy. What they promised then, and what we promise now, is not cradle-to-grave dependency but lifelong opportunity.

Inaugural address, Sacramento,
Jan. 5/Los Angeles Times, 1-6:(I)16.

Milovan Djilas
Author;
Former Vice President
of Yugoslavia

2

A Communist regime is not like the West's democratic systems in which, though you lose a political battle and lose also your position, you can still carry on in politics. A Communist system has an institutionalized power structure with a tightly closed milieu at the top, in which anything like that is totally excluded. Once you leave that milieu, you are completely outside.

Interview, Belgrade/
The Christian Science Monitor, 8-31:8.

Robert J. Dole
United States Senator, R-Kansas;
Candidate for the 1988
Republican Presidential nomination

3

You can learn a lot from [President] Reagan as far as personality, the way he handles people, and I could learn some of that delegation of authority [should I become President]. But I don't think I can delegate that much. I do dele-

gate, so long as I have competent people. But sometimes it's like turning your life over to a committee. I'll never just say here's a blank check. I like to know where I'm going before I get on an airplane.

Interview, Washington/
The New York Times, 1-27:24.

4

[On the first anniversary of televised coverage of Senate proceedings]: One year ago today, the American people were finally plugged in to their democracy. When we began the experiment last year, there were fears of abuse: members playing to the cameras, endless prime-time filibusters, and rumors of makeup in the chamber. Let's face it, there has been some grandstanding. But the botton line tells us that the people's government—the House and the Senate—can now be seen in millions of households around the country.

June 2/Los Angeles Times, 6-3:(I)4.

5

I deeply fear that we are moving in the direction, politically, of tying the hands of the President . . . Legitimate concern about breaking the law, misdeeds, excesses—and the Iran-contra mess is certainly an example of all these—is not only warranted, but necessary. Legitimate exercises of Congressional power are not only warranted, but necessary. But let us remember that we need a strong President.

Interview/The Washington Post, 6-13:(A)13.

Kenneth Duberstein
Deputy Chief of Staff to
President of the United States
Ronald Reagan

6

I think one of the major jobs of a good staff person is to paint a full canvas for the President. You need to present the ups and downs, the nuances, the realities, the full spectrum of practical ideas so that the President can make the best-informed decision.

The Washington Post, 5-11:(A)11.

Michael S. Dukakis
Governor of Massachusetts (D);
Candidate for the 1988
Democratic Presidential nomination

1

When people come to me and say, we've got to spend billions on this and billions on that, I say to them, look, unless and until we get somebody in the White House—and I think Michael Dukakis can do this job—who can get our fiscal house in order, we can't spend all of these billions. And I've said and I will continue to say it. And that's the test of Executive leadership.

Broadcast interview/
"This Week with David Brinkley,"
ABC-TV, 12-20.

Glenn English
United States Representative,
D-Oklahoma

2

The Reagan Administration came into office with the intention of controlling information to the greatest extent possible, to prevent information that is not flattering to it from getting to the public . . . One could certainly argue that previous Administrations also tried to control information, but the Reagan Administration has gone to far greater lengths than any other to achieve those ends.

Los Angeles Times, 8-30:(I)4.

Mervin Field
Public-opinion analyst

3

Americans have always expressed ambivalent desires about the role of government. We ask, "Why doesn't the government just get off our backs?" And then we demand, "Why doesn't the government do something about this?" Today, in several ways, the government *is* off the public's back. Taxes are down. Inflation is down. Interest rates are down. But at the same time, our polling data show growing public anxiety about both the national and local economies. The layoffs are hitting close to home. So

are the growing numbers of the homeless. More people are now asking, "Why doesn't government do something about this?"

Time, 3-30:31.

Marlin Fitzwater
Assistant-designate
for Press Relations to
President of the United States
Ronald Reagan

4

There are so many people who come to a problem from different angles. The diplomat sees an issue one way, the military genius sees it from a different perspective, the politician sees it from a third. That's why in this job access to the President is so important. The President's feeling is the only right one.

Interview/The Washington Post, 1-16:(B)4.

5

I've been chasing leaks in this business for 20 years, and I have found it's the most unproductive thing in the world. It never pays off, and the two or three occasions that I was successful, they've always turned out to be somebody I didn't want to know . . . somebody higher than me, usually the principal himself.

USA Today, 3-30:(A)4.

Thomas S. Foley
United States Representative,
D-Washington

6

[Addressing former Presidential National Security Adviser John Poindexter on his actions in the U.S. Iran-contra scandal]: If the view that you have . . . is that the National Security Council is surrounded by a media that often deliberately distorts and deliberately misreports on the news and events, that the Congress is reflecting attitudes that are in bad faith in the attempt to confront the President's policies, that the normal agencies of government are lacking in enthusiasm and sort of affected by a cancer, a bureaucratic unwillingness to take risks, that leaves a very small group of people . . . to whom you would feel comfortable sharing your plans and proposal for Presidential action.

At Iran-contra hearings, Washington,
July 21/Los Angeles Times, 7-22:(I)13.

John Hope Franklin
Professor of legal history,
Duke University

1

[On the celebration of the bicentennial of the U.S. Constitution]: Celebration is the wrong word. We should "observe" the Constitution. This country is so childish that it has to "celebrate" something. You observe something, you take note of the way in which it has been effective, you take note of the way in which it's been ineffective, and you try to make it more effective in the future. That's the way you observe it, not celebrate it.

Interview/USA Today, 2-4:(A)9.

Betty Friedan
Founder,
National Organization for Women

2

Ideally, the President's wife should be a role model, reflecting the evolution of women's full participation in our society. Today we can no longer expect a woman to hide her strength and her assumption of equality. If we are going to recognize this strength and equality, perhaps we should elect a President and his wife as a team, judging the qualifications of both for office. For instance—I hate to give this tip to Republicans—if Bob and Elizabeth Dole ran as a team, it would be marvelous; I bet they would get elected.

Ladies' Home Journal, August:69.

Craig L. Fuller
Chief of Staff to Vice President
of the United States George Bush

3

Any Vice President faces a certain quandary which has to do with his ability to emerge as a

leader when he is elected in office, and exists to function in support of the President.

The New York Times, 4-27:9.

Richard A. Gephardt
United States Representative,
D-Missouri; Candidate for the 1988
Democratic Presidential nomination

4

The days for leadership by rhetoric are over; the days for leadership by example and role model are here. I want to be the kind of President that people look at and say that's the way we ought to act, that's the way we ought to be. No more shredding and lying, no more secret military operations. I want to be a President who lives by the Constitution . . . The tone, the ethic, the morality of this country, what we are really all about, starts at the top.

Los Angeles Times, 10-31:(I)28.

Ira Glasser
Executive director,
American Civil Liberties Union

5

Even as we celebrate the bicentennial of the Constitution, its values are under enormous attack from people who believe that modern problems require individual liberty be curtailed. We must find solutions to today's emergencies without sacrificing fundamental rights, or on the next anniversary the Constitution will be honored as a historic relic, not as a living document.

News conference, Philadelphia,
June 18/The New York Times, 6-19:10.

Barry M. Goldwater
Former United States Senator,
R-Arizona

6

Republicans elect a President, and he doesn't know a thing about picking a staff. Right back to Eisenhower, we've had nothing but problems with White House appointments. But particu-

(BARRY M. GOLDWATER)

larly Reagan. Reagan has . . . picked some of the worst we've ever had.

*Interview, Scottsdale, Ariz./
The Christian Science Monitor, 8-25:1.*

Albert Gore, Jr.
*United States Senator, D-Tennessee;
Candidate for the 1988
Democratic Presidential nomination*

1

[On the U.S. Iran-contra scandal]: I think Americans are shaken by the betrayal of the public trust [by the Reagan Administration]— the shredding of public documents, stealing of public money, the dishonesty of public officials. I believe the next President must make a pledge, and I make it now: "Any public official who steals from the American people or lies to the United States Congress will be fired immediately."

*Panel discussion, Houston/
"Firing Line," PBS-TV, 7-1.*

William H. Gray III
*United States Representative,
D-Pennsylvania*

2

In the old days, you only voted against the Speaker [of the House] if you were willing to lose the vote, your parking space, and everything else. Now the members are more independent, and the young get an opportunity to lead. It's made possible my quick elevation, too.

The Christian Science Monitor, 2-6:18.

Fred I. Greenstein
*Professor of politics,
Princeton University*

3

There's been a terrific shift since the '30s. [Today,] the whole national agenda hinges on

what comes out of the White House—the budget, the State of the Union messages, and so on. It makes for [Presidential] potency but also vulnerability. So the Presidencies that have not been in trouble are the rare ones.

The Christian Science Monitor, 5-8:6.

Alexander M. Haig, Jr.
*Former Secretary of
State of the United States;
Candidate for the 1988
Republican Presidential nomination*

4

The President's pre-eminent task is to lead. To lead, a President must be a driven man, driven by the force of his conviction in the rightness of his cause . . . To lead, a President must realize that his popularity is his greatest strength, yet also his greatest temptation. He cannot mistake his standing in the polls for the real quality of his policy.

*At news conference announcing
his candidacy, New York, March 24/
Los Angeles Times, 3-25:(I)15.*

Lee H. Hamilton
*United States Representative,
D-Indiana*

5

We cannot advance United States interest if public officials who testify before the Congress resort to legalisms and word games, claim ignorance about things they either know about or should know about, and at critical points tell the Congress things that are not true . . . The Congress cannot play its Constitutional role if it cannot trust the testimony of representatives of the President as truthful and fully informed. The President cannot sustain his policy if he tries to carry that policy out secretly and his representatives mislead the Congress and the American people.

*At Iran-contra hearings,
Washington, June 3/
The New York Times, 6-4:6.*

WHAT THEY SAID IN 1987

Gary Hart
Former United States Senator,
D-Colorado; Candidate for the 1988
Democratic Presidential nomination

1

I have been very frustrated around here [Washington] . . . particularly under the [President] Reagan years. I don't think that people with my point of view have been getting much done . . . My career in the last five or six years has been to oppose what I think are bad policies, and that's not why I got into government in the first place.

The Washington Post, 1-20:(A)6.

2

This [Presidential] election in 1988 is not a question of whether our country should move left or right. It's an issue of recapturing our basic principles, beliefs and values. I believe our leaders in the future must match reason with rhetoric and policy with passion, and foresight with hindsight.

Announcing his candidacy for
the nomination, Denver, April 13/
Los Angeles Times, 4-14:(I)20.

Orrin G. Hatch
United States Senator, R-Utah

3

[President Reagan's Chief of Staff] Howard Baker does believe that almost everything can be compromised. I believe in compromise. [But] I don't think everything can be compromised, nor do I believe in compromising your principles . . .

To reporters, Nov. 9/
Los Angeles Times, 11-11:(I)22.

Harold C. Heinze
President, ARCO Alaska, Inc.

4

Every dollar spent in the public sector is a dollar taken from the private sector. State government doesn't create wealth. It's one of the users [of available resources].

The Christian Science Monitor, 3-18:4.

Jesse Helms
United States Senator,
R-North Carolina

5

[On his losing the Agriculture Committee Chairmanship to a Democrat]: I can be flippant and say that it's a lot easier to throw grenades than to catch them. You spend a lot of time in a Chairmanship that even other Senators don't realize. It is like running a business.

The Wall Street Journal, 1-27:30.

Stephen Hess
Scholar, Brookings Institution

6

[Today] a President of the United States must be prepared to become a public person . . . The people have the right of inspection, and those places that are put off limits are automatically suspect . . . The loss of privacy is nearly total. When Presidents are ill, their bodily functions are the subject of news briefings; their friends become celebrities by definition; their families [become] monuments on which the public can scrawl graffiti; even their dogs [are] the First Dog.

The Christian Science Monitor, 5-7:8.

Gordon Humphrey
United States Senator,
R-New Hampshire

7

[On an $87.5-billion Senate highway bill]: I don't know why the people of Toledo need better access to an amusement park when they can come to Washington and watch some of the world's biggest clowns for free.

U.S. News & World Report, 3-30:7.

Henry J. Hyde
United States Representative,
R-Illinois

8

When you have a liberal Democratic Congress—God bless them all, the people elected them and that's democracy and all that good

(HENRY J. HYDE)

stuff—and you have a conservative Republican President, you've got a recipe for gridlock. Nothing will happen.

At Iran-contra hearings, Washington,
July 13/The New York Times, 7-14:8.

Marvin Kalb
Moderator, "Meet the Press,"
NBC-TV; Director-designate,
Barone Center on the Press,
Politics and Public Policy,
Harvard University

1

We have now, in our political process, reached a point where the press, politicians and the formulation of policy have become so intertwined that we are dealing with one large process.

March 22/The New York Times, 2-23:9.

Thomas H. Kean
Governor of New Jersey (R)

2

The most important thing now is going on in the states, not in Washington. You now have a "debating society" in Washington, so a great deal of power is devolving on the states because they are the units that can solve problems and are closest to the people.

The Christian Science Monitor, 2-12:18.

Edward M. Kennedy
United States Senator,
D-Massachusetts

3

[Addressing Supreme Court nominee Robert Bork]: Whenever Congress has tried to curb abuses, you always seem to side with the President. The Constitution calls for checks and balances. You seem to feel that when it comes to the relation between Congress and the President, instead of checks and balances, the Presi-

dent has a blank check and the Congress exerts no balance at all.

At Senate Judiciary Committee hearing on
Bork's confirmation, Washington, Sept. 17/
The Christian Science Monitor, 9-18:3.

Joseph Kennedy
United States Representative,
D-Massachusetts

4

I've had a tough time learning how to act like a Congressman. Today I accidentally spent some of my own money.

Newsweek, 2-9:21.

Bill Kovach
Editor,
"Atlanta Journal and Constitution";
Former Washington bureau chief,
"The New York Times"

5

Washington produces very little except words. Congress produces words, the Administration produces words, the journalists produce words . . . An idea may get trapped among all those words every now and then. But generally, it's just a lot of words. I welcomed the opportunity to get out of there.

Interview/
The Washington Post, 4-13:(B)1,6.

Robert Kuttner
Author, Journalist

6

To somebody 35 years old today, what is the government? Well, the government is the Post Office, and it does a lousy job. And it's the motor-vehicle bureau, and it does a lousy job. And it's the IRS, and they have their palm out. There's no affirmative link.

Interview/
The Christian Science Monitor,
11-6:6.

169

WHAT THEY SAID IN 1987

Stephen J. Markman
Assistant Attorney General,
Office of Legal Policy,
Department of Justice
of the United States

1

[There is a] persistent tendency of government officials in Washington—well-meaning officials—to act as if only we [in government] can fully understand and remedy the problems confronting 240 million Americans. It is this attitude that in recent decades has been responsible for the mushrooming growth of a national government that not only has undertaken unmanageable responsibilities, but also has usurped the decision-making authority of private citizens and of the levels of government closest to those citizens—the states and their localities.

Before Senate Labor subcommittee,
Washington, Oct. 29/The Washington Post,
11-7:(A)23.

Charles McC. Mathias, Jr.
Former United States Senator,
R-Maryland

2

The nature of the problems since World War II has stretched the 18th-century base. The Senate used to be more conceptual. Now It's bogged down in trivia, which obstructs the deliberative function.

The Christian Science Monitor, 2-6:18.

Forrest McDonald
Professor of history,
University of Alabama

3

The government of the United States interferes on a level in ordinary people's lives in a way [the Founding Fathers] would have regarded as the most vicious form of tyranny imaginable. George the Third and all of his ministers could not have imagined a government this big, this intrusive and this powerful.

Interview, Washington/
The New York Times, 2-12:14.

4

Those who want to tinker with the [U.S.] Constitution are thinking in terms of making the government of the United States more effective, more efficient, less wasteful, less a totally deadlocked mess, and so on. It could be done: You could fix it so that it would work. [But] if it worked, it would be devastating! It would so restrict the operations of the spontaneous market that it really would interfere in a very deadly fashion . . . There are certain things about the national government which I think ought to be done and done well—like defending this country. The military is a legitimate function of the national government, and the better it works, the better we are. But on the other hand, given everything, it's better that [government] doesn't work.

Interview, Washington/
The Christian Science Monitor, 5-12:1,6.

Robert C. McFarlane
Former Assistant to President
of the United States Ronald Reagan
for National Security Affairs

5

The concept of accountability is firmly rooted in our political history for a very good reason. While in time of war one might imagine a justifiable transgression of law by a President to avoid a catastrophe, even the limited exercise of this license has been a matter in which Presidents have traditionally been very careful to enlist the support of members in Congress who would be there to share the blame if something goes wrong. The other reason for assuring accountability is also compelling. Without accountability, the temptation for a President to go beyond prudent limits to salvage a failing policy—especially if the majority in office is of the opposite party—will be virtually irresistable. And in circumstances of distress, while relying upon private parties who may not be competent or incorruptible, the margin for not just failure but for the establishment of a climate of enduring hostility with the Congress is dangerously high.

At Iran-contra hearings, Washington,
July 14/The New York Times, 7-15:6.

Ann Dore McLaughlin
Secretary of Labor
of the United States

1

[On her new position as Labor Secretary]: People have told me to expect a particular scrutiny because I am a women . . . If that proves to be the case, so be it. But I will do my part to make that attitude a thing of the past. Simply by doing my job responsibly, I shall perhaps make everyone understand that women running the government's business is business as usual.

At her swearing-in ceremony,
Washington, Dec. 17/
The New York Times, 12-18:11.

Edwin Meese III
Attorney General
of the United States

2

A president is always beholden to and bound by the law . . . [But] if the Congress operated un-Constitutionally, passed a law which was un-Constitutional to bind the President, and which would limit him in an un-Constitutional manner from performing his duties under the Constitution, then that's the kind of thing that would not be binding on a President because it was not a valid law . . . It may well be decided by the Supreme Court.

Broadcast interview, May 28/
Los Angeles Times, 5-28:(I)20.

George J. Mitchell
United States Senator,
D-Maine

3

. . . there's a substantial body of law developed over the last half-century, primarily by Americans, that there are circumstances in which government officers have a positive duty not to obey orders. And so the situation all government officers find themselves in is generally the presumption that orders are legal. But they have to also be conscious of the fact that there are circumstances in which they are not re-

quired to obey the law and, indeed, have a positive duty, as I said, not to obey it. And there's no clear line. There's no easy way to make that. It depends, really, upon the situation and the sensitivity of the individual.

At Iran-contra hearings,
Washington, May 28/
The New York Times, 5-29:4.

4

Although He is regularly asked to do so, God does not take sides in American politics. And in America, disagreement with the policies of the government is not evidence of lack of patriotism.

At Iran-contra hearings, Washington,
July 13/Los Angeles Times, 7-14:(I)1.

Jim Moody
United States Representative,
D-Wisconsin

5

[Saying House members' salaries are not commensurate with their responsibilities]: Corporate executives in my community make between $200,000 and $700,000 a year and exercise probably less important decisions than many of us are asked to exercise. School superintendents, and a number of other jobs which are important but have no less importance than we have, make far, far more.

The New York Times, 2-6:28.

Bill Moyers
Commentator,
Public Broadcasting Service

6

Like a soft, steady backlight, the spirit of this [U.S. Constitution] illuminates the letter on the page. No issue we face today, no matter how new or threatening, is unapproachable in its glow.

TV broadcast/
"Moyers: In Search of the Constitution,"
PBS-TV, 6-18.

WHAT THEY SAID IN 1987

Daniel P. Moynihan
United States Senator,
D-New York

1

When I was [U.S. Ambassador] at the United Nations, there were 148 countries represented. Of those which even existed as far back as 1914, only seven had not had their form of government changed by violent revolution. The marvel to me is the extraordinary stability of the arrangements the [U.S.] Constitution put in place.

The Washington Post, 1-7:(A)14.

Ralph Nader
Lawyer; Consumer advocate

2

[Criticizing House members for giving themselves a pay raise of over 15 per cent]: This vote crystallizes in the minds of millions of people, liberal or conservative, the arrogance and insensitivity of official Washington generally. The maneuver by House Speaker Jim Wright to adjourn today [thus allowing the pay raise to take effect without actually voting on it] added an element of parliamentary treachery to the leadership's arrogance on this salary-grab issue.

Feb. 3/Los Angeles Times,
2-4:(I)1.

Sam Nunn
United States Senator,
D-Georgia

3

They [Reagan Administration officials] are taking the position they can do anything they want without Congress. That's intolerable to me. I don't go looking for fights, but when someone forces me into a fight, I don't walk away . . . They're very cooperative so long as you agree with them. Their idea of bipartisanship is doing it all their way.

Interview/
The Washington Post,
10-6:(A)3.

William E. Odom
Lieutenant General,
United States Army; Director,
National Security Agency
of the United States

4

[On the leaking of intelligence information to the press]: I don't want to blame any particular area for leaking. There's leaking from Congress . . . there's more leaking in the [Reagan] Administration because it's bigger. I'm just stuck with the consequences of it. Leaks have damaged the [communications-intelligence] system more in the past three to four years than in a long, long time . . . [As far as the press is concerned,] when I'm with a group of journalists, I can usually look at the group and see two or three people who fall into the category of those who probably could be successfully prosecuted.

To reporters, Sept. 2/
The Washington Post, 9-3:(A)4.

Norman J. Ornstein
Resident scholar,
American Enterprise Institute

5

The experience of both [First Lady] Nancy Reagan and [former First Lady] Rosalynn Carter has sensitized people to the fact that you elect a team, not just President and Vice President.

USA Today, 9-29:(A)10.

Tom Petri
United States Representative,
R-Wisconsin

6

[Criticizing House members for giving themselves a pay raise of over 15 per cent by adjourning and thus allowing the raise to go into effect without a vote]: The House leadership acted like a thief in the night, skulking away with its ill-gotten gains.

USA Today, 2-5:(A)4.

Kevin P. Phillips
Republican Party political analyst

1

In the 1986 election, you saw the desire around the country for candidates who could make government work, for defining some government roles. It was flowing from parts of the country where people began thinking, "Hey, we need something from government after all." It was coming primarily from areas dependent on mining, timber, agriculture, energy, textiles, steel. They stopped thinking of government as something that just took care of muggers and Detroit welfare mothers, the whole conservative rhetorical syndrome.

Time, 3-30:30.

Nelson W. Polsby
Visiting professor,
Kennedy School of Government,
Harvard University

2

Congress used to rely on the President and Executive Branch for information. Today it relies on its staffs . . . Specialization is the genius of Congress. It's the only competent legislature in the world.

The Christian Science Monitor, 2-6:19.

3

[On the Vice Presidency]: The plus side is that the Vice President frequently becomes President. Why it tends to be a liability is that all the authority a sitting Vice President has is at the pleasure of the President he serves. Therefore, he can't influence policy in a way to enhance his future.

The New York Times, 5-13:16.

William Proxmire
United States Senator,
D-Wisconsin

4

The Congress of the United States always—and I mean always—takes a bum rap . . . No one—and I mean nobody—ever defends the Congress. In more than 30 years in this branch

of the Congress, and in literally tens of thousands of conversations back in my state, with people of every political persuasion, I have yet to hear one kind word, one whisper of praise, one word of sympathy for the Congress as a whole.

Before the Senate, Washington/
The Washington Post, 9-16:(A)21.

David H. Pryor
United States Senator,
D-Arkansas

5

In the cruel world of the bureaucracy, most government whistle-blowers can expect extraordinary efforts by their own agency to shut them up, to discredit them, or to eliminate them. In most cases, they can also expect little protection from the Inspector General, or from the agency Congress created to help and protect whistle-blowers, the Office of the Special Counsel.

The Washington Post, 7-21:(A)19.

6

The Senate is a great place. But the Senate is a place, right now, that reminds me of a huge giant lumbermill, with all the high technology and the biggest saws in the world, which is making toothpicks. Here in the Senate, we've kind of turned ourselves into a toothpick factory . . . While this is said to be the most exclusive club in the world, no one ever said it's the most productive.

Interview, Washington/
The New York Times, 12-21:12.

Nancy Reagan
Wife of President of
the United States Ronald Reagan

7

[On her position as First Lady]: Although I don't get involved in policy, it's silly to suggest my opinion should not carry some weight with a man [President Reagan] I've been married to for 35 years . . . In spite of a White House full

(NANCY REAGAN)

of people taking care of various aspects of a President's life, you're the one who knows him best. You don't give up your right to an opinion just because you're married to the President . . . I'm a woman who loves her husband, and I make no apologies for looking out for his personal and political welfare. We have a genuine, sharing marriage. I go to his aid. He comes to mine. I have opinions. He has opinions. We don't always agree. But neither marriage nor politics denies a spouse the right to hold an opinion or the right to express it.

At American Newspaper Publishers Association luncheon, New York, May 4/ The Christian Science Monitor, 5-6:4.

1

[On reports that she exerts a lot of influence on her husband's policies]: This morning, I had planned to clear up U.S.-Soviet differences on intermediate-range nuclear missiles, but I decided to clean out Ronnie's sock drawer instead.

U.S. News & World Report, 5-18:11.

Ronald Reagan
President of the United States

2

The Federal government needs to provide essential services that are truly public in nature and national in scope. It has no business providing services to individuals that private markets or their state or local governments can provide just as well or better.

Budget message to Congress, Washington, Jan. 5/ The Washington Post, 1-6:(A)7.

3

Much has been said about my management style, a style that's worked successfully for me during eight years as Governor of California and for most of my Presidency. The way I work is to identify the problem, find the right individuals to do the job and then let them go do it. I've found this invariably brings out the best in

people. They seem to rise to their full capability, and in the long run you get more done.

Broadcast address to the nation, Washington, March 4/ The New York Times, 3-5:12.

4

[On whether business people should run for public office]: You're asking a fellow who went into politics after serving six terms as president of a labor union. Before that, though, I was in business for myself—the canoe business. I used to rent out my canoe for 35 cents an hour when I was a lifeguard on the Rock River in Dixon, Illinois. Government needs the qualities of common sense and commitment that make men and women successful in business. Those who demonstrate these qualities should run for office, and they should draw on their experience in the private sector to make them more effective as communicators and candidates.

Interview/ Nation's Business, September:74.

5

[Comparing being President with his previous job as Governor of California]: I found a certain excitement and pleasure in both of them, but being Governor was the best training school for this job. Earlier in our time, that was normally the source of Presidents. It is the nearest thing to this job; the only addition that you have here is the national-security part of the job, which is supposed to be the most important, according to the Constitution. But Governors are the chief executives in their states, and we have to remember that. Our government was created to be a Federation of sovereign states.

Interview, Washington/ USA Today, 9-11:(A)11.

6

I would like to remove the amendment to the Constitution that limits the President to two terms, once I'm not in this job. I think it's an invasion of the democratic rights of the people to tell the people that they can't vote for whoever they want to vote for and for as long as

(RONALD REAGAN)

they want to. A Congress has people who have been there for 30 or 40 years telling the American people they can't have a President they might want for more than two terms. I'd like to see that changed.

Interview, Washington/
USA Today, 9-11:(A)11.

1

If our Constitution has endured, through times perilous as well as prosperous, it has not been simply as a plan of government, no matter how ingenious or inspired that might be. This document that we honor today has always been something more to us, filled us with a deeper feeling than one of simple admiration—a feeling, one might say, more of reverence. One scholar described our Constitution as a kind of covenant. It is a covenant we have made not only with ourselves, but with all of mankind. As John Quincy Adams promises, "Whenever the standard of freedom and independence has been or shall be unfurled, there will be America's heart, her benedictions, and her prayers." It is a human covenant, yes, and beyond that, a covenant with the Supreme Being to whom our Founding Fathers did constantly appeal for assistance.

At celebration of U.S. Constitution's
200th anniversary, Philadelphia,
Sept. 17/The New York Times, 9-18:19.

2

[Announcing his nomination of Anthony Kennedy for the Supreme Court]: Judge Kennedy is what as many in recent weeks have referred to as a true conservative, one who believes that our Constitutional system is one of enumerated powers, and that it is we the people who have granted certain rights to the government, not the other way around; and that unless the Constitution grants a power to the Federal government or restricts a state's exercise of that power, it remains with the states or the people. Those three words, "we the people," are an all-important reminder of the only legitimate

source of the government's authority over its citizens.

Washington, Nov. 11/
The Washington Post, 11-12:(A)38.

George E. Reedy
Professor of journalism,
Marquette University;
Former Press Secretary to
the President of the United States
(Lyndon B. Johnson)

3

The filibuster got a very bad name because, for a long period of time, it was the device used by the Southerners to block civil rights. But it's the way the minority prevents itself from being overridden at a time when action might very well lead to a serious split in the country. It means at least 20 or 25 Senators who are willing to speak for 10, 12, 15, 20 hours a day. Most of those men are rather elderly. That's a terrible strain on their health. Now, if they are willing to subject themselves to that kind of an ordeal, it's probably the point of wisdom to lay off passing that bill for a while. This country is so big that to decide everything on the basis of 51 per cent versus 49 per cent is an extreme course. This little 49 per cent might just revolt.

Interview/USA Today, 1-20:(A)9.

4

The real work of the Senate you don't see, because it consists of personal contacts. The real work of the Senate happens when two Senators are walking down a corridor, or when they meet for a cup of coffee in the cafeteria. Or when they go home and talk to some influential constituents. The trouble with this . . . is that the Senate operation is one which the press cannot cover adequately, no matter how hard it tries.

Interview/USA Today, 1-20:(A)9.

5

The press conference is the one thing a President has where he really gets a concept of how people feel. Everything else that comes

175

(GEORGE E. REEDY)

into the White House is tailored to please him
or anger him as much as possible.

Los Angeles Times, 10-13:(I)17.

William Bradford Reynolds
Assistant Attorney General,
Civil Rights Division,
Department of Justice
of the United States

1

The 14th Amendment does offer support for
Justice Marshall's claim that the Constitution is
"a living document," but only in the sense that
the Constitution itself provides a mechanism—
namely, the amendment process—to reflect changing social realities. Indeed, this orderly process
for Constitutional "evolution" is a part of the
original Constitution's genius, for it provides a
mechanism to correct flaws while safeguarding
the essential integrity of our Constitutional
structure.

At Vanderbilt University,
May 23/The Washington Post,
6-11:(A)22.

Elliot L. Richardson
Former Attorney General
of the United States

2

[Criticizing the Justice Department's contention that the statute permitting outside special
prosecutors and counsels in controversial government investigations violates the separation
of powers]: This is pushing notions of separation of powers out of shape. The way to get an
impartial [inquiry] is to draw on the experience
of people deemed to be beyond political influence . . . That ought to prevail over mechanis-
tic notions of separation of powers . . . I would
never have believed in '73 that there would
arise in the subsequent decade-and-a-half so
many situations involving sleazy conduct by
highly placed people [in government].

The Christian Science Monitor,
6-19:5.

A.M. Rosenthal
Former executive editor,
"The New York Times"

3

The whole First Lady business is a piece of
creaky condescension. It just means that because you married the right man [the Presi-
dent], it makes no difference whether you are
clever or stupid—you are our Number 1 "girl."
Simply raising the possibility of First Gentlemen shows what an insult to women the title
and concept of First Lady is.

Ladies' Home Journal, August:130.

William V. Roth, Jr.
United States Senator,
R-Delaware

4

Too often the problem in Washington is that
we try to throw too much money at a problem
without considering how it is being spent. How
do we get agencies to cooperate rather than to
fight for their own turf?

The Washington Post, 4-28:(A)21.

Warren B. Rudman
United States Senator,
R-New Hampshire

5

History is full of the frailties of men and
women. Every major [government and political]
scandal, be it Pearl Harbor, be it Teapot Dome,
be it Watergate, be it this [current U.S. Iran-
contra scandal]—people generally fail long before the systems they are supposed to operate
fail.

At Iran-contra hearings, Washington,
July 31/The New York Times, 8-1:7.

6

The real heroes [in government] are people
who speak up to their President, make their
views known, and are willing to take great personal risks in confronting their President.

At Iran-contra hearings,
Washington/Time, 8-3:12.

William Safire
Political columnist

1

[President Abraham] Lincoln had a terrific provocation, a civil war, as an excuse for straining the Constitution's limits. Today, there's much less excuse. We're not in a crisis, and there's too much weight toward national security and away from individual liberty. I think that [government] secrecy is abused and that a great many politically embarrassing secrets that should not be kept are kept under the guise of keeping genuine national-security secrets. So some of the precedents that were set in Lincoln's day are being used wrongly today.

Interview/
U.S. News & World Report, 8-24:57.

Richard Scammon
Public-opinion analyst

2

The idea of the lazy American voter is mythology. The percentage of those on the [registration] list who vote is around 75 per cent . . . The point is that law-makers are always attentive to the people—because they know where power rests.

The Christian Science Monitor, 2-13:22.

William S. Sessions
Director,
Federal Bureau of Investigation

3

This is the age of automation. The entire business community, the entire communications industry—everybody relies strongly upon electronic capability . . . The government seems generally to be one of the last . . . You can go over to [Federal] departments throughout Washington, and you will not be able to find the latest word-processing equipment; you will not find the latest dictation equipment; you will not find the latest electronic equipment.

Interview/
The Washington Post, 11-27:(A)16.

Lottie Shackelford
Mayor of Little Rock, Ark.

4

Once the thrill and excitement of serving people vanishes, get out [of government]. Otherwise, you stop working for the public good and start taking care of yourself and your friends. That's how most politicians get involved in corruption. I've seen it happen. They start to believe they are some kind of kings and can do no wrong. They start thinking, "Well, wait a minute, I've got to make this work for me. I've made all these sacrifices for people, now it's time for me to get something out of this." I get my high off serving people. Once that stops, I'm gone.

Esquire, December:126.

John S. R. Shad
Chairman,
Securities and
Exchange Commission
of the United States

5

[On his greatest frustration over the past six years]: It's probably the time it takes to get things done in government. On Wall Street, if we were working on a financing or merger and somebody had a problem, I'd grab the phone and I could resolve a lot of things almost instantly. But here [in government] it's different. I hear about a problem on the [Capitol] Hill, and I pick up the phone and I call a Congressman. He says he doesn't want to talk about it, and that he wants to have a hearing. Well, this becomes a big, you know, brouhaha. Instead of, "Let's get to the nuts and bolts of it and see if we can resolve it now," too often it's, "Let's have a hearing." On the other hand, the time here is justified because the rules and regulations here affect all the securities markets, and so they deserve a very deliberative process. I've mellowed a bit on this one.

Interview, Washington/
The New York Times,
6-24:27.

177

WHAT THEY SAID IN 1987

John Shannon
Director,
United States Advisory Commission
on Intergovernmental Relations

1

For 50 years—through the Great Depression, the New Deal, World War II, the Korean war, the Great Society, and Vietnam—the pendulum was swinging toward Washington because of its strengthened fiscal hand and national crises. Now the pendulum is swinging the other way— toward the state and local governments and a "do-it-yourself" Federalism.

The Christian Science Monitor, 2-12:19.

George P. Shultz
Secretary of State
of the United States

2

Nothing ever gets settled in this town [Washington]. It's a seething debating society in which the debate never stops, in which people never give up, including me.

The Washington Post, 11-5:(A)23.

3

I want to send a message out around our country that public service is a very rewarding and honorable thing, and nobody has to think they need to lie and cheat in order to be a public servant or work in foreign policy. Quite to the contrary, if you are really going to be effective over any period of time, you have to be straightforward.

At Iran-contra hearings,
Washington/Time, 8-3:14.

Terence Smith
White House correspondent,
CBS News

4

It seems to me that [Presidential] news conferences are justified as a kind of Presidential theatre because it's the only time this President [Reagan] is not scripted. This is the one moment when the public gets to see Ronald Reagan's mind at work as he copes with par-

ticular questions, even if all they are really seeing is his ability to remember the way he practiced it at the drill the day before.

The Washington Post, 3-19:(A)4.

Larry Speakes
Principal Deputy Press
Secretary to President of
the United States Ronald Reagan

5

Our ability to try to control leaks has been misrepresented in the press throughout the [Reagan] Administration. It's been represented that we were trying to stem the flow of information in general. We've been trying to stem the flow of top-secret documents, out of national-security agencies and departments into the newspapers, that are harmful to the national interest. The only real way to stop a person who had leaked national-security documents is to fire that person and then punish him to the fullest extent of the law.

Interview, Washington/
The New York Times, 1-26:12.

6

Too much government policy is decided on how it will play on the evening news . . . Let government decide policy on the basis of what's good for the people, not what's good for television.

On leaving his post as
Press Secretary, Washington,
Jan. 30/Los Angeles Times, 1-31:(I)20.

Arlen Specter
United States Senator,
R-Pennsylvania

7

In this city [Washington], regrettably, people are frequently more interested in claiming victory for what is happening than they are in the substantive *result* of what is happening.

Before the Senate, Washington, Oct. 30/
The Washington Post, 11-3:(A)22.

178

A. Knighton Stanley
Minister,
Peoples Congregational
United Church of Christ,
Washington

1

It is painfully and dangerously lonely at Washington's top, where cloak-and-dagger forces lurk in dark corners to assassinate your character and beat up on you night and day. How can I tell my children to aspire to Washington's political top when it is so dangerous and painful and destructive for anyone to be there?

Sermon, June 7/
The Washington Post, 6-17:(A)22.

Curtis Tarr
Dean,
Johnson Graduate School
of Management,
Cornell University

2

I've worked for the Federal government, state, city and county governments, and I've always been appalled at how little intelligent businessmen know about how governments work, how their laws are passed, or how legislators are influenced.

The Christian Science Monitor,
10-20:12.

Elizabeth Taylor
Actress

3

[On her experiences when she was the wife of a U.S. Senator]: Washington, D.C. is a very difficult place for a woman to live. I think there are more unhappy wives in that city than any place else in the world . . . You have to live through your men, and they don't pay too much attention. You help them get elected, and then the Senate becomes the wife, the mistress. That was one lady I couldn't begin to fight. She was too tough.

Interview/Cosmopolitan,
September:242.

Richard L. Thornburgh
Former Governor
of Pennsylvania (R)

4

The tide is turning toward more responsibility and a greater role for the states. The reasons are a recognition that our resources are finite and that you can no longer provide the enormous sum of Federal support for a lot of programs. Also, there is a sense of alienation from a government that has become remote and Washington-centered.

The Christian Science Monitor, 2-12:20.

John Tower
Former United States Senator,
R-Texas; Chairman,
Tower Commission investigation
of National Security Council

5

President Reagan has a particular type of management style of delegating authority. And that style, to work, means that the President must be surrounded by experts who will act responsibly. At the same time, the President must from time to time monitor the actions of those to whom he delegates authority. Now, there are other Presidents that have had different styles. Some have gotten heavily involved in the details of operations to the point where they failed to see the big picture. They lose vision and concept. I think that President Reagan is a man of great vision and concept.

News conference, Washington,
Feb. 26/The New York Times, 2-27:6.

Paul S. Trible, Jr.
United States Senator,
R-Virginia

6

Republicans in the Senate are parties in the governing process. Republicans in the House are, frankly, irrelevant. They can hoot and holler and raise a fuss, but they have no influence whatsoever over what goes on.

The New York Times, 10-27:7.

WHAT THEY SAID IN 1987

Gore Vidal
Author

1

[On today's press scrutiny of Presidents and Presidential candidates]: [In the 1960s,] the press then loved him [President John Kennedy], and protected him, and we had more of a tradition of privacy. And look what we've had since [as Presidents]: ideologues, crooks, rhetoricians, actors . . . we haven't had anyone capable of running a dry-cleaning establishment, let alone the Presidency. The media can only deal in personalities. And the public has been led to believe that if they just elect a nice person, everything will turn out all right. But the chances are that a "nice person" will not make a very good President.

Interview, New York/
Los Angeles Times, 10-7:(VI)4.

Paul A. Volcker
Former Chairman,
Federal Reserve Board

2

The Federal government . . . is increasingly unable to attract, retain and motivate the kinds of people it will need to do the essential work of the Republic in the years and decade ahead.

Upon receiving American Enterprise
Institute award, Washington, Dec. 2/
The Washington Post, 12-4:(A)25.

George F. Will
Political columnist;
Commentator, ABC News

3

[President] Ronald Reagan has done what a serious President does: force the country to ask and answer tough questions. To the question, how conservative are you, the American people have given the answer that they talk a very much more conservative game than they are prepared to see played. They have a voracious appetite for government. They just have a negligible willingness to pay for it.

Interview/Esquire, January:91.

Charles Vert Willie
Sociologist,
Harvard University

4

[On the 200th anniversary of the U.S. Constitution]: What we should be celebrating is how we overcame the [Constitution's] early defects, and even continuing defects; . . . how we overcame the defect of thinking that women were not worthy of being counted; . . . and how we overcame the defect of not thinking that blacks represented a whole person. As a teacher, I continuously try to teach my students to reflect upon, to review, their failures. It's only by understanding one's failures, and why one fails, that one really can discover ways of overcoming them.

Interview, Boston/
The Christian Science Monitor, 6-10:6.

Pete Wilson
United States Senator,
R-California

5

[Criticizing the recent pay increase Congress gave itself, and saying he will give his away to charity]: We could all use some more money. I'm not independently wealthy, but I knew what the job paid when I ran for it. I have sympathy with those members who have young families, but this is the wrong time, when we're asking others to take in their belts.

Interview, Sacramento, Calif.,
Feb. 10/Los Angeles Times, 2-11:(I)23.

Timothy E. Wirth
United States Senator,
D-Colorado

6

What immediately strikes you [about the Senate] is the emphasis on collegiality and consensus. There's much less confrontation and obvious partisanship than in the House. What you hear all the time is "Working it out, working it out."

The Washington Post, 1-20:(A)17.

Jim Wright
United States Representative,
D-Texas

1

We [in Congress] offer ourselves to the President not just as a rival center of power, but as a partner—not a junior partner, but a full and equal partner. That's what the Constitution intends. We ask no more. We'll settle for no less . . . The nation does not want an imperial Presidency but does not want or need an enfeebled Presidency.

Los Angeles Times, 1-7:(I)14.

2

If there is one basic change in the thrust in the House, I should think it will be our effort to establish a limited but achievable agenda—to establish time schedules with which the various principal components of our legislative program will be brought to the House. I hope we can do this in an orderly way which will let us consider the important matters in a logical succession, rather than waiting for everything to get all jammed up at the end of the session—when legislative craftsmanship sometimes suffers in the logjam.

Interview, Washington/
The Christian Science Monitor, 2-24:15.

3

[On his being Speaker of the House]: I don't mind being a lightning rod. You can finesse an issue only so long. Ultimately, the role of leadership is to see it and have sufficient steady nerve to come to grips with it before it becomes unmanageable.

Interview/
The New York Times,
4-7:12.

4

The [U.S.] Constitution did not ordain instant utopia. It was a creature of its time. But it was not bound to the mores of its time, and therein is its genius. It set in motion the machinery for achievement in each succeeding age of a continuous social revolution through peaceful means.

To Constitutional
scholars and historians,
Washington/
The New York Times, 5-25:8.

5

[On the investigation into the U.S. Iran-contra scandal]: If we have learned anything from the last seven months, it is that no one man in this country is above the law. If there is a bottom line to our Constitution, it is that we are a nation of laws, not a small circle of men with a cause.

At celebration of
bicentennial of U.S. Constitution,
Philadelphia, July 16/
Los Angeles Times, 7-17:(I)18.

Law • The Judiciary

Howard H. Baker, Jr.
Chief of Staff to
President of the United States
Ronald Reagan

1

[On the Senate's role in the confirmation of a Supreme Court Justice]: The role of the Senate in the advise-and-consent process is not defined in the Constitution. It simply says that the Senate will either give its consent or withhold its consent. As a result, it varies, and I expect it has throughout the history of the country. The long and short of it is that the role of the Senate is whatever the Senate decides the role is. And that depends on the Senate at any given moment and any given nominee.

Interview/USA Today, 9-16:(A)15.

Paul Bator
Professor of law,
University of Chicago

2

[On the Senate process of confirmation of a Supreme Court nominee]: The trouble with ideological questions is that they are always today's ideological questions. Ten years from now who knows what the big issues will be? The questions of creativity and intellectual distinction are much more important than how [a nominee] will vote on a specific case next week.

U.S. News & World Report, 9-14:20.

Gary Bauer
Assistant to President of the
United States Ronald Reagan
for Domestic Policy

3

[On the controversial Senate Judiciary Committee confirmation hearings on the nomination of Robert Bork for the Supreme Court]: There could be a backlash among the public about the tactics used [by anti-Bork members of the Com-

mittee] in this confirmation fight . . . Beyond that, even if we lose the [Senate] vote, we win in the long term in establishing certain principles—ideas about what kind of judiciary we want, as compared to our political opponents, and something about what the confirmation process for the highest court in the land ought to be.

Los Angeles Times, 10-10:(I)23.

Griffin B. Bell
Former Attorney General
of the United States

4

[Supporting Robert Bork's nomination for the Supreme Court]: If we don't get Judge Bork, who will we get? He is a very bright person. We have to be very careful in this country; we do it from time to time; we've become anti-intellectual. It would be easy to get somebody confirmed who's never done anything, who's never taken a controversial position on anything. But that's not the kind of person we want.

At Senate Judiciary Committee hearing
on Bork's confirmation, Washington,
Sept. 28/The New York Times, 9-29:1.

Mary Frances Berry
Member,
United States Commission
on Civil Rights

5

[On liberal opposition to President Reagan's nomination of Robert Bork to the Supreme Court]: The President said Bork shares his judicial philosophy, and he certainly is entitled to make the nomination on that basis. The Senate has an equal right to oppose the nomination on the same basis. Based on what I know about Bork now—and we may get additional information during the confirmation hearings—I'd oppose him for the same reason the President

(MARY FRANCES BERRY)

proposed him. Just as the President believes Bork is not only qualified but is guided by an ideology he finds compatible, any Senator could say, "Here's a guy exceptionally well-qualified, but I, unlike the President, do not agree with his ideology."

Interview/
The Washington Post, 7-3:(A)27.

Joseph R. Biden, Jr.
United States Senator,
D-Delaware; Candidate for the 1988
Democratic Presidential nomination

1

[On the Senate's right to block a Presidential Supreme Court appointment]: There are obvious costs to a political fight over the Supreme Court, [but] a Senator has not only the right but the duty to respond [when] the President attempts to use the court for political purposes.

Before the Senate, Washington,
July 23/Los Angeles Times, 7-24:(I)19.

2

[On the controversy over the nomination of Robert Bork for the U.S. Supreme Court]: Racially restrictive covenants, the sterilization of criminals, the prior restraint of freedom of the press—is it true, as Judge Bork has written extensively, that the Constitution does not forbid them? [Although] we can't be certain these are among the dozens of precedents that Judge Bork might or might not overturn, we can be certain, if Judge Bork has meant what he has written for the past 30 years, that had he been [Supreme Court] Justice Bork during the past 30 years and had his view prevailed, America would be a fundamentally different place than it is today. For all Americans, particularly those in the Senate . . . the issue [of Bork's nomination] is what will America look like if I have even remotely gotten the meaning of what Judge Bork's Constitutional view would dictate.

Before American Bar Association,
San Francisco, Aug. 11/
The Washington Post, 8-12:(A)9.

3

[On the Senate Judiciary Committee's rejection of Robert Bork for the Supreme Court]: I would assume the President [Reagan] would understand the reason for the rejection of Robert Bork. I predict to you, if he sends up a mainstream conservative who has very strong views on basic conservative philosophy, but acknowledges the progress that has been made thus far and does not seek to turn it around, I think that person would be confirmed.

Broadcast interview/
"Face the Nation," CBS-TV, 10-11.

4

[On the controversy surrounding the nomination of Robert Bork for the Supreme Court]: As we approach the Senate's moment of action on this nomination . . . we have been told that the judiciary is being dangerously politicized [by Bork's opponents] and that, as a result, the independence of the judiciary, and the Supreme Court in particular, is in great jeopardy. Well, I'll acknowledge there has been politicization, but any politicizing has been driven by President Reagan's single-minded pursuit of a judiciary packed with those who are his ideological allies [such as Robert Bork].

Before the Senate, Washington,
Oct. 21/The New York Times, 10-22:12.

Charles Black
Professor of law,
Columbia University

5

In a world that knows that a man's social philosophy shapes his judicial behavior, that philosophy is a factor in a man's fitness to be a [Supreme Court] Justice.

U.S. News & World Report, 9-14:20.

John R. Bolton
Assistant Attorney General
of the United States

6

[Criticizing the special-prosecutor system of the Federal government]: To the extent that the

WHAT THEY SAID IN 1987

(JOHN R. BOLTON)

present statute authorizes a prosecutor to investigate and prosecute Federal crimes without such accountability [to the President], and makes such a prosecutor subject to the direction and control of a court rather than the Executive, we believe it is un-Constitutional . . . These independent counsels, as presently operating, are utterly without review . . . utterly without supervision. Nothing is too trivial for these people to investigate. And the proof of that lies in what we already know about their expenditures.

News conference, Washington, June 16/
The Washington Post, 6-17:(A)18.

David L. Boren
United States Senator,
D-Oklahoma

1

[Advocating confirmation of Robert Bork for the Supreme Court]: Judge Bork is clearly qualified by intellectual ability, character and experience to serve on the Court. While some of his detractors have argued that he would not follow precedent in protecting the rights of all citizens, a careful evaluation of his record does not support these concerns. My study of the record leads me to predict that if Robert Bork becomes a member of the Supreme Court, he will surprise many of his strongest critics and staunchest supporters by being more moderate than either expects.

The New York Times, 10-6:10.

Robert H. Bork
Judge,
United States Court of Appeals
for the District of Columbia;
Nominee for Associate Justice,
Supreme Court of the United States

2

Most people would probably say I am a conservative. But political outlook has little to do with judicial philosophy.

Interview/USA Today, 7-2:(A)2.

3

The position I have taken in public—that you can find in my writing—is that the judge's task is to take the intentions of the legislatures and apply [them] to the circumstances. It's a view that has been taken by liberals and a view that's been taken by conservatives—and it's a view that's been denied by both.

Interview/USA Today, 7-22:(A)9.

4

I think it's possible as an academic to toss out ideas with some freedom. But when you're a judge, what you're doing is important to people. You don't feel the same kind of intellectual freedom that you might as an academic. I think you become very careful about the application of a principle to facts. In a classroom, nobody gets hurt; in a courtroom, somebody does.

Interview/USA Today, 7-22:(A)9.

5

I think the best a judge can leave behind is a number of examples of a process of reasoning and hope, if his process of reasoning is good, that that will become in some sense constructive to others coming along in the law. Laws are constantly evolving in culture and intellectual enterprise, and what one would like to do is leave some influence upon the intellectual enterprise.

Interview/Newsweek, 9-14:36.

6

It is one thing as a legal theorist to criticize the reasoning of a prior [judicial] decision, even to criticize it severely, as I have done. It is another and more serious thing altogether for a judge to ignore or overturn a prior decision. That requires much careful thought.

At Senate Judiciary Committee hearing
on his confirmation, Washington,
Sept. 15/Los Angeles Times, 9-16:(I)20.

7

The judge's authority derives entirely from the fact that he is applying the law and not his personal values. That is why the American public accepts the decisions of its courts, accepts

(ROBERT H. BORK)

even decisions that nullify the laws a majority of the electorate or of their representatives voted for. The judge, to deserve that trust and that authority, must be every bit as governed by law as is the Congress, the President, the state Governors and legislatures and the American people. No one, including a judge, can be above the law. Only in that way will justice be done and the freedom of Americans assured. How should a judge go about finding the law? The only legitimate way, in my opinion, is by attempting to discern what those who made the law intended . . . Where the words are precise and the facts simple, that is a relatively easy task. Where the words are general, as is the case with some of the most profound protections of our liberties in the Bill of Rights and in the Civil War Amendments, the task is far more complex . . . If a judge abandons intention as his guide, there is no law available to him, and he begins to legislate a social agenda for the American people. That goes well beyond his legitimate power. He or she then diminishes liberty instead of enhancing it.

At Senate Judiciary Committee hearing
on his confirmation, Washington,
Sept. 15/The New York Times, 9-16:16.

1

[Defending himself against criticism that he is against privacy rights of individuals]: Suppose a Senator introduced a bill that said every man and woman and child in this country has a right to privacy. Period. I don't think that bill would go anywhere until he had to tell everybody exactly what the right of privacy protected. Did it protect incest? Did it protect beating your wife in private?

At Senate Judiciary Committee hearing
on his confirmation, Washington,
Sept. 16/USA Today, 9-17:(A)8.

2

[Refuting charges made by his critics who do not want him confirmed for the Supreme Court]: I have not asked that either the Congress or the courts be neutral in the face of ra-

cial discrimination. I have upheld the laws that outlaw [it] . . . I have never written a word hostile to women . . . hostile to privacy . . . I have never complained about the reasoning of one Supreme Court case. I have never written a word or made a decision from which you can infer that I am pro-big business at the expense of other people . . . Nothing in my record suggests I have a political or ideological agenda.

At Senate Judiciary Committee hearing
on his confirmation, Washington,
Sept. 18/The Washington Post, 9-19:(A)10.

3

I've changed my mind in major ways through my life. I don't see anything wrong with it. That's the business I'm in—trying to think things out. Most of the changes had nothing to do with confirmation hearings [by the Senate on his nomination to the Supreme Court] or anything other than honest intellectual effort. Some people say I'm closed-minded. Others criticize me for changing my mind. I find it all very unfortunate.

Interview/Time, 9-21:18.

4

Liberal, moderate, conservative shouldn't apply to judging. The correct philosophy is to judge according to the intent of the legislature or the intent of the Constitution's framers. Judges are overwhelmingly from a very narrow segment of society, and if they begin to read their own ideals into the law, then most of society isn't represented.

Interview/Time, 9-21:18.

5

[Criticizing his treatment by members of the Senate Judiciary Committee during his confirmation hearings and the organized public campaigns against his confirmation]: The process of confirming Justices for our nation's highest Court has been transformed in a way that should not and indeed must not be permitted to occur again. The tactics and techniques of national political campaigns have been unleashed on the process of confirming judges. That is not simply disturbing, it is dangerous . . . The

(ROBERT H. BORK)

most serious and lasting injury in all of this, however, is not to me. Nor is it to all of those who have steadfastly supported my nomination and to whom I am deeply grateful. Rather, it is to the dignity and the integrity of law and of public service in this country . . . A crucial principle is at stake. That principle is the way we select the men and women who guard the liberties of all the American people. That should not be done through public campaigns of distortion.

Washington, Oct. 9/
The New York Times, 10-10:12.

Bill Bradley
United States Senator,
D-New Jersey

1

[Arguing against confirmation of Robert Bork for the Supreme Court]: A law-school professor dissects precedents. A circuit-court judge applies precedents. A Supreme Court Justice sets precedents. If a professor slips back temporarily into the blank spots of racial insensitivity, it hurts only his immediate friends who believe him to be a different person. If a Justice of the Supreme Court slips back, it could hurt generations of Americans. Ask yourself [if you are a Senator who votes for Bork's confirmation] how you will feel 5, 7 or 10 years from now if the Supreme Court, with Judge Bork as the decisive vote, issues a series of decisions that effectively ends 32 years of progress in civil rights. Ask yourself how you will face your neighbors and supporters who believed in you.

The New York Times, 10-6:10.

James R. Browning
Chief Judge,
United States Court of
Appeals for the 9th Circuit

2

All judges confronted with prior precedents, if they don't like it, will try to find a way to dis-

tinguish it [from the prior precedential case]. But my feeling is, that's the way the law grows. You move a little bit here, then a little bit there and, bit by bit, you move the law along—like building a coral reef.

Los Angeles Times, 8-24:(I)16.

Warren E. Burger
Former Chief Justice
of the United States

3

[Supporting the nomination of Robert Bork for the Supreme Court]: It would astonish me—astonish me to think that he is an extremist [as Bork's opponents have charged] any more than I am an extremist . . . the most important things for examination are, first, integrity; if you don't pass the integrity test you're finished. And then, training, and then, experience, and then, temperament. Now, we all remember that the Constitution doesn't require that a Justice of the Supreme Court be trained in the law, but all of them have been. I have said, before the American Bar Association, and have no hesitation in repeating here, in the half century since I was a law student following these things, I know of no person who meets those qualifications better than [Bork] does.

Before Senate Judiciary Committee hearing
on Bork's nomination, Washington,
Sept. 23/The New York Times, 9-24:12.

George Bush
Vice President
of the United States

4

[On those who criticize President Reagan's nomination of Robert Bork for the Supreme Court]: [Some] say Judge Bork would upset the "balance" on the Court. You know, when liberals talk about "balance," I'm reminded of the line from *Animal Farm:* "All animals are equal, but some animals are more equal than others." When close votes go their way, liberals say the Court is balanced; when close votes go against them, it's the end of the world.

The Washington Post, 7-18:(A)4.

Robert C. Byrd
United States Senator,
D-West Virginia

1

. . . the Senate has both the right and the duty to scrutinize as carefully as possible the individuals who are nominated to serve on the Supreme Court of the United States. Unlike the case when we consider legislation, the Senate has no second chance in passing on lifetime appointments. As an equal partner with the President in making these appointments, the Senate should consider the nominee's integrity, candor, tempermanent, experience, education and judicial philosophy.

At Senate Judiciary Committee hearing
on the Supreme Court nomination of
Robert Bork, Washington, Sept. 15/
The New York Times, 9-16:16.

Charles M. Carberry
Lawyer; Former Chief,
Securities and Commodities
Fraud Unit, U.S. Attorney's office.

2

The legal profession is very competitive, and attorneys too often waste energy measuring their careers and their progress against everybody else. It seems to me, based on my dealings with senior lawyers I really respect, that you can't see your career as a sprint. It's a long race, a thirty-five-year-race, maybe more. When you reach your mid-sixties or early seventies, then you can look back and see what you've done. But not before.

Esquire, December: 97.

Erwin Chemerinsky
Professor of Constitutional law,
University of Southern California

3

[Criticizing the nomination of Robert Bork for the Supreme Court]: He is critical of virtually every Supreme Court case protecting individual liberties. Judge Bork's Constitutional decisions can be explained by a single principle: Where there's government versus the individual, the government always wins.

News conference, Los Angeles,
Aug. 28/The New York Times, 8-29:6.

Jesse H. Choper
Dean,
University of California
Law School

4

You get no written money-back guarantees with a Supreme Court appointment, and one of the good illustrations of that is Justice [Lewis] Powell, who was appointed by a President [Richard Nixon] who went out of his way to change the Court.

Los Angeles Times, 6-27:(I)26.

Warren Christopher
Lawyer;
Former American diplomat

5

[Saying he is frequently a secretive person]: I'd have to confess to playing it close to the vest most of the time. When you're dealing with people's lives, I think that's a lawyer's obligation.

Interview, Los Angeles/Los Angeles Times, 9-29:(I)3.

Ronald K. L. Collins
Visiting professor of law,
Syracuse University;
Former judicial fellow,
Supreme Court of the United States

6

With some exceptions, thanks to [Justices] Louis Brandeis and Oliver Wendell Holmes, this [U.S. Supreme Court over the centuries] has not been a Court that protected individual rights or minority rights. This was a Court that protected business rights, corporate rights, economic rights, the rights of the vested, the rights of the few.

Interview/
The Christian Science Monitor, 10-22:6.

Alan Cranston
United States Senator,
D-California

1

[Criticizing President Reagan's nomination of Robert H. Bork as Associate Justice of the U.S. Supreme Court]: He [Bork] seems to have many of the qualifications one would want in a Supreme Court Justice, but a deeply held ideological [conservative] attitude constitutes a conflict of interest . . . And that, to me, can be disqualifying.

July 1/Los Angeles Times, 7-2:(I)22.

Mario M. Cuomo
Governor of New York (D)

2

It is wrong, in my opinion, for a judge to go on the Supreme Court . . . bench with his mind made up on abortion or any issues. If it becomes clear that he has already made up his mind, then he should not be on the bench. Can you call a strike before the pitch is thrown? How can you make a decision before reading the evidence?

Before National Association for
the Advancement of Colored People,
New York/The Washington Post, 7-8:(A)4.

Lloyd N. Cutler
Former Counsel to the President
of the United States (Jimmy Carter)

3

[Supporting the nomination of Robert Bork to the Supreme Court]: I'd like to make one particular statement, if I could, to the Democratic members of the [Senate Judiciary] Committee, who are understandably chafing under eight years of a Republican President. And given our growing national penchant for ticket-splitting and lack of party sensitivity and loyalty on the part of voters, a Democratic President may well come to office with a Republican Senate. It's necessary for Democrats who would vote against a moderate conservative nominee to the Court [such as Bork] to recall, or remember, that they are giving a hostage to

the time when a Democratic President will be appointing a moderate liberal, or perhaps a very liberal, member to the Court who will be judged by the same standard in reverse that you would be applying, in my view, if you rejected Judge Bork today.

At Senate Judiciary Committee hearing
on Bork's confirmation. Washington,
Sept. 23/ The New York Times. 9-24:12.

Dennis DeConcini
United States Senator,
D-Arizona

4

[On the controversy surrounding the nomination of Robert Bork for the Supreme Court]: Why has this single nomination aroused such whirlwinds of passion and rhetoric? Because more than any other legal thinker in America, Judge Bork has become a symbol of a return to the days when our legal system protected only the rights of the haves and not the have-nots. A time when going to court meant your rights and liberties were being taken away, not protected. Judge Bork is different from [other conservatives such as Supreme Court Justice] Sandra Day O'Connor, Chief Justice Willian Rehnquist and Justice Antonin Scalia. He has spent his career as a legal scholar criticizing in the harshest terms the Court and its decisions. He has used inflammatory terms to criticize the decisions that most people in this country credit with giving some measure of equality and respect to all of us. In my judgment, no other Supreme Court nominee in history has been as strident in his criticism of the way the Constitution has been used to protect individual liberties. His career indicates a lack of understanding of the effect of judicial decisions on real people.

Interview/USA Today, 10-9:(A)11.

Robert J. Dole
United States Senator,
R-Kansas; Candidate for the 1988
Republican Presidential nomination

5

[Criticizing the opponents of Robert Bork's nomination for the Supreme Court]: The

(ROBERT J. DOLE)

stark—and to his opponents disconcerting—fact is that Judge Bork's views are well within the acceptable range of legal debate and, if Presidential elections mean anything at all, are probably much closer to the mainstream of American thought than that of most of his political critics . . . [Bork] has in large part made his formidable reputation by arguing for a neutral, non-political and non-personal kind of judging, for a reaffirmation of the great principle of judicial restraint. His opponents fear only that the application of that traditional principle will not result in judicial decisions that will advance their own political and social agendas.

Before the Senate,
Washington, July 23/
The Washington Post, 7-24:(A)3.

Robert F. Drinan
Professor of law,
Georgetown University;
Former United States Representative,
D-Massachusetts

1

I like to think that the new generation of lawyers has a higher ethical standard than the lawyers who went before them. Furthermore, they're confronting situations which are infinitely more complex than their predecessors ever faced in the legal profession. When you deal with insider [stock] trading, and junk bonds, and all of the new problems, the lawyer's dilemma becomes a great deal sharper than it ever was before . . . There will always be a tiny minority of lawyers and other professionals who will disgrace the profession. But I am inclined to think now that the level of expectation of all lawyers is higher, and you have more supervision and more punishment of lawyers than ever before. I don't think there's more sin or avarice now. It's just that we're more conscious of it.

Interview/
USA Today, 6-23:(A)11.

W. Clark Durant III
Director,
Legal Services
Corporation of
the United States

2

[Saying non-lawyers should be allowed to handle much of the routine work that currently must be done by lawyers]: When I came to the Legal Services Corporation, I made a commitment that my whole thrust would be to find ways to maximize access to justice. The problem is not a shortage of lawyers. The problem is that the organized bar has built a dam across the river, and now it is complaining about the shortage of water in the fields . . . If a person wanted to take a bar exam and hold himself out as a specialist, I'd say more power to him. But if someone is demonstrating the ability to deliver a product in the ordinary course of things, and that person has not gone to law school, I would not stop them. I would encourage more such people to get into the business. You shouldn't have to spend three years in law school at a cost of many thousands of dollars, and then pass a comprehensive bar examination, if all you want to do is handle landlord-tenant disputes or domestic disputes.

Interview/
The Washington Post,
6-22:(A)11.

Monroe H. Freedman
Professor of law,
Hofstra University

3

[On "ambulance-chasers," lawyers who rush to the scene of accidents to try to obtain clients]: The lawyers who are making these trips are earning their living, just the way reporters earn their living by going to accident scenes, and doctors and medical technicians earn their living by going to accident scenes. The question is whether they are serving a positive social function, and it is clear to me that they are.

The Washington Post,
1-9:(A)20.

189

Leonard Garment
Lawyer;
Former Adviser to
the President of the United States
(Richard Nixon)

1

[On the controversy surrounding the nomination of Robert Bork for the Supreme Court]: If this [anti-Bork political] process is permitted to go forward without a full airing and debate on the floor of the Senate, then we can all hang our heads in shame and watch the inevitable politicization of the centerpiece of American liberty, which is a free and independent judiciary. Future judges will be selected, nominated and confirmed on the basis of political campaigns rather than their judicial qualifications. This would be a tragedy. The issue, in a very real sense, transcends Bork.

Interview/USA Today, 10-9:(A)11.

Jake Garn
United States Senator, R-Utah

2

[On the controversy surrounding the nomination of Robert Bork for the Supreme Court]: In the past, I have always voted for judges—liberal or conservative—as long as they have been well-qualified nominees with character and integrity. In the future, because of the way the process has been subverted [by anti-Bork forces], we will no longer vote for nominees on this basis. We will most likely play the political games of judging nominees on their political philosophies rather than on their merits.

Interview/USA Today, 10-9:(A)11.

Paul D. Gewirtz
Professor of law,
Yale University

3

[Saying the Constitution provides that the President shall make Supreme Court appointments with the advice and consent of the Senate]: [That] seems pretty clearly to make the Senate an equal partner. It's hard for me to see why a factor that is relevant for the President [the political orientation of the appointee] is somehow off limits for the Senate . . . If Senators talk openly about the relevance of [a Supreme Court nominee's] views, then the Senators have to . . . make some judgments about what the Constitution means. That means the Senators have to get into some of the most controversial value questions facing the country. It's easier to say the only value that's important here is that you [the nominee] shouldn't be corrupt. Everyone agrees on that.

Los Angeles Times, 7-3:(I)28.

Stephen Gillers
Professor of legal ethics,
New York University Law School

4

[On the effect of malpractice suits against lawyers]: As it begins to sink in that lawyers are vulnerable, they will take greater precautions to the point that they will worry about themselves first and their clients second. Self-preservation is a natural instinct.

The New York Times, 5-25:18.

Douglas H. Ginsburg
Judge,
United States Court of Appeals
for the District of Columbia;
Nominee for Associate Justice,
Supreme Court of the United States

5

[On revelations that he used marijuana when he taught at Harvard Law School in the 1970s]: Earlier today, I was asked whether I had ever used drugs. To the best of my recollection, once as a college student in the '60s, and then on a few occasions in the '70s, I used marijuana. That was the only drug I ever used. I have not used it since. It was a mistake, and I regret it.

Nov. 5/The New York Times,
11-6:1.

Ira Glasser
Executive director,
American Civil Liberties Union

_1_

[Opposing Robert Bork's nomination for Supreme Court Justice]: Judge Bork's writings make it crystal clear that he thinks the highest right in this society is the right of local majorities to make law and to impose their morality on the rest of society. [In this view,] the Bill of Rights is an intrusion on a democratic society.
News conference, Washington,
Aug. 31/The New York Times, 9-1:7.

Robert W. Gordon
Professor of ethics and history,
School of Law, Stanford University

_2_

Corporate law firms are increasingly sacrificing all other goals of professional life toward the single goal of making as much money as possible. This has been very bad for the profession, and a lot of lawyers are concerned because many believe ethics are sinking rapidly under the stress of competition.
Los Angeles Times, 10-19:(I)16.

_3_

The reputation of lawyers for honesty and forthrightness and good service has never been particularly high in Western culture . . . On the other hand, one has to look at the prestige of being a lawyer. The paradox is that people fear and distrust lawyers as a group, but may still want their kids to go to law school.
Los Angeles Times, 10-19:(I)16.

Albert Gore, Jr.
United States Senator,
D-Tennessee; Candidate for the 1988
Democratic Presidential nomination

_4_

[Arguing against the confirmation of Robert Bork for the Supreme Court]: Judge Bork does not understand the Constitution. He says he would interpret the Constitution exactly as the

framers would have 200 years ago. But 200 years ago, black people were property and women couldn't vote . . . Not only have we added amendments to our Constitution, we have changed the context in which it should be read.
Oct. 7/Los Angeles Times, 10-8:(I)24.

Phil Gramm
United States Senator,
R-Texas

_5_

[Advocating confirmation of Robert Bork for the Supreme Court]: In America, we hold Presidential elections to choose between candidates representing differing philosophies of government, but we appoint people to the Supreme Court based on their integrity, experience and ability. Because Judge Bork's critics cannot successfully attack his talent and character, they instead attack the President's [Reagan] philosophy [by criticizing Bork's philosophy]. Broad public approval of that philosophy—strict construction of the Constitution, a belief that the courts should interpret the law rather than make the law, and a high concern for the rights of victims as well as criminals—manifested itself in Ronald Reagan's two landslide elections. Critics of Robert Bork and Ronald Reagan seek to gain a philosophical victory in the Senate [which must approve or reject Bork] that they were denied by the American people in the last two Presidential elections.
The New York Times, 10-6:10.

Charles E. Grassley
United States Senator, R-Iowa.

_6_

[Criticizing the Senate Judiciary Committee's handling of its confirmation hearings for Supreme Court nominee Robert Bork]: I've been in public office 28 years of my lifetime, and never have I seen such an unjustified and untrammeled assault on a distinguished American citizen as I have witnessed these last few weeks. Words are very inadequate to express

(CHARLES E. GRASSLEY)

my shame at the [negative] distortions [of Bork] that I have heard in this room.

At Senate Judiciary Committee hearing on Bork's confirmation, Washington, Oct. 6/The New York Times, 10-7:12.

Alexander M. Haig, Jr.
Former Secretary of State of the United States; Candidate for the 1988 Republican Presidential nomination

1

[On the Senate's turn-down of the nomination of Robert Bork to the Supreme Court]: I've known Bob Bork since the early '70s. I considered him to be—before his nomination—the most highly qualified jurist in America who should have been nominated. That he wasn't confirmed was a travesty of our confirmation process. As much as I love and admire Bob Bork, if I had been his choreographer, I'd have taken him to the barber, cut that beard, cut that hair and not have him look like the reincarnation of some of the extremists the history books have taught us to be wary of.

Interview/USA Today, 12-21:(A)13.

Orrin G. Hatch
United States Senator, R-Utah

2

[On the controversy surrounding the nomination of Robert Bork for the Supreme Court]: . . . I would like to honor Judge Robert H. Bork, one of the most qualified and impressive individuals it seems to me ever nominated to the Supreme Court. In the unlikely event that he is confirmed, history is likely to remember him as one of the greatest jurists of the latter half of this century. In the event that he is not confirmed, history will remember him in two senses. First, as an individual who did more than almost any other in the latter half of this century to restore legal honesty and integrity to the interpretation of the Constitution. And sec-

ond, as an unfortunate and undeserving victim of political [anti-Bork] circumstances [in the Senate and in organized public protests against his nomination].

Before the Senate, Washington, Oct. 21/The New York Times, 10-22:12.

Carla Hills
Former Secretary of Housing and Urban Development of the United States

3

[Supporting the nomination of Robert Bork for the Supreme Court]: [While working together in the Justice Department in the Nixon and Ford Administrations,] we grappled with a broad menu of complex and controversial legal issues, many of them matters of first impression. And during that period, Judge Bork displayed an uncommon capacity to listen with an open mind, a relentless fairness in all of his actions, and an enormous dedication to intellectual effort. Given my deeply held views of Judge Bork's splendid character and capacity, I was startled and saddened by the proliferation of reports from interest groups contending that his presence on the Court [would threaten] that group's particular interest. Rather than reason with his considerable intellect, too many [who oppose him] have used highly selective quotations from his writings, and skewed tabulations of his opinions, to brand him anti-labor, anti-First Amendment, anti-feminist and, in particular, anti-the-social-objective of the writer.

At Senate Judiciary Committee hearing on Bork's nomination, Washington, Sept. 22/The New York Times, 9-23:15.

Shirley Hufstedler
Former Federal judge; Former Secretary of Education of the United States

4

[Arguing against confirmation of Robert Bork for the Supreme Court]: I oppose Judge Robert Bork's confirmation as Associate Justice of the Supreme Court because in my view he is

(SHIRLEY HUFSTEDLER)

not a moderate Constitutional architect that the country requires at this time in the Court's history . . . the evidence discloses his quest for certitudes to resolve the ambiguities of the Constitution and of the Supreme Court's role in Constitutional adjudication, and an effort to develop Constitutional litmus tests to avoid his having to confront the grief and the untidiness of the human condition.

At Senate Judiciary Committee hearing
on Bork's confirmation, Washington,
Sept. 25/The New York Times, 9-26:8.

Jesse L. Jackson
Civil-rights leader;
Candidate for the 1988
Democratic Presidential nomination

1

[Criticizing President Reagan's nomination of Robert Bork for the Supreme Court]: Judge Bork's political direction is a threat to the credibility of the Court. We don't need the nominee of a jilted Justice Department confirmed so that we can end up with a tilted Court. President Reagan nominated Judge Bork because of his conservative political ideology, and the Senate ought to reject him for the same reason.

At National Association for
the Advancement of Colored People
convention, New York, July 8/
The Washington Post, 7-9:(A)4.

2

What you have today is prosecutors leaking news of sweeping indictments, and then relatively few convictions. [Mayor] Ken Gibson of Newark, indicted but not convicted in the courts—yet tried and convicted in the press beforehand. You get a combination of an ambitious state attorney and a hostile press, and you have a dimension of power to struggle against. Every bark is not a bite. Every indictment is not a conviction.

Interview/Mother Jones, October:30.

Barbara C. Jordan
Professor of public values and ethics,
University of Texas, Austin;
Former United States Representative,
D-Texas

3

[Arguing against Senate confirmation of Robert Bork for the Supreme Court]: Judge Bork has this theory: "If you can't find that right within the letters of the Constitution explicitly, it's not there, it doesn't exist." I believe that the presence of that point of view on the Supreme Court of the United States places at risk individual rights. It is a risk we should not afford— we don't have to. I like the idea that the Supreme Court of the United States is the last bulwark of protection for our freedom. Would the membership of Judge Bork alter that altogether? I don't know whether that's the case, but that is not the question. I don't want to see the argument made that there is no right to privacy on the Court. I don't want that argument made. And the only way to prevent its being made is to deny Judge Bork membership on the Court.

At Senate Judiciary Committee hearing
on Bork's nomination, Washington,
Sept. 21/The New York Times, 9-22:13.

Yale Kamisar
Professor of law,
University of Michigan

4

[On whether the Senate should not confirm a Presidential nomination for the Supreme Court because of ideology of the nominee]: The modern view is that a President should get his pick once you satisfy considerations of ability, integrity and competence [of the nominee]. People only recently have made a contrary argument. But it never came to a test before because Presidents really never gave much weight to ideology. With all respect, a Supreme Court appointment was not considered that important until 20 years ago.

The Washington Post,
7-1:(A)9.

193

WHAT THEY SAID IN 1987

Anthony M. Kennedy
Judge,
United States Court of Appeals
for the Ninth Circuit;
Nominee for Associate Justice,
Supreme Court of the United States

1

It is a fact . . . not a perception, that courts have become more active in the public dialogue and in policy-making than at any other time in our Constitutional history. This expanded role of the courts tends to erode the boundaries of judicial power and also threatens to permit the individual biases of the judge to operate. Life tenure is in part a Constitutional mandate to the Federal Judiciary to proceed with caution, to avoid reaching issues not necessary to the resolution of the suit at hand, and to defer to the political process.

Reply to Senate
Judiciary Committee questionnaire,
Dec. 1*/The Washington Post, 12-2:(A)3.

2

It would be highly improper for a judge to allow his or her own personal or religious views to enter into a decision respecting a Constitutional matter . . . A man's or a woman's relation to his or her God and the fact that he or she may think they're held accountable to a higher power may be important evidence of a person's character or temperament. It is irrelevant to his or her judicial authority.

At Senate Judiciary Committee hearing
on his confirmation, Washington,
Dec. 14/Los Angeles Times,
12-15:(I)24.

Edward M. Kennedy
United States Senator,
D-Massachusetts

3

[Criticizing President Reagan's nomination of Robert Bork for the Supreme Court]: We are not prepared to sit by while a lame-duck President attempts to reach out beyond the end of his Administration to tilt the balance of the Su-

preme Court for the next generation. Robert Bork is wrong on civil rights, wrong on equal rights for women, wrong on the First Amendment, wrong on one-man-one-vote, and Ronald Reagan is wrong to try to put him on the Supreme Court.

At "We the People" rally,
Los Angeles, July 12/
Los Angeles Times, 7-13:(I)4.

4

[Arguing against Senate confirmation of Robert Bork for the Supreme Court]: Robert Bork's America is a land in which women would be forced into back-alley abortions, blacks would sit at segregated lunch counters, rogue police could break down citizens' doors in midnight raids . . . No justice would be better than this injustice.

U.S. News & World Report, 9-14:18.

5

[Arguing against confirmation of Robert Bork for the Supreme Court]: Time and again, in his public record over more than a quarter of a century, Robert Bork has shown that he is hostile to the rule of law and the role of the courts in protecting individual liberty. He has harshly opposed, and in public, itching to overrule many of the great decisions of the Supreme Court that seek to fulfill the promise of justice for all Americans. He is instinctively biased against the claims of the average citizen and in favor of concentrations of power, whether that is governmental or private. And in conflicts between the Legislative and Executive Branches of government, he has repeatedly expressed a clear contempt for Congress and an unbridled trust in the power of the President. Mr. Bork has said many extreme things in his comments of a lifetime in the law. We already have a more extensive record of his work and writings than perhaps we have had for any other Supreme Court nominee in history. It is easy to conclude from the public record of Mr. Bork's published views that he believes women and blacks are second-class citizens under the Constitution. He even believes that in the relation to the Executive that members of Congress are second-

(EDWARD M. KENNEDY)

class citizens. Yet he is asking the Senate to confirm him.

At Senate Judiciary Committee
hearing on Bork's confirmation,
Washington, Sept. 15/
The New York Times, 9-16:15.

1

[Arguing against the confirmation of Robert Bork for the Supreme Court]: . . . in a lifetime of writings on the public record, Mr. Bork has shown his bias against women and minorities and in favor of big business and Presidential power. And it's small comfort to minorities to know that some years after the Civil Rights Act was passed over his opposition, Mr. Bork changed his mind and said that it had worked all right . . . Again and again on the public record, he's suggested that he's prepared to roll back the clock, return to more troubled times, uproot decades of settled law in order to write his own ideology into law. And in these hearings this week, he's asked us to believe that he can make a U-turn in these areas of fundamental importance to the kind of America we are and hope to be. The question all of us are asking is who is the real Robert Bork? And what risks are we taking for the future if he becomes a Justice of the Supreme Court, with the last word about justice in America?

At Senate Judiciary Committee
hearing on Bork's confirmation,
Washington, Sept. 18/
The New York Times, 9-19:9.

2

[On President Reagan's nomination of Judge Douglas Ginsburg for the Supreme Court]: [Ginsburg] is one of the least experienced nominees ever submitted by a President to the Supreme Court [and is] an ideological clone of Judge [Robert] Bork [whose nomination to the Court was recently voted down by the Senate], a Judge Bork without a paper trail.

Oct. 29/Los Angeles Times,
10-30:(I)15.

Carl M. Levin
United States Senator,
D-Michigan

3

[Criticizing the Justice Department's attack on the special-prosecutor system of the Federal government]: This is the first direct assault by the Justice Department against the independent-counsel statute, but the Department's position against reauthorizing the law, sadly, comes as no surprise. The Department would have us return to the days of Watergate and [then-President Richard] Nixon's "Saturday night massacre," when public trust in our criminal-justice system hung in the balance. We don't want to go to the brink again.

News conference, Washington, June 16/
The Washington Post, 6-17:(A)1.

Michael McConnell
Professor of law,
University of Chicago

4

[Supporting the nomination of Robert Bork for the Supreme Court]: Some nominees in the past have been accused of being rigid ideologues, who will have some set and unacceptable view of Constitutional law. Others have been accused of being shifting sands, changing their opinions all too often, and not being rooted in any firm principle at all. I think I can confidently say that Judge Bork is the first nominee ever to be accused [by those testifying against his nomination] of both of these things at the same time. I think that there's a reason for this impression as well, which is that the criticisms of Judge Bork have tended to be so extreme, so inflated as to create an impression coming into this chamber that the nominee is some kind of a monster, some kind of a threat to our civil liberties. And then, when you see Judge Bork in the flesh and you find out that he's in fact a moderate, sensible, intelligent liberal—in the sense of honoring liberty—sort of person, there is an inclination to assume that he's the one who has changed. And also, he has indeed changed his mind on some matters. I think that in general [though], if you follow his

195

WHAT THEY SAID IN 1987

work through the 30 long years that he's been contributing in the field, you will find that these broad themes have been far more consistent than all of that.

At Senate Judiciary Committee hearing on Bork's confirmation, Washington, Sept. 22/The New York Times, 9-23:15.

Forrest McDonald
Professor of history,
University of Alabama

1

[On the critical and often harsh questioning of Robert Bork during the recent Senate Judiciary Committee hearings on his confirmation for the Supreme Court]: [The hearings were] Mc-Carthyism and trial by innuendo . . . Bork was being judged by crooks, cheats, frauds, liars and philanderers. Do you think that's fair?

Los Angeles Times, 10-10:(I)1.

Edwin Meese III
Attorney General
of the United States

2

[On the qualifications for appointees to the U.S. Supreme Court]: I think it ought to be someone who has demonstrated competence, obviously intellectual ability, probably some extensive judicial experience, someone who has judicial temperament and integrity and someone who has an understanding and adherence to the role of the judiciary under the Constitution; that is, as a judge or justice who would apply the law and interpret the law, not make the law.

Broadcast interview/
"This Week with David Brinkley,"
ABC-TV, 6-28.

3

[On the Senate vote not to confirm Robert Bork for the Supreme Court after the Judiciary Committee's controversial handling of Bork during his confirmation hearings]: The distortion of the [confirmation] process was done completely by this small band of special-interest lobbyists and left-wing groups who engaged in a highly organized, well-financed political campaign outside the normal processes. The important thing now is to be sure the public and the Senate recognize the kind of gutter politics that was played by some of these left-wing groups. There's never been anything like this in history . . . The defeat really is for the confirmation process rather than the President [Reagan]. Judge Bork's courageous stand to try to return this to an orderly Constitutional process . . . will provide a cooling-off period for some of the Senators who have been influenced by the outside political circus to think seriously about how future confirmation processes ought to be carried out.

Interview/
U.S. News & World Report, 10-19:20.

Abner Mikva
Judge,
United States Court of Appeals
for the District of Columbia

4

[The terms conservative and liberal, when applied to judges on the D.C. Court of Appeals,] confuse more than they explain. Most of the time judges are trying to resolve cases on neutral principles. More recently we've had more dissents than in the past, but that may be a reflection of the newness of some of the judges—a desire to reinvent the wheel.

The Christian Science Monitor, 6-9:4.

George J. Mitchell
United States Senator,
D-Maine

5

The rule of law is critical in our society. It's the great equalizer. Because in America, everybody is equal before the law. We must never allow the end to justify the means, where the law is concerned, however important and noble an objective.

At Iran-contra hearings, Washington,
July 13/The New York Times, 7-14:8.

Ralph Nader
Lawyer; Consumer advocate

1

Where is the evidence that higher pay [for judges] secures higher quality [judges]? . . . Political loyalty, ideology and the right connections [are more important].

The Washington Post, 2-3:(A)4.

Eleanor Holmes Norton
Professor of law,
Georgetown University;
Former Chairman,
Federal Equal Employment
Opportunity Commission

2

[On the controversy surrounding the nomination of Robert Bork for the Supreme Court]: I don't think the issue was whether he was mainstream. On the bench today, there are judges who are either very liberal or very conservative and not in the mainstream, but no one would say they should be disqualified. The opposition to Bork went beyond the ordinary political differences between conservative and liberal. He simply has not accepted 20th century Constitutional law, on equal protection, for example. Only at his confirmation hearings did he concede that women should enjoy the protection of the 14th Amendment and even then used a weak standard.

Interview/USA Today, 10-9:(A)11.

David O'Brien
Constitutional scholar,
University of Virginia

3

That's one of the remarkable things about the [U.S.] Constitution: We have a basis for an independent judiciary and for a government of law and not of men. That's why the judiciary is so important and why the justices are constantly being attacked.

The Christian Science Monitor,
2-11:18.

William Proxmire
United States Senator,
D-Wisconsin

4

[On Supreme Court nominee Robert Bork]: I think very highly of Bork's personality and intellect, and I have often voted for people like him in the past, even though I did not agree with them. However, I think Judge Bork is dead wrong on civil liberties, civil rights and antitrust—some of the proudest accomplishments of the Congress. And I would not want to see his vote begin to reverse this process.

The New York Times, 9-28:12.

David H. Pryor
United States Senator,
D-Arkansas

5

[Saying he is against confirmation of Robert Bork for the Supreme Court]: Having gone from extreme positions in his youth to unexplainable positions in later life, Robert Bork continues to wrestle with what he believes. Today, he remains an unknown man with unknown beliefs. There is something sad about the whole issue of Judge Bork's nomination. Here is a brilliant scholar, going through the agony of public hearings and public scrutiny. And yet we don't know him any better now than we did months ago. I would even submit the respectful opinion . . . that he does not know himself.

Oct. 1/The New York Times, 10-2:13.

Ronald Reagan
President of the United States

6

. . . when it comes to crime and safety of our citizens, it's so important for our courts to take a tough, clear-eyed look at the Constitution's purpose to establish justice and insure domestic tranquility. Judge [Robert] Bork, whom I nominated [for the Supreme Court] nearly eight weeks ago, would be just such a Justice. His guiding principle is one of judicial restraint. And Judge Bork believes that judges should not make the laws; their function is to

197

WHAT THEY SAID IN 1987

(RONALD REAGAN)

interpret the laws based on the Constitution and precedent. It's time we reassert the fundamental principle [that] the purpose of criminal justice is to find the truth, not to coddle criminals.

> To law-enforcement officials,
> Los Angeles, Aug. 28/
> The New York Times, 8-29:6.

1

The genius of our Constitutional system is its recognition that no one branch of government alone could be relied on to preserve our freedoms. The great safeguard of our liberty is the totality of the Constitutional system, with no one part getting the upper hand. That is why the judiciary must be independent.

> At celebration of U.S. Constitution's
> 200th anniversary, Philadelphia,
> Sept. 17/The New York Times, 9-18:1.

2

[Criticizing those who are against the confirmation of Robert Bork for the Supreme Court]: It's clear now that the charges that Robert Bork is too ideological are themselves ideologically inspired, and that the criticism of him as outside the mainstream can only be held by those who are themselves so far outside that they've long ago lost sight of the moderate center.

> Before Concerned Women for America,
> Arlington, Va., Sept. 25/
> The New York Times, 9-26:9.

3

[On the controversy and criticism of his nominee for the Supreme Court, Robert Bork]: This is no longer a battle over whether the most qualified man nominated in a century is confirmed to the Supreme Court. At stake here is the integrity and independence of the American system of justice. [Those who have been] distorting [Bork's record] have said over and over he's going to turn back the clock on civil rights. It's amazing they can find a room big enough

for them to get in front of the cameras. Their noses must be so long by now.

> At White House ceremony,
> Washington, Oct. 2/
> Los Angeles Times, 10-3:(I)18.

4

[Criticizing the Senate Judiciary Committee's hostile handling of Supreme Court nominee Robert Bork]: What's at stake is that we make sure the process of appointing and confirming judges never again is turned into such a political joke. If I have to appoint another one [in place of Bork, if Bork is not confirmed by the Senate], I'll try to find one that they'll object to just as much as they did to this one.

> Before New Jersey
> Chamber of Commerce, Whippany, N.J.,
> Oct. 13/Los Angeles Times, 10-14:(I)16.

5

[On the recent Senate Judiciary Committee hearings on the confirmation of Robert Bork for the Supreme Court]: During the hearings, one of Judge Bork's critics said that among the functions of the Court was reinterpreting the Constitution so that it would not remain, in his words, "frozen into ancient error because it is so hard to amend." Well, that to my mind is the issue, plain and simple. Too many theorists believe that the courts should save the country from the Constitution. Well, I believe it's time to save the Constitution from *them*. The principal errors in recent years have had nothing to do with the intent of the Framers.

> Broadcast address to the nation,
> Washington, Oct. 14/
> The New York Times, 10-15:15.

6

In our democracy, our elected representatives make laws and un-elected judges interpret the laws, and that's the foundation of our system of government. Above all, judges must be guided by our most fundamental law, the Constitution. Every judge that I appoint must

198

(RONALD REAGAN)

understand that he or she serves under the Constitution, not above it.

Speech nominating Douglas Ginsburg
for the Supreme Court, Washington,
Oct. 29/The Washington Post, 10-30:(A)20.

William H. Rehnquist
Chief Justice
of the United States

1

[Saying a second national tribunal is required to handle the expanding Supreme Court caseload]: The Supreme Court today is much like an airport built 60 years ago with 150 "landing slots" to accommodate incoming traffic.

U.S. News & World Report, 6-1:11.

2

There has been considerable criticism over the perceived excesses of the confirmation process [for Supreme Court Justices]. Without in any way depreciating that criticism, I think that in the United States, at any rate, we recognize that there is apt to be some inquiry by the Senate as well as by the President into what may be called the "judicial philosophy" of a nominee to our Court.

At Columbia Law School,
New York, Nov. 19/
The New York Times, 11-20:9/.

William Bradford Reynolds
Assistant Attorney General,
Civil Rights Division,
Department of Justice
of the United States

3

. . . it [is] abundantly clear that the Framers [of the Constitution] gave no license to judges— members of the branch regarded, to borrow from Alexander Hamilton, as the "least dangerous" of the three—to construe Constitutional provisions as they see fit. There is good reason for this confluence of restraints on judicial activism. The Constitution is not a mass of fungi-

ble, abstract principles whose meaning varies with time; rather, it comprises a broad societal consensus on certain fundamental, absolute principles necessary for the protection of individual liberty . . . Accordingly, the Constitution was structured so as to require that any change reflect the broadest expression of societal consensus . . . Judges are not free to disengage from our Constitutional moorings in furtherance of their own social agendas; they are not free to determine that the Constitutional principles themselves are unwise or obsolete.

At Vanderbilt University, May 23/
The Washington Post, 6-11:(A)22.

Aubrey E. Robinson, Jr.
Chief Judge,
United States District Court
for the District of Columbia.

4

[Ruling in favor of the Constitutionality of the independent-counsel law used by Congress to investigate wrongdoing by government officials]: [It is an appropriate response by Congress] to the recurrent question of how to enforce the laws of the United States when they are violated by high government officials . . . For the United States, the act represents a landmark effort to instill public confidence in the fair and ethical behavior of public officials.

Washington, July 22/
The Washington Post, 7-23:(A)1.

Terry Sanford
United States Senator,
D-North Carolina

5

[Criticizing President Reagan for continuing to push for Robert Bork's confirmation for the Supreme Court, even though Senate sentiment appears clearly against such confirmation]: It is at least imprudent that the President of the United States is fighting a rear-guard action against the clear mandate of the Senate to move on with the process of selecting a new Supreme Court nominee. One mark of a great leader is

WHAT THEY SAID IN 1987

(TERRY SANFORD)

not only being gracious in victory but being gracious in defeat.

Oct. 14/The Washington Post,
10-15:(A)6.

Antonin Scalia
Associate Justice,
Supreme Court
of the United States

1

[In 1960,] the Federal courts were the forums for the big cases . . . [Today, Federal courts are] fast becoming a vast judicial bureaucracy . . . This is not the system you and I learned to love. I wanted to be a judge, not a case processor . . . The question is not whether the Federal courts should be changed, but rather whether that change, through inaction, will take the form of continuing deterioration, or of some structural alteration that will preserve the essence of a valuable institution. I hope the bar will have the foresight to give thoughtful consideration to this.

Before American Bar Association,
New Orleans, Feb. 15/
Los Angeles Times, 2-16:(I)19;
The New York Times, 2-16:9.

Sol Schreiber
Lawyer;
Former Federal magistrate

2

[Saying high starting salaries paid by law firms to new lawyers may increase pressures to raise revenues through more billable hours]: My concern is that the increase may lead to even more controversy than necessary in complex litigation cases, because controversy generates more billable hours. Of course, a young lawyer ought to be paid a living wage that takes into account the nature of the profession he is in. But to pay someone a salary that equals, if not surpasses, the salary of a Federal judge that the young associate might not even get to argue before, merits more serious attention.

The New York Times, 2-23:20.

Herman Schwartz
Professor of Constitutional law,
American University, Washington

3

[In the future,] we will have a [Supreme] Court that's probably a bit to the right of the current Court. Justice [Antonin] Scalia is somewhat to the right of Chief Justice [Warren] Burger, whom he replaced. Justice [Sandra Day] O'Connor seems to be roughly where Justice Potter Stewart was, except on issues like abortion—she seems to be to the right of him. She seems to be more sympathetic to women's rights, discrimination issues. So we have a Court that's somewhat tipped to the right. The big difference, of course, is there is a solid core of those people who are in their 50s and 60s, and those will be there for a long time. And that may be the most significant Supreme Court legacy of [President] Ronald Reagan— that he tipped the Court slightly to the right and may well keep it there for the next 20 years.

Interview/USA Today, 11-12:(A)9.

Whitney North Seymour, Jr.
Lawyer;
Former United States Attorney

4

The position of U.S. Attorney is the finest public-service position that exists. U.S. Attorneys carry the responsibility that the law is firmly enforced, but with compassion and consideration.

The New York Times, 6-8:9.

Paul Simon
United States Senator,
D-Illinois; Candidate for the 1988
Democratic Presidential nomination

5

[On Robert Bork's nomination for the Supreme Court]: Certainly my tilt at this point . . . is to say this man should not be on the Court. [Bork is] mentally qualified, no question, academically qualified. [But] when you say closed-minded, there is a serious question. I do not

(PAUL SIMON)

want someone who is a rigid ideologue, and this man appears to fit that mold.

The Washington Post, 7-8:(A)5.

Alan K. Simpson
United States Senator,
R-Wyoming

1

[Criticizing those on the Senate Judiciary Committee who he says went beyond reasonableness in their criticism of Supreme Court nominee Robert Bork]: To really believe that this lumbering, Neanderthal, hideous, bestial man [Bork] is somehow going to go to the Supreme Court and wrench four of those remarkable eight people [on the Court] off their noodle and make them all go his way and just destroy America—now, they [the critical Committee members] really lost their lunch on that one; they lost their marbles.

At Senate Judiciary Committee hearing
on Bork's confirmation, Washington,
Sept. 21/The Washington Post, 10-2:(D)4.

2

[Criticizing the Senate Judiciary Committee's handling of its confirmation hearings for Supreme Court nominee Robert Bork]: [There has been] an element of tyranny [in the tactics of Bork's opponents. His defeat] will set a tone for future Supreme Court confirmation procedures that are sure to jade and gall us for years to come.

Washington, Oct. 6/
The New York Times, 10-7:12.

Chesterfield Smith
Former president,
American Bar Association

3

[Arguing against confirmation of Robert Bork for the Supreme Court]: I oppose the nomination of Judge Bork. I believe that in America, quite properly, there are large segments of the people who believe that he has a

knee-jerk reaction . . . As a trial lawyer, I'd like to have a Court up there with two good conservatives like Justice Scalia and Justice Rehnquist on one hand, two good liberals like Justice Marshall and Justice Brennan on the other, and I'd like to feel that there's somebody there in the middle that I can talk to, I can tell about, that I wouldn't feel a knee-jerk already was going to decide things in a certain sort of way.

At Senate Judiciary Committee hearing
on Bork's confirmation, Washington,
Sept. 25/The New York Times, 9-26:8.

William French Smith
Former Attorney General
of the United States

4

[Criticizing the Federal law that authorizes the use of special prosecutors]: In my opinion, this legislation has not served the ends of justice, is cruel and devastating in its application to individuals—falsely destroying reputations and requiring the incurring of great personal costs—has applied artificial standards unrelated to culpability, and to that extent has prevented the use of normal standards of prosecutorial discretion, has been used more for political purposes and media appetite than to achieve justice, has been a nightmare to administer and has caused a needless and substantial waste of taxpayers' money.

Letter to Senate subcommittee*/
The New York Times, 3-13:12.

5

[Supporting the nomination of Robert Bork for the Supreme Court]: . . . I think he's a very fair-minded individual. I think he's very principled. I think he would apply, for lack of a better term, neutral principles in coming to conclusions he comes to. There has been so much talk here [at the confirmation hearings] which seems to lead to the conclusion that if a right is not protected here, [by the Supreme Court], it won't be protected anywhere else. That is not the way our system works. A right which is not protected here may very well be protected

WHAT THEY SAID IN 1987

somewhere else. . . . what you [Bork's critics] are saying is, and the impression you're creating is, that Judge Bork wants to control the use of contraceptives in the bedroom. That is the image you are projecting through the kind of propaganda and distortion that's being thrown out. That is not true and I suspect and I am willing to say you know it's not true. But [it] is the impression that's being created and you can multiply that by every single issue—race relations, women, everything—that's come before this group.

At Senate Judiciary Committee
hearing on Bork's confirmation,
Washington, Sept. 21/
The New York Times, 9-22:13.

Thomas Sowell
Senior fellow,
Hoover Institution

1

[Supporting Robert Bork's nomination for the Supreme Court]: This may be the most important Supreme Court nomination of our time, not simply because the present Court is so closely divided or even because Judge Bork is the most highly qualified nominee of this generation, but because this is an historic crossroads as regards the expanding power of judges, which is to say, the erosion of people's rights to govern themselves democratically . . . It is both ironic and appalling that Judge Bork's own record is being judged on a myopic basis of an issue-by-issue statistical box score on how he has allegedly voted for or against one class of litigants or another, as if he liked chemical companies more than he liked pregnant women or liked asbestos manufacturers better than he liked bereaved widows. Surely, no responsible person thinks that this is what law is all about. Yet such shrill propaganda from special-interest groups is repeated in respectable quarters as if the statistics represented some objective facts.

At Senate Judiciary Committee hearing
on Bork's confirmation, Washington,
Sept. 25/The New York Times, 9-26:8.

Arlen Specter
United States Senator,
R-Pennsylvania

2

[Arguing against confirmation of Robert Bork for the Supreme Court]: I am troubled by his writings that unless there is adherence to original intent, there is no judicial legitimacy; and without such legitimacy, there can be no judicial review. This approach could jeopardize the most fundamental principle of U.S. Constitutional law—the supremacy of judicial review—when Judge Bork concedes original intent is so hard to find and major public figures contend that the Supreme Court does not have the last word on the Constitution.

The New York Times, 10-6:10.

Eugene C. Thomas
President,
American Bar Association

3

[Criticizing advertising by lawyers]: The better services are being provided by those [lawyers] who are not advertising.

USA Today, 7-1:(A)10.

James S. Todd
Senior deputy
executive vice president,
American Medical Association

There's a mentality out there these days that there is no longer any "chance," no longer ill fortune, no acts of God. If something doesn't go right in an automobile, in a hospital, in a factory, on a playground, even in a church, it must be malpractice. If something goes wrong, somebody must be at fault, somebody has to pay. Trial lawyers have capitalized on this. They hear a siren song that is very hard to resist.

Interview/USA Today, 1-14:(A)11.

Laurence Tribe
Professor of Constitutional law,
Harvard University

4

[Attorney General Edwin] Meese's attacks [on the judiciary] have been politically moti-

(LAURENCE TRIBE)

vated and not sound. He is in favor of court restraint on affirmative action but not on abortion. It's a result-oriented, not a principled, set of objectives.

The Christian Science Monitor, 2-11:19.

1

[On Supreme Court nominee Robert Bork]: It's disservice [to Bork and other conservatives] to call Bork a moderate. He clearly has a [conservative] program. However, the President has a right to choose somebody with a program. The question is: Is the Senate willing to sign on to those views? [But] Bork is not some sort of robot whose decisions are predictable.

The Christian Science Monitor, 10-5:6.

Stephen S. Trott
Associate Attorney General
of the United States

2

The overwhelming number of cases prosecuted in the grand-jury system come out well. Do grand juries screw around and play fast and loose? Hell, no. We ought never to take a case to a grand jury unless we're convinced of it.

U.S. News & World Report, 6-8:24.

Lowell P. Weicker, Jr.
United States Senator,
R-Connecticut

3

I will vote no on the nomination of Robert Bork [to the Supreme Court]. The basic reason relates to my unwillingness to accept several months of seemingly innocuous sophisticated banter [during the confirmation hearings] by an eager nominee as substitute for that nominee's lifetime of unrelenting criticism or disdain for landmark laws giving our Constitutional ideals their highest and best meaning. Certainly, nominee Bork is correct when he prods a nation to legislative and executive rather than judicial resolution of its problems. But as a commentator of 15 years vintage, Robert Bork knew that

if it were not for the courts, much of our dreams would lay trashed by the political hesitancy of our leaders.

The New York Times, 10-6:10.

Byron R. White
Associate Justice,
Supreme Court
of the United States

4

In a republic like ours, where the people are supposed to govern through their public officials, there is something to be said for the notion that judges, who decide matters of life or death, should also be chosen periodically by the people. [However,] if people are to have the brand of justice to which they are entitled, judges must have sufficient protection against political or other pressures that threaten to distort their judgment . . . Judges should not feel compelled or be tempted to decide cases so as to please those who are . . . responsible for them being on the bench, whether it be the appointing authority, political parties who nominate and help elect, or those who make critical contributions to judicial election campaigns, which have become very costly.

At American Bar Association
convention, San Francisco, Aug. 10/
The Washington Post, 8-11:(A)5.

Robert Wilentz
Chief Judge,
New Jersey Supreme Court

5

Attorney advertising is one of the best ways to foster price competition.

USA Today, 7-1:(A)10.

Charles Vert Willie
Sociologist,
Harvard University

6

If we want our laws to continue to be beneficial to all, we have to make sure that the lawmaking structures are diversified. Diversity is

WHAT THEY SAID IN 1987

(CHARLES VERT WILLIE)

our source of security. It was our source of security when our Constitution was formed, and it will continue to be our source of security even today. That is the lesson to be derived from the Constitution . . . One racial minority [Thurgood Marshall] and one female [Sandra Day O'Connor] have been appointed to the Supreme Court. That is almost blasphemous in a society where half of the people are racial minorities. We should never have had a situation in which their representation was not present over the highest law-making structure of our nation.

Interview/
The Christian Science Monitor, 6-10:6.

Andrew Young
Mayor of Atlanta

1

[Arguing against Senate confirmation of Robert Bork for the Supreme Court]: I think that what we have here is not only the appointment of a judge, but we have an attempt to transform the Court. And I would contend that there's no mandate in the 1986 elections to give the President [Reagan] the power to so completely transform the judiciary that substantive changes in the life-style of the people of the United States would ensue. But I don't have anything against Judge Bork personally. I don't know enough law to argue with him. But just listening to him and reading his opinions, I have the feeling that here is a very amiable and intelligent man who is extremely well educated but not necessarily wise. And it seems to me that somewhere in this—this list of qualifications a certain kind of wisdom, a certain kind of sensitivity and compassion—for us the Supreme Court has never been just about issues and cases. It really could never be an intellectual feast. It's about people. It's about Rosa Parks wanting the seamstress to sit down in the bus and not have to stand up when a white man comes on. It's about Charlayne Hunter and Hamilton Holmes wanting to go to the school in the University of Georgia.

At Senate Judiciary Committee hearing
on Bork's confirmation Washington,
Sept. 21/The New York Times, 9-22:13.

Jeffrey Archer
Author;
Former deputy chairman,
Conservative Party of Britain

1

[On the forthcoming 1988 U.S. Presidential election]: I'm very distressed to think that the truly greats are not willing to be involved in that mad system of yours. [New York Governor] Mario Cuomo won't stand [for the Presidency]; I hope he'll be willing to change his mind. Why won't [Chrysler Corporation Chairman Lee] Iacocca stand? I think your [American] candidates are very average. The most important job in the world is going to end up with people not worthy of it.

Interview, London/
Los Angeles Times, 6-11:(VI)9.

Bruce Babbitt
Former Governor of Arizona (D);
Candidate for the 1988
Democratic Presidential nomination

2

[Criticizing President Reagan's leadership]: America does not have to leave arms merchants in charge of our diplomacy, terrorists in charge of our security, soldiers of fortune in charge of our Central America desk, Japanese traders in charge of our markets, embezzlers in charge of Wall Street, bigots in charge of our social agenda, pollsters in charge of our politics, and amateurs in charge of the White House.

Announcing his candidacy
for President, Manchester, N.H.,
March 10/The New York Times, 3-11:14.

3

The Democratic Party is crossing, however uncertainly, into some post-New Deal configuration . . . I celebrate the confusion . . . Let a thousand flowers bloom.

Los Angeles Times, 3-11:(I)18.

4

This business of [Presidential election] campaigning—I'll tell you it's a real circus. I've been watching [candidate] Joe Biden's difficulties with emotion and sadness over the last week, because I'll tell you, it's tough. It's a long road; its alleys are long; the stresses on families are very, very difficult.

At campaign breakfast,
Studio City, Calif., Sept. 22/
Los Angeles Times, 9-23:(I)18.

5

We've evolved a cycle of dishonesty in our national discourse. Politicians don't tell the necessary but unpleasant truths because they are afraid that the voters will kill the messenger. So people learn not to expect the truth from politicians.

Time, 11-9:19.

6

[Criticizing Gary Hart's decision to re-enter the race for the 1988 Democratic Presidential nomination after withdrawing earlier in the year because of a sex scandal]: Mr. Hart is going around saying he feels bound to run because nobody else is addressing the vital issues of the day. I resent that. It seems to me that Gary Hart has a hell of a long way to go before he has anything to teach this candidate about grappling with hard choices and standing up for the truth. I think anyone is entitled to make a comeback. [But] I don't know if the appropriate model is [boxer] Sugar Ray Leonard or [controversial evangelists] Jim and Tammy Bakker.

Chicago, Dec. 17/
The Washington Post, 12-18:(A)1.

James A. Baker III
Secretary of the Treasury
of the United States

7

[Election] campaigns have degenerated into a series of 30-second [TV] spots. You can't ex-

WHAT THEY SAID IN 1987

(JAMES A. BAKER III)

plain the budget deficit, the trade deficit and arms control in 30 seconds.

The Christian Science Monitor, 2-13:22.

Joseph L. Bernardin
Roman Catholic Archbishop
of Chicago

1

Bishops should not be political partisans. But they can specify, examine and press in the public debate the moral dimensions of issues.

USA Today, 11-16:(A)8.

Joseph R. Biden, Jr.
United States Senator,
D-Delaware; Candidate for the 1988
Democratic Presidential nomination

2

The standard of judgment [in politics] is no longer results but the flickering image of seriousness, skillfully crafted to squeeze into 30 seconds on the nightly [TV] news. In this world, emotion has become suspect—the accepted style is smooth, antiseptic and passionless.

Announcing his candidacy
for President, Wilmington, Del.,
June 9/The New York Times, 6-10:10.

3

[Announcing his dropping out of the Presidential race because of a controversy over his using sections of speeches of others, and over his college and law-school record]: Although it's awfully clear to me what choice I have to make, I have to tell you honestly I do it with incredible reluctance, and it makes me angry. I'm angry at myself for having been put in the position—put myself in the position—of having to make this choice. And I am no less frustrated for the environment of Presidential politics that makes it so difficult to let the American people measure the whole Joe Biden and not just misstatements I have made.

News conference, Washington,
Sept. 23/The New York Times, 9-24:1.

Merle Black
Professor of political science,
University of North Carolina

4

In the South, the Democratic candidates [for the 1988 Presidential nomination] have to combine enough progressive positions to turn out both blacks and blue-collar whites with enough conservative positions to keep from alienating middle-class whites. How you do that without appearing philosophically inconsistent is the million-dollar question.

Los Angeles Times, 11-22:(I)1.

David L. Boren
United States Senator,
D-Oklahoma

5

[Supporting legislation designed to bring down and equalize the cost of political campaigns]: Can [opponents of the legislation] honestly say it is healthy for the system that competition for the highest offices in this land . . . are based on which candidate can raise the most money?

Los Angeles Times, 9-16:(I)8.

Vince Breglio
Campaign manager for
Alexander Haig's bid
for the 1988 Republican
Presidential nomination

6

Al Haig has not learned the subtleties of political speech. He says what's on his mind. It's the only way he knows how to behave. He doesn't equivocate. He doesn't back away. He doesn't slide along an ideological scale to hit a particular group because they may be available. He calls issues like he sees them . . . To me, Al Haig is like the Boston *Celtics* [basketball team]. He doesn't panic, he knows who he is, he keeps coming back at you.

Interview/The New York Times,
10-21:7.

David Broder
Journalist

1

Every good politician will attempt to work the press. If you live in a country where public opinion ultimately decides public policy, any politician who's at all serious is going to try to manage public opinion, and that means working the press. So they all do it . . . [The late President] John Kennedy was the most successful manipulator. He knew the press inside and out, he knew most of the reporters who were covering him inside and out, and he was diabolically clever about using friendship, and skill, and charm, and humor, and the targeted release of information to manage the press.

Interview/USA Today, 8-13:(A)13.

Dale Bumpers
United States Senator,
D-Arkansas; Candidate for the 1988
Democratic Presidential nomination

2

This [Reagan] Administration, like the Nixon Administration, clearly flouts the law, rather than tries to change it or live with it. I doubt seriously whether any Administration has had more people leave under disgrace or indictment.

The New York Times, 5-15:10.

Clair Burgener
Former chairman,
California Republican Party

3

Politics has become one giant cash register. I think that undermines confidence in the political process.

The Christian Science Monitor, 3-17:7.

Walter Dean Burnham
Professor of political science,
Massachusetts Institute
of Technology

4

In general, people choose to abstain [from voting] when politics is of no particular interest to them. It's not a question of ideology or of the masses wanting to break free, but of the fact that we have a system organized in such a way that it simply has no relevance to everyday life, especially at the bottom of the social scale.

The Christian Science Monitor, 2-13:21.

James MacGregor Burns
Historian, Williams College

5

Millions of Americans just don't think it makes much difference whom they vote for. They are cynical about the system and feel they are not provided with big contrasts. There's so much emphasis on consensus [that] voters see both sides working together against them. So there's apathy.

The Christian Science Monitor, 2-13:21.

6

[President] Reagan has brilliantly regenerated the Republican Party by making it into an ideological party . . . The Democrats could learn a great deal from the Republicans. The Republicans decided fundamentally who they were, and they made that work.

At American Political Science
Association meeting, Chicago/
The Washington Post, 9-7:(A)14.

Robert C. Byrd
United States Senator,
D-West Virginia

7

[On last year's Democratic Party victories in the Congressional elections]: Clearly, something happened on Election Day last November. The American people voted for change. And change they will have. The time of business as usual is over. I believe we Democrats were placed back in the leadership of the chamber [the Senate] for a very specific reason: to begin the task of fitting political actions and rhetoric to the reality of the world in which we live.

The New York Times, 1-7:12.

WHAT THEY SAID IN 1987

Jimmy Carter
Former President
of the United States

1

I think the crimes of the Iran-contra affair are much more serious than those of Watergate, but I don't think there's a desire on the part of the news media or the American people to punish President Reagan as there was against [former President] Richard Nixon [in the Watergate affair] . . . We've been through one impeachment episode with Watergate. I don't think we want to see our nation go through that experience again. And also, there's an inclination to protect [Reagan] from his own mistakes, his own foibles, his own misleading statements, his own improprieties. So I don't think we'll pursue the Iran-contra revelations to a punitive stage, as it relates to Reagan.

Interview, Washington/
The Christian Science Monitor,
6-5:3.

2

[On the 1988 Presidential race]: I think the American people will be looking for someone who will tell the truth and be competent and compassionate. There is a lot of similarity between what has occurred this time and in 1976 . . . I think everyone in the 1988 Presidential campaigns has to realize that the American people are fed up with constant misstatements of fact that have been coming from the White House for the past six years . . . I think it is very good for the American people and the press to be very demanding: "Are you telling the truth? Are you a person of integrity? Can we depend on the history of your past life?" . . . I have personally always been in favor of a long, difficult testing campaign because it requires candidates to learn a lot more about this country than they would otherwise learn, and it lets the American people learn a lot about the candidates.

Plains, Ga., Oct. 4/
Los Angeles Times,
10-5:(I)19.

Shirley Chisholm
Chair,
National Political Congress
for Black Women;
Former United States Representative,
D-New York

3

Unless we [black women] can show that we can deliver delegate votes at [political] conventions, that we can really have some determination over the issues on the national agenda or the platform of the party, we will continue to be nothing but workhorses for the political parties and not be considered an important part of the American political scene. Our mission is to empower black women to run for office from small municipalities to the Congress. We must become visible at all levels. Since I left Congress, only one black woman—Cardis Collins, D-Illinois—remains, and most political offices held by black women are on the lower echelons. Black women are moving sideways on the lower end of the ladder.

Interview/USA Today, 8-26:(A)9.

John E. Chubb
Senior fellow,
Brookings Institution

4

[On Vice President George Bush, who is a candidate for the 1988 Republican Presidential nomination]: You can't create a vision out of whole cloth. His great weakness is that he does not stand for anything clear at all . . . It's not clear that Bush ever stood strongly for any portion of the Republican set of ideas. And for him to try at this point to identify clearly with any portion of Republicanism would be fruitless . . . It's artificial. You either stand for something and it's authentic, or eventually people are going to see through it.

The Christian Science Monitor, 10-13:36.

Clark M. Clifford
Former Secretary of Defense
of the United States

5

[On the use of TV by candidates in an election campaign]: Someday some very dangerous

(CLARK M. CLIFFORD)

fellow could be enormously appealing on television and we would fear for our country. If we've gotten to the point where the tube is so important, the presentation of the candidate, his charm, his voice—and these are what impress people—then we may have run into trouble.

The Christian Science Monitor,
2-13:22.

Tony Coelho
United States Representative,
D-California

1

The one thing that sold [President Reagan] was his super-integrity. He has lost that [because of the Iran-contra scandal], and now everything—his inattention to detail, his age, his health—becomes an issue.

U.S. News & World Report,
1-26:20.

Mario M. Cuomo
Governor of New York (D)

2

In 1982, when [New York City] Mayor [Edward] Koch was ahead of me by 38 percentage points, people said I couldn't win [the Governorship] because I could never get the Jewish vote. I won the Governor's race over Koch, who up till then was the most popular politician in the state. So I reject this line that an Italian can't be President. Ethnicity is part of our strength. Americans relish it . . . I say it's a lot of baloney that this country is still so crude that people won't vote for a Jew, an Italian, a black person.

Interview, Jan. 7/
The Washington Post, 1-9:(A)23.

3

Words and phrases like "conservative," "liberal" may be unavoidable habits of our expression, but they are not useful as meaningful descriptions of the complex forces with which our policies must contend.

At Tulane University, Feb. 16/
The New York Times, 2-17:7.

4

[On the current candidates for the 1988 Democratic Presidential nomination]: To be trite but terribly true, it is much too early to make any significant judgment on this field of candidates. A good deal of the analysis is presumptuous, premature and evidences to me a lack of knowledge of history. It does not take a great deal to make a person a celebrity. Stars are born in every primary.

Interview/
The New York Times, 6-29:13.

5

[On his current visit to the Soviet Union]: I wouldn't do this because I was trying to get ready for a Presidential bid [in 1988]. There is no Presidential bid for me. There never will be, because we [Democrats] will win in 1988, and the person who wins will be there for eight years. And eight years from now, no one will remember my name.

Interview, Moscow, Sept. 23/
The Washington Post, 9-24:(A)35.

6

I really don't want to be President in the sense that this is my objective. I really don't have it as my objective, and from the beginning I have not had it as my objective. They, the [current announced] candidates, have it as their objective. They felt that destiny called them or they wanted it or they were needed, whatever their personal motivation, which I am sure was the very best motivation. I did not have the same motivation. I did not feel I was called by destiny. I did not feel it was essential for the good of the country [that] I run [for President in 1988]. I did not feel I was the best or the only [one] and I did not feel I needed it for myself, and that is the truth of it, and I am not embarrassed by that. That doesn't mean I am not self-confident . . . But I have never felt this powerful impulse. That does not mean I am

(MARIO M. CUOMO)

afraid of it or I wouldn't do it if I felt I must do it. I just don't feel that way, never have.

Interview/
Los Angeles Times, 10-25:(I)9.

Robert J. Dole
United States Senator,
R-Kansas; Candidate for
the 1988 Republican
Presidential nomination

1

Public financing of Senate [election] campaigns impinges on an individual's right to support voluntarily those political candidates of his or her choice; public financing diminishes—not increases—an individual's opportunity to participate in the political process . . . Right now, budget conferees—at least the Democratic ones—are struggling to come up with a fiscal 1988 budget. I believe if you ask them, what would you think of creating a new government "entitlement program" costing millions of dollars, they would not look kindly upon it. And yet that is what public financing of Senate campaigns would be—an outright subsidy for those seeking re-election.

June 16/
The Washington Post,
6-18:(A)22.

2

I'd like to see 50 wheelchairs in this audience. I'd like to see 50 black faces, 50 Hispanics, 50 Asian-Americans. We [Republicans] get a rap that we don't care about people who have real problems. We turn our back on the disabled. We don't like low-income Americans. We don't like old people. We don't care much for black people or brown people or Asian-Americans or white people. We're sort of a hard-hearted party. The upper crust. You don't want to be in the upper crust, you can't be a Republican. The bottom line is how you treat others. And we [Republicans] have an obligation

and a responsibility and, above all, an opportunity to open up the doors of this Party.

At Young Republican
National Federation convention,
Seattle, July 11/
The New York Times, 7-13:1

Michael S. Dukakis
Governor of Massachusetts (D);
Candidate for the 1988
Democratic Presidential nomination

3

[On the difficulties for Governors running a state and running for the Presidency at the same time]: I don't like the idea that, somehow, public servants are disqualified from seeking the Presidency. I don't want an America where only full-time professional candidates are eligible. If that's what the system is becoming, then now may be a very good time to start changing the system.

News conference, Boston, March 16/
The New York Times, 3-17:8.

4

If there are three unique qualities I bring to this [Presidential] campaign, they are, first, a track record on economic issues . . . secondly, I have been a chief executive . . . and . . . thirdly, no Republican is going to hang a tax-and-spend label on Mike Dukakis. I've balanced nine budgets in a row; I've cut taxes five times in the last four years, and we still commit a lot of resources in Massachusetts to economic development, health care and education.

At Hispanic Presidential Forum,
Los Angeles, Aug. 24/
Los Angeles Times, 8-26:(I)12.

Richard J. Durbin
United States Representative,
D-Illinois

5

[The 1984 election was] the first time since we have extended the vote to 18-year-olds that a Republican candidate for President [Reagan] won a substantial majority of the 18-to-29 voting block . . . Many [Democrats in Congress]

(RICHARD J. DURBIN)

have [had] their eyes opened about what young people are thinking about, about their attitudes toward issues. We have a tendency to think that most young people have the same values we did when we were their age. That isn't true. Things have changed.

The Christian Science Monitor, 4-29:1,4.

Frank J. Fahrenkopf, Jr.
Chairman,
Republican National Committee

1

Compassion [is] a word we [Republicans] should never be afraid to use. Despite what the Democrats think, compassion doesn't belong just to them. The Republican Party does not need solutions to problems bound by hard-nosed approaches with little or no concern for people . . . Concern over budget deficits will not override the concern of even the most conservative voter worried about losing the family farm, sending a child to college, or the need to clean up a toxic-waste site.

At Republican National
Committee meeting, Washington/
The Washington Post, 1-24:(A)3.

2

Democratic politicians may definitely stroke the soft keys of moderation and conservatism back home, but when you cut them to the bone, they bleed red ink, the red ink of the big-spending, big-government liberal Democrat . . . To Southern Democrats, we say, "Your patience and your steadfast loyalty [to the Democratic Party] is admirable." But after George McGovern, after Jimmy Carter, after Walter Mondale, after Gary Hart, consider the choices your Party is again offering.

At Meeting of Republican
National Committee, New Orleans,
June 26/The New York Times, 6-27:7.

3

[Addressing Southern state legislators]: The national Democratic Party is a liability to you,

a fracture point between you and your constituents. How much longer can you support a Party so much at odds with the beliefs, the values and the traditions of the South? . . . The people of the South are fed up with the national Democratic Party.

At Southern Legislative Conference,
Little Rock, Ark., Aug. 18/
The Washington Post, 8-19:(A)4.

4

[On Gary Hart's decision to re-enter the race for the 1988 Democratic Presidential nomination after withdrawing earlier in the year in the wake of a sex scandal]: It seems only fitting that during the Christmas season . . . the Democrats would be visited by the ghost of candidate past. What it really shows is the disarray of the Democratic Party going into 1988, when a man who, in effect, resigned from the race in disgrace feels that he can come back and win the nomination.

Dec. 15/
Los Angeles Times, 12-16:(I)14.

Dianne Feinstein
Mayor of San Francisco

5

Our [Democratic] Party has a much more difficult time because it is a much broader and much more diverse party. It takes in the interests of many groups of people. It is very difficult to work out a program that appeals broadly to America. And that's what has to be done. That's a challenge.

Interview, San Francisco/
Los Angeles Times, 3-8:(I)27.

David Frost
Interviewer

6

There are problems with [interviewing] politicians who play safe. The most fearless thing they'll do is come out against road accidents. Ask some politicians their favorite color, and they'll say "plaid." I once had a Senator who actually said at one point, stepping into safe pa-

211

WHAT THEY SAID IN 1987

triotism: "Where would this country be without this great land of ours?" Isn't that wonderful?

Interview/USA Today, 3-26:(A)11.

Curtis B. Gans
Director,
Committee for the Study
of the American Electorate

1

If you have lower and lower voting, the more our politics becomes the province of the intensely interested. Whether they are anti-abortion or anti-gun control, they exercise a much bigger influence. Also, if we do not participate, we weaken the spirit of voluntarism that is so necessary for society.

The Christian Science Monitor, 2-13:22.

Richard A. Gephardt
United States Representative,
D-Indiana; Candidate for the 1988
Democratic Presidential nomination

2

I stand before you as a member of the Party that has won the White House only once in the last five elections [the Democratic Party]—a Party that has been equated, fairly or unfairly, with soft-headedness and faint-heartedness. The person Democrats nominate to carry our standard next year must be someone who has the record of resolve . . . to reclaim our rightful position as the Party of a strong America.

Campaign address, Washington,
Sept. 25/The Washington Post, 9-26:(A)3.

David R. Gergen
Editor,
"U.S. News & World Report";
Former Director of Communications
for President of the United States
Ronald Reagan

3

[On political candidates who give up their candidacy because of an embarrassing revela-

tion revealed by opponents or in the press]: The single most important rule of damage control is to know all the damage before the rest of the world does. When you're in a running story and you don't know where the bottom is, more often than not it will fall out from under you.

The New York Times, 9-28:12.

Albert Gore, Jr.
United States Senator,
D-Tennessee; Candidate for the 1988
Democratic Presidential nomination

4

[Announcing his candidacy for President]: [The U.S. needs a leader to match Soviet leader Mikhail Gorbachev,] who combines youthful energy and innovation with experience . . . a leader who can match him, test him, bargain with him, and make the most of this historic opportunity for a safer, saner world. Twenty-seven years ago, the voters of America, looking for the strength and hope of a new generation, replaced the oldest man ever to serve in the office of the Presidency [Dwight Eisenhower] with the youngest ever to be elected to that office [John Kennedy]. I believe they are ready to do so again.

Carthage, Tenn., June 29/
The Christian Science Monitor, 6-30:3.

Alexander M. Haig, Jr.
Former Secretary of State
of the United States;
Candidate for the 1988
Republican Presidential nomination

5

[On his decision to run for the 1988 Republican Presidential nomination]: If the Republican Party picks its candidate on pedigree or pecking order instead of an assessment of who can win [the race] is irrelevant. Since World War II we have elected three Republicans. If they have any common characteristic, it was their ability to attract traditional Democratic and independent voters. That means [being] something more than simply "Mr. Republican." And where we

(ALEXANDER M. HAIG, JR.)

have gone that route [nominating "Mr. Republican"], we take a bath.

The Christian Science Monitor, 6-15:6.

1

I am taking a distancing position from the Reagan Presidency. I don't think a business-as-usual Republican candidate who goes around the country telling the American people how good they have it [provides any solutions to national problems]. Don't tell that to somebody in the energy sector of America. Don't tell that to somebody in the agricultural sector of America. Don't tell that to the rust-bucket manufacturing belt along the Great Lakes who have been experiencing down times and dislocation. Don't tell that to our friends abroad, who look to America's foreign policy for consistency and reliability.

News conference, Los Angeles,
Aug. 24/Los Angeles Times, 8-25:(I)4.

2

[Arguing against Presidential candidates discussing their personal lives during a campaign]: I've always held that the Presidency as an institution is something more than just the qualifications of the candidate and professional talent. It's also a very important measure of the character of the individual, and anyone who throws his helmet in the ring, as [humorist] Mort Sahl said I did, can and should expect probing questions. But if I'm secure in my assessment of myself, my answer to you [about his personal life] is going to be, "It's none of your damn business."

Interview/USA Today, 12-21:(A)13.

Michael Harrington
Co-chair,
Democratic Socialists
of America

3

[On his organization]: It is democratic socialist, as that would be defined, let's say, by

railroad labor leader Eugene Debs, who founded the Social Democratic Party of America in 1905; by people like Willy Brandt, the former Chancellor of West Germany; by the Prime Ministers of Spain, Sweden and Norway; and by Neil Kinnock of Britain's Labor Party. That is to say, we are for democracy with a small "d." We are against any dictatorship, even if it calls itself socialist . . . I regard the Soviet Union as a dictatorship over the working people, which I'm against. Most Communists regard it as a society run by the workers. I would say the main thing that distinguishes socialists and Communists is that socialists are the most consistent democrats in the world, whereas Communists defend dictatorships as being a way to have a democracy. I think that's just a little too much.

Interview/
USA Today, 10-7:(A)11.

Gary Hart
Former United States Senator,
D-Colorado; Candidate for the 1988
Democratic Presidential nomination

4

[On suggestions in the press of his involvement in a recent extra-marital affair and its effect on his candidacy for President]: Last month, when I announced my candidacy for the Presidency, I said that all candidates should be tested and that all of us should hold ourselves to the highest possible standards—of competence to govern, of character, of vision and of leadership. I believe that even more today than I did then. And I had a very good idea of what I meant when I made that statement. Since the very first day I entered public life, I have always held myself to a high standard of public and private conduct, and I always will. But the events of the past few days have also taught me that for some of us in public life even the most commonplace and appropriate behavior can be misconstrued by some to be improper. This just means that I have to raise my own personal standard even higher. Did I make a mistake by putting myself in circumstances that could be misconstrued? Of course I did. That goes with-

(GARY HART)

out saying. Did I do anything immoral? I absolutely did not.

*Before American Newspaper
Publishers Association, New York,
May 5/The New York Times, 5-6:16.*

1

[Announcing his withdrawal from the race for the 1988 Democratic Presidential nomination because of suggestions in the press of a recent extra-marital affair]: We're all going to have to seriously question the system for selecting our national leaders, that reduces the press of this nation to hunters and Presidential candidates to being hunted, that has reporters in bushes, false and inaccurate stories printed, photographers peeking in our windows, swarms of helicopters hovering over our roof, and my very strong wife close to tears because she can't even get in her own house at night without being harassed . . . Politics in this country—take it from me—is on the verge of becoming another form of athletic competition or sporting match. We all better do something to make this system work, or we're all going to be soon rephrasing Jefferson to say: I tremble for my country when I think we may in fact get the kind of leaders we deserve.

*News conference, Denver, May 8/
Los Angeles Times, 5-9:(I)27.*

2

[On his decision to re-enter the race for the 1988 Democratic Presidential nomination after withdrawing earlier in the year in the wake of a sex scandal]: I intend to resume my Presidential candidacy and let the people decide. This will not be like any campaign you've ever seen, because I am going directly to the people. I don't have a national headquarters or staff. I don't have any money. I don't have pollsters or consultants or media advisers or political endorsements. But I have something better. I have the power of ideas and I can govern this country. Let's let the people decide. I'm back in the race.

*Concord, N.H., Dec. 15/
The Washington Post, 12-16:(A)1.*

Howell Heflin
*United States Senator,
D-Alabama*

3

Southern politics are changing. Basically, it's become a situation of groups. You've got about 25 percent blacks, and they're liberal Democrats; about 25 percent Republicans, and they're hard-core conservatives; and the rest I call independents. They aren't as right-wing, but they're basically conservative in nature.

*Interview, Rainbow City, Alabama/
The Washington Post, 9-7:(A)5.*

Stephen Hess
Scholar, Brookings Institution

4

[On the press' scrutiny of the private lives of Presidential candidates]: There are appropriate actions by the press, given different levels of political office. We do not need to hold the candidate for water commissioner up to the same kind of scrutiny that we do [a candidate] for President. Some of the criticism [of the press] comes up because of the question, "Would you want your neighbor to get this level of scrutiny?" The answer would be no. But we are talking about very few people, a dozen out of 243 million, who say, "I want to be leader of the Free World." Those people do lose their right of privacy. They are self-annointed.

The Christian Science Monitor, 5-12:3.

Harrison Hickman
*Democratic Party
political analyst*

5

[On the proliferation of debates among candidates for the 1988 Democratic Presidential nomination]: We have a race where even the front runners are midgets in the public's mind. Every one of them needs as much exposure as they can get. Remember who the audience is [at the debates]: people who tend to be opinion leaders, the press, or local pols and contribu-

(HARRISON HICKMAN)

tors and activists. For a formless, leaderless field, that is a critical group right now.

The Washington Post,
8-31:(A)4.

Henry J. Hyde
United States Representative,
R-Illinois

1

[On the Republican situation in the 1988 Presidential election with the departure from office next year of President Reagan]: That's a tough one because there's only one Ronald Reagan. His philosophy is transferable, his persona is not.

The New York Times,
6-17:12.

Jesse L. Jackson
Civil-rights leader;
Candidate for
the 1988 Democratic
Presidential nomination

2

[On his quest for the Presidential nomination]: They say I'm leading in New York because of high name recognition. I'm leading in California because of high name recognition. I'm leading in North and South Carolina because of high name recognition. Well, that's true. But I wasn't born with high name recognition! I earned high name recognition! Jesse Jackson, your name is Number 1 because of just recognition. People don't recognize the stepson of a janitor born to a teen-age mother. If my name was Jesse J. Rockefeller, that might mean something. If my name was Jesse Joe Kennedy, that might mean something. But I'm Jesse Jackson from Greenville, South Carolina, and what does my name mean? My name doesn't mean money. My name doesn't mean oil. My name means service.

At Labor Day rally,
Brooklyn, N.Y., Sept. 7/
The Washington Post, 10-5:(A)3.

3

The party did not decide in 1932 that a man in a wheelchair [Franklin Roosevelt] could win [the Presidency], but the people did, and it worked. The party did not decide in 1960 that a Catholic [John Kennedy] could win, but the people did, and we prevailed . . . If one does not vote for me because I do not make sense, then they have a right . . . If one does not vote for me because I'm black, I leave that in God's hand.

Sept. 7/
The Washington Post, 9-8:(A)11.

4

I have a much bigger following now [than in 1984], a bigger responsibility. Last time my rhetoric was sufficient to do what I had to do— open up the [political] process, demand room for progressive-thinking people, register new voters. You know, there's a right wing and a left wing, and it takes both to fly a plane. My concern is about 85 million voters in neither wing: They're in the belly of the plane. If one perceives that some changes have taken place, they have. I do not resist growing. I do not resist maturing. I do not resist expanding.

Interview/Mother Jones, October:31.

5

If I can win [the Presidency], family farmers can win . . . If I can win, any American can win. If I cannot win, most Americans cannot win . . . Together, we are the people. Together, we are the majority.

Campaigning in Iowa/
Los Angeles Times, 12-7:(I)20.

John E. Jacob
President,
National Urban League

6

The black vote [in the 1988 Presidential election] will hinge on whether the parties and the candidates are convincing in their policies regarding racism, equity in education and aggressive reforms that meet the health, housing and survival needs of the poorest among

215

(JOHN E. JACOB)

us . . . For both parties, the road to the White House leads through Houston's Third Ward, through Watts [in Los Angeles], through [New York's] Harlem, through Chicago's South Side. The major parties are in peril if they ignore that fact.

*At National
Urban League convention, Houston,
July 19/The New York Times, 7-20:8.*

Jack Kemp
*United States Representative,
R-New York; Candidate for the 1988
Republican Presidential nomination*

1

Somewhere along the way, my [Republican] Party blundered. It strayed from the principles of Abraham Lincoln. And I hope today to lead it back to those principles. I want my Party to be a Lincoln party, not a Hoover party.

*Before League of United States
Latin American Citizens,
Corpus Christi, Texas, June 26/
The Washington Post, 6-27:(A)3.*

2

I don't think it is right to defend the status quo, because not everybody has access to the status quo. I favor change. I take teasing over using words like "progressive" and "conservative" [in describing himself] at the same time. On foreign policy, defense and fiscal responsibility, you can probably pick where Kemp is going to be conservative. But on things like taxes, was I a conservative, progressive or a reformer? I think I was a reformer. On trade, I think I would probably come down as liberal, with a little "L."

*Interview/
Los Angeles Times, 6-29:(I)16.*

3

The difference in the Republican Party is between the conservative who believes in the status quo and the conservative who believes in traditional values, change, progress, reform,

the future, technology, unlimited opportunity, equal opportunity for everybody. While I have conservative values and am conservative on fiscal policy and on defense policy, I am progressive with regard to my belief in the Republican Party being a Lincoln party. I don't believe in turning my back on the poor, the aged and minorities.

Interview/USA Today, 12-14:(A)13.

Edward M. Kennedy
*United States Senator,
D-Massachusetts*

4

[Giving advice to 1988 Democratic Presidential candidates]: Speak of a vision of the future, work hard, and get a good road map of Iowa.

USA Today, 7-1:(A)4.

5

I don't think about being President any more. I don't think about it any less, either.

Newsweek, 10-12:23.

Paul G. Kirk, Jr.
*Chairman,
Democratic National Committee*

6

[Calling for an end to Democratic political infighting, as occurred in the 1984 nomination campaigns]: My memory of the 1984 Democratic nomination contest is one of self-inflicted political wounds, of meaningless straw polls, of campaigns devoting . . . effort to tearing down the opposing Democratic candidates, to trashing our traditional base constituencies, to bashing the Party itself, and to bickering about nominating rules and internal procedures . . . I'm aware of the pressures of a Presidential campaign . . . [But] the bottom line is, how much do you want to win in 1988?

*At National Press Club,
Washington, March 11/
The Washington Post, 3-12:(A)1,7.*

(PAUL G. KIRK, JR.)

1

[On Democratic-Republican agreement to hold four candidate debates during the 1988 Presidential election campaign]: The agreement . . . takes [the Commission on Presidential Debates] a long step toward the permanent institutionalization of debates in the general-election process and . . . in fulfilling our roles as political parties in educating the electorate about the views and philosophies of our two parties.

Washington, July 7/
The Christian Science Monitor, 7-8:3.

2

I hope those who are listening today will record it as a sign of political maturity for the national Democratic Party to acknowledge that there have been too many good, solid Democrats of the South who have split the ticket in recent national elections . . . The Democratic Party will prevail nationally in 1988 only if it is truly competitive in America's South. And before expecting the voters of the South to respond to the national Democratic Party next November, I believe the Democratic Party must first listen to the voters of the South between now and then.

Atlanta/
The Washington Post, 7-21:(A)5.

3

The cherished principles of the Democratic Party cannot embody a single issue. A majority candidate has never won and no President can successfully govern from an agenda or with policies seen as elitist, or extreme or bound to rigid ideologies or narrow interests.

Atlanta/
The Washington Post, 7-21:(A)5.

Jeane J. Kirkpatrick
Former United States
Ambassador/Permanent Representative
to the United Nations

4

Probably for the first time ever, there are about as many people, women, prepared to vote for you because you are a woman, as people, meaning men, ready to vote against you because you are a woman . . . For better or worse, women have to be prepared to play by the same criteria as men are judged by. And when [former Presidential candidate] Ed Muskie cried in the snow, everybody thought it hurt him. And I'm afraid that when [aspiring Presidential candidate] Pat Schroeder cried, a lot of people concluded that was inappropriate. I think everybody's wrong in both cases. I think that's really wrong. There is nothing wrong with crying, men or women. It's a perfectly civilized way to express emotion.

Interview, Washington/
The New York Times, 11-2:14.

Edward I. Koch
Mayor of New York

5

Some Democrats seem to be straining for an image which avoids association with the cities. But I maintain that there is, in fact, nothing to be embarrassed about at the core of the Democratic Party's traditional political strength—and that is the urban Northeast and Midwest, the poor and lower-middle and middle classes, ethnic and minority groups, and regions which are most severely affected by economic change and dislocation. We are the party of the cities. If we are ashamed of that, or ignorant of that, it will come home to haunt us in [the] November [elections].

Before Economic Club of Detroit,
April 27/The New York Times, 4-28:10.

6

With respect to [President] Reagan, I happen to like him. He's a very decent human being. When I was out at Ellis Island this week, I was sitting there, rather cold, and he had a coat on, and he says, "You shouldn't be here without a coat!" I think that's rather sweet. He's going to go down in history as a President who acted positively on the country, and moved it in his philosophical direction. Now, you can describe the move as good, bad, indifferent, but that he

(EDWARD I. KOCH)

moved the country philosophically, there's no question about it.

Interview/USA Today, 5-8:(A)11.

Richard D. Lamm
Former Governor of Colorado (D)

1

Politics, like theatre, is one of those things where you've got to be wise enough to know when to leave.

Jan. 13/USA Today, 1-14:(A)2.

Jim Leach
United States Representative,
R-Iowa

2

If the trend toward more expensive [election] races, and thus heavier financial obligations for candidates, is not curbed, individuals elected to Congress will increasingly become indebted to either big business or big labor.

Washington, June 18/
Los Angeles Times, 6-19:(I)19.

Ann F. Lewis
Director,
Americans for Democratic Action;
Former director,
Democratic National Committee

3

[On Gary Hart's recent withdrawal from the Presidential race because of a sex scandal]: From the moment you enter the world of a Presidential campaign, the normal rules no longer seem to apply. You're in a vacuum-sealed universe where everyday concerns no longer exist. It's easy to forget the rules of the real world. But they are neither expired nor suspended—they're waiting for you right out-side the door.

The New York Times, 5-19:17.

4

[Saying a woman should run for President]: Presidential campaigns are too much the last locker room of American politics.

USA today, 6-15:(A)8.

Ken Maddy
California State Senator

5

[On the increasing exposure of politicians' private vices by the press]: There is a growing awareness by politicians at all levels . . . that a new era of journalism has been coming. When I first came up here in 1970, it was [known but] unwritten that we had our drunks—and the womanizing fell into that same category. Now all of us recognize anything is fair game for the press.

Interview, Sacramento/
Los Angeles Times, 6-1:(I)1.

Paul Maslin
Democratic Party
public-opinion analyst

6

[President] Reagan's personal popularity, as evidenced in the 1986 elections, can no longer sting the Democratic Party. There is no elec-toral worry any more about Ronald Reagan. That was certainly not the case for the first five or even six years of his Presidency. It only dawned on people last year that he would not have a major impact on the outcome of the elec-tions, and in fact he didn't.

The New York Times, 1-27:9.

Terence R. McAuliffe
Finance chairman,
1988 Presidential campaign
of Representative Richard Gephardt

7

[On the growing difficulty of obtaining fi-nancing for political campaigns due to in-creased costs and inability of some candidates to repay loans]: There is a general feeling out there in all the campaigns that it is really diffi-

(TERENCE R. McAULIFFE)

cult to repay campaign debt. If the money isn't there, I think a lot of candidates are going to have to look at bowing out rather than going into debt. The horror stories about creditors coming out after debts would certainly not be a pleasant experience.

The New York Times, 6-16:35.

Ann McBride
Senior vice president,
Common Cause

1

Traditionally, honoraria are supposed to be given a member [of the U.S. Senate] giving a speech. What one is hearing more and more about, however, is a Senator simply going and having breakfast or lunch with 10 or 12 people and being paid $2,000. Very often, the honorarium is given in a beautiful location where, in addition, expenses are paid. What the Senator does for the money varies, but the ultimate impact is the same: Special interests gain access through money.

Interview/USA Today, 5-20:(A)15.

Gary McDowell
Former Associate Director
of Public Affairs,
Department of Justice
of the United States

2

Ultimately, the libertarian and conservative approaches to law and Constitutional interpretation are irreconcilably different . . . The fact is that the economic libertarians are much closer to liberal activists on the left than they are to the conservative advocates of restraint on the right. Their objective is not to forsake judicial activism but only to redirect it to include their main objective—an expansive notion of property rights. As a result, the Constitution is currently beset from both the left and the right by those who would like to see it transformed through judicial interpretation into what they think it should mean . . . The premises of judi-

cial activism implicit in the Constitutional theories of those on the libertarian right are fundamentally at odds with the Constitutional theories of those within the traditional conservative fold.

At discussion of
the Federalist Society, April 4/
The Wall Street Journal, 11-10:34.

Joshua Meyrowitz
Professor of communications,
University of New Hampshire

3

[On political candidates' use of TV as a campaign tool]: [TV in general] fools us into thinking that we know our candidates . . . [The video approach is] brilliant from the practical stance of getting one's candidate across. But the question is, how good is it for the country and getting leaders in the White House? . . . The very things that might look good—quick thinking, running and throwing a football—are not things that make a good President. Those are good characteristics for a public-relations person.

Los Angeles Times, 11-22:(I)38.

Walter F. Mondale
Former Vice President
of the United States;
1984 Democratic Presidential nominee

4

[On his being out of politics since he lost the 1984 Presidential election]: I miss people. I miss the fight on issues. In our system, at about 11:30 on election night, they just push you off the edge of the cliff—and that's it. You might scream on the way down, but you're going to hit the bottom, and you're not going to be in elective office. It's so abrupt.

Interview, Washington/
The New York Times, 3-4:24.

5

[On deciding to run for the presidency]: It's the toughest decision in the world, and there are no manuals . . . You're going to get hurt unless you go into it all-out, with a singleness

WHAT THEY SAID IN 1987

of concentration that defies human nature. And then you have got to be able to ask that most arrogant of all questions. You have to look in the mirror and say, "I'd be the best President." Boy, that's hard for an honest man to do.

Interview/
The Washington Post, 3-17:(A)14.

1

I certainly think [liberalism has a future]. The genius of the country is its ability to adjust to change. We go through periods in which we become convinced that some politicians with old ideas wrapped in some new rhetorical package will save us. Then we open the package, and it is the same old conservative policies that cost us before. And people decide that they want a change from that.

Interview/USA Today, 9-28:(A)15.

Sid Morrison
United States Representative,
R-Washington

2

We [Republicans] need to get away from dependence on the far right and come back a little closer to where America really is. If we're ever going to be a majority party, we have to lead where America wants to follow.

At conference of Republican
House members, New York/
Los Angeles Times, 3-28:(I)21.

Daniel P. Moynihan
United States Senator,
D-New York

3

If the Democratic Party doesn't win the Presidency in 1988, we're going to have to look for a new country.

Broadcast interview/
"News Forum," NBC-TV,11-29.

Irene Natividad
Executive director,
National Women's Political Caucus

4

One of our missions is to transfer the political expertise we have developed on a national level to the state and local levels. We want to train women to run for local offices because if we don't feed that pipeline, we won't have state winners. We have to insure that we have more wins [by women] at the local level, for that is where it all starts.

Interview, Washington/
The New York Times, 11-18:14.

Sam Nunn
United States Senator,
D-Georgia

5

When I ran for the Senate, I sat down one night after doing a good bit of thinking about it. And I wrote on a yellow pad all the reasons I should run, and I wrote on the other side of the sheet all the reasons I shouldn't run. The final analytical product—after going through all of that—came down not to those factors but whether I would be happy the rest of my life sitting back, wondering what would have happened had I run. And I concluded that that would be a prospect I didn't want to go through. I wanted to know that I'd either run and lost and had given it my best—or that I had decided not to. In that case, I wanted to run bad. It was an intuitive type of thing. At that stage, I had very little chance of winning, but I did not want to sit back and be haunted the rest of my life. If I ever conclude that about the Presidency, then I'll have my answer [about running for that office].

Interview/
U.S. News & World Report, 1-19:20.

6

When it comes to Presidential aspirations, those of us in Congress can be divided into five separate groups. The first group includes five members who are actively running for the job of President of the United States. The second

(SAM NUNN)

group includes two members who are stealthily testing the waters for the same job. The third group consists of one lonely member who has stated categorically that he will not run. The fourth group consists of four members who are under the age of 35 and are barred by the Constitution from being President. The fifth and last group contains the remaining 535 members of Congress. They all have sufficient egos to believe they are eminently qualified to be President. But while they are not preparing to run for President, they have not completely closed the door.

At Jefferson-Jackson Dinner,
Atlanta, Feb. 20/
The Washington Post, 3-3:(A)22.

Kirk O'Donnell
President,
Center for National Policy

1

The Democrats found out under the Reagan Administration that they could no longer take the support of young people for granted . . . One of the things that [Congressional Democrats] discovered is that [the late President] John F. Kennedy was not a relevant political figure to college students today. They were rather surprised by that . . . Between 1980 and 1984, the Democratic Party began to be perceived as the party of the past; the Republican Party began to be perceived as the party of the future . . . Under those circumstances, it was inevitable that young people would begin to move to the Republicans.

The Christian Science Monitor, 4-29:1,4.

Thomas P. O'Neill, Jr.
Former United States Representative,
D-Massachusetts

2

The [political] ethics of today are different from the ethics of 30 years ago. In fact, until 1962, I never saw a [funding] check in a [election] campaign. Nobody ever gave you a check.

Everybody gave you cash. And back in the '60s, nobody had to report it, and so you gave a candidate cash. He paid for the gasoline for the people driving the automobiles to bring the voters out. You paid for the person who stayed at the polls.

Interview/USA Today, 10-5:(A)7.

Norman J. Ornstein
Resident scholar,
American Enterprise Institute

3

[On Gary Hart's decision to drop out of the 1988 Presidential race because of allegations of a recent extra-marital affair]: If character can force a front-running candidate out of the race in five days, then character is going to be raised as an issue whenever and however people can raise it.

Los Angeles Times, 5-9:(I)24.

Kay Orr
Governor of Nebraska (R)

4

It's time that a woman should be considered by both parties [when choosing its Presidential-election ticket]: I was amazed in 1984 when . . . the question was asked, because Geraldine Ferraro was running [for Vice President on the Democratic ticket]: "Do you think the Republicans in 1988 ought to consider a woman for a Vice Presidential candidate?" I said, "Good God, they ought to consider one for the Presidency."

Interview/USA Today, 6-19:(A)11.

Kevin P. Phillips
Republican Party
political analyst

5

[On Senator Robert Dole, who may seek the Presidency in 1988]: His negatives are he's a micro-manager, a hands-on guy, who is obviously having difficulty giving up his one-man-band status. He's done terrifically well so far,

WHAT THEY SAID IN 1987

(KEVIN P. PHILLIPS)

but people who are one-man bands don't often get to play.

The New York Times, 2-25:10.

1

Mark my words, there will be much more attention to management style for the next two years. Management style has suddenly become an issue for Presidential candidates, people who want to run Presidential campaigns, and politicians at lower levels.

Los Angeles Times, 3-12:(I)21.

2

Incumbency can probably be shown as a net benefit for most Presidents, but not for Vice Presidents. Presidents tend to get re-elected unless they have major economic problems, while Vice Presidents tend to get nominated [for President] but not elected.

The New York Times, 5-13:16.

3

It's clear that we're looking at the growing Republican realization that the social Darwinish state of conservatism—the dog-eat-dog, survival-of-the-fittest economics—has breathed its last. Even if we don't have a stock-market crash, the heyday of uncaring capitalism is over. There's a sense that too many people have been left out and the conservative cycle has passed its peak.

The New York Times, 10-22:24.

Austin Ranney
Political scientist,
University of California

4

I don't see the [political] parties coming back in voters' minds, because television focuses on individuals and not on parties and groups. Elections now are almost non-partisan, with the stress on personality and individuality.

The Christian Science Monitor, 2-13:21.

Ronald Reagan
President of the United States

5

All those who talk about lame ducks and the post-Reagan era are dead wrong. I can't help but noticing that they're the same gurus whose mantra for the last six years [of the Reagan Administration] has been, "This, too, shall pass." There will be no post-Reagan era, because there's been no Reagan era in the way those people mean it. This has been the era of the American people. Leaders may come and go. When it comes to the American people, their truth keeps marching on.

To Republicans, Washington, June 29/
The Washington Post, 6-30:(A)5.

6

Critics have claimed that in opposing our Administration on the issues, they're at some kind of an unfair disadvantage—that this Presidency is somehow based more on personality than on policy. Well, the truth is no President can remain popular unless he retains the fundamental support of the American people on the issues. So I invite my critics—I welcome my critics—to go after me on the issues just as hard as they please. We'll let the people decide who's right and who's wrong.

Before National Association
of Counties, Indianapolis, July 13/
The Washington Post, 7-14:(A)6.

George E. Reedy
Professor of journalism,
Marquette University;
Former Press Secretary to
the President of the United States
(Lyndon B. Johnson)

7

It was Winston Churchill who said that when you're going to kill a man, it costs nothing to be polite. The issues before [U.S.] Senators are hard, sharp, divisive issues. And if they started to snarl at each other, you'd never get anything done. Every Senator must be aware that the man he absolutely hates today, the man who might be his bitterest opponent, may tomorrow

POLITICS

(GEORGE E. REEDY)

be his strongest ally. And, in the Senate, they do not like the burned bridges.

Interview/USA Today, 1-20:(A)9.

1

[On the leadership style of Presidential candidates and its effect on their election prospects]: A man could say one thing on Monday, be elected on Tuesday and change his mind on Wednesday. But if a man is bent on Monday, he will still be bent on Wednesday.

Los Angeles Times, 5-9:(I)24.

Howard Reitman
Associate professor
of political science,
University of Connecticut

2

[On suggestions that Presidential candidate Gary Hart is having an extra-marital affair and whether that should count against him as a Presidential candidate]: I don't think it means anything about the ability to govern. F.D.R. and John Kennedy were unfaithful, but very effective Presidents. Just because a person is putting on a false image about his private life doesn't mean he's also putting on a false image in his public life.

USA Today, 5-4:(A)2.

Charles S. Robb
Former Governor of Virginia (D);
Chairman,
Democratic Leadership Council

3

[Democrats would] gain almost instant credibility by identifying with a basic philosophy and approach and value system. To a certain extent, that's what the success of [President] Ronald Reagan is all about. He articulates a value system. People may not agree with every element of it. But they know that it sustains him.

Interview, Fairfax, Va./
The Christian Science Monitor, 1-30:6.

Pat Robertson
Evangelist;
Candidate for the 1988
Republican Presidential nomination

4

[The Republican Party represents a] philosophy of life and government that mirrors the hopes and dreams and aspirations of a majority of the American people. If we are bold enough to speak out against Communist tyranny, bold enough to speak out for free enterprise and against the encroachment of big government, bold enough to speak out for the family and social values that are tugging at the heartstrings of the American people, then the Republican Party will not be the minority party but the one that is destined to govern the United States for the rest of the 20th century.

Before National Federation
of Republican Women, Orlando, Fla.,
Sept. 20/The Washington Post, 9-21:(A)6.

5

. . . I am keenly aware of the deeply held belief in this nation that there should not be an established religion in the United States of America, nor should the government prohibit the free exercise of religion by any of the people. For this reason, I recognize that although the overwhelming majority of the American people desire leaders with strong religious faith, to many of our citizens the election of an ordained clergyman of any faith—Protestant, Catholic or Jewish—to as high a public office as the Presidency of the United States would, in their opinion, be tantamount to a preference of one religious denomination over all others.

Announcing his resignation as a minister
in preparation for his running
for President, Sept. 29/
The New York Times, 9-30:13.

Michael Jay Robinson
Professional lecturer
in government,
Georgetown University

6

Character is singularly important [for Presidential candidates], more important in the Pres-

223

WHAT THEY SAID IN 1987

(MICHAEL JAY ROBINSON)

idency than in any other office. Not only do I believe it's proper focus for press scrutiny, but I am absolutely convinced that the question of Presidential character is more important than a candidate's position on any issue or set of issues.

Los Angeles Times, 5-9:(I)1.

1

[On the withdrawal of Gary Hart from the 1988 Presidential race after allegations in the press about his infidelity]: Candidates are going to be rushing to show how faithful they have been, to show how much in love they are with their wives. It will make family life front and center as a campaign issue. In 1986, we had urine tests. In 1988, we'll have fidelity tests.

U.S. News & World Report,
5-18:24.

Terry Sanford
United States Senator,
D-North Carolina

2

[On President Reagan]: This is the President who states that he will bear full responsibility for his actions, and yet this is the same President who always seems to find a fall guy for the bad things that happen on his watch. Have you no shame, Mr. President? The American people can see through your act.

Before the Senate,
Washington, June 24/
The Washington Post, 6-25:(A)4.

Richard Scammon
Public-opinion analyst

3

The primary [-election] system gives us a winner even before the party meets. So the convention is a coronation, not a point of decision.

The Christian Science Monitor,
2-13:20.

Patricia Schroeder
United States Representative,
D-Colorado

4

[On the possibility of her running for the 1988 Democratic Presidential nomination]: I have to keep asking myself why I am in politics . . . And one sure thing I know is that I don't have any interest in being a Presidential candidate, like all the other guys I see out there. I'm not a normal candidate. I've never been a traditional candidate. If I had a traditional campaign manager, I would drive them nuts, and they'd drive me nuts.

The Washington Post, 9-15:(A)4.

5

[Saying she will not be a candidate for the 1988 Democratic Presidential nomination]: I could not figure out how to run and not be separated from those I serve. There must be a way, but I haven't figured it out yet . . . I feel that [I] could compete in the popular vote. It is the part of having your delegates selected, and if other people already have the delegates, you can have the votes and they've got the delegates, and all that counts in Atlanta [at the Democratic convention] is delegates. I could not find any way that we could really run the kind of campaign I wanted to run if we were targeting delegates and still trying to talk to people, which is what keeps me going as a human being. It's hard to do the grass-roots thing and the delegate thing simultaneously. I want to find a way to break through that process, but at this moment I don't see it today.

News conference, Denver, Sept. 28/
The New York Times, 9-29:9.

6

There are no more women in the House and Senate than there were in 1964. So we don't have a big farm club [for potential Presidential candidates] on either side. Neither party is really encouraging women. They may not be discouraging them, but they certainly aren't going out of their way. We have numerous Mayors and women in city councils. But your Presidential

(PATRICIA SCHROEDER)

farm club comes out of the House, the Senate and the Cabinet.

Interview/USA Today, 9-30:(A)13.

John Sears
Republican political analyst

1

You know, 20 or 25 years ago, when the [Presidential] nomination system was different . . . the press probably didn't have to play as active a role as it does today because a lot of people who might think of running for President were really screened out by the party leaders. Today, there really are no party leaders. There are no guys who can take you in a back room and get real answers out of you. If there are weaknesses in your candidacy or personal things about you that might be difficult if you were to run for President, there is no group of people who can sit you down and say, "Well, unless that is solved . . . we can't support you."

To reporters, Washington, Sept. 24/
The Christian Science Monitor, 9-25:3.

Paul Simon
United States Senator,
D-Illinois; Candidate for the 1988
Democratic Presidential nomination

2

[Announcing his candidacy for the 1988 Democratic Presidential nomination]: To become fashionable, some people tell me to get rid of my bow tie and my horn-rimmed glasses and, most of all, to change my views. Well, [the late President] Harry· Truman wore a bow tie and horn-rimmed glasses, and he didn't knuckle under to pressure to change his views. Nineteen eighty-eight is not going to be the year for a candidate slickly packaged like some new soft drink.

Announcing his candidacy
for President, Carbondale, Ill.,
May 18/The Washington Post, 5-19:(A)1.

3

Some advise us [Democrats] to adjust our sails to the prevailing winds, however they may be blowing. I do not join those who want the Democratic Party to forget its heritage in order to become more acceptable to the wealthy and powerful. If we do that, we will lose our soul and do a great disservice to the nation. I'm glad there is a Republican Party, but one Republican Party is enough.

Announcing his candidacy
for President, Carbondale, Ill.,
May 18/The New York Times, 5-19:8.

I.F. Stone
Author, Journalist

4

Some people become politically radical out of hatred. Others become radical out of love and sympathy. I come out of the second class—I have hated very few people.

Interview, Washington/
The New York Times, 12-24:20.

Robert S. Strauss
Former chairman,
Democratic National Committee

5

The battle for the political support of the South is now on. The nomination of a Democrat [for President in 1988] who cannot make inroads in the South would be the nomination of a loser.

Aug. 27/Los Angeles Times, 8-28:(I)4.

Clarence Thomas
Chairman,
Equal Employment Opportunity
Commission of the United States

6

The problem of the post-Reagan Republican Party . . . is making conservatism more attractive to Americans in general. In fact, our approach to blacks has been a paradigm of the Republican Party as a whole. The failure to assert principles—to say what we are "for"—

WHAT THEY SAID IN 1987

plagued the 1986 campaign. Everyone was treated as part of an interest group.

At Heritage Foundation, June/
The Wall Street Journal, 8-25:28.

Robert G. Torricelli
United States Representative,
D-New Jersey

1

[On Gary Hart's withdrawal from the 1988 Presidential race because of allegations of a recent extra-marital affair]: [Politicians,] sadly I think, are going to hesitate in their professional relationships with women on their staffs, women who work on their campaigns. There's going to be a caution that is not good for getting women involved in public life.

Broadcast interview/
"Face the Nation," CBS-TV, 5-10.

Morris K. Udall
United States Representative,
D-Arizona

2

[Saying the Democrats must win the 1988 Presidential election, after losing four of the last six such races]: We've got to win this one or we are through. If you were a baseball manager with that record, you sure would want to make some changes . . . Maybe we need to go back to the smoke-filled room.

To reporters, Nov. 5/
The New York Times, 11-6:12.

Richard Viguerie
Conservative political analyst

3

[Criticizing President Reagan, saying he has deserted the conservative cause]: One thing is unanimous among the President's long-time supporters: that he has quit the fight and left the field of battle in many important matters. In other important matters, he has changed sides and he is now allied with his former

adversaries—the liberals, the Democrats and the Soviets.

News conference, Dec. 4/
Los Angeles Times, 12-5:(I)12.

Stephen J. Wayne
Professor of political science,
George Washington University

4

[On suggestions that Presidential candidate Gary Hart is having an extra-marital affair, and whether that should count against him as a Presidential candidate]: The public wants Presidential candidates to be larger than life, and to set examples. If a man cheats on his wife, or a wife cheats on her husband, and that person is running for public office, it's part of the judgment people make. [It shows] they're not trustworthy.

USA Today, 5-4:(A)2.

Fred Wertheimer
President, Common Cause

5

[On the private-financing system, including PACs, for election campaigns]: This is a rotten, awful, terrible system for the country.

Los Angeles Times, 4-8:(I)13.

Paul M. Weyrich
President,
Free Congress Foundation

6

[White House Chief of Staff] Howard Baker is strategizing and thinking like the moderate that he is. He genuinely has the disposition of somebody who doesn't like conflict and really comes down in the middle. This is essentially an Administration that's scared. Howard Baker's automatic reaction is a yellow light. He doesn't understand the national [conservative] coalition that put [President] Reagan in office. The price is a Presidency without punch.

Los Angeles Times, 10-9:(I)15.

(PAUL M. WEYRICH)

1

Conservatives make a mistake in identifying with a politics that says it really doesn't matter what happens to the community as long as those who can survive get theirs. There is a wonderful tradition in this country of serving others. It is time we [conservatives] develop a conservative doctrine of service.

The New York Times, 11-30:11.

Elie Wiesel
Historian;
Professor of humanities,
Boston University;
Winner, 1986 Nobel Peace Prize

2

Fanaticism is gaining ground in our midst. As does rancor. And hate. Extremism on the right is matched by extremism on the left. Some have turned politics into religion. Others have transformed religion into politics.

At 92nd Street Y, New York,
Jan. 21/The New York Times, 1-22:16.

Hugh Winebrenner
Professor of political science,
Drake University

3

It's very hard to deny incumbent Vice Presidents the [Presidential] nomination [when the incumbent President leaves office], but it's very hard to elect them.

USA Today, 10-12:(A)4.

Jim Wright
United States Representative,
D-Texas

4

[President Reagan is a] charming person, a well-meaning person, not an evil person, [but one who] hasn't the faintest idea of the contents of legislation or the application of real facts to real problems. [He] has the ability to psych himself up to reject factual data if they don't conform to his preconceived notions . . . He's smart but he's ignorant of the facts a President ought to know, and willfully so . . . I like him personally, but not as President.

To reporters, Washington, Sept. 17/
The Washington Post, 9-18:(A)17.

5

[President] Ronald Reagan is a man who shoots the arrow first and then draws the target where the arrow hit. If you say, "But the target was over here, Mr. President," he says "Not so, not so."

U.S. News & World Report, 9-28:17.

Andrew Young
Mayor of Atlanta

6

If [the Democrats] want to win the Presidency, they've got to campaign in the black community now. If you don't build any ties to a constituency in the primaries, no group of endorsements can get people excited after the convention for a big turnout.

The New York Times, 4-27:9.

227

Social Welfare

Bruce Babbitt
*Former Governor
of Arizona (D);
Candidate for
the 1988 Democratic
Presidential nomination*

1

Government can't do everything for everybody. Do we really need to give a mortgage-interest deduction to mansions and vacation homes? Do we really need to pay subsidies to corporate mega-farms? Do we really need three new generations of nuclear missiles—all at once? Do the Vanderbilts and the Mellons really need just the same tax-exempt Social Security benefits as a widow in a cold-water flat?

*Speech/
The Washington Post,
5-1:(A)18.*

2

One American child in four lives in poverty. One in four! That is unacceptable. We have children who lack for medicine, children who go unsupervised while their parents are at work, children who pass from grade to grade without ever learning to read. We must have an affirmative program to bring our children into the 21st century.

*Interview, Oak Creek Canyon, Ariz./
The Christian Science Monitor, 10-16:6.*

3

[Calling for a tax on Social Security payments to the wealthy]: Why do we have a system in which the Mellons and the Vanderbilts get tax-free income? I'd set a "needs test," a threshold of $100,000 or $75,000 a year, somewhere in there, above which Social Security benefits are taxable.

*At forum sponsored by
American Association of
Retired Persons, Des Moines, Iowa,
Nov. 19/The Washington Post,
11-20:(A)4.*

William J. Bennett
*Secretary of Education
of the United States*

4

In the last year, we have seen a good deal of attention paid to the problems of the poor in our nation's inner cities. This attention is good; there are problems that need to be addressed. But there is an attitude often accompanying this attention that is not a good one. I believe that in many quarters we have seen a sort of resignation to the plight of the urban poor; there are some who today speak despairingly of a "permanent under-class." In looking at the inner cities . . . they see no hope.

*At Martin Luther King Center,
Atlanta, Jan. 15/
The Washington Post, 1-29:(A)24.*

Joseph R. Biden, Jr.
*United States Senator,
D-Delaware; Candidate for the 1988
Democratic Presidential nomination*

5

[Saying many welfare programs serve to promote the continuing dependence of recipients on welfare]: It should have been no surprise that taxpayers would become resentful of the way that we not so much *spend* on poverty in this country as much as we *finance* it.

*At Princeton University, May 22/
Los Angeles Times, 5-23:(I)27.*

Larry Brown
*Professor,
School of Public Health,
Harvard University*

6

[On hunger in America]: People obviously are not dropping like flies. The epidemiology is not like the Third World, where you go around and count bodies. But if you look at Census Bureau data on household income, you find people

(LARRY BROWN)

can't cope. Families miss meals, cut down, go without for a couple [of] days. The typical profile is one fairly well-rounded meal a day, but even that falls short of RDA.

Boston, Oct. 26/
The New York Times, 10-27:12.

George Bush
Vice President
of the United States;
Candidate for the 1988
Republican Presidential nomination

1

Prosperity with a purpose means, in short, helping your brothers and sisters, whoever they are, whatever their needs. There are those who would say it's soft and insufficiently tough to care about these things. But where is it written that Republicans must act as if they do not care, as if they are not moved? I say to my fellow Republicans: We are the Party of Lincoln. Our whole history was protecting those who needed our protection and making this a kinder nation.

Announcing his candidacy
for President, Houston, Oct. 12/
The New York Times, 12-13:10.

Michael N. Castle
Governor of Delaware (R)

2

Welfare has always been simply a financial support system. Now people are ready to see it as something that should be a vocational, training and education program. From Governor Kean in New Jersey to Governor Dukakis in Massachusetts, there is clearly a genuine consensus that crosses all layers and ideologies. I think in the next two- or three-year period we're going to see some fundamental changes . . . We may have to invest more money up front, but we believe that the states and the Federal government can, over time, reduce public expenditures for welfare by targeting resources which

reduce the need of children and their families to resort to the welfare system.

Interview, Washington, Feb. 2/
The New York Times, 2-3:10.

Mario M. Cuomo
Governor of New York (D)

3

Need must be a criterion with respect to the entitlement programs. Medicare, Social Security, pensions—the people who don't really need enhancements should be willing to forgo them. Now you get a cost-of-living increase without regard to your wealth. We need to calibrate that somehow so that wealth is a factor. And, politically, I think the country is ready for that kind of truth.

Interview, Albany, N.Y./
U.S. News & World Report, 12-14:20.

Christopher J. Dodd
United States Senator,
D-Connecticut

4

[On the difficulty of getting companies to invest in such things as day care for children of working mothers]: The problem is getting them to invest in a generation they won't be around to be CEO of. They get very involved in universities because universities turn out hireable people. But infant care—that just doesn't tie together for them. Business views it as a wimpish subject, kind of a cute issue. [When business groups meet Senators on family issues,] they always give some woman the morning off. "Send the *gals* out on this one." It's never the chief financial officer or the senior vice president.

At Senate hearing, June/
The New York Times, 7-1:10.

Robert J. Dole
United States Senator,
R-Kansas; Candidate for the 1988
Republican Presidential nomination

5

I am not prepared to support a guaranteed family income financed through the welfare

WHAT THEY SAID IN 1987

(ROBERT J. DOLE)

system, but I am prepared to put money into state efforts to increase opportunities for people to get off welfare and to encourage the states to redirect any resulting savings toward increased benefits.

Interview/
Los Angeles Times, 11-16:(I)13.

Thomas R. Donahue
Secretary treasurer,
American Federation
of Labor-Congress
of Industrial Organizations

1

In America today, one family out of every five with children under 18 is headed by a woman, with no husband or father present. Among black Americans, it's one family out of two. Scarcely one family in 20 fits the old pattern of one breadwinner, one homemaker, two children and possibly a dog. But a one-parent family is a family nonetheless, and it should be helped and encouraged to provide all the benefits of family living it can.

At National Conference
on Work and Family Life, March 30/
The Washington Post, 4-8:(A)20.

Eugene Dorsey
Chief executive officer,
Gannett Foundation

2

It's true that those with the smallest income give the largest percentage of their incomes to charity. Perhaps that's a sense of people being much closer to the problems and having a considerable amount of empathy for those who don't have even as much as they do.

Interview/USA Today, 8-5:(A)9.

Thomas J. Downey
United States Representative, D-New York

3

There's a growing understanding of the serious problems of poverty in this country that we

simply haven't been addressing. People realize there are more important things than personal wealth, and that even a healthy, growing economy would not be enough to help these people.

Washington, Jan. 23/
The New York Times, 1-24:7.

Michael S. Dukakis
Governor of Massachusetts (D);
Candidate for the 1988
Democratic Presidential nomination

4

What we [Democrats] are saying now is that if we are going to help people lift themselves out of poverty, there is a kind of mutual responsibility here. There is responsibility on the part of government to provide day care and job training. But there is also the responsibility on the part of the recipient and on the part of the absent father to support his kids. Democrats weren't talking that way 10 years ago.

Announcing his candidacy
for President, Boston, March 16/
Los Angeles Times, 3-17:(I)16.

5

The conscience of the nation is beginning to be troubled. People in every city see the homeless lying around on grates, even a few blocks from the White House. And they wonder, does this have to be?

Time, 3-30:37.

Pierre S. du Pont IV
Former Governor of Delaware (R);
Candidate for the 1988
Republican Presidential nomination

6

The programs of [the late President Lyndon] Johnson's Great Society sought to pay people so that they wouldn't be poor, and instead paid people so that they wouldn't work. The result is, today we have a subculture that is generations deep and growing at a frightening pace and which has no familiarity with or respect for the traditional work ethic . . . The Great Society's programs also told families to break up. It

(PIERRE S. du PONT IV)

is a dismal fact that America pays poor families only when the father leaves home.

Nashua, N.H./
The Washington Post, 3-14:(A)4.

Marian Wright Edelman
President,
Children's Defense Fund

1

[President] Reagan's callousness has given us a new political base. We've learned the importance of the budget process—whoever controls the money, controls the policy. We've been forced to do tough state and local organizing. The opposition Reagan presented has encouraged children's advocates to overcome their political timidity. And we've learned, all of us, the need to work together. Finally, Congress is at last realizing the wisdom of preventive investment: One dollar up front prevents the spending of many dollars down the road. It's taken 15 years to get people to hear, frankly, but we have more child-health bills going into Congress this year than we can keep up with.

Interview/"Ms.," July-Aug.:100.

2

There is a new recognition that someone has to do something about families and soup kitchens and the homeless. It is clear, after eight years of [President] Reagan rhetoric, that these problems can't be solved by volunteers. Government clearly has a role.

The New York Times, 8-20:12.

David T. Ellwood
Labor economist,
Harvard University

3

If you gave me just two facts for any year between 1960 and 1980—the average wage rate in the United States and the unemployment rate, that's all—I can tell you the poverty rate for that year for children in two-parent families within half a percentage point. It runs perfectly. And

the disturbing fact is that these full-time working poor, after counting in all the government transfers, are actually the poorest of the poor. That's nuts.

Brainerd, Minn./
The Washington Post, 10-12:(A)19.

Daniel J. Evans
United States Senator,
R-Washington

4

[Calling for a national minimum benefit level for Aid to Families With Dependent Children]: In a wealthy nation like ours, it is a disgrace that a poor family of four in one region of the country can receive assistance up to five times as great as a poor family in another region. After all, to be poor and hungry in New York or California is not much different than being poor and hungry in Mississippi, Maine or Missouri.

Before Senate Subcommittee on
Social Security and Family Policy,
Washington, Jan. 23/
The New York Times, 1-24:7.

Raymond L. Flynn
Mayor of Boston

5

If the people [living] on America's streets and soup kitchens had been driven there by a natural catastrophe, many parts of our country would be declared disaster areas.

USA Today, 12-28:(A)12.

Don Fraser
Mayor of Minneapolis

6

[Saying additional welfare benefits should be barred to welfare mothers who have a second child]: Those who increase their dependency by having additional children while on welfare are not likely to work very hard to get off of it.

Time, 2-16:20.

WHAT THEY SAID IN 1987

Rudolph W. Giuliani
United States Attorney for
the Southern District of New York

1

The worst possible thing to do is to try to solve the problem of poverty by using a system that doesn't create a sense of responsibility. You have to try to encourage the best in human beings . . . A lot of the programs that we've enacted are built on no understanding of the weaknesses in human nature.

Interview, New York/
The Christian Science Monitor, 3-31:4.

Barry M. Goldwater
Former United States Senator,
R-Arizona

2

If we don't solve the problems of the welfare state, then we are going the way of all other nations that have tried it. Bankruptcy, then dictatorship . . . We have today nearly 50 per cent of our people [to some degree] dependent on the Federal government for their livelihood.

Interview, Scottsdale, Ariz./
The Christian Science Monitor, 8-25:6.

Stanley Greenberg
Electoral analyst

3

Democrats are in a position to acknowledge the reality of the modern family and the problems of parenting. The Republicans, ideologically trapped in the traditional family, may be left with a family rhetoric that is precious, but increasingly anachronistic.

U.S. News & World Report, 9-14:30.

Alexander M. Haig, Jr.
Former Secretary of State
of the United States;
Candidate for the 1988
Republican Presidential nomination

4

[The] welfare problem is best handled on a local and state basis [because the problems of

the poor] cannot be managed from Washington. Work is the way out of welfare, and required work is one way to encourage social responsibility.

Interview/
Los Angeles Times, 11-16:(I)13.

Dorcas Hardy
Administrator,
Social Security Administration
of the United States

5

If I have one responsibility, it's to remind [the baby-boom generation, heading toward retirement] that the one with the primary responsibility to the individual's future is that individual. Somewhere along the line we came up with the idea that Social Security is the entire retirement ticket. It's not. The ticket is a combination of Social Security, savings and pension.

Interview, Washington/
The Christian Science Monitor, 3-5:31.

Augustus Hawkins
United States Representative,
D-California

6

For some 8 million of America's working poor, a higher minimum wage will help break the vicious cycle of poverty they have been living in for the past six years. Since 1981, the cost of living has risen about 27 per cent, but the minimum wage has been frozen.

Nation's Business,
May:30.

John Heinz
United States Senator,
R-Pennsylvania

7

When the Office of Management and Budget computer is programmed "cut," operators automatically punch "Medicare."

USA Today, 2-19:(A)6.

John Paul II
Pope

1

Service to the poor also involves speaking up for them, and trying to reform structures which cause or perpetuate their oppression . . . we must realize that social injustice and unjust social structures exist only because individuals and groups of individuals deliberately maintain or tolerate them. It is these personal choices, operating through structures, that breed and propagate situations of poverty, oppression and misery. For this reason, overcoming "social" sin and reforming the social order itself must begin with the conversion of our hearts.

At mass, San Antonio, Texas,
Sept. 13/The New York Times, 9-14:14.

Judith Jones
Associate professor of public health,
Columbia University;
Director, National Resource Center
for Children in Poverty

2

We have not yet acknowledged the fact that poverty among our children, our most valuable resource, should be unacceptable. It's an urgent problem because it's growing. The disparity between the rich and the poor in this country is growing . . . [But] we haven't been able to capture [that it is] totally unacceptable in a wealthy country like this to have children going to bed hungry at night, to have children have a poor education, poor health, who start life poorly because their mothers don't get prenatal care in a timely fashion. We have not said, "Listen, America, this is unacceptable."

Interview, New York/
The Christian Science Monitor, 7-15:3.

P. X. Kelley
General and Commandant,
United States Marine Corps

3

Fifty per cent of the mothers today work. And that means that a number of our children are not getting the kind of upbringing in their homes that you and I had. Instead, their moral upbringing is being dictated by some nameless, faceless child-care center. A lot of people aren't going to like that remark, but I'm going to say it anyway.

To reporters, Washington, June 25/
The Washington Post, 6-26:(A)3.

Edward I. Koch
Mayor of New York

4

[On those who criticize his new policy of forcibly hospitalizing homeless people who cannot care for themselves]: If the crazies want to sue me, they have every right to sue; and by crazies, when I say crazies, I'm not talking about the people we're going to be helping by removing them from sleeping on the streets or defecating in their own clothing; I'm talking about those who say "No, you have no right to intervene to help these people." Those are the crazies.

Before American Psychological
Association, New York, Aug. 31/
The New York Times, 9-1:11.

Richard D. Lamm
Former Governor of Colorado (D)

5

Social Security and Medicare take money out of the pockets of some Americans, many of whom are quite poor, and pay it to other Americans, many of whom are quite rich.

USA Today, 4-17:(A)10.

Mike Lowry
United States Representative,
D-Washington

6

A decision to eliminate or cap the Social Security COLA in 1988 [to help balance the Federal budget] will have much the same impact as when proposed in 1985. The American Association of Retired Persons . . . estimates an additional 272,500 individuals age 62 or older will fall below the poverty line if the COLA is

(MIKE LOWRY)

withheld . . . These individuals depend on Social Security for their very survival, and to deny them the COLA or limit its size leaves them little hope of maintaining their already minimal standard of living.

Before the House,
Nov. 9/
The Washington Post,
11-12:(A)22.

Peter McPherson
Former Administrator,
Agency for
International Development,
Department of State
of the United States

1

The permanent salvation of the hungry [around the world] is not the feeding of individuals but the economic growth of nations.

USA Today,
11-27:(A)8.

George Miller
United States Representative,
D-California

2

Just this year, President Reagan's budget proposed a massive rescission in the temporary emergency food program; advocated underfunding the Women, Infants and Children Feeding Program by 50,000 people; endorsed a cut of up to 40,000 from the Commodity Fundamental Food Program which serves children, the elderly and mothers; and demanded over a billion-dollar reduction in food-stamp and child-nutrition programs. We don't need Herbert Hoover, and we don't need "Poor Richard." We need leadership from the President and from the Congress to attack the real issues underlying our fiscal misfortune. And while we spend so much time worrying about the Dow Jones, let's not forget Mr. and Mrs. Jones—tens of millions of working-class and poor Americans who have endured Mr. Reagan's voodoo economics for the past seven years, while the stock market soared.

Before the House, Washington, Oct. 27/
The Washington Post, 10-29:(A)24.

Daniel P. Moynihan
United States Senator,
D-New York

3

At this point, for the first time in our history, the poorest group in our population are children. A child under 6 is seven times more likely to be poor than someone 65 or older. I think older persons are fairly secure because of the mature social insurance system, private pensions and the ability to save. But marriages are so unstable that it's the children who are ending up the poorest group.

Interview/USA Today, 2-18:(A)15.

Richard Muth
Chairman,
department of economics,
Emory University

4

[Rent control] is as bad as the income-tax deduction for home ownership . . . All the beneficiaries [of the deduction] are high-income earners, not simply some of them. It leads to extra-large swimming pools, extra bedrooms in Beverly Hills, but no housing for the people who need it most. Still, when this issue was last voted on in Congress, 85 out of 85 Senators present voted for it. The only surprising thing, given the number of beneficiaries, is that somehow the other 15 Senators didn't manage to get their names on the roll call.

At forum sponsored by
Manhattan Institute, May 6/
The Wall Street Journal, 7-9:28.

Ronald Reagan
President of the United States

5

I think truly that the bulk of people on welfare aren't just lazy bums or cheaters. They

(RONALD REAGAN)

want nothing more than to be independent, free of the social workers and out on their own once again. [The welfare system has become a] poverty trap.

Feb. 9/
The Washington Post,
2-10:(A)8.

James D. Robinson III
Chairman,
board of governors,
United Way of America

1

The Federal government cannot do everything—certainly not in the face of massive budget deficits. Many of the Great Society programs haven't worked—and won't work. More money has often gone into overhead than to the needy. So state and local governments have no choice; they must tackle the problems. But they can't do it alone. So what's left? What's left is us [private charitable organizations]. When it comes to our social problems, government should neither be the answer, nor the enemy, nor a bystander—but a partner.

Washington/
The Washington Post,
5-1:(A)22.

Felix G. Rohatyn
Senior partner,
Lazard Freres & Company

2

We have created hundreds of paper millionaires and quite a few billionaires. But alongside the wealth and glamour of Manhattan and Beverly Hills, we have seen the growth of a semipermanent or permanent under-class. In the inner cities and in the rural areas, blacks and Hispanics, poor whites and immigrants are falling further behind because of inadequate education, drugs and a welfare system that systematically destroys family structures. Meanwhile, jobs that can provide a future require higher and higher skills. These diverging paths

condemn more and more people to a permanent condition of need. A democracy cannot flourish half rich and half poor, any more than it can flourish half free and half slave.

At Long Island
University commencement/
The New York Times, 6-3:27.

Edward R. Roybal
United States Representative,
D-California

3

Especially for the elderly living alone, the risk of long-term-care-induced impoverishment is great and totally unacceptable. With annual nursing-home costs averaging over $22,000 and elderly median annual income being just over $11,500, a host of personal catastrophes are in the making. Unless concrete action is taken quickly, all lower- and middle-income elderly and non-elderly Americans will remain at great risk of impoverishment due to the high and sustained cost of long-term care.

Nov. 8/
The New York Times,
11-9:12.

Patricia Schroeder
United States Representative,
D-Colorado

4

[Saying child-care-leave legislation should include men as well as women]: Otherwise, you start making people mad. You go back to male versus female and to "what do women want now?" The whole reason the bill hasn't moved is that it's been seen as establishing a right for women. It's important to make it a family program.

The New York Times, 2-3:26.

5

It's not only the stock market that crashed [recently]. The American family crashed a long time ago. You do better in America raising

WHAT THEY SAID IN 1987

thoroughbred racehorses than you do raising children under the tax code.

Interview, Coronado, Calif./
The Christian Science Monitor, 11-30:3.

Haskell G. Ward
Authority on community
and economic development;
Former Deputy Mayor of New York

1

If people were to look at what was happening in community development . . . people's attitudes about the poor and about low-income neighborhoods would shift, because they would see that the people they think are simply interested in receiving government handouts are really working beyond their capacity. They want to solve the problems themselves with their own solutions . . . [Community-based groups] provide a framework that begins to deal with the strengths of people . . . and this can be a way for those at the Federal level to begin to look at ways of providing assistance, without taking in [a Federal] solution to the problem.

The Christian Science Monitor,
6-29:6.

Transportation

John Albertine
Chairman,
President's Commission
on Aviation Safety

1

Yes, the [air-transportation] system is incredibly safe. The $64 question is: Is the system getting less safe? That is a very tough question. Since there are so few fatalities, it's hard to get an index which correlates whether the system is getting more safe or less safe . . . You've got to look at maintenance [of aircraft]. I happen to think that deregulation, from an economic point of view, is a good idea. [But] I've got to believe when you're under a lot of competitive pressure that there could be an incentive to meet the letter of the requirements and maybe not all of the spirit. So I think we have to look at whether or not there ought to be beefed-up requirements with regard to maintenance.

Interview, Chicago/
The Christian Science Monitor, 9-3:3,4.

, 2

Part of what people think about [airline] safety really does relate to how comfortable they are in flying. If you go to an airport that's crowded and congested, you tend to think that the airspace is crowded and congested, and maybe unsafe. You get on the plane, and the coffee's cold. You say, "Well, if they can't keep the coffee hot, how are they going to keep the engines in repair?"

Interview/USA Today, 11-16:(A)13.

John Baker
President,
Aircraft Owners and
Pilots Association

3

[On restrictions being placed on private aircraft around major airports to help keep private and commercial planes from flying too close to each other]: We're pinning the tail on the wrong donkey. We ought to be going after the people who were charged with making sure that the system grew to accommodate the demand. We ought to be looking at the politicians who deregulated the system when we didn't have an infrastructure that would accommodate demand. The hard reality is that the air-traffic-control system won't accommodate any more data or any more airplanes than they curently have.

Broadcast discussion/
"This Week With David Brinkley,"
ABC-TV, 8-23.

William E. Brock
Secretary of Labor
of the United States

4

[On whether President Reagan's firing of striking air-traffic controllers in 1981 has adversely affected the safety of air travel]: We have problems like everybody else, but we're flying the safest skies in the world. The people who were fired back in 1981 broke the law [by striking]. But the fact is that we have some of the world's finest people who are air controllers [now]. Some of them are even talking about organizing [in a union] again . . . If they want to do that, they have an absolute right to do that. It's a matter of being sure that we as a country keep our priorities focused on the Number 1 job of government, and that is to keep this thing safe.

Interview/USA Today, 9-3:(A)9.

James H. Burnley
Secretary of Transportation
of the United States

5

We've had an explosion in the number of people who want to fly in this country. It's time to take a look at how the Federal government

WHAT THEY SAID IN 1987

does business in its relationship with aviation. Maybe the problem is that even though we have some very dedicated people over at the FAA, we haven't given them the flexibility that they need to keep up with changes in the industry.

Broadcast interview/
"Good Morning America,"
ABC-TV, 12-3.

Robert L. Crandall
Chairman and president,
American Airlines

1

The time has come to end the quibbling, public and private, about how much [flight] capacity can or cannot be handled safely. We don't have time to bicker any further. The public's confidence in air travel cannot help but be eroded by endless acrimonious debate . . . If we are to have optimal safety, for instance, it may not be possible to offer the lowest ticket prices. Safety does not come free, nor even cheap. Service is deteriorating; complaints are rising; the skies and airports are crowded; and the entire system is creaking as we seek to accommodate the waves of customers brought to our ticket counters by deregulation and cheap fares.

Interview, Evanston, Ill., June 23/
Los Angeles Times, 6-24:(IV)1.

2

In the airline industry, one priority overrides everything else. That priority is safety. Unfortunately, at least some elements of the aviation community—like many in the general public—aren't yet prepared to accept the reality that to have optimum safety, lower priorities must be assigned to other elements of the air-transportation equation, such as convenience . . . If we are to have optimal safety, for instance, it may not be possible to offer the lowest possible ticket prices. Safety does not come free, and it certainly doesn't come cheap . . . Nor may it be possible to be totally unyielding in our dedication to the principle of open skies. Even though

we are committed to and believe in free-market competition, that goal, too, must take a back seat if it conflicts with our foremost priority. I am not advocating a return to public-utility-type economic regulation. I am simply arguing that, to achieve the promise of deregulation, we must do a better job of deciding which goals are more important than others. In other words, we cannot give the same priority to every goal. We can't have an absolute commitment to safety and simultaneously assign top priority to all the other things on our wish list.

Before Aviation
Safety Commission, July 23/
The New York Times, 8-7:10.

James E. Daust
President,
Commercial Vehicle
Safety Alliance

3

Economic deregulation at the Federal level has had an adverse effect on the entire motor carrier industry with regard to safety on the public highways. One of the most understated causes for large traffic crashes today is driver fatigue. Detailed studies indicate the problem is more widespread than ever before. Driver-related causes, coupled with poor vehicle maintenance programs, are by far the largest contributing factor in the rise of heavy truck fatalities and severe-injury crashes.

At transportation safety conference,
Northwestern University/
Los Angeles Times, 6-29:(IV)6.

Elizabeth Hanford Dole
Secretary of Transportation
of the United States

4

[On her plan to require airlines to disclose such matters as on-time performance, flight cancellations and other passenger complaints]: The Department [of Transportation] will do whatever is appropriate to insure that consumers are treated fairly and are adequately informed. At the same time, we will take no

(ELIZABETH HANFORD DOLE)

action that compromises public safety. Over the course of the past year, airline passengers have been experiencing increasing levels of flight delays, which are not only costly to consumers but cause considerable inconvenience. Growing dissatisfaction by consumers is reflected in complaints to the Department, which reached 4,893 in the first quarter of 1987, a 43 percent increase over the same period in 1986.

Washington, June 4/
The New York Times, 6-5:12.

Hank Duffy
Director,
Air Line Pilots Association

1

Hell, every week that goes by, it's almost accepted as a common event, a near midair [collision]! Near midairs, runway incursions, delays—every indicator in the system says that we're hanging by our fingernails.

Time, 1-12:25.

Michael S. Dukakis
Governor of Massachusetts (D);
Candidate for the 1988
Democratic Presidential nomination

2

There's nothing quite like running for the Presidency for six months to awaken one to the chaos that currently afflicts transportation in this country, especially our airports. There is one thing we can do . . . That is to use an extraordinary and under-utilized resource in this country, and that is rail.

Oct. 14/
Los Angeles Times, 10-15:(I)20.

John H. Enders
President,
Flight Safety Foundation

3

Scheduled air transportation safety has improved [since deregulation], and air travel is

safe. But the margin-of-safety levels over that required by law is vulnerable to erosion. Investment in such research is diminishing, thus threatening continued progress in safety improvement. It is possible to skate on thin ice and it is possible to skate on thick ice. Let's not let the ice get too thin.

At transportation safety conference,
Northwestern University/
Los Angeles Times, 6-29:(IV)1.

Donald D. Engen
Administrator,
Federal Aviation Administration

4

I can't deal with somebody claiming that "the margin of safety [in the air] has decreased." I deal with real facts, the accidents in hundreds of thousands of hours flown. These rates are continuing to go down.

Time, 1-12:26.

5

Only in aviation do you see people counting near-accidents.

USA Today, 4-28:(A)10.

6

There's a lot of room in our skies. One of the problems has been that airplane manufacturers have designed planes that fly most efficiently between 28,000 and 30,000 feet. We need to design engines and airplanes that fly higher. My hope is we can trade on military technology for civil technology.

Interview/USA Today, 6-30:(A)9.

7

The airports today are the bus stations of the 1950s. You see people flying in cut-offs. You see people with babies on their backs. It is the U.S. flying.

At National Press Club, Washington,
June 30/The Washington Post, 7-1:(A)17.

239

WHAT THEY SAID IN 1987

Newt Gingrich
United States Representative,
R-Georgia

1

[On the congested, de-regulated U.S. air-transportation system]: We have now stretched the old system to its limit. We will either develop a new and more effective air-transport system to accommodate the economic growth and the desire for customer choice, or we will start re-regulating to cramp the economic system to fit the government's comfort zone.

At Presidential Aviation Safety
Commission hearing, Washington,
July 23/The New York Times, 7-24:9.

Ted Harris
President,
Airline Industry Resources

2

As [air] carriers have grown both internally and through the merger route, they have stretched their management resources incredibly thin. They have encountered serious labor problems integrating work forces of merged carriers and serious communication problems, all of which have resulted in a diminution of the service product, which is the only product that airlines offer in the final analysis.

Interview/USA Today, 8-18:(A)11.

Richard Hillman
Vice president
for flight operations,
Continental Airlines

3

[Comparing Continental's pilot program with a baseball team's farm system]: We will hire a guy fairly young—21 or 22 who may have 800 or 900 hours of flying time—out of one of the aviation schools. We would hire him for Continental and let him fly in the third seat [flight engineer] for about a year. Then he could go to one of our commuters as a co-pilot for a couple of years till he built up 2,000, 3,000 or 4,000 hours of flying time. He would then come back to Continental. What you basi-

cally have is like a baseball farm club system. You need someone, and you can call him up quickly. If he had trouble for any reason, he could go back to the commuters.

Los Angeles Times, 5-29:(I)24.

Ernest F. Hollings
United States Senator,
D-South Carolina

4

Plain and simple, the fact is economic pressures brought about by deregulation have eroded the margin of safety in the skies. As long as I am Chairman of this [Commerce] Committee, I will accept no knee-jerk reactions against the possibility of reimposing government regulations in the interest of safety.

At Senate Commerce
Committee hearing, Washington,
Oct. 15/The New York Times, 10-16:8.

James J. Howard
United States Representative,
D-New Jersey

5

[Criticizing a House vote to allow an increase in the speed limit from 55 m.p.h. to 65 m.p.h. on some rural highways]: Are we willing to kill and maim thousands of people just so we can have one extra minute a day? . . . [The Western states that support the increase in speed limits are] against the Federal government on everything. I don't know why they stay in the Union.

To reporters, Washington, March 18/
Los Angeles Times, 3-19:(I)1.

Lee A. Iacocca
Chairman,
Chrysler Corporation

6

[On charges that Chrysler has sold cars as new that it had lent to its executives to test drive, and had disconnected the odometers on those cars]: Did we screw up? You bet we did. We're human, and sometimes people do some

(LEE A. IACOCCA)

pretty dumb things . . . The first thing was just dumb. We test-drove a small percentage of our cars with the odometers disengaged and didn't tell our customers. The second thing, I think, went beyond dumb, and reached all the way out to stupid—a few cars were damaged in testing badly enough that they should never have been sold as new. Those are mistakes we will never make again. Period . . . [But] the only law we broke was the law of common sense.

News conference, Detroit, July 1/
Los Angeles Times, 7-2:(IV)1.

Alfred E. Kahn
Professor of political economy,
Cornell University;
Former Chairman,
Civil Aeronautics Board
of the United States

1

[If re-regulation of the airline industry means] the government doing the things it should always have been doing all through these years, then clearly there is a need. But that's not re-regulation. That's the government fulfilling its responsibilities . . . deregulation did precisely what we wanted it to do. People who couldn't fly before are flocking to these low fares, with all the inconvenience, the advance reservations, the penalties, the crowding, the narrow seating. That's giving people what they want.

The Christian Science Monitor, 8-24:1,14.

2

[Criticizing the U.S. Department of Transportation's handling of airline mergers, which critics now say has been too permissive]: It seems to me, DOT never met a merger they didn't like. What they did, in effect, was let the elephants go through, and now they're straining at a gnat [the possible turn-down of the proposed USAir-Piedmont merger].

Interview/
The Christian Science Monitor, 9-25:3.

Richard Lally
Vice president
in charge of security,
Air Transport Association

3

It's the nature of the beast when it comes to aviation—we have a single aviation incident, and there is a tremendous [public] response, whether it's an accident, hijacking or whatever. On the other hand, we can have a pipeline explosion or thousands of deaths on the highway, and we don't get the same reaction. Aviation occupies a special niche in our society. And probably deservedly so. People expect a higher standard of performance from aviation than they do from other activities in our society.

Interview/USA Today, 12-10:(A)11.

John Lauber
Member, National
Transportation Safety Board
of the United States

4

As we go into more highly automated [aircraft] cockpits—rather than eliminating human error, which was the intent—all we're doing is creating new opportunities for even worse kinds of human error . . . It's extremely important to take a look at where we are with pilot training, especially with regard to . . . crew coordination and communication. We have not, as an industry, done an adequate job in training people in those skills . . . [or] given adequate recognition to the central role of human . . . error.

Interview, Aug. 24/
USA Today, 8-25:(A)3.

Frank Lautenberg
United States Senator,
D-New Jersey

5

There are questions about whether there's a sufficient penalty system to deter railroads from careless or sloppy procedures, whether the fines that are imposed are significant enough, whether all of the violations of safety rules are appropriately reported. Apparently there are al-

(FRANK LAUTENBERG)

most 300,000 violations established each year, and only 3,000 or 4,000 of those are seriously considered, and fined. So the safety shield for rail safety seems to be full of holes.

Interview/USA Today, 1-22:(A)11.

Michael E. Levine
Professor of management,
Yale University; Member,
Federal Aviation Safety Commission

1

Aviation safety is a serious business. Only the fanatic few among us are prepared to die for the right to buy a deep-discount ticket. And it is natural to worry that the same system that is giving us the discounts must be cutting corners on safety.

At transportation safety conference,
Northwestern University/
Los Angeles Times, 6-29:(IV)6.

2

Any look at the statistical record would suggest that aviation has gotten safer and safer since 1978. [But] the public seems very conscious of the way the system is running, partly because there have been a lot of delays and there is a widespread perception that service quality has gone down. When the public sees things a little disorganized—they get to the airport and the flight is delayed or canceled or they see that service isn't what they expect it to be—they may wonder whether the things they can't see, like maintenance and traffic control, are deteriorating as well.

Interview/USA Today, 8-18:(A)11.

John Leyden
Spokesman
for the Federal
Aviation Administration

3

We [the FAA] invented air-traffic control and made it the best system in the world. Now all of a sudden everybody says, "Hey, the FAA can't be trusted to run the air-traffic-control system." They say: "You guys have lost your commitment to public safety." Again, that's nonsense. Safety is always job one.

The Christian Science Monitor, 6-4:3.

T. Allan McArtor
Administrator,
Federal Aviation Administration
of the United States

4

The executive management of every air-carrier certificate holder [airline] is hereby on notice. If you do not comply with your obligations to maintain your fleets and fulfill the obligations of your operating certificates, you will not operate in the national airspace. This goes for large carriers as well as small ones. Pilots, co-pilots, flight engineers and other crew members also are on notice. If you are not drug-free, if you are not technically proficient, if you cannot demonstrate your skills, you will not fly in the national airspace.

At his swearing-in,
Washington, July 27/
The Washington Post,
7-28:(A)13.

5

[Saying airlines and pilots should get back to the basics when it comes to air safety]: I'm talking about [problems of] landing on the wrong runway, landing at the wrong airport, taxiing across runways without clearance, turning left instead of turning right, dialing in wrong way-points in a navigational computer, inadvertently shutting down engines in flight . . . It is necessary to ensure that every pilot in the system, every day, is earning his wings that day . . . I want to create a sense of individual responsibility on the part of [airline] executives . . . every bit as much as they feel accountable for putting out the precise financial condition of the airline.

News conference, Aug. 5/
USA Today, 8-6:(A)1.

Herbert R. McClure
Deputy Director,
General Accounting Office
of the United States

1

Additional [air-traffic] controllers should reduce the concern [about air safety]. The problem remains, however, that based on what's known to us and the public, it's impossible to tell how many controllers the FAA actually needs . . . The fact is that the FAA simply hasn't established a standard that it believes. It has really only been in the last several months that it's been clear to us why this issue has been so controversial and cloudy. This is because nobody has anything to go on, because the FAA hasn't defined these things.

The Christian Science Monitor, 6-5:3.

W. Allen Moore
Chief of Staff
for the Republican minority,
U.S. Senate Commerce, Science
and Transportation Committee

2

Today, members of the traveling public have little assurance when they board a plane, a train or a bus, or get into a car, that they will not be putting their lives into the hands of a drunk or drugged pilot, engineer, bus driver or trucker. We do not routinely test these transportation employees whose alertness and judgment may separate us from safety and disaster.

At transportation safety conference,
Northwestern University/
Los Angeles Times, 6-29:(IV)6.

L. Fletcher Prouty
Railroad consultant
to government

3

The 200,000 miles of railroad in this country are in the hands of the freight operators,

and an American freight train travels at an average speed of 20.1 miles an hour. Tracks throughout the country therefore have small-radius curves and are flat—they are not banked on the curves. The whole geometry is wrong for high-speed trains. Since the late 1970s, when the Department of Transportation decreed that Northeast Corridor tracks must in perpetuity carry freight as well as passenger trains, the corridor has been a Russian roulette game. Fatal crashes are inevitable.

The New York Times,
1-12:14.

Frank Spencer
Professor
of transportation studies,
Northwestern University

4

[On the new labor union for air-traffic controllers, coming six years after President Reagan fired all controllers who went on strike and thus ruined the previous union]: It was the *permanent* firing that was such a blow to the nation's labor movement. Nobody had ever done that before. Even murderers serve their time in prison and are released. These controllers, though, were ostracized from careers for life . . . [The government] said the whole strike was due to some misguided missiles in the leadership of the controller group who convinced the masses through hysterics that they were being mistreated. But such wasn't the case . . . It was only a matter of time before we had a union all over again, because the basic problems of dealing with people were not settled very well. You can't have a group that large without anybody to speak for them.

Interview/
The Christian Science Monitor,
6-16:23.

Urban Affairs

Alan Beals
Executive director,
National League of Cities

1

We [in the cities] are worried about what lies ahead. Most of the quick solutions—capital cutbacks, new fees, hiring freezes and contracting out—have been wrung dry. The signals are pointing to tougher times and more stress on local government finances. Our national leaders would be well advised to study this report [on city fiscal matters] carefully and heed these warning signals . . . [Cities are maintaining balanced budgets] through cutbacks and postponements that are eroding their capacity just to maintain current services, not to mention their ability to deal with future problems and stresses.

The New York Times, 6-30:1,18.

Pierre S. du Pont IV
Former Governor of Delaware (R);
Candidate for the 1988
Republican Presidential nomination

2

[Addressing Mayors]: I'll leave to the others the idea that they can curry favor with promises of more money [for cities]. We will never create more opportunities for people if we all assume that the only thing we can do is paper over the problems of urban America by asking the Federal government for a bigger check each year.

At United States Conference
of Mayors, Nashville, Tenn.,
June 16/The New York Times, 6-17:11.

Richard A. Gephardt
United States Representative,
D-Missouri; Candidate for the 1988
Democratic Presidential nomination

3

The trouble with American cities today is that the people in our cities are in trouble, deep

trouble, and that is what [President] Ronald Reagan doesn't care to see. Millions are living in or on the edge of desperation.

At United States Conference
of Mayors, Nashville, Tenn.,
June 15/USA Today, 6-16:(A)8.

John Gunther
Former executive director
and general counsel,
United States
Conference of Mayors

4

The pay for Mayors in cities that have city managers, except for a few California cities, is almost non-existent. The Mayor of Dallas—I don't know if they've just changed it or not—he'd get paid $10 a week. And the Mayor of Boulder, Colorado, was paid nothing. Zero. So what you have is people can't stay in office very long. And that's bad, I think, for the system.

Interview/USA Today, 6-18:(A)9.

Truman A. Hartshorn
Chairman,
department of geography,
Georgia State University

5

The American metropolis today no longer consists of a dominant central city surrounded by a ring of dormitory suburbs. That residential belt of the recent past has been swiftly transformed during the last 10 years into a curvilinear outer city, which is now home to an ever-increasing majority of the urbanized area's economic activities.

Los Angeles Times, 5-21:(I)24.

Paul G. Kirk, Jr.
Chairman,
Democratic National Committee

6

The Democratic Mayors can be assured that the Democratic Party will have a national mes-

(PAUL G. KIRK, JR.)

sage for a national audience in 1988. And you can also be assured that the voices and the values of the families of America's cities will be part of that message and a part of that audience . . . The Republican policy toward the cities of America has been the same as toward the people of America—a "survival of the fittest" approach. They deprived the Mayors of needed revenues and gave you all the responsibilities. But . . . you can't go it alone any longer. The time for a new American partnership is now.

At United States Conference
of Mayors, Nashville, Tenn.,
June 14/Los Angeles Times, 6-15:(I)4.

Edward I. Koch
Mayor of New York

1

I sense that the spirit and imagination of American politics have, once again, somehow disengaged from city life. What I worry about is this: Who will speak for the cities? Who will speak for Detroit and New York? Who will speak for what, in reality, if not in memories and dreams, is still the true political, social and economic heartland of America?

Before Economic Club
of Detroit, April 27/
The New York Times, 4-28:10.

2

The urban agenda will never be addressed by Republicans. They just don't believe in it.

At United States Conference
of Mayors, Nashville, Tenn./
USA Today, 6-18:(A)4.

Peter O. Muller
Professor of geography,
University of Miami

3

The recent changes of the American metropolis have transformed "bedroom suburbia" into the burgeoning outer city that is well into its way to urban dominance in every region of the

United States. Thus, in the late 1980s, the outer city is no longer "sub" to the "urb" and its re-examination is overdue. That can only elevate this newest urban form to its rightful place—for the suburbs today have clearly become the essence of the contemporary city.

At "Suburbia Re-Examined"
conference, Hempstead, N.Y./
The New York Times, 6-15:16.

Joseph P. Riley, Jr.
Mayor of Charleston, S.C.;
President, United States
Conference of Mayors

4

Our message is that the Federal government is really proposing to abandon many of its very legitimate, very appropriate responsibilities to the citizens of our cities . . . We've [the cities] removed the fat. We've removed the muscle. And now we're cutting into the bone.

News conference/
The Washington Post, 1-7:(A)14.

5

We must make certain that the urban agenda is part of the agenda of the next President of the United States. The programs of this [Reagan] Administration have really, to a large extent, ignored the needs of our cities.

At United States Conference
of Mayors, Nashville, Tenn./
The New York Times, 6-15:13.

Pat Robertson
Evangelist;
Candidate for the 1988
Republican Presidential nomination

6

[Proposing a 10 per cent income-tax credit for public contributions to officially authorized urban projects]: I do not think the Mayors of our nation should be coming like mendicants, hat in hand, to the Federal government asking

245

WHAT THEY SAID IN 1987

(PAT ROBERTSON)

for your share of money that's already been taken from your communities and taken to Washington.

At United States Conference
of Mayors, Nashville, Tenn.,
June 16/Los Angeles Times, 6-17:(I)16.

Harold Washington
Mayor of Chicago

1

[The late President] John F. Kennedy used to say there's no school for Presidents. Well, there's no school for Mayors, either. Before I was elected, I thought I understood city government. And I did—academically. But there are still some things you can't know until you do it.

Interview/
The New York Times, 5-4:12.

Walter B. Wriston
Former chairman,
Citicorp
(Citibank, New York)

2

[Saying it is important for corporations to remain in big cities]: The basic reason that you stay is that all of the great ideas of the world were formed in urban centers: Athens, Rome, Paris, London, New York. The reason is that in New York you can meet 10 fellows or women who are smarter than you are every day of the week. The intellectual stimulation of New York is what it is all about. If you go out in the woods somewhere and eat lunch in some company dining room, the first thing you know, you think you know all there is to know in the world.

The New York Times, 6-9:15.

PART TWO

International Affairs

Africa

Moshe Arens
Minister
without portfolio
of Israel

1

[Defending Israel's arms sales to South Africa despite that country's apartheid system]: Israel has to export arms to maintain a defense industry without which this country could not survive. In 1973, Israel found itself isolated and beleaguered in Africa with countries which long benefited from relations with us cutting ties in hope of Arab cash from the oil boom. To find a country then that would be helpful to us in our hour of need was not easy. But the South African government was one such government which was ready to help.

To American Jewish leaders,
Jerusalem, March 20/
Los Angeles Times, 3-21:(I)11.

Richard L. Armitage
Assistant Secretary
for International
Security Affairs,
Department of Defense
of the United States

2

[On Chad's recent military victories over Libya in the war between those two countries]: [Libyan leader Muammar] Qaddafi has always put great stake in his military machine, and this is clearly the most significant military and psychological defeat since the Chad war began. In the Arab world, and in Africa, the fear of Qaddafi is lessening daily . . . I predict Qaddafi will be seen as almost a comic parody. But none of these setbacks mean his imminent demise is on the horizon. He is very competent, and if our information is correct, so are his security forces.

March 27/
The New York Times, 3-28:3.

Elijah Barayi
President,
Congress of South
African Trade Unions

3

[Criticizing South African President Pieter Botha and that country's apartheid system]: I'm here to bury P.W. Botha, not to praise him . . . There can be no freedom in this country unless the [banned] African National Congress is involved . . . I know that by [my] saying this, the Botha regime will one day lock me up, but let them do so. This intransigent government will not hand over power. The black majority will have to seize power from the intransigent government.

At South African
Trade Unions conference,
Witwatersrand University, July 15/
Los Angeles Times, 7-16:(I)8.

Pieter W. Botha
President
of South Africa

4

Discussions with the ANC are possible only if it severs its ties and terminates its subservience to the South African Communist Party, abandons violence and participates, as peaceful South African citizens, in constitutional processes in South Africa . . . I must warn those who have committed themselves irrevocably to the violent overthrow of the state and the disruption of society that the government will not for a moment hesitate to act decisively against them. The government would like to lift the state of emergency, but it will maintain its basic responsibility to uphold law and order purposefully at all times.

Before South African
Parliament, Cape Town,
Jan. 30/Los Angeles Times,
1-31:(I)1,10.

WHAT THEY SAID IN 1987

(PIETER W. BOTHA)

1

The demand is often made here and abroad that South Africa should adopt a so-called one-man, one-vote non-racial democracy. In our circumstances, this demand cannot lead to a just dispensation in a multi-cultural society.

Before South African Parliament,
Cape Town, Jan. 30/
Los Angeles Times, 1-31:(I)10.

2

[Criticizing U.S. economic sanctions against South Africa to protest that country's apartheid system]: The Kremlin has had its work done for it in Washington. South Africa is the scapegoat for America's bad conscience on race relations . . . These [Americans supporting sanctions] are not only blind to reality, but they will be satisfied with nothing less than total capitulation to the revolutionary forces in South Africa . . . But we are not prepared to surrender.

Election campaign address,
Lichtenburg, South Africa, March 25/
Los Angeles Times, 3-26:(I)5.

3

South Africa is standing in the front line of the international war against terrorism, and we are experiencing a total onslaught against us [by those fighting apartheid], a total strategy that includes both military and propaganda campaigns and an effort to disrupt our economy . . . It's easy for people to shout about reform, but it's another thing to deal with the realities of this country. But despite our problems with security, with the economy, and with international sanctions against us, we are busy with a spirit of renewal . . . Liberals always scream and denounce, but they can never build.

At rally, Stellenbosch,
South Africa, April 22/
Los Angeles Times, 4-23:(I)1,14.

4

[On his party's victory in the recent national elections]: The outside world must now have a clear picture that they cannot dictate to South Africa [regarding the apartheid system]. South Africans want to solve their own problems, and South Africans believe in moderate reform, well-balanced reform. But South Africa's white electorate is not prepared to accept and follow a policy that will lead to one group [blacks] dominating the other [whites]. The outside world must accept that the white electorate believes they are here to stay . . . and are determined to follow their convictions.

Interview, May 7/
Los Angeles Times, 5-8:(I)12.

5

[On the apartheid system in South Africa]: My government and I have the power and the desire to negotiate with [black] leaders who reject violence and intimidation as instruments for achieving political ends. These negotiations will be honest meetings of men of peace and good-will, determined to find peaceful solutions to our common problems.

Speech, Sebokeng,
South Africa, June 4/
The New York Times, 6-5:3.

6

[Saying he is extending the state of emergency imposed last year in response to violent anti-apartheid protests]: On June 12 last year, here in Parliament, I referred to the background against which deeds of violence and unrest were being planned and executed. According to information provided to me, I am of the opinion that this background still exists . . . We will fight them [the ANC], for the simple reason that they are part and parcel of the terrorist curse besetting the world today . . . You cannot talk with the ANC without talking to its present leaders [and] we reject them for their philosophy of violence and terror . . . Considering the safety of the public and the maintenance of public order, I have decided to proclaim a state of emergency once more in the whole of the republic.

Before South African Parliament,
Cape Town, June 10/
The Washington Post,
6-11:(A)25,26.

Roelof F. Botha
Foreign Minister
of South Africa

1

[Criticizing the U.S. imposition of economic sanctions against South Africa to protest the apartheid system]: It is time to show the American Congress that they will not determine our future. The Congressional legislation [imposing sanctions] was an outside intrusion trying to solve our problems, and almost any South African will reject any attempt to tell us what we need to do. There is a strong anti-American feeling in this country now . . . and in this way the United States has become more and more irrelevant in the whole of southern Africa.

To foreign correspondents,
Cape Town, South Africa, Feb. 3/
Los Angeles Times, 2-4:(I)5.

2

[Criticizing the African National Congress' fight against apartheid in South Africa]: It is unacceptable to the South African government that the ANC should be permitted to get away with murder, while no stone is left unturned to criticize the government every time steps are taken to protect our people against violence . . . the ANC and its fellow travelers want to gain power through violence and death. The ANC and its front organizations in the republic, which operate under the guise of priestly hypocrisy, do not care in the least for democracy or for fundamental human rights . . . In fact, they abuse democracy to destroy freedom.

To reporters, April 14/
The Washington Post, 4-15:(A)27.

Gatsha Buthelezi
Chief Minister of KwaZulu
(black South African homeland);
Leader, South African
Zulu people

3

The ANC does not talk to me and attempts to isolate me. That is foolish, because I have millions of supporters . . . We are not cowards.

Rather, we continue the tradition of nonviolence in which the ANC was founded [but which it has abandoned in favor of a more militaristic fight against apartheid] . . . I am dissatisfied with the pace of progress [against apartheid in South Africa], but it would be irresponsible to assert that nothing had happened during the past few years. The President [Pieter Botha] has shown courage by coming before Parliament and calling apartheid outdated.

Interview/
World Press Review,
January:34,35.

4

Black-on-black violence [in South Africa] does nothing but create a vicious circle of death and despair. The struggle for black unity and liberation is being set back time and again . . . Blacks must show each other that we have not been so dehumanized by the [apartheid] system that all that is left is to turn on each other like a pack of rabid dogs. What future have we if our dignity and our decency is destroyed in ongoing orgies of hate and revenge?

Los Angeles Times, 9-29:(I)9.

Joaquim A. Chissano
President of Mozambique

5

Some would say that terrorism does not allow development. But development is a fight against terrorism. The United States and others cannot just cross their arms and say, "We can't help Mozambique [financially] because of [antigovernment rebel] terrorism." They have to get rid of terrorism, and development would contribute to its decrease.

Interview/
The New York Times, 1-28:3.

Venancio de Moura
Deputy Foreign Minister
of Angola

6

[On the presence of Cuban forces in Angola]: The Cubans are our friends indeed, and

(VENANCIO DE MOURA)

they are helping us solve many problems, including health, education, construction and manpower training, and not just assisting with defense. A time will come when they are not necessary for our security, but that is not yet the case.

Interview/
Los Angeles Times, 7-2:(I)8.

Jose Eduardo dos Santos
President of Angola

1

[On Cuban troops in Angola]: No country in southern Africa can feel secure as long as apartheid exists [in South Africa]. As long as apartheid continues to threaten, the Cuban forces must remain.

News conference,
Luanda, Angola, June 29/
The New York Times, 6-30:2.

2

[On when he will ask Cuban forces to leave his country]: From our point of view, there will be total peace and tranquility only when Namibia is free and apartheid [in South Africa] is ended. As long as apartheid continues to threaten us, Cuban forces will remain in Angola . . . No country of southern Africa will feel secure as long as apartheid exists. But every time the military situation shows relative improvement, the Cuban forces are pulled back. The timetable for their withdrawal is a function of the military situation.

News conference,
Luanda, Angola/
Los Angeles Times, 7-2:(I)8.

Colin Eglin
Leader,
Progressive Federal Party
of South Africa

3

[Criticizing the state of emergency imposed by the ruling National Party in response to anti-

apartheid violence in South Africa]: The state of emergency, with its police powers, its abrogation of the rule of law . . . is proof that the National Party, after 39 years in office, is incapable of governing this country by democratic means . . . If a government that has ruled for nearly 40 years has to resort to these measures to maintain peace, law and order, it deserves to be thrown out of office . . . This wonderful country of ours is in a mess, thanks to the incompetence of a government that has lost its way and which now, mercifully for South Africa, is starting to lose both members and supporters.

Before South African Parliament,
Cape Town, Feb. 2/
Los Angeles Times, 2-3:(I)5.

Bobby Godsell
Chief labor negotiator,
Anglo-American Corporation
(South Africa)

4

There is a continuing romanticism in the minds of people inside and outside South Africa which thinks that the trade-union movement is the short-cut to [anti-apartheid] revolution. They are wrong. If the trade-union movement devotes its resources to a head-on confrontation with the South African state through a national strike, the government will smash the trade-union movement. The trade-union movement is a beachhead for incremental change toward a non-racial society. But when you mistake a beachhead for incremental change for a short-cut to revolution, you destroy that beachhead.

The New York Times, 8-25:4.

Anton Harber
Editor,
"Johannesburg Weekly Mail"
(South Africa)

5

[Because of government emergency restrictions on the press,] we cannot discuss the most vital subjects [in South Africa]. In fact, if you want to discuss security-force actions at the

252

(ANTON HARBER)

dinner table—whether favorably or unfavorably—
you technically need permission . . . In South
Africa, people will be making decisions about
their future without being told about the real
situation. It is frightening to consider the consequences, because I fear that people will die of
ignorance.

Interview/
World Press Review,
March: 38.

Jesse L. Jackson
Civil-rights leader;
Candidate for the 1988
U.S. Democratic
Presidential nomination

1

[Criticizing the apartheid system in South
Africa]: Every moral and ethical imperative
that made us say "no" to [Adolf] Hitler and the
Third Reich [in Germany during World War II]
should make us say "no" to South Africa's
[President] Pieter W. Botha in the Fourth
Reich. One difference in the Third Reich is that
so much of Hitler's dirt was in the dark. In the
case of Botha, he is bold, public, has nuclear
power, an open relationship with America . . .
It is that entanglement that makes a very complicated and yet morally challenging situation.

Interview/
The Washington Post,
10-15:(A)11.

Kenneth D. Kaunda
President of Zambia

2

[Criticizing violence by the government of
South Africa against blacks in that country]:
Why is it that when there was a Hitler . . . killing whites, the Western world got up to fight?
Here we are told that we must be patient. [The
reason is that] the black man is not worth anything in their minds. They're happy, as long as
they get their gold, platinum, copper.

Interview, Lusaka, Zambia/
The Christian Science Monitor,
8-18:7.

Alan L. Keyes
Assistant Secretary
for International Organizations,
Department of State
of the United States

3

I think that it's terribly important that the
idea that democracy can work be vindicated in
South Africa . . . All the things that the black
people of South Africa have been denied [be-
cause of apartheid] can be realized if they can
establish a real democracy. But they won't do it
through a cataclysmic violence or revolution.
Out of the barrel of a gun has not grown freedom. Out of the barrel of a gun, when you look
around the world, has grown tragedy—in Ethiopia and in Uganda and in Cambodia. It is the
betrayal of the democratic aspiration, not its
realization.

Interview, Washington, Sept. 17/
The Washington Post, 9-18:(D)9.

Stephen Lewis
Canadian Ambassador
to the United Nations;
Special representative
of the UN Secretary General
for African economic growth

4

Despite Herculean efforts by all the African
governments, there has been a calamitous decline in economic circumstances. Either the
world mounts an effort with the scope of the
Marshall Plan—or the continent breaks.

The Washington Post, 10-16:(A)36.

Tom Lodge
Political scientist and
specialist in black politics,
University of Witwatersrand
(South Africa)

5

[The militant anti-apartheid African National Congress] may continue to use the rhetoric of the seizure of power, and the military
struggle will still play a role; but I think they
have recognized that, in the end, the ANC's

WHAT THEY SAID IN 1987

(TOM LODGE)

victory is going to come as a result of shifts of mood which will affect people in decision-making positions within South Africa.

The Washington Post, 1-19:(A)1.

Johnstone Makatini
*Director
of international affairs,
banned African National
Congress (South Africa)*

1

The illegitimacy of the apartheid regime [in South Africa] is self-evident. Everyone is agreed that apartheid as a system cannot be reformed . . . and so our challenge is to build up a replacement. It is not enough to say apartheid must go. We must say what and who will replace it . . . We should have a clear program of action in various capitals on the position of the ANC as the incontestable vanguard of the broad democratic movement in South Africa, even as the sole authentic representative of the oppressed people of the country. Once they understand it, no one can fault the position of the ANC—not even the [U.S.] Reagan Administration—when we say that South Africa belongs to all who live in it, black and white, and that the birthrights of all should be guaranteed, regardless of race, creed or color . . . We sound like the American Founding Fathers.

*At anti-apartheid conference,
Arusha, Tanzania/
Los Angeles Times, 12-7:(I)8.*

Govan A. Mbeki
*Former chairman,
banned African National
Congress (South Africa)*

2

[On his being released from South African prison after serving 23 years for plotting to overthrow the government]: I am a member of the African National Congress. The ideas for which I went to jail and for which the ANC stands I still embrace . . . I am still a member

of the [South African Communist Party]. I still embrace Marxist views . . . We all belong to South Africa. South Africa belongs to all of us. With this as a premise, it appears to me that it should not be difficult to find solutions.

*News conference,
Port Elizabeth, South Africa,
Nov. 5/The New York Times, 11-6:4.*

Thabo Mbeki
*Top official,
banned African National
Congress (South Africa)*

3

One myth that we want to kill off is that we do not want the United States involved in southern Africa, and that the ANC is involved in some clever conspiracy to put the Soviet Union in the best position in this region. This is definitely not so, not at all. We want the United States involved. And we want Americans to know that . . . It is important the United States be seen by countries like the United Kingdom, West Germany and Japan to have shifted and to be taking a strong and consistent anti-apartheid position [against South Africa] and not acting timidly with U.S. companies finding clever ways to "disinvest" without leaving [South Africa].

*Interview, Gaborone, Botswana/
Los Angeles Times, 1-26:(I)8.*

Robert S. McNamara
*Chairman of the jury,
1987 Africa Prize for Leadership
for the Sustainable End of Hunger;
Former President,
International Bank
for Reconstruction and
Development (World Bank)*

4

Part of the [economic] problem in Africa is of their own doing. They have had inadequate pricing policies, particularly in agriculture. They haven't provided incentives to farmers to produce more. They had over-valued exchange rates, which penalized their exports. They've had fiscal deficits, resulting from wasteful ex-

(ROBERT S. McNAMARA)

penditures. They've had inefficient public enterprises. They've had over-regulation of their economies. So, they have made mistakes.

Interview/USA Today, 9-14:(A)15.

Smangaliso Mkhwatsha
General secretary,
South African Catholic
Bishops Conference

1

[Criticizing apartheid in South Africa]: I feel that it is very important to create a new climate in this country—a climate conducive to dialogue—where people can really sit down and listen to one another and try to find a solution to the problems that face us . . . I don't think that any of us opposed to an unjust system, such as exists in this country, can do any different. I don't think that anyone can choose not to struggle against an unjust system or tyranny . . . I think it is our duty to fight for a new society that is truly non-racial and truly democratic.

News conference,
Pretoria, June 12/
Los Angeles Times, 6-13:(I)6.

Daniel Arap Moi
President of Kenya

2

[On the apartheid system in South Africa]: I reminded [U.S.] President Reagan that in South Africa the values of human dignity our two countries cherish are being abused daily. An end to apartheid is inevitable, and the sooner it comes, the less will be the bloodshed and violence. The world community in general, and Africa in particular, look upon the United States for a deeper commitment to this cause.

Washington, March 12/
Los Angeles Times, 3-13:(I)5.

Rapu Molekane
General secretary,
South African Youth Congress

3

[Urging black youths to isolate black policemen, local officials, soldiers and others whom they view as collaborators with apartheid in South Africa]: Do not talk with them, do not mix with their children, do not let them in your shops. If you allow an informer in, you are aiding and abetting apartheid. We must isolate these people. Only if they resign and march step by step with us in the struggle can we accept them . . . We need to involve each and every youth on every street in every block and intensify the struggle for peace, freedom and liberty. When we achieve this, we will be able to fly the [ANC's] green, gold and black flag, to see the face of [imprisoned apartheid foe] Nelson Mandela and to listen to [ANC leader] Oliver Tambo speak.

At rally, Soweto,
South Africa, June 16/
Los Angeles Times, 6-17:(I)9.

James Motlatsi
President,
National Union of Mineworkers
(South Africa)

4

Comrades, the answer to our problems on the mines is clear. We need to take control. Nineteen eighty-seven is the year we march in that direction . . . Under capitalism, we will never find a solution to our problems. It is only with a democratic socialist South Africa that the working class and all the oppressed people will have the wealth which they produce under their control.

At National Union
of Mineworkers congress, February/
The Christian Science Monitor,
8-11:28.

Dirk Mudge
Minister of Finance
of Namibia

5

In this country, political parties are normally based on ethnic groupings. But it's one thing to have a political party based on ethnicity and another thing to have a government based on ethnicity. Personally, I would not participate in ethnic elections. We want nation-wide elections.

The Washington Post, 6-17:(A)27.

WHAT THEY SAID IN 1987

Beyers Naude
General secretary,
South African Council
of Churches

1

[On the apartheid system in South Africa]: There is a long and deep-rooted fear in the mind of the Afrikaner of being overwhelmed by alien religious, political and cultural forces . . . of loss of language, identity and economic security. Over decades, the Afrikaner was made to believe his deliberate separation from the black community was divinely ordained and approved, and as long as there is that divine justification for separation, it is very difficult to break through that barrier. Because of their religious background, there is almost a schizophrenic fear of anything to be seen as Marxist or Communist, and any propaganda exploiting that fear for political goals can be very effective. As far as other South African whites are concerned, they know that if the situation worsens there is a back door to Britain, Germany or Holland. But the Afrikaner has nowhere to go and that has a double effect. It can strengthen the laager mentality, but it can also force other Afrikaners to say that if eventually we are pushed into a corner we will have to find an acceptable compromise for us and the blacks. They want to postpone that as long as possible. But the blacks are no longer prepared to hear those words, "be patient."

The Washington Post, 2-10:(A)18.

Julius K. Nyerere
Former President of Tanzania

2

[Saying apartheid reforms recently instituted by the South African government are merely to dupe blacks into abandoning the fight against apartheid[: We are told there are [South African] moderates who have to be supported. We are told by the [U.S. President] Ronald Reagans and the [British Prime Minister] Margaret Thatchers of the world that we should negotiate with the apartheid government to get more reform. [But] all these reforms are merely an attempt to confuse the people and delay the

inevitable . . . All that the so-called reforms amount to is an amelioration of the prison house called apartheid.

At anti-apartheid conference,
Arusha, Tanzania, Dec. 1/
The Washington Post, 12-2:(A)34.

Olusegun Obasanjo
Former Head of State
of Nigeria

3

If Africa becomes a positive contributor to peace, security, economic cooperation and economic development in the world, [then] that part of the world will to a large extent cease to be a destabilizing factor in the equation of international peace and security. [Improvements in African living standards] will have implications for America, Europe, the socialist bloc and the Third World as a whole. With more position and power, Africa can then contribute more meaningfully, more actively and more positively to the economic progress of the world through world trade.

Interview, New York/
The Christian Science Monitor,
3-18:17.

Harry Oppenheimer
Former chairman,
Anglo-American Corporation
(South Africa)

4

[On the apartheid system in South Africa]: What's wrong is that we've got a government— and largely, a white public—which does not want to share power in a meaningful way with black people. More has been done than most people would give this government credit for. But the fear of giving blacks a genuine share in political power is very great. [Still,] this is something which has got to be done, both because I don't believe in the long run that it can be resisted or ought to be resisted . . . I've never thought that [foreign economic] sanctions would simply have no effect [in changing apartheid policy in South Africa], but I also don't

(HARRY OPPENHEIMER)

think the government has been in the least influenced in a better direction. The whole sanctions campaign is predicated on the idea that you can turn South Africa into a real democracy in a year, and you can't. It's going to take time, and we've just got to see it through.

Interview, Johannesburg/
Newsweek, 9-14:53.

Edward J. Perkins
United States Ambassador
to South Africa

1

[Criticizing new South African regulations prohibiting demonstrations that protest detention of those involved in anti-apartheid actions]: It is said that a government which claims to uphold the values of human dignity, and which portrays itself as secure and strong, should be so intimidated by the peaceful protestations of its citizens that it declares those protestations to be illegal. The new regulations banning any public appeal for the release of detainees simply point to the erosion of fundamental liberties in this country. Freedom of assembly, the freedom to speak out, and the freedom to give and receive information which are deemed vital to the community are in serious jeopardy.

Written statement, April 13/
The Washington Post, 4-14:(A)16.

2

[There is a need for] more inventive ways to manage our relationship with the government of South Africa and with the South African people. We have to make abundantly clear in almost any way we can our abhorrence of a system [apartheid] which has a minority of the population enjoying economic and political rights at the expense of the majority.

Speech, Oregon/
The Christian Science Monitor,
6-25:11.

3

The imposition of sanctions [by the U.S. against South Africa to protest that country's

apartheid system] was largely the result of frustration with the current situation and our hope to positively influence it. But, in practical terms, the effect of sanctions is much harder to assess . . . In the long run, however, I doubt that the sale of assets or the withdrawal of Western businesses will add to a solution here.

Before Executive Women's Club,
Johannesburg, Aug. 19/
The New York Times, 8-20:5.

Jonas Savimbi
Leader,
National Union for the Total
Independence of Angola

4

The day the Angolan problem [Communist rule] is solved, six months later Namibia will be independent. This is within reach of daring minds. As long as the Cubans remain in Angola, there will always be the "Cuban problem" blocking Namibian independence. If they were withdrawn, South Africa would no longer have a pretext for delaying Namibian independence . . . I am convinced that the South Africans, against their will, would then have to relinquish Namibia.

Interview, Jamba, Angola/
Los Angeles Times,
12-26:(I)1,16.

Rachid Sfar
Prime Minister of Tunisia

5

We have urged the opposition [in Tunisia] to be a responsible opposition. Tunisia cannot create a democracy like America's straight away. It has to be done in stages . . . I have urged the opposition to accept that President [Habib] Bourguiba remains the final arbiter and that his decisions, his personal decisions, are final. There are other Tunisians, persons who learned democracy in the Bourguiba school, and we can make democracy with them.

Interview/
The New York Times,
6-25:4.

WHAT THEY SAID IN 1987

George P. Shultz
Secretary of State
of the United States

1

Over the course of the 1980s, the Soviets have sent 20 times as much arms to nations of sub-Saharan Africa as the United States [which concentrated on economic aid]. These figures capture the difference between two very different visions of Africa's future. In one, the continent becomes an outpost of militarism and strategic designs. The other vision sees Africa . . . as a collection of nations whose people . . . are paramount.

To Senegalese business leaders
and Cabinet officials,
Dakar, Senegal, Jan. 8/
Los Angeles Times, 1-9:(I)11.

2

[Criticizing South African restrictions on press reporting by American and other newspapers]: My reaction is very negative, and we've said that in our diplomatic channels. We think it's important that our news organizations have an opportunity to report what's going on. It is more of a kind of self-imposed isolation. It [South Africa] is becoming isolated diplomatically, it's becoming isolated financially and it's isolating itself from the stream of world opinion when [by expelling some foreign reporters] it takes away from its country people who are reporting to the world what's going on.

Nairobi, Kenya, Jan. 9/
The New York Times, 1-10:4.

3

[Criticizing the apartheid system in South Africa]: The time has come for South Africans to act on their hopes, not their fears. They will find a friend in the United States when they do so, a friend that is realistic in its understanding, hopeful in its expectations and optimistic in its vision of what they can achieve. If the contending parties in South Africa are ready to take risks for peace, they may be assured of the active political, diplomatic and economic support of the United States and its allies . . . Apartheid has succeeded all too well in its design of keeping the races apart. South Africans of different races may talk *about* one another all the time, but they all too rarely talk *to* one another. As South Africans move toward meaningful negotiations, the United States would be willing to encourage this process.

Before Business Council
for International Understanding,
New York, Sept. 29/
Los Angeles Times, 9-30:(I)12.

4

[On U.S. policy toward South Africa's apartheid system]: It would be counter to the objective of ending apartheid if we were to isolate South Africans and withdraw our influence from that society. That is why we strongly support the continued presence of American business in South Africa. American companies have been in the forefront in the business community in promoting equal opportunity for their employees and in developing the managerial skills of blacks.

Before Business Council
for International Understanding,
New York, Sept. 29/
The New York Times, 9-30:4.

Ian Smith
Former Prime Minister
of Rhodesia (Zimbabwe)

5

I would like to get out of politics. Forty years is enough for any man. But when you've been in a position of great prestige and dignity and respect, standing up against the whole of the world and creating a country that was the most efficient in the world, it's easier said than done. People still look to you for leadership.

Los Angeles Times, 8-1:(I)10.

Helen Suzman
Member of South
African Parliament

6

[Criticizing the continuing state of emergency imposed by the South African govern-

(HELEN SUZMAN)

ment in response to anti-apartheid violence]:
Long ago, we predicted that if laws were enacted without the consent of the mass of the
people, normal measures would not be sufficient to maintain law and order. South Africa
has as a result been sliding down that slippery
slope toward a fully fledged police state, and
emergency rule has now become a permanent
feature of our lives.

Los Angeles Times, 6-12:(I)8.

Theunis J. Swanepoel
Former chief interrogator,
South African
intelligence agency

1

[On anti-apartheid violence by blacks in
South Africa]: The only way to stop them is to
use as much force as is necessary. If you have
to shoot one person, or wound one person in
the leg to stop him, you do so. But if it is necessary to shoot a hundred to get the situation
under control, do it. There are no half measures when you deal with riots. Law and order
must be restored at all costs. Lose that and you
might just as well chuck in the towel.

The Washington Post, 3-28:(A)29.

Oliver Tambo
President,
banned African National
Congress (South Africa)

2

[On the fight against apartheid in South Af-
rica]: We must pay the greatest possible attention to the mobilization and activization of the
white population, which should fuse with and
become part of the motive forces of the democratic revolution. Our white compatriots have to
learn the truth that it is not democracy that
threatens their future. Rather, it is a racist
tyranny which poses a dire peril to their very
survival.

Radio address, Lusaka,
Zambia, Jan. 8/
The New York Times, 1-9:2.

3

[On why his organization uses violence in its
fight against apartheid in South Africa]: I can
think of no conditions in which we would suddenly call it off while apartheid continues . . . If
it was possible to obtain our political objectives
without violence, I would denounce [violence].
[But in the] practical situation [prevailing in South
Africa today], of course, it's not thinkable.

Washington, Jan. 26/
The Washington Post, 1-27:(A)10.

4

We [the ANC] go to the Soviet Union to ask
for assistance, as we go to Sweden, Norway,
Holland, Italy, and we get assistance there. For
us, support is very important, and we must get
that support from everywhere in the world, including the socialist countries.

News conference,
Los Angeles, Feb. 2/
Los Angeles Times, 2-3:(I)5.

5

We [the ANC] seek to create a united, democratic and non-racial society. We have a vision
of a South Africa in which black and white
shall live and work together as equals in conditions of peace and prosperity . . . We want to
see a political system in which all South Africans will have the right to vote and to be elected
to any elective position without reference to
color, race, sex or creed. We are committed to
the birth of a society in which all democratic
freedoms would be guaranteed, including those
of association, of speech and religion, the
press, and so on. We wish to guarantee the rule
of law, and ensure the protection of the rights of
the individual as a fundamental feature of any
new constitutional arrangement.

Speech/
The Washington Post,
2-19:(A)27.

6

[On the South African government's invitation to the anti-apartheid ANC for peace talks if
that organization renounces violence]: [The
South African government is starting] a wide-

(OLIVER TAMBO)

ranging propaganda campaign whose aim is to give racial tyranny a new face, and thus to divert attention away from the ugly reality of the continuing system of apartheid. To hide this reality and shift the focus of our offensive away from the objective of our advance toward people's power through struggle, the racist regime has been making all manner of noises about the issue of negotiations. At the same time, it hopes to give sufficient grounds for its international allies to be able to claim that the basis for negotiations exists and thus to try to undermine and destroy the campaign for sanctions [against South Africa]. The fact of the matter is that [South African President Pieter] Botha's regime is not interested in any genuine negotiation that would lead to the transfer of power to the people through a system of one-person, one-vote in a united, democratic and non-racial South Africa.

At anti-apartheid conference,
Harare, Zimbabwe, Sept. 24/
Los Angeles Times, 9-25:(I)14.

Desmond M. Tutu
Anglican Archbishop
of Cape Town
(South Africa)

1

All these artificial barriers separating blacks from whites and whites from blacks will fall with one-man, one-vote. When we solve the fundamental problem, all these lesser questions will be quite easily dealt with if, in fact, they still remain. And whites need not worry; when there is a democratic and non-racial government in this country, they will not be put into ghettos or made to ride at the back of the bus, or subjected to the discrimination we [blacks] have had to endure.

To reporters, Cape Town/
Los Angeles Times, 2-17:(I)13.

2

[Saying he will not obey new restrictions on anti-apartheid protests in South Africa]: I warn

the government again; just remember one thing: You are powerful, perhaps even very powerful, but you are not God. You are mere mortals. Beware when you take on the church of God. Others have tried and come a cropper. Others have tried and bitten the dust.

At St. George's Cathedral,
Cape Town, April 13/
The Washington Post, 4-14:(A)16.

3

[On the recent election victory of South Africa's governing National Party]: Now we have a right-wing government that has been confirmed in its right-wing views with an extreme right-wing opposition. I believe what we are going to see now is an escalation in the [pro-apartheid] intransigence of this government, an escalation in oppressive intolerance of any dissent.

Cape Town, May 7/
Los Angeles Times, 5-8:(I)12.

4

[Saying the South African government is prohibiting peaceful protests against apartheid]: They are saying that the only thing they can accept is for the victims of apartheid to become the doormats on which people can wipe their feet. My own concern is how heartless the rulers have become . . . Yet there is a promise about our land, for it is remarkable that people are not hate-filled. They are not bitter, but they are angry, and I expect them to be.

Prayer service,
Cape Town, June 12/
Los Angeles Times, 6-13:(I)6.

Stoffel van der Merwe
Deputy Minister
of Constitutional Development
and Information of South Africa

5

[Criticizing anti-apartheid violence in South Africa]: We are adamant that in South Africa a real democracy must be created. A democracy, of which the essence is a peaceful negotiated settlement of political disputes, cannot be cre-

(STOFFEL VAN DER MERWE)

ated by the use of violence . . . A system created by violence has to live by violence, and that is the exact opposite of what is envisaged by the notion of democracy . . . [The anti-apartheid African National Congress should] accept the peaceful rules of a democratic contest and come home and assist other peaceful South Africans to build a democratic society for all our peoples . . . The original grounds advanced by the ANC for their decision to opt for violence, whether or not they were valid at the time, are most definitely not valid today. No other reason advanced by them for the continuation of violence can bear the scrutiny of logic. There is no valid reason for the ANC to continue with its policy of violence.

Before South African Parliament,
Cape Town, Sept. 9/
Los Angeles Times, 9-10:(I)14.

Kobus van Rooyen
Chairman,
Publications Appeals Board
of South Africa

1

[On South African security laws which ban certain anti-apartheid publications and activities]: The government should not be above criticism; that's not the intention of the law. We have allowed works that criticize detention without trial, the forced resettlement of blacks, the new Constitution, the tricameral Parliament, and government policies in general. To ban a work on security grounds, there must be a real threat, not just an ideological threat. For example, we have banned T-shirts calling for black retribution against whites, but approved

T-shirts with the slogan, "The people must govern."

Interview/
Los Angeles Times,
5-18:(I)4.

Jacinto Veloso
Minister of Cooperation
of Mozambique

2

In the United States there is a sense that we [Mozambique] are satellites of the Soviet Union. There were, of course, errors on our part. Perhaps because of our poor understanding we didn't encourage the West, maybe the West didn't understand what we were doing. It was only in 1983 that we introduced a platform of cooperation with the West. We are still in the process of developing, of understanding, of learning, of realizing our mistakes.

The New York Times, 2-19:6.

Alan Woods
Administrator, Agency
for International Development
of the United States

3

[On the famine in Ethiopia]: There is very little reason for people to die in this world today. The world can now more than feed itself; 10 years ago, people didn't think that would be true. Today, we have vast surpluses. In Ethiopia, you have a combination of two things: You have drought and you have government policies that discourage the growing of food which would allow them to create reserves.

Interview/USA Today,
12-22:(A)11.

The Americas

Elliott Abrams
Assistant Secretary
for Inter-American Affairs,
Department of State
of the United States

1

A process of negotiation [with the Sandinista government of Nicaragua] can be achieved only through pressure on the Sandinistas. [If the pressure continues,] either they will be forced to compromise or, refusing to compromise, the Nicaraguan people will rise up and get rid of them, just as the Nicaraguan people got rid of the dictatorship which preceded them, the Somoza dictatorship.

Newsweek, 1-19:24.

2

[Supporting private individuals who provided financing for the contra rebels of Nicaragua after Congress denied U.S. funds for that purpose]: Is there something wrong with the [Reagan] Administration, having lost the vote in the Congress, appealing directly to the people? We want to be a great power on the cheap. No Administration wants to undertake unpopular actions. In the case of Central America, this Administration did want to undertake that responsibility, but we were stopped by the Congress. But there were a lot of Americans who felt that there was such an enormous danger to the country [from the Sandinista government of Nicaragua] that they were willing to act on their own. As long as they didn't violate the Neutrality Act or the Arms Export Control Act, how can anyone say what they did was wrong?

The New York Times, 1-20:6.

3

[On the U.S. Iran-contra scandal]: U.S. policy and U.S. laws have changed over the last two years, but certain fundamentals have remained constant: support for peace and democracy in Central America, and opposition to the consolidation of a Communist regime in Nicaragua. These are views which the Executive and Legislative branches share. As an official of the Department of State, I have tried to promote those views . . . The disclosures on November 25, and since, have been surprising and sobering to me, and I have followed closely the accounts—some accurate, some inaccurate—of my own activities. It is important to me to set the record straight and I look forward to discussing with you now the conduct of U.S. policy in the region, and my role in it.

At Iran-contra hearings,
Washington, June 2/
The New York Times, 6-3:6.

Raul Alfonsin
President of Argentina

4

[On U.S. relations with Latin America]: I think the U.S. has abandoned the idea that authoritarian governments are a kind of a dam against left-wing subversives. [They know] the solution is in democracy. In this sense, what we want is more imagination to encourage and protect the development of our countries . . . For example, on the theme of the [Latin American] debt. We are in a situation similar to that of Europe when after [World War II] it was necessary to reconstruct Europe . . . with imagination, with new measures and new policies, the situation in Europe was saved [by the Marshall Plan]. This is not seen in regards to Latin America, which makes me think that it is not noticed what Latin America means for the security of the hemisphere . . . Consider the problems in Central America and the concern they raise in the U.S.—multiply that by a thousand, and you'll get an idea of what the convulsion of Latin America as a whole would mean.

Interview,
San Diego, June 20/
The Christian Science Monitor,
6-25:10.

(RAUL ALFONSIN)

1

[Saying the U.S. and other Western countries should adjust their policies to help debt-ridden Latin American nations]: Those nations which constitute the center of the West must recognize and understand to what extent current economic conditions impede our development and condemn us to backwardness. We cannot accept that the south pay for the disequilibrium of the north.

*At Latin American
summit conference,
Acapulco, Mexico, Nov. 27/
The New York Times, 11-28:17.*

Oscar Arias
President of Costa Rica

2

[On his plan for a peace agreement that would end the guerrilla war between the contra rebels and the Sandinista government of Nicaragua they are fighting]: I want to call the bluff of the Sandinistas. They've told the world that they can't fulfill the pledges of democracy they made in the past because they are under siege by the United States [-backed contras], that it's absolutely nonsense to ask them to democratize when there are thousands of contras inside Nicaragua. I want to test their sincerity. According to my plan, within 60 days of signing, they'd have to open their country to a free ¬ ¬ess and to free political expression . . . What I want to prove is that I'm right, that they've [the Sandinistas] deceived everybody, that they've lied for eight years, that people have been wrong to give them the benefit of the doubt.

U.S. News & World Report, 6-1:39.

3

[Criticizing U.S. support for the contra rebels of Nicaragua]: [Nicaragua] can't become a pluralistic country if there is war. We believe the contras cannot do the job; we believe the contras are the best excuse for [Nicaragua's] Sandinista government. So I propose to get rid of the contras . . . [The U.S. and Costa Rica have the same objective for democracy [in Nic-

aragua], but we disagree on the means on how to obtain this democracy. I don't think the contras are the answer.

*News conference,
Washington, June 18/
Los Angeles Times, 6-19:(I)9.*

4

The peace accord [for ending the war in Nicaragua between the Sandinista government and the contra rebels] is a means, a procedure whereby we have all committed ourselves to work for peace . . . It is time to focus on the positive. War signifies the failure of politics. Let us restore faith in dialogue and give peace a chance. Let us not allow fear to prevail. If we work together, we will achieve peace. It will be difficult. But has progress ever been easy? Here in the United States it was a hard-won struggle to wrest a living from the land, to win equality for all people, to preserve freedom, and to conquer space itself! Yet the more difficult the obstacle, the greater the satisfaction in overcoming it.

*Before joint session
of U.S. Congress,
Washington, Sept. 22/
The New York Times, 9-23:8.*

5

It is true for the *comandantes* [Nicaragua's Sandinista leaders] that it is not easy to advance toward a pluralistic society being Marxists, but there is always a first time. The alternative is war, and they don't want war. We [Costa Ricans] don't want war. And the whole of Latin America is very much against war . . . It is not possible to have durable peace unless there is democracy in all our countries. And Nicaragua is no exception.

*Interview/
The Christian Science Monitor,
9-29:7,8.*

6

As long as Washington is convinced that the only way to achieve democracy in Nicaragua is by military aid to the contras [rebels fighting Nicaragua's Sandinista government], [the U.S.]

(OSCAR ARIAS)

will remain isolated [throughout] all Latin America.

Interview/Newsweek, 10-26:44.

1

I say to [the super powers] with the utmost urgency: Let Central Americans decide the future of Central America . . . Support the efforts for peace instead of the forces of war. Send our people plowshares instead of swords, pruning hooks instead of spears.

Accepting 1987 Nobel
Peace Prize, Oslo, Dec. 10/
Los Angeles Times, 12-11:(I)4.

Ricardo Arias Calderon
Leader,
Christian Democratic Party
of Panama

2

[Criticizing Panamanian leader Manuel Antonio Noriega]: Each day we are living in a more typical repressive dictatorship led by a military chief who is rejected by society but who maintains himself by force.

Interview/
The New York Times, 7-28:1.

Jose Azcona
President of Honduras

3

[On aid to the contra rebels of Nicaragua during the current period when a peace accord is to be implemented between the contras and Nicaragua's Sandinista government]: For now, I don't think there should be lethal aid . . . We have to wait for the agreement to take its course. But we shouldn't use the ban on lethal aid as an excuse for permitting non-compliance [by the Sandinistas]. It is one thing not to help the contras right now and another to call off aid completely. That would preclude the use of the contras as a lever to force compliance . . . What should definitely not be done is to make a

decision to close out all possibilities for aid to the contras in the future.

To reporters, Washington,
Oct. 21/The Washington Post, 10-22:(A)36.

Harry Barnes
United States Ambassador
to Chile

4

[On those who say the U.S. should apply more pressure on the Chilean government to move toward democracy]: The best way not to achieve something [in Chile] is to press too much for it. The perception of the influence of the United States is one I find quite exaggerated. From the standpoint of the opposition, it's "if only [the U.S. would] do something more." And those who support the government say that if we'd only stop what we're doing, everything would be okay.

Miami/
The Christian Science Monitor,
4-9:12.

Alexandre Barros
Brazilian political scientist

5

The old-time politicians [in Brazil], long used to a system of interlocking favors, depend on the government for survival. But modern-minded reformers want to trim government, which controls over half of the Brazilian economy, and give more dynamism to small and middle-sized business and farms. The political structure belongs to an era 40 years ago . . . Lags exist in all societies. Society changes first, and then it's reflected in the political structure. When you read history in a book, the interval is one paragraph. When you are living it, it takes a longer time.

The Christian Science Monitor,
10-6:10.

Perrin Beatty
Minister of Defense
of Canada

6

One of the points we'll be making to our allies is that if it's abhorrent that a square centi-

(PERRIN BEATTY)

meter of European soil is lost, it should be equally abhorrent to NATO that a square centimeter of Canadian soil be lost, and that any activity that we [Canadians] undertake in defense of Canada's north, or in the Pacific, is also a contribution to NATO and should be seen to be so by our allies.

Interview, Ottawa/
The Christian Science Monitor,
3-23:10.

Jaime Bengoechea
President,
Nicaraguan Chamber
of Industry

1

The [ruling Nicaraguan] Sandinistas use three means to enforce obedience. They control the press, they apply the law in an irregular way so that the ordinary citizen feels insecure, and they distribute food and other necessities through outlets that only certain card-holders can use. The whole system is very subtle. Those of us who have stayed here want a transformation of this country, but not one that disrupts our cultural or economic traditions. We are trying to build democracy in a country where democracy has never existed.

Interview/
The New York Times, 8-11:6.

Harry E. Bergold
United States Ambassador
to Nicaragua

2

I don't think we consider the internal situation [in Nicaragua] a lost cause. The Nicaraguan people are generally very pro-American. Despite the historical realities of our Marine occupation of Nicaragua and our government's support for the Somoza dictatorship, most people here like the United States and respect its institutions and its culture. They are difficult subjects for the agit-prop machinery [of the Nicaraguan Sandinista government], which at-

tempts to portray a more negative image of the United States. The opportunities for catalytic change inside the country are real. But the Communist Party and the Communist state are extant, and are not lightly to be dismissed or easily to be changed.

Interview, Managua/
The New York Times, 7-1:3.

Enrique Bermudez
Military commander
of the contras,
rebels fighting
the Sandinista government
of Nicaragua

3

[Criticizing a peace plan developed by Central American leaders to bring an end to the contra war against the Sandinistas]: The worst impact of all would be seeing the United States Congress cut off aid to an army [the contras] fighting for democracy, while Cuba and the Soviet Union keep aiding the Sandinistas . . . [The Sandinistas] are looking for a way to stop our aid and make our troops lose faith. They won't comply with the treaty. The plan doesn't favor us. It offers us the chance to put down our guns and join a totalitarian process—which is absurd . . . It's demonstrated that, due to our presence, the Sandinistas had to sit down and negotiate. To take us away is to take away the pressure.

Interview, Sept. 4/
The New York Times, 9-7:5.

David E. Bonior
United States Representative,
D-Michigan

4

The resignation of [contra leader] Arturo Cruz [from the contra organization] reflects not only the military failure of the contras, but also their unwillingness to move toward democracy. It really reflects the bankruptcy of the whole contra program.

News conference,
Washington, March 10/
The New York Times, 3-11:6.

WHAT THEY SAID IN 1987

L. Brent Bozell III
President,
(U.S.) National Conservative
Political Action Committee

1

Now that Round I of the Iran-contra hearings is over, it is time for [the U.S.] Congress to focus on abuses by the left. An almost identical scandal has occurred under the guise of humanitarian aid to the victims of violence in Central America. [At the Iran-contra hearings,] there is a kangaroo court in progress, as star-struck members of Congress attempt to destroy the Reagan doctrine while purposely ignoring subversive efforts by some Americans to help overthrow a duly elected democracy in El Salvador.

New conference,
Washington, June 11/
The New York Times, 6-12:9.

Jack Brooks
United States Representative,
D-Texas

2

[Criticizing the testimony of U.S. Assistant Secretary of State Elliott Abrams about his role in the Iran-contra scandal]: I'm very troubled with the job that you did, because you would have us believe that you just had no idea about private fund-raising [for the Nicaraguan contra rebels], about solicitation to governments for a few million dollars; you had no idea about how the contras were operating or where they were getting their supplies; you had no idea about a large number of people who were commuting almost daily between the United States and your area of surveillance [Latin America]. And I can only conclude after this that you're either extremely incompetent or that you are still, as I say, deceiving us with semantics or, three, maybe the [Reagan] Administration has intentionally kept you in the dark on all these matters, so then you could come down and blatantly mislead us.

At Iran-contra hearings,
Washington, June 3/
Los Angeles Times,
6-4:17.

Adolfo Calero
President,
national directorate,
Nicaraguan Democratic Force

3

[On his lack of curiosity regarding the sources of funding for his contra rebels]: When you're in the desert and you're dying of thirst, you don't ask if the water they are giving is Schweppes or Perrier.

Newsweek, 3-16:17.

4

[On funds his contra rebels received which may have come from secret U.S. arms sales to Iran]: It did not interest me [where the money came from]. I had an inkling that it came from a Middle Eastern source. And I understood this to be a covert thing. And . . . I didn't want to be privy to information that I do not need . . . What mattered was that, frankly, we had the money, and not who had given it to us.

At Iran-contra hearings,
Washington, May 20/
Los Angeles Times,
5-21:(I)29.

Fernando Cardenal
Minister of Education
of Nicaragua

5

[The Sandinista government of Nicaragua is] not a revolution that wants to copy the Soviet model, where atheist science is taken as a principle . . . For so many years we fought against the North American government, which had taken from us our independence and self-determination. How could you imagine that the revolution would turn itself over to another foreign power [the Soviet Union]? We did not betray the blood of 200,000 for someone else. If that were the intention, it would have been better to stay with the U.S.

Interview/
The Christian Science Monitor,
11-10:17.

Frank C. Carlucci
*Assistant to President
of the United States
Ronald Reagan for
National Security Affairs*

1

[On the Sandinista government of Nicaragua]: This is a self-avowed Marxist-Leninist regime . . . that just yesterday, after espousing the principles of democracy, used cattle prods and dogs to break up a peaceful demonstration. No agreement signed with them is self-implementing. You have to keep the pressure up.

*Broadcast interview/
"Meet the Press,"
NBC-TV, 8-16.*

Fidel Castro
President of Cuba

2

[On free-market experiments in his country]: The peasant with the peso sign in his head makes his living from our scarcity, from the government's mediocrity. Of course, that's the easy way for well-to-do bureaucrats who want to avoid headaches. But things bring terrible results. Socialism isn't worth a thing—I say this with an absolutely straight face—if it can't produce parsley, gentlemen.

*At Communist Youth congress/
The Washington Post, 4-24:(A)22.*

3

[On whether he will follow Soviet leader Mikhail Gorbachev in pursuing more "openness" in his country]: We are not obliged to copy . . . the socialist countries' experience. Often when you get into the habit of copying, you make grave mistakes.

*Speech/
The Christian Science Monitor, 6-22:7.*

Joaquin Cuadra Chamorro
*President,
Central Bank
of Nicaragua*

4

If we cannot contain it quickly, inflation is going to become unmanageable, like a boy who

grows up and defies his parents. The danger at that point is that the revolutionary program, which is supposed to ease the people's burdens, would have failed.

Los Angeles Times, 9-20:(I)1.

Tony Coelho
*United States Representative,
D-California*

5

[On the proposed cease-fire/peace plan for the contra war against the Sandinista government of Nicaragua]: There are senior officials in the [U.S. Reagan] Administration who are trying to sabotage this [agreement]. We know that. Let's quit playing games and let's give peace a chance.

*Interview/
Los Angeles Times,
8-19:(I)10.*

Arturo Cruz
*Former leader of contras,
rebels fighting
the Sandinista government
of Nicaragua*

6

I feel tremendously frustrated because we Nicaraguans are going in circles. We started in 1967 with one dictatorship, only to have a new dictatorship led by the Sandinistas emerge in 1979. It would be terrible to create a new dictatorship if we defeat the Sandinistas. For me, it is the duty of Nicaraguan democrats to see this does not happen . . . The contras have to show that they don't just want to win power but that they want democracy. I left [the contras] because I found that there was not political will to make changes, but I believe that others will try to bring reform and I hope they are successful.

*Interview,
Costa Rica, March 10/
The New York Times, 3-11:6.*

7

In the end, the factor which most undermines Sandinista rule is their continuing and growing unpopularity with the Nicaraguan people. If the contras maintain themselves as a via-

(ARTURO CRUZ)

ble force, and strengthen their activities in Nicaragua, we will begin, perhaps in a few years, perhaps sooner, to see serious insurrectional activity breaking out . . . The other factor which will continue to undermine Sandinista rule is that, by their very nature, they pose a threat, a serious threat, to their Central American neighbors. I believe that when insurrectional activity breaks out in Nicaragua, these countries will find it to their advantage to support that activity by launching a joint military invasion of the country.

Interview, Miami/
The Christian Science Monitor,
3-11:32.

Miguel de la Madrid
President of Mexico

1

[On U.S. criticism of Mexico for the illegal-drug problem]: The narcotics traffic is a crime that originates in, is fed by, and benefits from the large industrialized markets, principally those of the United States. We cannot accept attempts to blame our country for this matter. How can those of the north see the mote in our eyes with the beam that is in their own?

Sinaloa, Mexico, June/
The New York Times, 7-17:3.

2

Ours is no longer a time of emergency [in Mexico], but one of renewal. There are already promising signs on the horizon this year . . . We prevented the collapse of the nation's economy . . . The results are there for all to see. We have full enjoyment of our freedoms and exercise our rights; the natural problems of our life together are resolved through dialogue and negotiation; essential social and public services are provided at adequate levels, and their coverage and quality have improved.

State of the nation address
before Mexican Congress,
Mexico City, Sept. 1/
Los Angeles Times, 9-2:(I)6.

Robert J. Dole
United States Senator,
R-Kansas; Candidate for the 1988
Republican Presidential nomination

3

I've got a feeling a little three-day invasion [of Nicaragua] wouldn't make anybody unhappy down there, if you just overthrew [President Daniel] Ortega. But that's just my guess.

Newsweek, 9-21:21.

Michael S. Dukakis
Governor of Massachusetts (D);
Candidate for the 1988
Democratic Presidential nomination

4

[Criticizing U.S. policy in Latin America]: We played footsie with [the late Cuban dictator Fulgencio] Batista, we got [current President Fidel] Castro. We supported [the late Nicaraguan dictator Anastasio] Somoza for 50 years, we've [now] got the Sandinistas. We overthrew the government of Guatemala in 1954, and we consigned those people to years of the most repressive brutality any nation has ever undergone. When does it stop? . . . We need a new alliance for progress in Latin America where we go after the real problems that cause radical revolution, which are poverty and injustice and exploitation and death squads and all the rest of it.

Interview/USA Today, 5-18:(A)9.

Pierre S. du Pont IV
Former Governor
of Delaware (R);
Candidate for the 1988
Republican Presidential nomination

5

The problem of a long-term Communist presence [the Sandinista government of Nicaragua] in Central America is the United States' problem. It is ours to solve or suffer . . . As the Sandinistas persist in ignoring their commitments to their own people, and ours, the U.S. must renew its policy of freeing the Nicaraguan people from its new oppressors, and

(PIERRE S. du PONT IV)

make the long-term strategic commitment needed to achieve that goal. We must make every effort to isolate the Sandinistas diplomatically, beginning by breaking diplomatic relations with their government and encouraging our allies to do the same. If we are to bring democracy to Nicaragua, we must state openly and clearly that we are willing to talk, but are equally prepared to support those who are willing to fight.

Before Los Angeles
World Affairs Council, Aug. 3/
The Washington Post, 8-5:(A)4.

David Durenberger
United States Senator,
R-Minnesota

1

[Criticizing the U.S. Iran-contra scandal, in which military aid was given to the contras, rebels fighting the Sandinista government of Nicaragua]: In retrospect, when we [Congress] shut down the United States involvement in the contra thing, we should have nailed it down. I'm sorry about not dotting the i's or crossing the t's, but at some point you trust the Administration to get the message. We said no lethal aid, and we meant it.

The New York Times, 1-15:4.

Carlos Escude
Professor
of international relations,
Belgrano University
(Argentina)

2

The most positive element [in Argentina] is that the Army realizes public opinion is monolithically in favor of democracy. You must realize, in Argentina, [military] coups have always had an important margin of civilian support. And [President Raul] Alfonsin was able to get written support of every significant political party, industrial union and rural group. And it left the military without any support at all.

The Christian Science Monitor,
4-21:36.

Joao Figueiredo
Former President
of Brazil

3

[Criticizing the current Brazilian government of Jose Sarney, to whom he turned over the Presidency in 1985]: I gave that opening, which I thought would lead to a democracy, and it led to a thing that—I don't know what it is. They used to talk about dictatorship. I ask: Which is the biggest dictatorship, mine or this "economic dictatorship" that is there [now]?

To reporters/
Los Angeles Times,
4-2:(I)26.

David Fleischer
American political scientist,
University of Brasilia
(Brazil)

4

Everyone from the left to the right [in Brazil] agrees that the Constitution is just a piece of paper, and that the military has the coercive force to do what it wants to do. That's a reality that everybody accepts.

Los Angeles Times, 7-6:(I)7.

John R. Galvin
General,
United States Army;
Commander-in-Chief,
Southern Command;
Supreme Allied Commander/
Europe-designate

5

[On the contras, rebels fighting the Sandinista government of Nicaragua]: The contras are insurgents. An insurgency normally takes 15 years to go from the building of ideology, of infrastructure, of logistics, of training and so forth, until they get up to the stage of violence. The Sandinistas themselves were 15 years old in 1977, when they reached the shooting and violence stage, and they had 5,000 people. The contras are less than six years old. They are up to 15,000 people. Yet people think that's a failure. I can't understand it.

Interview/USA Today, 3-31:(A)9.

269

WHAT THEY SAID IN 1987

(JOHN R. GALVIN)

1

[Criticizing the U.S. Congress for its impatience with, and putting time requirements on, the contras, rebels fighting the Sandinista government of Nicaragua]: When you start telling a guerrilla that it has to be done quickly, it costs lives because the essence of guerrilla warfare is slow, careful planning. I don't think there's a contra out there that is not aware that he had better get some good action done by September [the next Congressional vote on contra aid] . . . That is why I hope we not only support the contras but we will give some indication that we're going to sustain that support for some time . . . [If U.S. aid stops,] the contras won't have the wherewithal to fight at the levels they are now. The Sandinistas will have more time to undermine their neighbors, and that's what they will do. The contras are the cheapest and most effective way that we can achieve our goals and protect our allies in Central America.

Interview, Panama City,
Panama/Los Angeles Times,
5-20:(I)6.

Manuel Gamero
Editor, "Tiempo"
(Honduras)

2

[On U.S. activities in Central America aimed against the Sandinista government of Nicaragua]: We used to believe in "the Virginian," in the American cowboy-style Don Quixote, the man who always told the truth. Now we have watched the United States pull us [Honduras] into a lot of questionable activities, and we see that we're equal: You are just like us!

The Washington Post, 2-6:(A)19.

Alan Garcia
President of Peru

3

[On the Sandinista government of Nicaragua]: I appeal, on behalf of Latin America, to all peoples of the world to take notice of the monumental step that is being taken here [in

Nicaragua] and to extend their solidarity to this democracy growing even stronger. We call on all people of good faith in the world to put aside all doubt, preconceptions and mistrust. Our American voice calls out to the free socialists of the world who sing in chorus, "Arise ye wretched of the earth," to let them know that the majority of the world's poor do not live in the developed countries. They live in the Third World, threatened with economic colonialism. They must understand that our anti-imperialism is a struggle entirely consistent with their socialist ideals.

At celebration of Nicaragua's
new Sandinista Constitution,
Managua, Jan. 9/
The Wall Street Journal, 2-10:38.

Samuel Gejdenson
United States Representative,
D-Connecticut

4

At a time when Central America is exploding, when the policy of this [U.S. Reagan] Administration, in aiding the [contra rebels in Nicaragua], is at an impasse, it seems to me to be absolutely imprudent to supply advanced aircraft to Honduras [where the contras are based]. We may soon find ourselves with a region as well-armed as the Middle East.

Washington, June 4/
Los Angeles Times, 6-5:(I)16.

Richard A. Gephardt
United States Representative,
D-Missouri;
Candidate for the 1988
Democratic Presidential nomination

5

The contras [U.S.-backed rebels fighting the Sandinista government of Nicaragua] are not democrats. Their senior military leaders were officers in the [late dictator Anastasio] Somoza [National Guard]. They seem more interested in burning villages and blowing up power lines than in the well-being of the Nicaraguan

(RICHARD A. GEPHARDT)

people . . . I believe that we should give our unequivocal, unwavering support to the [Costa Rican President Oscar] Arias peace plan. To be sure, there are no guarantees and there are many questions and details that must be addressed. But our friends and allies in the region have embarked on an effort that warrants our full support.

Survey interview/
Los Angeles Times,
10-11:(I)29.

Mikhail S. Gorbachev
General Secretary,
Communist Party
of the Soviet Union

1

I have to smile when I hear [from certain segments in the U.S.] that the security of the United States is being threatened by the Sandinista regime [of Nicaragua]. That's not serious . . . I think now even in [the U.S.] Congress they have understood that. Surely the Americans understand that Nicaragua cannot threaten, pose a threat to the United States.

American broadcast interview,
Moscow, Nov. 28/NBC-TV, 11-30.

Paul Gorman
General,
United States Army (Ret.);
Former commander of U.S. forces
in Central America

2

[On the contras, rebels fighting the Sandinista government of Nicaragua, saying they cannot defeat the Sandinista army]: [The contras] are largely a cross-border raiding force, not an unconventional warfare force . . . You're not going to knock off the Sandinistas with a conventional armed force and that's what the contras are. [The $100-million approved by the U.S. Congress last year for the contras] is not

going to do it; the money you're going to be asked to spend this year isn't going to do it.

Before Senate
Armed Services Committee,
Washington, Jan. 28/
The Washington Post, 1-29:(A)20.

Clemente Guido
Nicaraguan author
and physician;
Runner-up in 1984
Presidential election

3

At this moment, political freedom in Nicaragua is quite limited. People are afraid to speak out because they risk not only going to jail, but also losing their farms or property if they are convicted as counter-revolutionaries. We [the opposition to the Sandinista government] can't take our views to the people because we have no access to newspapers or television. We are in a system that is not democratic in the Western sense, but that could evolve into a democracy. People like me are losing now, but if we give up, it would be disastrous for our country's future.

Interview/
The New York Times, 8-11:6.

Alexander M. Haig, Jr.
Former Secretary of State
of the United States;
Candidate for the 1988
Republican Presidential nomination

4

On some of the questions of Central America, I have differences with the [U.S. Reagan] Administration. I never supported the covert program [of U.S. aid to the Nicaraguan contra rebels], but now that we are there, I do support aid to the contras because the consequences of suddenly terminating the aid once we started it would be devastating.

At news conference
announcing his candidacy
for President, New York, March 24/
Los Angeles Times, 3-25:(I)15.

WHAT THEY SAID IN 1987

(ALEXANDER M. HAIG, JR.)

1

What gives Central America its strategic dimension? Marxism in Nicaragua? Come on. If the people of Nicaragua freely choose Marxism, of their own sovereign free will, we Americans would have no other course to follow but to let them stew in their own juice. If it were not for the Soviet Union and Castro's Cuba, and their proximity, the people of Nicaragua would have thrown Marxism out or never have established it in the first place.

Interview/
USA Today, 12-21:(A)13.

Albert A. Hakim
Iranian-born
U.S. businessman

2

[On his involvement in alleged secret U.S. funding of the contra rebels in Nicaragua]: I was told that our contra activities were being undertaken not only with approval by, but at the request of, the President of the United States [Reagan]. We were dealing directly with the White House staff. Consequently, it never occurred to me, as a private citizen, independently to investigate the legality of the President's policy.

At Iran-contra hearings,
Washington, June 3/
Los Angeles Times, 6-4:(I)16.

3

[On his involvement with Lt. Col. Oliver North in alleged secret U.S. funding of the contra rebels in Nicaragua]: He's got two loves: One, his country; and, to a point, *that* is, in my mind, the biggest satisfaction that can be given to him: if he would enter into an environment [in which] he could get killed for his country; I sensed that so many times. And the other love that he has is his family . . . I witnessed him being torn apart between these two loves.

At Iran-contra hearings,
Washington, June 3/
Los Angeles Times, 6-4:(I)16.

Gary Hart
Former United States
Senator, D-Colorado;
Candidate for
the 1988 Democratic
Presidential nomination

4

[On the debt owed by Latin American countries to U.S. banks]: The United States government should act more like a champion of global growth and less like a collection agency for the over-extended banks. If we help expand Latin American economies rather than squeeze them, we can increase U.S. exports as we strengthen southern democracies—and our mutual security . . . The banks should know that full repayment of these loans is no longer tenable as a primary goal of U.S. policy.

Before American
Chamber of Commerce,
Sao Paulo, Brazil, March 17/
The New York Times, 3-18:13.

Orrin G. Hatch
United States Senator,
R-Utah

5

[On the covert diversion of funds, from the secret sale of U.S. arms to Iran, to contra rebels in Nicaragua]: I don't think the [U.S.] NSC should ever operate covert operations; I just don't think they should. And frankly, I don't think that we should have had a diversion of funds here, even though I have to confess I kind of think it's a neat idea, too, to take money from [Iranian leader] Ayatollah [Khomeini] and send them over to the [contra] freedom fighters in Nicaragua. What a nice use of those funds, except . . . I don't think [the covert diversion of the funds] was right . . . I think you [U.S. Lt. Col. Oliver North] were right—at least well-motivated—in your desires to help [the contras], because we weren't helping them like we should up here. We weren't supporting this policy in our own hemisphere.

At Iran-contra hearings,
Washington, July 13/
The New York Times, 7-14:8.

272

Howell Heflin
United States Senator,
D-Alabama

1

[Addressing U.S. Assistant Secretary of State Elliott Abrams on his involvement in the U.S. Iran-contra scandal]: . . . your testimony today concerning your monitoring of [U.S.] Colonel [Oliver] North [who is implicated in the scandal]—as a responsibility imposed upon you by Secretary [of State George] Shultz to, in effect, be his eyes and ears on North, and to report to him on activities concerning him—[it is] one interpretation that you did it rather nonchalantly and not very aggressively. Another interpretation would appear to be that when it came to Colonel North, you could see no evil, hear no evil, speak no evil, inquire of no evil, concerning Colonel North.

At Iran-contra hearings,
Washington, June 2/
The New York Times, 6-3:6.

Rafael Hernandez Colon
Governor of Puerto Rico

2

The reality [of Puerto Rico] is that of two different cultures. Here we have to take the laws and regulations of the United States, the richest society in the world, and try to apply them to Puerto Rico, which doesn't have the economic infrastructure to support them. We need help, like tax exemptions, to attract businesses to Puerto Rico, or why else would they locate here with the geographic disadvantage of being 1,600 miles away from New York or more than 1,000 miles from Miami?

Interview, San Juan/
The New York Times, 1-28:10.

Jack Kemp
United States Representative,
R-New York; Candidate
for the 1988 Republican
Presidential nomination

3

[On proposed cease-fire/peace plans for the contra rebel war against the Sandinista govern-

ment of Nicaragua]: . . . any plan that halts [U.S.] aid to the [contra] freedom fighters before the Soviet colonial presence is out of Nicaragua, before democracy comes to Nicaragua, is a plan that is flawed at its core and that is doomed to fail.

News conference,
Washington, Aug. 18/
Los Angeles Times,
8-19:(I)10.

4

The Communists who rule in Nicaragua will say whatever they have to say, will sign whatever they have to sign, but will never stop exporting Communism by force. If the Communist Sandinistas [who rule Nicaragua] remain in unchallenged dictatorship . . . there will be no peace in Nicaragua or Central America.

Survey interview/*
Los Angeles Times,
10-11:(I)10.

Jeane J. Kirkpatrick
Former Unites States Ambassador/
Permanent Representative
to the United Nations

5

The future of Nicaragua depends as much on the people as on the [Sandinista] government, because liberty has to be demanded and used, and democracy has to be built by the very people who are going to enjoy it.

At U.S. Columbus Day rally,
Managua, Nicaragua, Oct. 11/
Los Angeles Times, 10-12:(I)12.

6

[What President of El Salvador Jose] Napoleon Duarte . . . is always saying about El Salvador and about Latin America generally, and Central America, is that there are two revolutions abroad. One is a democratic revolution and one is a Marxist revolution. Both of them reject the old, oligarchic, traditional military model. I think the old traditional military dictator model is finished in Latin America and that

273

WHAT THEY SAID IN 1987

(JEANE J. KIRKPATRICK)

the two places it lives on are Chile and Paraguay, and they are on borrowed time.

Interview, Washington/
The New York Times, 11-2:14.

Edward I. Koch
Mayor of New York

1

[On his just-concluded tour of Central America sponsored by Central American Peace and Democracy Watch]: Public opinion polls are illegal in Nicaragua, and have been since [the newspaper] *La Prensa* sought to measure the extent of popular support for the [ruling] Sandinistas in 1981. My impression, which is based on personal observation in Managua, where between one-third and one-half of the population resides, is that if an election were held today, the Sandinistas might well be able to carry the day. However, such an election would not reflect a free choice in a society where news broadcasts are restricted, opinion polls can't be taken, political rallies are against the law, and opposition parties are not well organized.

Speech, Nov. 12/
The Washington Post,
11-17:(A)26.

Gabriel Lewis Galindo
Former Panamanian Ambassador
to the United States

2

[Criticizing Panamanian leader Manuel Antonio Noriega]: I am going to travel to every country to tell people that we have a delinquent in charge of Panama. I have appointed myself international representative of the Panamanian opposition, and I am going to charter a plane and use every penny at my disposal . . . We are in a crusade to overthrow these military officers and establish a democracy. There is room in our society for a professional, non-corrupt military, but not for the kind of repression Noriega is using. The selling point of Panama is our stability,

and if this government stays in power, we are going to lose that.

Interview/
The New York Times,
6-16:3.

Dan Lungren
United States Representative,
R-California

3

[Criticizing the U.S. Congress' off-on approach to funding the contras, rebels fighting the Sandinista government of Nicaragua]: What kind of legislative farce is this? When we asked for help in our Revolution from Lafayette, did he send a delegation of accountants? At Bunker Hill, did they say don't shoot till you see the bottom line?

Before the House, Washington/
The New York Times, 3-12:6.

Rodrigo Madrigal
Foreign Minister
of Costa Rica

4

The problem is that Nicaragua has never wanted to talk seriously about democratic principles. They will . . . negotiate something cosmetic, to speak about peace and not about democracy, so they can have a peace that protects their kind of regime for as long as they want. This is not the kind of peace that interests Central Americans.

Interview,
San Jose, Costa Rica/
Los Angeles Times,
3-26:(I)10.

Francisco Martin Moreno
Mexican author;
Political commentator

5

Everyone is seeking an explanation for the current crisis [in Mexico]. To do that, we have to go back, find where we began to go wrong as a nation and clarify what happened so that it

(FRANCISCO MARTIN MORENO)

doesn't happen again . . . When a country loses its historical memory, as I believe Mexico has, it loses its way. It becomes incapable of knowing whether it should be Marxist or capitalist, a republic or a monarchy, nor can it know who its enemies are.

Interview/
The New York Times,
5-4:4.

Robert C. McFarlane
Former Assistant to President
of the United States
Ronald Reagan for
National Security Affairs

1

[On the U.S. Iran-contra scandal]: The President [Reagan] repeatedly made clear in public and in private that he did not intend to break faith with the contras [rebels fighting the Sandinista government of Nicaragua]. He directed that we make continued efforts to bring the movement into the good graces of Congress and the American people, and that we assure the contras of continuing Administration support, to help them hold body and soul together until the time when Congress would again agree to support them. Congressional restrictions made it impractical for either the Defense Department or the Central Intelligence Agency to function even as liaison with the contras. The State Department has always been disinclined to be associated with a covert action, but the President had made clear that he wanted a job done. The net result was that the job fell to the National Security Council staff.

At Iran-contra hearings,
Washington, May 11/
Los Angeles Times, 5-12:(I)15.

2

[On the U.S. Iran-contra scandal, which involved covert transfer of funds to the contra rebels fighting the Sandinista government of Nicaragua]: There's little doubt in my mind that if we could not muster an effective counter to

the Cuban-Sandinista strategy in our own backyard, it was far less likely that we could do so in the years ahead in more distant locations. There's a corollary to that proposition: For if we did prevail in Nicaragua, [U.S. President Reagan] might go far toward inhibiting Soviet pursuit of this strategy in other areas. In short, there was a powerful, and to many a persuasive, case that to lose in Nicaragua would invite the Soviets to step up their investment in aggression significantly in other developing nations of the world. We had to win this one. And this is where the [Reagan] Administration made its first mistake. For if we had such a large strategic stake, it was clearly unwise to rely on covert activity as the core of our policy.

At Iran-contra hearings, Washington,
May 11/The New York Times, 5-12:6.

3

[On Lt. Col. Oliver North's involvement in the U.S. Iran-contra scandal]: I don't doubt for a minute that Ollie would have offered to step forward to protect me or his Commander-in-Chief, or both [in this scandal]. It would be as much in character for him to do this as it would have been for him to throw himself upon a grenade to protect his comrades, colleagues in battle. But surely we can agree on one thing: Ollie North should not be the fall guy or scapegoat or sacrificial lamb for anyone [in the scandal]. Ollie acted at all times without regard to personal gain and was motivated by devotion to the people that he loves—the freedom fighters [contras fighting against the Sandinista government] in Nicaragua.

At Iran-contra hearings,
Washington, July 14/
The New York Times, 7-15:6.

Richard Millett
Authority on Central America,
Southern Illinois University

4

[On the new Central American peace plan designed to end the war between the contra rebels and the Sandinista government of Nicaragua]: The contras have been very, very badly

WHAT THEY SAID IN 1987

(RICHARD MILLETT)

hurt by all of this [since the plan calls for cessation of U.S. aid to them], and the hurt will get worse rapidly. The Sandinistas have played this [peace efforts] very cleverly, the contras very stupidly, and the [U.S.] Reagan administration dumbest of all.

USA Today, 9-30:(A)4.

Brian Mulroney
Prime Minister of Canada

1

The biggest trading partner of the United States is not West Germany or Japan; it's right here [in Canada], by a long shot. And the government of Canada, and Canadians, don't want to be on anybody's back burner, or taken for granted at any time.

To visiting U.S.
Vice President George Bush,
Ottawa, Jan. 21/
The New York Times, 1-22:1.

2

[On the signing of an accord giving Canada's provinces more local authority, which ended Quebec's boycott of the Canadian Constitution]: Today we close one chapter in Canadian history and open another. Today we welcome Quebec back into the Canadian Constitutional family. Tomorrow we get on with the business of building a new Canada for a new decade and a new century.

At signing of accord,
Ottawa, June 3/
The New York Times, 6-4:4.

James Nielson
Former editor,
"Buenos Aires Herald"
(Argentina)

3

The first 40 months of democracy (in Argentina) occurred under the shadow of military power. All were conscious of its existence; nevertheless, it was possible to minimize its impor-

tance, to try to believe that the military would conform to a secondary role. But since Easter week, no one can assume such a luxury. The pendular swings, so typical of Argentine politics over the past half century in which power has oscillated between strong military and weak civilian regimes, have not been overcome. On the contrary, the pendulum is newly in motion, and stopping it will not be easy.

The Washington Post, 6-4:(A)38.

Daniel Ortega
President of Nicaragua

4

[On Nicaraguan-Soviet relations]: We give this visit [by Soviet officials] great value because it ratifies our good relations. These respectful and friendly relations are the kind we want to have with all countries of the world, including the United States . . . Have the Soviets come to destroy hospitals [as the U.S.-backed contra rebels do]? To destroy health centers? Cooperatives? Have they come to assassinate children, to kill peasants? . . . The Soviet brothers and sisters have invaded Nicaragua with tractors, trucks for transporting goods and harvests, with wheat and oil. This is the way we would like the United States to invade us.

To reporters,
Managua, March 5/
Los Angeles Times, 3-6:(I)6.

5

[Saying other Central American governments would face criticism from the U.S. if they made peace agreements with Nicaragua]: If they take a real step toward peace, that will mean confrontation with the United States. If they don't have the firmness to confront this risk, which could include reprisals by the [U.S.] Reagan Administration, the only alternative is economic and military disaster in Central America . . . As long as the United States is not willing to negotiate . . . the proposals made by Nicaragua and other Central American countries will remain only proposals. If there is a desire on the part of the United States to reach an agreement [with Nicaragua], one could be

(DANIEL ORTEGA)

reached quickly, and it would respond to the major security concerns of the United States. The most reasonable thing President Reagan could do would be to listen to Central America, to Latin America and to his own Congress, and change his [anti-Nicaragua] policy.

Interview,
Managua, March 17/
The New York Times, 3-18:1.

1

Washington's policy—to destroy the [Nicaragua] revolution by using mercenary forces—is falling apart. The contras [rebels fighting Nicaragua's Sandinista government] are being defeated, so we are closer to the danger of a direct U.S. invasion. Nicaragua is militarily encircled by the U.S. The only thing the U.S. needs is to provoke an incident so it can justify a direct military intervention. The danger will remain as long as [U.S.] President Reagan is in office.

Interview/
World Press Review,
April:22.

2

The type of regime that we are establishing is a socialist regime with its own particular characteristics. It is based on a mixed economy, political pluralism and a non-aligned foreign policy. We have private property in the cities and in the countryside. There are many political parties. The solution to our economic problem does not lie in the liquidation of private property.

Interview/
World Press Review,
April:22.

3

I cannot deny that with regard to the movement of arms [between countries], which all revolutionary movements carry out, like those we undertook in the past, some [shipments] cross all the countries that are necessary to cross in order to reach their destination and don't necessarily cross these countries with the consent of governments. It could be that a quantity of arms passes through Nicaragua to [the rebels in] El Salvador, but they are the smallest quantities of armaments.

Interview/
Los Angeles Times,
6-25:(I)15.

4

The principal cause of our economic problems is the terrorist policy of interventionist war which the United States has launched against Nicaragua. The United States does not want any kind of negotiation, and this is something the Nicaraguan people and the international community must see clearly. At this moment, there is no prospect or possibility of negotiation with the United States. This is not because Nicaragua does not favor it, but because the United States government does not want a political solution, does not want this [Sandinista] revolution to live, wants to destroy this revolution whatever the cost.

At rally,
Matagalpa, Nicaragua, July 19/
The New York Times, 7-20:6.

5

[Saying he is willing to speak with U.S. President Reagan about ending the war between U.S.-backed contra rebels and Nicaragua's Sandinista government, but not to the contras]: We have nothing to discuss [with the contras] because the owner of the circus is Ronald Reagan. There is no need to speak to the clowns.

Newsweek, 8-24:25.

6

[U.S.] President Reagan dreams every day of the collapse of the Nicaraguan economy, and we cannot deny that it has been seriously battered [by the current guerrilla war against the Sandinista government]. If it weren't for the ideological consciousness of the revolution, Reagan would certainly have won this battle years ago.

Speech/
Los Angeles Times, 9-20:(I)1.

277

WHAT THEY SAID IN 1987

(DANIEL ORTEGA)

1

[Saying his government's decision to allow more press and political freedom in Nicaragua should cause his Sandinista government to be more forceful in defending itself]: [We Sandinistas should] prepare for an ideological struggle, because the combat does not end at the war front. It is easier to struggle against an enemy who has no possibility for expressing himself. But it is richer for the revolutionary process to fight an ideological struggle against the enemy if we give him the possibility to express himself.

Speech, Oct. 1/
Los Angeles Times. 10-2:(I)14.

2

From the Bronx, I want to make a new call to the President of the United States [Reagan]: that he will end the war against Nicaragua [the U.S. support for Nicaraguan contra rebels] and will accept our friendly hand, because we have never been and never will be enemies of the United States.

At rally, Bronx, N.Y., Oct. 9/
The New York Times, 10-10:10.

3

We are willing to give assurances on the non-establishment of foreign military bases [in Nicaragua], and on negotiating the withdrawal of foreign military presences in the region. In the first stage, we would seek only a regulation of this foreign military presence because we're pragmatic and we know that the [U.S.] Reagan Administration right now would not agree to a total withdrawal of its forces . . . such as exist in Honduras, for example. On the other hand, we Central Americans undertake by signing the accords . . . not to install foreign military bases or have military maneuvers with forces from outside the region.

Interview, Washington/
Newsweek, 11-23:36.

4

This country [Nicaragua] will never vote for any party other than the Sandinista National Liberation Front. But in the hypothetical case that [the] Sandinista Front lost an election, the Sandinista Front would hand over government, not power.

To labor unions,
Managua, Dec. 13/
The New York Times,
12-14:6.

Robert W. Owen
Courier for U.S. Marine
Lt. Col. Oliver L. North

5

[On the scandal involving covert funding of the Nicaraguan contra rebels by members of the U.S. Reagan Administration, including Lt. Col. North, and foreign governments, individuals and arms sales]: Why did the Administration have to turn to our allies and people outside of government to carry out some aspects of a stated foreign policy? And why did private American citizens choose to risk their lives, their fortunes and their sacred honor to help a ragtag army [the contras], the majority of whom are poor *campesinos*? . . . Many of us got involved because we cared about those Nicaraguans, willingly fighting, bleeding and dying in the jungles so that some day they might be able to enjoy some of the freedoms we Americans take for granted every day. And, in truth, taking the long view, they, we, are fighting for our freedom, too. The totalitarian dictatorship in Communist Nicaragua is a strategic threat to the rest of Central and Latin America and to the United States . . . After these hearings, the problem with how to deal with Nicaragua will still be there. The Sandinistas and their Soviet, Cuban, East German, North Korean and Vietnamese advisers . . . will be ensconced in Managua while controlling the reins of power in Nicaragua . . . As Churchill . . . said: "You cannot feed all around you to the crocodiles on the hopes they'll eat you last."

At Iran-contra hearings,
Washington, May 14/
Los Angeles Times,
5-15:(I)23.

Claiborne Pell
United States Senator,
D-Rhode Island

1

I'd like to see a normalization in our [U.S.] relations with Cuba. It's very disagreeable and against our interests to have right on our doorstep a hostile power. I'm not saying we have to be palsy-walsy with them. But why can't we have the same kind of relations with them that we have with, say, Romania or Bulgaria?

Interview, Washington/
The New York Times,
2-3:26.

2

[On the contras, U.S.-backed rebels fighting the Sandinista government of Nicaragua]: In my judgment, the military strategy represented by the contras is headed for disastrous results which offer the stark prospect of deepening U.S. military involvement. We need to redirect our policy toward exploring every political and diplomatic path available, which I frankly do not believe the [U.S. Reagan] Administration has done.

At Senate
Foreign Relations Committee
hearing, Washington, Feb. 5/
The New York Times, 2-6:3.

Augusto Pinochet
President of Chile

3

[Addressing Pope John Paul II on the threat of Communism in Chile]: Your Holiness knows well, and can appreciate as few others can, the most grave aggression and siege that Chile has suffered and continues to experience before an expansionist action of the most extreme materialistic and atheistic ideology ever known by mankind.

On the arrival in Chile
of Pope John Paul II,
Santiago, April 1/
The New York Times, 4-2:6.

John M. Poindexter
Former Assistant to President
of the United States
Ronald Reagan for
National Security Affairs

4

[On his participation in the covert diversion of funds to Nicaraguan contra rebels in the U.S. Iran-contra scandal]: The point was, and still is, that the President has the Constitutional right, and in fact the Constitutional mandate, to conduct foreign policy. His policy was to support the contras. Congress had put some restrictions on the use of appropriated funds. Those restrictions didn't apply to private funds; they didn't apply to third-party funds. And the restrictions in the Boland Amendment, as I've said, did not apply to the NSC staff.

At Iran-contra hearings,
Washington, July 17/
The New York Times, 7-18:4.

5

[On his and U.S. Lt. Col. Oliver North's involvement in the U.S. Iran-contra scandal]: I have always felt that if the American people, the average American citizen out there, understood all of the issues involved, that they would support the President's [Reagan] program [of aid to the contra rebels of Nicaragua]. People don't want a Communist government on the mainland of the Americas [in Nicaragua]. The response [from the people] to Colonel North's appearance [at these hearings] and the responses that I have received since I've been up here just simply confirm that for me.

At Iran-contra hearings,
Washington, July 17/
The New York Times, 7-18:5.

Sergio Ramirez
Vice President of Nicaragua

6

If we assume that the United States stops supporting the counter-revolution [the contra rebels fighting the Sandinista government of Nicaragua], that the counter-revolution accepts a cease-fire, that the counter-revolution begins

279

(SERGIO RAMIREZ)

the process of giving up arms, that the government of Honduras closes the contra bases and prohibits the use of Honduran territory for contra operations, then parallel with that, the state of emergency [in Nicaragua] will end. Full Constitutional freedoms will be restored. [the opposition newspaper] *La Prensa* will reopen, the Catholic radio station will reopen, there will be no prior censorship of the press, there will be no restrictions on political-party activity, the people's tribunals will be closed and all counter-revolutionary prisoners will be freed. I hope it happens.

Interview, Managua, Aug. 12/
The New York Times, 8-14:7.

Ronald Reagan
President of the United States

1

[On U.S. backing of the contras, rebels fighting the Sandinista government of Nicaragua]: It is both in our national interest and consistent with our traditions as a free people to assist those brave souls who are struggling for freedom and national independence. That's especially true when it comes to those fighting Soviet-backed tyranny in Central America. We must not and will not abandon them. If you hear anyone any more talking about the danger of Nicaragua becoming a Communist totalitarian state, correct them. It *is* a Communist totalitarian state, and we are helping the people who are trying to change that.

At American Legion conference,
Washington, Feb. 10/
The Washington Post, 2-11:(A)18.

2

Soon the Communists' prediction of a "revolutionary fire"— their words—sweeping across all of Central America could come true. [Lenin said that] the road to America leads through Mexico. This Administration's support of the Nicaraguan freedom fighters [the contra rebels] in their struggle for peace and democratic government will not change unless the regime in

Nicaragua accedes to the democratic aspirations of the Nicaraguan people. The democratic Nicaraguan resistance, including the freedom fighters, today offers the only political alternative to the dictatorship of the past and the Communism of today. That alternative is democracy, and it is winning increasing support from the people of Nicaragua. For as long as I am President, I have no intention of withdrawing our support for these efforts by the Nicaraguan people to gain their freedom and the right to choose their own national future.

Before American Newspaper
Publishers Association, New York,
May 3/The New York Times, 5-4:8.

3

[On U.S. involvement in the covert funding of the contras, rebels fighting the Sandinista government of Nicaragua, and the restrictions of the Boland Amendment as it applies to such fighting]: There is nothing in the [Boland Amendment] that prevents citizens—individuals or groups—from offering aid [to the rebels] of whatever kind they wanted to . . . And my interpretation was that it was not restrictive on the National Security Adviser [to the President] or National Security Council . . . I believe the NSC is not an intelligence operation; it's simply advisory to me. And there is nothing that has ever been in the Boland Amendment that could keep me from asking other people to help [the rebels]. The only restriction on me was that I couldn't approve the sending of help or arms out of our [Federal] budget.

To reporters, Washington/
U.S. News & World Report, 5-25:25.

4

[On other countries and private individuals who have covertly contributed funds or material to the contras, rebels fighting the Sandinista government of Nicaragua]: I knew that there were individuals and groups in America which on their own, privately, were contributing. I didn't know who they were and I never asked and I never asked how they did it. And at the same time, I had expressed a belief that other democratic nations in the world—it might be to

(RONALD REAGAN)

their best interest also to lend support to the freedom fighters [contras]. And other countries did. But, again, I never solicited any country and asked it to do that, and I never knew who was or who wasn't, until one—the head of state of one of those countries told me that they were contributing and were going to increase their contribution. Now, that is the truth. But that's not the way the image is portrayed. I'm being portrayed as having, behind the scenes, violated the law and done all sorts of shady things to try and violate the [U.S.] Congress' restriction on aid to the freedom fighters. And it just isn't true.

Interview, Washington, May 27/
The New York Times, 5-29:9.

1

The polls now suggest that the American people are waking up to the threat of a Communist power grab in their own neighborhood [Central America]. Let me pledge to you here today, we are not about to stand by and see our neighbors in Central America added to the list of captive nations . . . The threat is too close to home . . . to tolerate an on-again, off-again, vacillating Congressional policy toward that region. All indications suggest that the more people know about what's happening in Central America, the more they support a strong stand for freedom.

At Captive Nations Conference,
Washington, July 24/
Los Angeles Times, 7-25:(I)21.

2

[Addressing the contras, rebels fighting the Sandinista government of Nicaragua]: Your struggle has and always will have our support because our goal is the same. Until the people of Nicaragua are guaranteed basic liberties, I know you will keep on with the struggle. And the United States will be with you. The journey's end is Nicaragua Libre [Free Nicaragua] . . . The Sandinistas are now promising democracy, with the world as a witness. Like you, I hope they keep their promise. But

like you, I also know that the civil war in Nicaragua began when the Sandinistas promised you democracy but failed to meet their commitment. The Sandinistas have agreed that the repression must stop at the same time the fighting stops. The Sandinistas have told us this before, and no one believes the Sandinistas any more. Simultaneity must mean freedom up front and no deals.

Broadcast address to contras,
Aug. 24/Los Angeles Times,
8-25:(I)6.

3

To the [Nicaraguan ruling] Sandinista delegation here today I say: Your people know the true nature of your regime. They have seen their liberties suppressed. They have seen the promises of 1979 go unfulfilled. They have seen their real wages and personal income fall by half—yes, half—since 1979, while your party elite live lives of privilege and luxury. This is why, despite a billion dollars in Soviet-bloc aid last year alone, despite the largest and best-equipped army in Central America, you face a popular revolution at home. It is why the democratic resistance is able to operate freely deep in your heartland . . . The goal of United States policy toward Nicaragua is simple. It is the goal of the Nicaraguan people and the freedom fighters [the anti-Sandinista rebel contras] as well: It is democracy—real, free pluralistic, constitutional democracy. Understand this: We will not, and the world community will not, accept phony "democratization" designed to mask the perpetuation of dictatorship.

At United Nations,
New York, Sept. 21/
The New York Times, 9-22:6

4

Anything short of true democracy in Nicaragua will at best bring only a false peace to Central America. The wound will fester and the infection will break out once again . . . Open up the jails [of Nicaragua] and let the thousands of political prisoners free; let the exiles come home; allow freedom of worship, free labor unions, a free economy. And last but not least,

WHAT THEY SAID IN 1987

(RONALD REAGAN)

2

send the Soviets and the Cubans home. We'll not be satisfied with mere show. Until these conditions are met, democratization will be no more than a fraud. And until they're met, we'll press for true democracy by supporting those [the contra rebels] who are fighting for it.

Before Concerned Women
for America, Arlington, Va.,
Sept. 25/Los Angeles Times,
9-26:(I)3.

1

There are now well over 15,000 Nicaraguan freedom fighters [contra rebels]—three times the number that overthrew [the late dictator Anastasio Somoza]—operating throughout the entire length of Nicaragua [fighting against the Sandinista government]. They would not have survived without the friendship and help of the Nicaraguan people. For seven years now, the freedom fighters have prevented the consolidation of totalitarian power in Nicaragua [by the Sandinistas]. For now, the billions of dollars in Soviet-bloc military aid pouring into Managua have been aimed primarily at defeating the freedom fighters—so that later [the Sandinistas] may attack the surrounding democracies. All of us in public life should remember it is the freedom fighters—most of them poor farmers fighting against overwhelming odds in the jungles of Nicaragua—it is their blood and courage that have stemmed the tide of Communist expansion in Central America. Without the freedom fighters, the Sandinistas never would have signed the Guatemala accord, and there would be no pressure on the Sandinistas to reform. Their totalitarian grip on Nicaragua would only grow tighter and, with all dissent quashed at home, the Sandinistas would soon turn their attention to their neighbors. The huge Sandinista military machine—equipped and staffed by Cubans and Soviet-bloc "advisers"—would spread its shadow across all of Central America.

Before Organization
of American States, Washington,
Oct. 7/The New York Times, 10-8:8.

The Sandinistas [who rule Nicaragua] must learn that democracy doesn't mean allowing a rally to take place and then arresting those who take part—it means hundreds of such rallies, free from harassment, either by the secret police or by what the Sandinistas call the "divine mobs." Democracy doesn't mean opening one [opposition] newspaper and one [opposition] radio station—but opening them all. Democracy doesn't mean releasing a few political prisoners—but all 10,000 of them, some of whom have been imprisoned as long as 8 years. Democracy doesn't mean selectively granting temporary freedoms in order to placate world opinion—but permanent, across-the-board human rights, guaranteed by a constitution and protected by the checks and balances of democratic government. Ultimately—and this is the most important lesson of all—democracy means returning power to the hands of the people. The Sandinistas have to understand that they do not have the option of being dictators. Their only option is to lead a political party, and serve for limited terms of office, if chosen by the people in free and fair elections.

Before Organization
of American States, Washington,
Oct. 7/The New York Times, 10-8:8.

3

[On the contra rebels fighting the Sandinista government of Nicaragua]: Year upon year for seven years now, they have fought and sacrificed and endured. It is the resistance—the brave members of the [contra] resistance, many of them no more than teen-agers—who have kept the Communist Sandinistas from consolidating their power and forced them into the current peace plan. It is the resistance, in short, that has given Nicaragua at least a chance for true freedom. My friends, I know you agree: We must not abandon these courageous men and women, these soldiers. So let me promise: Nicaragua will have its freedom. And we will help the resistance [the contras] carry on its brave fight until freedom is secure.

At U.S. Military Academy, West Point, N.Y.,
Oct. 28/The New York Times, 10-29:8.

Charles E. Redman
Spokesman
for the Department of State
of the United States
1

[Criticizing the wave of violence that disrupted and postponed Haiti's national elections last Sunday]: We remain deeply distressed and saddened by the events that occurred there. The will of the Haitian people to establish democracy was thwarted by violence. The failure of the Haitian government to protect innocent civilians attempting to vote was extremely disappointing. And the dismantling of the electoral authority was unjustified. It is now incumbent on the government to take dramatic and credible steps to demonstrate that it has the will and the ability to arrest, prosecute and punish those who struck this blow against democracy.
Washington, Dec. 1/
Los Angeles Times, 12-2:(I)5.

Raul Roa
Deputy Minister
of Foreign Affairs
of Cuba
2

Counter-revolutionary prisoners in Cuba are not imprisoned because they are against the ideas of socialism but because they have violated Cuban laws, either by planning to sabotage the economy or harm our leaders.
News conference, Geneva,
Feb. 23/The Washington Post,
2-24:(A)18.

Humberto Rubin
Owner,
Radio Nanduti (Paraguay)
3

[On the Paraguayan government's forcing his radio station off the air]: The circle is closing. I believe that to inform and to be informed is a basic human right. Therefore, I'm subversive, and a threat to the government. When people are informed, they begin to lose their fear, to assert themselves. That is what bothered them

[the government] most: People were losing their fear. They were learning that not in every country is crime legal . . . It's an old story. What dictatorship can endure a free press?
Interview/
Los Angeles Times,
3-17:(I)1.

Jose Sarney
President of Brazil
4

Interest rates are at unbearable levels. Our economic growth is threatened. Millions of businesses are engulfed in an unsustainable situation. Over our workers looms the shadow of unemployment, the fear of losing the purchasing power of their salaries. I know that in these past months there has been much perplexity and suffering, mainly among the most humble Brazilians. This situation, without doubt, cannot continue, and it will not continue. We are aware that right now we are making decisions that will improve the lives of Brazilians.
June 12/
Los Angeles Times,
6-13:(I)14.

5

Each of us [in Latin America] is witness, in the anguished course of our daily life, to the perverse effects of an international situation which we have not created but which falls on us and has converted us into net exporters of capital. Adjustments are demanded of us which the developed countries give no signs of being willing to undertake in their own economies.
At Latin American summit
conference, Acapulco, Mexico,
Nov. 27/The New York Times,
11-28:18.

George P. Shultz
Secretary of State
of the United States
6

[On the Sandinista government of Nicaragua]: The *commandantes* have a choice: They

WHAT THEY SAID IN 1987

can keep the promises [of democratic reforms] they made to their people and the international community to get into power, or they can accept the risk of more violent and less voluntary changes down the road. But this much is certain: Nicaragua will change. The tyranny there is out of step with the aspirations of the Nicaraguan people and the realities of this hemisphere. Nicaragua . . . is on the wrong side of history.

Before American Bar
Association, New Orleans,
Feb. 12/Los Angeles Times,
2-13:(I)8.

1

The Central American situation is vastly different than it was when the [U.S.] President [Reagan] came into office. [Then] we had one democracy in Central America and there was a kind of assumption lying around that the Communists were going to take things over and that nothing could be done about it. That has been turned around completely. We now have elected civilian presidents in Honduras, El Salvador and Guatemala . . . There is broad bipartisan readiness to help those four countries [including Costa Rica] . . . That's a gigantic change right there . . . [Our goal is to have] five democratic governments [including Nicaragua], not four, in Central America.

Interview, Washington/
The Christian Science Monitor,
5-4:7.

2

[On the U.S. Iran-contra scandal]: I think it's important to keep the [Nicaraguan contra] freedom fighters alive. But I don't . . . think that desirable ends justify means of lying, of deceiving, of [Americans] doing things that are outside of our Constitutional processes. That's not in the picture as far as I'm concerned.

At Iran-contra hearings,
Washington, July 23/
USA Today, 7-24:(A)5.

Denny Smith
United States Representative,
R-Oregon

3

[On the possibility of U.S. military involvement against the Sandinista government of Nicaragua]: I'm wary of a direct American involvement if we don't have a commitment to win. We have a lot of things to do before we get our own people into combat there. But on the other hand, we don't just want to let the Soviets continue to support these people [the Sandinistas]. They foment revolution throughout the area. And I think there will come a time, after all is said and done, when we will have to get involved militarily there. What is important is that the Russians want Mexico, because Mexico is right next to the United States. So I think if it is important to us to keep Mexico free, then we need to do something in Central America militarily . . .

The New York Times, 5-28:12.

Rafael Solis
Nicaraguan Sandinista legislator

4

Under the state of emergency [in Nicaragua], we have restricted the right to hold outdoor meetings and we have suspended freedom of expression. When people criticize us in sensitive areas like the military draft, we react. There are things that cannot be tolerated in Nicaragua while there is a war going on [with the U.S.-backed contra rebels].

The New York Times,
8-11:6.

Alfred Stepan
Professor
of political science,
Columbia University

5

[On the military's continued influence in Brazil]: The military has six Cabinet members [and] runs the state intelligence agency and the National Security Council. There is no other

(ALFRED STEPAN)

democracy in the world where the military has that sort of presence.

U.S. News & World Report,
7-13:41.

Clyde D. Taylor
United States Ambassador
to Paraguay

1

We believe democracy is the best defense against instability [in Paraguay], so U.S. policy is supporting those who are working toward a transition to democracy, recognizing that how they get there and in what form they arrive will be determined by Paraguayans. We believe that essential to this policy is respect for human rights.

Interview/
The New York Times,
3-24:3.

Mauricio Vargas
Colonel, Army of
El Salvador; Commander,
Fourth Army Detachment

2

[On the guerrilla war in El Salvador]: In this war there can be no strictly military solution, because the problem is not of a military nature . . . The politicians have to become aware of the realities. In this country, three-quarters of the peasants are landless. An agrarian reform is indispensable. There are people in power who will neither leave nor share, but they are going to have to choose. All of these sumptuous mansions, swimming pools, luxury cars, jewel-bedecked women—all of this pleasure is indecent when so many people lack the means to survive. It is with all of that in mind that I am making war here. If I wanted to, I could stage a destruction operation in the Pequin sector, where there are [anti-government] terrorists, and kill 2,000 people. That is not my method. I prefer to re-open the schools that have been closed, rebuild power lines, set up

medical clinics. That is how I gained control of this region.

Interview/
World Press Review, August:25.

Mario Vargas Llosa
Peruvian author

3

I am convinced—although I am not sure whether to be happy or sad about it—that when a Latin American nation chooses democracy, it not only chooses freedom and the rule of law but the most extreme form of independence as well. This is because no other type of government receives less support from the West . . . than those regimes in the Third World that try to live the ideals of freedom and pluralism which are the West's greatest contribution to the world. I doubt that any democratic nation in the under-developed world has received the credits and subsidies Cuba has received from the Soviet Union. And it is certainly true that no Latin American nation fighting to live in peace and freedom within the law ever before aroused the militant sympathy that [Marxist] Sandinista Nicaragua has inspired in liberal and progressive circles in the West.

Before Trilateral
Commission, San Francisco/
The New York Times, 3-23:17.

Pete Wilson
United States Senator,
R-California

4

[On the U.S. Iran-contra scandal]: I don't think the privatization of foreign policy is a good idea. But what do you think of a Congress . . . that says "Yes, we will help the freedom fighters of Afghanistan" but doesn't do the same thing when the Marxist oppressor [the ruling Sandinistas in Nicaragua] is a couple of hours from their doorstep? If [American officials] have broken the law [in the Iran-contra scandal], they obviously have to be dealt with. But the more important issue is the wisdom of the policy.

Interview, Los Angeles, June 22/
Los Angeles Times, 6-23:(I)3.

285

WHAT THEY SAID IN 1987

Jim Wright
United States Representative,
D-Texas

1

[On the war between U.S.-backed contra rebels and the Sandinista government of Nicaragua]: [U.S. President Reagan has to deal with] a virulent right-wing faction [in the U.S.] which is deeply mistrustful of the peace process. Some of them don't want . . . anything but a military solution. On the other hand, at the other extreme . . . there is a similar situation in Nicaragua in which the far-left hard core doesn't really have any faith in the peace process. All they want is a military solution. If there is ever going to be any peace, those extremes have to be pacified to a degree.

To reporters,
Washington, Aug. 25/
Los Angeles Times 8-26:(I)8.

2

[Criticizing U.S. President Reagan for reaffirming support for the contras, rebels fighting the Sandinista government of Nicaragua, while at the same time seeming to support a peace plan to end the fighting]: It seems counter-productive to me, if peace is our goal, to be continually waving the red flag of military conquest. One doesn't say with one hand extended, and an olive branch offered, "Come, let us reason together," when at the same time you're hitting a person up-side the head with a crowbar. You've got to do one or the other . . . Obviously the Sandinistas have not been struck by a bolt of lightning . . . they haven't undergone an enormous conversion. But I believe the realities of death and degradation and poverty that have afflicted that land have brought home

to them the necessity of . . . beginning to democratize and open up.

To reporters,
Washington, Sept. 17/
Los Angeles Times, 9-18:(I)19.

3

Some people in the [U.S. Reagan] Administration are scared to death that peace will break out [in the war between the U.S.-backed contra rebels and the Sandinista government of Nicaragua]. There is a small cadre, which I hope does not include [President Reagan], who don't want a negotiated settlement. They want a military solution.

To reporters,
Washington, Nov. 16/
The New York Times, 11-17:1.

4

[Arguing against U.S. military aid to the contras, rebels fighting the Sandinista government of Nicaragua]: I am not prepared to say that the contras' military effort should be funded, because that presumes that we [the U.S.] have the right to dictate the form of [Nicaragua's] society and to enforce that dictate at the end of a bayonet . . . There are circumstances in which U.S. aid can be warranted. But, simply on our own volition, to decide that we have the right to kick other people around and tell them what they've got to do and force them to do it, I believe is fundamentally flawed. It is that attitude that has reaped a whirlwind of resentment in the Hemisphere, and we should demonstrate a willingness to be a part of the family rather than trying to be landlord of the neighborhood.

Interview, Washington,
Nov. 20/Los Angeles Times,
11-21:(I)1,19.

Asia and the Pacific

Sergei F. Akhromeyev
Chief,
Armed Forces General Staff
of the Soviet Union

1

[On the Soviet military involvement in Afghanistan]: It was not a mistake. The limited contingent of Soviet troops was introduced in Afghanistan at the persistent, repeated request of the government of Afghanistan to help defend that country from outside interference. The Soviet soldiers in Afghanistan are helping the Afghan people with whom we are bound not only by a common border but also by many years of good-neighborly relations. As for withdrawal of Soviet troops, this question is settled. We are in favor of having a shorter timeframe of withdrawal. But the withdrawal of forces depends not only on us. The sooner the military interference of the United States and Pakistan [their backing of Afghan rebels fighting the Soviet-backed government] in the internal affairs of Afghanistan has been ended and its non-resumption guaranteed, the sooner the Soviet troops will be withdrawn to our territory.

Interview*/
The New York Times, 10-30:4.

Corazon C. Aquino
President of the Philippines

2

The answer to the terrorism of the left and the right [in the Philippines] is not social and economic reform but police and military action . . . I told you when we were discussing the peace initiatives that when they fail, as we feared they would, and when it becomes necessary to take out the sword of war, that I want a string of honorable military victories. I want this victory . . . As I came to power peacefully, so I had hoped to keep it. God knows I have tried. But my offers of peace and reconciliation have been met with the most bloody and insolent rejections by the left and right. It is clear

that the forces of the extremes will not leave us in peace to achieve the recovery and progress we so badly need.

At Philippine Military
Academy commencement, March 22/
The New York Times, 3-23:1.

3

[On the Communist insurgency in her country]: To our enemies, let me say: Give up your futile struggle if you have a drop of humanity and patriotism in your veins. Democracy is here to stay. It is your people you are killing. We will spare no effort and adopt any measure to protect them.

At Philippine Military
Academy commencement, March 22/
The Washington Post, 3-23:(A)13.

4

[On the recent attempted coup by military rebels against her government]: The aim of the rebels was clearly to kill the President and her family. The size and ruthlessness of the attack, the treachery that marked it, the brutality of the rebels who fired on civilians, and the timing . . . prove beyond a doubt their murderous intentions . . . For the past 18 months, it has become clear to me that [Armed Forces Chief of Staff] General [Fidel] Ramos and I have begun to share common enemies. And also for the past 18 months, I and General Ramos have crushed every threat to this government and our democracy.

Heroes Day holiday address, Manila,
Aug. 30/The Washington Post, 8-31:(A)17.

5

Henceforth, I shall rule directly as President. To the ad-hoc committees and commissions created to inform me on their special areas, I now add one more: an action committee with a single member—me.

To businessmen, Manila, Oct. 20/
The New York Times, 10-21:3.

287

WHAT THEY SAID IN 1987

(CORAZON C. AQUINO)

1

The question you all really want to ask [is], "Can she hack it? Isn't she weak?" These are the questions that were asked by all those who have openly challenged my power, authority and resolve, and who have suffered for it. Well, they can forget it. Although I am a woman, and physically small, I have blocked all doors to power except elections in 1992 . . . The facts speak for themselves. With the military, we have crushed every challenge to the supremacy of civilian authority. They fought me, I fought back. Surrender would have been neater, but it is not in me to yield.

To businessmen, Manila, Oct. 20/
Los Angeles Times, 10-21:(I)9.

2

There has been more talk than work in our country today . . . When all the talk is about coups and strikes, it is worth remembering that it is work, by all of us, that is going to lift us to better times. When politics gets in the way of work, we have a problem. And there's been too much politics.

To businessmen, Manila, Oct. 20/
The Washington Post, 10-21:(A)25.

Richard L. Armitage
Assistant Secretary for
International Security Affairs,
Department of Defense
of the United States

3

[On the Communist insurgency in the Philippines]: I would say that the most serious problem confronting both ourselves and the Philippines is complacency. This is a subtle threat that tempts us to underestimate the dangers that confront the Philippine democracy. Certainly the story of [Philippine President] Cory Aquino and democracy in the Philippines should have a happy ending. But regrettably, I must say that such an outcome is by no means assured.

Before House Asia Subcommittee,
Washington, March 17/
The Washington Post, 3-18:(A)14.

Philippe Berges
Senior political adviser
to the French High Commissioner
in New Caledonia

4

If [New Caledonia] becomes an independent country, the teachers will go and there will be no one to teach; the army will go, and there will be no one to provide security; the civil servants will go, and there will be no one to run the government.

Los Angeles Times, 7-3:(I)10.

Stephen Bosworth
United States Ambassador
to the Philippines

5

[On the Communist insurgency in the Philippines]: Economic improvement and restoring credibility and effectiveness of government can, combined with appropriate military action [by government forces], offer the prospect, over time, of reducing the insurgency to a point at which it is no longer as serious a national problem as it is today.

News conference,
National Press Club,
Manila, March 27/
The Washington Post, 3-28:(A)28.

Zbigniew Brzezinski
Professor of government,
Columbia University;
Former Assistant to the President
of the United States (Jimmy Carter)
for National Security Affairs

6

I think that while the Chinese want to have a more normal relationship with the Soviet Union, they're likely to be far more cooperatively involved with the United States and Japan. They know that their modernization depends on closer technological and economic cooperation with the most advanced countries, notably the United States. They also need to have a good relationship with the United States to balance the immediately contiguous presence of Soviet military power.

Interview/USA Today, 11-3:(A)11.

Vu Can
Acting editor,
"Vietnam Courier"

1

Even though we call ourselves the Socialist Republic of Vietnam, we have only opted for a socialist orientation. After the war [with the U.S.], we acted as if we were socialist. That was forcing it too much. The whole [Vietnam Communist] Party wanted to go fast, until we hit reality . . . We are a rather peasant people with peasant problems. As peasants, we thought that with only our will we could go fast on industrialization. We have not made good investments . . . The old guard of the Vietnamese revolution was very experienced in national liberation . . . But for building socialism, it is quite a different story. [The late President Ho Chi Minh] is a national hero, but as for building the institutions of a modern country, he was a little simplistic.

Interview/
The Christian Science Monitor,
5-20:10,11.

Chun Doo Hwan
President of South Korea

2

[Announcing Roh Tae Woo as his successor when he steps down as President next year]: This is the first time in our 40-year Constitutional history that the government party has chosen a Presidential nominee while the incumbent President was still in office. This simple fact alone constitutes a firm cornerstone in the establishment of new democratic traditions.

At Democratic Justice
Party convention, Seoul, June 10/
Los Angeles Times, 6-11:(I)1.

3

[On the violent protests against his government and in favor of democracy]: Citizens of no country are fully satisfied with their basic law. What is important is a respect for the Constitution and for law and order. The observance of

even an unsatisfactory law until it is amended is basic to democracy.

At meeting with opposition
leader Kim Young Sam, Seoul,
June 24/The New York Times, 6-25:8.

4

. . . the key to democratic development in our country lies in establishing a tradition of the President peacefully handing over the reins of government to a successor at the end of his term of office, and then retiring with the blessing of the public . . . I clearly recognize the fact that, regardless of the possible merits and demerits of a particular system, and irrespective of the preferences of any specific political parties, the general public has an ardent desire to choose the President directly. No matter how good a system may be, it is of no use if the people do not want it. I believe that the intrinsic function of politics is to carry out the public will, if only on a probational basis, and to make sure it works well . . . Democracy is implemented not by word but by action. We can no longer ignore the fact that the only means democracy has are dialogue and compromise within the framework of law and order . . . Let us work another miracle by developing Korea into a model of political development deserving to be so recorded in world history. We must not be content with having merely become a model of economic development.

Broadcast address to the nation,
Seoul, July 1/The New York Times,
7-1:6; Los Angeles Times, 7-1:(I)1.

5

[On the forthcoming democratic elections in South Korea]: . . . our aspiration to build a solid foundation for Korean democracy by banishing, once and for all, the specter of protracted unreasonable one-man rule . . . is now being successfully fulfilled . . . [But] we must always keep in mind that a good system does not necessarily guarantee a good result. To use a metaphor, the same clean water that becomes milk when drunk by a cow becomes venom when drunk by a poisonous snake. We must not forget that lesson, which can be learned from

289

(CHUN DOO HWAN)

our own past experience and also from many foreign examples.

Seoul, Sept. 21/
The Los Angeles Times. 9-22:(I)8.

Diego Cordovez
United Nations mediator
in the Afghan-Soviet war
against Afghan rebels

1

I think everyone is tired of this situation, particularly the Afghans themselves, and want to see a speedy end to the whole thing . . . The only major issue remaining to be solved is the timetable for the withdrawal of the [Soviet] troops. Both sides have brought new proposals here, and I'm going to listen to them. Agreement on a time-frame for withdrawal of the troops means that there is, in effect, an agreement. So this, of course, means that the position of both sides becomes more difficult, because they know these talks are the crux of the whole negotiation.

To reporters, Geneva, Feb. 25/
The Washington Post, 2-26:(A)32.

Robert K. Dornan
United States Representative,
R-California

2

I do not know how we are going to get across to [Soviet leader Mikhail Gorbachev] that although many of us support the [new U.S.-Soviet] INF treaty, as I do, we have severe reservations about the validity of a promise made by the head of a government which maintains occupation troops in Afghanistan. When the General Secretary [Gorbachev] told [British Prime Minister] Margaret Thatcher . . . yesterday that Afghanistan is an "internal problem," then I have doubts about his sincerity. If this Afghan war, which is in its ninth year, is not something that Mr. Gorbachev can withdraw his troops from, then he is not worthy of being called a leader of any country, even a communist country. Those Russian tanks do have reverse gears, and those flying helicopter gunships can be grounded whenever the General Secretary says so.

Before the House, Washington, Dec. 8/
The Washington Post, 12-10:(A)26.

Rajiv Gandhi
Prime Minister of India

3

We do not have nuclear weapons. We do not want nuclear weapons. And we certainly do not want nuclear weapons in our neighborhood. We have watched with concern developments in our immediate vicinity. Nuclear stockpiles have multiplied. Yet another country [Pakistan] seems on the threshold of fulfilling a long-time goal of acquiring nuclear weapons. On our part, let me assure you . . . that we have no intention of producing nuclear weapons unless constrained to do so.

Washington, Oct. 20/
The Washington Post, 10-21:(A)10.

Richard A. Gephardt
United States Representative,
D-Missouri; Candidate for the 1988
Democratic Presidential nomination

4

[The U.S. is] supporting a military dictatorship in South Korea that deprives its own people of basic rights—and by its predatory trade practices deprives our people of jobs. We can no longer accept a situation in which they can invade our market with Hyundais [cars] sold cheap because we are paying dearly for the tanks that defend their borders.

Announcing his candidacy
for President, St. Louis, Feb. 23/
Los Angeles Times, 2-24:(I)14.

Mikhail S. Gorbachev
General Secretary,
Communist Party
of the Soviet Union

5

[On the Soviet involvement in Afghanistan]: After the well-known revolution in Afghanistan, where an attempt was made to make some inter-

290

(MIKHAIL S. GORBACHEV)

nal reforms and to bring that society out of its ancient system . . . a different government came to power. But at the same time, certain processes were building up connected with, first and foremost, interference from outside, in order to undermine that new regime. And they [the new Afghan government] appealed to us, as to their neighbors, some say 11 times, others say 13 times . . . Meeting their desire, we introduced our limited Soviet contingent of troops, and have never increased it. But we see today that the situation does require some solutions. We are looking for ways to bring about the prompt solution of that problem.

American broadcast interview,
Moscow, Nov. 28/NBC-TV, 11-30.

1

[On the Soviet intervention in Afghanistan]: We are not seeking any outcome under which there has to be a pro-Soviet regime in Afghanistan, but the American side must clearly say that it is not seeking to install a pro-American regime in Afghanistan. In a free, non-aligned neutral Afghanistan there must be set up a government on the basis of reconciliation and on the basis of taking into account cooperation among all elements and national reconciliation. And our two countries can do a lot. On Afghanistan we said this: The political decision on a withdrawal of Soviet forces has been taken. We've named the time limit—12 months, maybe less . . . But as we see it, we can name the beginning of the withdrawal of Soviet forces, but this must at the same time become the start, the beginning of an end to arms and financial supplies to the insurgency forces.

News conference,
Washington, Dec. 10/
The New York Times, 12-11:12.

Jack Grayson
Author; Chairman,
American Productivity Center

2

The only [competitor] that really is a challenger for the United States' Number 1 position

is Japan. The average Japanese citizen is not only richer than we are in real terms, he is better educated than the average American, he works harder than the average American—more hours of work—and he saves more . . . Those are powerful ingredients.

Interview, Oak Brook, Ill./
The Christian Science Monitor, 7-3:5.

Tom Harkin
United States Senator,
D-Iowa

3

As [South] Korean politics become more polarized, as prospects for a peaceful democratization become more remote, the frustrations of the Korean people will fuel anti-Americanism, and our security in the region will suffer as a result.

The Christian Science Monitor, 6-22:5.

Bob Hawke
Prime Minister of Australia

4

[On his ordering Libya to close its Embassy in Australia]: The government [of Australia] has previously voiced concern about the nature and direction of Libyan activities in the South Pacific region. Libya has begun to intrude into our domestic affairs, too . . . There is no plausible explanation in terms of geography or legitimate national interest for Libyan activity in this region. The Australian government has concluded that a continuing official Libyan presence in Australia serves no Australian interest or purpose, and indeed is serving to facilitate Libya's destabilizing activities.

May 19/The New York Times, 5-20:7.

Bill Hayden
Minister of Foreign Affairs
of Australia

5

We support the continued presence of France as an influential factor in maintaining the [South Pacific] region as part of the Western

(BILL HAYDEN)

community. But we maintain that it should be the kind of presence that the people of the region consider acceptable and constructive. My abiding concern—and I don't say this lightly—is that a major factor in the force for unification in the region will be opposition to France, brought on by its policies on nuclear testing and New Caledonia. This would be inimical to Australian and Western interests.

Speech, Sydney, Australia/
Los Angeles Times, 7-3:(I)10.

Richard C. Holbrooke
Former Assistant Secretary
for East Asian
and Pacific Affairs,
Department of State
of the United States

1

[On whether North Korea would ever invade South Korea]: In the real world, none of this is going to happen . . . If it really happened and North Korea made a lightning attack, they'd probably reach Seoul. There would be enormous disruptions, the end of the South Korean economic miracle for several years. But as a result of that, the United States would undoubtedly use massive air power against North Korean targets, and the North Korean economy would be wrecked, too. And the North Koreans would not end up in control of a unified South Korea because the United States would not walk away from it. They just wouldn't—they couldn't—because it would be the end of our position in the entire Pacific.

The New York Times, 4-8:6.

Hun Sen
Premier of Cambodia

2

[Saying he invites the Khmer Rouge to negotiations about improving conditions in Cambodia]: We will allow the Khmer Rouge party to have a role to play in the negotiations and a role to play in the solution . . . The Pol Pot regime has left upon us only suffering, destruction and separation. Right now, the major object to reconstruction is the war. Our enemies get together to oppose us, inside and outside the country. But they just realize they cannot strangle us to death. So right now what is most important is to find a solution to put an end to the situation of war, which has lasted for 17 years.

Interview,
Phnom Penh, Cambodia,
Sept. 21/Los Angeles Times,
9-22:(I)7.

3

[On Cambodia's experiment with a free-enterprise economy]: The point that we should be afraid of is not that we have a free-market economy. What we should fear is the poverty of the population . . . If we are giving the population the opportunity to exercise freedom in the economy, in business, construction, in small industry, that is not as dangerous as the fact that poverty still exists . . . You have seen our markets are filled with goods from Japan, Thailand and Singapore . . . If the government cannot conduct this kind of trade, the people can do it, and we will allow them to do it.

Interview/
The Washington Post,
4-9:(A)38.

4

Any faction except the Khmer Rouge can negotiate for a future government. We have already declared that we are willing to negotiate with the other factions, based on the elimination of [Khmer Rouge leader] Pol Pot. Our demand for the elimination of Pol Pot means we ask for the elimination of their [Khmer Rouge] political and military organizations. Once this Pol Pot organization has been disbanded, [the Khmer Rouge forces] will be welcomed as ordinary citizens.

Interview,
Phnom Penh, Cambodia/
The Washington Post,
4-11:(A)28.

Rafael Ileto
Minister of Defense
of the Philippines

1

The inescapable fact in [the Philippines' Communist] insurgency problem is [that] it is tied to our economy. Business must break the cycle simultaneously with our peace-keeping effort. One cannot come before the other . . . We are caught in a vicious cycle of no peace, no profit, no relief from poverty, so no peace, no profit, and so on.

To businessmen's association, Manila,
June 19/Los Angeles Times, 6-20:(I)10.

Kim Dae Jung
A leader of opposition to
the government of South Korean
President Chun Doo Hwan

2

[On government promises to hold free elections next year]: There are still all sorts of possibilities [that the government will again resort to oppressive measures]. For instance, there are no labor unions in any big business, or, if they exist, they are company-controlled unions. Laborers will begin to rise up. That alone will create a big problem. Then, if freedom of expression is given, newspapers will take up all sorts of scandals that have been covered up until now. If they [the government] suppress the press, trouble will occur. If someone wants to stage a demonstration, they could suppress it, and the people will get angry. The path ahead is not so simple . . . Lack of principle is their [the government's] only principle. The only thing that has remained consistent is that, whatever happens, they intend to keep their grasp on power.

Interview, Seoul, July 2/
Los Angeles Times, 7-3:(I)14.

Kim Young Sam
Leader, Reunification
Democratic Party of South Korea

3

I agree that the essence of politics is dialogue. In the United States dialogue is, say, about particular tax policies, and so forth. But the American people need to understand that here in Korea, the essential question is dictatorship versus democracy.

Interview, Seoul/
The Christian Science Monitor,
6-10:9.

4

[Addressing South Korean President Chun Doo Hwan on the violent protests against the government and in favor of democracy]: The government appears to think that the middle class is supporting [the government]. But we do not think so. To insure national security and preserve the republic's foundations, nothing must be done that would give a pretext to the radical minority or push the situation beyond the control of the law-enforcement authorities. The scheduled peaceful transition of power [to a new President in 1988] is, per se, an excellent thing. There must be a political modus operandi by which everyone can retire honorably, which will preclude retribution and which will assure a better future. Mr. President, if you decide to lay a solid foundation for democracy before you leave office, you will leave an illustrious imprint on history.

At meeting
with President Chun, Seoul,
June 24/The New York Times, 6-25:8.

Mochtar Kusumaatmadja
Foreign Minister of Indonesia

5

[Saying Indonesians give too many parties and spend too much time on the toilet]: If you go to the toilet, do not sit there too long. That is not necessary. That kind of attitude is not what Indonesia wants . . . When you go dating, you make a party. When you get married, you hold a gala. When your wife becomes pregnant, you hold a party. Some people hold a series of parties to celebrate a pregnancy . . . All these parties do not have to be held at all.

Los Angeles Times, 4-7:(I)2.

WHAT THEY SAID IN 1987

Nguyen Cao Ky
Exiled former Premier
of South Vietnam

1

We must free and unify all Vietnam. They are waiting for us in North Vietnam. To make Vietnam free again is not only a dream but a duty and a responsibility. [The people of Vietnam] realize after 12 years [of Communist rule] that this is not the way of life they want.

At parade
of U.S. Vietnam veterans,
New Orleans, June 28/
Los Angeles Times, 6-29:(I)4.

David Lange
Prime Minister
of New Zealand

2

[Saying he is concerned by Libya's attempts to woo South Pacific nations]: [If people in Vanuatu and New Caledonia are frustrated] because they haven't had what they see as proper solidarity and support from regional nations, the temptation is that they do go ahead and flamboyantly forge what could be quite detrimental linkages with other countries [such as Libya]. . . . We're working to see that they do not get driven into romantic and peculiar liaisons with countries whose interests don't coincide with our region.

News conference,
Wellington, New Zealand, March 9/
Los Angeles Times, 3-10:(I)8.

3

French nuclear testing in the South Pacific has been condemned by successive New Zealand governments for more than 20 years. This activity by a nuclear-weapon state, in blatant disregard of the conditions of the South Pacific Nuclear Free Zone Treaty, adds an element of insecurity to our lives . . . Despite France having ignored our protests for so long, we have no intention of becoming complacent about their testing program. We shall continue to press, internationally, for the commencement of practical work on a nuclear test-ban treaty.

May 6/Los Angeles Times, 5-7:(I)9.

Li Peng
Acting Premier of China

4

Just because I studied in the U.S.S.R., it doesn't mean I'm pro-Soviet. The allegation that I'm in favor of central planning is a misunderstanding. [China's] present economic system must be restructured.

The New York Times, 11-25:3.

Li Yining
Chinese economist

5

A limited role for private enterprise should be permissible [in China]. But people with ossified brains think differently. In economics, they argue as though China had already entered the final stage of Communism. Hence, their insistence on "total" state ownership of property. In politics, they seem to believe the country is still battling capitalism and imperialists. Hence, the insistence on "persistent struggle."

World Press Review, September:27.

Nguyen Van Linh
General Secretary,
Communist Party of Vietnam

6

[On Vietnam's occupation of Cambodia]: I don't think it was a mistake for us to go in there. Even in the worst hours of the war with America, there was no such brutal massacre of Vietnamese civilians as occurred when [Khmer Rouge leader] Pol Pot invaded our land [in 1978]. We had no choice but to fight back. China gave the Pol Pot forces support, weapons and money. After we got them out and they went into Thailand, I should add, they received assistance from the [U.S.] CIA. Under such circumstances, the people of Kampuchea [Cambodia] asked us to remain. As soon as the situation is stabilized and the Pol Pot regime cannot begin again to massacre at will, the volunteers from Vietnam will come home.

Interview/Time, 9-21:40.

(NGUYEN VAN LINH)

1

We want to forget the past, forget that under several American Presidents we were engaged in a brutal war we did not start. We would like to see the U.S. embargo lifted and the two sides sit down and talk over the problems that are left from the war—problems like both cooperating to find the remains of Americans missing in action. We want the Amerasians, all of them, to go to America, if the father wants his child. If the Vietnamese mother wants to go, she will be allowed to go. There is no interest, none, for either country to maintain a gap between us. Step by step, we should move to restore diplomatic relations. Let us put the war behind us and work for a peaceful future.

Interview/Time, 9-21:40.

Ferdinand E. Marcos
*Exiled Former President
of the Philippines*

2

What I would like to be remembered for is the human-resources development program, the transformation of the indolent, the weak, the enslaved, resigned, fatalistic and unproductive Filipino into a spiritually regenerated and highly motivated, productive unit who has learned a livelihood, who has learned that he has a name of which he can be proud, who has acquired some dignity which he has obtained from knowledge of his past, his tradition, his heroes, his culture. And the slow transformation of the country into a country of free men, spiritually regenerated, possessing what he needs for his livelihood instead of begging. This is what I would like to be remembered for.

*Interview, Honolulu, Hawaii/
USA Today, 2-19:(A)9.*

3

There will be peace in Asia only if the American bases at Clark and Subic Bay [in the Philippines] remain firmly in place and we maintain a military balance of power not only between the two superpowers [the U.S. and Soviet Union] but between all the nations that

have legitimate interests in Asia. The danger is that while Madame [Philippine President Corazon] Aquino claims she is still "non-committed" about the future of the bases, it is her government's policy to get rid of them. Why is everyone afraid to ask her for a clear commitment?

*Interview/
U.S. News & World Report,
8-3:33.*

Najibullah
*Chief of State
of Afghanistan*

4

[Criticizing U.S. support for Afghan rebels fighting against his government]: The basic problem is that the U.S.A. and counter-revolutionary banditory leaders, protected by the U.S.A., have not realized the true situation in Afghanistan and had never paid attention to the balance of forces. In response to our peaceful offers, these counter-revolutionaries persistently demand from us only one thing: unconditional surrender. They call our national-democratic state a "Communist" government. They consider our existence a *casus belli*. People of the world need peace, not *Stingers* [missiles].

Interview/Newsweek, 10-12:48.

Yasuhiro Nakasone
Prime Minister of Japan

5

[On when Japan will recognize itself as an affluent country and be ready to contribute to the well-being of the outside world]: Don't forget that Japan was a developing country at least until 1955, and [a newly industrialized country] until 1964 [when the International Monetary Fund recognized Japan as a fully developed country]. You can't expect us to feel an affluence of the heart in such a short space of time. It's only from now on that we are having to accustom ourselves to the feeling. Japan is going to change a lot.

*Interview, Tokyo/
The Christian Science Monitor,
11-5:14.*

WHAT THEY SAID IN 1987

(YASUHIRO NAKASONE)

1

We [Japanese] have not yet won international respect. For that, we must correct [our faults]. We must expand efforts to associate with foreigners and we must make appropriate donations [to the world] . . . Japan must carry out reforms at home to win a voice in diplomacy.

News conference, Nov. 4/
Los Angeles Times, 11-7:(I)13.

Phyllis Oakley
Spokeswoman for the Department
of State of the United States

2

[On the current violent demonstrations in South Korea against that country's government]: We [the U.S.] have often repeated our support for basic human rights, such as freedom of speech and peaceful assembly, as well as our opposition to violence and abuse of force . . . The only solutions likely to last are those which are worked by and for Koreans themselves and enjoy the broad support of the Korean people. We think that real progress can come only through dialogue and a willingness of all sides to compromise. Events of the past week demonstrate once again the pressing need for such a process.

To reporters, Washington, June 16/
Los Angeles Times, 6-17:(I)7.

Blas Ople
Former Minister of Labor
of the Philippines

3

[Philippine] President [Corazon] Aquino has spent so much of her time balancing herself against the forces of the left and the right that her tendency has been to stay all the time in dead center, where nothing happens. What we have is a chronic stalemate and, as a result, you have only two highly organized power centers in the country—the armed forces of the Philippines and the Communist Party of the Philippines, along with its military wing, the New People's Army. So what we are seeing now is a

symptom of the internal breakdown and deterioration of the Aquino government as a buffer between these two far more powerful forces. We believe the process is irreversible—barring, of course, future miracles.

Los Angeles Times, 9-21:(I)9.

Tomas Padilla
Philippine Ambassador
to South Korea

4

[Comparing the political change in the Philippines last year, when dictator Ferdinand Marcos was forced to leave the country, with the political reforms recently announced by the South Korean government]: I would say it [the South Korean reforms] is a triumph of people-power. The people [of South Korea] were able to clearly manifest what they wanted, and the government was smart enough to oblige. We have a political miracle here, in that the ruling party just accepted almost everything the opposition wanted, with almost no bloodshed. But, of course, it was all in a very different way. In the Philippines, people-power overthrew a government and, of course, the [South Korean] government is still in power . . . President Chun [Doo Hwan] has improved the economy of the South Korean nation. He can take credit for that, and, of course, the credit also belongs to the Korean people. Whereas in the Philippines, the economy was, and still is, in bad shape. As the quality of life improves, the South Koreans want to be more involved politically. But there's a risk. They don't want to push beyond the point where it will begin to hurt their economy. There's too much at stake for them . . . [In South Korea] you have a Communist state [North Korea] with a larger army just the other side of the demilitarized zone . . . Every South Korean is aware of that threat, and for many of them it is the bottom line. The people's wishes were clearly manifested here in recent weeks, no question about that. But I think many of them believe that is quite enough for them right now.

Interview, Seoul, South Korea/
Los Angeles Times, 7-1:(I)12.

Sitiveni Rabuka
Lieutenant Colonel and leader
of recent military coup
taking power in Fiji

1

I hereby proclaim that from this day forth Fiji is declared a republic. I reaffirm the indigenous Fijian race is empowered [over the Indian majority] with the land and right to govern themselves and their advancement and welfare.

Broadcast address
to the nation, Oct. 6/
The New York Times, 10-7:2.

Ruth Richardson
Member of
New Zealand Parliament

2

[Criticizing the New Zealand government's proposed school "peace studies" program]: There is already substantial anti-Americanism among young people here. This exercise will fuel this. The message of peace studies is this: If you are for peace, you must be against nuclear weapons. Who has nuclear weapons? America.

The Christian Science Monitor, 4-6:30.

Roh Tae Woo
Chairman,
ruling Democratic Justice
Party of South Korea;
Candidate for President
of South Korea in 1988 election

3

[There must be a better balance] between the authority of the government and the checking ability of the people, between big business and small business, between urban and rural communities [and] . . . between those who have and those who have less. [South Korea's youth] should duly appreciate the achievements of the established generation whose members sacrificed their lives to defend the nation, endured hunger and hardship and have finally managed

to build a solid basis for economic development . . . We, the members of the established generation, must respect the pure sense of justice and the ideals of young people. I plead with you [young people] to end your intellectual wandering and join the grand endeavor to create a new era.

At Democratic Justice
Party convention, Seoul, June 10/
Los Angeles Times, 6-11:(I)19.

4

With the sacred right to vote at hand, let us all work together to create a society where young people develop their capabilities to realize their ideals, where workers and farmers can work free of anxiety, where businessmen exert even greater creative efforts and where politicians exercise the art of debate and compromise to work out the nation's future . . . This country belongs to us. It is our historic duty to exert our efforts and exercise restraint and wisdom to more successfully develop the country that was nurtured with the blood of our forefathers and the lives of our patriots to proudly hand it over to the next generation. I sincerely hope that national wisdom will be pooled to demonstrate to the world that the Korean people will not go backward but will move forward to make a contribution to world history.

Broadcast address
to the nation, Seoul, June 29/
Los Angeles Times, 6-30:(I)8.

5

[On the violent demonstrations protesting his recent election as President]: Of course, peaceful demonstrations should be allowed. However, what we see are protests using firebombs and other violent means, and these are against the national consensus. After all, we have elected the new President through a fair and open process, and the majority of public opinion favors the outcome. In order to make democracy work, it's necessary to use police power to curb the violence. Lawlessness has to be distinguished from the exercise of free expression.

Interview/Newsweek,
12-28:24.

Sarwono Kusumaatmadja

Secretary general,
political party of
Indonesian President Suharto

1

[The Indonesian] concept of democracy is different from the concept of democracy in the West. In the West, democracy has something to do with decision-making. But here, democracy would be best described as a process of participation. If somebody in a leadership position gives you a good sense of participation, that would be democracy. If he is sensitive to your needs, your aspiration, that would be democratic. It has nothing to do with decision-making.

The New York Times, 2-2:3.

Paul Seabury

Professor of political science,
University of California,
Berkeley

2

It must be recalled, if only by diplomatic historians, that the initiative to the creation of NATO in the late 1940s came from European statesmen in concert, appealing to America to lead in the framing of a common system of cooperative security; the national elements of it are interlocked in a common strategic posture—naval, air and ground forces. The nations of the Pacific Basin share today no such "networked communality" as did, and do, the Atlantic partners. Some of America's intimate Pacific partners fear each other nearly as much as they may fear a common hegemonic threat from the Soviet Union. Others are reluctant even to significantly contribute to a common defense. Still others are too insignificant to contribute much to it. Others, such as Taiwan, are regional pariahs. Still others, like some New Zealanders such as [Prime Minister David] Lange, wander off happily, like Little Bo Beep, to tend their sheep [and not allow U.S. nuclear warships into their harbors].

Fulbright lecture, Australia, April/
The Wall Street Journal, 9-30:36.

Eduard A. Shevardnadze

Foreign Minister
of the Soviet Union

3

[On the war in Afghanistan between rebels and the Soviet-backed government]: By countering reconciliation with irreconciliability, [the rebels] have demonstrated once again what has long been obvious, namely, that the cease-fire is opposed by those who are backed by imperialism, the forces who aren't in the least concerned about what will happen to Afghanistan and which make their policy on Afghans' blood . . . We believe that a political settlement is not a remote prospect but a reality of today. The issue of withdrawing the Soviet troops is being considered by us and the government of democratic Afghanistan accordingly. This event is not far off; it is only needed that in neighboring countries they also realize what is in their interests and what isn't . . . A settlement in Afghanistan will benefit both Pakistan and Iran, which should be vitally interested in the existence of a non-aligned and independent friendly neighboring country.

Interview, Jan. 7/
Los Angeles Times, 1-8:(I)13.

George P. Shultz

Secretary of State
of the United States

4

[Saying the U.S. has not lived up to its obligations to give financial help to the Philippines since Corazon Aquino took office there as President]: We've done ourselves a disservice. We haven't come up with the money . . . It is in our strategic interest to do all we can to support the efforts of President Aquino's government to restore democracy, stability and prosperity to the Philippines. That will take money on our part—but we will pay a far higher cost, later on, if we do not act effectively now.

Before House Appropriations
Committee, Washington, Feb. 11/
Los Angeles Times, 2-12:(I)5.

(GEORGE P. SHULTZ)

1

What Japan has to realize is that their economy is exceedingly vulnerable. It is heavily dependent on the willingness of the world to take a gigantic excess of Japanese exports over Japanese imports, mostly the United States. Now, when that stops, where does that leave the Japanese economy?

To reporters, Hot Springs, Va.,
May 8/The New York Times, 5-9:17.

Gaston J. Sigur, Jr.
Assistant Secretary
for East Asian
and Pacific Affairs,
Department of State
of the United States

2

The Republic of [South] Korea's security relies as much upon responsive political institutions that promote the aspirations of its people as upon the mighty military capability it possesses. Domestic political practices up to now—however well-suited they may have been for a simpler, slower-moving past—simply are inadequate to meet Korea's complex present and future needs.

Speech, February/
Los Angeles Times, 5-2:(I)12.

3

[On the promised December Presidential election in South Korea]: I firmly believe—strongly believe—that the duly elected President of this country in the coming election will take his seat as the President of [South] Korea . . . We believe that the way to solve problems that arise in the political process is not through military intervention. We believe that is not the way to go, and it is very difficult to foresee any kind of a situation in Korea which would necessitate anything of the sort. As far as the rumors of something happening in September and October [to interfere with the elections], I would say that what I received universally from all the political leaders of both the major parties with whom I spoke was that the democratization pro-

cess in Korea is on track, it will stay on track, and it will be handled in such a manner as not to upset anything.

News conference, Seoul, Sept. 15/
Los Angeles Times, 9-16:(I)14.

Stephen J. Solarz
United States Representative,
D-New York

4

We do have solid reason to believe that the Vietnamese have been less than forthcoming in the return of the remains of those [American] servicemen who died [in the U.S.-Vietnam war in the 1960s and '70s]. Why? I suppose they may feel there's a certain amount of mileage in doling them out. It's a ghoulish business, very cynical, but we have good reason to believe they could be more forthcoming.

The New York Times, 7-31:10.

5

There is no question that the Philippines faces serious problems which have helped to fuel a Communist-led insurgency. But we must not allow these very real difficulties to obscure the remarkable progress that has been made [since President Corazon Aquino took over after the dictatorship of Ferdinand Marcos] . . . Not all Filipinos believe that these reforms have been proper . . . But military coups and armed rebellions have no place in a democracy. Those who are dissatisfied with the policies of the present government must work to change those policies through the peaceful democratic means that are now, for the first time in many years, available to them, rather than by seeking to overturn the democratic system itself.

Before House Asian
and Pacific Affairs Subcommittee,
Washington, Sept. 10/
The Washington Post, 9-16:(A)20.

Gerald Solomon
United States Representative,
D-New York

6

[On the Soviet intervention in Afghanistan]: All of the Soviet abuses aside, their puppet re-

WHAT THEY SAID IN 1987

gime in Afghanistan is a notorious human-rights violator in its own right. Summary executions, torture, censorship, wiretaps, house-to-house searches, the complete suppression of all rights to peaceful assembly, public expression and religious worship—all of these horrible things become part of daily life for those Afghanis who live in areas of the country that are under effective control of the Soviets and their puppets . . . There can be no resolution of the crisis in Afghanistan until the Soviet forces are out and their puppets are gone with them. Afghanistan will be at peace only when the Afghanis themselves are in charge of their own destiny.

Before the House,
Washington, Oct. 20/
The Washington Post, 10-23:(A)22.

Juwono Sudarsono
Professor of political science,
University of Indonesia

1

What ASEAN does not have, and what the European Community does have, is NATO. The Europeans have a real sense of imminent danger—that's what made the economic positions more forthcoming. Here [in Southeast Asia], there is no common denominator of sufficient urgency to have economic cooperation put into the context of regional cooperation.

The Washington Post, 12-14:(A)37.

Ha Xuan Truong
Editor,
"Communist Review"
(Vietnam)

2

Our ideology is Marxism-Leninism, but we also seek the most productive elements of other ideologies. The best way of thinking is the kind that deals with the reality of living. Our leaders thought that cooperatives were socialism. But when they finished creating a cooperative, we found out that peasants only received 40 to 50 per cent of their income from the cooperative.

The rest came from the small family plots. For a long time, no one wanted to see this. But now we ask what really encourages the farmer to work . . . We thought before that socialism was either a cooperative or the state. And if you were not a socialist, then you were a capitalist. But private ownership can serve socialism or capitalism as long as the main means of production still officially belong to the state, benefits are guaranteed, and there is no exploitation of man by man.

Interview/
The Christian Science Monitor,
11-9:13.

Vernon A. Walters
United States Ambassador/
Permanent Representative
to the United Nations

3

[On whether the U.S. should establish diplomatic relations with Vietnam]: Perhaps politically we should, but personally and emotionally, no . . . My answer is let them fry for a while . . . In Vietnam, when American bombs were falling everywhere [during the U.S.-Vietnam war], when there was fighting in every village and all the young men were being drafted into the South Vietnamese Army, there were no boat people [trying to escape from the country]. It took the coming of this gang [the victorious North Vietnamese] to Saigon to drive 2 million people out to sea in open boats . . . As far as we know, 200,000 have been lost at sea doing that. And you expect me to deal with this government . . . as though it's an ordinary government?

Broadcast interview,
"John McLaughlin's One on One,"
July 31/Los Angeles Times, 8-1:(I)4.

Jusuf Wanandi
Director,
Center for Strategic
and International Studies
(Indonesia)

4

[In Indonesia,] the people vote to please the government. They want to be on the bandwagon

(JUSUF WANANDI)

with the government, which is the most respected institution they face in their daily lives. For most people, voting is still an obligation— not a right.

The Christian Science Monitor,
3-24:12.

Leonard Weiss
Staff director,
United States Senate Committee
on Governmental Affairs

1

If Pakistan builds an atomic bomb, India would probably build a thermonuclear weapon, and China would definitely be alarmed. The whole balance of power in Asia could be affected, and the result would be to sabotage the U.S.-Soviet arms agreement, and you could eventually wind up with a nuclear standoff in the Mideast.

March 13/
Los Angeles Times,
3-14:(I)34.

Clayton K. Yeutter
Special Trade
Representative for President
of the United States
Ronald Reagan

2

[Japan] must now play a significant role in the economic system of the world. They can't sit on the sidelines and simply be the beneficiaries of all of the good things and accept none of the responsibilities in a purely mercantilist approach any more—where they export everything and import nothing, take advantage of every market opportunity but keep everyone out of the Japanese market. That kind of self-serving stance, and one that is pure self-interest in the short-term sense, has to change.

Interview/
The Christian Science Monitor,
6-15:8.

Ying Ruocheng
Vice Minister
of Culture of China

3

China cannot adopt democracy as . . . Jefferson saw it. That simply doesn't work. China has never had a true bi-party system. What we are faced with in China is stability or chaos . . . To have a unified country with reasonable stability will always be the main concern of any Chinese government.

Interview, Peking, March 2/
The Washington Post, 3-3:(A)16.

Yu Kuo-hua
Premier of Taiwan

4

[On Taiwan's plans to allow some of its citizens to visit Communist mainland China]: We are now ready to launch an offensive, not of weapons, but of something much more powerful—ideas. It seems clear to us that the most effective tactic in this war of ideas is to offer the people of the mainland an alternative more viable and attractive than the Communist system . . . namely freedom, democracy, the prosperity of free enterprise, and stability and security under the rule of law.

To foreign journalists,
Taipei, Taiwan, Oct. 12/
Los Angeles Times, 10-13:(I)1.

Zhao Ziyang
Premier of China

5

The Chinese Communist Party has not only proposed and led the economic structural reform, but also set forward, at an appropriate time, the task of political structural reform. Many people have been concerned about elections, and this year election methods at the county level will be further improved, including nominating more candidates for election than required for each post . . . For the process to continue, it needs a stable political and social environment, which in turn needs a powerful core of leadership. Only under the leadership of

301

WHAT THEY SAID IN 1987

(ZHAO ZIYANG)

the Party can the national situation be stable and the people's will and strength be concentrated on reform and construction. Of course, the Communist Party's successful leadership in the Chinese revolution and construction were mixed with mistakes, and there are still shortcomings within the Party. But it is the Party itself that has openly exposed and corrected these mistakes and shortcomings.

At celebration of Chinese New Year, Peking, Jan. 29/ The New York Times, 1-30:3.

1

We cannot give up reforms, opening to the outside world and invigoration of the economy—and return to the closed working conditions of the past, just as one cannot go hungry because one once choked on food.

Before Chinese Communist Party, Peking/ Los Angeles Times, 6-4:(I)14.

2

We do not intend to change the socialist system in China. We do not intend to change the system of leadership by the Communist Party. Of course, in implementing the policy of reform and opening to the outside world, there is the question, which way should we go? We will criticize that thinking which is conservative, ossified, and which does not support reform in China. And, at the same time, we will also criticize that thinking which maintains that, by carrying our reform and opening up to the outside world, the socialist system in China should be changed . . . Maybe there are some people in the United States who view this as a crackdown or oppression of the intellectuals. I do not agree. If there is a writer or intellectual who happens to be a Communist Party member, then, as an intellectual, he is respected and he can play his role. But as a Party member, he is required to observe the Party Constitution and Party program.

Broadcast interview, Peking/ "Meet the Press," NBC-TV, 9-27.

Mohammed Zia ul-Haq
President of Pakistan

3

You can virtually write today that Pakistan can build a [nuclear] bomb whenever it wishes. What's the difficulty about a bomb? . . . Once you have acquired the technology, which Pakistan has, you can do whatever you like. You can use it for peaceful purposes only; you can also utilize [it] for military purposes. We have never said we are incapable of doing this. We have said we have neither the intention nor the desire. Pakistan has the capability of building the bomb.

Interview/ The Washington Post, 3-24:(A)22.

Europe

Kenneth L. Adelman
*Director, Arms Control
and Disarmament Agency
of the United States*

1

[On the recent release from Soviet prisons of some Soviet dissidents]: What we have seen thus far is a release of a few of the most famous dissidents—individuals who have been the subject of intense publicity in the West and continual Western pressure on the Soviet regime. For releasing these few conspicuous individuals, the Soviet regime has received a lot of good publicity. However, this is hardly the tip of the iceberg. Literally thousands of prisoners remain. Right now, according to our best estimates, there are between 4,000 and 10,000 prisoners of conscience in the Soviet Union. The names of only about 900 of these are known in the West. The rest suffer in anonymity, their plight hidden from world opinion. Forgotten people in the cold . . . We must be clear about what is at stake here: In the Soviet Union, you don't even have the option of leaving. The Soviet Union is a country in which even application for permission to emigrate is likely to bring the full weight of the state security apparatus down upon you and your family.

*Before Chicago Bar Association,
Jan. 22/The Washington Post,
2-12:(A)26.*

Christoph Bertram
*Diplomatic correspondent,
"Die Zeit" (West Germany)*

2

Not the least because of the megalomania of (Adolf) Hitler's Reich and the fate it suffered, Germans harbor a deep uneasiness about being powerful. West Germany's post-war experience has been that of an applicant who wishes to be accepted, not that of a leader who seeks to impress others. Yet, power has caught up with Germans whether they like it or not.

Los Angeles Times, 2-23:(I)9.

Gordon B. Beyer
*President,
George C. Marshall Foundation*

3

[On the 40th anniversary of the Marshall Plan]: In the spring of 1947, George C. Marshall, then [U.S.] Secretary of State, and other key advisers, became increasingly concerned by the state of disintegration of the European economy. The costs of World War II, in terms of physical destruction, the liquidation of assets, and general economic dislocation, threatened to cause a complete breakdown of normal social and commercial life. European governments were quickly exhausting their last reserves in order to import the necessities of life for their people. At a Council of Foreign Ministers' meeting in Moscow in April 1947, Marshall became convinced the Soviet Union was doing everything possible to achieve an economic breakdown in Europe. Mr. Marshall decided Europe needed help . . . Our world was fundamentally changed for the better by the Marshall Plan. Americans did that, and the success of the Marshall Plan is well known. But it was also a seminal idea. With the recovery of democratic nations in Europe, these free European countries and the U.S. turned to help the countries which were to become independent in the developing world.

*At Penn State
University-Fayette commencement/
The Christian Science Monitor,
6-4:17.*

Anders Bjoerck
Member of Swedish Parliament

4

We [in Sweden] have had 170 years with no war, a high standard of living, a quiet country with a welfare state. That tends to make you much less suspicious than you should be. It worries me that Sweden wants to go back to the

(ANDERS BJOERCK)

same kind of life we lived when we were still a remote part of Europe. But the outside world has come closer to Sweden. We have been used as a base for some terrorists; we have seen our Prime Minister assassinated. It has been a painful time, but I think we are waking up.

Interview/
Los Angeles Times,
11-11:(I)12.

Bill Bradley
United States Senator,
D-New Jersey

1

Americans are mystified by Soviet denial of many basic freedoms of expression. We do not understand why Mstislav Rostropovich could not conduct an orchestra or play his cello in his motherland [and had to leave for the West], why pianist Vladimir Feltsman had to emigrate to perform, why [ballet dancer] Mikhail Baryshnikov felt he had to leave in order for his artistry to grow.

At conference on
Soviet-American relations,
Chautauqua, N.Y., Aug. 27/
The New York Times, 8-28:4.

2

[Soviet leader Mikhail] Gorbachev cannot accomplish his domestic priorities unless the West is doing well, economically. To import technology, he must raise cash by borrowing more from the West or by exporting more to it. Whether he relies on Western capital markets or export markets, he will benefit from a healthy Western economy. So a serious economic downturn could doom his modernization plans. This degree of economic interdependence is new. It gives the Soviets an unprecedented stake in Western growth.

At conference
sponsored by Institute
for East-West Securities Studies/
The New York Times, 10-15:27.

Joseph Brodsky
Exiled Soviet poet;
Winner, 1987 Nobel Prize
in Literature

3

What's really bad about Russia, about the political system in the Soviet Union, is that it curbs the human potential. The genuine crime there is not the concrete political crime, but the cumulative aspect of it which has a reductive influence upon man's ability to evolve. In a sense, in the Soviet Union you are more likely not to think the thought that may have crossed your mind precisely because you think that it may be: [a] not applicable, [b] dangerous. As soon as this is realized by an individual, it slows him down, curbs him. When the people realize they must keep themselves, so to speak, down, they restrict their mental processes.

Interview, New York/
The Christian Science Monitor,
10-23:3.

George Bush
Vice President
of the United States

4

It is not for me to try to tell [Poland] what road to take. That is a matter for Poles themselves to decide. But I can tell you what has worked in our country [the U.S.] and in many other countries. It is respect for human rights. It is the right to form independent and self-governing organizations for many purposes, including the protection of workers' interests. It is an economic system that encourages people to reach their full potential.

Broadcast address·
to Polish nation, Sept. 28/
The New York Times, 9-29:3.

David P. Calleo
Director of European Studies,
School of Advanced
International Studies,
Johns Hopkins University

5

The nightmare [for Europeans] is that there will be a war [with the Soviet Union] limited

(DAVID P. CALLEO)

entirely to Europe. They [European leaders] feel that the best way to prevent that is to make sure that if there should be a war, the Americans would retaliate against the Soviet Union with nuclear forces, so that neither superpower would be tempted to try out their toys at the expense of the Europeans. The U.S. interest is far different: If a war starts, it should be kept as small as possible so it would stay in Europe.

Los Angeles Times, 5-25:(I)6.

Nicolae Ceausescu
First Secretary,
Communist Party of Romania

1

[Criticizing reforms introduced in the Soviet Union by Soviet leader Mikhail Gorbachev]: No one can conceive of a revolutionary party saying that it will let enterprises or economic sectors manage themselves and no longer interfere in the management of the enterprise or of scientific, cultural or other activities . . . One cannot speak of a socialist economy and not assume the socialist ownership of the means of production as its basis.

Los Angeles Times, 4-9:(I)23.

Julian Critchley
Member of British Parliament

2

[Speaking, as a Conservative, about Denis Healey, longtime Labor Party stalwart, who is retiring from the front-line of the Party following Labor's loss in the recent national elections]: The Labor Party has moved steadily to the left, leaving poor Denis stranded. You could see this in the election. He was running on his rims. He despaired in private, but did his best in public. Had the Labor Party won, the prayers of the rest of the nation would have been focused on Denis as Foreign Secretary. He would have been the last hope we had that [current Labor Party leader] Neil Kinnock would have been educated into the facts of life.

The New York Times, 7-3:5.

Mario M. Cuomo
Governor of New York (D)

3

This is the time to deal [with the Soviet Union]. The Soviets are vulnerable, in their economy and in their souls. There's a survival mentality now, and the people want more. [Soviet leader Mikhail] Gorbachev didn't invent *glasnost* [openness] because it was an inspiration; it's a response to an observed need of the population. So far, though, they haven't paid a significant price for *glasnost*—but they will. You can't give people a few liberties and expect their appetites to be satisfied. Of course, there's a flip side. Many people feel threatened by changing a system of guarantees even if those guarantees add up only to bare survival. So Gorbachev may not last.

U.S. News & World Report,
10-12:29.

Dominique David
Secretary general, Foundation for National Defense Studies (France)

4

The majority of French public opinion today thinks that French arms should help Germany if it is attacked . . . I think we made a lot of progress since '80, '81, '82—progress more political than military. Today, it is possible in France to say things about Germany and the [NATO] alliance which could not have been said 20 years ago [when France withdrew from NATO's military command]. There has been an important evolution in the political class and public opinion, and in Germany, too, there has been an evolution.

The Christian Science Monitor,
7-29:14.

Herve de Charette
French Cabinet Minister

5

The French at heart are monarchists. They like to prostrate themselves in front of the monarch, whom they now call President, and, every seven years or so, they guillotine him.

The New York Times, 1-26:4.

305

Ernesto Galli Della Loggia
Professor of history,
University of Perugia
(Italy)
1

[In Italy,] it's our best time when we don't have a government. You see, we Italians think the best government is the government that doesn't govern.

Interview/
The Christian Science Monitor,
6-4:15.

Donal Dewar
Member of British Parliament
from Scotland
2

The [Prime Minister Margaret Thatcher] government has taken the position that the reason Scotland has done so badly is that it hasn't embraced Thatcherism. But the whole self-help, grab-for-yourself ethics of Thatcherism is generally unpopular with Scots and, inevitably over time, the Tories have come to look more and more like an alien party. [Thatcher herself] looks almost from another planet.

The New York Times, 9-5:4.

Milovan Djilas
Author;
Former Vice President
of Yugoslavia
3

[On Soviet leader Mikhail Gorbachev's program for reform in the Soviet Union]: Gorbachev still has to show he contemplates more than reform *within* the system—i.e., simply to improve it—instead of reform *of* the whole system, which is essential. He talks only in general terms about improving democracy, but nothing specific about broadening it, by admitting new ideas and approaches. Yet, without that—as we see increasingly in Yugoslavia—there can be no true reform . . . Remember that, though Gorbachev is both younger, more dynamic and flexible than his predecessors, he faces the same problems—traditional Russian

mentality, the habit and inertia generated by enormous bureaucracy, and the highly closed nature of the system.

Interview, Belgrade/
The Christian Science Monitor,
8-31:8.

James Eberle
Director, Royal Institute
of International Affairs
(Britain)
4

[The American-run NATO alliance existed] not because the U.S. necessarily wanted to be the dominant partner, but because Europeans lay on their backs with their legs in the air and said, "please defend us." This relationship has got to change, and management of that change is the greatest task which now faces us—management of West-West relations rather than West-East relations.

The Christian Science Monitor,
7-31:19.

John Edmunds
Leader of General,
Municipal & Boilermakers Union
of Britain
5

We [in the Labor Party] have to re-establish our competence and credibility in the eyes of the electorate. Working people may not like [Conservative Prime Minister] Margaret Thatcher, but sure as hell they seem to have lost faith in the Labor Party.

At Labor Party convention,
Brighton, England/
Los Angeles Times, 9-30:(I)6.

Valentin Falin
Director,
Novosti Press Agency
(Soviet Union)
6

We don't want democracy [in the Soviet Union] to exist as a mere slogan, a label. It

(VALENTIN FALIN)

must be visible. What is happening with us is a revolution, in its depth, its quality and also in its consequences. It could be that the transformation in thinking and behavior will take until 1990, before quantity transforms into quality. Perhaps longer. One needs time to raise the younger generation to leading positions. In the future, everything will be by election—directors of factories, heads of departments, leaders of brigades, directors of institutes and the first secretaries of regional [Communist] Party organizations. The logic of [Soviet leader Mikhail] Gorbachev's policy would not contradict a secret ballot for the [Communist Party] Central Committee secretaries.

Interview/
The Washington Post, 2-9:(A)14.

Amintore Fanfani
Prime Minister of Italy

1

Centuries of invasions and tyrannies have taught the Italian not to waste time with formal resistance. Instead, we serenely invent home-made defenses and wait for the difficulties to blow over.

Interview/
The Christian Science Monitor, 6-4:15.

Joachim Fest
Co-publisher, "Frankfurter
Allgemeine" (West Germany)

2

The outside world cannot believe what it is seeing because the Germans have been responsible for so much unrest in the past 100 years. Now the Germans appear to be a relatively contented nation going through a non-intellectual period. We have made peace with reality.

Los Angeles Times, 2-23:(I)9.

Lorenzo Frassoldati
Political editor, "Il Resto
del Carlino," Bologna (Italy)

3

The [Italian] Communists are a little democratic and a little authoritarian. They say they

are like all other parties, and then they say they are different. In the last analysis, people here don't trust the Communists.

The Christian Science Monitor,
10-2:16.

Hans-Dietrich Genscher
Foreign Minister
of West Germany

4

[On Soviet leader Mikhail Gorbachev's plans for reform in the Soviet Union]: If there should be a chance today that, after 40 years of East-West confrontation, there should be a turning point in East-West relations, it would be a mistake of historical dimension for the West to let this chance slip just because it cannot escape a way of thinking that invariably expects the worst . . . [The West should declare itself ready] to launch large-scale economic cooperation that will help the Soviet Union modernize its economy.

At economic forum, Switzerland/
The New York Times, 2-18:5.

5

[On the proposed U.S.-Soviet INF arms-control treaty affecting missiles in Europe]: There are voices in the United States, those critical of the deal, who maintain that the Europeans are skeptical, that the Europeans feel themselves ignored. I cannot imagine that any reasonable and responsible person can oppose the removal of such a destructive capacity threatening us.

Los Angeles Times, 12-6:(I)13.

Andre Giraud
Minister of Defense
of France

6

There can be no security in Europe unless conventional defense is linked to nuclear deterrence.

At armed-forces seminar,
Paris. July 6/
Los Angeles Times, 7-7:(I)5.

WHAT THEY SAID IN 1987

Marshall I. Goldman
Associate director,
Russian Research Center,
Harvard University

1

The ultimate goal of all the changes [Soviet leader Mikhail] Gorbachev is talking about—the reforms, secret elections, changes in personnel—is to reshape the Soviet economic system to bring it into the 20th century so that it can be ready to go into the 21st century. The hard fact is that the system simply is not up to what is happening everyplace else in the world. That doesn't mean it is about to collapse. It isn't. Soviet economic growth has increased slightly since Gorbachev came in, but it's in the wrong areas, the wrong industries. To reform the economy, he must cut back on heavy industry, which means he's got to cut back on military expenditures. That's the only way he can devote resources to light industry, as China has done, to make things better for consumers, for the peasants.

Interview/
U.S. News & World Report,
2-9:38.

2

[On Soviet leader Mikhail Gorbachev]: I don't think he can last four years. I think Gorbachev himself recognizes how dangerous it is [to try to implement his reform program]. He's moving so fast [with the program], he's stepping on so many toes . . . so my prediction is he won't last four years.

March 24/
Los Angeles Times,
3-25:(I)17.

Mikhail S. Gorbachev
General Secretary,
Communist Party
of the Soviet Union

3

[On his plans for reform in the Soviet Union]: Reorganization is possible only through democracy and due to democracy. It is only in this way that it is possible to give scope to so-cialism's most powerful creative force—free labor and free thought in a free country . . . The point at issue is, certainly, not any breakup of our political system . . . Socialist democracy has nothing in common with permissiveness, anarchy or irresponsibility . . . Of course, the principle of [Communist] Party rules, under which the decisions of the higher bodies are compulsory for all lower Party committees, including those on personal matters, should remain unshakable in the Party.

Before Soviet Communist
Party Central Committee, Moscow,
Jan. 27/Los Angeles Times, 1-28:(I)1.

4

Those who have doubts about the expediency of further democratization [in the Soviet Union] apparently suffer from one serious drawback which is of great political significance and meaning—they do not believe in our people. They claim that democracy will be used by our people to disorganize society and undermine discipline, to undermine the strength of the system. I think that we cannot agree to that. Democracy is not the opposite of discipline. It is a conscious discipline and organization of working people based on a sense of really being master of the country, on collectivism and the solidarity of interests and efforts by all citizens. Democracy is not the antithesis of responsibility. It means no absence of control, no mentality that anything goes. Democracy means, rather, self-control by society, confidence in the civic maturity and awareness of social duty in Soviet people. Democracy is the unity of rights and duties.

At Soviet Trade
Unions Congress, February/
The Washington Post, 3-11:(A)18.

5

You have arrived in the Soviet Union at a time when essentially revolutionary changes are under way here. They are of immense significance for our society, for socialism as a whole, and for the entire world. It is only by understanding their content, meaning and aims that one can form a correct opinion about our inter-

(MIKHAIL S. GORBACHEV)

national policy. Before my people, before you and before the whole world, I state with full responsibility that our international policy is more than ever determined by domestic policy, by our interest in concentrating on constructive endeavors to improve our country. That is why we need lasting peace, predictability and constructiveness in international relations. It is often said—we still hear it—that there is some threat stemming from the U.S.S.R., a Soviet threat to peace and freedom. I must say that the reorganization that we have launched on such a scale, and which is irreversible, shows to everyone: This is where we want to direct our resources, this is where our thoughts are going, these are our actual programs and intentions, on this we intend to spend the intellectual energy of our society.

At "For a Nuclear-Free World,
For the Survival of Humanity"
forum, Moscow, Feb. 16/
The Christian Science Monitor, 3-18:14.

1

We [Soviets] do not think that we know the best answers to all questions. We are far from asking anyone to copy us. Every socialist country is unique, and fraternal parties shape their policies proceeding from national specifics.

Speech,
Prague, Czechoslovakia, April/
The Washington Post, 10-12:(A)30.

2

I disagree with what is sometimes said that the course toward the renewal of socialism [in the Soviet Union] is personally associated with the name of Gorbachev. If there were no Gorbachev, there would have been someone else . . . The point at issue is not a breakup of our political system, but fuller and more effective use of its potential.

Interview/
Los Angeles Times,
5-21:(I)17.

Under the effects of the present [Soviet economic] system, producers find it disadvantageous to use cheap raw materials and inexpensive products; they find it disadvantageous to improve output quality; they find it disadvantageous to introduce the achievements of scientific and technical progress. Such an economic system virtually eliminates the dividing line between enterprises that work well and those that are systematic laggards . . . Our economic mechanism, whether we like it or not, is geared to mediocre and even substandard work.

Before Soviet Communist
Party Central Committee, Moscow,
June/Los Angeles Times,
10-27:(I)15.

4

[On his program for reform in the Soviet Union]: Our enemy has figured us out. They are not afraid of our nuclear might. They are not going to start a war. They are worried about one thing: If democracy develops under us—if that happens, then we will win.

To Soviet writers, Moscow,
June 19/Newsweek, 10-5:20.

5

We must realize that the time when management [of the Soviet economy] consisted of orders, bans and calls has gone. It is now clear to everybody that such methods can no longer be employed, for they are simply ineffective. To create a powerful system of motives and stimuli encouraging all workers to fully reveal their capability, work fruitfully, use production resources most effectively—such is the requirement of the times . . . The system of pay and labor incentives must be arranged in a new way. The law on enterprise guarantees enterprises the right to raise wage rates and wages, to establish bonuses. The possibilities of effective stimulation are dramatically expanded. But it is particularly important that actual pay of every worker be closely linked to his personal contribution to the end result, and that no limit be set

(MIKHAIL S. GORBACHEV)

on it. There is only one criterion of justice: whether or not it is earned.

Report to Soviet Communist Party Central Committee, Moscow, June 25/The New York Times, 6-26:7.

1

There is now much discussion about the role of [the late Soviet leader Josef] Stalin in our history. He was an extremely contradictory person. To remain faithful to historical truth, we have to see both Stalin's incontestable contribution to the struggle for socialism . . . and the abuses committed by him and those around him, for which our people paid a heavy price and which had grave consequences for the life of our society . . . The guilt of Stalin and his immediate entourage before the Party and the people for the wholesale repressive measures and acts of lawlessness is enormous and unforgiveable. This is a lesson for all generations. We now know that the political accusations and repressive measures against a number of Party leaders and statesmen, against many Communists and non-Party people, against economic executives and military men, against scientists and cultural personalities, were a result of deliberate falsification.

Speech on 70th anniversary of Bolshevik Revolution, Moscow, Nov. 2/Los Angeles Times, 11-3:(I)12.

2

I think that right now we have among those who have not received permission [to leave the Soviet Union] only those who cannot leave because of state security reasons. There are no other reasons, and we will continue to act in that way.

American broadcast interview, Moscow, Nov. 28/NBC-TV, 11-30.

3

Soviet foreign policy today is most intimately linked with *perestroika*, the domestic restructuring of Soviet society. The Soviet people have boldly taken the path of radical reform and development in all spheres—economic, social, political and intellectual. Democratization and *glasnost* [openness] are the decisive prerequisites for the success of those reforms. They also provide the guarantee that we shall go a long way, and that the course we are pursuing is irreversible. Such is the will of our people.

At welcoming ceremony for him, Washington, Dec. 8/ The New York Times, 12-9:6.

Giovanni Goria
Prime Minister of Italy

4

[On the proposed U.S.-Soviet INF arms-control treaty affecting missiles in Europe]: We greeted this chance of an agreement with great joy. But we can't ignore the new problems this poses in European defense. It would be dangerous, following this accord, to think in terms of some kind of reduced involvement by the United States in Europe's defense.

Interview/ Los Angeles Times, 12-6:(I)13.

Karoly Grosz
Prime Minister of Hungary

5

The political atmosphere and public feeling [in Hungary] are noticeably worse than a few years ago, even worse than is justified by the average living standards. The public mood is deteriorating as the living standards of considerable strata of society have stagnated over the last years and even decreased for a not negligible segment of society. Confidence in the leadership has dwindled, and sometimes the viability of socialism is put in doubt.

Budapest, Sept. 16/ The New York Times, 9-17:2.

Arthur A. Hartman
United States Ambassador to the Soviet Union

6

[On Soviet leader Mikhail Gorbachev's program for reform in the Soviet Union]: The So-

(ARTHUR A. HARTMAN)

viet system rejects those who are not true supporters. Once Gorbachev begins to move away from centralized direction and control by the [Communist] Party elite and gives more power to managers of enterprises, then the central corps of Party people will feel uncertain about their positions. They will fight back. People whose power and privileges depend on their continuing role at the center of the Party are not going to give up easily. This is something Mr. Gorbachev is discovering.

Interview, Moscow/
U.S. News & World Report,
2-2:39.

1

[On the release of some political prisoners by the Soviet government]: In the last little while, the Soviet government has recognized that their treatment of individuals has had an effect on the over-all relationship of the Soviet Union with other countries. They have been moving to dampen down that effect. I don't think it is because they have yet changed their basic approach to the relationship of the individual with the state.

To U.S. reporters,
Moscow, Feb. 11/
The New York Times, 2-12:4.

Roy Hattersley
Deputy leader,
Labor Party of Britain

2

[On British Prime Minister Margaret Thatcher]: The idea that she may be wrong doesn't cross her mind. It's a formidable asset.

Los Angeles Times, 5-26:(I)10.

Erich Honecker
First Secretary, Communist
Party of East Germany

3

The German Democratic Republic [East Germany] is an active member of the Warsaw Pact, and the Federal Republic of Germany [West Germany] is firmly anchored in the Western Alliance. Under these conditions, that the borders are not as they should be [between the two Germanys] is only too understandable. But I believe that if we work together toward it, in accordance with the communique that we have just signed in Bonn, and if, in connection with this, we demonstrate further peaceful cooperation, then the day will come when the borders will no longer divide us, but when the borders will unite us, as the border between the German Democratic Republic and the Peoples Republic of Poland unites us.

At reception in his honor,
Neunkirchen, West Germany, Sept. 10/
The Washington Post, 9-11:(A)30.

Ivan Iliev
Chairman, commission to
develop economic and social
policies, Central Committee,
Communist Party of Bulgaria;
Former Chairman,
State Planning Commission

4

. . . we [Bulgarians] use as much ferrous metal, as much electricity per capita as any developed country, but our results are considerably lower. Our quality, technology and equipment are less good. Our capacity to introduce more raw materials, more manpower is exhausted. Our old methods of management were good enough when we had more resources to inject. No more. We have to give up our old methods. We need new technologies, high labor productivity and structural changes in the economy.

Interview, Sofia, Bulgaria/
The New York Times, 10-7:6.

Renzo Imbeni
Mayor of Bologna, Italy;
Member, Communist Party
of Italy

5

The Italian Communist Party is unlike any other Communist Party, anywhere. When we

311

WHAT THEY SAID IN 1987

(RENZO IMBENI)

think of socialism, we don't think of the Soviet Union, of Yugoslavia, of Cuba, or of any other orthodoxy. We think of Italy.

Interview, Bologna, Italy/
The Christian Science Monitor,
4-17:9.

Max Jacobson
Finnish diplomat

1

Western Europe's Communist engine has run out of fuel. After the war, the Communists had a constituency and an appealing message. Today, no one believes in their promise of a better future . . . The Soviets understand the big change taking place in Europe and have no illusions about a rise of Communist support in Europe. They want to improve their relations with Europe as it is, and that means downplaying ideology and improving state-to-state ties . . . As long as the Finnish Communist Party was strong, Moscow could hope to gain power. Now the Soviets must accept Finland as she is, a place where Soviet Marxism plays no role.

The Christian Science Monitor,
10-2:16,17.

Wojciech Jaruzelski
Prime Minister of Poland

2

[On Soviet leader Gorbachev's program of openness and reform in the Soviet Union]: We support all that Mikhail Gorbachev is doing. His energy, courage and farsightedness deserve our deep respect and honest Polish sympathy. It is our great satisfaction and at the same time our great chance that we are moving in the same common current. There is a full convergence of our class-ideological, state and international interests. We have never had such a happy convergence in a millenia.

Speech/The New York Times, 3-27:4.

3

The United States has very often encouraged us in reforms. We will be very interested to find

out if the fact that we are now pursuing them will affect United States policy in economic and financial matters. Will we find support in America, or will it be made difficult? I don't even want to think about that latter possibility.

Interview, Warsaw, Nov. 11/
The Washington Post, 11-12:(A)34.

Michel Jobert
Former Foreign Minister
of France

4

[Criticizing what he says is West Germany's over-desire for reunification with East Germany]: [West] Germany intends to go its own way in Mitteleuropa. It is a people that thinks it can make a deal with the Soviets, relying on the economic strength and current wealth of the Federal Republic to buy back its unity—in whatever form.

Newsweek, 9-14:50.

Paul Johnson
British author and journalist

5

[British Prime Minister Margaret Thatcher] has taken nationalized industries and said: "They're not sacred cows; they're just cattle to be slaughtered." In doing that, she has created a trend toward privatization and democratic capitalism, persuading a large number of working-class people to buy shares in public corporations. The total number of individual shareholders, which was under 2.5 million in 1979, is now over 10 million and expanding quite quickly. This represents not merely economic and political change, but a cultural shift. Most members of the British working class had not known how to buy shares in a public company. They were afraid to. They have now crossed the Rubicon. Once across, they're never going back. This ends the old-fashioned notion of the proletariat. The Marxist proletariat can't exist in a country where most people own homes and shares in the capitalist economy.

Interview/
U.S. News & World Report,
6-22:68.

Milton Katz
Former European Administrator
of the Marshall Plan

1

In the 40 years since the end of World War II, the Marshall Plan stands out by common consent as the most conspicuous success in the conduct of American foreign policy. Europe is what it is today in considerable degree because the Marshall Plan made the revival of Europe possible.

Interview/
The Christian Science Monitor,
6-5:6.

Neil Kinnock
Leader, Labor Party
of Britain

2

I do not know anybody [in Britain] who does not want [U.S.] cruise missiles out. I do not know anybody who has not opposed their coming in. And I do not know anybody who can suggest where cruise could be redeployed. The Germans will not take them. The Italians would not. The Spaniards even want the American conventional forces out; they do not want any nuclear forces. The Greeks would not take them. Neither would the Dutch, nor the Belgians, nor the Norwegians, nor the Danes. What we [in the Labor Party would] do, as I repeatedly have made clear, is to follow the pattern established within every other country remaining in NATO that has changed its disposition within the strategic structure of NATO: to discuss it in its process of implementation with the other allies.

Interview/World Press Review,
May:15.

3

Democratic socialism [the Labor Party doctrine] has got to be as attractive and as beckoning and as useful to the relatively affluent and secure as it is to the less fortunate in our society who are referred to as our [Party's] "natural vote." Any citizen in our society who has got

the franchise is a citizen to whom we could and should be able to make an appeal.

At Labor Party conference,
Brighton, England, Sept. 29/
The Washington Post, 9-30:(A)24.

Jeane J. Kirkpatrick
Former United States
Ambassador/Permanent Representative
to the United Nations

4

[On Soviet leader Gorbachev's avowed plans for reform in the Soviet Union]: The leaders of the Soviet Union, including Mikhail Gorbachev, attach a great deal of importance at this stage to what they are calling in English "the new thinking." The specifics of change are less clear at this point than what is apparently a will to new approaches.

Geneva, Feb. 6/
The New York Times, 2-7:4.

Helmut Kohl
Chancellor of West Germany

5

[Criticizing the Berlin Wall]: The arbitrary division of Berlin, Germany and Europe will not stand the test of history. Unity and justice and freedom for our German fatherland and its old capital—for this we want to work with all our power.

At ceremony marking 750th
anniversary of Berlin, West Berlin,
April 30/The New York Times, 5-1:7.

6

[While seeking better relations with East Germany,] there is no price we will ever be ready to pay or . . . would be ready to accept which would divide us from our [Western] friends . . . We do not wander between two worlds. We are part of the free world.

To visiting U.S. Vice President
George Bush, Bonn, West Germany,
Sept. 30/The Washington Post, 10-1:(A)38.

313

WHAT THEY SAID IN 1987

Valtr Komarek
Director,
Institute for Forecasting
of the Academy of Science
(Czechoslovakia)

1

The key question is the role of the creative forces of the people [of Czechoslovakia]. If up to now our society has shown a strong trend to centralized manipulation of human beings as objects, this has to be changed into a situation where human beings become sovereign subjects. Without this, at this stage of technological change, no modern society is possible. We need a greater radius of action for each individual, because the greatest of the few competitive advantages we have is the thinking people of Czechoslovakia, who know how to adapt themselves. It is our centuries of democratic traditions that has enabled them how to work in non-standard conditions. We must give these people all chances for that, or the economy cannot recover.

Interview/The New York Times, 11-7:4.

Leonid Kozlov
Exiled Soviet ballet dancer

2

[On the new *glasnost*, or openness, policy in the Soviet Union]: We must learn to tell the difference between gestures and real change. I just saw the Bolshoi [Ballet] perform in London and there are still the same KGB faces around, and my friends still were afraid to talk frankly to me. What does it mean that [exiled Soviet ballet dancer Mikhail] Baryshnikov was invited [to the Soviet Union]? It's the same old Russian story. One person is invited, and everybody thinks this is something huge. It's a lot of noise, this *glasnost*. It's advertising—"We're a new country." I don't believe it at all.

The Washington Post, 3-25:(C)8.

Spyros Kyprianou
President of Cyprus

3

[Turkey] has yet to abandon her expansionist and partitionist designs against Cyprus. It is

high time that Turkey be reminded of the mandatory nature of the [UN] Security Council resolutions and of the relevant provisions of the Charter in case of failure to conform with these resolutions. There has been a tendency, in light of the difficulties created by the intransigence of Turkey, to either avoid or postpone the tackling of the substance of the Cyprus problem. I believe all will agree with me that no problem can be solved by avoiding or postponing the tackling of its substance. The method of avoiding the real issue has not worked. It could not have worked in any case. Nor is it fair and realistic to rely for a solution on the weakness of the one side instead of pressuring the country that is acting contary to the Charter and the resolutions of the United Nations.

At United Nations,
New York, Oct. 9/
The New York Times, 10-10:40.

Ronald S. Lauder
United States Ambassador
to Austria

4

[Saying he is quitting as Ambassador because of Austrians' attitudes toward Jews, reflected in their election of accused Nazi collaborator Kurt Waldheim as President]: If somebody sat down at a computer to find the worst possible time to be an American Ambassador here, it is now . . . [In a letter last May written by the city of Linz's Deputy Mayor,] he said, I quote, "You Jews got Christ, but you're not going to get Waldheim the same way." [The letter was written to the president of the World Jewish Congress and] I jumped out of my chair and wanted to react to it, even if it was not addressed to me. I was told indirectly, "Don't worry, the Austrian people will react to it." The interesting thing is the Mayor, the Governor of the area and his party, the People's Party, did not react. They found nothing wrong with it. The government never condemned it, never said anything. This would not have happened any place in the Western world. The Deputy Mayor of Linz would not have lasted 15 minutes any place in the Western world. He is still in office

(RONALD S. LAUDER)

today . . . The interesting thing is, I believe the Austrian people don't consider themselves anti-Semitic; someone else is, but they themselves [say they] are not. They have a potential of being anti many things. The word "envy" would be the best word by which I could describe them. They feel envy for anyone who is successful. They feel that the Jewish people have always been successful. In my point of view, within a short period of time, the question of Kurt Waldheim and Austria's role in World War II and the Holocaust will be once again swept under the carpet. Except this time, there might be a little lump in the carpet.

Interview, Vienna/
The New York Times, 10-9:8.

Ronald F. Lehman
United States
arms-control negotiator;
Former Deputy Assistant Secretary
of Defense of the United States

1

There is some concern that the removal of U.S. missiles from Europe would somehow be a signal that the United States was decoupled from Europe. But, let me say, we are coupled. And we must remain coupled, because our security and our prosperity and our freedom are inseparable from that of Western Europe. The missiles were a concrete symbol of that commitment. But we have other commitments in Europe, including other nuclear weapons in Europe.

Interview/USA Today, 3-12:(A)9.

Jean-Marie Le Pen
Leader,
National Front Party
of France

2

[On his running for the Presidency of France]: I have decided to enter this decisive battle for the future of France because I have a deep conviction that the fatherland faces a great danger and that Frenchmen are under the threat of being ruined, submerged and enslaved. Traditional political parties, even institutions, are incapable of halting, or too weak to halt, this sinister destiny. The demographic crisis, immigration, unemployment, lack of security, bureaucratic and fiscal statism and degradation of morals are clinical signs of a mortal decadence.

Announcing his candidacy,
La Trinite-sur-Mer, France, April 26/
The Washington Post, 4-28:(A)20.

Yegor K. Ligachev
Chief ideologist,
Politburo, Communist Party
of the Soviet Union

3

It is essential to expand the rights and powers of creative organizations [in the Soviet Union] and to enhance their activities, but state agencies' responsibility for the state of affairs in artistic creativity must not be diluted . . . the creative milieu sometimes gives priority to the artistic side of a work, but one must not forget the ideological content.

To writers and artists,
Saratov, U.S.S.R., March/
The New York Times, 6-12:5.

4

We do not hide the fact that the Soviet people experienced the bitterness of temporary defeats and difficult and complicated stages, as well as magnificent accomplishments. Everything did happen, but the important thing is that it happened at all—the 70 years since the October Revolution have been, above all, a period of the triumph of socialist construction. No one can strike out the incontrovertible fact that it was precisely in the years of Soviet power, and thanks to it, that the country turned into one of the world leaders.

To broadcast journalists,
Moscow, March 23/
The New York Times, 3-24:8.

5

According to our Marxist-Leninist theory, it is impossible to make the economy progress

(YEGOR K. LIGACHEV)

without democratization, and democracy without *glasnost* [openness] is a joke . . . The objective of criticism, as we understand it, consists in finding ways that permit correction of existing flaws, acceleration of forward progression. In other words, criticism must be constructive . . . Everyone must be able to be criticized, for criticism is not a refusal of confidence. We have criticized the *Moscow News* and *Ogonyok*, but the editors are still in place and their work has improved.

Interview, Dec. 3/
The Washington Post,
12-4:(A)16.

Claude Malhuret
Secretary of State for
Human Rights of France

1

[On the release of some political prisoners in the Soviet Union]: One can only be glad at the liberation of dissidents and refuseniks. But one cannot forget that these liberations remain just as arbitrary as were the arrests, in a system that does not respect rule by law.

Feb. 17/
The Washington Post,
2-18:(A)12.

Jack F. Matlock, Jr.
United Stated Ambassador
to the Soviet Union

2

[On Soviet leader Mikhail Gorbachev's plans for reform in the Soviet Union]: It could be significant, but it's too early to tell. We went through the same emotions in the '60s with [then Soviet leader] Nikita Khrushchev, though the reforms were more modest. But a lot of things that were started then did not come off. So nothing is certain. But that makes it fascinating.

Interview, Washington/
The Christian Science Monitor,
3-31:6.

Sean McManus
Roman Catholic priest;
Director,
Irish National Caucus

3

The issue in Northern Ireland is not about Catholic or Protestant, fundamentally . . . No person is fighting in Northern Ireland over the interpretation of the Bible, or the Trinity, or any great religious truth. The issue at bottom is that England is illegally and violently oppressing part of Ireland. As England did in this country [the U.S.], in Africa, in the Mideast, wherever the butcher's apron flew. That's what we call the Union Jack in Ireland—the butcher's apron.

Interview/USA Today, 3-17:(A)13.

Marian Orzechowski
Foreign Minister of Poland

4

The United States has not shed at all—has been shedding very reluctantly—its stereotype of Poland as a country that is allegedly not sovereign, lacks stability and is weak. The Americans believe many myths.

Interview/
The Washington Post,
9-26:(A)17.

David Owen
Leader, Social Democratic
Party of Britain

5

[Criticizing the Labor Party's proposal to dismantle British nuclear weapons and force the U.S. to remove American nuclear weapons from Britain]: If the British electorate votes [Labor Party leader Neil Kinnock] in [as Prime Minister], the Americans will withdraw, and quickly. They will shake their head in amazement that we can voluntarily emasculate the British lion; but as good democrats they will accept the verdict and move out of Britain, leaving us to look after ourselves as a toothless, shorn and neutered lion.

Campaign address, Glasgow, Scotland,
May 25/The New York Times, 5-28:4.

Turgut Ozal
Prime Minister of Turkey

1

Turkey has as much right as Portugal, Spain or Greece to be part of the [European] Common Market. Our economic system is freer than that of some European countries, and we have a lot to offer. As an Islamic nation, we would add ethnic diversity to the Market. Turkey would also give Western Europe new dynamism through opportunities for investments in roads, harbors, power plants and many other things.

Interview/
U.S. News & World Report,
2-16:36.

Andreas Papandreou
Prime Minister of Greece

2

[On the future of American military bases in his country]: You [the U.S.] have to prove to us that your presence serves our own highest national interests. If you prove it, then we will go to the people for a referendum. If you don't, then you will go home. It is clear cut.

Nov. 7/
The New York Times,
11-10:2.

Karolos Papoulias
Foreign Minister of Greece

3

The question of Cyprus is not a Greek-Turkish issue. It is between the Republic of Cyprus and Turkey. Greece has a very clear position on this. In Cyprus, there was an invasion by Turkey against an independent country and member of the United Nations. When the United States or Greece or any other country talks about the principle of withdrawal of military forces in other areas of the world, such as Soviet troops in Afghanistan, the issue of Turkish troops in Cyprus cannot be omitted.

Interview/
The New York Times,
6-22:32.

Rupert Pennant-Rea
Editor, "The Economist"
(Britain)

4

Britain's labor market is stagnant, by American standards. If people in the U.S. lose their jobs, they move elsewhere to find work, or retrain, or start their own business. Those forms of behavior exist in Britain, but on a very small scale. As a result, although we have had fairly rapid economic growth in the past four years, little of it has penetrated the labor market. Instead, that market delivers big wage increases to those with jobs—partly because the unions and managers tend to think only of the current work force, and to deal only with them and exclude outsiders. That is, partly, alas, because a lot of the outsiders are poorly trained for some of the new industries where the jobs are. We have high unemployment figures and at the same time severe skill shortages. Companies say, "We could create 2,000 jobs tomorrow, but we do not have enough computer-literate people to fill them." It goes back to the educational system. The only way you can equip people to switch from one industry to the next is through more education, particularly in the maths and sciences.

Interview/
World Press Review,
January:31.

Richard N. Perle
Assistant Secretary for
International Security Policy,
Department of Defense
of the United States

5

Turkey . . . is a NATO ally . . . It has been badly treated at times by the United States. Turkey has the absolutely vital military mission within the alliance of controlling the straits through which the Soviet Black Sea fleet could pass into the Mediterranean. It is very much in our interest to assist Turkey.

Interview/
The New York Times,
3-13:12.

Rinaldo Petrignani
*Italian Ambassador
to the United States*

1

The Italian style—the well-known standards of quality and taste—has become the symbol of the new Italian presence in the world and increasingly in the United States. But the Italian economy is made also of advanced technologies and research in many strategic sectors; it means $10-billion of exports to the U.S. in 1986, including computers, telecommunication systems and military technologies; it also means an increasing network of industrial cooperation and joint ventures with American firms that would be too long to list here. The participation of some of our leading industries in the ambitious SDI research program—for which an agreement [with the U.S.] was signed in September of last year—is enough evidence of this.

*Interview/
The Washington Post,
3-25: (Special)1.*

Vladimir F. Petrovsky
*Deputy Foreign Minister
of the Soviet Union*

2

[On the reform program in the Soviet Union instituted under Soviet leader Mikhail Gorbachev]: It was not sudden. People in the [Communist] Party and in government felt that something [was] wrong, that depressing developments were taking place; there was not much economic development; social justice had been violated in the country . . . And we see in *glasnost* [openness], democratization and in a democratic people the only remedy against all of this. A democratic people will make bureaucrats behave properly and observe certain rules of behavior . . . Our intention is to have a period in which we would be able to concentrate on domestic affairs. This is the categorical imperative of our time. The best way to prove which system and which way of life is better is by putting your own house in order. Sometimes some people here thought that foreign policy could compensate for domestic shortcomings,

and this is wrong. The roots of foreign policy are at home; for foreign policy to be effective, it must rely on a well-organized domestic order.

*Interview, Moscow/
Los Angeles Times,
5-14: (I)1,29.*

Lucas Pires
*Secretary general, Christian
Democratic Party of Portugal;
Member, European Parliament*

3

[On Portugal's joining the European Community in 1986]: Joining Europe gave us our identity, making us a bigger, better country. We can help mediate between Europe and Africa, but we first and foremost belong to Europe.

*The Christian Science Monitor,
7-17:12.*

Imre Pozsgay
*Member,
Central Committee,
Communist Party of Hungary*

4

I don't think of establishing a multi-party system in a socialist system. There is one historical fact we cannot ignore. Our political stability and the integrity of the system is linked with the one [Communist] Party. I think it would be too easy to destroy this stability. For this reason, the most important matter would be for the Party to withdraw itself from its present relationship with the state and society—and to establish a new relationship.

*Interview, Budapest/
The Christian Science Monitor,
10-13:14.*

Ronald Reagan
President of the United States

5

Forty years ago, the United States said that if Europe were ever to see an end to the specter of war that had haunted that great continent over the centuries, all of its peoples would have

(RONALD REAGAN)

to know freedom, democracy and justice. And so we extended both to allies and former enemies a helping hand, a hand of compassion, a hand of hope . . . At this economic summit, I will look around the table and see—thanks in part to the generosity and wisdom of our nation over the past 40 years—not the leaders of broken, desperate and despotic nations, but the leaders of strong and stable democracies, countries that today are our partners for peace on the world stage.

Before departing for economic
summit conference in Europe,
Washington, June 3/
The Washington Post, 6-5:(A)33.

1

[Soviet] General Secretary Gorbachev, if you seek peace, if you seek prosperity for the Soviet Union and Eastern Europe, if you seek liberalization: Come here, to this gate [the Brandenburg Gate at the Berlin Wall]. Mr. Gorbachev, open this gate. Mr. Gorbachev, tear down this wall. This wall will fall. For it cannot withstand faith. It cannot withstand truth. The Wall cannot withstand freedom.

At rally, West Berlin, June 12/
Los Angeles Times, 6-13:(I)1.

2

[On Soviet leader Mikhail Gorbachev's program of openness and reform in the Soviet Union]: Are we entering a truly new phase in East-West relations? Is far-reaching, enduring change in the post-war standoff now possible? Do we have at last the change envisioned by Churchill to end the agony of the 20th century? Surely, these are our hopes. But let honesty compel us to acknowledge we have fears and deep concerns as well. And while we acknowledge the interesting changes in the Soviet Union, we know, too, that any Western standard for democracy is still a very distant one for the Soviets; we know what real democracy constitutes; we understand its implications. It means

the rule of law for the leaders as well as the people.

At Town Hall,
Los Angeles, Aug. 26/
Los Angeles Times, 8-27:(I)26.

3

We hear much about changes in the Soviet Union. We're intensely interested in these changes. We hear the word "glasnost," which is translated as "openness" in English. "Openness" is a broad term. It means the free, unfettered flow of information, ideas and people. It means political and intellectual liberty in all its dimensions. We hope, for the sake of the people of the U.S.S.R., that such changes will come. And we hope, for the sake of peace, that it will include a foreign policy that respects the freedom and independence of other peoples.

At United Nations,
New York, Sept. 21/
The New York Times, 9-22:6.

4

The commitment of the United States to the [Atlantic] Alliance and to the security of Europe—INF treaty [with the Soviets] or no INF treaty—remains unshakable. Over 300,000 American servicemen with you on the continent and our steadfast nuclear guarantee underscore this pledge. Those who worry that we will somehow drift apart or that deterrence has been weakened are mistaken on both counts.

Broadcast address to Europe, Nov. 4/
The Washington Post, 11-5:(A)10.

Joe Rodgers
United States Ambassador
to France

5

France has changed since the Second World War, when 35 per cent of the French were farmers. Today, less than 7 per cent are farmers. France after the war was an inward-looking, protectionist country. Today, they are competing with the world in high technology, ground transportation, space. Their nuclear industry is one of the best if not the best in the

WHAT THEY SAID IN 1987

(JOE RODGERS)

world. France has changed so much—from a 30 per cent Communist vote after the war to less than 10 per cent now, and reducing. I think France has come more to the center. We can understand the French better today. We really do understand the French—it's not a radical right or radical left. It's a more centrist country, and I think that's why we're better friends.

Interview, Paris/
TWA Ambassador, December:58.

Bernard W. Rogers
General,
United States Army (ret.);
Former Supreme Allied
Commander/Europe

1

[Criticizing the U.S. Soviet INF arms-control treaty which affects missiles in Europe]: This treaty puts Western Europe on the slippery slope to denuclearization. The Soviets want to make Western Europe safe again for conventional war and, with massive conventional forces as the backdrop, to be able to intimidate, coerce, blackmail and neutralize Western Europe without firing a single shot.

Speech/
Los Angeles Times,
12-11:(I)27.

Nikolai I. Ryzhkov
Premier of
the Soviet Union

2

As far as the planned economy is concerned, we are for that. We are not going to destroy the planned economy [in the Soviet Union]. At the same time, we are granting more authority to our enterprises. They will also have more responsibility. This is the direction we are taking. We are for state monopoly of the economy but, at the same time, we will give the right to large-scale enterprises to negotiate directly with foreign companies.

News conference,
Helsinki, Finland, Jan. 8/
The Washington Post, 1-12:(A)16.

Andrei D. Sakharov
Dissident Soviet physicist

3

I think the reasons for my release from internal exile [as a political prisoner] began to ripen a long time ago—in the broad international campaign on my behalf among foreign scientists and officials, and also in certain changes that have taken place in this country over the past five years. An especially important factor was the desire by the U.S.S.R. for international scientific and technical cooperation. I know that academics and scientific organizations throughout the world make their participation in such cooperation conditional on my release. It is possible that some elements in the [Soviet] government will try to use my release as window dressing to convince the world that the human-rights situation here has improved radically, when that is not the case. Persistent efforts of people in the West and in the U.S.S.R. will be needed to preserve reality.

Interview, Moscow/
U.S. News & World Report,
1-12:30.

4

[On Soviet leader Mikhail Gorbachev's program for reform in the Soviet Union]: I don't know what Gorbachev wants personally, but there are a number of people at the top who understand that without democratization, all of his goals in the economic sphere [and] international sphere cannot succeed.

Time, 2-23:52.

5

There is no turning from *glasnost,* [Soviet leader Mikhail Gorbachev's] new policy of openness. But it is just a start . . . The first taste of freedom will produce demands for more. That could accelerate to the point that the regime feels threatened and forced to clamp down. Still, *glasnost* is a greater threat to Gorbachev's opponents than to him, for it is they who are being exposed for inefficiency and corruption and drunkenness.

Interview, Moscow/
U.S. News & World Report, 4-20:31.

Carlo Santoro
Political scientist,
Milan University (Italy)

1

[On Italy's current election campaign, which features Prime Minister Bruno Craxi using TV interviews as a campaign tool]: One of the great unknowns in this campaign is the degree to which Italy has moved toward a more personalized form of politics, something closer to U.S.-style politics. Craxi's fate will be an important test . . . Craxi is fighting the system. He is gambling that the dynamics of Italian society have changed sufficiently for personality to outweigh party affiliations.

The New York Times, 6-8:4.

Carl-Christoph Schweitzer
Political scientist,
Bonn University
(West Germany)

2

[On former West German Chancellor Willy Brandt, who recently resigned as leader of the Social Democratic Party]: He will be remembered as the statesman after World War II who achieved a breakthrough in our relations with the East. Historians will also make him in some ways responsible for the state of affairs the SPD is in now, and there is no doubt that the SPD is in a mess.

Newsweek, 4-6:39.

Brent Scowcroft
Former Assistant to
the President of the
United States (Gerald Ford)
for National Security Affairs

3

The Europeans really don't want a conventional [non-nuclear] defense of Europe. The Europeans rely heavily, psychologically at least, on what they consider the deterrent value of nuclear weapons. They don't want a nuclear war which would be fought solely on European territory, nor do they want to fight World War II over.

Los Angeles Times, 5-25:(I)6.

4

[On the proposed U.S.-Soviet INF arms-control treaty affecting missiles in Europe]: Our fundamental objectives in Europe are twofold: to do everything possible to dissuade the Soviets from any notion that an attack would be profitable, and to reassure the Europeans that we will do what we say we will do. On both counts, the INF treaty is deficient. But if we now turn around, after persuading the Europeans to go along with the treaty and change direction again, we would really traumatize them. It is symbolically bad. It is potentially militarily bad. If we treat [the treaty] as a glorious achievement, that can be damaging. But if we say there are dangers inherent in this, and we have to take steps to compensate for it, then it may not be too bad.

Interview/
Los Angeles Times,
12-8:(I)11.

Gennady Seleznev
Editor,
"Komsomolskaya Pravda"
(Soviet Union)

5

One particular phrase that comes up often may be misunderstood by the West. [Soviet leader] Mikhail Gorbachev says repeatedly that we need to carry out our reforms within the framework of socialism in our country. What he means is that we will not change the principles of socialist government upon which our system is based but, instead, we will move to insure that the system works at its full potential. We will then be able to use reserves that have been untouched so far. There are a number of bills under consideration. One is aimed at improved productivity; another calls for changes in our electoral system. Such reforms are intended to strengthen the socialist system, not change it.

Interview/
World Press Review,
April:17.

321

WHAT THEY SAID IN 1987

Georgi K. Shakhnazarov
Member, Central Committee,
Communist Party
of the Soviet Union

1

[On democracy in the Soviet Union]: If violations of the democratic order take place for 10 to 15 years and the democratic system is not applied in full, then it gradually begins to rust. A whole generation of people appears which does not know how to use its rights. These may be educated people—they may read Shakespeare and are fond of Bach—but they are not citizens because they cannot defend their own rights and do not even understand very well what these rights are. That is why the cardinal problem has become to foster in people the feeling of being the masters of life, to make them understand again—and maybe even to explain for the first time—that they are the masters.

Interview/
Los Angeles Times, 1-12:(I)1.

Natan Sharansky
Exiled Soviet dissident

2

[On Soviet leader Mikhail Gorbachev's plans for reform in the Soviet Union]: The danger is that the West mistakes every step Gorbachev makes as real fundamental change. Gorbachev is very talented. He has developed the image of being liberal. [Sometimes] it looks like the West wants to be deceived, rather than analyzing what's really happening and looking at the bottom line, seeing that on the question of human rights there is not only no progress, but serious regression.

To reporters, Los Angeles, Jan. 28/
Los Angeles Times, 1-29:(II)6.

Nikolai P. Shmelev
Soviet economist

3

[On Soviet leader Mikhail Gorbachev's plans for reform in the Soviet Union]: We do not live so badly. We have food; we have flats [apartments]; we have work and some cultural life. Of course, not everyone is satisfied with the political life, but in a material sense we have an acceptable—but not very good—level of living in our country. We do not feel disaster here. And I can understand why some people say, "Why all this fuss about *perestroika* [reconstruction]? Why should they change everything in our economy, in our political life and so on?" Life was acceptable.

Los Angeles Times, 12-25:(I)10.

George P. Shultz
Secretary of State
of the United States

4

We have told the Soviets, time and time again, that significant progress on emigration is critical to improving our relations in other areas. The Soviets may be beginning to understand that our commitment to this issue is not only a cornerstone of the approach of this President [Reagan] and this Administration, but that it commands the broadest bipartisan support in the Congress . . . We have made clear to the Soviets that, while family reunification is vitally important, there is also a right to freedom of movement, which applies whether or not someone has relatives in another country.

Before Anti-Defamation League
of B'nai B'rith, Washington, March 24/
Los Angeles Times, 3-25:(I)11.

5

For the last 40 years there hasn't been a war in Europe. Why? It's because NATO got organized, had a deterrent capability, and that deterrent capability included, most importantly, a nuclear deterrent. That is what has kept the peace.

News conference, Oslo, Dec. 13/
Los Angeles Times, 12-14:(I)1.

Thomas W. Simons, Jr.
Deputy Assistant Secretary
for European Affairs,
Department of State
of the United States

6

[On Soviet leader Mikhail Gorbachev's program for openness and reform in the Soviet

(THOMAS W. SIMONS, JR.)

Union]: There has been a very important step forward as far as cultural policy is concerned. You have a cultural thaw under way which is quite serious. Things are being printed, things are being shown, things are being taken out of the can and made available to a degree that had not taken place in the Soviet Union for 30 years . . . I think most of us in the [U.S.] government have a basically positive attitude toward what he seems to be trying to do in the Soviet Union. Like any government, I think, the Soviets are going to try to give as little as possible to get as much as possible for anything they do. Mr. Gorbachev has shown himself to be more skilled than his predecessors in projecting an image of modernity, of liberality, of understanding. The way you deal with the problem is to insist that he perform before you make your judgment, to say that 140 or 500 political prisoners released is a good thing; but there are a lot more out there and we don't think they should have been in jail in the first place . . . [One danger is to declare,] "Everything that he is doing is just a sham and a delusion, a public-relations thing, which should be rejected. We are not going to be suckered; we are not going to be taken in." [The other danger is to believe,] "Hey, here is a real liberal that you can work with."

At symposium for educators,
Washington, Feb. 11/
The New York Times, 2-12:5.

Mario Soares
President of Portugal

1

[On Portugal's change from dictatorship to democracy]: The issue was whether Portugal was going to become another Cuba, where freedoms would have been abolished and where the pluralist system and the free market would have been done away with—whether all this was going to be destroyed or whether we were going to continue to be a Western nation . . . If democracy had not won out in Portugal at that time, it would not have been possible for the demo-

cratic transition to take place in Spain. I think the whole course of events in Europe would have been different.

Interview/
The Christian Science Monitor,
5-19:6.

David Steel
Leader, Liberal Party
of Britain

2

If you are unemployed in [Prime Minister Margaret] Thatcher's Britain, or poor or struggling on the bread line, or without hope for the future, then God help you, because a Conservative government won't.

The New York Times, 5-25:2.

Franz Josef Strauss
Premier of Bavaria,
West Germany

3

We have to end the attempt to limit German history to the 12 years of [Adolf] Hitler—the representation of German history as an endless path of Germans' mistakes and crimes, criminalizing the Germans. We must emerge from the dismal Third Reich and become a normal nation again . . . The historical truth shows that Germans in monstrous numbers committed terrible crimes—and whoever denies this has lost his connection with reality. But it would be the same loss of reality to say that the Germans and their allies did not suffer horrible crimes at the end of the war and after it!

At Christian Democratic
Party rally, Auggen, West Germany/
The New York Times, 1-13:5.

Klemens Szaniawski
Professor,
Warsaw University
(Poland)

4

[On the Pope's recent visit to Poland]: The Pope certainly left people with a sense of pride [in being Polish], but at the same time I'm

WHAT THEY SAID IN 1987

(KLEMENS SZANIAWSKI)

rather pessimistic. What we now need most is some kind of a social contract between the government and the people, some kind of understanding, and I see no evidence that this is forthcoming. My own best hopes were shattered, because I had hoped that the Pope might act as a kind of mediator between the government and the people . . . People [in Poland today] don't care about doing their regular work. They're just concerned about where they might make some extra money, where they can find some scarce item. They've given up hope of any real change. They mark time and try to get by.

Warsaw/Los Angeles Times, 6-19:(I)16.

Margaret Thatcher
Prime Minister
of the United Kingdom

1

[On her just-concluded meetings with Soviet leader Mikhail Gorbachev]: When I first met Mr. Gorbachev in December, 1984, I said he was someone I could do business with. Well, we were able to do a lot of business yesterday . . . When you have talked that length, it's investment in the bank. You begin to understand how someone else's mind works; you begin to understand their objectives and they begin to understand yours.

News conference, Moscow, March 31/
Los Angeles Times, 4-1:(I)1,12.

2

For much of the 20th century, it seemed that socialism [in Britain] was advancing and conservatism in retreat . . . How old-fashioned that [socialistic] vision now seems. It has the smell of the late 1940s about it—the atmosphere of shortages, rationing, the black market and the endless restrictions. Today it is socialism which is in retreat and conservatism which is advancing . . . in tune with [Britons'] own hopes and dreams.

At Scottish Conservative
Conference, Perth, Scotland, May 15/
The Washington Post, 5-16:(A)20.

[On her opposition saying she and the Conservative Party do not care about the needy]: All decent people care about the sick, the unfortunate and the old, and it is false and wicked to suggest otherwise. The real choice is between the opposition parties, which wring their hands because their economic failure has destroyed any hope of better care, and the Conservative Party, which cares effectively because it can first deliver economic success.

The New York Times, 5-25:2.

4

[On why she feels she will win the forthcoming national election by defeating the Labor Party]: People are afraid of the prospect of Britain left defenseless . . . of a return to roaring inflation . . . of the union bosses running the show again.

London, June 10/
Los Angeles Times, 6-11:(I)17.

5

[On her third straight election victory]: It's wonderful to be entrusted with the government of this great country once again. We have a great deal of work to do, so no one must slack . . . We were told that our [election] campaign was not sufficiently slick. I regard that as a compliment.

At Conservative Party
headquarters, London, June 12/
Los Angeles Times, 6-12:(I)1.

6

The United States will never become a laughingstock [in Europe]. We know just how much we owe to the United States. We owed it immediately after the last war in the generosity of the Marshall Plan; we owed it during the last war as she came to liberate countries in Europe from the tyranny under which they had been. We know how much we owe to the United States. Sometimes we don't always show it. I try to. We are very much aware of this debt.

Broadcast interview/
"Face the Nation," CBS-TV, 7-19.

(MARGARET THATCHER)

1

[Praising Soviet leader Mikhail Gorbachev's program of reform in the Soviet Union]: He's a bold, a determined and courageous leader, and I hope that he succeeds in his colossal task, for in doing so he will enhance the sum of human freedom and happiness.

After meeting with Gorbachev,
Brize Norton Air Force Base,
England, Dec. 7/
The New York Times, 12-8:8.

Jerzy Urban
Spokesman for
the government of Poland

2

In a matter of a few weeks from now, we shall be declaring quite revolutionary changes in our economy. These changes will include the replacement of the whole leadership of the Polish economy and replacement of methods of managing the economy. The whole program has not yet been published, but it will definitely mean stepping out from the way of the centrally subsidized industry. We would like the government to cease managing enterprises and instead conduct economic policy on the basis of economic rules. New enterprises should be established freely on the basis of competitive balance.

To reporters, Stockholm, Sweden,
April 6/Los Angeles Times, 4-7:(I)8.

Vladimir Voinovich
Exiled Soviet author

3

[On the reform program of Soviet leader Mikhail Gorbachev]: Ideology died during the [former Soviet leader Leonid] Brezhnev era. With so much corruption, with the invasion of Czechoslovakia and Afghanistan, Brezhnev could not count on ideology the way Stalin could. Ideology, when it is strong, can substitute for a real economy. People may even sacrifice their lives for it. But when it ends and no one believes in it, people suddenly notice how bad things are around them. Gorbachev under-

stands this. When [former Soviet leader Nikita] Khrushchev fell, it was said that he had tried to leap across the abyss in two jumps. Gorbachev is more of a tightrope walker. I think Gorbachev understands that in order to compete economically with the West, you have to set people free . . . The process may not go very far. In Russia, we say sometimes that it's too late to wish someone good health at their funeral. Gorbachev's intentions are serious, but the system resists and will resist. It may be an impossible mission.

Interview/
The Washington Post, 6-3:(D)15.

Richard von Weizsaecker
President of West Germany

4

[On the Marshall Plan after World War II]: The plan was visionary, as great victors seldom are . . . The aim of the United States was to restore the confidence of the Europeans in their own strength, in their own political future . . . The Marshall Plan is and will remain the most fundamental achievement of the Western world since the war.

At Harvard University commencement,
June 11/Los Angeles Times, 6-12:(I)9.

Andrei Voznesensky
Soviet poet

5

[On Soviet leader Mikhail Gorbachev's policy of reform and *glasnost*—openness—in the Soviet Union]: There is a practical side to *glasnost,* to the freedom that has been put in our hands. You can't just lie on the stove and rejoice, "Oh, how free we are!" You have to do something. This is the time for people of a new type, for decisive people who know what they want, who have a program . . . These people are leading a cultural revolution—let me correct myself, a revolution by culture. It is a revolution of consciousness. [But] there's a struggle [about these issues], and it is enormously difficult because there's a reactionary layer that is very strong and that opposes this—sometimes silently, sometimes not silently, but always

(ANDREI VOZNESENSKY)

fiercely. Nothing is happening of its own. This is a fight to the death. There's no way back, and this must become an irreversible process. It is a matter of life or death for the country. The process will become irreversible only when people are shaken from their inertness, their passivity.

Interview, New York/
The New York Times, 3-16:4.

Franz Vranitzky
Chancellor of Austria

1

Forty years have passed since the end of World War II. Today, already the grandchildren of those who were too young to incur guilt at that time are growing up. In Europe we enjoy security, stability and prosperity to a degree never known before, and relations between our countries are well-ordered and peaceful. Yet the shadows of remembrance still hang over us, the memory of moral failure deeply burned into our collective consciousness. In many European countries, not only in [Austria], there is a lively and emotional debate going on today under the concept of "coming to terms with the past." It cannot be our maxim to bury the past in order to be better able to work for the future. On the contrary, we shall only be able to work for this better future if we remember what happened to us in the past, and the guilt we incurred there. This is a debate and a recognition that we must not evade. We owe this debt not only to the victims of that war but also, on behalf of those victims, to future generations.

At World Meeting of War Veterans,
Resistance Fighters, War Victims
and Victims of Fascism, Vienna/
Los Angeles Times, 1-8:(II)5.

Lech Walesa
Former chairman, now-banned
Solidarity (independent Polish
trade union); Winner,
1983 Nobel Peace Prize

2

The most important thing . . . is the necessity of pluralism in Poland. Without it, Poland

won't make it . . . There is no pluralism of organizations. There is no pluralism at work, because we all have to work and then go home; not in the church, because you are told only to pray; not in the streets, because what you have there are only truncheons and riot police. It is time to put an end to this. Our goal is not to take over power, nor do we want to fight the regime. We want progress. We want structural changes which will allow Poland to develop economically.

To reporters,
Gdansk, Poland, June 11/
Los Angeles Times, 6-12:(I)11.

3

This [Poland] is an absurd society, where 90 per cent of the people are Catholic, and atheists hold power.

Interview, Gdansk, Poland/
The Washington Post, 7-21:(A)21.

Vernon A. Walters
United States Ambassador/
Permanent Representative
to the United Nations

4

If there is no agreement on [continuing to have] U.S. [military] bases in Spain and we are told to leave, we will leave. If we are not wanted, we will go . . . But we Americans will not forget . . . an unfriendly gesture toward us.

Interview/
Los Angeles Times,
12-24:(I)8.

Caspar W. Weinberger
Secretary of Defense
of the United States

5

[Saying peace in Europe can be sustained only through Western military strength and preparedness]: We [of the Western Alliance] have not always followed that advice. Complacency has taken its toll on our alliance. Today we face threats from within again, and they stem para-

(CASPAR W. WEINBERGER)

doxically in many cases from the very democratic spirit that defines our nations.

Before English Speaking Union
of the Commonwealth, London,
June 3/The New York Times, 6-4:3.

Charles Z. Wick
Director, United States
Information Agency

1

[Soviet] General Secretary [Mikhail] Gorbachev's ascent to power has encouraged a new and more dynamic leadership. Moscow is marketing a new image of openness to the world. They call this product *glasnost*. But *glasnost* is more than a product. It is a public-relations campaign. The Soviets are trying to win the war of symbols. If they win, they will have won the war of public diplomacy. And what would we lose? Most dramatically, we could lose our security . . . In the [long] term, if we lose the "war of ideas," we could jeopardize the very soul of the free world, its life today and its promise of security tomorrow. Thus the following question has a seriousness unparalleled, perhaps, in history: Does this new image portend a change in Soviet objectives? Or are they merely wrapping themselves in a Messianic mantel of false justice, a false economy, false fraternity and false promises? . . . Is *glasnost* truth-in-packaging? Or is it deceptive promotion?

Washington, March 13/
The Washington Post, 3-26:(A)26.

Elie Wiesel
Historian;
Professor of humanities,
Boston University; Winner,
1986 Nobel Peace Prize

2

It is in the name of memory [of the Nazi years] that I address myself to Germany's youth. "Remember" is the commandment that dominates the life of young Jews today. Let it dominate yours as well . . . Of course, I understand, for you [today's German youth] it is not easy to remember. It may even be more difficult than it is for us, Jews. We try to remember the dead; you must remember those who killed them. I appeal to you, young German men and women, [to] be our allies. Justify the faith we have in your future. Fight forgetfulness. Reject any attempt to cover up the past.

At conference on
the Wannsee Villa, West Berlin,
Nov. 10/The New York Times, 11-11:2.

Manfred Worner
Minister of Defense
of West Germany

3

The decisive security problem for Europe lies in the conventional arena. That is where the danger is. The Soviet Union has such superiority that if we had no more nuclear weapons, there could be attempts at excessive political influence or even military action.

World Press Review, June:11.

Alexander Yakovlev
Member, Politburo,
Communist Party
of the Soviet Union

4

[On the reform program in the Soviet Union instituted under Soviet leader Mikhail Gorbachev]: This does not mean we are going closer to your [U.S.] system of democracy. We are going further apart. Workers in your country will never be able to replace the owners and directors of a plant by secret ballot, because that would mean socialist revolution. The democracy we envision is much more radical than anything you have. You cannot just paste a mouse's tail on a crocodile and turn it into one.

Interview, Moscow/
Los Angeles Times,
5-14:(I)29.

WHAT THEY SAID IN 1987

Horace J. Zammitt
*Minister of Tourism
of Gibraltar; Member,
House of Assembly of Gibraltar*

1

Most people would tell you, if Gibraltar were Spanish it would lose its value. It would just be another three miles of Spanish land, and 25,000 more unemployed to add to the 3 million they [Spain] already have.

The Washington Post, 10-7:(A)28.

Warren Zimmerman
*United States Ambassador
to Vienna conference on
European security and cooperation*

2

The true test of *glasnost* [Soviet openness] as far as the Vienna meeting is concerned is whether the Soviet Union can continue and increase the positive trends we have observed, and can give them institutional stability . . . We want to see a faster rate of release of political prisoners [in the Soviet Union]. We want an eradication of the problem of reunification of families, of wives joining husbands and children, of refuseniks allowed to leave the Soviet Union to join their parents. We want an increase in the rate of emigration, which is higher than it has been but is lower than it was in the 1970s. Why not eliminate the security provision as a bar to emigration, annul those articles in the criminal code which are used for political arrests, close down the police-run psychiatric hospitals that imprison sane but critical individuals and abolish jamming [of foreign radio broadcasts], and dismantle the jamming equipment?

*At Vienna conference, July 31/
Los Angeles Times, 8-1:(I)5.*

The Middle East

James Abourezk
Chairman, American-Arab
Anti-Discrimination Committee;
Former United States Senator,
D-South Dakota

1

The Israeli government lives off the United States. They have to try to maintain a high level of support for them, and of course any time they see Arab countries becoming more friendly with the United States, they try to cut that down, because they see themselves as the exclusive benefactor of American taxpayers' largesse. And they believe, maybe properly so, that any lessening of that support for Israel would cut down the amount of money they get from the United States, which is a tremendous amount every year.

Interview/USA Today, 1-26:(A)15.

Tariq Almoayed
Minister of Information
of Bahrain

2

Twenty years ago, we [Persian Gulf nations] were in the Middle Ages. Oil wealth has brought us progress, education, modernity. Now all is threatened by the fighting among our neighbors [Iran and Iraq]. It is a dangerous time.

The New York Times, 8-14:1.

Yasir Arafat
Chairman, Palestine
Liberation Organization

3

We will maintain our armed struggle against Israel, not because we seek war but because we want peace, a just and comprehensive peace on the basis of the Palestinian right to self-determination, and to an independent state with Jerusalem as its capital.

At Palestine National Council
conference, Algiers, Algeria,
April 20/The New York Times, 4-21:3.

Michael H. Armacost
Under Secretary of State
of the United States

4

[On the U.S. decision to protect Kuwaiti oil shipments from Iranian attack in the Persian Gulf]: Kuwait is a friendly country, an oil-producing country, a moderate Arab country. Protection of the oil means the protection of access to oil, it means protection and a solid relationship with a friendly oil producer, and it means preventing the Soviets from acquiring a foothold from which they would acquire a protective role over oil destined for the West. That was the interest that we had engaged when we offered to help the Kuwaitis.

Broadcast interview/
"Meet the Press," NBC-TV, 8-30.

Robert H. Asher
President,
American-Israeli
Public Affairs Committee

5

[On recent foreign scandals Israel is alleged to have been involved in]: Did something go wrong? What happened? Well, what happened was very complex. Survival in the face of constantly hostile neighbors, the toll of fighting terror alone, both physically and psychologically, the draining military budget, the cost of absorbing 1.3 million Jews from Arab countries, created a life that was difficult to deal with, and yes, some mistakes were made. Some of the altruism got shipwrecked on the rocks built by the pressure of daily living and the hope for an easier life. Israel developed an incredible bureaucracy; the country seemed to lose some of its direction, and the politicians pursued their own goals.

Before American-Israeli
Public Affaires Committee,
Washington, May/
Los Angeles Times, 6-11:(I)12.

329

Les Aspin
United States Representative,
D-Wisconsin

1

[On the planned U.S. reflagging of Kuwaiti oil ships to protect them against attacks by Iran in the Persian Gulf]: Congress has been put in, I think, a very tough position. A vote to go ahead with the reflagging carries a lot of risk, and a vote against the reflagging, pulling the [U.S. Reagan] Administration back from the reflagging, I think carries enormous risk, too, of Iranian terrorist actions . . . So, in a sense, the two obvious options—yes and no—are not very good.

Broadcast interview/
"Face the Nation," 6-21.

2

The [U.S. Reagan] Administration policy of shunning the Soviets [in dealing with the Iranian threat] simply encourages them to play the spoiler role and make life tougher for us . . . If we are going to contain Iran, we have to do it with the Soviets. They are simply too important, too large and too close to Iran to exclude.

Before National
Women's Democratic Club/
The Washington Post, 10-14:(A)22.

Hafez al-Assad
President of Syria

3

There is no serious and direct reason which would have caused the deterioration in relations between [Syria and the United States]. Israel always has an interest in creating such divisions . . . [It] looks at the United States as a treasure and fears that any other side may compete to get this treasure.

Interview/Newsweek, 9-28:32.

Shlomo Avineri
Professor,
Hebrew University
(Israel)

4

Israel and the Soviets have a real love-hate relationship. On the one hand, the Soviets are vilified in Israel, maybe more than in any Western country, because of their support for the Arab armies and their persecution of Soviet Jews. But on the other hand, there is a real longing here for a restoration of ties with Moscow and a real fascination with the Soviet Union. One reason is the fact that so many Israelis are from Eastern European or Russian origin. Another reason is the similarity between Israeli and Soviet political cultures. It is true we may be a democracy with eight different parties, but each one of our parties is Bolshevik in both style and organization. Also, many Israelis were raised on the socialist dream and the revolutionary traditions. Even our songs come from there. To this day, when Israelis really want to create a nice atmosphere around the campfire, they start singing Russian Red Army songs.

The New York Times, 7-15:8.

Louis Awad
Egyptian political analyst

5

Out of this chaos [in Egypt after the 1967 Arab-Israeli war] I have the feeling something will come, maybe in 10 years' time. We are passing through a vacuum and the country is groping for balance. If the regime reaches it, then a new kind of intelligentsia will develop that expresses itself freely and makes its own dreams.

Interview, Cairo/
The Christian Science Monitor,
6-10:12.

Howard H. Baker, Jr.
Chief of Staff to
President of the United States
Ronald Reagan

6

[On U.S. statements that it will protect oil shipments, particularly by Kuwait, in the Persian Gulf from possible attacks by Iran]: It seems to me the United States has two choices. The United States can say, "Oh, I'm sorry about that—we were just full of bluster and

(HOWARD H. BAKER, JR.)

didn't mean we were going to protect free transit," or the United States says, "Yes, you bet—you're not going to stop us and you're not going to stop other nations of the world from having freedom of the seas to transport oil from the Persian Gulf, even though Iraq and Iran are at war" . . . [U.S. protection] should not be terminated as long as the Kuwaitis want it and as long as the Soviets are still playing in this game. As long as the Soviets are there, I don't want to see us pick up our marbles and go home.

Broadcast interview/
"Face the Nation," CBS-TV, 6-7.

Amatzia Baram
Lecturer in
Middle East studies,
Haifa University (Israel)

1

[Favoring an Israeli tilt toward Iraq in the Iran-Iraq war]: If you are ready to risk an Iranian victory in the war, then you could be risking the very existence of the state of Israel. After an Iranian victory, the atmosphere in the countries around us would be so unstable and paranoid no Arab leader would dare enter into a peace with Israel. The same pressures which pushed Iraq toward the Americans and the Arab moderates—the threats from Iran—are going to be there for a long time . . . We cannot change the size of the Iraqi Army. We are going to have to learn to live with it and to work hard for an understanding with Baghdad. I don't think we have tried very hard yet.

The New York Times, 10-31:4.

Tahsin Bashir
Egyptian political analyst
and former diplomat

2

If all the man-made theories failed [in Egypt], then the only real belief—of the generation that came to awareness after [the 1967 Arab-Israeli war]—was Islam. Twenty years [later], the most active, dynamic political force on the Egyptian scene is Islamic fundamentalism. And everyone is dancing to their tune.

Interview, Cairo/
The Christian Science Monitor,
6-10:12.

Robert A. Basil
President,
American Lebanese League

3

Two weeks ago, Syria started the next-to-final phase of its long-held dream of hegemony over Lebanon. Seven to ten thousand Syrian troops, backed by Soviet-furnished tanks, entered West Beirut to stop the intense and bloody conflict between warring militias, and to establish control and order . . . There appears to be little concern that Syria expects de facto control over the Lebanese government and institutions . . . Most nations appear to be considering the idea that maintaining a free, sovereign, democratic, pluralistic Lebanon has simply cost too great a price in regional instability and international terrorism. The truth is that Syria, over the past 11 years, has cynically created all these problems in Lebanon, and then postured itself to be the only salvation against the very problems it created.

Before House Foreign Affairs
Committee, Washington, March 11/
The Washington Post, 4-1:(A)22.

Zaid Ben Shaker
General and
Commander-in-Chief,
armed forces of Jordan

4

[Criticizing the covert sale by the U.S. of arms to Iran]: It is very difficult to be a friend and an ally of the United States now. We would like to be close to the United States. We train our officers in the United States. Ninety per cent of our equipment is from the United States. [But as a result of the U.S. current refusal to sell Jordan more modern equipment,]

(ZAID BEN SHAKER)

we have now to look for alternatives. Obviously, our alternative is Western Europe.

Interview, March 30/
The Christian Science Monitor,
3-31:32.

1

The United States has made Israel the strongest country [militarily] in this area. There is no military threat to Israel posed by any country in this region today. [Syrian President] Hafez al-Assad's theory of needing to deal with the Israelis from a position of strength is very credible, I think. His drive for parity with the Israelis is based on that and I would not criticize it. It is the only way to approach the Israelis. You want to be credible when you deal with them . . . One of many possible scenarios for peace is that there would be a demilitarized zone for the West Bank that could ensure Israel's security. There is no potential danger for Israel from any combination of Arab countries. The best security for any country is a friendly neighbor.

Interview, Amman, Jordan/
The Christian Science Monitor,
4-8:10.

Joseph R. Biden, Jr.
United States Senator,
D-Delaware; Candidate for the 1988
Democratic Presidential nomination

2

[On indications that President Reagan made covert arms deals with Iran in return for the release of American hostages in Lebanon]: I'm not angry with the President, because I think his action was one from the heart. I think his action was not one that was political. I think his action was not one done with any malevolence. I think he bled for those hostages.

To reporters,
New Hampshire, Feb. 26/
The New York Times, 2-27:11.

James Bill
Director-designate,
Center for International Studies,
College of William and Mary

3

In the Middle East, patience and time and low-key contacts are very important and are part of the political terrain. We [in the West] are not very patient. We do not understand that a policy of ignorance and arrogance is counterproductive.

Los Angeles Times, 2-16:(I)14.

Hyman Bookbinder
Washington representative,
American Jewish Committee

4

Resolving the West Bank issue is the big challenge to Israel, and any feeling that you can just stall and delay, and in time everything will be all right, is just absolutely wrong, in my judgment. We will have de facto if not de jure annexation. It's a demographic threat, a military threat and a threat to democratic values. Retaining it indefinitely in the absence of a real agreement on how to live together will compel Israel to be less democratic than it is.

Interview/
Los Angeles Times,
6-11:(I)14.

David L. Boren
United States Senator,
D-Oklahoma

5

[Saying the U.S. Reagan Administration made a mistake in selling arms to Iran in what turned out to be a deal for the release of Arab-held American hostages in Lebanon]: Even though the President [Reagan] to this good day may believe and sincerely think that he was trying to [improve relations with Iran . . . Administration officials] were so focused on the release of these hostages that they forgot to think what will happen if we undermine the credibility of our whole anti-terrorism policy . . . You cannot deal effectively with a hostage-type

(DAVID L. BOREN)

situation, or other terrorist incident, if you let the people on the other side know that you are so obsessed with the situation that you are willing to pay any price to get it ended. You almost doom your actions to failure.

Washington/
The Christian Science Monitor,
1-22:1,32.

Dale Bumpers
United States Senator,
D-Arkansas; Candidate for the 1988
Democratic Presidential nomination

1

[On U.S. reflagging of Kuwaiti oil ships in the Persian Gulf to protect them against Iranian attack]: How much is Kuwait paying [the U.S. for this protection]? Kuwait, whose tankers we have reflagged and, in my opinion, have thereby demeaned our flag in the process—and that is not to denigrate Kuwait; it is simply saying we ought not put the American flag on the ships of everybody who asks us. So what is Kuwait putting up? So far as I know, the answer is zip, zero, none. What kind of landing rights for our fighter planes and our helicopters and what kind of berthing rights do our ships have in Kuwait? Zip, zero, none. Yes, we will put our flags on your [Kuwaiti] ships, and we will put not six warships, as [U.S. President Reagan] said, but 30 to 40 warships in there to protect them. And Kuwait says, "We really appreciate that, and we would like to let your ships berth in our ports, but we can't. We would like to let your planes land on our soil, but we can't" . . . What kind of nonsense is this?

Before the Senate, Oct. 9/
The Washington Post, 10-16:(A)22.

George Bush
Vice President
of the United States

2

[On U.S. President Reagan's covert selling of arms to Iran]: I think history has to prove

whether it's wrong. I think it is debatable, and I think on the surface you can make the case that it's wrong. [However,] having said that, when you look at the whole policy and look at Iran's geographic standing and look at the problems facing them, if a small [arms] shipment establishes contact with moderate elements [in Iran], and if it results down the line in a solution to the Iran-Iraq war . . . I think we could argue that it was right. On the surface, selling arms to a country that sponsors terrorism, of course, clearly, you'd have to argue it's wrong. But it's the exception sometimes that proves the rule.

Broadcast interview/
"Good Morning America,"
ABC-TV, 1-28.

Robert C. Byrd
United States Senator,
D-West Virginia

3

[Criticizing the U.S. Reagan Administration's covert sale of arms to Iran]: The Administration's recent dealings with Iran have cast a long shadow over this country. There's a gathering sense of mistrust [of the government by the U.S. public]. The sale of arms to Iran—in direct contradiction to our stated foreign policy—raises real questions about trust. But it also raises real doubts about competence. Without competence—and a good measure of common sense—government will have a tough time earning the nation's trust. And government without trust is government without power.

Broadcast address to
the nation, Washington, Jan. 27/
The Washington Post, 1-28:(A)8.

4

[On U.S. Reagan Administration plans to reflag Kuwaiti oil tankers to provide American protection against possible Iranian attacks in the Persian Gulf]: We [in Congress] have a responsibility to try to help the Administration by making it see that this is a questionable, highly visible, highly provocative action, and that we ought to stop and look and listen . . . before the Administration gets deeper and deeper into a

WHAT THEY SAID IN 1987

(ROBERT C. BYRD)

policy which might prove, in the end, quite disastrous.

To reporters, Washington, June 29/
The Christian Science Monitor, 6-30:8.

Frank C. Carlucci
Assistant to President of
the United States Ronald Reagan
for National Security Affairs

1

[On U.S. plans to place the American flag on Kuwaiti oil tankers in the Persian Gulf to protect them from Iranian attacks]: We cannot afford to let hostile powers—either the Soviets or the Ayatollah [Khomeini of Iran]—gain a chokehold on so central a region. The President [Reagan] understands that's at stake, and like seven Presidents before him, is determined to prevent it. He knows the consequences of retreat from our offer to reflag Kuwaiti ships: [U.S. allies in the Gulf would] be faced with either giving in to Iranian intimidation or accepting Soviet offers of protection, and not just for shipping.

Before National Association
of Arab Americans, Washington,
June 15/The Washington Post, 6-16:(A)8.

Dvora Carmil
Researcher, Wolfe Center for ,
the Study of Psychological Stress,
Haifa University (Israel)

2

Israel is a small country, so when something happens, everybody is involved . . . The American is worried about himself and his job and his children, and whatever. But he doesn't worry about America as such. Israelis are worried about themselves—they want to achieve a lot; they're very, very ambitious and competitive. But [an Israeli is] also worried [about] . . . the Israeli situation. He's worried about the country's future—not only his own future.

Los Angeles Times, 7-29:(I)1.

Jimmy Carter
Former President
of the United States

3

I would like to see the peace process in this region pursued more vigorously [by the U.S.]. I'm not here to criticize my own government, but I think it is accurate to say that most of the initiatives [toward negotiations] have had to originate in this region [such as those by Egyptian President Hosni Mubarak and Jordanian King Hussein]. But these efforts are almost doomed to failure without a strong central core of partnership and encouragement from Washington. The mediation or negotiating role has to be played by some entity.

Before American Chamber
of Commerce, Cairo, March 19/
The New York Times, 3-20:4.

4

[I have] been surprised and angered by some leaders in the present [Israeli] government who speak with a degree of arrogance and even condemnation of the United States for "inadequate" support, for pursuing "unattractive" peace efforts, for general criticisms of Israel's policies relating to the West Bank, Lebanon or Gaza. I think that the more certain the prospect of [U.S.] economic aid [for Israel] is—and it is quite certain—the lesser inclination there is on the part of many Israelis to take it [as] other than the expected obligation by the United States to continue it or even to extend the present level of aid.

Los Angeles Times, 7-20:(I)13.

Dick Cheney
United States Representative,
R-Wyoming

5

[On revelations of Israeli spying against the U.S.]: I don't think it was a rogue operation. I think it was a major, very successful penetration of the U.S. government and our intelligence agencies by the Israeli government . . . behavior that doesn't behoove an ally. I don't think we've heard the last of it . . . On the one

334

(DICK CHENEY)

hand, Israel pleads a special relationship with the United States. On the other hand, they run a major intelligence operation against us. There isn't much they couldn't get if they asked for it. But they chose not to do it that way. I think the Israeli government ought to know that some of us are deeply concerned about that kind of conduct. [However,] it wouldn't be in our national interest to significantly reduce aid levels just because the Israelis made a dumb mistake.

Washington, March 4/
The Washington Post, 3-5:(A)24.

Jacques Chirac
Premier of France

1

How can other peoples, and more specifically the Palestinian people, avail themselves of the right to self-determination, that imprescriptible right that the Jewish people were among the very first to champion? Israel's right to existence and to security must be unambiguously guaranteed. But the Palestinian people's right to determine and ensure their future must equally be recognized and carried out.

Speech, Jerusalem, Nov. 1/
Los Angeles Times, 11-2:(I)7.

Ramsey Clark
*Former Attorney General
of the United States*

2

[Criticizing the U.S. bombing raid on Libya last year in retaliation for that country's involvement in international terrorism]: The dead and injured for whom claims are being filed were all civilians. Most, as far as we know, were asleep in their beds when the bombs struck . . . Whatever [Libyan leader Muammar] Qaddafi or his government may have done, there was no legal right [for the U.S.] to bomb Libya. If there were a robbery today in Washington, D.C., we wouldn't send the police out to a part of town where we thought they might have come from and just shoot it up. You

don't kill 3-month-old children because you labeled someone a terrorist, rightly or wrongly.

News conference,
Washington, April 15/
Los Angeles Times, 4-16:(I)8.

William S. Cohen
*United States Senator,
R-Maine*

3

[On last year's covert U.S. arms sales to Iran]: I think it's clear, at least to me, that [U.S. President Reagan's] decision to include arms as a part of the package . . . came over the strong objection of his two top foreign and military or defense policy advisers. And no one, no one on this committee, can challenge the President's sentiments or motives. I think it's clear . . . that he made a mistake and that his heart overruled his head. But I think it's also clear . . . that the American people do not want to see him pilloried or politically paralyzed for being human. They simply want, and I think they deserve, an acknowledgment of the truth.

At Iran-contra hearings,
Washington, July 24/
The Washington Post, 7-25:(A)9.

Alan Cranston
*United States Senator,
D-California*

4

Israel is a stable democracy and a reliable ally in a troubled region of the world. It shares values Americans hold, natural ties exist between us, and it deserves our whole-hearted support . . . The Israelis may not be allies in the technical sense—that is, through a treaty alliance—but they are allies in every other sense. They are the most powerful military force in the region, it is of vital importance for our country to keep them that way, and I would say our relationship with Israel is wholesome.

Interview, Washington/
Los Angeles Times, 7-20:(I)12.

WHAT THEY SAID IN 1987

William J. Crowe
Admiral, United States Navy;
Chairman, Joint Chiefs of Staff

1

[On U.S. plans to protect Kuwaiti oil shipping from attacks by Iran in the Persian Gulf]: The Gulf today is an uncertain place, and it can be dangerous, but it is not a war zone in the accepted use of the word. It is not a no-man's land . . . We have the capability to keep the oil line to Kuwait open, to assure our Arab friends of our commitment and to keep the risk low. [But] there are no absolute guarantees such an operation will be casualty-free.

Before Senate Armed Services
Committee, Washington, June 5/
Los Angeles Times, 6-6:(I)1.

Macabee Dean
Reporter,
"Jerusalem Post"
(Israel)

2

If Protestants in the U.S. pray: "Give us this day our daily bread," in Israel the prayer must run: "Give us this day our daily crisis." It is part of our Jungian makeup, our atavistic responses. We are a people addicted to a daily crisis.

Los Angeles Times, 7-29:(I)1.

Robert J. Dole
United States Senator,
R-Kansas; Candidate for the 1988
Republican Presidential nomination

3

[Questioning the U.S. plan to reflag Kuwaiti oil vessels so as to provide them with U.S. protection against attack by Iran]: I have been traveling around the country, and I think there are a lot of reservations on the part of the [American] people. We get [only] about 7 per cent of that oil . . . I don't believe they [the Reagan Administration] have yet explained any real reason that we should be providing free escort service to every country that depends on that part of the world for its oil supply.

To reporters, Washington, May 28/
Los Angeles Times, 5-29:(I)1.

David Durenberger
United States Senator,
R-Minnesota

4

[On the scandal about the covert sale of U.S. arms to Iran]: There was a need on the part of the Israelis to get the U.S. to sell arms to Iran, and there was a need on the part of the Iranians to get them, and a need on the part of some folks to make money. And you put that together with a very well-intentioned effort to find a long-range opening to Iran, and there you've got the whole bloody mess.

Los Angeles Times, 1-6:(I)12.

Abba Eban
Member of Israeli Knesset
(Parliament); Former
Foreign Minister of Israel

5

[On recent foreign scandals Israel is alleged to have been involved in]: We Israelis think that because we were aggrieved by the Holocaust that we can do what the hell we like, that we can go around like this Iranian involvement and the Pollard [U.S. spy involvement]—there is always some headline, like stealing British passports. There's a kind of feeling that the normal restraints of the international community don't apply. I think American Jews are getting a little bit fed up being asked to support things that are hard to support, like our involvement in Iran and like this recent espionage case [against the U.S.]. They feel they are entitled to make their views known. They are not being what I call the Jewish mother, and that's good. I think they are more outspoken, and it's a good thing they are being more critical . . . We [Israel] are not a very beautiful society at this moment, let's be frank. What's there for them [American Jews] to emulate or admire? This is not a very beautiful period in Israel's life.

Before American Friends of
Hebrew University, Palm Springs,
Calif./Los Angeles Times, 6-11:(I)1,12.

6

Our rule of the West Bank is more dangerous to us than any danger that comes from the So-

(ABBA EBAN)

viet Union, Syria, the Arabs, the PLO, because it is disruptive of our internal structure. We shall either become a Jewish minority or else we have to become a tyranny. We will either be Lebanon or we will be South Africa. The American Jews should join those of us in Israel who are fighting [these tendencies] and fight them in terms of American values. How do you support a state that intends to rule over 1.3 million people [in the West Bank] without rights, without votes?

Interview/
Los Angeles Times,
6-11:(I)13.

1

We have gotten so used to the idea that the Arabs were immobilized and frozen in their antipathy to Israel that when they do finally change we do not know how to take "yes" for an answer . . . All of this does not mean the Arab-Israeli conflict will be easy to solve, but it does mean that there is an opportunity. We should look at [the late Egyptian President Anwar] Sadat's visit to Israel a decade ago as the beginning of something and the [recent] Amman [Arab] summit meeting as the continuation of it.

Interview, Jerusalem, Nov. 16/
The New York Times, 11-17:4.

2

The notion that [Iranian leader the Ayatollah Ruhollah] Khomeini is a passing episode is nonsense. Those who have studied the history of Iran would be more inclined to believe that it was the [late] Shah's regime which was the passing episode.

Interview, Jerusalem, Nov. 16/
The New York Times, 11-17:4.

Ismail Fahmy
Former Foreign Minister of Egypt

3

It is not in the best interest of the U.S. that our [Egyptian] relations with the Arab world

should be rebuilt. If our relations improved, our dependency on the U.S. would diminish a great deal. Such dependency on a superpower affects the decision-making process here. The Americans should remember that in Egypt, superpowers come and go; there is no problem. The Russians were here; now they are out completely. Now the Americans are here.

The Christian Science Monitor,
2-18:15.

Marlin Fitzwater
Assistant to President of
the United States Ronald Reagan
for Press Relations

4

[On the controversial covert sale of U.S. arms to Iran]: The [Reagan] Administration was trying to open a dialogue with elements in Iran that were prepared to work with us, with the United States. And the question of [Iranian] moderates and radicals is a semantic difference. We were hoping for moderates in the sense of elements who were willing to work with us. But you can define moderates and radicals in hundreds of different ways, particularly in Iran.

Washington, Feb. 9/
Los Angeles Times, 2-10:(I)23.

5

It is simply not true that this [U.S. Reagan] Administration has neglected diplomatic channels in the Middle East. When you talk about the peace process in the Middle East, you talk about gains that come in inches and not miles, and there have been a lot of gains. There have also been setbacks.

Washington, March 20/
Los Angeles Times, 3-21:(I)7.

Elias Freij
Mayor of Bethlehem,
Israeli-occupied West Bank

6

[Criticizing Israel's plan to drill for water in the West Bank]: Israel has no right to do this

337

(ELIAS FREIJ)

project. With more water available, there will be more Jewish settlers, more settlements and more loss of our [Palestinian West Bank] land. And if they find big water, the Israelis will never under any condition withdraw from this area. This would seal our political future; it would be a very big nail in the coffin of the peace process.

The Washington Post,
10-1:(A)40.

Charles Glass
American journalist

1

[After escaping from his Lebanese captors]: I'm told by Syrian and American diplomats in Damascus [Syria] that the political environment between the U.S. and the Syrians is improving, that Syria is much more active on the ground in Beirut in trying to obtain release of hostages. But there is no movement in the sense of a new development. The movement is in the sense that [diplomats] are confident that Syria is doing a lot on the ground in Beirut to try to find out where these [hostages] are and [to] try to resolve the problem on a case-by-case basis.

To reporters, London,
Aug. 19/Los Angeles Times,
8-20:(I)18.

John Glenn
United States Senator,
D-Ohio

2

[Criticizing U.S. President Reagan for not complying with the Congressional War Powers Resolution in its use of force in the Persian Gulf while protecting ships from Iranian attack]: This is a textbook case of the situation in which the War Powers Act should be invoked. How anyone can say that hostilities are not imminent, when we are planning them and executing them ourselves, defies rationality. An

American President doesn't have the right to pick and choose the laws he will obey.

Oct. 19/Los Angeles Times,
10-20:(I)8.

Barry M. Goldwater
Former United States
Senator, R-Arizona

3

[Criticizing the current U.S. military protection of Persian Gulf oil shipments from attacks by Iran]: Personally, as one who has been through wars and lived with them most of my life, I don't like what the President's [Reagan] doing in the Persian Gulf. I think we're inviting disaster. In fact, I don't see how we can avoid it. One of these days, they're [Iran] going to sink . . . an American tanker or an American warship. Then what do we do? Now, if we don't do anything, we can kiss the whole world goodbye, because we are not held in great esteem around this world today. We're looked on as sort of a paper tiger . . . I don't believe in putting ourselves in a position that can result in war. And I think that's exactly what Reagan has done in the Persian Gulf.

Interview, Scottsdale, Ariz./
The Christian Science Monitor, 8-25:6.

George Habash
Founder,
Popular Front for
the Liberation
of Palestine

4

Israel is creating its own antithesis. Israel is digging its own grave by saying there is no such thing as the Palestinian people. This policy of saying they will crush the Palestinians will force the Arab people to say, "We will not accept." I will die in 10 years. By then, Palestinians will be 50 per cent of all the population [in Israel and the Israeli-occupied territories]. Today they are only 37 per cent. Scientifically, we can show that the present situation will change in our favor.

Interview, Damascus, Syria/
The Washington Post, 9-26:(A)2.

Alexander M. Haig, Jr.
*Former Secretary of State
of the United States;
Candidate for the 1988
Republican Presidential nomination*

1

[On the U.S. military presence in the Persian Gulf to protect oil shipping from Iranian attack]: You put me in the White House, and we won't be in the Persian Gulf. It makes [Iranian leader Ruhollah] Khomeini feel he can take a shot at our boys. The Soviets pull strings from the background and pick up all the goodies. That's the way they do it, and we're dumb enough to let them do it.

*Campaigning, Merrimack, N.H./
The New York Times, 11-21:6.*

Nizar Hamdoon
*Iraqi Ambassador
to the United States*

2

[On trusting Iran]: They can sell you and buy you at the same time.

USA Today, 8-27:(A)10.

Lee H. Hamilton
*United States Representative,
D-Indiana*

3

[Criticizing the U.S. Reagan Administration's covert arms sales to Iran which was followed by the release in Lebanon of some American hostages]: The President has acknowledged that his policy, as implemented, was an arms-for-hostages policy. And selling arms to Iran in secret was, to put it mildly, bad policy . . . It repudiated U.S. policy to make concessions to terrorists, to remain [uninvolved] in the [Persian] Gulf war, and to stop arms sales to Iran. We sold arms to a nation officially designated by our government as a terrorist state. This secret policy of selling arms to Iran damaged U.S. credibility . . . The policy achieved none of the goals it sought. [Iran's leader] the Ayatollah Khomeini got his arms; more Americans are held hostage today than

when this policy began; subversion of U.S. interests throughout the region by Iran continues. Moderates in Iran, if any there were, did not come forward.

*At Iran-contra hearings,
Washington, July 14/
Los Angeles Times, 7-15:(I)10.*

James Hayes
*United States Representative,
D-Louisiana*

4

[After visiting Israel]: I don't think I'll ever forget the impact that 40 years of imminent war has had on that country. Once you've seen the Golan Heights, you think harder about every vote you cast [on Middle East issues in the U.S. Congress].

Newsweek, 10-19:46.

Selim Hoss
Prime Minister of Lebanon

5

Lebanon's crisis has become self-perpetuating. It has formed into an entity all its own. It has its institutions, its generations, its manners and values. There are the militias, the illegal radio stations, illegal television stations, illegal taxes—these are the institutions of the crisis. When I grew up . . . it was unimaginable that someone who liked your car would simply take it, that someone who liked your apartment would break in and squat in it. That happens all the time now.

*Interview, Beirut/
The Christian Science Monitor,
6-19:12.*

Hussein I
King of Jordan

6

Israel has succeeded in diverting the role of the United States from that of a superpower with a special responsibility for world peace into the role of sponsor of Israel and its interests.

*At Arab League summit conference,
Amman, Jordan, Nov. 8/
The Washington Post, 11-9:(A)20.*

WHAT THEY SAID IN 1987

Saddam Hussein
President of Iraq

1

[On what he says was an accidental attack by Iraq on the U.S.S. *Stark* in the Persian Gulf, killing 37 American sailors]: On the occasion of the funeral ceremony of the victims lost in the grievous and unintentional incident that has happened to the American frigate *Stark*, I would like to express to you once again my condolences and feelings of grief . . . All the Iraqis and I feel most profoundly the sorrow of moments such as these, since we have ourselves lost a great many of our dear ones in this [Iran-Iraq] war, which has been raging for seven years; while the Iranian government still persists in perpetuating death and destruction and in rejecting our appeals and those of the international community for a just and honorable peace; an objective no doubt that is long desired by all those who believe in God, and in justice and brotherhood amongst peoples.

Letter to U.S.
President Reagan, May 22/*
Los Angeles Times, 5-23:(I)10.

John Paul II
Pope

2

[The Jewish people] have a right to a homeland, as does any civil nation, according to international law . . . What has been said about the [Jewish] right to a homeland also applies to the Palestinian people, so many of whom remain homeless and refugees. While all concerned must honestly reflect on the past—Muslims no less than Jews and Christians—it is time to forge those solutions which will lead to a just, complete and lasting peace in that area.

Speech to Jewish leaders, Miami,
Sept. 11/Los Angeles Times, 9-12:(I)21.

Ali Khameini
President of Iran

3

[On the Iran-Iraq war]: If the world wants peace in the region . . . the way to achieve [this] is to name the one who threatens security [Iraq], the one who began the war, the one who started the [oil-] tanker war and the one who launched air strikes against civilian areas. Unless this source is named, the war will continue.

Radio broadcast, Teheran, Sept. 11/
Los Angeles Times, 9-12:(I)3.

4

[On the Iran-Iraq war]: [As] we look back at the irrecoverable cost of this imposed war, we . . . believe that without punishing the aggressor [Iraq], any other achievement would be a loss for our people. As a nation who has borne the burden of a seven-year war, we long for peace more than anybody else. But we believe that peace, a lasting peace, can only be established in the light of punishing an aggressor who has added many other sins to the original sin of aggression.

At United Nations,
New York, Sept. 22/
The Christian Science Monitor,
9-23:32.

5

[Condemning an attack by an American military ship against an Iranian vessel said to be mining the Persian Gulf]: American television stations announced yesterday that the U.S. ship fired at this ship while it was laying mines, and thereby as usual told a pack of lies to the American people. But I declare here the [Iranian] ship was a merchant vessel called *Iran Ajr*, not a military speedboat. This is a beginning for a series of events, the bitter consequences of which shall not be restricted to the Persian Gulf, and the United States as initiator of the trouble shall bear responsibility. Should we now believe the United States' passionate claims for peace and tranquility in the Persian Gulf, or this open, flagrant and concrete measure to fan the flames of war? I declare here the United States shall receive a proper response for this abominable act.

At United Nations,
New York, Sept. 22/
The New York Times,
9-23:6.

Ruhollah Khomeini
Spiritual leader of Iran

1

[On the Iran-Iraq war]: Families and children are now being killed [in Iran], and this is hard for us and brings pressures to bear . . . Almost every day, Iran is hit and many children, youngsters, old men and ordinary people see their homes fall in on them. But as soon as they clamber from the rubble, they speak of the need for us to make war until victory.

Speech, Jamaran, Iran, Feb. 10/
The New York Times, 2-11:6.

2

[Criticizing the U.S. military presence in the Persian Gulf to allegedly protect oil shipping against attacks by Iran]: The United States and [U.S. President] Reagan . . . should remain assured that any continuation of the show of force in the Persian Gulf will lead the region into a hotbed of danger and unwanted crisis to themselves. If the world has prepared itself for an oil crisis, as well as the disruption of all economic, commercial and industrial activity, then we are ready also. We have tightened our belts; everything is ready for such a situation. The United States should conclude that military intervention in the Persian Gulf is not simply an experiment. It is a big step, a dangerous game. We, along with all the Moslems of the Persian Gulf region, interpret the superpowers' military presence as a prelude for invading the Islamic countries and the Islamic Republic of Iran. We interpret this as an extension of their support.

Radio broadcast/
The New York Times, 8-4:8.

3

As I have often warned both before and after the revolution, I once again remind everyone of the danger of the prevalent, festering and cancerous Zionist tumor [Israel] in the body of Islamic countries. I declare my own as well as the unreserved support of the Iranian nation, government and authorities for all Islamic struggles of nations and courageous and Moslem young people toward the liberation of Jerusalem. I express my gratitude to the dear

Lebanese youth, who have made Islam proud and world devourers abject. I pray for the success of all those dear ones who continue to deal blows to Israel and its interests in the [Israeli-] occupied territories or next to that usurped country by relying on the weapons of faith and jihad. I assure you that the Iranian nation will not abandon you.

Radio broadcast/
The New York Times, 8-4:8.

Henry A. Kissinger
Former Secretary of State
of the United States

4

[On proposed U.S. military protection for Kuwaiti oil tankers in the Persian Gulf against possible Iranian attack]: I think it's a bad idea to get ourselves militarily involved . . . By getting involved on—in effect—the Iraqi side [in the Iran-Iraq war], we are taking on a belligerent commitment [without knowing the outcome]. If the American national interest is involved, of course we should be prepared to fight Iran. But it's not something one likes to slide into, one tanker at a time, when one cannot define what the war aim is and what the terms are . . . [As far as U.S.-Soviet cooperation in defending the Persian Gulf,] I think that would be a disaster, because the Soviet aim, and the Russian aim, for a century and a half has been to establish a foothold in the warm-water area in the Persian Gulf. We have an interest in keeping Iran from winning the war, but we do not have an interest in establishing the Soviet Union in the Persian Gulf . . . We may have a very short-term common interest, but I would not consider that an area for superpower cooperation.

Broadcast interview/
"Meet the Press," NBC-TV, 6-14.

Robert H. Kupperman
Senior adviser,
Center for Strategic and
International Studies,
Georgetown University

5

[Saying Iran may be planning terrorism against American interests because of U.S. re-

(ROBERT H. KUPPERMAN)

flagging of Kuwaiti oil tankers in the Persian Gulf to protect them against Iranian attacks]: There is good reason to believe that Iran, the foremost sponsor of terrorism today, is planning terrorist operations against U.S. citizens and facilities, particularly in the Middle East, certainly in Europe, and possibly even in the U.S. . . . It is strongly believed by the intelligence community in this government and a number of allied governments that the potential for terror increases as we proceed down this path. Everybody's scared to death of this. The [U.S. Reagan] Administration has got to focus on the intelligence and how we're going to respond.

The Christian Science Monitor,
6-29:3,8.

Muhammad Javed Larijani
Foreign Minister of Iran

1

[On spreading the Iranian Islamic revolution to other countries]: I tell you frankly that once a revolution is under way, it will immediately be propagated beyond its borders. That happened to the French Revolution, to the revolution in the Soviet Union. And this is true for our revolution [which] from the day of inception was out of its border. It's not because it was us who want to export it. It goes by itself. Islamic revolution is . . . a renaissance in the Islamic world. Nobody can stop it. I think for the West it is better to cope with it, to live with it, rather than stand in front of it.

Interview, United Nations, New York/
The Christian Science Monitor, 8-25:8.

Gene R. La Rocque
Rear Admiral,
United States Navy (Ret.);
Director, Center for
Defense Information

2

[Criticizing the U.S. decision to protect Kuwaiti oil tankers in the Persian Gulf from attack by Iran]: [The policy is] leading us into a very

dark tunnel, through which we can't see the light of day. We're all alone . . . [U.S. President] Reagan has gone one step too far this time for even his best friends.

USA Today, 8-4:(A)1.

John F. Lehman, Jr.
Former Secretary
of the Navy
of the United States

3

We [the U.S.] have an enormous carrying charge for meeting the commitment of the Carter Doctrine; we will go to war to save the world's supply of oil out of the Persian Gulf. It's costing us about $40-billion a year. Europe and Japan totally depend on Persian Gulf oil. We get five times as much oil from Alaska as we have from the Persian Gulf, yet we are the ones paying $40-billion. The Brits keep a token force three months of the year. They go out and show the flag; they don't go in the Gulf. The French never go in the Gulf, either. We are the only ones risking lives to keep the oil flowing.

Interview/Newsweek, 6-1:26.

Samuel W. Lewis
Former United States
Ambassador to Israel

4

[On Palestinians who live in the Israeli-occupied West Bank]: They're better educated. They benefit economically, even though it's a bit of a colonial system in terms of the way it works . . . But there's really no good example anywhere where economic well-being takes the place of political satisfactions. Though they've gotten wealthier, [they] haven't gotten in any sense more ready to accept permanent Israeli rule.

Interview/
Los Angeles Times, 6-1:(I)16.

Paul N. McCloskey
Former United States
Representative, R-California

5

If you use the term "even-handed" in connection with American policy in the Middle

(PAUL N. McCLOSKEY)

East, let alone suggest that talks with the PLO might contribute to the peace process, you get into deep trouble with a lot of Jewish voters [in the U.S.]. To supporters of Israel, the term "even-handed" equates as anti-Semitic, and woe be to any American politician at election time who takes that approach.

Interview/
Los Angeles Times, 7-20:(I)12.

Hussein Moussavi
Prime Minister of Iran

1

If Kuwait thinks that by putting itself under the protection of the big powers it can continue to help Iraq [in the Iran-Iraq war] without being exposed to danger, it is wrong. The presence of the superpower navies in the [Persian] Gulf cannot prevent the Iranian people from answering one blow with another.

The Christian Science Monitor,
5-19:32.

2

[On U.S. plans to protect Arab oil shipping from Iranian attack in the Persian Gulf]: We will use our forces against the superpowers if they conspire against us. They're completely mistaken if they think they will not fall into the fire they are fanning for us. It will engulf them all.

June 5/Los Angeles Times, 6-6:(I)12.

3

The Persian Gulf States are permanent neighbors which should care more about good relations with each other rather than with the United States. However long the U.S. may linger in the Gulf [protecting oil tankers against Iranian attack], it will eventually pull out of the waterway and let those states bear the consequences of their hostility with Iran.

Teheran, Sept. 6/
The Washington Post,
9-7:(A)23.

Daniel P. Moynihan
United States Senator,
D-New York

4

[Criticizing President Reagan for not advising Congress of his plans involving arms shipments to Iran]: When you get to the point where you can trust a [Manucher] Ghorbanifar [a middleman in the arms deals], a man the career intelligence service did not trust, before you trust the Speaker of the House; or when you decide to pass on intelligence information to the Ayatollah [Khomeini, Iran's leader] but will not inform the Chairman of the [U.S. Congressional] Intelligence Committee of a Presidential finding, then matters are confused.

Los Angeles Times,
4-2:(I)32.

5

If we wish the Persian Gulf to become a Soviet lake, that fact of geopolitics, that irreversible fact of geopolitics, is upon us at this hour. The Soviets have, with astonishing dexterity and deftness, moved in on Kuwait, now head of the Islamic Conference, and offered to protect Kuwait against its non-Arab neighbor, the massive state of Iran . . . [Pakistan is] alarmed at the Soviet penetration in the Middle East. They see it as directly affecting their capacity to support the *mujaheddin* rebels in Afghanistan. They see the possibility of being outflanked completely and the United States being effectively excluded from the region. I need not remind . . . that Aden, the British protectorate that defined east of the Suez for a century and more in world politics, has fallen to a pro-Soviet, Soviet-supported, Soviet-maintained regime that, in effect, approaches the Persian Gulf . . . I would like to add the Afghanistan dimension, the Pakistan dimension, the Islamic Conference dimension. And, I repeat, if you would like to see the Persian Gulf become a Soviet lake, here is the place for the United States Congress to commence that process.

Before the Senate,
Washington, May 28/
The Washington Post,
6-2:(A)18.

343

Richard W. Murphy
*Assistant Secretary
for Near Eastern and
South Asian Affairs,
Department of State
of the United States*

1

Iran is trying to use the oil weapon to threaten the lifelines of the states in the [Persian] Gulf. It is focusing this time on Kuwait. If it is successful, it would employ the same strategy on the other states. [If Iran's strategy succeeds,] it would lead to actual or psychological interruption [of oil supplies,] causing a major surge in oil prices, global inflation and recession—including in the United States—with adverse security and political ramifications for the West, as happened in 1973 [during the Arab oil embargo].

*News conference, Washington,
May 21/Los Angeles Times, 5-22:(I)1.*

Robert G. Neumann
Former American diplomat

2

The issue is no longer whether we should invite the Soviets to a conference [on the Middle East] but whether *we* [the U.S.] are still players. There's a passivity and lack of drive on the part of our government. By our policy we have achieved the thing we wanted to avoid, i.e., making the Russians a major player in the area.

*The Christian Science Monitor,
5-13:32.*

Oliver L. North
*Lieutenant Colonel,
United States Marine Corps*

3

[On his involvement in the U.S. Iran-contra scandal]: I saw that idea, of using [Iranian leader] the Ayatollah Khomeini's money [paid to the U.S. for American arms] to support the Nicaraguan [contra] freedom fighters as a good one. I still do. I don't think it was wrong. I think it was a neat idea . . . We did it on three occasions . . . [in] February, May and October.

And in each one . . . we got three Americans [hostages held in Lebanon] back. And there was no terrorism while we were engaged in it, against Americans. For almost 18 months, there was no action against Americans, until it started to come unraveled. I believed then, and I believe now, that we had a chance to achieve a strategic opening [with moderates in Iran]. And right up until the last minute that I left the NSC, I was in communication with the Israelis and others who were working on the second channel to achieve that end.

*At Iran-contra hearings, Washington,
July 8/The Washington Post, 7-9:(A)26.*

John Cardinal O'Connor
*Roman Catholic Archbishop
of New York*

4

[On Palestinians in the Middle East]: They don't have a real identity; they don't have a passport; they don't have a piece of land they can call their own. They can hardly be called a people who have the right of self-determination.

*News conference, Tel Aviv, Israel,
Jan. 5/The New York Times, 1-6:6.*

Reza Pahlavi
*Exiled son of
the late Shah of Iran*

5

[On his desire to return to lead an Iran based on the 1906 Constitution]: It's the only democratic document we have in Iran today. It is a Constitution that has never been abrogated legally by the present regime [of the Ayatollah Ruhollah Khomeini]. It is the fruit of a revolutionary upheaval that took place in Iran in 1906, where the majority of the Iranian people, from all levels of society, participated. They asked for the end to an oppressive regime and asked for a democratic institution. My task is to see that this Constitution returns to Iran.

*Interview/USA Today,
9-22:(A)13.*

Claiborne Pell
United States Senator,
D-Rhode Island

1

[On the U.S. reflagging of Kuwaiti oil vessels in the Persian Gulf to protect them from Iranian attack]: An Iranian attack on United States-escorted vessels will clearly lead to United States retaliation. But what next? Suppose Iran responds to a United States retaliation attack by an assault on one of the poorly defended and sparsely populated Gulf states? Are we prepared to commit young American lives to the defense of Persian Gulf Arab nations? American military force can be a powerful tool to defend American interests. It should be used, however, where the interests are clear, where the consequences are understood and where the benefits justify the costs. The provision of a naval escort of reflagged Kuwaiti ships serves no clear interests, could have consequences we are not prepared to face and yields minimal gain as opposed to potential costs. Quite simply, it should not be done.

June 4/The Washington Post,
6-9:(A)20.

Shimon Peres
Foreign Minister,
and former Prime Minister,
of Israel

2

As long as the Soviet Union continues to pour arms into the Arab world, Israel will need another power to supply her with arms. Of course we must take America's views into account, because no other nation shows more consideration for Israel.

Before Israeli Knesset
(Parliament), Jerusalem, March 19/
Los Angeles Times, 3-20:(I)10.

3

Israel prefers that Egypt will become part of the Arab world, as it should be, and as it used to be, because it will change the Arab world in a positive direction. The Arabs are not our enemy, and Egypt is not our enemy. The only enemy we have is belligerency, hatred and war.

Radio broadcast, March 26/
The New York Times, 3-27:6.

4

Whoever wants [Arab-Israeli] war will turn to [PLO leader Yasir] Arafat. Whoever wants [peace] talks will turn to Jordan. Whoever wants to live in eternal terror will turn to the PLO. Whoever wants to find another road, the way is in the direction of [Jordan's] King Hussein . . . If Arafat thinks that by returning to terrorism he threatens us, he is mistaken. The return to terror will only unite us and strengthen us. He will bring disaster on the Palestinian people.

Jerusalem, April 21/
Los Angeles Times, 4-22:(I)9.

5

[On the Holocaust]: We [Jews] will learn not to rely on anything but our own strength. We will learn that nothing exists but our land, and we must cling to it so that it doesn't disappear from under our feet. Six million people, 2 million children, 5,000 communities. The same Europe which was witness to the greatest flowering of the spirit of our time is for Jews today an enormous cemetery. Here in Jerusalem, the capital of eternal Israel, we shall perpetuate those who are no longer among the living, and we will be able to carry on life to ensure the eternal presence of the Jewish people.

At new Valley of the Destroyed
Communities memorial, Jerusalem,
April 26/Los Angeles Times, 4-27:(I)5.

John M. Poindexter
Former Assistant to President
of the United States Ronald Reagan
for National Security Affairs

6

[On the revelation of covert sales of U.S. arms to Iran] . . . Iran is in a very strategic location that is critical to the security of the free world. It is important that we not simply ignore Iran and the coming succession to power

WHAT THEY SAID IN 1987

(JOHN M. POINDEXTER)

in that country . . . I think there's a recognition amongst many Iranian officials that things can't go on the way they've been going on. The economy is in a shambles. They're in a no-win war that Iraq started. And they're grasping for help . . . The confidence-building measure that the United States thought would be effective, and also we believed that the Iranians thought it would be effective, was to sell them a small quantity of essentially defensive arms.

At Iran-contra hearings, Washington,
July 20/The New York Times, 7-21:4.

Vladimir Poliakov
Director,
Middle East Department,
Foreign Ministry of
the Soviet Union

1

[On the Iran-Iraq war]: Both the U.S. and the U.S.S.R. want to restore peace in the [Persian] Gulf. In this area of the world our interests overlap . . . Iran's intransigency in its war against Iraq worries us a lot. We keep on warning the Iranians, but they're adamant. They just want [Iraqi] President [Saddam] Hussein's head. I think difficult days lie ahead in this area of the world.

To journalists, Brussels/
The Christian Science Monitor, 5-28:9.

Yevgeny Primakov
Director, Soviet Institute
of World Economics and
International Relations

2

[Soviet-Israeli] relations were broken off under certain circumstances, and they can only be restored under certain circumstances—the political settlement of the situation in the Middle East. And I am not certain that the whole U.S. leadership would like us to restore these relations.

Interview, Moscow, July 15/
The Christian Science Monitor, 7-16:10.

Muammar el-Qaddafi
Chief of State of Libya

3

The U.S. is aiming at encirclement of the Soviet Union through us [Libya]. As a result, we and the Soviets find ourselves facing a common enemy . . . We are needed as a springboard against the Soviets, who are the real object of American policy . . . Our relations with the Soviet Union are the natural consequence of American actions . . . We are now involved in a joint struggle . . . [U.S. actions] have resulted in promoting and even strengthening Soviet-Libyan relations.

Interview, Sirte, Libya/
The Christian Science Monitor, 2-6:14.

4

[Saying that U.S. actions against Libya could lead to Libyan military pacts with the Soviet Union]: Libya [would] in fact declare that it is a Communist country and join the Warsaw Pact and deploy Soviet missiles on the coast of the Mediterranean . . . When we become one military camp, nothing will be prohibited. That means when Libya becomes a Communist country, then that's final. The United States knows if it continues its aggression, this could lead Libya to join the Soviet side, and that's going to overturn the balance of power in the region.

American broadcast interview,
March 22/The New York Times, 3-23:3.

William B. Quandt
Senior fellow,
Brookings Institution

5

The exaggerated rhetoric [from the U.S. Reagan Administration] about how much we achieved by bombing Libya [last year] has to be discounted. This has not been a good year for [Libyan leader Muammar] Qaddafi, but his defeats have not necessarily been because of the bombing we carried out last April. The single most important setback was in Chad. It makes him look foolish in Africa, it alienates his army and it makes the Russians mad at him. But he is

(WILLIAM B. QUANDT)

still in the business of trying to act against American interests.

Los Angeles Times, 4-12:(I)31.

Yitzhak Rabin
*Minister of Defense,
and former Prime Minister,
of Israel*

1

Iran today is a bitter enemy of Israel in its philosophy. I believe that as long as [Iranian leader Ayatollah Ruhollah] Khomeini is in power there is no hope for any change. But, at the same time, allow me to say that for 28 of 37 years Iran was a friend of Israel. If it could work for 28 years . . . why couldn't it once this crazy idea of Shiite fundamentalism is gone?

Oct. 28/
The Washington Post,
10-29:(A)38.

2

[On the violent anti-Israeli protests in the Israeli-occupied West Bank]: We will fight with all our power against any element that tries by violence to upset our full control over Judea, Samaria and the Gaza Strip. I know that the description of what is going on in the territories, the way it is interpreted in the media, is not helping the image of Israel in the world. But I am convinced that above and beyond the temporary problem of an image, the supreme responsibility of our government is to fight the violence in the territories and to use all the means at our disposal to do that.

Before the Knesset
(Parliament), Jerusalem, Dec. 23/
The New York Times, 12-24:1

Hashemi Rafsanjani
*Speaker of
the Iranian Parliament*

3

[U.S.] President Reagan has said he would like to re-establish relations with the Islamic

Republic [Iran]. We believe he is serious. But Reagan is not feeling well. He is old and weak and under a lot of pressure from members of his own party. The Administration is corrupt inside, so it cannot make the right decisions at the right time.

News conference, Teheran,
Jan. 28/USA Today, 2-12:(A)10.

4

[On the continuing kidnappings of foreigners in Lebanon]: The people of Lebanon are so ignored and so oppressed that they have no other defense for themselves other than this.

News conference, Teheran,
Jan. 28/The New York Times, 1-29:1.

Said Rajaie-Khorassani
*Iranian Ambassador to
the United Nations*

5

[On U.S. armed protection of oil tankers against possible Iranian attacks in the Persian Gulf]: We will do our best in order to avoid confrontation. On the other hand, we see that the United States is conducting as many—and as often—provocative acts as possible. These provocations are nothing but dangerous, and we believe that they can easily lead to an all-out war. If the United States continues with this sort of actions taken [attacking suspected Iranian mine-laying ships, for instance], we have to react, and that would be the outbreak of war.

Broadcast interview/
"Meet the Press," NBC-TV, 10-11.

Ronald Reagan
President of the United States

6

[On his covert sale of arms to Iran and the subsequent release of U.S. hostages in Lebanon]: I undertook the original Iran initiative in order to develop relations with those who might assume leadership in a post-Khomeini [Iranian] government. It's clear . . . however, that I let my personal concern for the hostages spill over into the geo-political strategy of reaching out to

WHAT THEY SAID IN 1987

(RONALD REAGAN)

Iran. I asked so many questions about the hostages' welfare that I didn't ask enough about the specifics of the total Iran plan.

Broadcast address to
the nation, Washington, March 4/
The New York Times, 3-5:12.

1

[On the U.S. policy of protecting oil shipping in the Persian Gulf from attacks stemming from the Iran-Iraq war]: Every American President since World War II has understood the strategic importance of this region. It is a region that is a crossroads for three continents and the starting place for the oil that is the lifeblood of much of the world economy, especially those of our allies in Europe. Even more important, this is a region critical to avoiding larger conflict in the tinderbox that is the Middle East, and our role there is essential to building the conditions for peace in that troubled, dangerous part of the world. And it is this objective that has guided us as we have sought to end the brutal war between Iran and Iraq, a war that has gone on for over six and a half terrible years and taken such an awful toll on human life. Peace is at stake here; and so, too, is our own nation's security, and our freedom. Were a hostile power ever to dominate this strategic region and its resources, it would become a choke point for freedom—that of our allies and our own. And that's why we maintain a naval presence there. Our aim is to prevent, not to provoke, wider conflict; to save the many lives that further conflict would cost us.

At memorial service for those killed on
the U.S.S. Stark in attack in
Persian Gulf, Mayport Naval Station, Fla.,
May 22/The New York Times, 5-23:5.

2

I want to speak directly this afternoon on the vital interests of the American people, vital interests that are at stake in the Persian Gulf area. It may be easy for some, after a near-record 54-month economic recovery, to forget just how critical the Persian Gulf is to our national security. But I think everyone in this room, and everyone hearing my voice now, can remember the woeful impact of the Middle East oil crisis of a few years ago: the endless, demoralizing gas lines [due to the cut-off of Middle East oil], the shortages, the rationing, the escalating energy prices, double-digit inflation and the enormous dislocation that shook our economy to its foundations. This same economic dislocation invaded every part of the world, contracting foreign economies, heightening international tensions and dangerously escalating the chances of regional conflicts and wider war. The principal force for peace in the world—the United States and other democratic nations—were perceived as gravely weakened. Our economies and our people were viewed as the captives of oil-producing regimes in the Middle East. This could happen again if Iran and the Soviet Union were able to impose their will upon the friendly Arab states of the Persian Gulf, and Iran was allowed to block the free passage of neutral shipping. But this will not happen again, not while this President serves. I'm determined our national economy will never again be held captive, that we will not return to the days of gas lines, shortages, inflation, economic dislocation and international humiliation. Mark this point well: The use of the vital sea lanes of the Persian Gulf will not be dictated by the Iranians. The lanes will not be allowed to come under the control of the Soviet Union. The Persian Gulf will remain open to navigation by the nations of the world, and I will not permit the Middle East to become a choke point for freedom or a tinderbox of international conflict.

Press briefing, Washington,
May 29/The New York Times, 5-30:5.

Bernard W. Rogers
General (ret.),
United States Army;
Former Supreme Allied
Commander/Europe

3

[On the U.S. military presence in the Persian Gulf to protect shipping from Iranian attack]: I

348

(BERNARD W. ROGERS)

happen to believe that no matter which of the reasons we take for being there, they're all correct. Whether it's freedom of navigation, or trying to keep the Soviets from getting greater influence, or keeping the flow of oil going, or assisting the Gulf nations, any one or a combination of those is sufficient reason to be there. Whether or not the instrument of 11 Kuwaiti ships with American flags is the appropriate one to exercise that, I'm not sure. But what we're attempting to deter is the Iranians from messing over the area.

Interview/USA Today, 10-30:(A)11.

Amnon Rubenstein
Minister of Communications
of Israel

1

[Criticizing Israeli leaders who may have been involved in approving Israeli spying in the U.S.]: They cannot leave us in the dark about this—not any more. To place, or to agree that an Israeli spy should be placed, in the heart of the defense establishment of the superpower that is friendly to us and to endanger U.S. Jews [by using them as spies for Israel]—whoever decided on this is deficient in his decision-making. And I'm speaking in understatement.

Los Angeles Times, 3-9:(I)1.

Dean Rusk
Former Secretary of State
of the United States

2

People sometimes refer to Israel as an ally [of the U.S.]. Israel is not an ally. One becomes an ally through a treaty of alliance, and allies take special pains to try to coordinate their policies as much as possible. I don't think the Israelis have ever wanted that kind of obligation. They prefer to take their chances on going their own way and expecting Jewish support in [the U.S.] to force the United States to go along. So there have been some very disagreeable situations.

Interview, University of Georgia/
Los Angeles Times, 7-20:(I)12.

Ali Khalifa Sabah
Minister of Oil of Kuwait

3

[On the possibility of the U.S. reflagging Kuwaiti oil ships in order to provide protection against attacks on the ships by Iran]: It is up to [the U.S.] Congress and the Administration to decide whether it is in the interest of the United States to reflag Kuwaiti tankers. After giving everybody a chance, we would be satisfied to get our tankers reflagged by the Soviet Union. We will turn to other countries to reflag our ships if [the U.S.] Congress denies us this.

News conference/
The Washington Post,
6-23:(A)12.

Saud Nasir al-Sabah
Kuwaiti Ambassador to
the United States

4

[On the current U.S. military escort of Kuwaiti tankers in the Persian Gulf to protect them from Iranian attack]: Anytime they [the U.S.] see fit that such protection is not useful and would like to withdraw it, let them withdraw it. We are not asking them for the military escort to remain with the ships. It's a U.S. decision; it's not responding to our request. Sometimes we feel very uneasy about this whole thing.

Interview/
U.S. News & World Report,
11-2:40.

Jim Sasser
United States Senator,
D-Tennessee

5

[On the U.S. commitment to protect oil tankers in the Persian Gulf from Iranian attack]: Why should young Americans be defending this oil if it is not valuable enough to our allies that they will try to defend it themselves? Do we see any of them operating in the Gulf? How much is Japan contributing to the protection of its Persian Gulf lifeline? The answer is: nothing at all.

U.S. News & World Report, 6-8:20.

WHAT THEY SAID IN 1987

(JIM SASSER)

1

[Criticizing U.S. President Reagan's plan to protect Kuwaiti oil vessels in the Persian Gulf against attack by Iran]: Many American-owned ships will be left unprotected while we marshal our [naval] forces in defense of a country that has cynically played our interests off against the Soviets . . . Now, I ask, where is the logic, where is the moral backbone behind that approach? . . . If the [Reagan] Administration forgets the lessons of Beirut [where 241 Americans were killed in an attack against a Marine barracks in 1983], we will be condemned to repeat one of the darkest and most painful moments in recent American history.

Broadcast address to
the nation, July 11/
Los Angeles Times, 7-12:(I)27.

Harold H. Saunders
Visiting fellow,
Brookings Institution

2

[On Soviet influence in the Persian Gulf area]: The Soviets are already in the area, and they have interests there. Keeping the Soviets out of the Middle East may be an American interest, but it is not a real-world possibility.

Los Angeles Times, 6-3:(I)17.

Alexander M. Schindler
President, Union of
American Hebrew Congregations

3

[On the anti-Israeli violence in the Israeli-occupied West Bank]: . . . a tense political situation cannot continue indefinitely without some kind of movement, whether it be violent, as we are now witnessing, or peaceful, in the form of political accommodation. Israel simply cannot sit in the territories and wait for peace to come. The status quo sows the seeds of endless conflict . . . and it is a time-bomb ticking away at Israel's vital center.

Dec. 22/The Washington Post,
12-23:(A)10.

Suleiman Majid al-Shaheen
Under Secretary for
Foreign Affairs of Kuwait

4

[Calling on the world to help to militarily protect Kuwait's oil shipping in the Persian Gulf from attacks by Iran]: We have approached all our friends. We don't want any country to have an upper hand with Kuwait. The Soviet Union is ready to cooperate, and it is the right of any country to increase its economic activities . . . We hope the attention of the world, sharing the responsibility of the burden, will contribute to an end to the [Iran-Iraq] war. I think the [UN] Security Council is also going parallel to what we think is the right way. I think that the Iraqis clearly are ready to cooperate in a peaceful settlement. We hope that, with pressure, Iran will, too.

Interview, Kuwait, June 7/
The New York Times, 6-8:6.

Yitzhak Shamir
Prime Minister of Israel

5

[Saying improved Soviet relations with Israel should be a separate issue from Jewish emigration from the Soviet Union]: It is in our interest to have normal relations with [the Soviets]. It is in our interest to change their attitude toward Israel, toward our policy in the Middle East. But I don't think we have to put all that together with the problem of Jewish emigration from Soviet Russia. I don't think the Soviet Jewish people have to be hostages because of our policy in the Middle East.

Radio broadcast, March 26/
The Washington Post, 3-27:(A)30.

6

We are self-confident, and we know that we are on the right track. We have our difficulties, of course. Who has not? But there is no doubt that we are making progress in our economy, in our military strength, in our security. Peace is making progress . . . We have to proceed according to the Camp David [peace] agreements. This is the most realistic way. In spite of all initiatives and trends, nobody has found a better way to get a solution . . . In my opinion, [an international peace conference] will not serve the cause of peace [in the Middle East]. We believe we can only get peace by talks between the parties. An international conference will make things worse.

Interview, Jerusalem/Time, 4-20:36.

1

[For the PLO,] the goal has always been the same. They want *all* of Israel. The PLO was founded years before the Six Day War [during which Israel took the West Bank from Jordan]. Their intention then—and it is still their intention; just listen to them and read their documents—is to liberate *all* of Israel. If we give back [the West Bank], they will use it as a base to strike for the rest of the territory they want, no matter what they say. And they would have an easier time of it because they'd be closer in.

Interview, Jerusalem/
U.S. News & World Report, 6-29:14.

2

[Arguing against an international Middle East peace conference]: The sooner we drop this harmful international-conference proposal from our agenda, the closer we will come to the road that is likely to bring peace—direct [Arab-Israeli] negotiations. Everyone knows my stand—that I am willing to meet with the head of any Arab state. Such meetings can only bring peace closer and improve our ties with our Arab neighbors.

Radio broadcast, July 23/
Los Angeles Times, 7-25:(I)10.

3

[On the Iran-Iraq war]: It is a crazy war, initiated by [Iraqi President] Saddam Hussein—he has to admit it. But the other side is also crazy. We have no reason to wish either of the parties success. I know only one thing: Both of them are enemies of our country.

Interview, Jerusalem, Nov. 17/
The New York Times, 11-18:4.

4

I don't believe territorial compromise is a realistic solution for the conflict between us and the Arabs. Therefore, we have to look for other ways to make peace through other compromises and I think there are ways. If we will come to direct negotiations . . . we will find such solutions.

Washington, Nov. 20/
Los Angeles Times, 11-21:(I)6.

5

Our people . . . fought for 3,000 years for its land, for its freedom, for the right to observe its culture and heritage, and it is certainly continuing to fight. There is no end to this war [against those who want to get rid of Israel], and it is a war in which we must triumph, in each and every generation.

At Hannukah ceremony, Jerusalem,
Dec. 21/Los Angeles Times, 12-26:(I)1.

Farouk Shareh
Foreign Minister of Syria

6

Israel shall never enjoy peace in our region, irrespective of the extent of its military strength, as long as it continues to occupy any part of Arab lands.

At United Nations, New York,
Sept. 30/Los Angeles Times, 10-1:(I)12.

Ariel Sharon
Minister for
Industry and Trade,
and former Minister
of Defense, of Israel

7

[On the scandal of alleged Israeli spying in the U.S.]: Israel does not receive from the U.S. all the information it needs; certainly not. If we compare what we gave over the years with what we got, we without doubt gave much more in much more important fields than we received.

Time, 3-23:31.

WHAT THEY SAID IN 1987

Rashid Shawa
Former Mayor of
Israeli-occupied Gaza

1

[Lamenting the plight of Arabs who live in Israeli-occupied Gaza]: We are sweeping their [Israelis'] streets, washing their dishes, collecting their garbage, being second and third waiters in their restaurants and cleaning up their hospitals. All the dirty work in Israel is being done by us here.

Los Angeles Times, 6-2:(I)14.

George P. Shultz
Secretary of State
of the United States

2

[Saying there may be a basis for the U.S. and Iran to work out a new relationship]: We recognize the Iran revolution as a fact of life. It has its own needs and problems and to a certain extent there is a kind of inherent aspect to Iran's geographical position that causes them to look to other countries for some support. They have a long border with the Soviet Union. They see the Afghan problem on their doorstep. And so those are things that perhaps we can work with them on.

To reporters,
en route to Africa, Jan. 6/
The Washington Post, 1-7:(A)17.

3

While we [the U.S.] have an interest in improving our relations with Iran, the Iranians have an interest in normal dealings with us as well, and until they recognize their own interests and act upon them, our relations are unlikely to improve.

Congressional testimony, Washington/
Los Angeles Times, 2-16:(I)14.

4

[On the revelation of Israeli spying in the U.S.]: I am deeply distressed about [it], and I think it is very disheartening to find that Israel has been spying on the United States. Perhaps it

hurts especially when it's Israel . . . I think the process of investigation, although it is painful, in a democracy has a cleansing effect, and perhaps would help all of us who are deep friends of Israel to handle the situation.

Before House Operations
Subcommittee, Washington, March 11/
The New York Times, 3-12:7.

5

Could [the Soviet Union] be a constructive presence [in the Middle East]? Yes, it could be. And there have been some interesting developments recently. But are they now a constructive presence? No. Look what they do. They encourage the PLO to turn ever more radical and rejectionist. They align themselves with the worst terrorists and tyrants in the region. They refuse to re-establish diplomatic recognition to Israel. Their treatment of Jews and the practice of the Jewish religion in the Soviet Union is not acceptable by any standard.

Before American-Israeli Public
Affairs Committee, Washington,
May 17/The New York Times, 5-20:6.

6

What is making peace [in the Middle East] all about? Well, to me it's really simple. It's sitting down with people who want to make peace, and who are qualified and ready to negotiate. That's how you make peace. So you have to look for people who are qualified and ready. So let's ask a few questions. Is the PLO qualified? Hell, no! . . . Look at what they're just done. Their alliance involves the most violent and radical elements around, and they just put it together again. They showed once again that they don't want peace; they want the destruction of Israel, so they're not qualified. Palestinians? Certainly, they have to be part of peace-making. There are Palestinians who know that the only answer is through a non-violent and responsible approach to direct negotiations for peace and justice. We have to continue to find them, help them and support them.

Before American-Israeli
Public Affairs Committee, May 17/
The Washington Post, 6-4:(A)22.

(GEORGE P. SHULTZ)

1

[On the planned reflagging of Kuwaiti oil vessels so as to provide them with U.S. protection against attacks by Iran]: We believe freedom of navigation through the Gulf and the Strait of Hormuz is of vital interest to us and our allies in the West, and we will stand up for that . . . It is very important to us and to the West generally that that pool of oil, which is basically the largest in the world, not be dominated by hostile powers . . . The United States has no intention and will not get directly involved in the Iran-Iraq war. We are not going to war with either party . . . We are saying that we stand for freedom of navigation in the Persian Gulf and the Strait of Hormuz . . . [But] if our ships are attacked anywhere, including the Persian Gulf, we will defend ourselves. That's not going to war; that's defending ourselves.

To reporters, Washington, May 28/
Los Angeles Times, 5-29:(I)1,12.

2

We don't want to see the Persian Gulf become a place where the Soviet Union has any major role. That oil flows to the West. And so maintaining the ability of that oil to flow is something that we need to step up to . . . Oil is an internationally traded commodity . . . In a sense, it flows into a world oil pool. We are the biggest consumer of oil in the world, and we're the biggest importer of oil in the world, so we have a big stake in all of this.

June 2/Los Angeles Times, 6-3:(I)17.

3

We have grave concerns about policies and practices of the Iranian government outside its borders. While we respect the right of the Iranian people to determine their own form of government, the actions of the government in Teheran—including support of terrorist activities—are inimical to the interests of our country and citizens, as well as to other countries and their citizens.

At United Nations, New York,
July 20/The New York Times,
7-21:6.

4

If you [Israel] are a very small country in an area that is hostile to you, you have to be careful . . . and not allow your desire [for peace] to overtake your common sense. On the other hand, you have to find out if you can devise common-sensical ways to get to that objective . . . because if you never do, that, too, carries tremendous risks . . .

To reporters enroute to Israel,
Oct. 15/Los Angeles Times, 10-17:(I)8.

5

[Criticizing the PLO]: The enemies of peace and purveyors of violence, what have they achieved for the Palestinian people? Nothing. You can achieve more by dialogue, by constructive work . . . I just hope the enemies of peace will have second thoughts and that they will find themselves increasingly in the minority. They are part of the problem that prevents the people they allegedly represent from expressing their views.

News conference,
Jerusalem, Oct. 18/
Los Angeles Times, 10-19:(I)8.

Hanna Siniora
Palestinian newspaper editor

6

[On criticism by other Palestinians of his announced intention to run in the next municipal elections in Jerusalem]: I did it because I care for the future of my people, to focus the issue on the crucial point that will make or break any peaceful resolution of the Palestinian conflict [with Israel]—the future of Jerusalem. I wanted to show Israelis that there are not 135,000 ghosts in East Jerusalem—there are Palestinian people, and they will use tools to exert their political influence if Israel continues to hold on to Jerusalem . . . We have been in the same cycle for too long. I hope my idea [of running in the elections] will break this cycle. I could have stayed silent many times, followed the official [PLO] line and safeguarded my position. [But] I made up my mind that I would undertake to inject something new. Staying silent is being neg-

WHAT THEY SAID IN 1987

ligent of your national duties to start some change.

Interview, Jerusalem/
The Christian Science Monitor,
6-15:11,14.

Earl Sullivan
Political scientist,
University of Cairo (Egypt)

1

[The late Egyptian President Anwar] Sadat was government by shock and surprise. [Current President Hosni] Mubarak is steady as you go. It's partly his personality and partly almost deliberate dullness. His pitch is continuity. He's uninterested in ideology.

The Christian Science Monitor,
10-5:10.

Amir Taheri
Exiled former
editor-in-chief,
"Kayhan" (Iran)

2

If we can understand the solar system and the mentality of the lost tribes of the Amazon, why should we be incapable of understanding what goes on in the mind of [Iranian leader Ruhollah] Khomeini? He is a killer, and for that reason we should not deal with him. We need not buy his oil, or sell him arms, or maintain embassies in Teheran, or invite his representatives to visit Western capitals. The head of a group that has been involved in kidnapping hostages was served tea recently at the Elysee [Presidential] Palace in Paris. These people are international outlaws, and they must be treated as such. What do we have to show for our many efforts at negotiating with them? After all the money given to the kidnappers, and all the arms transferred to them in the past year, they now hold exactly 16 hostages—no fewer than a year ago. And the situation will get worse, because they have confirmed that they can extort millions of dollars for every hostage.

Interview/World Press Review, May:18.

354

John Tower
Former United States
Senator, R-Texas; Chairman,
Tower Commission investigation
of U.S. National Security Council

3

[On President Reagan's covert sale of arms to Iran and the subsequent release of U.S. hostages in Lebanon]: The President made mistakes. I think that's very plain English. The President did make mistakes. A lot of his subordinates made mistakes. I might note that every President has made mistakes from time to time, some of far greater consequences than the ones that President Reagan has made. I think that whole initiative could be justified on the grounds of a geo-strategic opening [to Iran], but that the arms-for-hostage exchange cannot be justified. And it was actually counterproductive of the long-term objective of a geo-strategic opening.

News conference, Washington,
Feb. 26/The New York Times, 2-27:6.

Vernon A. Walters
United States Ambassador/
Permanent Representative
to the United Nations

4

I would think in a general way the Soviet Union would have an interest in stability in [the Persian Gulf] area. The impact of a victorious Iranian regime [in the Iran-Iraq war] would have repercussions within the Soviet Union that would not be in their interests.

Interview, Washington/
The Christian Science Monitor,
6-17:8.

James Webb
Secretary of the Navy
of the United States

5

[On U.S. Naval presence in the Persian Gulf to protect oil tankers from Iranian attack]: When we have faced down the Iranians in a quiet way and make them understand that those

(JAMES WEBB)

waterways are open to all nations . . . and when we have brought the allies, again under their own initiative, to live up to their own obligations [in defending the Gulf], then we can downsize our presence.

USA Today, 9-17:(A)4.

Caspar W. Weinberger
Secretary of Defense
of the United States

1

[Criticizing last year's covert U.S. arms sales to Iran]: I was . . . against the whole idea. I did not think and do not think there's any moderate element in Iran that is still alive, and I think that it was not a good idea in any sense of the term . . . I didn't think there was

anybody we could deal with [in Iran] that was not virulently anti-American.

At Iran-contra hearings, Washington,
July 31/Los Angeles Times, 8-1:(I)24.

Sam Zakhem
United States Ambassador
to Bahrain

2

We would like to see an Iran that improves and builds. An Iran that uses its resources for the good of its people rather than to wage war. We would like to see an Iran that would not meddle in the affairs of its neighbors. We are cognizant of the constructive role that Iran is capable of playing in keeping the [Persian] Gulf safe, and free from Communist domination.

Interview, Manama, Bahrain/
The Christian Science Monitor, 8-25:9.

War and Peace

Oscar Arias
President of Costa Rica

1

Peace is a never-ending process, the work of many decisions by many people in many countries. It is an attitude, a way of life, a way of solving problems and resolving conflicts. It cannot be forced on the smallest nation or enforced by the largest. It cannot ignore our differences or overlook our common interests. It requires us to work and live together. Peace is not only a matter of noble words and Nobel lectures. We have ample words, glorious words, inscribed in the charters of the United Nations, the World Court, the Organization of American States and a network of international treaties and laws. We need deeds that will respect those words, honor those commitments, abide by those laws. We need to strengthen our institutions of peace like the United Nations, making certain they are fully used by the weak as well as the strong. I pay no attention to those doubters and detractors unwilling to believe that a lasting peace can be genuinely embraced by those who march under a different ideological banner or those who are more accustomed to cannons of war than to councils of peace.

Accepting 1987 Nobel
Peace Prize, Oslo, Dec. 10/
The New York Times, 12-11:3.

Mikhail S. Gorbachev
General Secretary,
Communist Party of
the Soviet Union

2

Mankind is beginning to realize that it has had enough of wars, that an end must be put to wars for good. The two world wars, and the grueling cold war, along with minor wars which cost and continue to cost millions of lives, are too exhorbitant a price to pay for adventurism, ambition, disregard for the interests and rights of others, the unwillingness or inability to reckon with reality and with the legitimate right of all nations to make their own choice and seek their own place under the sun.

At U.S. State Department luncheon
in his honor, Washington, Dec. 9/
The Washington Post, 12-10:(A)32.

Leonid A. Ilyin
Vice president,
Soviet Academy of Sciences

3

The aftermath of the Chernobyl [Soviet nuclear power plant accident] was coped with in peacetime and cannot even be compared with what will happen during a nuclear war, which would be a general catastrophe for mankind. There will be as good as no physicians left to treat the victims because out of the 3 million doctors now working in the world, hundreds of thousands will be among those killed. Besides other misfortunes, death from starvation will be quick to come. According to experts, the planet's population has only enough food reserves to last it for three months.

At Congress of
International Physicians for the
Prevention of Nuclear War, Moscow,
May 31/Los Angeles Times, 6-1:(I)11.

Jesse L. Jackson
Civil-rights leader;
Candidate for the 1988
Democratic Presidential nomination

4

I think we ought to modernize our approach to the world . . . It is significant that we have adequate and effective weapons in the field, but our real weapons are in our minds . . . The great breakthroughs for peace and security came through leadership initiatives . . . One cannot do that with a modern weapon; one has

(JESSE L. JACKSON)

to do it with a developed mind and a will for peace.

At Democratic Presidential
candidate debate sponsored by
Stop The Arms Race political-action
committee, Washington, Sept. 27/
The Christian Science Monitor, 9-29:3.

Olusegun Obasanjo
Former Head of State
of Nigeria

1

Can we be secure when our adversaries are insecure? Shouldn't we now be considering security in terms of what we call *common* security—which makes you secure because your seeming adversary feels secure? You cannot talk of peace without security. If you feel threatened, you are not going to really feel in harmony with your neighbor.

Interview, New York/
The Christian Science Monitor,
3-18:16.

Daniel Ortega
President of Nicaragua

2

The world cries out for peace, a vital necessity of all nations . . . To speak of peace is to speak of the health of our nations, to speak of the life of our nations, to speak of the future of our nations. And when we fight for peace and desire peace, it is because we want to create conditions that will allow us to meet the most vital needs of our nations; that is, the problems which particularly affect the health of children, mothers, men and workers.

Videotape prepared by
Pan American Health Organization,
April 5/The Washington Post, 4-22:(A)18.

Ronald Reagan
President of the United States

3

Teddy Roosevelt reminded us long ago that the cry of the weakling counts for little in the move toward peace, but the call of a just man armed is potent. To put Teddy in modern terms, speak softly but keep the battleship *Iowa* close at hand.

Before American Legion/
USA Today, 2-11:(A)5.

4

[Addressing visiting Soviet leader Mikhail Gorbachev]: Like the people of your country, we [Americans] believe our country should be strong, but we desire peace. Have no doubt about that. The longing for peace runs deep here, second only to our fervency for the preservation of our liberty. Americans believe people should be able to disagree and still respect one another, still live in peace with one another. That is the spirit, the democratic spirit, that I will bring to our meetings.

Washington, Dec. 8/
The New York Times, 12-9:6.

George P. Shultz
Secretary of State
of the United States

5

No one . . . improves the chances for peace by doing nothing at all, by just sitting around. Those who are reluctant to explore new ideas, or even revisit old ones, have an obligation to offer something different as an alternative to the status quo.

At Weizmann Institute of Science,
Jerusalem, Oct. 18/
The Christian Science Monitor, 10-19:12.

Charles Z. Wick
Director, United States
Information Agency

6

We need not be reminded that, if there be a war [between the West and the Soviet Union], there will be no winners. The loser will lose, and the winner will lose. That will be the ultimate penalty for miscalculation.

Washington, March 13/
The Washington Post, 3-26:(A)26.

357

PART THREE

General

The Arts

Andreas Alariesto
Finnish painter

1

I never called myself an artist in the beginning. I just always had a very, very strong will to save stories and life on pictures. So I painted and painted. For a long time people told me I was wasting my time; whenever I picked up my brush they would say, "Andreas is painting again; he is doing nothing." Some have changed their minds.

Interview/
The Christian Science Monitor,
7-21:19.

Mario Bellini
Architect and designer

2

A design career is a process of learning better and better what you know instinctively. I designed [a bench of Indian sandstone] in a few moments. But, of course, it took me 25 years to do it in five minutes.

Interview/
The New York Times,
6-25:21.

Allan Bloom
Author;
Professor of philosophy,
University of Chicago

3

There are plenty of opportunities in our society to see the advantages and pleasures of business, the law and medicine. But it's really hard to find living examples of a serious intellectual life . . . We don't have to teach kids that television exists. But the joys of classical music or classical literature—those are things that don't come immediately on the breezes.

Interview, Chicago/
Los Angeles Times,
6-10:(V)6.

Mario Botta
Architect

4

All architecture inflicts violence on nature. But I'm not talking about a negative violence. It is, rather, a rapport, a reciprocal tension. Nature needs architecture to become a more human landscape, so one creates a mutual relationship. I have too much respect for nature to try to imitate it—but only through confrontation can nature and architecture be given their true value.

Interview/Horizon, October:66.

Hortense Calisher
President,
American Academy and
Institute of Arts and Letters

5

In some countries—for instance in Russia—what writers write is important; so important that they can be shot for it. And, while I don't crave that, I would like my country to realize, as it sometimes does, that art has a real connection with life. We still haven't the recognized connection with a large part of our nation.

Interview, New York/
The Christian Science Monitor,
2-19:21.

Leo Castelli
Art promoter and
gallery owner

6

[On today's art scene]: I never thought it would come to this. I've always believed in development, one movement following another—the Cubists on the heels of the Fauves, Minimal after Pop, and so forth. But everything today is very much in flux. There's so much happening now that it's difficult to sort things out.

The New York Times,
2-5:20.

WHAT THEY SAID IN 1987

Howard Chapnick
President, Black Star
photographic agency

1

In photojournalism, we are seeing more manipulated, preconceived imagery, where the impact of the annual-report, commercial kind of photography is being transmitted to journalistic photography . . . As a result, the pictures have very strong graphic quality and great imagery, but the substance and content are secondary. It is making images for the sake of making beautiful, slick images. Many picture editors are asking photographers also to light their color pictures. Once we introduce artificial lighting, the spontaneity of the real moment is lost. The great era of candid photography is being threatened by this manipulated, art-directed, jazzily lit, pre-conceived, posed imagery. It is rare you get a picture of anybody who *moves* in magazine photography today.

Los Angeles Times, 3-26:(I)24.

Edo de Waart
Conductor,
Minnesota Orchestra

2

Nothing in the arts has ever been accomplished with thinking whether it will sell.

Newsweek, 1-5:54.

Elliot W. Eisner
Professor of
education and art,
Stanford University

3

Artists speak to us in a language that carries meaning that cannot be conveyed through words. Will our children be able to understand what they have to say? Even more, will they know their messages exist?

The Christian Science Monitor,
4-24:19.

Vladimir Feltsman
Exiled Soviet pianist

4

Russia has a number of outstanding musicians, no question about it. Maybe the problem is they have too many musicians, artists and writers. They think they're rich with them, and when they lose a few [who flee the country for the West], they think it's no big loss. But they are losing the best people—Rudolf Nureyev, Mikhail Baryshnikov—the pride of the Russian culture.

Interview/USA Today, 11-13:(A)11.

Allen Ginsberg
Poet

5

Artistic marginal people are unacknowledged legislators of the race, picking up new vibrations and absorbing them. It's a great social function. It's a great job. It doesn't pay so well, but the rewards of work well done and the quality of feeling are amazing. Yet everybody goes down the same hole of old-age sickness and death. So it doesn't get you anywhere in the long run, except you might do others some good by enriching their environment.

Interview/
U.S. News & World Report,
2-16:74.

Nikki Giovanni
Poet

6

I reject the concept of mentorship. It might work in the business world, but in the arts, it can't work and never has. No matter how often people want to say, well, so-and-so made it because so-and-so helped him or her . . . it just isn't so. The work had to be there. The talent has to be there. You're doing it, and you cannot let anyone take that away from you. All you have is yourself, and if you don't own yourself there's nothing there. I reject the concept of role models. The whole system is largely overblown.

Interview/Writing, January:14.

Mary Gordon
Author

7

You don't see a lot of Catholics in American writing, and that's not an accident. The whole

(MARY GORDON)

history of the arts has a shocking absence of Catholics. That kind of creativity was not valued in the American Catholic Church; it was seen as a threat because it would get you outside the parish, open you to the world and let you think in ways that could be threatening and dangerous. I don't think I could have been a writer if my father hadn't been a Jew.

Interview/
U.S. News & World Report,
10-5:74.

Frank Hodsoll
Chairman,
National Endowment for
the Arts of the United States

1

[Saying he does not believe high ticket costs are pricing the arts out of business]: I don't think ticket prices generally are the problem. The Metropolitan Opera, the Los Angeles Music Center, they fill up the hall. It's the place to be. I do think there is a major problem with regard to the cultural heritage and those things that lie outside the popular culture in America. There are whole segments of our population that simply don't go. And I don't think it's because they can't afford it. Rock concerts cost $40. You go to the Kennedy Center in Washington, in a city that's well over 50 per cent black; I was there the other night for the Joffrey Ballet . . . It has 2,000 seats and there were 10 to 20 black people in the audience, and barely any young people. People are making choices not to go.

News conference,
Salt Lake City, April 30/
Los Angeles Times, 5-2:(VI)6.

John Paul II
Pope

2

[Addressing entertainment-industry executives and artists]: . . . you must cultivate the integrity consonant with your own human dig-

nity. You are more important yourselves than success, more valuable than any budget. Do not let your work drive you blindly; for if work enslaves you, you will soon enslave your art. Who you are and what you do are too important for that to happen. Do not let money be your sole concern, for it, too, is capable of enslaving art as well as souls.

Universal City, Calif.,
Sept. 15/Daily Variety, 9-16:9.

Paul Johnson
British author and journalist

3

Perhaps the most important thing that will happen in the 21st century is a rebirth of classical cultural values and civilization—after a century of frenzied experiment which hasn't really produced very much.

Interview, London/
The Christian Science Monitor,
3-12:17.

Thomas Lawton
Art scholar;
Former director,
Freer Gallery of
Smithsonian Institution

4

There are so many demands put on museum directors now. There simply isn't a moment left to intellectually refresh yourself. You can go on being a PR man, and a fund-raiser and an after-dinner speaker. But at some point you have to go back to the objects and the research, which is the core of any great museum.

Oct. 1/The New York Times, 10-2:18.

Norman Mailer
Author

5

When people start asking what something's about, the critics come along and start saying, "It's a tough-guy murder mystery with elements of horror, or it's a surrealistic novel that derives from the *roman noir* of the French," so

363

WHAT THEY SAID IN 1987

(NORMAN MAILER)

forth and so on . . . That's all very nice, but you try to write something that defies—no, not defies, that straddles—categories. Categories are just critics' attempts to bring order to a complex esthetic universe. I've always resisted that, because I feel it's up to the working artist or craftsman to create their own order. If they pay too much attention to categories, that can really get in the way. You see that happening to young movie-makers all the time. They confuse their own opportunity to create order with an order created generations before, and sacrifice creation for homage.

Interview/Film Comment, August:13.

Alexander Melamid
Painter

1

There's no question that painting is visual, but it depends on talk no less than any other part of our activity, even love. Love talk. The only universal medium in human life is words. It's an illusion that we can make art without words. Modern art is based to some degree on this illusion, but it's a pure lie.

Interview, New York/
The New York Times, 10-2:18.

Melina Mercouri
Minister of Culture
of Greece; Former actress

2

All is politics, even cultural exchanges. But I am here to work for friendship between people. Cultural exchanges are a new language that we must explore. In the day in which we live, with ideologies and war everywhere, perhaps the artists of the world can do more than soldiers.

Washington, Oct. 1/
The New York Times, 10-2:10.

3

I am a political person; I am not artistic. What is art, if it is not politics? Art is not apart

from life, it is everywhere, even in the workers in an industry. Art is a political act.

Interview, Washington/
The Christian Science Monitor, 10-23:21.

Elena Obraztsova
Soviet opera singer

4

Politics are politics and art is art. The two shouldn't be mixed; it's impossible . . . When politics helps art, that's fine. But no politician can do as much as an artist can. Everybody talks about world peace. Well, the first people who can help this are the artists. Beauty is the thing that will save the world.

Interview, New York/
The New York Times, 11-21:10.

Anthony Quinn
Actor, Painter

5

[On his painting and sculpting]: The Spanish have a wonderful word: *duende* . . . the demon that's inside of your gut. He drives you and drives you. You don't know why you're driven . . . If I don't get up here and paint, if I don't get up here and work on some kind of sculpture, I don't feel that I'm living. The *duende* says, "Come on: *Do* it! *Do* it! *Do* it!"

Interview, New York/
USA Today, 8-5:(D)2.

Georg Solti
Music director,
Chicago Symphony Orchestra

6

Nothing is [culturally] easy in these times. Bloody TV and movies run everything. People don't want to hear music. They want to sell condoms on TV.

Interview, Newport Beach, Calif./
Los Angeles Times, 2-8:(Calendar)4.

Andrei Voznesensky
Soviet poet

7

. . . I'm so for art—not realistic art, but very modern art, experimental art, because this art will give us a new kind of thinking. When

(ANDREI VOZNESENSKY)

you see classics like [the paintings of] Salvador Dali, or Picasso, or my friend Robert Rauschenberg, you [perhaps] cannot agree with them, but immediately they give you another possible [way] to look at the world. That is why I am fighting in Russia for modern art—not because I am an artist but because these modern paintings [and works of] literature show people how to think [about] economics, politics and agriculture.

Interview, Cambridge, Mass./
The Christian Science Monitor, 4-17:16.

Silvia Williams
Director,
National Museum of
African Art, Washington

1

It is the art historian's paradise when you track everything right back to the earliest moment. You don't hit that often. If you achieve it once in your life, either on a minor or major scale, it keeps you going, and you never forget it.

Interview, Washington/
The Washington Post,
9-28:(B)1.

Journalism

Howard H. Baker, Jr.
Chief of Staff to President
of the United States
Ronald Reagan

1

There is a difference in [Washington news] reporting [today compared with the 1950s], and that difference is television. There's a higher premium on the spectacular now, and that really began with the Kefauver hearings. Television discovered the value of conflict and controversy and has a way to make that conflict more vivid than the printed page could do. The players aren't very different, just the stage.

Interview, Washington/
The New York Times,
5-12:12.

Alexander Baranov
Editor,
"Sotsialisticheskaya Industria"
(Soviet Union)

2

As editors, we have the right under [Soviet] law to publish what we see fit and to write what we consider necessary. There are no directives from the upper echelons of the [Communist] Party or from government organizations that pressure us to write in a particular way or on a particular subject. But we are not free from criticism . . . In [Soviet leader Mikhail Gorbachev's] discussions with media leaders, he leaves the impression: "We will not tell you what to write. You know how and what to write. What we need for you to show is initiative." The editors then decide what they will or will not do regarding coverage of any policies or problems. The editors are members of the Central Committee [of the Communist Party], and they have quite a bit of authority.

Interview/
World Press Review,
April:16.

Joseph R. Biden, Jr.
United States Senator,
D-Delaware; Candidate for the 1988
Democratic Presidential nomination

3

The only thing worse than bad taste on your [the media's] part would be for us to start to meddle in your First Amendment right to exercise your bad taste.

USA Today, 5-11:(A)10.

David Broder
Journalist

4

As reporters, we do the best with the information that we have, but that information is always less than complete, and in some cases it's just really a bare sketch of what the reality is. If we were honest with our readers, we'd say, at the end of each story, "subject to revision and amplification" . . . I think the readers sometimes expect more from newspapers. The very fact that something is in print gives it a sort of authority in people's minds, and the fact that it's something that comes into their home every day, that they have accepted as part of their lives, involves a relationship of trust. Judge us critically, but judge us by realistic standards. And, realistically, our best efforts will almost always fall short of the truth.

Interview/USA Today, 8-13:(A)13.

Les Brown
Editor-in-chief,
"Channels" magazine

5

I'm one of those who doesn't believe the networks will lose their newscasts. While local stations can interview the President or have people in the Senate, they are really not equipped . . . They don't have the expertise, especially for the international news and the

(LES BROWN)

very sophisticated stuff. Just because local news is more popular doesn't mean it's better.

The Washington Post, 2-9:(A)4.

Richard Burt
United States Ambassador
to West Germany

1

If there's a problem with the electronic [news] media in this country [the U.S.], in my view, it's superficiality . . . The Germans go into far greater detail . . . They will put on prime-time a discussion program where they will go into great detail on a problem like the environment or U.S.-Soviet arms control—hours of talking-head shots, which the networks in this country would not tolerate . . . We simply don't understand the impact it [the electronic media] is having on our lives. I'm quite convinced that because of television, our attention span is shorter than it once was. There's a tendency for news today to be sequential in nature, and people have forgotten the problems that were raised the week before. As a result, there is a lack of continuity in understanding news. There is a lack of context. It concerns me.

Interview, Los Angeles,
Feb. 24/Daily Variety, 2-26:40.

Jimmy Carter
Former President
of the United States

2

There have been a few Presidents in my lifetime who have been treated with kid gloves by the press. I would say [Franklin] Roosevelt, [Dwight] Eisenhower, [John] Kennedy, and [Ronald] Reagan. And all the rest of us have been treated quite harshly by the press: [Harry] Truman, [Richard] Nixon, [Lyndon] Johnson, [Gerald] Ford, and me. I have never understood the difference, but there is a sharp difference . . . It still hasn't been studied adequately, but the sum total of it is that I was the one who failed

in my dealings with the press, in spite of my best efforts. I never was able to form a reasonable relationship with the press.

Interview, Washington/
The Christian Science Monitor, 6-5:6.

3

The White House press corps, in the main, are a bunch of prima donnas. I thought that kids in high schools asked better questions when I was President.

Broadcast interview,
USA Today, 6-22:(D)2.

John Chancellor
Commentator, NBC News

4

[TV news] programs ought not to try to be *everybody's* news program but take into account that people already know the basic elements in the news. The evening news should explain, interpret, analyze those stories.

The Christian Science Monitor,
12-1:22.

Charles
Prince of Wales

5

The thing that appalls me about the newspaper business is the number of trees it consumes.

To reporter
at a reception, London, Oct. 29/
The New York Times, 11-2:7.

Connie Chung
Broadcast journalist,
NBC-TV

6

What I like to see in [news] anchors is a naturalness. I don't like anchors who look like they're posturing or who look unnatural. I think you have to convey a feeling of confidence, credibility, fairness and balance. But I think the test of a good anchor is not when he or she is doing a half-hour program but when a tough story breaks and the anchor has to ad-lib. I've

(CONNIE CHUNG)

done that, and I find it most difficult because then the adrenalin starts going and your heart starts beating in your ears—*poom, poom*! It's beating so loudly you can't even hear yourself talk. That's when you really show your mustard.

Interview/Emmy Magazine,
July-Aug.:44.

Walter Cronkite
Former anchorman,
CBS News

1

. . . we've got to reassume the responsibility that is ours on the networks to help inform and educate the public. I think it'd be great if the evening news broadcast, for instance, were unsponsored and unrated. But that's like dreaming of nuclear disarmament next Friday afternoon. It ain't gonna happen.

Interview, New York/
Los Angeles Times, 1-1:(VI)16.

2

I think there's a different philosophical thrust in the production of CBS News [now]. There is a feeling that it should be more interesting, more entertaining. I think they are fairly hard-hitting when they're reporting the *news*. But there is certainly the intention to lighten the broadcast with more feature material. That could be interpreted as being softer.

Interview/
The Christian Science Monitor,
12-1:21.

3

I worry about the fact that more and more people are getting all their news from television. There's no way in the world that any network news can tell you in 22 minutes all you need to know about your world that day. If you're going to be well-informed, you've got to be a multi-media customer.

Interview/
The Christian Science Monitor,
12-1:22.

Morton Dean
Broadcast journalist

4

Over the years, young people like yourselves have come to me seeking advice about how to break into the business. I always ask the same question and I always get the same answer. I ask, "What do you want to do in the business?" What do you think the answer is? It is always the same answer, the same answer that two-thirds of the recent Miss Americas have given about careers: "I want to be an anchorperson." And they want it now. The "anchorman syndrome" is such that rarely do these people say that they want to become an anchorperson in the old-fashioned way by earning it, by learning the tools of the reporter's trade, by rising up through the ranks, by covering the police beat in a small town, then moving on from that.

At Ohio
Wesleyan University commencement/
The Christian Science Monitor,
6-15:24.

Jerry Della Femina
Advertising-agency executive

5

[On why *The Reader's Digest* has such a large circulation]: A lot of its readers are of an age where they forget to cancel.

Newsweek, 1-12:8.

Ken Dodd
Executive editor,
"The Guardian" (Britain)

6

[Criticizing a British court ruling prohibiting the press from publishing excerpts of a revealing spy memoir by a former British agent]: [The decision] indicates this country is probably the least free and least democratic of any Western European country today. [The ruling's] potential for repression of the British press is enormous.

July 30/The New York Times, 7-31:7.

Sam Donaldson
White House correspondent,
ABC News

1

If you send me to cover a pie-baking contest on Mother's Day, I'm going to ask dear old Mom why she used artificial sweetener in violation of the rules and, while she's at it, could I see the receipt for the apples to prove that she didn't steal them. I maintain that if Mom has nothing to hide, no harm will have been done. But the questions should be asked. Too often, Mom, and Presidents—behind those sweet faces—turn out to have stuffed a few rotten apples into the public barrel.

Newsweek, 3-2:59.

2

[On the frequency of quick, shouting questions by journalists to President Reagan as he rushes from one place to another]: There's more of a need for it. Once in a while we shouted at [former President Jimmy] Carter, but no one really remembers shouting to Jimmy Carter. You could talk to him. You could ask him, "What do you think about . . .?" Most of [President Reagan's] answers are answers that in effect say, "Don't bother me, boy, I'm busy," as opposed to, "Here is a considered view from the top." I wish it weren't this way. If you ask, "Is this [shouting quick questions at Reagan] really a service to your viewers in watching democracy work?" I would say it is a very poor service. But it's all we have. I don't like it. I think it stinks.

The New York Times, 3-9:10.

3

The only use [the Reagan Administration] want of us [in the press] is as a conduit. If we don't docilely accept that fate, then they try to use us as foil to generate hostility to us and therefore support for them. It's Nixonian that way. The reason I keep excepting Ronald Reagan is not that I don't know he, too, has these feelings of frustration about the press . . . but that most of his public life . . . I've felt he has generally understood the role of the press.

Interview, Washington/
The Christian Science Monitor, 4-16:29.

Robert K. Dornan
United States Representative,
R-California

4

I have had my tensions with the press over the years, [but] those who risk their lives to bring us the news from combat areas . . . should be honored and remembered by their fellow Americans.

Congressional testimony,
Washington, June 18/
The Washington Post, 6-19:(A)6.

Douglas Edwards
Broadcast journalist,
CBS News

5

[On the high salaries paid to TV news anchormen]: Something got loose here a couple of years ago when anchormen could make $2.5-million a year. Of course, I suppose they could argue, "What good is happiness if you can't have money?" I don't subscribe to that exactly, but I understand the point.

Interview/
Los Angeles Times,
9-12:(VI)11.

Ray Ekpu
Editor,
"Newswatch" magazine
(Nigeria)

6

[On the government's closing down his magazine]: Publishing in the Third World is like walking through a mine field while blindfolded. When government can act by whim, it becomes more difficult to know where to stop, to see the safe cut-off points.

Los Angeles Times, 4-28:(I)1.

Marlin Fitzwater
Assistant-designate to
President of the United States
Ronald Reagan for
Press Relations

7

A good [Presidential] Press Secretary doesn't have to [lie to the press]. There are always

(MARLIN FITZWATER)

times when you have to say, "I can say nothing for national-security reasons," or "I can't tell you anything because we're still working on a decision that hasn't come out yet." There are ticklish times when you want to run out the back door, but I don't think there are any reasons to lie.

Interview/
The Washington Post,
1-16:(B)4.

1

I like my job. It forces an intellectual exercise in a way I've never had before. The challenge to learn about issues in a fast and thorough way is greater than I ever anticipated . . . I have to know more than I talk about. It's like running down an alley on every issue—you know you will get to the end and you will have to say, "I don't know any more." That's a very humiliating experience.

The Christian Science Monitor,
3-13:6.

Steve Friedman
Executive producer,
"USA Today's" TV newscast

2

[On his forthcoming TV version of the *USA Today* newspaper]: I know people call the newspaper "McPaper" [after the McDonald's fast-food restaurants]. I have no problems with them calling the television version "McTelecast." The paper is a quick read; we will be a quick watch.

Interview/
The Christian Science Monitor,
12-1:22.

Fred W. Friendly
Professor emeritus of journalism,
Columbia University;
Former president, CBS News

3

[Criticizing CBS for cutting the budget and personnel of its news division]: They can fire [veteran correspondent] Ike Pappas, and six

months from now they could say, "See, it didn't hurt at all." But the way you judge a news team is how it acts in a crisis. When President [John] Kennedy was shot, the country was on the edge of chaos. CBS held the country together with hundreds of reporters in five continents reporting on the meaning of it. They're (CBS) losing money? That's a big myth. They're just not making as much as they might make. But they're not cash registers or pork bellies. They're licensed to operate in the public interest, and that's all been forgotten.

The New York Times, 3-14:18.

4

[Lamenting today's news broadcasts]: The public sees a 90-second piece on arms control . . . two minutes on AIDS . . . the newscasters giggle at each other. It looks like news. It smells like news. But it's so thin, it's not.

At House subcommittee hearing,
Washington, April 28/
Los Angeles Times, 4-29:(VI)8.

Edward O. Fritts
President,
National Association
of Broadcasters

5

[Criticizing the Congressional vote to make the broadcast Fairness Doctrine into law]: We regret the House saw fit to join the Senate in voting to legislate government intervention in the presentation of controversial issues by broadcast journalists. Broadcasters are committed to fairness, but we believe government second-guessing of the content of news and public-affairs programming is unconstitutional. If the Fairness Doctrine becomes law, we will immediately challenge its constitutionality in court.

June 3/Los Angeles Times, 6-4:(VI)11.

Julian Goodman
Former chairman,
National Broadcasting Company

6

The Fairness Doctrine needs to be eliminated, not made into law. Putting it into law, re-

(JULIAN GOODMAN)

quiring that all sides of a controversial question be covered, puts editorial judgments into the hands of a government department. Fairness should be decided by trained journalists.

At House subcommittee
hearing, Washington,
April 28/Los Angeles Times,
4-29:(VI)8.

Fred Graham
Broadcast journalist

1

[On his being fired by CBS News along with other on- and off-air personnel as a cost-cutting move]: I think the layoffs are a symptom of something deeper. To me, it's not altogether a coincidence that I'm going to [work at] a local station [in Nashville, Tenn.]. I think that maybe that's where the future is in broadcasting. [In the years ahead,] we may be seeing network news operations becoming a little more like a wire service—like the Associated Press—and it may be that those of us in the good local stations will be more like the good local papers around the country.

Los Angeles Times,
3-11:(VI)10.

2

[On the high salaries paid to TV network news personalities]: I think some of these executives in TV in recent years were pushovers for these people. I think it started with this high, wide and handsome style that they had. Some of our executives at CBS were among them. [Former CBS News president] Van Gordon Sauter invented the term "infotainment," you know. A part of that was a pretty swinging style with money contracts. I was a beneficiary of that for a while and I didn't put it down. But I think there is a cause and effect here. When you bring entertainment values to news, this is what happens . . . Before [TV journalist] Barbara Walters [who commands a million-dollar salary] the mentality was that a journalist, for so many years, was

this scruffy ink-stained type with a pencil behind the ear. I think that when you confuse the journalistic values of Hollywood with the news, you can't blame anyone when the price goes up.

Los Angeles Times, 3-12:(VI)12.

George J. Green
Executive vice president,
Hearst Magazines;
Former president,
"The New Yorker" magazine

3

I think the magazine that's only serious and literary has little chance in this era. Who has the time to read long articles? People have so many options. Where 20 years ago the talk at dinner parties might be about what was in *The New Yorker* that week, now it's about TV and movies.

Los Angeles Times, 2-12:(I)30.

Gary Hart
Former United States
Senator, D-Colorado;
Candidate for
the 1988 Democratic
Presidential nomination

4

[Criticizing the press for spying on him and suggesting he had a recent extra-marital affair]: You, ladies and gentlemen [of the press], have the honor of leading the only industry singled out for protection under the Constitution of the United States. That signifies enormous power. But it also places upon each of you a very heavy responsibility. In that spirit, I hope you'll ask yourselves some searching questions: about what is right and what is truthful; about the propriety of a newspaper conducting a questionable and inadequate surveillance of one Presidential candidate; about whether the urgency of meeting a deadline is subordinate to hearing the truth; and about whether it's right or good journalism to draw an extraordinary

(GARY HART)

conclusion before hearing some rather ordinary facts.

Before American Newspaper
Publishers Association, New York,
May 5/The New York Times, 5-6:16.

Jesse L. Jackson
Civil-rights leader;
Candidate for the 1988
Democratic Presidential nomination

1

I have an analysis of the role the media plays in the power structure of this country. Our press is privately owned by wealthy people who have substantial investments in the world economy. And they have power without accountability. Any publisher can make a political judgment and unleash the hounds—or redirect the hounds. That power is very real.

Interview/Mother Jones, October:30.

Peter Jennings
Anchorman,
"World News Tonight,"
ABC-TV

2

[On TV news programs]: This is a business that is incorrectly, unfairly and unwisely, I think, judged by ratings rather than content. You get the ratings every Tuesday morning. If they're not good, Tuesday mornings are a little depressing. But by one o'clock, you've gone back to work and decided you can't spend the rest of the day worrying. I don't keep the ratings around to stare at all day.

Interview, New York/
Emmy Magazine, March-April:54.

3

The information business is an absolutely key component of democracy. It's also a key component of Fascism, Communism and suppression of various ilks around the world. That should tell us something about the great value of having a free press.

Interview, New York/
Emmy Magazine, March-April:56.

Marvin Kalb
Moderator, "Meet the Press,"
NBC-TV; Director-designate,
Barone Center on the Press,
Politics and Public Policy,
Kennedy School of Government,
Harvard University

4

There's a perception on the part of policy-makers that the press is one of the things they just have to put up with . . . They hold the institution of journalism in low regard.

Interview, Washington/
The Christian Science Monitor,
4-30:28.

5

Press people like to think of themselves as independent, as above the fray. Yet, if you widen your lens and examine the process with some dispassion, you must almost inevitably come to the conclusion that major press figures are inextricably part of the process of politics and governance.

The New York Times, 9-17:9.

6

[On the controversy about a new book by reporter Bob Woodward in which he reveals a possible death-bed admission by CIA Director William Casey that he knew of a diversion of funds in the U.S. Iran-contra scandal, an admission Woodward and his newspaper, *The Washington Post*, withheld even during the Congressional Iran-contra hearings]: Are we then to use two standards of judgment? Is a book fact to be seen one way and a newspaper fact to be seen another? Are there different standards to be applied? For me, there has to be a single standard of truth. If it's true in a book, it's true in a newspaper story.

The New York Times, 9-30:12.

Michael Kinsley
Editor,
"The New Republic"

7

[On *USA Today*'s fifth anniversary]: No one who reads a real newspaper is going to rely on

(MICHAEL KINSLEY)

USA Today. But then, most places in the country don't have access to a real newspaper.

Time, 10-12:63.

Ted Koppel
Anchorman,
"Nightline," ABC-TV

1

There is only one thing that keeps some of us still working at the network, and that is a commitment on the part of the network to do things in a more professional fashion, to use the extraordinary resources that only exist at a network. That includes overseas bureaus; that includes a lot of old and tried-and-true producers and correspondents, who may not be as pretty as they once were but who sure have institutional memory, who can put things into context; that includes a vast library of hundreds of thousands of tapes that some of these newer organizations simply do not have. [But] if all the networks are going to be doing is looking at the bottom line, then they are going to find that, for a while, they will seem to be competing economically very well. But there will be a gradual erosion, and I would not want to be part of it.

Interview, Washington/
The Christian Science Monitor,
9-16:21.

Bill Kovach
Editor, "Atlanta Journal
and Constitution";
Former Washington bureau chief,
"The New York Times"

2

[On Presidential press conferences]: The press has got to find a way to examine carefully, deeply the President's policy positions without appearing to badger him. They've got to figure out a way to ask tough, sensitive questions and follow-ups without that whining, accusatory tone that, instead of making it a press conference, makes it a contest of personalities.

The Washington Post, 3-19:(A)4.

Lewis H. Lapham
Editor,
"Harper's" magazine

3

[On writers at *The New Yorker* who are protesting new editor Robert Gottlieb's ideas for changes in the magazine]: The writers want everything to stay like 1956, and I'm sympathetic. They have been very comfortable for a very long time. So it's like the first day Mary Poppins arrives on the job; she makes them take their medicine, and Gottlieb's going to make them cut their articles. But the truth is that magazines need periodic revision. It's good for them.

The New York Times, 1-16:18.

Patrick J. Leahy
United States Senator,
D-Vermont

4

I sometimes feel that [Congress'] way of getting intelligence briefings might be better if they took the newspapers, marked them Top Secret, and handed them to us. First, we'd get the intelligence material in a more timely fashion. Second, it would be more complete. And third, there'd be a crossword puzzle.

USA Today, 3-30:(A)4.

Lee Kuan Yew
Prime Minister of Singapore

5

We do not want our journalists to model themselves on the Americans or the British and take an adversarial, anti-establishment role. Our journalists have a responsibility to help, not hinder, national unity and solidarity.

Los Angeles Times, 5-4:(I)6.

Bill Leonard
Former president,
CBS News

6

Congress has traditionally made [TV] its business because TV gets its license through the

(BILL LEONARD)

FCC, which is a child of Congress. But government has no business in [TV] journalism. We ought to be free to practice it without even a helping hand from them. Beware of the smile on the face of the tiger.

Interview/USA Today, 4-30:(A)9.

G. Gordon Liddy
*Former Special Assistant to
the Secretary of the Treasury
of the United States
for Organized Crime;
Convicted Watergate conspirator*

1

The press is like the peculiar uncle you keep in the attic—just one of those unfortunate things.

Newsweek, 1-12:8.

Nackey Loeb
*Publisher, Manchester (N.H.)
"Union Leader"*

2

We print more letters in the paper than any other paper in the country. We allow people to spit in our eye, so to speak. If they disagree with us, they can tell us so in no uncertain terms. We want people to be involved and to be concerned. This is what the Founding Fathers had in mind when they established the government of this country, and I think that one of the dangers in this country is that a lot of people don't really care.

Interview/USA Today, 5-22:(A)9.

Edward J. Markey
*United States Representative,
D-Massachusetts*

3

[On the Congressional vote to make the broadcast Fairness Doctrine into law]: The vote sends two powerful messages—one to the American public and the other to President Reagan. it tells the public that Congress is back and that the public-interest standard will be restored to

communications policy; and it tells President Reagan that he can no longer gut the concept of broadcasters' public-interest responsibilities . . . The Fairness Doctrine is not a censorship doctrine. [The policy] only requires broadcasters to do what any good broadcaster would do anyway—address important issues in a fair and impartial manner.

*Washington, June 3/
Los Angeles Times, 6-4:(VI)11.*

Eileen McNamara
*Reporter, "Boston Globe";
Winner, Nieman Fellowship
of Harvard University*

4

It's been said that a newspaper reporter's job is to comfort the afflicted and to afflict the comfortable. Tell the stories of ordinary people, the people that reporters, on our best days, remember that we're there to serve. Newspapers nowadays are filled with young careerists, kids in pinstripe suits with master's degrees who don't know how to cover a three-alarm fire. And don't want to learn. They all want to be [investigative reporters like] Woodward and Bernstein [and uncover sensational scandals]. Better they should go into another line of work because they have no feel for people. The worst thing that happened was when somebody decided journalism was a profession instead of a trade. People got kind of full of themselves.

Esquire, December:116.

Bill Moyers
*Commentator,
Public Broadcasting Service;
Former commentator, CBS News*

5

When people come home, they don't need headlines any more [on their TV newscasts]. They need insight, analysis, commentary, interpretation, explanation—fair, balanced, but journalistic . . . CBS News has been dying slowly from terminal irrelevance. The critical 5 to 10 percent of the viewers who came to rely on CBS News for important reporting were turned

(BILL MOYERS)

off by finding their precious time being wasted on inconsequential or amusing pieces that they could have gotten on *Entertainment Tonight*.

The Christian Science Monitor,
12-1:22.

Thomas S. Murphy
Chairman,
Capital Cities/ABC

1

The network news is the glue that keeps the network together. Otherwise you are just a distribution system for entertainment programming, most of which is supplied by outside producers in Hollywood. You might as well be the Palace Theatre. There are businessmen at all three networks who have been looking at costs, and the costs did escalate substantially over the past half-dozen years. But any network that fools around with their cost structure to the point where they damage the potential of that network news for being Number 1 is making a great economic mistake. It's just pure business logic which demands that they maintain the best, the highest-quality, network news operation.

The Christian Science Monitor,
12-3:24.

Martina Navratilova
Tennis player

2

In Czechoslovakia there is no such thing as freedom of the press. In the United States there is no such thing as freedom *from* the press.

Los Angeles Times, 2-2:(III)2.

Andrew Neil
Editor,
"The Sunday Times"
(Britain)

3

[Criticizing a British court ruling prohibiting the press from publishing excerpts of a revealing spy memoir by a former British agent):

Clearly, this country now needs a bill of rights. It needs a First Amendment freedom of speech, as the Americans have. Otherwise, the Law Lords will be able to gag us.

July 30/The New York Times, 7-31:7.

Allen H. Neuharth
Chairman, Gannett Company

4

Newspapers generally across the U.S.A. in the last five years have changed more in appearance and content than in any previous time period like that. I believe *USA Today* [which he publishes and which is now five years old] has been some of the cause . . . Maybe some years down the road when the critics accept *USA Today* as the Nation's Newspaper, they may even say there was a contribution to journalism. But that will take awhile.

Los Angeles Times, 10-8:(I)1,21.

William E. Odom
Lieutenant General,
United States Army; Director,
National Security Agency
of the United States

5

[On leaks of sensitive information to the press by people in government]: The press is not a wholly innocent bystander. Many in the media try unrelentingly to pry loose highly classified information. Then they blame the leakers, refusing to accept any responsibility. If we do not save our intelligence capabilities, if we fritter away through leaks and publicity, we may pay a very large price in blood to save not only the First Amendment but also the Constitution. What I am saying is that there is something called the "national interest" which can and should limit, from time to time, the unbridled exercise of individual rights. [In the case of journalists] their invocation of the First Amendment inevitably includes incantations regarding the public's "right to know" included, either explicitly or implicitly, within the First Amendment. The notion that the media stands as an unelected ombudsman with a constitution-

WHAT THEY SAID IN 1987

(WILLIAM E. ODOM)

ally conferred mandate to extract all information on government activities and disseminate it to the uninformed citizenry has neither historical nor legal foundation.

Before Association of
Former Intelligence Officers,
Oct. 10/The New York Times, 10-14:12.

Don Ohlmeyer
Television producer-director

1

I happen to think network [TV] news is one of the most dangerous things in this country. I mean, it is absolutely dangerous, to the degree that it is driven by ratings, driven by advertising. It doesn't have the checks and balances of a newspaper. When [President] Reagan was shot, you had people saying [Presidential Press Secretary] James Brady was dead . . . he was alive . . . he was dead . . . alive. Just totally irresponsible broadcasting. I mean, James Brady's cousin is sitting in Louisville and hears his cousin is dead. That's dreadful.

Interview, New York/
Emmy Magazine, Jan.-Feb.:24.

Dennis Patrick
Chairman, Federal
Communications Commission

2

[On the FCC's scrapping the Fairness Doctrine]: By this action, we introduce the First Amendment into the 20th century.

U.S. News & World Report, 8-17:9.

Rupert Pennant-Rea
Editor, "The Economist"
(Britain)

3

[On whether the British press is undergoing significant change]: It certainly is. We recently saw the arrival of *The Independent*, the first new quality daily in 131 years, and there is a new tabloid, *Today*. There is the prospect of a new London evening paper and of a Sunday newspaper. All of these things are changing the shape of British journalism, and they are driven mostly by technology. For many years we had ossification in journalism because of the problems of introducing new technology, especially in printing. Those problems have not disappeared, but there is a new willingness by the unions to accept the new technology. So the economics of newspaper publishing suddenly look much more attractive, and the result has been this influx of new newspapers. Whether the quality of journalism will improve is another matter.

Interview/
World Press Review,
January:31.

Walter Pincus
Reporter,
"The Washington Post"

4

[Answering the question, "What keeps you going?" as a reporter]: All reporters want to have impact, so that's part of it. And all reporters want to take down the government, so that's a part of it, too. But I also believe in democracy. I really do. That's what makes this job interesting.

Interview/
The Wall Street Journal,
5-5:38.

Dan Rather
Anchorman,
"Evening News," CBS-TV

5

[On the fall in ratings for his news program]: The longer I go, the less I know. The ratings are a great mystery. I don't understand them. I can't find anyone who does . . . I don't get concerned about them. They are a false god. We have to put on the best broadcast we can put on. Naturally, I hope the ratings will be good. But if we put on a good broadcast, whatever the ratings are, I walk away feeling okay.

Interview, New York/
The Christian Science Monitor,
6-22:22.

(DAN RATHER)

1

The press should always be a good watchdog. It should be suspicious and inquisitive, but it should never be an attack dog or a lapdog.

At seminar, Fordham University/
McCalls, July:132.

Jonathan Rodgers
Manager, WBBM-TV,
Chicago

2

It is the nature of the business now that network news is no longer the premium it once was. You make more money, given the same rating, off a game show than you can off a news show because the advertiser would rather reach younger people—and younger women specifically—and those people tend not to watch news. The aged, 50-plus people watch news.

The Washington Post, 2-9:(A)1.

William Safire
Political columnist

3

I have the greatest job in the world. Somebody asked me, would I give this up to be Secretary of State? I said, "Why take a step down?"

Interview, New York/
The Christian Science Monitor,
8-28:28.

Van Gordon Sauter
Former president,
CBS News

4

[On the cutbacks in budget and personnel at CBS News]: At one time, the journalists who went out to cover the layoffs at steel mills and oil fields and auto plants returned to their offices with a rich, reassuring sense of "it will never happen here." But it has happened at the network, and many of those people are faced with the reality that they are dispensable employees just like those featured in the stories

with datelines such as Lackawanna or Midland or Dearborn . . . Under [the] green eyeshades [of the network owners], the tube to them—be it news or soap operas or the NFL—is a business. And, in their opinion, you can't be a business still within reason and meet what they consider to be the general expectations of a news employee. The tube, as Howard Beale [the fictional newsman in the film *Network*] said, may be an awesome force, but for the news people who service it, the tube has lost some of its focus. The owners don't think that [is] adverse and the viewers don't care.

At California State University,
Northridge, Los Angeles Times,
3-14:(VI)12.

Antonin Scalia
Associate Justice,
Supreme Court of
the United States

5

[On how the Supreme Court should rule in a case in which a TV network has information regarding a planned secret U.S. invasion of a foreign country in order to rescue hostages]: This is not a case that the press is going to win. I think where the President is conducting military operations, I think the Court, out of respect for the political branches, is not going to try to second-guess the need for secrecy in those military operations. It's a narrow situation, it's a troop-ship situation, and in these circumstances, and for a limited time period, a prior restraint [against the press announcing the secret operation] should issue.

At symposium,
Tulane University, Feb. 15/
The New York Times, 2-17:10.

Charles E. Schumer
United States Representative,
D-New York

6

[Criticizing broadcasters who say making the Fairness Doctrine into law infringes on their freedom to program]: This minimal require-

(CHARLES E. SCHUMER)

ment placed on broadcasters can in no way be construed as a form of censorship or an infringement upon the broadcasters' First Amendment rights. The Doctrine does not insinuate the government into a broadcaster's programming or editorial decisions.

Washington, June 3/
The New York Times, 6-4:1.

Eric Sevareid
Former commentator,
CBS News

1

When I was doing nightly commentary, I wasn't really trying to tell people *what* to think. I was trying to tell them what they should be thinking *about*, and *how* to think about these things that engulf us every day—that is, what historical importance to give these things, and how to separate out the minor issues from the truly major ones.

Interview, Washington/
The Christian Science Monitor,
1-28:1.

Yitzhak Shamir
Prime Minister of Israel

2

Scandals you have everywhere you have the press. They will discover scandals.

Interview, Jerusalem/
Time, 4-20:36.

George P. Schultz
Secretary of State
of the United States

3

Since the founding of our republic, American journalists have sometimes been a thorn in the side of government officials. But our history has also demonstrated their indispensable im-

portance in safeguarding freedom and justice and in insuring the health of our democratic system.

At dinner in his honor,
Peking, March 2/
The New York Times, 3-3:3.

Hugh Sidey
Political columnist,
"Time" magazine

4

I've never really thought of political reporting as the high calling of journalism. It's imprecise. You can get away with saying many things that can never be disproved. It's a business filled with leakers of all types. It's very appealing to a lot of nomadic characters in our trade. I do think that at the top of the field there are about a dozen people, like [columnist] David Broder, who have elevated it. But I also note that they are the ones who are the most modest and troubled about these things.

Interview/
The Christian Science Monitor,
10-23:16.

Alan K. Simpson
United States Senator,
R-Wyoming

5

[To reporters who try to question President Reagan during photo sessions]: You know very well that you're not asking him things so you can get answers. You're asking him things because you know he's off balance and you'd like to stick it in his gazoo.

Newsweek, 3-30:17.

Robert Sims
Spokesman for
the Department of Defense
of the United States

6

[Saying background checks will be tightened for many reporters wishing to enter and cover the Pentagon]: We will be going from a situa-

(ROBERT SIMS)

tion where we have 50 to 75 reporters whom we know and love, whom we have more or less vouched for, to a system where we have a large number of people, perhaps 1,000, whom we don't know, some of whom we may not even love, who will be coming in the building. And I certainly can't take responsibility for all of those without some [security] check.

The New York Times, 5-4:14.

Larry Speakes
Principal Deputy
Press Secretary to President
of the United States
Ronald Reagan

1

In my years in the White House, which began in the Nixon Administration in '74, the way a Press Secretary has to do business has changed dramatically. And it's largely based on the growth of television. The ratio in 1974 was probably 3-to-1 print press over electronic press. Now it's directly reversed. Television dominates the way the White House is covered. In 1974, the Press Secretary would prepare for eight or 10 subjects going into a briefing. Today, you prepare for eight or 10 subjects but you're only asked about one or two. And that, in my opinion, is because television covers, can cover, only one story a day from the White House beat. And that story tends to dominate. That's not to say the print press doesn't have influence. The lead story in the major morning newspapers is very often the television lead story on the evening news, and that means television follows the print press. So no White House can afford to ignore the newspapers.

Interview, Washington/
The New York Times, 1-26:12.

2

The Presidential press conference is an important institution because it's the one time that the public sees the President in what many times is a difficult and adversarial relationship, and they see how he performs. But the press

conference in its present form is in danger of outliving its usefulness because of the fact that it is boiled down to an East Room extravaganza, and the questions do not come in a coherent fashion and stay with a subject and explore the depth of the President's thinking. It boils down to more a battle of the wits.

Interview, Washington/
The New York Times, 1-26:12.

3

Clearly, the news media—mainly television—is the authoritative voice of the nation. The time has come for television to examine the way it covers the news, the way it goes about presenting it to the American people and the impact it is having on our nation.

Farewell address,
Washington, Jan. 30/
Los Angeles Times, 1-31:(I)20.

James D. Squires
Editor, "Chicago Tribune"

4

. . . if we [in the press] ever get to the point where the readers can't believe us [in the news columns] because we've given in to advertisers' pressure, that loss of credibility will transfer to the advertising, too. We don't mind telling the advertising department we're doing [a section] on the ski slopes in Colorado in six weeks, so they can go sell some [appropriate] ads. That brings down the walls [between advertising and news]. But we don't let them tell us they want us to do something on the ski slopes of Colorado because they've already sold three ads or they think they can sell some ads for it. They would compromise our integrity.

Interview/
Los Angeles Times,
2-16:(I)24.

Howard Stringer
President, CBS News

5

[On CBS' budget and personnel cutbacks in its news division]: I have to work night and day

(HOWARD STRINGER)

over the next weeks to convince everyone that we [in news] may be cherished, but we're not going to be protected from the outside world. We have to work our way through it. No leader of this institution can afford to let this happen again, because then you would destroy it, if indeed it hasn't been mortally wounded by this . . . There's nothing wrong with journalists being in the real world. You can't have rich correspondents and rich [news] producers saying, "How dare they treat us like a business?" It's a contradiction in terms. You can't have it both ways.

March 7/
The New York Times,
3-9:16.

1

[TV reporters today find that] to survive and do something valuable and successful is far harder than what our predecessors had to do. They invented television news, but they had the time to do it. Viewers today don't want lectures; they want to satisfy all their senses . . . It's the difference between air travel and ships. In the past, there was no worry that you might not have time to think about the story. Now you go right on the air. People today have to be faster and more facile. I'm not saying it's better, but that's the way it has to be . . . [Viewers] want the information when it's hot. We [in TV news] may have created this need, but we have to satisfy it.

Interview, New York/
Variety, 9-30:99,118.

Annalyn Swan
Editor, "Savvy" magazine;
Former senior editor,
"Newsweek" magazine

2

This is a very difficult time for newsweeklies. They do have to redefine themselves. Once they had their own turf carved out. Now the newspapers are making inroads into their territory; *USA Today* has had a major impact. [And

newsweeklies] are consistently beaten by television news.

The Christian Science Monitor,
6-25:21.

Tom Tauke
United States Representative,
R-Iowa

3

[Arguing against the broadcast Fairness Doctrine]: [It has a] chilling effect on sound journalism [and] inserts governmental control into the media. The Founding Fathers thought that liberty was more important than fairness, so they adopted the First Amendment.

Washington, June 3/
The New York Times, 6-4:1.

Laurence Tisch
Chief executive officer,
CBS, Inc.

4

I think it is incumbent upon CBS to deliver the news to the American people, regardless of cost. It does not have to make a profit. But it has to be run with some regard for money. Like every businessman, I am interested in running a semblance of an efficient organization. I know we can't achieve production line-like efficiency, but at least we should have an [news] operation where there is not abject waste. There is always a group of people in every walk of life that believes the old times were better. I don't buy that. I think if you compare our news programs today to the programs of 20 or 30 years ago, you'll find them much better today, with all due respect to the giants of the past.

Interview/
The Christian Science Monitor,
12-3:24.

Donald Trelford
Editor, "The Observer"
(Britain)

5

Fleet Street [London's newspaper-publishing district] went through a mad period when the

(DONALD TRELFORD)

traditional newspaper-owning families could not cope any more. Newspapers were sold to corporations, and they tended to be corporations where there was a dominant chief executive—often a man with great vanity. Fleet Street has benefited from that period, although we resented it when it started because these people proved equal to the print unions and have turned Fleet Street at last into a business. My view is that newspapers can be independent only when they are run profitably. Otherwise, you are dependent on somebody else's purse. If you are making a profit, it is hard for people to say you are doing something wrong. That is the language they understand. Curiously, the editorial test is ultimately commercial.

Interview/World Press Review,
November:28.

William Van Allstyne
Professor of law,
Duke University

1

The [broadcast] Fairness Doctrine, while never stringently policed by the FCC, just resting there among the government apparatus and enforced by the threatened death penalty of license revocation, is an uncomfortable First Amendment contradiction.

The New York Times, 8-5:20.

John Vinocur
Editor,
"International Herald Tribune"

2

The *Trib* today is a mixture of two things—the enormous journalistic resources of *The [New York] Times* and *The [Washington] Post*, and a tradition of really intelligent eclecticism and occasional eccentricity. Together, they make quite a combination.

On the 100th anniversary
of his newspaper/Time,
10-12:79.

George F. Will
Political columnist;
Commentator, ABC News

3

My popularity derives chiefly from putting into words what people are already thinking. I do not change minds, because I preach to the converted. The people who read op-ed pages are not blank slates looking to be written upon. They are people who have an interest in public affairs and hold settled opinions about them. And that is good. Who would want to live in a country where journalists had real power, where people would be blown around like leaves by the gusts of public opinion? That would be a silly country.

Interview/Esquire, January:92.

4

Journalism is usually a net subtraction to understanding.

Interview/Esquire, January:92.

Bob Woodward
Reporter,
"The Washington Post"

5

[On the controversy about a new book of his in which he reveals a possible death-bed admission by CIA Director William Casey that he knew of a diversion of funds in the U.S. Iran-contra scandal, an admission Woodward and his newspaper withheld during the Iran-contra hearings]: On a personal level, Casey's nod [that he knew of the diversion] meant a lot but, as a reporter, it's not a word, it's only a nod and I got to ask no follow-up questions. What do you write [in a newspaper]? A story saying that Casey nodded? Unfortunately, like lots of things in the book, like riding on the airplane with Casey, like dinners and discussions and so forth, it fit into the book to paint a cumulative portrait, but it didn't lend itself to a news story.

Interview, Sept. 29/
The New York Times,
9-30:12.

WHAT THEY SAID IN 1987

Robert C. Wright
*President, National
Broadcasting Company*

1

I think a network's news is a significant contributor to the image of the network . . . but it doesn't shape the image any more than sports does . . . I don't think NBC News can pay for itself. An awful lot of what we do on the news side falls into the category of public service. It's not something we can ever expect on its own to make money at. On the other hand, I think we have to have rational views as to how much we can afford.

The Christian Science Monitor,
12-3:24.

Literature

Martin Amis
British author

1

[Writers in America] are turned into oracular figures. If you don't watch out, you're going to get semi-deified there. In England, I've always thought writers are taken slightly less seriously than the average citizen. In America, they're rung up by newspapers and invited to give their views on things. They're much more famous, and that brings with it all sorts of risks. One tends to find that the novelists who last, are the ones who tuck themselves away somewhere, be it Boston of Chicago. I could agree with [American author] Saul Bellow when he said there were no writers to talk to in New York; there were only celebrities on exhibit. And that brings with it a lot more competitiveness. English writers tend to get on well together. In America . . . it's probably the size of America. They come from such distances—from Alabama, from California—so when they do run into each other, they look a bit odd to each other and they don't get on. They sue each other and beat each other up at parties.

Interview, London/
Los Angeles Times, 9-27.

Larry Ashmead
Executive editor,
Harper & Row, publishers

2

[On factual crime-story books]: It's always been a good area of publishing. When you have a success in this area—and there have been watershed successes—it's an editor's dream. It's a non-fiction subject, it's melodramatic and there's vast appeal to the public. They're exciting books to write for the writers, to edit for the editors, for the publishers to publish and for the salesmen to sell.

Los Angeles Times,
5-7:(V)12.

Virginia Barber
Literary agent

3

Big publishing houses are more cautious; they want "brand-name" writers [who guarantee profits]. It seems easier for eccentricity to survive in small publishing houses, and good literature thrives on being able to accept the eccentric, the new, the different.

Los Angeles Times, 3-13:(I)16.

John Barth
Author

4

In college, I decided I hadn't read anything, and therefore I would try to read everything. It was a wonderful apprenticeship for a person only beginning to realize that he was going to try to be a writer. I recommend it as an easy way to pick up the last thing a talented apprentice usually acquires in fiction writing—a sense of plot and pacing, of story, of complicating a situation, of beguiling the reader . . . I've realized more and more that at the core of what I do is a deep fascination with the process of storytelling. I also see that in Homer, in Shakespeare, in every writer I admire. Homer and Shakespeare and Cervantes kept more up their sleeves than the modernists. I've been trying to learn as I get older to stuff back some of that stuff up my sleeve. That's what I think of as post-modernism: returning to an emphasis on storytelling, on plot, on the exfoliation of situation.

Interview/
U.S. News & World Report, 8-31:55.

Saul Bellow
Author

5

I didn't start out to be successful. I started out to write. I didn't start scribbling at the age of 16 to win a prize. I would have been satisfied with much less. I didn't invent America's celebrity machinery, either, and I stay away from it

383

(SAUL BELLOW)

as much as I can. In between books, I have nothing at all to do with it. [Writing is] my path into life. I don't know what I am without it. It's inconceivable for me to picture myself without it. I don't have a full explanation for it, any more than birds do for bird song.

Interview, New York/
The New York Times, 6-3:22.

1

I'm tuckered out [writing] right now. There are things stewing inside my head. A writer in his 60s and 70s always has subjects laid aside. Will they be ripe when I'm 90? It's a good reason to hang in there.

Interview, New York/
Newsweek, 6-8:79.

Allan Bloom
Author;
Professor of philosophy,
University of Chicago

2

I don't care about literacy if people are not going to read good books. And if they're going to read good books without posing serious questions and taking them seriously for their lives, I don't particularly want them to read good books. We're always asking is this going to work, is it going to be understandable to a lot of people, and that's the wrong thing. The first and most important thing is the absolute, unabashed, total dedication to the truth without thinking about how relevant it's going to be or how many people can appreciate it.

Interview, Chicago/
Los Angeles Times, 6-10:(V)6.

Daniel J. Boorstin
Librarian of Congress
of the United States

3

Books liberate people outside of their time and place. Books awaken them to the delights of ideas, which are precious things.

Interview, Washington/
The New York Times, 1-31:8.

4

W. H. Auden once said that some books are undeservedly forgotten, but none are undeservedly remembered. And that goes to the heart of the problem. You can never tell whether a book has a claim to immortality by the number of people who read it at the moment. It's a cautionary experience to look back at books that have been on the best-seller list and are now remembered only to be forgotten.

The Christian Science Monitor,
5-28:21.

5

A wonderful thing about a book, in contrast to a computer screen, is that you can take it to bed with you. You can embrace a book. You can hide it. It becomes part of you. You own it in the best sense of the word—in the sense that it owns you, too, if it's a great book.

Interview/
Los Angeles Times, 9-17:(V)1.

6

We are not doing as much as we could to encourage people to read; but we must be wary of generalizations about what people do and don't read. Because one of the special charms of reading is that it's secret and private. Nobody knows how much you read or what you get out of your reading, or what you mean by reading something . . . we should be aware that reading is from its very nature not statistically verifiable in the same way as the prevalence of diseases can be described.

Interview/
Los Angeles Times, 9-17:(V)30.

Ray Bradbury
Author

7

The library is not a serious place. [In fact,] the library is a maelstrom. When I talk to students, I tell them, plunge into it like a bunch of apes; like you were climbing Kilimanjaro or going to Alpha Centauri. Libraries are joyful, explosive, hysterical! They're playgrounds!

Los Angeles Times, 1-17:(V)3.

Leo Braudy
Professor of literature,
University of
Southern California

1

We are living in an age in which people are looking to other lives for answers to questions about their own. People aren't clear what the norms of social behavior are—and biographies help provide answers. They are lessons in the etiquette of social being.

U.S. News & World Report, 8-3:50.

Joseph Brodsky
Exiled Soviet poet;
Winner, 1987 Nobel Prize
in Literature

2

[On his winning the Nobel Prize]: I'm the happiest combination you can think of. I'm a Russian poet, an English essayist and a citizen of the United States.

Interview, London, Oct. 22/
The New York Times, 10-23:8.

3

Literature is simply the most focused form of the demands on the evolution of the species. It imposes a certain responsibility, moral, ethical and esthetic responsibility, and the species simply doesn't want to oblige. Literature sort of makes your daily operation, your daily conduct, the management of your affairs in the society a bit more complex. And it puts what you do in perspective; and people don't like to see themselves or their activities in perspective. They don't quite feel comfortable with that. Nobody wants to acknowledge the insignificance of his life, and that is very often the net result of reading a poem.

Interview, New York/
The Washington Post, 10-23:(B)4.

4

[On the Soviets' decision to publish his work in one of their magazines as an aspect of the new *glasnost* or "openness" policy of Soviet leader [Mikhail Gorbachev]: About that I will not celebrate much . . . Poems, novels—these things belong to the nation, to the culture and the people. They've been stolen from the people and now the stolen things are being returned to their owners, but I don't think their owners should be grateful to receive them.

Interview/
The Wall Street Journal,
11-3:32.

Gwendolyn Brooks
Poet

5

I don't want to be obscure. I know a great many poets who try to be obscure because they feel that they should write to exclude those who they feel don't have the proper appreciation for poetry. That's a very snobbish attitude, and one, I think, that I never had.

Interview/Ebony, June:158.

Bill Buford
Editor and publisher,
"Granta" magazine

6

A great deal of pig shit, without putting too fine a word on it, goes under the banner of literary writing. I can never figure out why someone went through the labor of reading it, editing it, typesetting it, finding a cover for it, and printing it.

Esquire, December:97.

Charles Bukowski
Poet

7

The wine does most of my writing. I just open a bottle and turn on the radio, and it just comes pouring out. I only type every third night. I have no plan. My mind is a blank. I sit down. The typewriter gives me things I don't even know I'm working on. It's a free lunch. A free dinner. I don't know how long it is going to continue, but so far there is nothing easier than writing.

Interview/
Los Angeles Times Magazine,
3-22:13.

Hortense Calisher
President,
American Academy and
Institute of Arts and Letters

1

People stop reading [even recognized authors] when they die. They come back eventually, if they're good enough. But you don't hear [the late author Vladimir] Nabokov talked about now the way you did when he was alive.

Interview, New York/
The Christian Science Monitor,
2-19:21.

Harry Crews
Author

2

I get up in the morning, that's one of the hard parts, drag myself over to the old typewriter and sit down—that's even harder—and then I tell the Lord, "I ain't greedy, Lord. Just give me the next 500 words."

Interview/
The New York Times,
2-19:23.

Janet Dailey
Author

3

In the type of novel that I write, my first intention is to entertain. I want to tell them a good story. Secondly, I'd like to let them know something that maybe they didn't know before. But I want to do it in a way that never interferes with the entertainment. I don't ever want a passage in my book to be the kind that grabs you by the shirt collar, slaps you across the face and says, "Pay attention, you're going to learn something."

Interview/USA Today, 7-2:(A)11.

Robertson Davies
Author

4

All authors of any degree of acceptance are solicited to go on tour [on the lecture circuit].

The money is large and tempting, the schedules are demanding. But are you going to write or be a traveling show? Writing is an introverted act; you have to be a showman to be a successful actor.

At Wheatland Conference
on Literature, Washington/
The New York Times, 4-27:16.

5

I do not "get" ideas; ideas get me. I have written to countless aspiring writers that if they do not have any ideas that demand to be written about, perhaps they should seriously consider whether writing is the life for them.

World Press Review, November:53.

James Dickey
Author, Poet

6

I don't have any real idea about sitting down deliberately to concoct something that will sell a lot of copies. I've got a statement to make as a writer, and as a human being, and I want to make it as best I can rather than settle for a temporary amount of money, which the government gets anyway.

Interview/
Publishers Weekly, 5-29:63.

Joan Didion
Author

7

People think that if there are fewer [publishing] houses you have fewer chances [to get published]. I try not to think about the economics of publishing, because they are so bleak.

Los Angeles Times, 3-13:(I)16.

Gary Fisketjon
Editorial director,
Atlantic Monthly Press

8

I live with a book [when considering it for publication]. It takes me five hours to do 40 pages. I don't understand the people who say

(GARY FISKETJON)

you just go to lunch and then say "I love it!" into the phone. You have to get into the voice of the book and look to see where it wavers. The book is in the writing; it's in what's being written about; and either it comes together or it doesn't . . . You're looking at sentences. You're looking at how sentences fall together. Then you look back and see whether there are any tics in the style.

Interview, New York/
The Christian Science Monitor,
9-9:6.

Nikki Giovanni
Poet

1

[On what she looks for in a poem]: I look not to be bored. Can I get through it? If I'm reading a student's work, I'm looking to see what the central idea is and how it is developed. I listen for the sound of a poem. A poem is like a song. You don't read a song, you sing it, and you have to hear it to appreciate it. The same thing applies to poetry. It should be read aloud.

Interview/Writing, January:15.

Nadine Gordimer
South African author

2

The crackdown by the [South African] government on the press has affected me as a person. But it hasn't affected me in my work. You see, with writers of fiction what happens is a delayed process. Events have to be re-imagined, re-created before they come out as a poem, a play, a novel or a story. You may be in the middle of some tremendous political event. You could go off and write an article about it. But for it to become the core of a novel, that's going to take a year or two, because everything in the rest of the novel has to grow from it. I won't know how current events will affect my writing until I begin another book.

Interview/
U.S. News & World Report,
5-25:74.

[On writing]: Your whole life, you are really writing one book, which is an attempt to grasp the consciousness of your time and place—a single book written from different stages of your ability.

Interview/
World Press Review,
October:61.

Joanne Greenberg
Author

4

Most of what I do is re-writing. The pencil company's great act of genius was to put an eraser on the other end of a pencil. I'm always changing things, adding, subtracting. When I've finished writing a book in longhand, I read it all over. Then I type it and change it some more. Then I read it aloud to my husband, and, as I read, I change it again. Then I re-type it and mess around some more, and somewhere in this process I get to know the people I've written about well enough so that, very often, the trip itself changes.

Interview/Writing, February:21.

Joseph Heller
Author

5

[On reports that he will receive $4-million for his next two novels]: I will only confirm that I got less than I asked for and more than I deserve.

U.S. News & World Report, 4-20:13.

E. D. Hirsch, Jr.
Professor of English,
University of Virginia

6

Reading is a constructive act. What you bring to the text is all important in understanding it.

Interview, San Francisco/
The Christian Science Monitor,
4-13:23.

WHAT THEY SAID IN 1987

Josephine Humphreys
Author

1

I try not to use real people [as characters in novels]. I think that writers have to be good at imagining other people's experiences strongly enough to understand it. It was quite a shock to me when reviewers spoke of the novel's characters as though they were flesh and blood. I never—never!—looked at them that way. I was much more interested in the words. Storytelling is not my biggest talent, I'm afraid. It's necessary, of course, but I think of the story as a vehicle for words.

Interview, Charleston, S.C./
Publishers Weekly, 9-4:50.

P. D. James
Author

2

In 1930s mysteries, all sorts of motives were credible which aren't credible today. Especially motives of preventing guilty sexual secrets from coming out. Nowadays, people *sell* their guilty sexual secrets.

Newsweek, 2-2:17.

David S. Kaufer
Associate professor of rhetoric,
Carnegie-Mellon University

3

By emphasizing grammar, we give students the illusion that they are a dangling participle or sentence fragment away from becoming a Shakespeare or a Milton. As a writing teacher, I got tired of living that lie . . . Most composition courses are museum guides to great works, but students receive no formal training in writing. We want students to experience authorship, not just report on what the grownups are saying.

The New York Times, 4-7:19.

Stanley Kunitz
State poet-designate
of New York

4

The deepest thing I know is that I am living and dying at once, and my conviction is to report that dialogue. It is a rather terrifying thought that is at the root of much of my poetry. To have such a thought is, of necessity, to relate the imagination to primary issues—moral issues, spiritual issues—and that separates me from those who think of poetry as a literistic game.

Interview, New York/
The New York Times,
3-11:19.

Louis L'Amour
Author

5

This is the only period in [literary] history, except for one period in England during the Reformation, when anybody enlarged on the idea of sex. I don't know why everybody talks about it so much [in books], because Tolstoy got along fine [without writing about it]. So did Robert Louis Stevenson, and so did Victor Hugo, Alexandre Dumas, and thousands of others. It's only now that we're suddenly concentrating on it. We act like a lot of little boys who have suddenly discovered sex. They've been out behind the barn talking about it, so now they're writing about it, and it's the same as when they're talking about it behind the barn.

Interview/
USA Today, 2-13:(A)13.

6

I woke up the other morning with a complete story in my mind—a story I'd never even dreamt of writing, never even thought of before. This can happen to anybody. You have to give yourself material, though. You can't get something out of nothing. You've got to treat the mind constantly with ideas. Then the human mind, itself, will make the comparisons, the connections and the adjustments. Many times, when I'm writing a story, I start out with two characters in a situation. I have no idea how it's going to go. My subconscious mind takes care of the whole thing. The story just rolls out.

Interview/
USA Today, 2-13:(A)13.

Madeleine L'Engle
Author

1

It never occurred to me that it was easier to write a children's book than an adult one. I didn't realize that one was supposed to write differently when one wrote for children. I thought one was supposed to do one's best, regardless. It's a terrible fallacy that people think, "Oh, you're not good enough to write for adults. Write for kids; it's easier." I wrote several adult novels before I felt that I knew enough to write a book for children. This is the absolute truth: When I have something I want to say that's too difficult for most adults, I'll have a young protagonist and I'll write it for kids. They haven't closed their doors to new ideas yet.

Interview/Writing, March:13.

Elmore Leonard
Author

2

I find that I'm using more of what's going on around me . . . in my novels. To some extent, I've always drawn on the present, whether it's a reference to a soap opera, a movie or a song. I miss a sense of time in so many books. I was told once that putting such elements in a novel dates it because they won't mean anything to readers in years to come. But I'm not writing for years to come; I'm writing for next year, when another book will be out.

Interview/
U.S. News & World Report,
3-9:64.

Robert Ludlum
Author

3

[When writing,] I have a concept, and that's very strong. It's got to be very strong, because if you don't have that, you'd be writing a cartoon, not a novel. It's always present, and as I'm making up characters, I think they will take a stand one way or the other in terms of that theme, of that idea. As George Bernard Shaw

once said, give your antagonists the strongest arguments you can so that your theme doesn't revolve around straw people. But the major characters express their positions in terms of theme throughout the book.

Interview, Naples, Fla./
Writer's Digest, July:22.

Norman Mailer
Author

4

It takes two hours to get up for writing every day, then you work for three hours, and sometimes you have to go through this twice a day. It's exhausting beyond belief, and as you get older it gets tougher in a lot of ways. The writing itself gets a little easier, certain of the old anxieties go; but finally, writing is like going into jail. I have to live in a state of partial boredom in order to do it.

Interview/Daily Variety, 5-4:2.

5

Novel writing is so visionary . . . so obsessive. You love the novel, you hate it. The novel nags at you, accuses you, reminds you what you haven't done for its life. Terribly personal, like a mate; I repeat, a *wife*. It's total and sometimes has nothing to do with anything else in reality, but it has to claim you. It's confining in the same way marriage is confining. All the sides of yourself that don't fit the other person can't be used. I know. I've been doing it for 40 years.

Interview/Film Comment, August:16.

Andrew Malcolm
Author;
Chicago bureau chief,
"The New York Times"

6

To my mind, that's one of the most exciting things about writing, if not *the* most exciting thing—that I can sit down somewhere by myself and by selection and arrangement of words and sentences and language, rhythms and patterns, can make somebody feel exactly the same thing

(ANDREW MALCOLM)

somewhere else at another time, and cry . . . That just makes your day.

Interview/Publishers Weekly, 4-17:55.

Robert Maxwell
British publisher

1

. . . publishing, which comes out of a cottage industry, is a global business, and I'm in books, in England and other countries. But at the end of the day I know that what matters is a man or woman who sits down at a typewriter and works alone . . . All my life, if I've had a conflict of interest between the author and the publishing house, I've sided with the author. I love creative people, and I find nobody more creative than the writer. I also like books, including the way they smell when they come off the presses.

*Interview, New York/
The New York Times, 5-23:11.*

Alice McDermott
Author

2

Established writers should be very, very careful with their public praise of young and inexperienced writers. Too much praise and too much attention too early can cause young writers to take themselves far too seriously. Being accepted as part of the literary life so quickly can be damaging. The life alone becomes important. Going out and drinking wine and having your picture taken as you gaze soulfully into the camera, and being a writer with a capital "W"—all that is very appealing. But it drains your energy from where the energy should really be, and that's in the unromantic and seemingly unimportant daily working on a piece of paper with a pencil.

Esquire, December:114.

Ian McEwan
British author

3

My preferred form is fiction. I take it more seriously than any other kind of writing. The reason the novel is such a powerful form is that it allows the examination of the private life better than any other art-form. Our common sense gives us such a thin wedge of light on the world, and perhaps one task of the writer is to broaden the wedge.

*Interview/
Publishers Weekly, 9-11:69.*

Edmund Morris
*Pulitzer
Prize-winning biographer*

4

The problem in writing about living people is that sources are more guarded. You have always to consider the feelings of the subjects as well. I'm not saying that the biographer of a living person should be untrue to himself by writing flattering stuff; all biographers should be brutally honest. But it's a lot easier to do that when somebody is not around. Because of the need for honesty, it's wise to avoid writing about anybody you don't have some liking for. The ideal attitude is mild affection. If you choose a subject you dislike, you end up with a diatribe. And why spend four years of your life pouring out venom. It's equally dangerous to write about somebody you adore, because then you just write sycophantic nonsense.

*Interview/
U.S. News & World Report,
8-3:51.*

Toni Morrison
Author

5

Unlike all my other books, this one [*Beloved*], did not give me that sudden depression that follows when you're finished because you lose the company [the story's characters] you have been keeping all these years. This was different, because this book, I can see, is a longer story. I was under the impression that I had written a third of it when I turned this book in [to the publisher]. I was very apologetic, because I decided I couldn't make the deadline. And my editor said, "Well, that's too bad. Let

(TONI MORRISON)

me read it." And then he said, "Whatever else you're doing, do it, but this is a book; it's not a part." So I'm not finished with these people [the characters], and they are not finished with me. We have this hiatus right now. But I guess they are all waiting out there for me to come back.

Interview/
U.S. News & World Report,
10-19:75.

V. S. Naipaul
Author

1

I'm thought to be a tough writer, but I'm really a softie. I could meet dreadful people and end up seeing the world through their eyes, seeing their frailties, their needs. You refer to yourself in order to understand other people. That's the novelist's gift, isn't it? When I was young, I was always amazed that out of such profound rage, one could end by writing quite calmly. One reacts rather strongly, but, as a writer, one distills that down. If those responses were not strong, probably one would not be a writer.

Interview, New York/
The New York Times, 4-25:13.

2

My life has been extraordinarily dull. I think all writers' lives are boring, because writers do nothing but work . . . Their early lives tend to be rather interesting—and that is their capital. But it always breaks down with their first book. Nothing is as romantic in Dickens' life as that dropping of the first sketch by Boz into the mailbox.

Interview/
World Press Review,
October:33.

Marsha Norman
Author, Playwright

3

I found writing a novel much more satisfying than doing a play. I was more in control. I

didn't have to write lines and worry that an actor or the audience might not understand my intent. I wanted to be able to write the sentence, "Edith blinked," and know that Edith, by God, is going to blink every night at the same time for the same reason in the same way—forever.

U.S. News & World Report, 6-8:78.

Ivan Obolensky
Former publisher

4

Book publishing is more of an ego trip than most other professions. When you're a publisher, chiefs of staff and captains of industry sit at your desk and ask how they can write a book when they retire. That's very heady stuff . . .

The New York Times, 3-17:21.

Octavio Paz
Poet

5

[On poetry, especially modern poetry]: It is very elusive to define. If you asked me 40 years ago, it might be possible, but now modern poetry includes all kinds of verse. The important thing, for me, is rhythm, which has nothing to do with rhyme. Poetry is not a matter of good taste. It should not be confused with witticism or cleverness. You can be a good poet without being clever or fashionable or tasteful. I don't think that Donne or Milton were men of good taste . . . I think a great poet writes for himself. He doesn't see his reader very clearly. A great poet should travel and get experience—even go to dangerous places. Some poets have taken refuge in the university, but I think it is better to pass through a university than to stay there. If it happens that what you write for yourself becomes something for others as well, especially for a young reader, then you have achieved something. The great prize for me is to be read with the same passion that I read the older poets when I was young.

Interview, New York/
The New York Times 12-1:8.

Marge Piercy
Author

1

To show just how restrictive novels used to be, when I was growing up there were no Jews in fiction. All characters were Anglo-Saxon Protestants. All heroes were English gentlemen. I remember the excitement I felt when I was in my 20s and there began to be Jewish-American writers. They were all men, and after a while it became evident that when they wrote about women they showed the same contempt and the same lack of understanding others did when writing about Jews. Still, it was terribly exciting. It has been that constant creating of a literature of many more voices in which more people can find their families, their faces, their hopes and fears that has been important in creating a space in which writers like me can exist.

Interview/
U.S. News & World Report,
5-18:70.

Jonathan Raban
Author

2

The industrial boundary lines between fiction and non-fiction are drawn less rigidly in the [United] States than they are in England, where they are absolutely obsessed with labels. I don't recognize labor divisions. There is no fundamental difference when I sit down at the typewriter; whether it is "fiction" or "non-fiction" seems to me to be the problem of booksellers and library cataloguers.

Interview/Publishers Weekly, 2-13:77.

Jack Romanos
President,
Trade Publishing Group,
Simon & Schuster, publishers

3

Every publisher is chasing the big book because we have to have strong lead titles to pull the rest of our list along. They're the books that pay the rent and allow you to publish the first novel and the chancier books of non-fiction.

The New York Times, 3-26:21.

Philip Roth
Author

4

There is a typical process I follow in writing. I sit down and stick with it and put in regular hours and regular days. But each book throws up its own problems, and the previous book is not much help in solving the problems of the new one. In that way, writing is a singular profession. Other professionals who have been doing their jobs diligently for 25 or 30 years aren't faced with that dilemma. When the dermatologist opens the door to his waiting room where there are 10 people, I imagine he feels that he can handle everything that's there. If he can't, then it probably can't be done, especially after 25 years or so of practice. But in writing, when you begin a new project you really get very little help from all you've done in the past. You're accustomed to the discipline. You know what your process is, and if you follow it you're probably going to get through. Aside from that, there's very little to go on, because in a way you're trying to throw off the way you did it before. You can't treat the new patient like the old one.

Interview/
U.S. News & World Report,
2-2:62.

May Sarton
Author

5

Look at the great women writers. How many of them were married and had children? I realized that if I married I would not write what I could have. Of that I am quite sure . . . It would have taken the energy that would have gone into work. Of course, everything can be done. But art isn't cheap. You don't get it for nothing.

At 100th anniversary
celebration of Clark University/
The Christian Science Monitor, 12-18:23.

Sidney Sheldon
Author

6

Some [other best-selling authors] consider me a competitor, but I compete with myself.

(SIDNEY SHELDON)

There are writers today who are better than I'll ever be. If I compare myself to them, I might as well give up. I'm Sidney Sheldon, and whatever talent was given me is what I work with. The only thing I worry about is that next book.

Interview/Cosmopolitan, June:157.

1

I don't know what the hell [book] critics are looking for. Most critics are novelists—need I add *failed* novelists. If they weren't, they'd be doing it [writing] instead of tearing other writers apart.

Interview/Cosmopolitan, June:157.

2

[Writing,] next to being a doctor, is about the most important thing in the world anyone can do. We have so many problems in our lives, and if we—and I mean all writers—can bring a few hours or days of pleasure to people, and then leave this earth, we've contributed something that is worthwhile.

Interview, Los Angeles/
Beverly Hills (213), 11-11:13.

Charles Simmons
Author; Former editor,
"The New York Times
Book Review"

3

Publishers have always been commercial at heart. It's just that those [small, mid-list] books used to be more profitable; now the hunger the mid-list novel fed is being satisfied by movies and videocassettes. The people who still read novels want something guaranteed, so they go for the big best-sellers. Perhaps the sensitive novel of family life is simply not written in bright enough colors today to compete in the marketplace. At least the blockbusters mostly have some kind of new wrinkle, despite the formula approach; their writers are expert at injecting a journalistic kind of originality.

Interview/Publishers Weekly, 5-8:55.

Ted Solotaroff
Editor,
Harper & Row, publishers

4

Right now, we're in the middle of a feeding frenzy on yuppie fiction, brat-pack fiction. It's sort of like sun-dried tomatoes as the food of choice. What is getting attention? Right now, this kind of fiction by people in their 20s is in vogue. Last year, it was the revival of the short story. [These trends play havoc with] the slow accumulation of reputation . . . there just isn't the interest in building [authors'] careers any more.

Interview, New York/
The Christian Science Monitor,
10-1:21.

Debra Spark
Author; Artist-in-residence,
University of Wisconsin,
Madison

5

Some people think you have to have had an interesting life to write fiction, but I'm not sure that's true. Everyone can imagine stories. It's just a matter of pulling out and relating what is deepest and most sincerely felt. And it's also a matter of originality, seeing what others see but expressing it in a new way. That's craft, but it's also something you must feel within . . . Good literature, for me, should be well-written, with attention to style and detail; it should be "smart"—I don't think there are really any "dumb" writers, but I admire writers who try to make a reader think about a story; it should be sensitive; it should tell you something about the world you didn't know or that you did know but in a way you hadn't thought about. Sometimes a story can be just clever and be good, but that's not always enough to make it good literature. Good literature gives you insight.

Interview/Writing, May:20,21.

Wallace Stegner
Author

6

It took me until I was 60 or so to learn how a novel should be written. Short stories I have

393

(WALLACE STEGNER)

theories about, but novels elude any theory . . . Some [of my books] I wince at a little bit, some I wince at a lot. When you write books you get your education in public, especially when your enthusiasm outruns your experience—and mine did. [I have] a good deal of faith [in my latest book]. But would I want to go to heaven on it?

Interview, Vermont/
Publishers Weekly, 9-25:86.

Roger W. Straus
President,
Farrar, Straus & Giroux,
publishers

1

The so-called "middle book" is being eschewed [by publishers]. The book that Doubleday and Simon & Schuster used to be pleased to publish . . . is in danger of not finding a home. It's more and more difficult to publish the fourth and fifth work of an author of some distinction who never made it big.

The Christian Science Monitor,
5-28:22.

Peter Taylor
Author; Winner,
1987 Ritz-Hemingway Award
for literature

2

I am not a professional writer. I'm suspicious about professionalism, which I've always felt comes perilously close to commercialism. A serious writer must write out of compulsion.

Paris, April 6/
The New York Times, 4-7:25.

Leon Uris
Author

3

Talent isn't enough [to be a writer]. You need motivation—and persistence, too; what Steinbeck called a blend of faith and arrogance. When you're young, plain old poverty can be

enough, along with an insatiable hunger for recognition. You have to have that feeling of "I'll show them." If you don't have it, don't become a writer. It's part of the animal; it's primitive. But if you don't want to rise above the crowd, forget it. You have to evolve a permanent set of values to serve that function [of motivation]. For me, fighting the scourge of anti-Semitism—an apparently incurable cancer—became my ultimate motivation. As a writer, you've got a shot at making an impact on the world until your dying day, and even beyond. And that allows me to keep saying, as I have before, that wise old writers never die. They don't even fade away. They just snarl forever.

Interview, Aspen, Colo./
Writer's Digest, August:39.

Mario Vargas Llosa
Author

4

When we write novels, what we do is create a profoundly distorted manifestation of reality, which we impose on readers, on society. Real literature has never told the truth. It has imposed lies as truths.

At Wheatland Conference
on Literature, Washington/
The Washington Post, 4-25:(B)5.

5

As a writer, I have never considered literature an intellectual game. I admire [the late author Jorge Luis] Borges and his sophisms. But when I write, it is something else. Fiction is realism; it is invention that simulates reality . . . Writing is my entertainment; it completes my existence. Thanks to literature, my life is richer, more intense. When I am not writing, my world crumbles.

Interview/
World Press Review,
August:61.

Kurt Vonnegut
Author

6

Reading is extremely difficult. It always has been an elitist art-form. It's the only one that

(KURT VONNEGUT)

requires the consumer to be a performer. Unlike patrons of fine art or music, the reader has to create . . . It's miraculous anyone can do it.

Los Angeles Times, 1-17:(V)4.

Andrei Voznesensky
Soviet poet

1

I am not a powerful man. I have no high job; I have no motor car with a special telephone. But as a poet, if I ask an [official] in high authority—if I call and ask, "Please, look, we [the people] need [something]"—in Russia they love poetry. For them, poetry is something special. If I ask, they do it, [because] they want to do something for a poet.

Interview, Cambridge, Mass./
The Christian Science Monitor, 4-17:16.

Robert Penn Warren
Poet

2

I can remember when [poet] John Crowe Ransom, my old teacher, told me he was giving up writing poems. I was deeply shocked. He was only 45 or 50 then, and I couldn't believe my ears. A poet, as Jarrell once said, has to stand out in the storm. If he gets struck by lightning maybe six times in a career, he's a major poet. The point is, you've got to stand out there in the rain.

Interview, Vermont/
Horizon, June:37.

Elie Wiesel
Author;
Professor of humanities,
Boston University; Winner,
1986 Nobel Peace Prize

3

One should write out of his or her own experience. Every writer has a universe which is made up of experiences such as childhood memories, friends, family and school. The only

advice one can give to a writer is to open your eyes, open your ears, and listen. The writer sees. The writer hears. He sees that something occurs. He opens himself to what is surrounding him, and through his writing he causes others to open their eyes, and, sometimes, their hearts.

Interview/Writing, March:19.

Richard Wilbur
Poet Laureate
of the United States

4

I'm in danger of self-approval—if I write a first draft with slovenly words or leave blanks for clever words to fill in later, what I have written is likely to satisfy me too much. Writing involves lots of doubt, lots of groping around, waiting for a word that may not be there until next Tuesday. I don't want to go ahead until I'm certain lines 1, 2 and 3 are right. I do envy my friend, [poet] Dick Eberhart, who wrote eight poems in one night.

Interview, Washington/
Los Angeles Times, 10-13:(V)4.

George F. Will
Political columnist;
Commentator, ABC News

5

I gave up on Merriam-Webster [dictionaries]. Any dictionary that says "uninterested" and "disinterested" are synonyms deserves to be brought before an uninterested judge.

The Christian Science Monitor,
7-16:23.

A. N. Wilson
British novelist and critic

6

Tennyson said that to be a poet you have to have fire in your belly. Well, there's nobody around with fire in their belly at the moment. If you think of the effect on your life of the great poets, there's something consoling, uplifting and grand about great poetry. But when you sit

WHAT THEY SAID IN 1987

(A. N. WILSON)

on the London Underground and see one of these modern poets' work stuck up above your head [in the Underground car]—do you feel a sense of uplift? I don't.

The Christian Science Monitor, 5-13:22.

Tom Wolfe
Author

1

[On his decision to write a novel]: I guess there were a couple of reasons. First, I was curious, having spouted off so much about fiction and non-fiction, and, having said that the novelists weren't doing a good job, to see what would happen if I tried it. Also, I guess I subconsciously had the suspicion that, maybe, what if all this to-do I've made about nonfiction is all because I really, secretly think I can't do a novel. So I said, well, I've got to prove this to myself. But I also had the idea of trying to prove a point, which was that most of the theories about the contemporary novel were wrong, particularly the theory that I think Ortega y Gasset first promulgated, which was that the novel was like a quarry, and that the quarry had now been exhaustively mined. He was writing in the 1920s, and he said that after Flaubert and Henry James, there was nothing left to be done. I just felt that the contemporary novelists who were avoiding realism were missing the boat, and that realistic, even naturalistic, fiction not only could be but should be written in a period like this.

Interview, New York/
The New York Times, 10-13:25.

2

[Writer] Philip Roth had a theory in the '60s, when he was the hot young novelist. He said we live in an age in which the imagination of the novelist is helpless against what he knows he is going to read in tomorrow's newspaper. I never found this very convincing. It just seems to me that the novelist has to work harder. If it's a crazy age, the novelist has to jump into the craziness and see what's going on.

Interview/
Newsweek, 10-26:85.

3

I don't think writers can back off from realism, just as an ambitious engineer cannot back off from electricity. You can't say: "Ah, it's been done. I'm going to head off in another direction." It wouldn't work, because electricity gets down to the nature of matter. And realism in prose gets down to the nature of how writing triggers the memories of a reader.

Interview/
U.S. News & World Report,
11-23:58.

Yevgeny Yevtushenko
Soviet poet

4

If you read [the] history of Russia, you will find that all the political/social moments which changed our history began in poetry.

Interview, Beverly Hills, Calif./
The Christian Science Monitor,
5-15:1.

Medicine and Health

David Baltimore
Nobel Prize-winning
microbiologist

1

Quarantining [AIDS victims] will help no one. Most AIDS patients are too sick to be transmitting the virus. The virus is being spread largely by people who do not have AIDS but are infected with the virus, and they may or may not even know it. Quarantining would be totally futile.

Interview/
U.S. News & World Report,
1-12:70.

William J. Bennett
Secretary of Education
of the United States

2

Here's the heart of it: Most cases of AIDS result from behavior that can be avoided—and when it comes to the young, nothing more powerfully influences their behavior than their values, their internally held beliefs and convictions. The behavior of our nation's teen-agers is the product of the values they hold, not just the facts they have learned.

News conference, Washington,
Oct. 6/Los Angeles Times, 10-7:(I)4.

Otis R. Bowen
Secretary of Health
and Human Services
of the United States

3

[I have] always believed as a physician that the best and final guarantee of quality care is the physician. As long as we can maintain that strong tradition of the doctor who cares first and foremost about [a patient], then I say quality care is in good hands. Competition among private health plans extends to the quality of care those plans offer and, in the years to come, consumers will become much more savvy about differences in quality . . . This means that managed care systems will be competing among themselves for the best providers of care.

Speech to private health-maintenance
organizations, Washington, Jan. 12/
Los Angeles Times, 1-13:(I)18.

4

[AIDS] could well become one of the worst health problems in the history of the world. We may have to sacrifice some individual rights [to conquer the disease].

At National Governors' Association
conference, Washington, Feb. 22/
Los Angeles Times, 2-23:(I)12.

George Bush
Vice President
of the United States;
Candidate for
the 1988 Republican
Presidential nomination

5

We [in the U.S.] have the best medical-attention system in the world, and I don't want to see it go into the mode of England or this whole concept of socialized medicine where the government provides absolutely everything. You are going to break the government.

Broadcast interview/
"Meet the Press," NBC-TV, 12-13.

Robert Butler
Chairman,
department of geriatrics,
Mt. Sinai Medical Center,
New York

6

If you're confronted with a freeze on [Medicare] fees [to doctors], and your malpractice insurance is rising, and the cost of running an

WHAT THEY SAID IN 1987

(ROBERT BUTLER)

office goes up, how do you survive? You increase the number of patients, or the frequency you see them, or the procedures you do upon them.

Los Angeles Times, 9-28:(I)13.

Joseph A. Califano, Jr.
*Former Secretary of
Health, Education and Welfare
of the United States*

1

What we need is a minimum health-care law [in the U.S.], just as we have a minimum-wage law. Let's simply require that each employer assure its employees of a minimum level of health care: physician treatment, hospitalization, preventive services for the employee and his or her family . . . [The U.S. has] a pothole system of medical care . . . and they're savage potholes because they shatter people's lives.

*Before Senate Labor and
Human Resources Committee,
Washington, Jan. 12/
Los Angeles Times, 1-13:(I)18.*

John H. Chafee
*United States Senator,
R-Rhode Island*

2

Smokers' illnesses have to be paid for by all taxpayers, and it costs us $7-billion a year. Doubling the cigarette tax to 32 cents a pack would discourage people from smoking. It would also raise $3-billion in revenue. It's time to raise excise taxes on cigarettes and perhaps on other health-threatening items.

*TV spot/
The New York Times, 8-20:12.*

Ray Charles
Musician

3

[Calling for increased spending on fighting deafness, although he is blind]: My eyes are my handicap, but my ears are my opportunity.

*Congressional testimony/
U.S. News & World Report, 5-11:7.*

Jay Cohn
*Cardiologist,
University of Minnesota*

4

[Doctors] doing procedures with all this new equipment is glitzy. It's what many young doctors want to do, and have been trained to do, as medical education has moved away from teaching cognitive skills.

*U.S. News & World Report,
11-23:63.*

Norman Cousins
*Chairman, Task Force on
Psychoneuroimmunology,
School of Medicine,
University of California,
Los Angeles*

5

In 10 years at UCLA, I've seen 450 to 500 patients. To me, nothing is more striking about these patients than the fact that their illness intensified at the moment of diagnosis. Feelings of panic, helplessness, depression and loss of control set the stage for the advance of the disease. Panic is a disease in itself. It constricts the blood vessels, it can produce spurts of hormones that can rupture the heart . . . Physicians have conflicting interests. They are educated by their lawyers to lay it on the line. Telling a human being the worst may bring on the worst. One patient I talked to said his doctor told him, "We're still not sure, but we're pretty sure you've got cancer." He communicated panic to the patient before he had the definitive word.

*Interview, Los Angeles/
The Wall Street Journal, 4-24:(D)5.*

Michael E. DeBakey
*Surgeon;
Chairman of surgery,
College of Medicine,
Baylor University*

6

The patient must always come first, always. That is why we [doctors] are here. It is not the

(MICHAEL E. DeBAKEY)

money or the prestige, or anything else. It is to save lives, to heal. A scientist must be a humanist first, somebody who seeks to help humanity. That is fundamental. I don't think that is just some vague concept of philosophy. If you go back in history and study the great scientists, you'll see they were truly dedicated, compassionate, humanistic individuals. They were not detached from their fellow man.

Interview, Houston/
Los Angeles Times,
3-8:(I)38.

Lawrence DenBesten
Professor of medicine,
Fuller Theological Seminary

1

I've been in medicine 30 years and there's been an incredible change. The use of prayer in medicine is not a groundswell, but there is a willingness to recognize non-scientific interventions. Physicians are no longer bothered about using things whose mechanisms aren't understood. In my years in medical practice, there are many concrete examples where I would have to give prayer the credit for the outcome, rather than my own intervention as a physician.

The Christian Science Monitor,
12-29:16.

Richard Egdahl
Director,
Boston University
Medical Center

2

[Saying doctors are being squeezed by cost-cutting pressures, competition, etc.]: It's a painful shakeout. Steel has gone through it, farmers, computers. We doctors have always occupied a very favored position. Now it's our turn.

U.S. News & World Report,
1-26:44.

Richard Epstein
Professor of law,
University of Chicago

3

The [AIDS] disease is certainly being spread, in part, by deceitful behavior. I'm a Hobbesian: I believe there are probably enough bad apples in the barrel to make some measure of coercion necessary. The world doesn't work without coercion, and I'm suspicious of an exclusive reliance on voluntary behavior.

The Wall Street Journal, 6-17:24.

Jonathan Fielding
Professor of health services,
School of Public
Health and Medicine,
University of California,
Los Angeles

4

The difference in longevity that leads so many women to survive their male contemporaries is being abridged by an increase in the number of women who fall victim to their most deleterious habit—smoking.

U.S. News & World Report, 11-30:9.

Leo Fretz
Professor of philosophy,
Delft Institute of Technology
(Netherlands); Chairman,
Dutch Voluntary
Euthanasia Association

5

After years of debate, voluntary euthanasia has become accepted by broad segments of the [Dutch] population and by far the largest part of the medical profession . . . It would be a misunderstanding to state that we're pro-euthanasia, period. Every death is a drama. Killing someone in self-defense is a drama, but it's not considered immoral. We think it should be the same with voluntary mercy killing—a drama but not immoral.

Los Angeles Times, 4-12:(I)30.

Anne Geller
Director,
Smithers Alcoholism Center,
New York

1

[On fighting substance abuse in her patients]: It's being able to see yourself reflected in someone very different that helps bring home the disease [to the patients]. Otherwise, you can blame it on stress or overwork. You can blame it on poverty, or think that achievement immunizes you . . . It's not a class thing—we have many working-class patients—and it's certainly not a race thing. It has to do with the psycho-social assets that a person brings to treatment, with whether they have been able to achieve the basic competencies of adult life. The hardest patients to treat, and I can't treat them in such a short stay, are those being habilitated, not rehabilitated.

Interview, New York/
The New York Times, 7-3:12.

Albert Gore, Jr.
United States Senator,
D-Tennessee; Candidate for
the 1988 Democratic
Presidential nomination

2

History will deal harshly with the [U.S.] Reagan Administration for its failure to face up to the threat of AIDS. It is his policies that have left Americans groping for answers and blaming each other.

At United States Conference
of Mayors, Nashville, Tenn./
USA Today, 6-18:(A)9.

3

Three months ago the President [Reagan] finally addressed the issue of [the] AIDS [disease] for the first time in his Administration. Public-health experts recommended that he focus attention on expanded research and public education. But instead, the President made testing [for AIDS] a goal in itself—doing more to

set back AIDS policy by that one action than he had already done in six years of silence.

Interview/*
Los Angeles Times, 11-2:(I)13.

John Habgood
Anglican Archbishop
of York (England)

4

[On the AIDS disease]: There are people who say this is a problem for an immoral minority [homosexuals], and they are getting their just desserts. The church should hold back from applying that moral judgment to individuals and not add to their burdens. On the other hand, it's quite legitimate to say something about the character of a society which has allowed this disease to develop.

Interview, York, England/
The Christian Science Monitor, 7-15:17.

David Halberstam
Author, Journalist

5

AIDS is and will continue to be almost the most important story—the growing terror from it is extraordinary, not just of the disease itself but what it is likely to do to social and sexual mores. It will affect profoundly how we live in every aspect.

Interview/USA Today, 2-11:(A)11.

William Hembree
Director,
Health Research Institute

6

The way a good [health] benefit plan was defined in the past was that employees didn't need to pay anything. Today, the definition of a good plan is that employees do pay something. If that's not required these days, with so many two-income families, it means that the company puts too many of its compensation dollars into health benefits.

The New York Times, 6-9:30.

Katharine Hepburn
Actress

1

We're living in strange times when doctors practically go bankrupt buying insurance to protect themselves against [malpractice] suits. Lawyers and insurance companies and patients are all stirring up trouble—we've gotten crooked as a nation. If my doctor had failed in saving my leg after my car accident, would I have sued? Of course not. I wouldn't sue him, even if he was wrong, because he is a human being, and human beings do the best they can; but we all make mistakes.

Interview, Connecticut/
Ladies' Home Journal, October:216.

Donald R. Hopkins
Deputy Director,
Federal Centers for
Disease Control

2

The main public health objective in regard to AIDS is to prevent infection. Thus if the net effect of wide-spread mandatory testing would be to reduce the number of persons at higher risk who are in fact counseled and tested, because many others are scared away, then mandatory testing would not serve that crucial public health objective.

At AIDS conference, Washington/
The New York Times, 6-8:11.

Stephen C. Joseph
Commissioner of Health
of New York City

3

There will be no slowing of the transmission of the AIDS virus, or of preventing the seepage of the virus into the general population, without a meaningful war on drugs. The future of the AIDS epidemic in New York, and elsewhere in the nation, lies in the AIDS-intravenous-drug-use connection.

The New York Times, 6-12:11.

Edward I. Koch
Mayor of New York

4

[Calling for compassion and help for victims of the AIDS disease]: If you turn your back on these people, you yourself are an animal. You may be a well-dressed animal, but you are nevertheless an animal.

Interview/
The New York Times, 3-16:10.

5

AIDS is a catastrophe, but what people don't realize is that the largest group that will suffer from AIDS will be, ultimately, minorities. Why? Because the largest number of IV drug users are to be found in our minority population . . . You and I and every decent citizen in this country has to stand up when the push is on to deny medical aid and when the push is on to quarantine—segregate if you will, because that's what quarantine is—those two groups [homosexuals and IV drug users]. And it will come as sure as you and I are sitting here, and we must stop it.

Before Eastern Baptist Association,
New York, July 16/
The New York Times, 7-17:12.

C. Everett Koop
Surgeon General
of the United States

6

I think that the risk of AIDS is so great and the task is so huge, almost insurmountable, that you've got to pick what you can accomplish. You don't have to talk to the Medicare population about AIDS, but you've got to talk to the young, vulnerable people. I would hope that we could raise a generation of kids to understand that when you have a temptation for a heterosexual experience in the back seat of a car, or if a certain portion of the population has an opportunity for a homosexual experience, or teenagers are out some night and someone says let's go shoot drugs, that they would withdraw from that possibility, opportunity, temptation—withdraw with caution and ask themselves, is what I'm

(C. EVERETT KOOP)

about to do worth dying for? I think the answer is no.

Interview/
The Washington Post,
3-24:(Health)7.

1

Confidential AIDS testing? Not as long as people are people . . . There is associated with AIDS a very serious stigma at the moment. The knowledge [that] a person is carrying the virus of AIDS can be extremely detrimental to his life-style . . . If it suddenly were known . . . he could lose his job and insurance, he could lose his housing, his children or grandchildren might be asked to leave their school, or his pastor might ask him to stop attending church. Until we get over that stigma, we're going to continue to have controversy over who should be tested and who shouldn't.

News conference, Houston, June 15/
Los Angeles Times, 6-16:(I)4.

2

[On the AIDS disease]: It is a medical threat, because the diagnosis carries with it such a stigma. It is especially bad for people who have received the AIDS virus by what the rest of Americans consider to be improper behavior—drug abuse or homosexual behavior. That stigma now covers all of us, no matter how we got the AIDS virus. Therefore, although it is a medical problem, the social, economic, political, cultural issues will far outlast the day when we conquer this disease medically.

Interview/USA Today, 9-18:(A)13.

3

[Comparing health care in Europe with that in the U.S.]: I'm not saying they do it better in Europe, but if, for instance, you have a health problem in Finland, everyone speaks the same language, they all go to the same church, they all have the same kind of ideas, and 98 per cent of them are sort of clones of the others. If the government health officer says, "Do this; do that," everyone answers, "Okay, we'll do it." It

doesn't work that way here. When you want to do something in the way of an educational program in the United Kingdom, it comes out of the Department of Health. If you want to do it here, it comes out of 50 different places (the 50 states).

The Saturday Evening Post,
November:110.

Jeffrey Levi
Executive director,
National Gay and
Lesbian Task Force

4

[Criticizing President Reagan's call for routine testing for AIDS]: He fails to recognize the impact of testing and the value of testing. If he is opposed to discrimination, then he must be willing to put the force of the Federal government behind it. If he wants people to choose to be tested, he must also guarantee confidentiality. And if he wants a testing program to be successful, then he must be willing to put the resources into the counseling that makes a testing program valuable.

May 31/Los Angeles Times, 6-1:(I)7.

Susan M. Love
Assistant clinical professor
of surgery, Harvard University
Medical School

5

Surgery is the most male of medical specialties and the least friendly to women. A lot of women like surgery, but they ask themselves, "Am I willing to put up with the discrimination and five years of training, and what will my life-style be like afterward?" In private practice, there is a lot of nights call and emergencies.

The New York Times, 6-29:17.

Donald Ian MacDonald
Deputy Assistant to
President of the United States
Ronald Reagan for
Drug Abuse Policy

6

What we are talking about isn't so much introducing punitive measures [against illegal-

(DONALD IAN MacDONALD)

drug users] as changing our present attitude, which is enabling. Our present attitude, which allows drug abusers to blame someone else—"society"—for behavior that is destructive to themselves or others, enables them to continue that behavior. It's like having your teen-ager smash up the family car several times and you only say, "Be more careful." At some point, we have to think in terms of consequences. People talk about the failure of Prohibition. In my view, the mistake we made with Prohibition was that virtually all of the effort was directed against bootleggers. Use or possession of alcohol was rarely punished. Contrast that with Japan, which faced a major amphetamine epidemic in the 1950s. Japan's approach was user-based. They cracked down and arrested 54,000 amphetamine abusers, and in two years the epidemic was over.

Interview/
The Washington Post,
9-11:(A)25.

Barbara Melosh
Curator, division of
medical sciences,
Smithsonian Institution,
Washington

1

[On the Smithsonian's acquisition of the Jarvik-7 artificial heart for display in its collections]: It's possible 100 years from now that the artificial heart will be as routine as a blood transfusion or a hip implant. It's also possible that the artificial heart will be viewed as a curious quirk, a byway on the path of medical history that went in another direction.

Washington, June 17/
Los Angeles Times, 6-18:(I)4.

Thirman L. Milner
Mayor of Hartford, Conn.

2

[Criticizing the Reagan Administration for cutting back expenditures for anti-drug programs]: We [in the cities] established our pro-

grams based on what the President told us last year, and now we can't move ahead. I'm beginning to wonder if they're really serious about the drug program. Once communities became deeply involved, the Administration pulled the rug out from under us.

At U.S. Conference of Mayors,
Washington, Jan. 21/
The Washington Post, 1-22:(A)9.

Claude Pepper
United States Representative,
D-Florida

3

The Congress and the Administration are now committed to enacting catastrophic-health-care legislation this session of Congress. We must make sure that the plan they adopt is one which covers the real, bankrupting health-care needs of Americans—a plan which covers care in the home and care in a nursing home, instead of one which stops the moment one leaves a hospital.

Before National Council
on the Aging, Chicago, March 30/
Los Angeles Times, 3-31:(I)13.

Steven Piver
Chief,
gynecologic oncology department,
Roswell Park Memorial Institute,
Buffalo, N.Y.

4

Rather than putting so much money into research for the rare cancers, put it into education and early detection. [But cancer researchers resist that because] it's much more glamorous to write a grant for a rare disease like leukemia, than to write a grant for screening for rectal cancer.

Los Angeles Times, 4-17:(I)17.

Mitchell T. Rabkin
President,
Beth Israel Hospital,
Boston

5

[It is often inappropriate to go through] the massive exercise of cardiopulmonary resuscita-

(MITCHELL T. RABKIN)

tion [for] irreparably or irreparably ill patients [whose death is imminent]. Our goal is to avoid the useless prolongation of dying. This is not a quality-of-life issue, a question of what a patient's life will be like if he gets better. If you attempt resuscitation, knowing that it will not do any good, you are only abusing the patient, and you can create enormous emotional trauma for the family if any relatives are present.

The New York Times, 6-5:11.

Ronald Reagan
President of the United States

1

Let's be honest with ourselves: AIDS information cannot be what some call "value neutral." After all, when it comes to preventing AIDS, don't medicine and morality teach the same lessons? . . . All the vaccines and medications in the world won't change one basic truth: that prevention is better than cure, and that's particularly true for AIDS, for which right now there is no cure. This is where education comes in. The Federal role must be to give educators accurate information about the disease. How that information is used must be up to schools and parents, not government.

Before College of Physicians,
Philadelphia, April 1/
Los Angeles Times, 4-2:(I)1.

2

American medicine is the world's best because it is private, and it must stay that way . . . We need no second opinions . . . Our competitive system has produced the finest health-care in history.

Before College of Physicians,
Philadelphia, April 1/
USA Today, 4-2:(A)4.

3

Just as most individuals don't know they carry the [AIDS] virus, no one knows to what extent the virus has infected our entire society. AIDS is surreptitiously spreading throughout our population, and yet we have no accurate

measure of its scope. It is time we knew exactly what we were facing. And that is why I favor routine testing . . . As individuals, we have a moral obligation not to endanger others—and that can mean endangering others with a gun, with a car, or with a virus. If a person has reason to believe he or she may be a carrier, that person has a moral duty to be tested for AIDS. Human decency requires it.

At fund-raising dinner
sponsored by American Foundation
for AIDS Research, Washington,
May 31/The New York Times, 6-1:1;
Los Angeles Times, 6-1:(I)1.

Arnold S. Relman
Editor,
"The New England
Journal of Medicine"

4

[Criticizing claims that for-profit hospitals are more efficient]: The measures of efficiency are meaningless. If I'm making a standard product, a Xerox copier or a McDonald's hamburger, and you tell me you can turn it out 10 per cent faster and 10 per cent cheaper, that's more efficient. But if you tell me you can run a hospital with 20 per cent fewer nurses, the right question to ask is what it does to the quality of care.

Interview/
The New York Times, 4-2:32.

5

[Criticizing doctors who own or are partners in diagnostic laboratories to which they send samples or refer patients]: This is plainly unethical. It creates a clear conflict of interest. And it's not only the few crooked docs who are going to be influenced. All of them will.

U.S. News & World Report, 11-23:65.

John Rizzo
Research economist,
Center for
Health Policy Research,
American Medical Association

6

Those who say that defensive medicine is not a big problem or that these extra tests do some

(JOHN RIZZO)

good are now going to have to demonstrate the benefits and, frankly, I think they will be hard-pressed to do that. There are clearly things that are being done that don't deter claims, that don't do any good medically, and do cost money. They aren't making the patient any happier; they're just costing them more.

Chicago, May 21/
Los Angeles Times, 5-22:(I)28.

Sandra Scarr
Chairman,
department of psychology,
University of Virginia

1

When you ask parents what they want for their children, most will tell you they want them to be happy and satisfied with their lives. They're saying they value mental health, being able to function effectively in society, as well as being satisfied with oneself . . . If you aren't happy, you don't enjoy achievement.

USA Today, 2-18:(D)2.

Robert T. Schooley
Specialist in infectious diseases,
Massachusetts General Hospital

2

[On his research into the AIDS disease]: I don't think that in the year 2055 someone will pull out an encyclopedia, look up AIDS and find the names of most of the people doing the [research] work now. When you look at polio, you only see Jonas Salk and Albert Sabin. You don't see the several hundred others who were also doing research. Yet Salk and Sabin couldn't have done what they did without the work of those several hundred other people. I don't have any illusions about being remembered as the person who cured AIDS. I want to be remembered as one of the people who contributed.

Interview, Boston/
Los Angeles Times, 5-18:(I)1.

Anson Shupe
Chairman, department of
anthropology and sociology,
Indiana University-Purdue University
at Fort Wayne

3

The medical establishment must come to grips with the voluminous claims of those who have experienced spiritual healing and testify that it works. Simplistic mob psychology explanations about mass delusion will not do. For an unknown but seemingly significant proportion of the population, the medical profession's hard-won credibility has been called into question. The medical model has more limitations than its promoters wish to admit.

The Christian Science Monitor,
12-29:18.

Mervyn F. Silverman
President, American Foundation
for AIDS Research;
Former Commissioner of
Health of San Francisco

4

[Arguing against mandatory testing for AIDS]: It wouldn't control AIDS. It would have the reverse effect on the people you most want to get in. To encourage them to come in, there must be trust. There can't be trust when there's a risk of interfering with their livelihood, housing and other important issues. We're not trying to reach a 65-year-old monogamous male or female. We're trying to reach people from 20 to 49, sexually active, maybe shooting drugs. These are the key people, and you can't get to them if distrust and fear are present . . . Some of these people have already dropped out of sight. They won't get voluntary help or seek help from doctors. Some health centers have had people come in for testing who call themselves Ronald Reagan or Ed Meese—anything, rather than give their names. We lose sight of our goal; you don't educate by making something mandatory.

Interview/
U.S. News & World Report,
3-9:62.

405

(MERVYN F. SILVERMAN)

1

[On the Reagan Administration's call for mandatory testing of certain groups for AIDS]: There is one big question about all this testing. Since there is no cure or vaccine, what is the Administration planning to do with the person who's [infected]?

The Washington Post, 6-11:(A)16.

Harold S. Solomon
Assistant professor of medicine,
Harvard University Medical School

2

Exercise makes us healthy. It lowers our blood pressure. It reduces cholesterol. It helps to control our weight. But what is the best exercise? I am not a good one to ask. Everybody has his own, and we need to tailor our activities to our environments. What I know is that I feel better when I make my body perspire at least three times a week. Our bodies were built as beasts of burden. But in the past 50 years, we've gone to standing behind counters, sitting at desks, riding in cars.

Interview/USA Today, 3-26:(D)4.

Harold Sox
Chief of internal medicine,
Stanford University
School of Medicine

3

[On those who criticize doctors who own or are partners in diagnostic laboratories to which they send samples or refer patients]: There's nothing intrinsically bad about doctors having or running labs. It can be efficient and good for patient care. I don't think most doctors are consciously ripping people off.

U.S. News & World Report, 11-23:68.

James S. Todd
Senior deputy executive
vice president,
American Medical Association

4

[On doctors]: It is absolutely mindless that a group of 500,000 highly educated professionals

are now *the most* regulated group in this country. There seems to be this mentality in Congress: "We're going to tell you how much money you're going to get, and you just go ahead and take care of these people." There is no understanding that doctors have to educate their children, have to pay malpractice-insurance payments, have to maintain quality of care . . . Here is a group of 500,000 individuals with absolutely no leverage. They don't strike, they don't have organized labor unions, they don't have economic power in terms of withholding or dedicating their resources. But when you go to Washington to talk with the legislators, it all just falls on deaf ears.

Interview/USA Today, 1-14:(A)11.

Alexander V. Vlasov
Minister of the Interior
of the Soviet Union

5

[On drug abuse in the Soviet Union]: I wouldn't say we never had this evil before, but public discussion of such ulcers was not encouraged. We must admit that silence about the extreme danger of drug addiction blunted social awareness, weakened the attention and vigor of the police and the medical profession, lowered vigilance of parents, schools and public opinion. This silence actually encouraged the spread of drug addiction . . . We must give wider exposure to the obscene nature of the drug den, the ugly face of the pusher and the moral deformity of the user.

Interview, Jan. 6/
Los Angeles Times, 1-7:(I)6.

Henry Waxman
United States Representative,
D-California

6

The brand-name [pharmaceutical] companies argue that rising prices [of drugs] are necessary to fund their fast-rising costs of research and development . . . [But] the recent increases [in prices] are not producing new drugs; they are filling corporate coffers. If prices continue to

(HENRY WAXMAN)

skyrocket, the fundamental balance of our patent system will be distorted. We award monopolies in the form of patents to innovators. But when the innovation is an essential drug, we cannot allow a private enterprise to price sick people out of the market. In the immediate future, the public and health-care system are the losers from high prices, and in time I have no doubt that brand-name pharmaceutical companies will suffer as well. Their image as caring for the patients treated by their drugs is already tarnished, and at some point the public will turn to the government for help.

Speech, June 25/
The Wall Street Journal,
7-20:18.

Ted Weiss
United States Representative,
D-New York

1

GAO's findings raise serious questions about the performance over the past several years of the $1-billion-a-year national cancer program. While it is heartening that cancer-patient survival has improved for some cancer patients, we have apparently not done nearly as well in treating cancer as government officials have led us to believe. Neither Congressional policymakers nor the public is well-served by unwarranted expectations that we have turned the corner on this group of devastating diseases.

The New York Times, 4-16:12.

David Werdegar
Commissioner of Health
of San Francisco

2

[On fighting the AIDS disease]: There has been a lack of an organized response at the Federal level. We are at war against this disease, but we seem to have no real battle plan

and no money to fight with. I'm glad [President Reagan] is finally getting involved, but we need more than just words. We need real leadership on this issue.

April 1/USA Today, 4-2:(D)4.

Sheldon M. Wolff
Physician-in-chief,
New England Medical Center;
Co-chairman, Institute of
Medicine panel on AIDS

3

I don't thing anything in our lifetime has had the same kinds of overtones [as the AIDS disease]. AIDS is a disease that afflicts people outside the midstream of America: the gay population, minorities, intravenous drug users. You can't separate that from the equation. If we were able to look at things purely from a medical standpoint—accepting that the disease happens to occur in these people—it would be pretty simple. But nobody takes that attitude.

Los Angeles Times, 11-2:(I)1.

Joseph Zanaga
Physician,
Children's Medical Center,
Richmond, Va.; Former chairman,
Committee on School Health,
American Academy of Pediatrics

4

[Lamenting that children are becoming too fat]: It's funny. I look around my own neighborhood and see a generation of young adults desperately working to be physically fit and a generation of children working as hard as they can to avoid it . . . You'd think we're sending our kids the right message, but somewhere it's not getting through. Maybe they think you only become interested in physical fitness as an adult. Maybe they think, "As an adult, I will become interested in physical fitness." But that might be too late.

Interview, Richmond, Va., Aug. 25/
The New York Times, 8-27:12.

The Performing Arts

Ben Bagdikian
Dean,
Graduate School
of Journalism,
University of California

1

By far the majority of dollars in the astronomical purchase prices [of TV stations] is for the broadcast license issued by the U.S. government. Where else can you buy a piece of paper that gives you annual pre-tax profits of 40 per cent, that gives you a monopoly on your channel protected by the full police powers of the government, and with almost no obligation to do anything in return?

Before House
Telecommunications
Subcommittee, Washington/
The Christian Science Monitor,
12-2:22.

Robert Batscha
Director,
Museum of Broadcasting,
New York

2

[On how people should choose the TV programs they watch]: You don't walk down the street and see a cluster of movie houses and just walk into one to see what's showing. You check out the reviews, you read about it, you try to make sure you're not going to be wasting your time. [TV should be approached in a similar way.] If you sit down on Sunday night with your newspaper's TV supplement and pick out six hours [during the coming week] that you are going to watch, I think you're going to find an excellent six hours.

Interview,
New York/Los Angeles Times,
7-3:(VI)26.

Saul Bellow
Author

3

I don't mind entertainment. But literature is fighting for its life. All forms of literature have taken second or third place to TV. Television programs turn the stories of the world into cracker cheese.

Interview, Wilmington, Vt./
USA Today, 9-17:(D)5.

Merrill Brown
Executive editor,
"Channels" magazine

4

[On the FCC's recent warnings about obscenity on radio and TV]: I think it's clearly more of a symbolic move than it is a law-enforcement move. I think [FCC Chairman] Mark Fowler is making a political statement rather than a regulatory initiative, and he is entitled to do that as the [outgoing] Chairman of the FCC. He has that kind of "bully pulpit." It is a statement of our times and of the regime in power now.

Interview/
The Christian Science Monitor,
4-22:23.

James E. Burke
Chairman,
Johnson & Johnson Products, Inc.

5

[Saying TV presents too much of a negative image of business and businessmen]: The disenchantment in this country over the last 20 years in our institution [business] among the public is profound, and I think [it] will shock most of you . . . [TV] is very influential and

(JAMES E. BURKE)

very powerful. I'm not sure you realize how powerful it really is.

At "Television, Families and Work"
conference, Montecito, Calif./
Daily Variety, 6-8:4.

John Chancellor
Commentator,
and former anchorman,
NBC News

1

In the 1950s, a lot of television organizations were operated out of a system of paternal ownership. When CBS was Bill Paley's network and NBC, David Sarnoff's network, they held them in the palm of their hands, and there was that link of personal accountability that no longer exists. It has now been replaced by boards of directors who have a fiduciary responsibility under the law not to run risks, and to maximize profits. They can be sued by stockholders if they do certain things you and I might regard as courageous.

Interview/
The Christian Science Monitor,
11-30:22.

Bruce L. Christensen
President,
Public Broadcasting Service

2

I think you'll continue to see [on PBS] a mix of programs that will make both right, left and probably center unhappy at particular times. Ours is an attempt to find the standards by which we can judge those programs in such a way that they are not either unfairly kept off the air, or given air time when they don't really warrant it because they aren't . . . good, accurate, quality programs . . .

Interview/
The Christian Science Monitor,
4-16:4.

Barbara Corday
President,
Columbia/Embassy Television

3

When people criticize [commercial] television, I'm not sure what they're comparing it with . . . If Americans love *Masterpiece Theatre* [on PBS] so much, why doesn't it have any ratings? I mean, if you get a 30 share of the audience watching *Magnum P.I.*, and an 8 share of the audience watching *Masterpiece Theatre*, it must tell you something. It's like when they do telephone surveys and everybody says, "The only thing I watch on television is *60 Minutes*." Who are they kidding? It makes me furious. When I was working at the network, the one thing that made me angrier than anything was when some writer or producer walked into my office to pitch a show and said, "I don't watch television, but . . . " and then proceeded to pitch me something that was exactly like something already on the air. It is a put-down of the business that is keeping them fed. We certainly do make some bad shows, but we don't work any less on a bad show than we do on a good one.

Interview, Burbank, Calif./
Emmy Magazine, July-Aug.:22.

Norman Corwin
Former radio dramatist
and television producer

4

[TV] today is worse than I forecast. There are some bright areas, but you've really got to look for them . . . What is happening to the best? And what is happening to the worst? The worst is going to the top in terms of budgets and exposure, and the best is being cut back . . . Programs that are total trash and are acknowledged to be such, not only by the audience but by the makers, will never be taken off the air as long as they have good ratings. Conversely, programs of quality will die quickly if they don't [get] the ratings . . . There is something very basically and dramatically wrong when quality itself becomes suspect and a script that has literacy, wit and subtlety is immediately at a

(NORMAN CORWIN)

disadvantage when it arrives at the desk of the planners, along with something that is simple-minded and unimaginative, perhaps copied from some other successful format. These are given the red carpet and shown the way to the studio.

Interview, Los Angeles/
Emmy Magazine,
Sept.-Oct.:42,43.

Bill Cosby
Entertainer

1

There's nothing worse in comedy than looking at a comedian or a movie or a TV show where you see that these people are *trying* to be funny. It makes the viewer tired and it also depresses the viewer, because there's nothing worse than looking at failure.

New York/
USA Today, 8-31:(A)1.

2

[On his high salary for TV's *The Cosby Show*]: Nobody is over-paid. The people who pay me the money make a lot more from me than they give me. NBC is much richer than me, and so is everybody else who signs checks made out to me. I produce, so they pay me for it . . . Whenever I think of the really super-rich, I look at the *Fortune* [magazine] list, and I ain't anywhere near the top of that, baby.

Interview/
USA Today, 10-19:(D)2.

Patrick Cox
Chief executive,
Sky Channel
(private European TV network)

3

State [-owned] broadcasters are like the medieval church. They think their job is to teach and preach.

U.S. News & World Report,
5-25:52.

Dennis E. Eckart
United States Representative,
D-Ohio

4

[Saying TV networks should be licensed to insure they serve the public interest]: We are deeply concerned that with the rush to profits the public interest has been trampled . . . [A public-interest standard should apply to network control] much in the way that Congress, through the FCC, imposes a public licensing standard to own a television station. I don't suggest for a moment that the government ought to advocate censorship. But what I do believe, frankly, is that government ought to insure that the public interests are ultimately protected.

Washington,
March 12/The New York Times,
3-13:25.

John Erman
Director

5

I think that's the great thing about TV now—the networks are willing to tackle these controversial subjects. Sometimes I wish they would tackle them with more guts—we have to sugar-coat the pill a little too much. But at least we're getting them done.

Los Angeles Times,
5-25:(V)1.

Martin Esslin
British drama critic

6

America doesn't have radio and television. It has advertising. It is one of the most culturally under-developed countries in the world—below Ghana, I would say. The United States is the only country that spends billions and billions to make people more stupid than they were before.

At Wheatland Conference
on Literature, Washington,
April 23/The Washington Post,
4-25:(B)5.

Dan Filie
Vice president of
drama programs, NBC-TV

1

It used to be that if you watched TV, you watched one of the three networks. Independent stations and PBS were still marginal then. Now the indies have more product, there's cable and there's video—and for the networks to succeed, we're going to have to attract the best [creative] people we can, whether they're from television, the movies or the theatre.

American Film, April:52.

Fred W. Friendly
Professor emeritus of journalism,
Columbia University;
Former president, CBS News

2

[Arguing against current FCC philosophy of less regulation of broadcasting]: When there are more people who want to operate stations than there are stations to give out, you can't talk about an open marketplace. You can't talk about the rules of free enterprise in a closed marketplace.

The New York Times, 1-19:9.

3

Sadly I must tell you that the television networks, of which I was once a part, are mercantile shadows of what they once were. Those in Congress, those in the FCC and the people like myself who stand idly by, are as guilty as the Wall Street traders who have changed something licensed "in the public interest, convenience and necessity" into a midway of junk entertainment and headline-service news.

At House subcommittee hearing,
Washington, April 28/
Los Angeles Times, 4-29:(VI)8.

Leonard Goldberg
President, 20th Century
Fox Film Corporation

4

A newspaper person asked me a couple of week ago, "Why isn't television better? Whose

fault is it?" I said, "Well, if you know the guys at the three networks—Brandon Stoddard, Brandon Tartikoff, Bud Grant—they're nice men. They don't want to do anything bad. They'd like it to be better. So they're not the heavies. Most producers want to do better things." "Well then, why isn't it better?" I said, "I guess it's just really hard to do really good work in any form."

Interview/American Film, May:11.

Julian Goodman
Former chairman,
National Broadcasting Company

5

It is not uncommon for those new to the [TV] business, or for consultants brought in, to say to themselves, "All businesses are alike and I'm going to tackle this network like any other business." That's a mistake. Networks are not like other businesses, if evidenced only by the fact that we are invited to appear so frequently before committees of Congress to justify our behavior.

At House subcommittee hearing,
Washington, April 28/
Los Angeles Times, 4-29:(VI)8.

Lawrence Grossman
President, NBC News

6

[On public television, public radio and the other elements of the public broadcasting system in the U.S.]: What's wrong is that the structure of public broadcasting, as it has been designed in this country, is so diffuse, duplicative, bureaucratic, confusing, frustrating and senseless that it is a miracle [it] has survived at all.

At Public Radio Conference,
Washington/Los Angeles Times,
5-4:(VI)1.

Helen Hayes
Actress

7

[On TV]: Every time I turn it on to get to the station I want, I pass through stations as I

411

(HELEN HAYES)

punch the buttons, and there's a great screech and the car is being knocked over a cliff, bursting into flames or something. I never saw so many cars being wrecked as there are on television today. And it's monotonous and tiresome. I just don't want to see anymore cars wrecked, that's all.

Interview/USA Today, 1-9:(A)11.

Gordon Humphrey
United States Representative,
R-New Hampshire

1

[Criticizing the violence in TV programming]: Somehow, we have to turn off the torrent of rubbish pouring out of television sets into the living rooms of homes all across our nation.

Los Angeles Times, 6-26:(VI)26.

Jamie Kellner
President,
Fox Broadcasting Company

2

We [at Fox Broadcasting] are trying to provide very high-quality programming and target it a bit more narrowly than the three other networks do. They try to appeal to everybody, and we believe that has resulted in derivative, homogenized programming . . . We are going after the young-adult audience. A large percentage of the network audiences is over 50, and, in order to win the household ratings game and be Number 1, they must appeal to the older viewers. Fox is not in that household ratings game. We believe that the future of television is going to be directed toward pinpointed demographic audiences.

Interview, New York/
The Christian Science Monitor,
7-9:23.

Ted Koppel
Anchorman,
"Nightline," ABC-TV

3

You won't be surprised to learn that there is not a great deal of room on television for com-

plexity. We are nothing as an industry if we are not attuned to the appetites and limitations of our audience. We have learned, for example, that your attention span is brief. We should know. We helped make it that way. Watch *Miami Vice* some Friday night. You will find not only a pastel-colored world, which neatly symbolizes the moral ambiguity of that program, you will discover that no scene lasts longer than 10 or 15 seconds. It is a direct reflection of the television industry's confidence in your ability to concentrate. We require nothing of you. Only that you watch and say that you are watching if Mr. Nielsen [TV ratings] representatives happen to call.

At Duke University commencement/
The Christian Science Monitor, 6-15:24.

Frank Lautenberg
United States Senator,
D-New Jersey

4

Television can help educate and inform our kids and excite their curiosity about the world around them, or it can grow for the nation a crop of couch potatoes.

USA Today, 10-8:(A)10.

Norman Lear
Producer, Writer

5

[On TV's coverage of the U.S. Iran-contra scandal in which U.S. Lt. Col. Oliver North's testimony elicited sympathy from many of the viewing public]: TV eats up moist-eyed people . . . and at the minute it's eating up Ollie North. He gets tears in his eyes, he gets all teared up. TV loves moist. The camera loves moist.

Newsweek, 7-20:11.

6

Don't try to be socially relevant [when doing TV shows]. You are or you are not. I don't think anything turns out if somebody says "I will do something important [or] socially relevant . . . [With *All In the Family*,] I don't really

(NORMAN LEAR)

believe I was wanting to be socially relevant. [The show's main character], Archie, was my father. I was raised in a Jewish household, but my father was as bigoted as [Archie] Bunker. He used to call me the laziest white kid he ever met. So I'd say, "Why do you put down a race of people to call me lazy?" He argued and argued and argued, and he said, "You're the stupidest white kid I ever knew" . . . He never understood he was putting down a race of people by calling me lazy and stupid. I had to do that show because this was my father and me . . . [But] you don't start to tell the story of an issue. You just tell the story of a particular family . . . Just tell the story the best you can, and in the most responsible way you can. If you start with an issue, the emotional truth isn't there.

At Young Artists United seminar,
Santa Monica, Calif., Oct. 1/
Daily Variety, 10-5:8,18.

Kim LeMasters
President, CBS Entertainment

1

We've moved into a different era in TV. A network doesn't have the ratings power it once had to put on a show, promote it and have a hit. The fragmentation of the audience to pay-TV, and other media, has reduced the ability of network to manufacture a hit. You can't take the time to build, as you did formerly. It now requires extreme patience. We have got to look at the structure, at the writing.

Los Angeles, Nov. 17/
Daily Variety, 11-18:1.

Sidney Lumet
Director

2

[On TV]: The problem lies in the form itself. There's something about that 19-inch piece of glass, something about the solitary experience of viewing it, that defeats even the most ambitious TV project. One can ask oneself a simple question: Have I ever laughed as loud watching a comedy on TV as I have watching a movie or a play? As for drama, I find that pictures that are supposed to be emotional become only sentimental. It may be that TV will finally become the primary medium for seeing movies, and we'll simply have to make the best of it. But I sure as hell am going to keep trying to stay out of "the box."

American Film, April:54.

Newton N. Minow
Former Chairman,
Federal Communications
Commission

3

Today, children spend more time with television than they do with their teachers, even their parents . . . At some point we're going to say, no more ignorance about the responsibility to provide good programs for children on television. It may be 1990, it may be the year 2000, but at some point our society is going to say, no more inattention to the fact that most of our children are spending most of their time with a television set.

Panel discussion, Boston/
Los Angeles Times, 6-19:(VI)25.

John O'Toole
Executive producer,
"Modern Maturity," PBS-TV

4

We know television commercials distort reality. Actually, we know they *lie*—don't we? There are now Isuzu commercials featuring a man who looks us in the eye and lies *outrageously*, which makes us laugh. Watergate conspirator John Ehrlichman is currently featured in a commercial in which he asserts the truthfulness of the label, on the grounds that who knows more about truths and untruths than *he* does? Can a Rosemary Woods commercial for Memorex tape be far behind? Or perhaps Gary Hart for Rice-a-Roni? So, reality and television become harder and harder to separate.

The Washington Post, 5-26:(A)20.

413

WHAT THEY SAID IN 1987

Dennis Patrick
Chairman, Federal
Communications Commission

1

[On the FCC's fight against broadcast obscenity]: . . . this Federal Communications Commission is second to none in the history of the Commission in terms of its sensitivity to First Amendment rights. And therefore, we do not, as a philosophical matter, enjoy or look for opportunities to be involved in broadcast content . . . However, all of that having been said, obscenity has *never* been protected by the First Amendment and indecency is subject to reasonable time, place and manner restrictions, even in the print media, which is my standard for First Amendment jurisprudence. And it's the standard that I believe ought to be applied to the electronic press . . . The fact is that, whereas the Commission is *very* sensitive to First Amendment rights and is *very* disposed to give broadcasters a maximum amount of discretion generally with respect to how they program their stations, as a Constitutional matter, obscenity is excepted from that category of speech which enjoys First Amendment protection, Number 1. And Number 2 . . . there is a statute on the point. It's 1464 of the Criminal Code, which prohibits the broadcast of obscene and indecent speech, and the Constitutionality of that statute, even as applied to indecency in the context of the broadcast medium, has been upheld by the Supreme Court.

Interview, Monterey, Calif./
Los Angeles Times, 8-17:(VI)1.

Octavio Paz
Poet

2

The major obstacle to poetry [today] has been the stubborn indifference of television. Since poetry doesn't have a high commercial rating and resists being made an ideological tool of governments, it has been eliminated almost entirely from the TV screen. This mistake, compounded by ignorance and contempt, is deplorable.

Interview, New York/
The New York Times 12-1:8.

Stefanie Powers
Actress

3

Television uses things up like people go through a Kleenex box. Bingo, and you're out, for the most part. And yet, there's a certain amount of loyalty to people who have been on television over a period of years in successful series. The public has loyalty, and producers know they will be interested in watching those people again and again. There's no real loyalty in the industry though. I could give the most brilliant performance of my life, never to be duplicated, but after this show is on the air, no one will remember. There is so much product and we are inundated with all kinds of diversion . . . we can't absorb it.

Interview/USA Today, 1-6:(D)2.

Sharon Rockefeller
Member, Corporation for
Public Broadcasting

4

The Federal funds for public broadcasting were slashed 25 per cent in 1981. Why is this Federal commitment so important? Because it provides the leverage, the incentive, the "Good Housekeeping Seal of Approval" by which other sources of funding are secured. CPB dollars are the seed money that have the classic multiplier effect: They stimulate states, colleges, corporations, foundations and individuals to contribute four times again as much. The Federal portion provides the critical difference between our being a "mediocre" institution and a nearly "excellent" institution.

At Democratic Congressional
Wives Forum, Jan. 28/
The Washington Post, 3-4:(A)18.

Eric Sevareid
Former commentator,
CBS News

5

. . . broadcasting—radio and TV—is the only medium of information and entertainment in all time that ever tried to perform 18 to 24 hours a

(ERIC SEVAREID)

day, 365 days in the year. It can't be done at a decent level of quality.

Interview, Washington/
The Christian Science Monitor, 1-28:6.

Frank Stanton
Former president, CBS, Inc.

1

Now, as there's less emphasis by the FCC on a balanced [TV] schedule, as deregulation allows local stations to put on entertainment instead of public affairs, changes are coming about, because the men who were originally dedicated to broadcasting are now off the scene, and bottom-line-oriented MBA types, largely out of sales and business management, are taking over.

Interview/
The Christian Science Monitor,
11-30:22.

Barbara Stanwyck
Actress

2

The real problem with television is, of course, the writing, or the lack of it. They don't write scenes, they write radio. And they're never willing to listen to somebody like me who wants the material to be better. I went to the producers of *The Colbys* and said, "Look, I'm playing the same scene I did last week." And they said, "Don't worry, it'll work." Finally I had to go to [producer] Aaron [Spelling] and tell him flatly I'd never walked out on a contract before, but, reluctantly, I was going to leave the show. "I've played the same damn scene 24 times now!" He nicely asked me to reconsider, but we both knew it had been difficult enough for me to accept the series in the first place.

Interview/American Film, April:43.

Jack Valenti
President,
Motion Picture
Association of America

3

[Lamenting that five companies control 40 per cent of U.S. cable-TV subscriptions and thus dictate what viewers will get to watch]: Choice is to the cable monopoly what sunlight is to the vampire.

U.S. News & World Report, 5-11:7.

Henry Waxman
United States Representative,
D-California

4

[Criticizing TV networks that are reluctant to air condom advertising as a way to fight the AIDS disease]: While portraying thousands of sexual encounters each year in programming, and while marketing thousands of products using sex appeal, television is unwilling to give the life-saving information about safe sex and condoms. We cannot afford such selective prudishness.

At House subcommittee hearing,
Washington, Feb.10/
Daily Variety, 2-11:1.

Edward Woodward
Actor

5

When you say yes to a TV [series] offer, you've got to go for the role—not the money or the temporary fame. You have to say to yourself, "If the series is a success and I'm locked into it for five years, could I bear to be playing the same role all that time?" If the answer is no, then forget it, because all the money in the world won't make up for the boredom or the hard work.

Interview, Los Angeles/
Los Angeles Times, 2-15:(Calendar)34.

MOTION PICTURES

Jane Alexander
Actress, Producer

1

If you look at what's happening with the marketing of studio pictures in the past two to three years, you see they really can't support smaller stories . . . Because of their overhead, which is significant, they need to do block-buster films—action, adventure, sci-fi, comedies—with major stars, for the most part. So the rise of independents is not an accident. This year, the number of independent films surpassed that of studio pictures. They certainly didn't surpass studio pictures at the box-office—studios still rake in more than 85 percent. But something new is happening in the film market.

Interview, New York/
The Christian Science Monitor,
3-13:26.

Woody Allen
Actor, Director, Writer

2

Popular acceptance to me is never necessarily a mark of quality in a film. Sometimes it can be. But just as often it bears no resemblance to the quality of the film. You can be completely dissatisfied with a film you make, but it's very meaningful to people and very enjoyable. And you can be totally thrilled and fulfilled with something you've done and, you know, it's good for you—but it's just got no meaning for anybody else. The only thing you can do is try to have a philosophy about what films should be, and stick to that philosophy and when you achieve it, feel good, and when you don't . . . It's like playing poker. You want to play well, and even if you lose you can go home that night thinking, "Gee, I played very good and luck was against me," and it's the same with film.

Interview, New York/
Los Angeles Times,
2-8:(Calendar)38.

3

I wish somebody would come in and tell me I can't make films any more. I don't have the discipline not to make them. It's as though someone is saying to me, "Everyone wants to be in the film business and wants to make films. We'll bankroll you, give you eight million, nine million dollars. Make the films you want to make." So I feel, like, how can I say no to that? How often in life does that opportunity come to anybody, to be funded for that kind of money to do things? So I do it. But it would sort of relieve the anxiety and the ambivalence I have about it if someone would come to me and say, "That's it. It's over. You cannot make another film." I'd suddenly heave a huge sigh of relief.

Interview/Esquire, April:95.

4

[On the controversy over colorization of old black-and-white movies]: If a movie director wishes his film to be colorized, then I say by all means, let him color it. If he prefers it to remain in black-and-white, then it is sinful to force him to change it. If the director is not alive and his work has been historically established in black-and-white, it should remain true to its origin. The presumption that the colorizers are doing him a favor and bettering his movie is a transparent attempt to justify the mutilization of art for a few extra dollars.

At Senate subcommittee hearing,
Washington, May 12/
Los Angeles Times, 5-13:(VI)1.

Richard Attenborough
Director

1

I don't fool myself [that] I'm considered a great *auteur* film director or anything like that. What interests me is the narrative and telling the story through the actors. To me, they are the jewels of the film. It's not the camera angles or the pyrotechnics which touch an audience's heart; it's the actors. I never forget that.

Interview, Los Angeles/
Los Angeles Times, 10-25:(Calendar)23.

Claude Berri
Director

2

Like [director Francois] Truffaut, I don't think about what is more important, life or movies . . . In all my life, I am making only one movie. And that movie *is* my life.

Interview, New York/
The Christian Science Monitor,
7-3:20.

Bernardo Bertolucci
Italian director

3

It is dangerous in Italy now for film. In five years, the movies have lost 55 percent or 60 percent of the audience, because of television. Part of the trouble is that too often now the movies are *imitating* television. In Europe, they still want to go to see *movies*. Cinema will survive *if* it will be *cinema*. Once again, to be in the cinema must be like being in a cathedral, sharing the collective dream.

Interview, Los Angeles/
Los Angeles Times, 12-6:(Calendar)30.

Tony Bill
Producer

4

The history of success in our business is rejection. The history behind literally every successful film . . . is rejection. It's been turned down more than once by directors, actors, stu-

dios, writers, technicians. And the history of failure is "the sure thing" . . . Even the less-than-huge failures seem to be aimed at a market, or repeating history or catching a trend.

At Young Artists United seminar,
Santa Monica, Calif., Oct. 1/
Daily Variety, 10-5:18.

John Boorman
Director

5

It's a difficult time, I find, for me to make films, because there's a great resistance in the marketplace to quality films or films with ambition. I think 20 years ago, when the studios were making more pictures, they would throw in a quality film for prestige, and I fear that the kind of prestige films they make now are rather kind of "official art"—the kind of films that are not really art but people can convince themselves that they're seeing art when they go to watch it, but is, in fact, actually formula entertainment disguised as art to make them feel better. The whole film industry is incredibly depressing, isn't it? But whatever you say about films, somehow or other they go on being made, and every now and again a terrific film gets made and the whole thing is worthwhile.

Interview/
Films and Filming, September:7.

Martin Bregman
Producer

6

Most [film] executives don't understand the process of making films. Executives go to "dailies" and they have no idea what they are watching. If it's in focus, it's wonderful. That is why there is so much junk out there. This is the only business in the world where you can fail upwards: You can fail at one studio and then go to a better position at another one. If you hang in long enough, you'll become president of the world.

Interview/American Film, May:51.

WHAT THEY SAID IN 1987

Bernie Brillstein
Chairman,
Lorimar Film Entertainment

1

Don't use [stars] if they're too expensive. There are very few stars who guarantee you a hit, or even an opening weekend. Those are the ones who deserve that big money. There are a lot of middle people who are getting more money than countries in Africa make. I don't think any of us are going to rush to pay them that unless they're perfect for the role.

Panel discussion/
American Film, September:41.

Mel Brooks
Actor, Director, Writer

2

Most audiences only remember the ornaments of a comedy—the jokes. They don't see the tree. It's dark. It's all bark. But what would all the ornaments be without the tree for support? They'd just be a pile of shiny baubles on the ground.

Interview/
Los Angeles Times,
3-8:(Calendar)23.

Cyd Charisse
Actress, Dancer

3

[On the film musicals of the '50s]: This [today] is a different era. Art reflects that. I think it was a very charming period [the '50s]. A more romantic time than we have now. Naturally, it was lovely, and those films still have a wide audience [on pay-TV and videocassettes]. People are looking for romance and that wonderful feeling of beautiful music that we're lacking today. We're missing that. And I agree with you that the audience for them will get bigger because of the way they're available now. It's so easy to see it. As far as musicals being like that again, I think the more people who can buy it at home, the fewer people will go out and pay for it.

Interview, London/
Films and Filming, April:28.

Cher
Actress

4

I happen to think crazy people make good actors because they can suspend their belief systems so easily—and at making movies you have to go in and out of different realities very quickly. Like, I'm talking to you right now and in a few minutes I have to go out there and . . .

Interview, Brooklyn, N.Y./
Los Angeles Times, 3-1:(Calendar)17.

Jack Clayton
Director

5

I have to admit that when I take on a film I don't think about the audience at all. I just pick a subject I love and hope for the best.

Interview/
Los Angeles Times,
12-27:(Calendar)34.

Bill Conti
Composer-conductor

6

[On music in films]: Music [in films] brings out the feelings that aren't said. Music is much more subtle. We can show emotional feelings which aren't necessarily on the screen; we can, as in a Greek chorus, make further comments that the script has left out or would like exaggerated. We can take you psychologically in a different direction completely, or enhance the direction the film is going in. We [composers] have a lot of power.

The New York Times, 5-22:16.

Bette Davis
Actress

7

I think one of the things that has made my career different is that I've never avoided playing unpleasant characters. I've never had any vanity . . . [And] I always went with the changes . . . I did the early TV shows, like *Wagon Train*, and I was one of the first to go on

(BETTE DAVIS)

the talk shows. I knew TV was definitely the coming thing and, of course, TV kept all my old films coming to new generations. I think all of this kept my career going. [But] it will never be as exciting as the years when I was hoping to make it; you can't ever have that real thrill again.

Interview/
Los Angeles Times,
10-16:(VI)12.

1

We all need romance and sentiment. That's what motion pictures used to be a great contributor of, to people. The most important thing in the world is love, isn't it? We have no more of that [in films]. Terrible! Too bad. That's why so many people look at the old movies—because they loved them.

Interview, Washington/
The Christian Science Monitor,
12-28:20.

Sammy Davis, Jr.
Entertainer

2

[On the late film dancer-actor Fred Astaire]: . . . Bill Robinson, and the Nicholas Brothers, and Donald O'Connor [are] always mentioned with great respect, and Gene Kelly, my friend and a brilliant dancer and choreographer. But Astaire was . . . well, look. There was Astaire, and then there was everybody else. He did it over five decades. Only two men I've known have lasted that long: Astaire and Cary Grant. Fred Astaire was elegant, the ultimate athlete with elegance.

Interview, Hartford, Conn./
Los Angeles Times, 6-30:(III)2.

Kirk Douglas
Actor

3

I discouraged all of my sons from ever going into any phase of the entertainment business.

My theory is that if you can discourage someone from going into this business, they shouldn't be in it anyway. It's too painful, too full of rejection. And the rejection is personal: It's "I don't like *you*."

Interview, New York/
The New York Times, 4-2:19.

Jose Ferrer
Actor

4

You do the best you can [as an actor] and then you take the praise—which is often excessive—or the criticism—which is also often excessive. In this business, you have to be thick-skinned about humiliation, about rejection, about failure—all of which goes on, for your entire career. There isn't an actor alive today, successful or not, who doesn't every day encounter in some way, some form of wounding, some lesion, some trauma—and it can't be helped.

Interview/
Films in Review, March:137.

Albert Finney
Actor

5

When I read a script, I want my imagination to salivate. The first reaction I like to get is from the gut. But that doesn't mean every role I have played has stirred me. In a career in this game, if you are going to work fairly consistently, you say to yourself: "I've been sitting for three months waiting for a good script, and this is the best that has come in; I may as well do that. I've got to keep the engine running."

Interview/
U.S. News & World Report,
12-14:63.

Harrison Ford
Actor

6

My technique as an actor is to use as much of myself as possible in a part and to censor

(HARRISON FORD)

those parts of myself that are not appropriate to the character, and to invent where there is no overlap.

Interview/
Films and Filming,
February:26.

Leonard Goldberg
President,
20th Century Fox
Film Corporation

1

I have to believe very strongly that if you make good-quality films, finally you will succeed. I don't mean necessarily that every film has to be a work of art. You can make teen-age films, films for adults, action films, comedy films, wonderful dramas. You can run the gamut . . . As long as they are true to themselves and they are the best that you can make them, they will find an audience.

Interview/
Los Angeles Times,
2-11:(VI)6.

2

In a feature motion picture, when you bring in a director, you bring in someone who shares your vision, hopefully—or you shouldn't bring him in. Once he's there, you have to give him his room. I mean, you can't direct over his shoulder. I drop by the set once a day. Then I always see the "dailies" with the director, and we talk afterward. But basically, once you turn the script over to him, *he's* got to yell, "Action," and *he's* got to decide what works or not.

Interview/American Film, May:10.

Lee Grant
Actress, Director

3

An actor goes to another place that's unreal. To make real an unreality is a very hard job. As a director, my job is to protect my actors and

make sure that they're able to go to that place—with encouragement to take risks and with the knowledge that I won't let them make fools of themselves.

Interview/
Films in Review,
September:388.

Alec Guinness
Actor

4

What do I like about film? Very little. Of course, the money always comes as a lovely surprise. I never thought I'd have any money. On the other hand, I never did a film just for the money—except for one, which I won't mention. I've always regretted doing anything for the wrong reasons: money, popular success. It's madness, madness, to do things for the wrong reasons.

Interview, New York/
The New York Times, 4-27:18.

Paul R. Gurian
Producer

5

Movies are the last common basis for expressing noble ideas. They are still universal enough to transcend differences in cultures. And I believe if I ever got my Academy Award moment I would say to those two thousand bimbos out there, "Listen, you control the most powerful, intellectual, emotional expression of ideas available to man today."

Interview/American Film, May:52.

Dennis Hopper
Actor, Director

6

Probably a good actor is one who hasn't grown up yet. I remember Marlon Brando gave an interview years ago. He said he wanted to give up acting because he wanted to finally grow up. And everybody said, "Oh, that's terrible." At the time, I defended that because I understood it. It's hard work to stay like a child

(DENNIS HOPPER)

and have a child-like feeling, imagination and response. Acting, at best, is like playing in a vacant lot: "Bang, bang, you're dead." "No, I'm not, da da da da da." There's a lot of that.

Interview/USA Today, 2-12:(A)11.

James Ivory
Director

1

It's extraordinary how, during editing, one line or even one word can seem too much and can spoil the rhythm of the dialogue. So you can imagine how much we have to get rid of with [adapting something from] Henry James! It seems while you're doing it that you're making everything crude, and in a way you are: You're making everything much more obvious and broad. It seems that you're doing a disservice to the writer, but that's in the nature of doing an adaptation of any great book. We try to be true to the spirit and to what the writer is trying to say; we try to get his or her tone.

Interview/
American Film, Jan.-Feb.:14.

2

Most of the scripts that highly paid screenplay writers come up with from scratch are a chore to read—they're flat, there's no character development, the scenes aren't interesting. With a good novel, your imagination immediately gets to work. As a director, you can sometimes visualize a scene almost literally and film it to convey exactly what is on the printed page [of the novel], or you can take the words as a jumping-off place to carry the author's idea further, visually. But it's rare when film-makers do justice to the wonderful books that they turn into films. When you make a film out of a book, you at least owe the author gratitude and, in the case of a first-class novelist, living or dead, you owe him more. You have a responsibility to try and capture the author's tone of voice and to get into the film some sense of the atmosphere from the book. And it's well to remember that the book has been there for a long time and will continue to be, while the film is ephemeral and will literally disintegrate within 20 years.

Interview/
U.S. News & World Report,
12-21:68.

Norman Jewison
Producer, Director

3

Feature films drive television and all media. They reflect the country, sometimes reveal the truth its artists have discovered. They create a country's myths, celebrate its victories and its heroes and sweep across borders into the minds of others. The importance and scope of movies, television and videocassettes today is overwhelming. All of this industry is driven by talent.

Los Angeles/
Los Angeles Times, 5-2:(VI)2.

James Earl Jones
Actor

4

Nobody asks any artist to be an artist. So you don't enter that field with a great sense of reality of what's really going on there. You're a fool. So there is no room for bitterness about making it or not making it. Nobody said, "Please be an actor." And when you retire, nobody's going to say, "Please don't quit." They'll say, "Okay, we'll go find somebody else." But those are the realities.

Interview/USA Today, 9-21:(A)13.

Stanley Kramer
Producer, Director

5

. . . there is no rule or prejudice against films with content except against those films with content which do not make money. There is a very, very big difference there. I can't explain it to you, because I don't know what makes money or is commercial. As soon as you're sure of the place in the scheme of things

WHAT THEY SAID IN 1987

(STANLEY KRAMER)

that's commercial, they—those powers that be—move it.

Interview/American Film, March:16.

1

The dramatic actor cannot always do comedy, but the comedian can do drama. I think [comics] Buddy Hackett and Jonathan Winters and Sid Caesar can play the greatest heavies in the history of heavies. I mean evil. Comedy is cruel; it's an attack on society. No dramatic actor ever sweats like a comedian to trigger a laugh. I've never seen anybody work like these fellows.

Interview/American Film, March:17.

2

[On his return to film-making after nine years]: I decided that somewhere between films on outer space and Sylvester Stallone, there is a place for me. I was always associated with films that had an opinion. I don't believe films change anyone's mind, but I was spawned during the Roosevelt era, a time of great change, and I still believe in trying to get people to think. I'm very excited about being a participating mule again—that's mule, with a kick.

Interview/
The New York Times, 5-15:16.

Akira Kurosawa
Japanese director

3

Generally, the Japanese film industry is facing a very important crisis, and that's because, in the old days, film-makers themselves, the directors, used to occupy a prominent place. Now it's the commercial people, and they don't want risk. They just see their immediate profit. They don't want adventure. Every time I make a film, I want to take a step, and they are afraid; they don't want to do that.

News conference, Tokyo/
Daily Variety,
10-5:2.

George Lucas
Director

4

The underlying issues, the psychological motives, in all my movies have been the same: personal responsibility and friendship, the importance of a compassionate life as opposed to a passionate life . . . New technology—whether it's new film stock or electronic editing or special effects—enhances the tools you have available and expands your vocabulary. But they don't make a picture successful. A film is not about technique. It's about ideas.

Interview/
The New York Times, 5-21:22.

Shirley MacLaine
Actress

5

One of the most important things I've learned is that I've been playing myself ever since I was born. You see, life is what you perceive it to be . . . just like a play is, just like a movie is. And once I realized that Shakespeare was right—that all of life is a stage, and we're just actors writing, directing, producing and starring in our own plays—then on-screen I played the character I had been playing in life.

Interview, Malibu, Calif./
Ladies' Home Journal,
October:36.

Madonna
Singer, Actress

6

I think it's really difficult for Americans to express passion and desire in movies. Something *bad* always has to happen—violence—or the relationship doesn't last. I will not be attracted to making violent films. I'm attracted to roles where women are strong and aren't victimized. Everything I do has to be some kind of a celebration of life.

Interview, Burbank, Calif./
American Film,
July-Aug.:24

Norman Mailer
Author

1

[On his direction of a film of one of his books]: What I like about movie direction is that it's so different from novel writing. One's living free in the world in a funny way. It's like being in combat. Things happen every day as you inch forward from place to place. It's marvelous because it's combat without blood. We'll have a rout now, then we'll stop and eat, clean up the crumbs, and take the next hill.

Interview/Film Comment, August:16.

2

I think fiction can intensify the moral consciousness of a time. I think theatre can enlarge one's emotional appreciation of social situations. [But] film doesn't work on our minds. It works on all the places that have never been worked on by other art-forms—all the synapses between our memory and our emotions and our nerves and our sense of time.

Interview, Provincetown, Mass./
The Christian Science Monitor, 9-4:20.

3

. . . in a film, there's nothing more obscene than boredom. Because, with everything else, a film is a ceremony. It is the nearest thing to a religious experience that non-religious people are ever going to get. And so, imperfection or boredom in a ceremony is unpleasant. When I work on a script, the point is to move in an opposite direction from a novel. The point is to tighten the surface till your work resonates. That's the only way you're going to get depth in a film—through resonance. You can't go directly for profundity.

Interview/
The New York Times,
9-18:24.

Karl Malden
Actor

4

[On today's films]: It's all mechanics; it's flying saucers, it's robots, all that sort of stuff.

Maybe I'm too old to understand it, but I would rather see a story about relationships—a man and a woman, a husband and wife, a girl and a boy. To me, a relationship story with human beings is much more interesting than a flying saucer coming to earth.

Interview/USA Today, 1-15:(D)2.

Steve Martin
Actor, Comedian

5

As a comedian, you must do silly things, and silly things are not critically respected. But it is just as hard to do silly things as it is to do dramatic things. The easiest thing to play as an actor in the movies is anger. It's a strong emotion. Most people can get in touch with it. Yet, that's what you get Oscars for—crying and yelling.

Interview, Los Angeles/
Los Angeles Times, 6-30:(VI)9.

Marcello Mastroianni
Actor

6

When I make films, I am absolutely happy. That's why I make so many films. This is a most beautiful thing, to be with 60, 70 people on a set and to make stories. It helps me to act. I work seriously but never take myself seriously. I want to enjoy myself—really enjoy— like a child. Because all actors are children. If it is a limit that an actor is still a child, it is also a miracle. And when the film is finished, I am looking for another film. Otherwise, my life is a little more bored.

Interview, New York/Time, 10-12:80.

Roger L. Mayer
President,
Turner Entertainment Company

7

[Supporting the colorizing of old black-and-white movies and criticizing those who are against colorization]: This is not a contest between art and commerce. All those who worked on these movies were paid, and usually paid

WHAT THEY SAID IN 1987

(ROGER L. MAYER)

handsomely. Moreover, they didn't return their salaries with an apology if the movies flopped. It's hardly fair for anyone who ever earned big and risk-free money working on a movie to cry "Greed!," because the copyright holder also wants to earn money or recoup an investment.

At Senate subcommittee hearing,
Washington, May 12/
Los Angeles Times, 5-13:(VI)4.

Mike Medavoy
Executive vice president
of production,
Orion Pictures Corporation

1

I think [film] critics, at times, become vicious for no reason. A lot of them are basically frustrated by the kind of work that they do. It's as though they're almost in show business trying to become stars. I've had critics say to me, "Hey, I'll give you a good review if you'll use my name in your ad." And a lot of business journalists don't get the facts right, don't do their homework. They're basically pack followers.

Interview/Film Comment, June:60.

Ismail Merchant
Producer

2

Hollywood is what you would call a giant conglomerate of different people who are shuffling all the time from one place to the other. It's like a roundtable conference: Today there is this executive, tomorrow that executive. And for the director or producer who wants to make a commitment to his work, studios are really accountants and lawyers. There is no personal commitment . . . As Hollywood as an entity is concerned, films are made purely for the sake of money. And of all the films you see in a year, I would say about four or five are good. The others make money, but there is nothing to hold onto.

Interview/American Film,
Jan.-Feb.:15,54.

Nicholas Meyer
Director

3

Hollywood is making films I have no interest in seeing, machine-tooled, packaged, with a lot of numbers after their names. The studios don't just want home runs. They want grand-slams. Anything less than $100-million is not interesting to them.

The New York Times, 4-6:18.

Ronald Neame
Director

4

The most important thing you learn as a director is not to direct too much. You must force the audience to work, too . . . [Director] David Lean and I are fighting a rearguard action. We want movies to return to greatness, to touch audiences and teach them—and if that's being old-fashioned, then I stand condemned.

Interview/
Films in Review,
January:3,9.

5

I was brought up in a school [of directing] in which it was an unwritten law that there was no camera; I and others of my generation were brought up to disguise our camera movements. They were always there—my camera never stops—but I can't help disguising the movements. The whole thing was, you were telling a story, and you gave to the actors everything you could to let them convey the best of what they've got and develop their characters . . . [Today,] it's no longer "there is no camera"; it's become "I am a camera." What has happened is that directors draw attention to themselves. That to me is reprehensible; I want to draw attention to the actor. But that doesn't negate the director at all. I will fall over backwards to see that the subtleties of the actor are up there on the screen and not on the cutting-room floor . . .

Interview/
Films and Filming, April:26.

Paul Newman
Actor

1

[On his never having won an Academy Award]: . . . as for the Oscar, well, I don't know how I feel about that any more. It's like chasing a beautiful woman year after year and finally she says yes to your advances. And you say, sorry, I'm too tired now.

Interview/
Films and Filming,
March:13.

Kim Novak
Actress

2

[On why she left the motion-picture business]: The studios cared so much about how you looked, rather than how you got inside a character. It was all so surface, so slick. But I wanted to get under the façade. I left because I couldn't bring any of myself to my work.

At "Celebration of Women
in Film," San Francisco,
Jan. 17/Daily Variety, 1-20:29.

Sidney Poitier
Actor, Director

3

[Comparing acting with directing]: What am I doing [right] now? I'm acting. What does that mean? It means I'm sitting around a warm dressing-room talking to a couple of nice guys about matters that interest me. As a director, you can't do that for *months*. When you're directing, you work half the night on your shot list for the next day. You arrive with 10 or 15 shots to do to complete a sequence. But after two or three shots, other shots suggest themselves. Everybody is asking a million questions, and you are the one who gets to answer all of them. What's seductive about this work? Ah, well, if we didn't have very large egos, we wouldn't be directing. It's very heavy stuff.

Interview, Monrovia, Calif./
Los Angeles Times, 3-5:(VI)6.

Sydney Pollack
Director

4

[Criticizing the colorization of old black-and-white movies]: It is morally unacceptable to alter the product of a person's creative life without that person's permission. There is a difference between a film in black-and-white and a film in color. Black-and-white photography is not color photography with the color removed. It is not better or worse in general, but it is different. It is a choice. We are here to protect those choices.

At Senate subcommittee hearing,
Washington, May 12/
Los Angeles Times, 5-13:(VI)4.

David Puttnam
Chairman,
Columbia Pictures

5

I've developed a kind of formula. It has to do with the questions that you ask at different prices [of a film]. There is a certain film that we would make at two to two-and-a-half million dollars for which I'd only ask two questions: "Does the person attached appear gifted?" and "Is the subject matter interesting?" At six to eight million dollars, which is really the next bracket, you ask yourself: "Is this a subject which is *really* interesting and a script that could be made to work?" "Am I working with someone who I *really* think has talent?" And there the latitudes are different. Then you move on to the ten-to-twelve-million-dollar picture, where you are looking at a different level of proven skill. Then you get up to the twenty-five-million-dollar picture, and the questions are quite, quite different. And the irony—and you try to explain this to a banker—is that the twenty-five-million-dollar film with a big star probably represents a more risk-free situation than the two-and-a-half-million-dollar picture with unknown film-makers. Listen to the movie. The movie tells you, "This price with this director, yes." "That price with that person, no."

Panel discussion/
American Film, September:40.

425

WHAT THEY SAID IN 1987

Alain Resnais
Director

1

[In the 1940s,] my family, my friends, they all believed that film was not an art. One friend, a writer I admired very much, he asked me: "How can it be an art when you can't change anything? There's no interpretation there. You're just taking a picture." Well, it took me one week to discover the answer: What you could change is in the editing. You could manipulate time. That could be the art of film-making . . . I think first about editing. While I'm shooting, I imagine where I'd put the splice. And in the editing room, I try to change everything, if possible. I'm not saying it's the best way—it's just my way.

> *Interview, New York/*
> *The Wall Street Journal,*
> *3-24:30.*

Fernando Rey
French actor

2

I became a movie extra just to get money to eat—and to lose myself as a face in the crowd. I never had that ambition to be an actor, but it was like a chain reaction. One day a director asked me if I could say a line, and I did it. I had a "parenthesis" feeling in the first years— that one day the parenthesis would be closed— but here I am.

> *Interview, Los Angeles/*
> *Los Angeles Times,*
> *5-13:(VI)7.*

Cliff Robertson
Actor

3

Hollywood is a small but fat fiefdom, where the marrow of artists is gouged. It has been the burial ground of many creative hopes and dreams. Stucco mausoleums dot its fields, and the tanned corpses at Malibu wonder what hap-

pened to their dreams. They settle for fat purses as they drain their souls.

> *At Bradford College commencement/*
> *The Christian Science Monitor, 6-18:23.*

Ginger Rogers
Actress

4

[Criticizing the colorizing of old black-and-white movies]: It feels terrible [to see oneself in a colorized film]. It hurts. It's embarrassing and insulting. It's a violation of all the care and trust that goes into a work of cinematic art. In the movies, your face is truly your fortune. The studios spent months, even years, grooming us and carefully developing an image that looked just right on black-and-white film. Our appearances and expressions are the tools we use to create a character on the screen. It is a subtle and sensitive art that is completely obliterated by computer coloring.

> *At Senate subcommittee hearing,*
> *Washington, May 12/*
> *Los Angeles Times, 5-13:(VI)4.*

Mickey Rooney
Entertainer

5

The motion-picture business was killed purposefully—or weren't you aware of that? They paid a lot of money to have an antitrust law, paid a lot of money to kill Hollywood, so that only a few people would own it all. They said it was against the law for Metro-Goldwyn-Mayer to make a picture and show it in a Metro-Goldwyn-Mayer theatre. They said it was against the law for Warner Bros. to make a picture and show it in their theatre—or for Paramount, 20th Century Fox or Columbia. But it's *perfectly* all right for Chrysler, Chevrolet and Ford. It's all right for Kinney's to manufacture shoes and sell them in their stores. It's all right for Burger King, Wendy's and McDonald's to manufacture hamburgers and sell them in their stores. And yet you can't make a picture and show it in a theatre you own.

> *Interview, Los Angeles/*
> *Los Angeles Times, 5-28:(VI)1.*

Richard Schickel
Film critic,
"Time" magazine

1

I fear the [musical film] form is dead. Economically, they don't translate well to foreign markets. In the case of [the late musical director Vincente] Minnelli, the Arthur Freed unit he worked with at MGM was an extraordinary phenomenon, devoted to opening up the possibility of the post-Busby Berkeley musical from around 1942 through 1958. The presence of that unit—directors, conductors, designers, everybody—helped create the new musical genre which freed the form from the backstage lot and allowed it to move into non-theatrical settings, as in *Cabin in the Sky* and *An American in Paris* and *Gigi*. There cannot be a revival of the musical genre in movies unless something comes along like that Freed unit once again. Maybe we are forever destined to see the old musical films in repertory movie houses.

Interview/
The Christian Science Monitor,
3-17:27.

John Schlesinger
Director

2

I know nothing nicer than a [film] success in America. And there's nothing more certain than being dropped after an American failure. In England, it's rather unfashionable to be successful or to make any money. I live in England because, in many ways, I'm a little scared. I don't trust success and I don't trust failure. It is a constant struggle, and a question of really being a fighter. You've got to remain tremendously strong about what you know you can do. And never take no for an answer.

Interview/
American Film, November:17.

George C. Scott
Actor

3

I still feel the same about [acting] awards. I don't recognize them, nor accept them if offered. I don't like competition that pits actor against actor. It started with my first Academy Award nomination. I was up for best supporting actor in *Anatomy of a Murder* [1959]. I remember how much I wanted that Oscar. I lusted for it, craved it. And then I understood. This craving was demeaning to me, my profession, my fellow actors and actresses. I've never wanted one since.

Interview/USA Today, 10-19:(D)2.

Susan Seidelman
Director

4

I think there's a myth that women can direct only sensitive, emotional stories about the family . . . I happen to like those kinds of stories, so I don't say that in a negative way. But I think, also, there are women out there who can and probably will, even more so in the future, be able to direct a Western, . . . or a war film, or action-adventure . . . As more and more women make movies that are successful . . . I think it does benefit all of us. I really don't think it's because Hollywood is getting more liberal . . . If monkeys were directing movies that were successful, Hollywood would hire monkeys to direct. But one can discount the fact that, as more and more women get a chance to direct and some of those films go on to be successful, it's got to help other women.

Interview, Washington/
The Christian Science Monitor,
3-18:23,26.

Sylvester Stallone
Actor

5

[As an actor,] you drag your history with you. Audiences don't forget. Their memory is of the last film you did. And if it was big, they want more, like a fix. They don't want me to go off and do something weird.

Interview, Las Vegas, Nev./
USA Today, 2-13:(A)1.

WHAT THEY SAID IN 1987

Barbara Stanwyck
Actress

1

Whenever people ask me about the movies I've done, I always mention the writer first. I was very lucky, most of the time, in having good scripts. Good writers, directors, producers. To me, the words come first. If it ain't on paper, it ain't ever gonna get up there on the screen.

Interview/
American Film,
April:41.

Oliver Stone
Director, Screenwriter

2

[On directing his own scripts]: I don't see any conflict. I see it as a natural progression, to take it from writing to directing. Sometimes, as a director, I think you need another writer; it would be helpful to have a second voice. But the writer and the director are really two different people, two different parts of the self. The director is more the host, the emcee; the writer is the quieter side, the introspective side, the miserable, depressed and lonely side. Writing's probably the hardest of the two because it requires more loneliness and isolation, and that's harder to put up with. Directing is more arduous physically; but, mentally, writing is harder. It requires concentrated thought over a long period of time. But I don't see them in conflict. They go hand in hand.

Interview/
Film Comment,
February:60.

3

Movies are different from what you [as a journalist] do. You [in the press] try to clarify. In the movies, I think we deal more with obfuscation . . . You can be on the nose in print, but when you're on the nose in movies, it goes over the top. Movies always involve reduction.

Interview/
American Film,
December:26.

Tony Thomopoulos
Chairman,
United Artists Corporation

4

Today, there is this instant stardom, which is a disservice not only to the industry, but to the person who has become the instant star. Instant success brings with it, much of the time, long-term failure. I saw it in television for years; I see it today in the motion-picture business.

Panel discussion/
American Film, September:41.

Tom Tryon
Author; Former actor

5

If you write a book, it's you. A movie is never one person. It can be 100 people or more. I think that's why there aren't better movies. Too many cooks, too many viewpoints.

Interview/USA Today, 1-23:(D)2.

Lawrence Turman
Producer

6

I believe essentially there's one creative force on almost any film. It actually ought to be the director. And in those cases where he's very talented, you get wonderful films . . . But if you eliminate those directors who can do that, you're left with a lot of other directors who have an authority that exceeds their abilities.

Interview/
American Film, May:50.

Kathleen Turner
Actress

7

Hollywood is at least 10 years behind the real world. Just now, we're getting roles with women who work and raise children . . . Just now, we're getting an intimation of gay relationships in films. [Hollywood] is not supposed to be avant garde, but it should recognize what's going on.

Interview, Los Angeles/
Los Angeles Times, 3-11:(VI)4.

James Woods
Actor

1

[Actors] are either good at what they do or bad at what they do. And usually they're bad, not for lack of talent, but for lack of dedication. And that drives me crazy. The one thing that makes me want people to disappear from a set is that they're too busy doing something else and don't have time to do the job that they're getting paid for. You know, [they're] buying a string of condos in Marina del Rey or whatever else they have on their mind. My attitude is that when you make a film, you eat, drink and sleep it. And be thankful that you can go 24 hours a day, because if you're spending any time less than that, you're probably not giving it your best shot.

Interview, Beverly Hills, Calif./
American Film, May:43.

Robert Young
Actor

2

I know a lot of actors complain about it, but the studios and the networks don't typecast players. The public typecasts players, and if you fight that, you're fighting fate. Actors always want to express their versatility. At times I felt that and I tried playing a villain, and I played to empty theatres. I started out at the Pasadena Playhouse, and there they cast you in anything. You would be the romantic lead one night and a heavy the next night. That's great training for an actor. But when you get out into the professional world, a pattern or image is established quickly. You eventually find yourself in a little niche, and there's nothing you can do about it.

Interview, Los Angeles/
The New York Times, 1-10:12.

MUSIC

Stephen Albert
Composer

1

[On his winning the Pulitzer Prize in 1985]: It's not the Pulitzer that you wanted to achieve; it's some sort of parity with some of the composers of the past with whom you feel you are having a dialogue. You want to achieve something in that tradition, that's worthy of that tradition . . . The problem with this country [the U.S.] is that we're focused on these instantaneous hit things, these momentary gratifications, and we don't understand there's a continuity involved; there's a continuity to all great art. There's a continuity to our own character development. [But the Pulitzer] does allow you to exist on a more gratifyingly professional level with other musicians. It helps to bring you to the attention of people who are serious and good music-makers. They hear of you and there's a grapevine that starts up. If you've got the goods—if they think you've got the goods—it will open a door to their consciousness. But your music has to go through that door. Nobody should commission you if you write music they don't wish to play and their audiences don't wish to hear.

Interview/
The Washington Post,
5-30:(C)5.

Julie Andrews
Actress, Singer

2

I can't open my mouth and just sing like a bird. It needs work. It gets rusty, like an old engine, if I don't practice. I've always had to work at it all my life. I love it and I hate it . . . But the rewards are so phenomenal. There are only a few pleasures greater than singing with a big orchestra. To sing something luscious and beautiful with a big orchestra is such a turn-on.

Interview/USA Today, 1-30:(A)15.

Arleen Auger
Classical singer

3

I've found it a bit difficult to come to grips with the fact that classical music here [in the U.S.] is expected to be like Broadway. A performance is a "show," the orchestra is a "band." There's the "curtain going up" sort of thing. Everybody has to be glitzy, and look constantly 25 years old. I feel tainted. I'm not saying that classical forms are any better or worse than Broadway or operetta, but I think that each of the forms must retain its own identity. I want to maintain a certain amount of seriousness about orchestra concerts and the song-recital form.

Interview/Ovation, March:23.

Joan Baez
Singer

4

[On her using her music for political activism]: I'm absolutely arrogant about the quality of my voice. I could certainly be faulted for that attitude, except that the voice was given to me, and the best I can do with it is to use it as a vehicle for things that I feel strongly about: the betterment of people, and so forth. That may sound rather trite, but in the end . . . you're tallied up by what you did, and I hope that what I've done has lessened some grief. That's what I think I'm here for.

Interview, New York/
The Christian Science Monitor,
9-3:21.

Herbert Blomstedt
Music director,
San Francisco
Symphony Orchestra

1

Although I've made many recordings over the years, I never listen to them. I'm sure that I haven't heard all of them—and the ones I have heard have been by accident. Once the last bar is played in a recording studio, I lose interest. In recordings you can achieve technical perfection, but you risk, by constant repetition of a particular passage, losing its life in the over-all structure. You end up with a perfect, but lifeless, mosaic. A live musical performance is special because it's like a mayfly. It lives only in the moment, and that's what gives it its special quality. That's what makes it different from painting and sculpture.

Interview/Ovation,
February:26.

John Cage
Composer

2

What distinguishes my music is that it gives up intentionality. I'm not saying anything with it. Other music rests with discourse; mine strives to be non-discursive.

At California Institute of the Arts/
The Christian Science Monitor,
4-3:23.

Benny Carter
Jazz musician

3

The kids [new jazz musicians today] are fantastically endowed with technique. They do more today than I would have thought possible 50 and 60 years ago. But they sacrifice a lot of emotional content for technique. There's something to be said for street knowledge, for going around and sitting in at clubs, as I did when I was young, when they let me.

Radio broadcast/
The Wall Street Journal,
4-6:22.

James Conlon
Conductor,
Rotterdam (Netherlands)
Philharmonic Orchestra

4

[As a conductor, it is my job] not to impose my personality on the piece, but to surrender . . . to the piece so that it flows through me, from the composer, through the orchestra, to the listener . . . [But] orchestras have an almost immediate identification with their own music, stated or unstated, whether they know it or not. I've had the experience with the Orchestre National de France, of seeing a piece of Debussy or Ravel come alive without saying a word. Why? Because so much of that music [is] in their blood. It's just there . . . You might do the same piece in Germany and England and find yourself rehearsing to produce feelings and colors that the players are capable of playing, but don't come to idiomatically or naturally.

Interview/
Los Angeles Times,
10-16:(VI)4.

Bill Conti
Composer-conductor

5

[On his composing music for motion pictures]: I am a composer in the Baroque sense rather than the Classic and Romantic sense. The Baroque sense means that one composes because that is one's job description. Bach wrote a mass for Sunday's church service or a piece for someone's wedding—a composer wrote something because the king wanted it to be played for dinner that night, not the Romantic sense of composing in isolation for oneself to produce art.

The New York Times, 5-22:16.

Barbara Daniels
Opera singer

6

The artist will take it in the neck. You'll have, at absolute outside, perhaps 10 years of satisfactory singing, and then [the voice] will

WHAT THEY SAID IN 1987

(BARBARA DANIELS)

begin to shut down. And you will have the artist experiencing great difficulties. It has happened to the best of them. At one point or another, you don't feel you've gone the right route, yet you're powerless to turn yourself back, and *no one* is going to assist you. They assisted you swiftly enough to *get* you there. It's cruel.

Interview/Opera News, 1-3:18.

John DeMain
Music director,
Houston Grand Opera;
Music director,
Opera Omaha

1

[On his leaving New York in 1973 to become an associate conductor with the St. Paul Chamber Orchestra]: Until then, all I had experienced was a professional rat race that made me wonder if a person couldn't lose his love for music by always having to deal with the pressures of "making it." I remember once counseling a pianist at [New York] City Opera who wanted to conduct but did not want to go after building a career. He thought that just by playing the piano brilliantly he would be acknowledged for his work; but, unfortunately, when his work was *not* acknowledged, he was destroyed as a human being. So—instead of being a pianist in New York who suddenly had a chance to pick up a stick, conduct opera and *hope* that Julius Rudel might offer me another production six months later—when I was offered a chance to leave New York to perfect my craft, I took it.

Interview/Opera News, October:22.

Jean Fournet
Opera conductor

2

Naturally, a [opera] singer must strive to produce beautiful sounds, colored with emotion, but a singer must produce them within the proper framework. He or she must deal with declamation, articulation, the correct accents,

the qualities peculiar to the French tongue. I'm not speaking about linguistic facility. Certain artists have the gift, others don't. Americans are good in this respect—willing to accept the advice of coaches in stylistic matters. The difficulties start with experienced singers who have done a role for so many years that they have come to believe theirs is absolutely the only way.

Interview/
Opera News, 4-11:39.

James Galway
Flutist

3

[On his refusal to have some of his recordings released because he was not satisfied with them]: If I really don't like it, I don't see why anyone else should have to listen to it. I've been lucky in that I've had that power from the beginning. The first time I told RCA that I wanted to re-record something, I offered to pay for it myself if the new version wasn't better. And, of course, it was . . . I believe that making a recording is actually like trying to catch someone's soul. How else can you explain that, when you hear Callas sing, it gets to you every time? You can feel the pathos of this woman's soul. Or when you hear Heifetz play, and every note hangs on a tear or a smile. So it's no use making a recording when you don't feel up to it—your shortcomings will be fully exposed.

Interview,
Los Angeles/Ovation,
June:12.

Paul Gemignani
Conductor

4

Being a conductor is something like being a pacer in a horse race. If the pace horse has energy and communicates that, things happen. If you show you care about the music, the orchestra will care, too. That keeps it fresh over the long haul.

Interview/
Opera News, June:12.

432

Dizzy Gillespie
Jazz trumpeter

1

I definitely am a teacher. If somebody learns from you, you are a teacher. They listen, those young musicians—trumpet players, saxophone players, piano players. Teachers are the royalty, because they mold people. I like that role. As a matter of fact, when I can no longer play, that's what I'm going to do—teach.

Interview/
The Washington Post,
6-5:(B)3.

Richard Goode
Pianist

2

A performer is not a composer, but some performers re-compose music in a way that's quite marvelous. [Pianist Arthur] Schnabel's recordings are very vital that way. They leave a strong impression of shaping. You get the feeling he stepped back from the music to make complete, objective sense of it.

Interview/Ovation,
January:20.

Sofia Gubaidulina
Soviet composer

3

[On the new policy of openness in the Soviet Union as it reflects on music]: It is an extraordinary event in the country, this openness. I think that now in Moscow we have a situation beginning which is going to mean more hearing of new music, and promote creative achievement on the part of composers. New art in general has been lacking, but in Moscow there is a hunger for new music. In people's eyes, I can see how much they need people who are thinking about new things. It doesn't have to be avant-garde; it has to meet spiritual needs.

Interview, Louisville, Ky./
The Wall Street Journal,
10-20:38.

Hans Werner Henze
Opera composer

4

I write in order to make an immediate impact, an effect. To communicate is the social obligation of the artist. Yet I have never avoided complex musical structures or severe subject matter. I use the so-called traditional elements of syntax because these forms are not merely cultural artifacts, they resonate with truth. Furthermore, if you want to write an opera, you have to be able to represent human expression. Please tell me, how does one show a person laughing with joy? With a twelve-tone row, with a computer? Of course not . . . Like a Greek chorus, the music gives away the story behind the story. It gives opinions, it declares its sympathies, and it is always on the side of those who suffer. They get the best and most beautiful music. Those horrible people, the murderers, the torturers, the collaborators and traitors, get ugly music. I deride and denounce them. It is essential that an audience understand the emotional intention of a score . . . Music, the all-knowing wise woman, is at the heart of any opera.

Interview/Opera News, May:32,33.

Jerry Herman
Composer

5

Nobody loves a critic, and I think all critics know that. I also think they can be unduly harsh after seeing something only once that a group of people might have taken two years to accomplish. I don't know if it's possible to truly evaluate a score in one hearing. I don't think any critic can do it successfully. *I* can't do it, and I have the best ear in this business.

Interview, New York/
Cosmopolitan, October:144.

Milt Jackson
Vibist,
Modern Jazz Quartet

6

Not being able to replace all the great [jazz] innovators we've lost—that puts a real damper

WHAT THEY SAID IN 1987

(MILT JACKSON)

on the art-form itself . . . The media has played our music down so badly that youngsters are not interested in [jazz], especially young black kids. I read that some of these [rock and pop stars] get $100,000 for a one-nighter. I could keep a six-piece band going for a year with that kind of money.

Interview/
The Washington Post, 1-5:(D)7.

Raymond Jackson
Professor of music,
Howard University

1

Black music, in general, is educational—from an historical and social standpoint, as well as from an artistic standpoint. The music reflects social characteristics, the hardships people have gone through, people who are disappointed in life and love. The composer who is particularly attuned will take the characteristics and thread them through the composition.

Interview, Washington/
The Christian Science Monitor,
2-23:26.

Robert Kimball
Music historian

2

There has been a reaction against amplification and other ways in which music is distorted, increased dissatisfaction with the kind of music that has been written for Broadway in the last some years, and an increased desire to go back to the works of masters in the field and become reacquainted with them.

Interview/
The Christian Science Monitor,
4-16:31.

Yuri Lyubimov
Soviet director

3

All the major theatre directors of the world, when they come to opera, try to bring this dino-saur back to life! It's such a conservative genre. By itself, it doesn't want to look for anything new. But opera is theatre. I'm sorry to have to say such obvious things, but there is the musical theatre of Mussorgsky, of Richard Wagner, of Mozart, of Alban Berg. These are *not* concerts with people wearing costumes!

Interview/Opera News, November:36.

Eva Marton
Opera singer

4

People come to the theatre with different expectations, and many are tired after a day of work. They want to be refreshed with lovely melodies, to relax, perhaps to sink into sleep. With me, you are guaranteed not to get this. That damn Marton insists you work with her. I want every person to be Tosca, to suffer with her and me. I want to lift people out of themselves through my feelings, to bring them out from the dreary daily struggle—especially in America, the business, money, money, money! There is something else, such as art and beauty. People forget the wonderful release of showing emotions. They are glad to laugh at a TV comedy, but they forget they can also cry and be touched. When I am told "Oh, you sing so beautifully," that's fine. But when I hear, "This woman works and lives through her role, and we experience it with her," that's when I am satisfied and proud to be a singer.

Interview/Opera News, 3-28:19.

5

I don't like to be in an opera where everything is centered around me, where the other colleagues are not a match. I hate that. I feel like, in such conditions, you have a yoke on, and you have to pull everything—it's all depending on *you.* I believe opera is teamwork, and in teamwork everybody is equal.

Interview/Ovation, November:15.

John Mauceri
Conductor

6

Conducting is so complex, every choice you make, no matter how much it's based on study,

(JOHN MAUCERI)

is still subjective. When the performance is over, all that's left is the memory. Weeks of rehearsal and months of research are summed up with "That was too fast," or "That was too slow," and on occasion, "That was terrific." We deal in interpretation and opinion. A conductor's job is all about communication.

Interview/Opera News,
June:46.

James McCracken
Opera singer

1

People ask sometimes why this or that didn't happen, but it really doesn't matter. They wanted me to sing Wagner early in my career and kept telling me I had no voice for it. If I had sung Wagner then, I know I wouldn't be singing now. So that was definitely the right choice. Happiness, having the kind of life I wanted to have, prompted me to make the decisions I did. Some may think I made wrong moves, but I don't agree. There are crossroads that come during your career, and you have to choose. You can't go back years later and reverse your decision. You can never know what would have happened. I'm satisfied with the roads I did take.

Interview/Opera News,
October:41.

Mehli Mehta
Director and conductor,
American Youth
Symphony Orchestra

2

Too many young people see music as a matter of fact—they take it for granted. They had better see it as a matter of art. It must be nourished, cultivated, promoted and cherished—and nurtured.

Los Angeles Times,
5-3:(Calendar)48.

Yehudi Menuhin
Violinist

3

Not all music is equally understood . . . Bach is the most beloved composer—a man for all ages, all peoples, all instruments. You can whistle his music, grunt it, play it on electronic instruments or on the harpsichord, organ or piano. His music is fundamental in its laws, in its expression, in its faith, in its capacity to penetrate the human soul. It's part of every civilization. Yet, no matter how great the composer, he cannot escape his period. That is the global envelopment within which he is working, whether it's passionately religious like Bach, incredibly social like Mozart or an assertion of the individual like Beethoven.

Interview/
U.S. News & World Report,
4-13:68.

Edward Q. Moulton
President and
general manager,
Columbus (Ohio)
Symphony Orchestra

4

Society's dilemma is how it chooses to support the arts. We did a survey recently and the average age of our audience was well over 50 years. We're either fast becoming a dinosaur or we'd better get to the yuppies pretty fast. I think we've been a little smug.

The New York Times, 1-19:14.

George Moustaki
Greek-French singer
and composer

5

I have no important message. I am simply looking for the connection between the world and myself . . . I dramatize my life, my sorrows, my joys. This weave produces poetry and music.

World Press Review, April:52.

435

WHAT THEY SAID IN 1987

Riccardo Muti
Artistic director,
La Scala Opera, Milan

1

For me, music is not entertainment. It is a mutual exchange of culture and feelings between the orchestra and the public. It is a religious ceremony, a *communione*. If you can raise the understanding of the public, to listen to music and to receive something that brings them home in a better spiritual condition, you have achieved the purpose. The danger, especially today when we have become slaves of the media, is that concerts become showpieces, filled with fireworks, fortissimos and spectacular gestures. Loud, big, spectacular are a growing danger for the artist and for the art. If we play loud and spectacularly, public success will not fail. But the quality is often in the softness, the things left unsaid.

Interview, Ravenna, Italy/
Opera News, 1-17:42.

Ivo Pogorelich
Pianist

2

The important pianist is the one who makes discoveries. Discoveries that no one else has made. And if a discoverer becomes influential, and eventually gets copied, then suddenly there's a new tradition. History has changed. That's the ultimate goal of a performer: to have his interpretation beat the others.

Ovation, February:14.

Andre Previn
Music director,
Los Angeles
Philharmonic Orchestra

3

A lot of criticism about me is that I seem to under-conduct. But I like the style. I find—to put it an absolutely idiotic way—that if you jump up and down, they don't play any louder. So what's the point? . . . I don't know whether it's [my] 21 years with English orchestras, where they don't believe in [podium dramatics],

but I got over that a long time ago. And now I just work for the orchestra. If it's clear to them and if I make them play a certain way, then certainly, visually, I've got no time left to look good to an audience. They should just listen.

Interview, Los Angeles/
The Christian Science Monitor,
5-6:27.

4

The best repertoire in the world is written for the symphony orchestra. And the fact that you are involved in music that is better than any performance of it is a nice thought. It means you can't be bored, that every time you do Beethoven's Seventh, it's a premiere, because you are merely running after it, seeing if you can get a little closer.

Interview, Los Angeles/
The Christian Science Monitor,
5-6:30.

Kenny Rogers
Singer

5

I've always believed artists create their own demise when they reach a certain level of success by saying, "Boy, I'm not going to work *that* hard any more." So they stop touring, and people stop buying their records. My big goal is to have a top-ten record when I'm 50.

Interview/
Ladies' Home Journal,
January:44.

Manuel Rosenthal
Conductor

6

I thought often about what Wagner said of the French. He had no liking for them at all—didn't he refer to them as pigs?—but like Brahms, he believed they played his music better than anyone else. Why? Because the *Ring[des Nibelungen]* is so elegant, and elegance is something the French understand. They can give Wagner's music the right transparency and grace . . . Once I asked Andre

(MANUEL ROSENTHAL)

Gide what he thought the essential feature of the French artistic character was, and he said, "Rien de trop"—nothing in excess. I agree. That is what guides my work.

Interview/
Opera News, May:11,14.

Mstislav Rostropovich
Conductor, Cellist

1

You must play for the love of music. Sometimes I see my young colleagues who are more interested in being perfect technicians than they are in making music from the heart. Shostakovich told me once, "If you have friends, you can never be sure that your love is returned. If you have a wife, you can never be sure that your love is returned. But if you love music, it will always come back to you. Your love will always be returned." I tell that to young musicians.

Washington, March 27/
The New York Times, 3-28:10.

Carl St. Clair
Assistant conductor,
Boston Symphony Orchestra

2

I think first is [the question of] what motivates the conductor's movements? Does this movement look genuine or honest? Is it a choreographed move? Or is it inspired by an inner sound and an inner passion to have that sound be produced by the performers? . . . If the gesture is motivated through a choreographic "this would look good to the audience" kind of feeling, the musicians would know it's not honest, it's not genuine . . . Orchestras are fantastic about being able to read the hands of a conductor. Especially in almost any of the standard repertoire. They're so familiar with the parts and the music that they are really free to . . . listen carefully to the rest of their colleagues in the orchestra, to listen to a conductor speaking to them.

Interview, Boston/
The Christian Science Monitor,
6-10:27.

Nadja Salerno-Sonnenberg
Violinist

3

As a student, I did many things besides practicing. I wasn't obsessive. Juilliard students stay up there all day on the fourth floor. There are no windows, no circulation. Their approach is not an emotional approach. Of course, when you're practicing to learn a piece, you've got to be analytical, but even when they've learned the notes, their approach to performance is as if they were still in the practice room. I'm not saying going to the ballet is going to make you play great. But it's experience, seeing bums on the street, anything that happens to you that makes you better or worse as a person. At least something's happening inside. Entertainment is an emotional business. I have to pour out my soul every time I play. I'm not going to have much to pour out if I sit in that room all day long.

Interview/
The Wall Street Journal,
5-11:23.

Andres Segovia
Guitarist

4

First, I consider myself a normal man. After that, an artist. After the artist, a musician. After the musician, an instrumentalist. And among instruments, I play the most beautiful of all instruments, the guitar.

USA Today, 3-23:(D)4.

Michael Senechal
Opera singer

5

The process of recording [an opera], also of film, are distortions of reality. I have seen films where an opera is presented and sung in a way that would be altogether different and unacceptable if sung live on a real stage with the same singers. These are misleading media. Perfection on records—a false perfection—has falsified the ears and taste of the public.

Interview/Opera News, 2-28:26.

WHAT THEY SAID IN 1987

Artie Shaw
Former jazz bandleader

1

The kind of music I was making was not taken seriously at all. Now jazz has become, while not thoroughly understood, at least not totally misunderstood.

Interview,
Newbury Park, Calif./
Los Angeles Times, 3-27:(VI)10.

Paul Simon
Singer, Composer

2

Pop music is usually so pretentious when it tries to be political. That's because it usually operates on the most naive level. I've said it before: If your awareness of the world is based on pop music, you're probably not very aware.

Harare, Zimbabwe/
Los Angeles Times,
2-22:(Calendar)60.

Elisabeth Soderstrom
Opera singer

3

The sad thing is that so few people get inside the opera house. The [ticket] prices are so high. It's hard to explain opera to people who haven't had a chance to be exposed to it. Its sheer physical joy cannot be conveyed by television. I am against the idea that opera is elitist. All my life I have fought for music as drama. I have seen what it can mean to people who never dreamed they could enjoy an opera performance.

Interview/
Opera News, 2-14:11.

4

It is known to psychiatrists: You can reach a person through music when everything else fails. Music is the only art-form that reaches the heart without having to pass through the brain.

Interview/
Opera News, 2-14:45.

Georg Solti
Music director,
Chicago Symphony Orchestra

5

I try to make good music and leave some good music behind. That's all. What people think or say later on is not my concern. Posterity is only a composer's worry, not an interpreter's. An interpreter lives in the present.

Interview/Ovation, November:18.

Stephen Sondheim
Composer

6

One difference between poetry and [song] lyrics is that lyrics sort of fade into the background. They fade on the page and live on the stage when set to music.

At 92nd Street Y, New York,
March 26/The New York Times, 3-28:11.

Marilyn Thomas
Associate professor
of theory and composition,
Carnegie-Mellon University

7

I think discrimination against women composers still exists because the prestigious conducting positions are still held by men . . . The way most music gets performed on an orchestral level is political. There is a lot of friendship in the business—kind of a "good old boy" network. I guess what we are really talking about is how a woman reaches the level of Bach. Can a woman today really have the opportunity to reach the level of Beethoven? I say yes. I think the only problem remaining is a social one.

At "Turning the Page:
Women and Music" workshop,
West Virginia University/
The New York Times, 12-1:15.

Michael Tilson Thomas
Conductor

8

I think that in this day and age, with the pace of musical life getting faster and faster, the

438

(MICHAEL TILSON THOMAS)

greatest cause is to give a generous and personal expression in any performance. I guess this has something to do with being a bit older.

Interview/Ovation, December:16.

Andre Watts
Pianist

1

[Music] is my overriding passion and the most important thing in my existence. It's so hard to make music and to experience the kind of magic you feel when it's really done well. But once you experience it, you want to feel that magic again and again. That's what keeps me going.

Interview/Ebony, April:45.

Krystian Zimerman
Pianist

2

I absolutely disagree with recordings. They make some things simply impossible to capture.

You miss the special feeling of something that is happening *now*, at this moment. I try to record live, in concert, whenever it's possible. I need an audience for every phrase, for every note. I feel like a fool in the studio. It's as if you'd gotten all dressed up and then just looked at yourself in the mirror, with no one to respond to you!

Interview/Ovation, April:18.

3

At the end of the last century [when they didn't have note-perfect recordings], pianists like Liszt often read through the music in the afternoon and gave a recital in the evening. I don't believe they played all the right notes in the right places . . . but they were in the end much closer to art than we are now. [I] want to share whatever emotions a composer has put into the notes. It's as if each composer wrote a beautiful book, and I'm reading it to the audience.

Interview/
The Wall Street Journal,
4-13:24.

THE STAGE

George Abbott
Producer, Director, Writer

1

I'm often shocked when I go see a stock-company production of one of my shows. They've heard it's supposed to be "fast," so they say their lines fast. That's not it. What seems fast is really variety; I just try to keep the action interesting throughout. What's not interesting is broadness. My comedy comes from people and characters. The people have to be real to make their predicament real. I direct farce as if it were *Hamlet.*

The Christian Science Monitor,
5-13:24.

2

I didn't like producing; never liked it. Directing, writing, acting I loved. But I never liked deciding who got what dressing room.

Interview, Cleveland/
The New York Times, 6-2:24.

Jane Alexander
Actress, Producer

3

Theatre itself is never going to die, because you're never going to kill that one-to-one dimension. It only takes two people to do that: one to perform and one to watch. And there's plenty of street theatre going on, and the rise in community theatre across the country has been extraordinary . . . But the professional theatres are very, very sick dogs because it takes so much [money] to maintain them at this time. That's going to be a never-ending spiral downward, I'm afraid. The stories are being told in . . . other media, so I'm not worried about that. What I think we're going to lose is some kind of verbal skills that the playwrights gave to

us. The finest playwrights are poets: They have something wonderful to say and they have a beautiful way to say it.

Interview, New York/
The Christian Science Monitor,
3-13:26.

Robert Anderson
Playwright

4

I only go to the theatre to be shattered. With laughter or excitement or emotion. One thing that bothers me about a lot of contemporary theatre is that you go and you're mildly interested and you walk out with nothing. I always want to say to the playwright—"Were you there, Charlie?" . . . But I don't want people to feel that I've just dumped my emotions on the stage. They have been crafted. They have been written into a play.

Interview, New York/
Los Angeles Times,
12-6:(Calendar)53.

Frederick Ashton
Choreographer

5

Dancers today jump better than they used to, certainly. They can lift their legs higher, if that's what's important to you. But I like style. In the older days, people didn't have these brilliant techniques, but they had *great style.* They didn't exaggerate. Arabesques weren't so high, and they didn't have to be. Through concentrating too much on the technical side, dancers have lost that sense of style. It seems that dancers [today] want to do their fellow dancers one better and, as a result, dance has become a competition, with winners. And dancing be-

(FREDERICK ASHTON)

comes somehow hard. What do you do with a company of dancers like that? I imagine you do what you must. Everything becomes a bit abstract, doesn't it? But if a dancer is given a role in which he has to express something, then you have another matter. And that's where dancers fail nowadays.

Interview,
Dancemagazine, June:138.

Mikhail Baryshnikov
Ballet dancer

1

I know dancers who are intelligent, well-read, speak a lot of languages, have good family ties. It's true dancers know everything about the ballet and less about everything else, but it's not true they are some kind of funny creatures you wind up and they dance—and that's it.

Interview, Washington/
Cosmopolitan, November:293.

John Caird
Director

2

As to which of the creators [in a musical] are responsible for what, it is always impossible to disentangle the complexities of a true collaboration. You lose your contribution in everybody else's, which is one of the most exciting things about the musical theatre.

Interview/Time, 3-23:89.

Kenneth Cork
Authority on
the British theatre;
Former chairman,
Royal Shakespeare Company

3

We've [the British] got the best theatre in the world. It is our best export. At the same time, all the subsidized theatre companies in Great Britain are in a chronic disaster . . . When the

Arts Council was first set up in the 1940s, it was given a lot of money to fund companies. But once the companies are funded, there is very little option [about how to fund them differently] the next year. It's a bottomless pit, and the theatres lose face by constantly relying on this begging bowl [approach]. The whole [government funding] thing has to be rethought. The Arts Council must become more entrepreneurial in its approaches. We need to organize funding for theatre as a whole with new schemes.

Interview, London/
The Christian Science Monitor,
6-16:29.

Tyne Daly
Actress

4

The biggest difference between movies and theatre is the presence of the actor. In movies, you've got costumes, lights, sets, music—but the actor is a shadow on the wall. The best thing about theatre is that *I* get to be here.

Interview, Los Angeles/
Los Angeles Times, 4-22:(VI)6.

Gordon Davidson
Artistic director/producer,
Mark Taper Forum,
Los Angeles

5

One of the main problems facing us [is that] you have these [theatre] institutions, but they don't mean anything without the live blood in them. It's a question of who's coming into [the theatre field], and their vision of what's possible. If they don't have a hunger and an appetite to do extraordinary things, they're not going to do it. I don't feel that same hunger and appetite . . . I think we've created the possibility of a legacy, but there is some serious question about how to pass it on. I believe very strongly in the social function of art. But I'm not so sure that everyone believes that.

Interview/
The Christian Science Monitor,
6-30:19.

441

Alessandra Ferri
Principal dancer,
American Ballet Theatre

1

I like to be able to make an audience "live" something with me. I don't want to be a ballerina for balletomanes. I want people, especially people my own age, to respond to me as a human being—not just to the dancing, not just to an image—but to a person who is living out something on the stage. Aside from that, I have set very high standards for myself. If I compete, I'm always competing with myself. I get terribly depressed if I don't give as much as I know I can give. Then, I feel I'm wasting my time. The point is, dancing should be like life. It should be real and exciting and full of surprises. Watching dance should not be like going to a museum. It should be like going further and further into life.

Interview/Dancemagazine,
October:42.

Zelda Fichandler
Producing director,
Arena Stage, Washington

2

Theatre is elitist. No matter how many people it plays to, it will never reach as many as does film or television. [But] I don't think how [far-reaching] an art-form is any definition of its worth . . . The experience of witnessing, of participating [in a play], is just not reproducible in a technological medium . . . Our curiosity, our persistent interest to know what stuff we fools are made of—they will keep [theatre] alive. You see the impulse in every society to enact and examine its rituals in this magic space, to find out what it's all about.

Interview/
The Christian Science Monitor,
6-30:18.

Frank Gilroy
Playwright

3

[Saying dramatic plays are more and more being produced at regional theatres around the U.S., rather than on Broadway]: The whole game has changed and there is not sufficient audience to sustain a serious play on Broadway . . . You're going after something illusory [in trying to produce serious plays on Broadway]—it doesn't exist any more. I think ultimately this is a healthy thing.

Panel discussion, New School for
Social Research, New York, June 15/
The New York Times, 6-17:21.

Alec Guinness
Actor

4

I prefer the life of the theatre [over working in films]. I prefer to rehearse a month, five weeks. I prefer acting in the evening to acting at breakfast time. I like being among the same group of people day in and day out. In films, actors come and go. You do one scene, then another, usually not in sequence. You often don't begin at the beginning. Because the continuity is broken, I don't know which way to go emotionally.

Interview, New York/
The New York Times, 4-27:18.

Peter Hall
Producer, Director;
Former artistic director,
Royal Shakespeare Company and
National Theatre (Britain)

5

I've run theatre companies for 25 years of my life. The difficulty always has been that if you're the National Theatre, somebody's always saying, well, you're not doing enough Greek plays or there aren't enough German plays, and that's all right—everybody's busy grinding their own axes. The advantage of this new situation [having a privately run production company in which he is one of only three owners] is that I'm beholden to no one . . . My decision to leave [the National Theatre] was an artistic decision. A huge organization—the National Theatre is a 15-million-pound-a-year organization—has to make a lot of money, has

(PETER HALL)

to draw a huge audience. It's a big administrative task, and I've enjoyed that. But I think I'd like to spend my mature years doing my plays my way. It was a good time to leave. Time for somebody else to fight a few battles.

Interview, New York/
The New York Times, 4-22:20.

Vaclav Havel
Czech playwright

1

I consider the Theatre of the Absurd the most significant development in 20th-century theatre, largely because it shows modern human beings who have lost the basic metaphysical certainties. Absurdist plays shock us by confronting us with the question of meaning, by making us aware of its absence.

Interview/
World Press Review, May:25.

Helen Hayes
Actress

2

[On her advice for young actors starting out in the theatre today]: I would say stay home, stay home. The reason I'd say that is not to bury themselves in their own bedrooms and not pursue a career, but to try to work with their regional theatre, with their community theatre. New York [theatre] has shrunk to such alarming proportions that regional theatre, community theatre, has supplanted it. Young people should not make a dart at Hollywood or Broadway, because they'll just break their hearts.

Interview/USA Today, 1-9:(A)11.

Jerry Herman
Composer

3

[On whether it bothers him that some critics call his type of composing for the musical theatre "old-fashioned"]: I love it, I love it! I want to thank them, because . . . well, just look at

this room. This antique chair is old-fashioned. That table is old-fashioned. And they're the most beautiful things. Old-fashioned to me means beautiful, permanent, sturdy, all the things I'd like my work to be remembered as . . . [The current Broadway hit British musical *Me and My Girl* is] an absolute delight. And it's old-fashioned—there's that word again! *And* it's making a fortune. Which is a perfect example of why we must never let go of tradition and what we believe in.

Interview, New York/
Cosmopolitan, October:142,146.

Glenda Jackson
Actress

4

[If] everything has to be at a definitely commercial level, that's not exactly the best way to define a culture, is it? Even with 100 percent attendance, there are some things that won't pay for themselves, but no society can afford *not* to do some work like that. That's why you need subsidized theatre. It's the subsidized theatres that have created the great plank of serious work. The West End [London's commercial theatre district] is mostly froth and musicals. But the great [British] theatres—the National and the Royal Shakespeare Company—are in real trouble and the RSC has been facing bankruptcy. They've been saved temporarily by a grant from an insurance company, but they shouldn't have to go out hat in hand. And if the great theatres are in trouble, what about the small ones?

Interview, London/
Los Angeles Times,
9-20:(Calendar)3.

John Lithgow
Actor

5

The best thing about awards is that they build your self-esteem. And you needn't sulk any more if you're not nominated again. When I won the Tony for my Broadway debut I

443

(JOHN LITHGOW)

thought: Good, that's over with. Now I don't have to worry about it any more.

Interview/
Los Angeles Times,
5-2:(VI)5.

John Malkovich
Actor

1

A show may not be wholly humiliating, I suppose, but the theatre is an invitation to the blues. Every night, the playwright, the director and the cast have to prove that they're worth $35 and $40 a ticket. If I was good last night, at 8 p.m. tonight, that's meaningless; if I was bad last night, it's of no particular harm to me tonight.

Interview, New York/
The New York Times, 10-30:17.

Marcel Marceau
Mime

2

Words express feelings and provide images, and images give an understanding of people that creates philosophy. Unfortunately, you can also lie with words. In mime, you cannot lie. You have to go to the action directly, deliberately. You see quicker—the eye perceives better—because mime is beyond words. Mime is like smelling a flower, a moment of silently breathing in the perfumes of life—the best and worst. And the audience has to create in its minds the words that it heard in silence.

Interview/
U.S. News & World Report,
2-23:62.

Jackie Mason
Comedian

3

People, when they come into a theatre, see you in a whole new light. It's like taking a picture from the kitchen and hanging it in a mu-

seum. In a nightclub, people think of you as something that goes with a glass of liquor. If they see you in a theatre, they think you have something on the ball.

Interview/
The Wall Street Journal,
2-17:30.

Des McAnuff
Artistic director,
La Jolla (Calif.) Playhouse

4

Theatre is about the spiritual and moral health of a nation. [As] the mightiest nation the world has ever known . . . [we, the U.S.,] have a huge impact on the rest of the earth. We would be very ill-advised not to provide the best art that we know how. We don't want to snatch bread from babies' mouths, but there are a lot of places to get support. We don't need much.

At colloquy, Los Angeles, Feb. 21/
Los Angeles Times, 2-23:(VI)3.

5

In the theatre you are not going to get out as much verisimilitude as in film and TV. [But] you're getting reality . . . flesh and blood on the stage. Because it's not as powerful as TV in reaching masses of people, theatre tends to be a freer form, freer socially, politically, morally. There's a lot of dreary theatre out there, let's not kid ourselves . . . But on the point of [cultural] spiritual health, it's a great forum to exchange and examine opposing points of view. Because you get somebody who is alive representing with particular passion a particular point of view. Theatre is a great way to question ourselves, our times. Few other [art] forms do that as well.

Interview/
The Christian Science Monitor,
6-30:18.

Arthur Miller
Playwright

6

The hope was, and maybe it will come to pass someday, that through a Lincoln Center we

(ARTHUR MILLER)

could gradually develop an American way of keeping alive what is valuable in our theatrical heritage. I'm against creating a bureaucratic national theatre because it will throttle things all over again, but we must find some way to at least partially subsidize it. There's a lot of good and enjoyable work from the past that we should know about, but at the moment there's a far better chance of being able to see the past excitingly reinterpreted in countries like Great Britain. It's not just an artistic question, it's a matter of rooting us in our own time. You don't know where you are if you don't know where you've been—and theatrically we have no idea where we've been.

Interview, New York/
Publishers Weekly, 11-6:52.

1

[On critics]: [They are] a condition of the trade. It's terrific when you get praised, because it means all sorts of goodies, and it's painful when you don't. But even when the praise comes, you get the feeling that it's not reading the interior of the work. If one doesn't absorb one's own standards, then you're at the mercy of whoever happens to have the job that week of writing reviews. And I don't see the point in that. We expect too much from critics in this country, maybe because the run of a play has to be quite long to be regarded as successful. Ibsen's plays ran only a matter of a few weeks. Here, [in the U.S.], if you don't run a year, you're a failure. Well, who says that?

Interview, Roxbury, Conn./
Los Angeles Times,
11-15:(Calendar)54.

2

[As a playwright,] you're bound to get discouraged. I've been discouraged from time to time . . . if not all of the time. But then, suddenly, it changes. And I've got stuff running all over the world again. The human race uses what it feels like using at any particular moment. It's a little bit like when you go into your clothes closet and suddenly discover a suit you

haven't worn in seven years and it looks great. Or a pair of shoes. And I'm afraid a lot of the time the basis of the choice is as trivial as that.

Interview, Roxbury, Conn./
Los Angeles Times,
11-15:(Calendar)54.

Marsha Norman
Author, Playwright

3

Compared with writing a novel, putting a play together can be brutal. It's so tiring to search for actors and try to figure out when the actors and the director are likely to be in the same city so they can meet, look at their schedules and see when in the next five years they can get together to put the play on.

Interview/
U.S. News & World Report,
6-8:78.

Joseph Papp
Producer,
New York
Shakespeare Festival

4

[Saying he will allow his actors to approve the directors in his upcoming Shakespeare series]: Shakespeare was an actor. Everything was done by actors. I want to get away from all the other ideas of the way Shakespeare is done, in which other people have the main say. The humanization of the plays comes from the fact that these are actors.

Interview, New York/
The New York Times, 11-4:24.

Hildy Parks
Producer

5

The Broadway theatre today, for lack of leadership or showmanship, is turning out to be the part of show business in which there is no business. It's really true when compared with the television business, which shows an astonishing growth.

Interview, Los Angeles/
Emmy Magazine, May-June:15.

445

WHAT THEY SAID IN 1987

Maya Plisetskaya
Artistic director,
National Ballet of Spain;
Former prima ballerina,
Bolshoi Ballet (Soviet Union)

1

Everyone [young dancers today] is involved with technique rather than using technique as the means by which one dances. They approach dance like a sport. Instead of going step by step in their progress, young dancers have a tendency to leap forward into things they are not prepared to do. That leaves gaps in the education and training, and an uneven technique . . . Much will depend on choreographers to demand expressiveness over physicality. Jacobson and Goleizovsky, for instance, demanded these qualities, while Robbins and Balanchine demanded style. A dancer should be able to perform works that require pure technique as well as those that require expressiveness as expected from the choreographer.

Interview/
Dancemagazine, October:54.

Lloyd Richards
Dean, School of Drama,
Yale University;
Artistic director,
Yale Repertory Theatre

2

The [TV] networks say what is taste and, within the networks, taste is defined really by one person—the person who controls programming in that network that received the highest ratings. In the theatre, someone writes a play, sends it to seven directors, and all say no; the eighth guy says, "Yes, I love it." And he produces it. The control of taste is a more amorphous thing in the theatre.

Interview/
The Christian Science Monitor,
6-30:19.

Mickey Rooney
Entertainer

3

I love people. I love the public. They're the ones I work for anyway. Not the critics. Most [critics] show up with their write-ups already written. Look, we're not doing *Othello* here. I'm doing what I've found the public expects of me. I can't please all of them. But as Mr. Lincoln said, you *can* please some of the people some of the time. And I sure aim to try.

Interview, Los Angeles/
Los Angeles Times, 5-28:(VI)6.

George Rose
Tony Award-winning actor

4

I feel safer [working] in the theatre than anywhere else. It's comforting to have somewhere to go at night, to have the friendship of the cast, and not have to worry about what's on television or the movies, or if there's anything in the refrigerator. I look forward to coming here. It's quiet and peaceful.

Interview, New York/
The New York Times, 2-13:19.

Gerald Schoenfeld
Chairman,
Shubert Organization

5

[On criticism that dramatic plays are seldom seen in Broadway theatres]: In order for any playwright to achieve success, you need an audience. I know of very few plays that have been deprived of a forum, though not necessarily on Broadway.

Panel discussion, New School for
Social Research, New York, June 15/
The New York Times, 6-17:21.

Peter Sellars
Director

6

The least important part of the [theatrical] experience is what happens while the audience is in the theatre. You're planting a seed there, and what matters is how it grows later . . . It's all the same to me if they love it or hate it, because one way or another it enters their lives, and it's something they won't forget.

Interview/
The Christian Science Monitor,
12-15:22.

Red Skelton
Comedian

1

Today's comics use four-letter words as a shortcut to thinking. They're shooting for that big laugh and it becomes a panic thing, using four-letter words to shock people. You'll laugh, but when you leave and your dignity returns, you say, "Why?" I know more dirty jokes than any guy who ever lived. But I don't do them on stage. I have too much respect for my audience.

Los Angeles Times, 6-24:(VI)2.

Isabelle Stevenson
President,
American Theatre Wing

2

Top prices for tickets on Broadway are now around $50 for many plays. I constantly hear, when friends come here and ask me to recommend a play: "But is it worth the price?" Sometimes it's hard to say. Certainly we must bring ticket prices down. But we must also remind people that not everybody has to sit in the orchestra. There are often cheaper seats available in the balconies. I remember the thrill of seeing shows from high up when I was younger. But will prices come down? I really don't think so. Nothing ever comes down . . . the price of onions or the price of a bus ride. But we must at least try. Perhaps the unions and other organizations in the theatre will recognize that they may be pricing themselves out of jobs.

Interview, New York/
The Christian Science Monitor,
6-8:26.

Paul Taylor
Choreographer

3

A [dance] company is for people to pass through, it seems. You work with them. You get fond of them. You have a bond there. But they eventually go off, like children in a way, though I try not to call them kids. Nobody stays forever.

Interview/
The New York Times, 4-21:24.

Douglas Wage
Director

4

I have a great passion for directing and for the theatre. I grew up as a very religious young man, and I think in some ways the theatre has become for me personally, as a director, a public forum for expressing, reaffirming the potency of the human spirit and its capacity for great creativity, and in a cautionary sense its capacity for destruction. Theatre for me has to be a highly nourishing, spiritual experience.

Interview,
Washington/
The Christian Science Monitor,
11-20:26

Colm Wilkinson
Irish actor

5

Tyrone Guthrie is the great Irish director who said to [actor] Ian McKellen that the first and foremost obligation was to excite and move an audience—as an entertainer. And that's what I call myself. I mean, people come—and you're supposed to get withdrawn and not emote and not relate? I just don't understand that kind of approach . . . You know when you get it emotionally right, that's how it will affect people out there. And all this Brechtian thing about you must not be associated with your audience— well, that's the greatest lot of rubbish.

Interview, New York/
The Christian Science Monitor,
6-3:23.

August Wilson
Playwright

6

You can have problems writing if you recognize things like writer's block. I refuse to recognize any of that stuff. Nothing is sacred. You put a piece of paper in the typewriter, you type on it. You have something that wasn't there before. If it's not good, you tear [it] up and start over again if necessary; it's not that big a deal. If you're going to write a play, that's 80 to 100

WHAT THEY SAID IN 1987

(AUGUST WILSON)

be able to write two plays a year.

Interview, Los Angeles/
Daily Variety, 5-29:22.

[As a playwright,] you have to confront the
dark parts of yourself, and work to banish them
with illumination and forgiveness. Your willingness to wrestle with your demons will cause
your angels to sing. Use the pain as fuel, as a
reminder of your strength. When you're working on a play, it's like walking down this strange
road that is the landscape of the self. You simply have to be willing to confront whatever you
discover there. It's all a process of discovery.
What happens all too often is that we run from
the parts of ourselves that we least recognize.

You have to be willing to stand up to that and
push beyond it. That's where your writing takes
a leap.

Esquire, December:128.

Garland Wright
Artistic director,
Guthrie Theatre,
Minneapolis

Theatre is an antique art-form, and a lot of
theatre [professionals] are envious of the toys of
the other media. And we're in danger of losing
sight of 2,000 years of history of written theatre. [But] there is a timeless need for the actors and audience [to interact].

Interview/
The Christian Science Monitor,
6-30:18.

Philosophy

Vassily Aksyonov
Exiled Soviet writer

1

When I visited the West as a traveler, many times I found myself in bewilderment before the shop windows. Sometimes, it would seem a sort of immoral display of luxury. But then, when I became a Western person myself, I realized that this is a mass culture. It's the ultimate expression of common sense, this affluent consumerism.

Interview/
U.S. News & World Report, 8-17:49.

Yehuda Amichai
Israeli poet

2

It is the duty of the intellectual to express the right to doubt. Absolutely free utterance exists only in writing. That is the principal message of the intellectual . . . Intellectuals must be able to speak their lofty words, but . . . they must also descend to reality.

World Press Review, February:32.

Robert L. Bartley
Editor,
"The Wall Street Journal"

3

So far at least, the amazing thing about the [stock-market] insider-trading scandals is that they have found so little insider trading. No, we do not live in an age of moral collapse. We more nearly live in an age of moral zealotry.

At Babson College commencement/
The Christian Science Monitor, 6-18:23.

Saul Bellow
Author

4

At the beginning of modern times, women were promised love, as it were. They were told, you're going to be free, you're going to be well, you're going to love and be loved, and this will help you to weather the difficulties of life. This is Rousseau's plan—these free societies based on enlightened principles were not going to work unless people were trained in love, educated for it . . . Suddenly this was snatched away, and it was replaced by the sexual revolution, which has a very different foundation—namely, that you were a creature, you were an animal, you had certain creaturely needs, sex was one of them, you have a right to gratify these for the sake of your health, your well-being, your complexion, your personality, or whatnot else. All right, so people gave this a fling. Well, no human being takes another human being all that seriously any more, and when you have that happening at the very core of a society, then you're looking at a lot of trouble, a great deal of wretchedness, because something in human nature demands a constancy of connection, emotional constancy. There's a secret voice in us which says, "No, this is bad; this is wrong. I'm alone again, once more cast into outer darkness."

Interview, New York/
The New York Times, 6-3:22.

5

. . . people now are beginning to have a material, medical, literal vision of one another. I quote Freud as saying that love is an overvaluation. He means that from the point of view of a physician looking at patients with a clinical eye, one can't really see why they conceive mad passions for each other. So there has to be a sort of passionate illusion. Medical science has seen love for quite a while as having an evolutionary cause: It's for the procreation of the species. The view of the body as a machine has had a rather widespread effect. One machine falls in love with another—is that the story?

Interview, Wilmington, Vt./
U.S. News & World Report,
9-7:52.

449

WHAT THEY SAID IN 1987

Bruno Bettelheim
Child psychologist

1

I would never force a [toy] gun on a child, but parents think that if their children play with [toy] guns now they are going to be murderers. If they play with blocks, it doesn't mean they will become architects. If they play with trucks, it doesn't mean they will become auto mechanics or truck drivers. War games are as old as childhood. One learns how to socialize violence rather than repress it . . . Why do they want to play with guns? Because they feel defenseless. At least this is a symbolic defense.

Interview/
Newsweek, 6-22:79.

James H. Billington
Director, Woodrow Wilson
International Center for Scholars;
Librarian of Congress-designate
of the United States

2

I believe in highly interpretive scholarship—humanistic, synthetic, historical. If you read about what people have aspired to, you are somehow better fortified for your own path. The kind of scholarship I think we need more of is providing tentative answers to important questions rather than definitive answers to secondary ones. I'm a great fan of all kinds of analytic and methodical techniques; but we also need to put things together, not just take them apart.

Interview, Washington,
April 17/The Washington Post,
4-18:(C)4.

Allan Bloom
Author;
Professor of philosophy,
University of Chicago

3

There used to be an intellectual class in America. In the political realm, for example,

you had Dean Acheson and George Kennan; in journalism there was Walter Lippmann. These people kept the world of ideas alive. But today the distinction between intellectuals and non-intellectuals doesn't make any difference; celebrity is the only standard. If you had a direct descendant of George Washington in a class together with [rock singer] Mick Jagger's son, the students would probably be much more interested in Mick Jagger's son. The level of public taste—and taste is a good beginning point for serious thinking—really has declined. The cultivated person no longer has any public model.

Interview/
U.S. News & World Report,
5-11:78.

Derek C. Bok
President,
Harvard University

4

I think there are very broad cultural patterns that are resisting authority—that are resisting inhibitions on everyone living the way they want to live. It's not just that religion is less important. It's the tremendous emphasis that's placed on success, results—which puts more pressure on a certain shaving of the rules in order to achieve success.

Interview,
Cambridge, Mass./
The Christian Science Monitor,
7-27:21.

Daniel J. Boorstin
Librarian of Congress
of the United States

5

Historically, risk-takers are people who shatter the illusion of knowledge. They are willing to try something that everyone thinks is outrageous or stupid.

U.S. News & World Report,
1-26:62.

Ernest L. Boyer
President,
Carnegie Foundation for
the Advancement of Teaching

1

To sustain a culture, you need points of common memory, tradition and experience. If we don't have those, it's impossible to intellectually and socially engage with one another. [The risks for the nation are] disintegration, fragmentation and anarchy.

U.S. News & World Report,
9-28:86.

Joseph Brodsky
Exiled Soviet poet;
Winner, 1987
Nobel Prize in Literature

2

In the West you have every opportunity for civilization to triumph. But what do you do with the opportunities? This is a large issue. The species goofed long ago. One has a choice, either to learn or not to learn. And, invariably, the bulk of human beings choose not to learn. It's as simple as that. It's partly the fault of the institutions of education. But it's partly the decision to be relieved of responsibility.

Interview, New York/
The Washington Post, 10-23:(B)4.

David Brown
Motion-picture producer

3

I'm a very complicated older man who is knowing for the first time a certain degree of security and peace within himself owing to a great many mistakes. I've suffered many, many traumas, many bouts of joblessness, many bouts of being unloved. I'm not very secure socially. I'm always afraid of offending. I'm an incomplete person working against time.

Interview, New York/
The Wall Street Journal,
10-27:32.

Charles Bukowski
Poet

4

I've been run over, beaten up, jailed—I've picked up a *lot* of baggage along the way, everything from ex-wives to ex-jobs. I've always been worried about my damn soul—maybe I worry too much. But you carry in one hand a bundle of darkness that accumulates each day. And when death finally comes, you say, right away, "Hey buddy, glad to see ya!"

Interview, Los Angeles/
Los Angeles Times, 11-3:(VI)4.

George Bush
Vice President of
the United States;
Candidate for the 1988
Republican Presidential nomination

5

I am a practical man. I like what's real. I'm not much for the airy and abstract. I like what works. I am not a mystic, and I do not yearn to lead a crusade. My ambitions are perhaps less dramatic, but they are no less profound.

Announcing his candidacy
for President, Houston,
Oct. 12/The Washington Post,
10-13:(A)4.

Jimmy Carter
Former President
of the United States

6

Nothing better exemplifies the continuity of human life than the planting of a tree.

At ceremony of planting 39 trees
dedicated to the 39 signers
of the U.S. Constitution, at
the Carter Presidential Center,
Atlanta/USA Today, 10-12:(A)4.

Richard F. Celeste
Governor of Ohio (D)

7

Whether in science or in politics, whether in theory or in social policy, every accepted fact

451

WHAT THEY SAID IN 1987

(RICHARD F. CELESTE)

was once only a fond hope. Virtually everything now true was once simply someone's dream.

Inauguration address,
Columbus, Jan. 12/
Los Angeles Times, 1-13:(I)4.

Lynne V. Cheney
Chairman,
National Endowment
for the Humanities
of the United States

1

The humanities are important now, as they've always been, because what they deal with are questions that have to do with human nature and the state of the human condition that never change: What are the most important goals in life? What goals should one set for oneself? Questions about identity: Who am I? What's important to me? Questions about relationships: *King Lear*, for example—the questions it asks are about what parents and children owe to one another. Particularly in a world like today's, where everything seems to whirl into chaos at all times, where things are moving so quickly, the humanities that deal with eternal verities have a particularly important role to play. They are a rock for us to hold onto.

Interview, Los Angeles/
Los Angeles Times,
6-3:(V)2.

Warren Christopher
Lawyer; Former
American diplomat

2

There are not so many lessons in glad times. Adversity is by far the better teacher. Adversity will be a part of almost all our lives. So it is not in escaping adversity, but in answering it, that our character is defined.

Los Angeles Times,
9-29:(I)3.

Colleen Dewhurst
Actress

3

Don't go around the agony. It took me years to find out that trying to avoid it doesn't work. You must simply go through the middle of it . . . Someday, somewhere, this moment of agony will be useful to you. This horror will be useful. The killer is bitterness—the other killer is drive without real desire.

At Bryn Mawr College commencement/
The Christian Science Monitor, 6-18:23.

Joan Didion
Author

4

One of the most malignant aspects of the ['60s] was the extent to which everyone began to deal exclusively in symbols . . . Marijuana was a symbol; long hair was a symbol, of course, and so was short hair; natural food was a symbol—rice seeds, raw milk. Now, this was all very interesting. To be present at a moment when an entire society was so starved for meaning it made totems out of quite meaningless choices.

At Bard College commencement/
The Christian Science Monitor, 6-18:23.

Kirk Douglas
Actor

5

[On whether he feels "supplanted" by his son, actor Michael Douglas, because of his son's success]: On the contrary—I feel immortal. That's what immortality is all about. I think sons fight their fathers, and are sometimes intimidated by their fathers, but the love of a father is the only kind of love in which one wants the son to surpass him. It's not that I'm such a nice guy. It's narcissistic. But narcissism is a nice word. Self-love is important. Maturity means falling in love with yourself, in the sense of understanding yourself and saying, "Hey— I'm not such a bad guy." You change, and you have to come to grips with yourself—and make

(KIRK DOUGLAS)

peace with yourself. I think the most elegant form of narcissism is your children.

Interview, New York/
The New York Times, 4-2:23.

Vladimir A. Dzhanibekov
Soviet cosmonaut

1

There has been a great change in my own human philosophy. In routine life we don't pay attention to Earth. But when I'm in space and see the planet so beautiful and blue with no borders between, I realize the most serious thing of all is the life of the planet.

Los Angeles, April 9/
Los Angles Times, 4-11:(I)27.

Linda Ellerbee
Broadcast journalist

2

To this day I have trouble getting the word *career* out of my mouth. I'll talk about my job. After a couple of margaritas, I might even talk about my craft. But career, no. I don't think ambition is absolutely necessary. Some of the best people in this business are not terribly ambitious people . . . Let your ignorance shine, and ask people to help you. They will love it, and you will learn . . . Somehow, with words like *career* and *goal-oriented*, we've gotten away from the notion that kindness is a good thing and you can have it in the workplace, that you really can treat people as you would like to be treated, and have it work. And remember: Those who are jerks on the way up had better be prepared to wear false moustaches on the way down. And in my business there are a lot of ups and downs.

Esquire, December:100.

Mikhail S. Gorbachev
General Secretary,
Communist Party of
the Soviet Union

3

When I see breakthroughs in science or the economy at the same time that I see great hu-

man losses, spiritual losses, or if man is excluded from the process, then . . . that system should . . . be subjected to great questioning.

Interview, Moscow/
The Christian Science Monitor,
1-5:14.

4

Democracy is not the opposite of order. It is order of a greater degree, based not on implicit obedience, mindless execution of instructions, but on full-fledged active participation by all the community in all society's affairs . . . Democracy is not the opposite of discipline. It is a conscious discipline. Democracy is unity of rights and duties.

At trade-union congress,
Moscow, Feb. 25/
The Washington Post,
2-26:(A)32.

5

I have always held that my weakness is that I have always shown interest in many things in various fields. One might assent that people who concentrate on some specific field achieve much in life. But still, people with a broad outlook are more to my liking.

Interview/
Los Angeles Times,
5-21:(I)17.

Mary Gordon
Author

6

Even though life is quite a sad business, you can have a good time in the middle of it. I like to laugh, and I think the unsung, real literary geniuses of the world are people who write jokes. Both the Irish and Jews are very fatalistic, but they laugh a lot. Only the Protestants think that every day in every way, life is getting better and better. What do they know?

Interview/
U.S. News & World Report,
10-5:74.

WHAT THEY SAID IN 1987

Alec Guinness
Actor

1

When I was a boy, an adolescent driven to act, I envisaged thunderous applause for my every gesture. I still am attracted by the limelight, but I also rather despise it. After a lifetime of playing other people, there comes a time when I feel . . . oh, I'd just like to discover myself for a change.

Interview, New York/
The New York Times,
4-27:18.

Garrett Hardin
Ecologist

2

There's nothing more dangerous than a shallow-thinking compassionate person. God, he can cause a lot of trouble.

Interview/
The New York Times,
6-30:25.

Charles Henry
Chairman,
Amnesty International
U.S.A.

3

The toughest thing for anybody getting involved in human rights is to strike a balance between optimism and pessimism. You start out being very idealistic, but it's easy to become cynical. In my first political-science course in college, the first thing my professor said was, "Forget everything you learned in high-school civics. Things really don't work that way."

Esquire, December:104.

Chaim Herzog
President of Israel

4

[Addressing the victims of the Holocaust buried at Bergen-Belsen concentration camp in Germany]: At this awesome place, the vale of slaughter, and at the outset of my journey on this soil, I leave as a memorial to you, my brothers and sisters, victims of the Holocaust, a stone hewn from the rocks of Jerusalem. I do not bring forgiveness with me, nor forgetfulness. The only ones who can forgive are dead; the living have no right to forget. The mourning of your deaths will be kept in eternal memory in our hearts. Not to sustain an enduring enmity [against Germany], not to maintain a sterile, debilitating hatred, but to gain strength and steadfastness.

At site of Bergen-Belsen
concentration camp, April 6/
The New York Times, 4-7:8.

E. D. Hirsch, Jr.
Professor of English,
University of Virginia

5

Liberals want society to change fast. Cultural conservatives like myself think that if you want society to work, you have to change slowly, because the change has to be intergenerational. Everybody has to understand.

Interview, San Francisco/
The Christian Science Monitor,
4-13:24.

Soichiro Honda
Founder,
Honda Motor Company
(Japan)

6

I have some ideas. But I always find out that younger people have done them already. Young people are wonderful—I just can't beat them. They've learned from our experience, and then they add their own ideas. Many older people talk about "kids these days." I have never used that expression.

Interview, Tokyo/
The New York Times,
1-12:34.

Erich Honecker
First Secretary,
Communist Party
of East Germany

1

Socialism and capitalism cannot be united any more than fire and water.

At dinner in his honor,
Bonn, West Germany, Sept. 6/
The Washington Post, 9-7:(A)13.

Benjamin L. Hooks
Executive director,
National Association
for the Advancement
of Colored People

2

In a real sense there are "No Parking" places in life, as there are on busy streets. If one parks in life in the wrong place, he or she risks being ticketed, or fined by stunted growth or arrested development. Life is not a parking lot, nor a cemetery, nor a museum—rather it is a gymnasium, an arena, a thoroughfare. Nature itself demands that we either grow or we die; we move or we lose.

At NAACP convention,
New York, July 6/
The Wall Street Journal, 7-9:28.

John Houseman
Actor, Director

3

The only important thing when you've lived as long as I have [84 years] is what you've accomplished—a body of work . . . We all tend to talk about successes. At least as important are our failures.

At tribute to him, Los Angeles/
Los Angeles Times, 4-9:(VI)12.

Henry J. Hyde
United States Representative,
R-Illinois

4

Communism is the most sustained assault against the human spirit in human history.

At Iran-contra hearings,
Washington/Newsweek, 6-1:36.

John Paul II
Pope

5

[Criticizing divorce]: There are those who dare to negate and even ridicule the idea of a faithful commitment for all of life. How, with that hypothesis, could one continue to require of a man loyalty to his fatherland, to labor agreements, to the fulfillment of laws and contracts? . . . It is not strange at all that the spread of divorce in a society is accompanied by a diminishing of public morality in all sectors . . . True love does not exist if it is not faithful. And it cannot exist if it is not honest. Neither can it be in the concrete vocation of matrimony if there is no full promise that lasts until death. Only indissoluble matrimony will be firm and lasting support for the familial community.

Speech, Cordoba, Argentina,
April 8/Los Angeles Times,
4-9:(I)18.

6

I take this occasion to assure you of the Church's particular concern for those who leave their native countries in suffering and desperation. The frequent repetition of this experience is one of the saddest phenomena of our century. Yet it has often been accompanied by hope and heroism and new life.

At mass, Miami, Sept. 11/
Los Angeles Times, 9-13:(I)17.

Paul Johnson
British author and journalist

7

History is the most important thing to learn. It's more important than almost any other discipline if you're involved in high-level decisions.

Interview, London/
The Christian Science Monitor,
2-12:17.

Elia Kazan
Motion-picture director

8

You get more frankly interested in yourself as you get older, or at least I did. I've had an

(ELIA KAZAN)

interesting history. I've been an actor, a stage director, a film director, a novelist, and then I became an autobiographer. So now I've reached the end of the road, I'd like to make one more movie, if I can get the money for it, which is hard. I've got a wonderful script, I think. I wrote it.

Interview, New York/
The New York Times, 1-20:21.

Madeleine Kunin
Governor of Vermont (D)

1

One is responsible for one's own life. Passivity provides no protection.

The Christian Science Monitor,
9-4:21.

Fang Lizhi
Former vice president,
University of Science and
Technology (China);
Former member,
Communist Party of China

2

Marxism is obsolete. It is useful for understanding the past century but not the current one. It is like an old coat that must be discarded.

World Press Review, October:50.

Mary Martin
Actress

3

. . . for anyone who is having a rough time with anything, I think the most vital thing in the world is *encouragement* . . . although God can give you your talents, he may also take them away if you don't make full use of them . . . And it doesn't just apply to a talent like performing, but to everything—even the use of your arms and legs. I know that from the [1982 automobile] accident.

Interview, Philadelphia/
Good Housekeeping, July:164.

Forrest McDonald
Professor of history,
University of Alabama

4

When I think of bureaucracy, I think of Mark Twain's definition thereof. Bureaucracy, he said, is 50,000 ants on a log floating down the Mississippi River—and every one of them thinking they're running it!

Interview, Washington/
The Christian Science Monitor,
5-12:1.

Marvin Mitchelson
Lawyer

5

[On divorce cases]: I think that men are equally or more emotional [than women]. Generally speaking, there's a big ego there. Men hate to have their empire divided. They hate to think, I've got a $10-million business, and my wife's going to get half. They don't seem to understand the theory of partnership and sharing. Women share, generally speaking, their lives, their bed, their board, their spirit, their souls; but when it comes to sharing property, men don't like that.

Interview/USA Today, 9-1:(A)9.

Richard M. Nixon
Former President
of the United States

6

If you take no risks, you will suffer no defeats. But if you take no risks, you win no victories.

Eulogy for Ohio State
football coach Woody Hayes/
U.S. News & World Report, 3-30:9.

Donald O'Connor
Actor, Dancer

7

What makes people laugh most, I think, is the downfall of dignity. When a rich and pompous man, maybe someone who looks like a banker, slips and falls on a banana peel, that's

(DONALD O'CONNOR)

funny. But if you were to try this with a bag lady, it wouldn't work, because the context is all wrong.

At California Polytechnic University,
Pomona/The Christian Science Monitor,
7-30:24.

Cyril Northcote Parkinson
Author, Historian

1

The chief product of a highly automated society is a widespread and deepening sense of boredom.

Interview, Onchan, Isle of Man/
The New York Times, 9-25:7.

Diane Ravitch
Adjunct professor of
history and education,
Teachers College,
Columbia University

2

American parents believe their kids will get ahead if they're smart. Japanese parents believe kids will get ahead if they work hard.

U.S. News & World Report, 1-19:60.

Ronald Reagan
President of
the United States

3

The greatest challenge for those of us who live in freedom is to recognize the ties of common interest that bind us, to prove wrong those cynics who would suggest that free enterprise and democracy led to shortsighted policies and undisciplined self-interest.

Speech on 40th anniversary of
Marshall Plan, June 1/
The New York Times, 6-2:3.

4

In the 1950s, [then Soviet leader Nikita] Khrushchev predicted, "We will bury you [the

West]." But in the West today, we see a free world that has achieved a level of prosperity and well-being unprecedented in all human history. In the Communist world, we see failure. Technological backwardness. Declining standards of health. Even want of the most basic kind—too little food. Even today, the Soviet Union still cannot feed itself. After these four decades, then, there stands before the entire world one great and inescapable conclusion: Freedom leads to prosperity. Freedom replaces the ancient hatreds among the nations with comity and peace. Freedom is the victor.

At Berlin Wall, June 12/
The New York Times, 6-13:3.

5

. . . the old solution of the 20th century for the world's woes—solutions calling for more and more state power concentrated in the hands of smaller and smaller elites—have come under fire everywhere, especially among the intellectuals. The new idea of a nexus between economic and political freedom as the principal vehicle of social progress is catching on. In looking back over these past 6 1/2 years, then, I cannot help but reflect on the most dramatic change to my own eyes: the exciting new prospects for the democratic cause. A feeling of energy and hope prevails; statism has lost the intellectuals; and everywhere one turns, nations and people are seeking the fulfillment of their age-old aspirations for self-government and self-determination. Perhaps, then, we may finally progress beyond the post-war standoff.

At Town Hall, Los Angeles, Aug. 26/
Los Angeles Times, 8-27:(I)26.

William H. Rehnquist
Chief Justice
of the United States

6

Time is a wasting asset, and most of us realize it only too late to avoid spending a lot of it unwisely. Like any free-market economist, you ought then to look at what else might be done with the marginal few hours at the end of the

WHAT THEY SAID IN 1987

week that aren't really necessary to earning a living.

At Boston University commencement,
May 17/The New York Times, 5-18:17.

Cliff Robertson
Actor

1

There must be a place where hopes and dreams are nurtured, and that place is only within ourselves. A place to clean the grime of life, a place that waits for us to stay and look inside that we might see the truth.

At Bradford College commencement/
The Christian Science Monitor, 6-18:24.

Benno C. Schmidt, Jr.
President, Yale University

2

Privacy is absolutely essential to maintaining a free society.

USA Today, 10-16:(A)8.

Natan Sharansky
Exiled Soviet dissident

3

I've had to face a new reality, the reality of the Free World, which means that you have the problems of choices, the problems of making your own decisions. You have the problem of a big variety of views . . . and everybody wants you to become part of them.

Interview, Jerusalem/
Los Angeles Times, 2-14:(I)14.

B. F. Skinner
Psychologist

4

What's wrong with punishments is that they work immediately, but give no long-term results. The responses to punishment are either the urge to escape, to counter-attack or a stubborn apa-

thy. These are the bad effects you get in prisons or schools, or wherever punishments are used.

Interview, Cambridge, Mass./
The New York Times, 8-25:18.

Tommy Smothers
Comedian

5

[On comedy teams]: The comic is always kind of driven, involved in detail, the timing, the creation of the act. But the straight man enjoys life. Plays a lot of golf, gets around, has friends. Dean Martin. Bud Abbott. Oliver Hardy.

The Washington Post, 9-12:(D)1.

Javier Solana
Minister of Culture
of Spain

6

There is a generation in Spain that looks at politics with a bit of an epic feeling—the struggle for liberty, and all that. But in a democracy, politics is not so epic. It is daily life, solving daily problems with a view toward the future.

Interview/
The Washington Post,
5-7:(A)43.

Sylvester Stallone
Actor

7

I believe in a God force. I don't know if that God is in heaven or in your heart. But I believe there's an inner power that makes winners or losers. And the winners are the ones who really listen to the truth of their hearts.

Interview/
Cosmopolitan, August:199.

W. Clement Stone
Industrialist

8

You get a diploma at any elementary school or high school by using your memory. You get a degree at any university or seminary in the

(W. CLEMENT STONE)

behavioral sciences by using your memory. Knowledge is not power; it's potential power. You may have the knowledge, you may know what to do, you may know how to do it, but you may not know how to *motivate* yourself to do it.

Interview, Los Angeles/
Los Angeles Times, 5-20:(V)6.

Jule Styne
Composer

1

[On his being 81 years of age]: I'm working harder, thinking better, being able to listen to other people better—that comes from getting older. I never stop to think about my age. The whole name of the game is, you must have something to do every day so you just can't wait till you do it. You've got to go to a place where you sit down and do some work. Your brain *wants* to work. It worked all your life for you. If you want to retire, you're old. If you keep your brain working, you're young.

Interview, New York/
The New York Times, 6-10:23.

Elizabeth Taylor
Actress
/

2

I have a great passion for life, and passion is not just a word that indicates love-making or lust. I think it's passion that makes me a survivor. If you care about other people, it becomes a passion. If you can reach a natural high that is bliss—that's passion.

Interview, New York/
USA Today, 1-15:(A)1.

Twyla Tharp
Choreographer

3

Living, I am finding, is not letting the downside get the upper hand. As you become more experienced and adept, do not become blase. Boredom is our own doing. It is not done to us.

It is our responsibility to keep ourselves alive. No one does this for us . . . Do not hold back. Do not be tentative. Go for it full force or stay home.

At Pomona (Calif.)
College commencement/
The Christian Science Monitor,
6-18:24.

Margaret Thatcher
Prime Minister of
the United Kingdom

4

I don't feel sorry for people. Feeling sorry for someone does nothing.

Los Angeles Times, 5-26:(I)11.

5

Capitalism and enterprise is a system which only works by spreading ever more widely to more and more of the population what used to be the privileges of the few.

June 10/The New York Times, 6-13:4.

6

I am a naturally hard worker. I was brought up that way. It is a sin to be idle. The reason you are here is to use whatever talents and abilities you have to the greatest extent. If you do not at first do what you want to do, you just come at it another way and try again.

Interview, London/
Ladies' Home Journal,
November:193.

Dennis Weaver
Actor

7

[On his social work in the community]: . . . when you feel like you're of value, it is a very important part of your happiness. The moment we get to the point where we feel we're not useful, we're not very happy about it. We are all looking for happiness, so what I'm doing in that sense is not all altruistic. The wise person understands that his own happiness must include the happiness of others.

Interview/USA Today, 9-10:(A)9.

459

WHAT THEY SAID IN 1987

E. B. White
Author

1

When you plan and dream, choose a suitable decision and hold to it. Finish what you have begun.

To Cornell University graduates,
May 30/The New York Times, 6-1:15.

Elie Wiesel
Historian;
Professor of humanities,
Boston University; Winner,
1986 Nobel Peace Prize

2

I have never been a Nazi hunter, but I understand why Nazi hunters are hunting. They feel—and most of us feel—that something is wrong about these war criminals, that those who committed crimes against humanity should not live a peaceful life . . . It's not a question of vengeance. It's much more a matter of history and of justice. They should be brought before a court of law simply to enable us to know more. For instance, because of this [accused Nazi John] Demjanjuk trial, we have now a better understanding of [the] Treblinka [Nazi concentration camp]. What happens to him afterwards really is almost irrelevant . . . There can be no punishment for the person who was involved in mass murder . . . What really could one do to a Mengele or to a Demjanjuk or to Eichmann?

Interview/USA Today, 4-28:(A)11.

3

Woe to us human beings of the 20th century, that we have seen innocent children pay the price for the mistakes of adults.

Hiroshima, Japan, May 22/
The New York Times, 5-23:3.

Art Wolfe
Professor of business law,
Michigan State University

4

The yuppie generation are very good game-players, but morally, ethically, they have no idea what they're about. To them, justice is efficiency, not fairness.

U.S. News & World Report,
2-23:59.

Alexander Zinoviev
Exiled Soviet author

5

An economically flourishing and democratic Communist society is as possible as a flying crocodile.

At conference sponsored by
Foreign Policy Research Institute,
New York/The New York Times, 10-27:5.

Religion

Jan Achotte
Roman Catholic Archbishop;
Adviser to Pope John Paul II

1

The Church in the U.S. faces problems that are similar to those in other Western countries. Society shows signs of an increased secularism and materialism. There is also an increasing but gratuitous assumption that one can tailor one's Church to one's own desires and turn it into a "pick and choose" Church, where it is accepted that being Catholic has little to do with adhering to all the Church's teachings.

The Christian Science Monitor,
9-10:10.

Bruce Babbitt
Former Governor
of Arizona (D);
Candidate for
the 1988 Democratic
Presidential nomination

2

I grew up a very rigorous Catholic in a very Catholic family. I had a Catholic education, and am still a practicing Catholic. What I learned at [University of] Notre Dame was that there is a lot more to religion than just ritual observance. What I saw at Notre Dame was a broader background of Christian commitment in terms of community [and] social justice.

Interview,
Oak Creek Canyon, Ariz./
The Christian Science Monitor,
10-16:6.

Jim Bakker
Evangelist

3

[On the sex scandal that forced him to resign as head of the PTL ministry]: I guess it's free-for-all time right now. I can understand the media doing it [spotlighting him]; that's their

job. But I'm so surprised by people in the ministry . . . to hear such hatred directed toward me . . . I am so very, very sorry. I am so very sorry this happened. I ask God to forgive me every hour of every day.

Interview/
Los Angeles Times,
3-31:(I) 21.

4

[On the controversy over the high salaries paid to him and his wife by the PTL ministry]: I think we've made a lot of mistakes and I'm very sorry about it . . . but Tammy and I had nothing to do with our salary. We should have said no, but our board cared about us, and they would tell us, "Jimmy and Tammy, you earn every penny that we give you."

Broadcast interview,
Palm Springs, Calif./
"Nightline," ABC-TV, 5-27.

Joseph L. Bernardin
Roman Catholic Archbishop
of Chicago

5

It is . . . important to know that many Americans, given the freedom they have enjoyed for more than two centuries, almost instinctively react negatively when they are told [by the Church] that they must do something, even though in their hearts they may know they should do it. As a result, the impression is sometimes given that there is a certain rebelliousness in many American Catholics, that they want to "go it alone" . . . The practical question that must be addressed today . . . is how to maintain our unity while affirming the diversity in the local realizations of the Church; how to discern a proper balance between freedom and order.

Addressing Pope John Paul II,
Los Angeles, Sept. 16/
Los Angeles Times, 9-17:(I)6.

WHAT THEY SAID IN 1987

(JOSEPH L. BERNARDIN)   *1*

Our [Americans'] realization of the Church . . . is situated in the context of our American culture. We live in an open society . . . Many tend to question things, especially those matters which are important to them, as religion is. They want to know . . . why certain decisions are made, and they feel free to criticize if they do not agree or are not satisfied with the explanations. They see this as an integral part of the call to live their lives as responsible, educated adults.

The Washington Post,
9-17:(A)20.

Allan Bloom
Author;
Professor of philosophy,
University of Chicago

2

. . . there is the notion that reason can't provide values. So there is a turn to religion. I'm not suggesting religion is unnecessary, but there is a widespread belief that religion can decide values and reason can't.

Interview/
U.S. News & World Report,
5-11:78.

Edmund G. Brown, Jr.
Former Governor
of California (D)

3

[On Pope John Paul II]: . . . the central need of any church is the manifestation of spiritual experience, or what you might call depth of conviction or the presence of the spirit. I believe this man manifests this in his own life and in his way of presenting himself, in the Mass and in the ceremony and how he speaks . . . Here we have a man who is premodern in a sense, who is coming out of the very different reality of pre-war Poland and experiencing the war. We are getting a life experience very different from suburbanized, upwardly mobile, secularistic, consumeristic,

yuppie-ized America. And maybe that is what I am sensing here, and what I perceive is vital to a reawakening of the church, and the whole society for that matter.

TV commentary,
San Francisco, Sept. 18/
Los Angeles Times, 9-19:(I)20.

George Bush
Vice President of
the United States

4

I don't believe a person could be President of the United States without faith in God. It is universal. It is much more than we think. An amazing thing happened at the funeral of Soviet leader [Leonid] Brezhnev. Things were run to a military precision; a coldness and hollowness pervaded the ceremony—marching soldiers, steel helmets, Marxist rhetoric—but no prayers, no comforting hymns, no mention of God. I happened to be in just the right spot to see Mrs. Brezhnev. She walked up, took one last look at her husband, and there—in the cold, gray center of that totalitarian state—she traced the sign of the cross over her husband's chest. I was stunned. In that simple act, God had broken through the core of the Communist system.

The Washington Post,
7-18:(A)4.

John Tracy Ellis
Professional lecturer in
theology and church history,
Catholic University,
Washington

5

The only question to which 53 million Catholics would give an answer approaching unity is if you asked them about the divinity of Christ . . . You'd get something nigh to unanimity on accepting that one . . . But there are questions to which there are no certain answers this side of eternity.

Los Angeles Times,
8-23:(I)1.

462

Jerry Falwell
Evangelist

1

The local church is now more important than ever. A repudiation of a materialistic approach to Christianity is in order. God is no longer looked on as a slot machine, where you put in a dollar and get out $10. We can perform within our local churches our Christian responsibilities. And we can carefully support those media ministries like Billy Graham, Charles F. Stanley, and a host of others who are clearly operating in a biblical and honest fashion.

Interview/
USA Today,
11-23:(A)13.

Margaret Farley
Professor of
Christian ethics,
Yale University
Divinity School

2

[On the Vatican document condemning artificial means of human fertilization]: People making decisions will not take it seriously. It doesn't offer them the answers they need. The church, by acting in an authoritarian way, loses the kind of moral power regarding these issues.

The New York Times,
3-12:12.

Ronald Garet
Professor of religion
and Constitutional law,
University of Southern
California Law School

3

It seems to me that religion is part of life. To strike down laws because they are partially religiously motivated would be to strike down most laws.

The New York Times,
3-16:13.

Richard A. Gephardt
United States Representative,
D-Missouri; Candidate for
the 1988 Democratic
Presidential nomination

4

I pray every day. I ask for guidance, ask for help from God, and I think I receive that help. I ask for it, and I think it's there. I may not always understand it or see it, but I really feel that I am aided by that continuous effort at prayer, and I feel that's important in what I do.

Interview, Washington/
The Christian Science Monitor,
4-14:7.

George Gerbner
Dean, Annenberg School
of Communications,
University of Pennsylvania

5

[On the current sex and money scandals involving PTL evangelist Jim Bakker]: In view of the current controversy, the major theme on which most of [TV's evangelical] programs harp is the question of morality. Much of the attraction of these programs rests on the fact that they cultivate a notion that regular commercial TV is immoral, permissive, full of sex and violence. They say they provide fare that is moral, traditional, uplifting. That is why these claims, back and forth, are sending shock waves.

USA Today, 3-26:(D)5.

Stephen Jay Gould
Paleontologist,
Harvard University

6

[On whether science and religion can peacefully coexist]: They do, in most people. The way I like to reply to that question is that if you take all the evolutionary biologists in this country—a few thousand—and survey their religious views, you'd find everything—plenty of devout Christians, Jews, Muslims,—everything. So you have three thousand experts all agreeing on evolutionary theory but having radically dif-

WHAT THEY SAID IN 1987

(STEPHEN JAY GOULD)

ferent religious views. Religion is about values; science about the factual state of the world. They are different enterprises, and there's no more reason for them to be at loggerheads than music and ditchdigging.

Interview, Harvard University/
Cosmopolitan, February:132.

Paskal Haxhi
Instructor in
Constitutional law,
Tirana University (Albania);
Former Albanian
Supreme Court Justice

1

[On religion in Albania]: It is not illegal for people to have icons or to wear crosses, but the climate is hostile to such things, so people avoid it . . . Our Constitution doesn't forbid a religious conscience, but any organized expression of religion, such as a Mass, a baptism or religious funeral service, is prohibited. We think religion—any religion—poisons society and plays a negative role, slowing progress down.

Interview/
Los Angeles Times, 5-24:(I)6.

Samuel S. Hill
Professor of religion,
University of Florida

2

[On evangelist Jerry Falwell's intervention in the PTL ministry scandal]: It's not that Jerry Falwell has tried to become the intellectual leader of the religious right as much as its statesman. If [evangelist] Pat Robertson is a politician and [PTL's] Jim Bakker is an entertainer, then Jerry Falwell is a preacher. What he wants to do is apply the same set of ideals to religion and to America. That's why he got involved in PTL, not to try to take it over.

The New York Times, 6-4:9.

Jesse L. Jackson
Civil-rights leader;
Candidate for
the 1988 Democratic
Presidential nomination

3

In a real sense, our politics and our political ethics must match the moral imperatives put forth by the prophets and Jesus. Farmers and workers, that is the message of Jesus today. When your back is against the wall, and when you develop some of society's leprosy of unemployment, leprosy of inadequate medical care . . . leprosy of your job being taken to a foreign market, leprosy of rejection when your farm has been foreclosed on . . . there still is a Jesus who is willing to walk past the rich, the mighty, the powerful and the privileged, and stay with you . . . in the midst of rejection.

Springville, Iowa/
The Christian Science Monitor,
8-26:6.

Wojciech Jaruzelski
Prime Minister of Poland

4

We appreciate the grandness of the moral teachings of the church. Enterprise, laboriousness, co-ownerlike concern add power and wealth to nations. In this area, joint action of the state and the church could prove particularly fruitful.

Addressing Pope John Paul II,
Warsaw, June 9/
The Christian Science Monitor,
6-10:9.

John Paul II
Pope

5

It is the priest who shares the lot of his own country, the priest who is close to all its experiences, the priest who always remains nearby.

To Polish clerics,
Tarnow, Poland, June 10/
Los Angeles Times, 6-11:(I)16.

464

(JOHN PAUL II)

1

The Jewish religion is not "extrinsic" to us, but in a certain way is "intrinsic" to our religion. With Judaism, therefore, we have a relationship which we do not have with any other religion . . . In a certain way it could be said that you [Jewish people] are our elder brothers.

At synagogue, Rome/
Los Angeles Times,
6-25:(I)13.

2

The Catholic Church is not a democratic institution. It is an institution governed by Jesus Christ, a theocratic one. We are only servants of one chief, of one pastor. We are only his instruments, his envoys. It is difficult to compare the Catholic Church and her structure to a democratic state.

To reporters during flight
from Rome to Miami,
Sept. 10/Los Angeles Times,
9-11:(I)16.

3

The physical and emotional health of priests is an important factor in their over-all human and priestly well-being, and it is necessary to provide for these . . . Yet, the fulfillment that comes from our ministry does not, in the final analysis, consist in physical or psychological well-being; nor can it ever consist in material comfort and security. Our fulfillment depends on our relationship with Christ and on the service that we offer His Body, the Church. Each of us is most truly himself when he is "for others."

Before U.S. priests,
Miami, Sept. 10/
The New York Times, 9-11:12.

4

Dissent from Church doctrine remains what it is: dissent. As such, it may not be proposed or received on an equal footing with the Church's authentic teaching.

Los Angeles/Time,
9-28:87.

5

Religious freedom, an essential requirement of the dignity of every person, is a cornerstone of the structure of human rights, and for this reason [is] an irreplaceable factor in the good of individuals and of the whole of society as well as of the personal fulfillment of each individual.

New Year's peace address,
Vatican City, Dec. 15/
Los Angeles Times, 12-16:(I)6.

Leonard Levy
Professor of humanities,
Claremont (Calif.)
Graduate School

6

Our Constitutional system, by separating church and state, aids religion in the only way that government should aid religion—by keeping hands off . . . Historically, government has damaged religion. Whenever government intercedes in religious matters, it corrupts religion. Religion is a matter that is so personal—it is so intimate a thing, it is so fragile, it is so sacred, too—that this is not a place for government to be involved.

Interview, Claremont, Calif./
The Christian Science Monitor,
7-14:1,4.

Daniel C. Maguire
Professor of
moral theology,
Marquette University

7

[Criticizing a Vatican document that condemns new birth technologies such as test-tube fertilization as well as surrogate mothers, etc.]: The Vatican is squandering its moral authority on issues where it has no privileged knowledge or expertise. This is another example of celibate men pronouncing on the reproductive rights of women, when women's voices have not been heard. If the Vatican tended to stick to issues of justice and peace—issues where they

WHAT THEY SAID IN 1987

(DANIEL C. MAGUIRE)

have a clear biblical mandate—their credibility could be maintained.

March 10/
The New York Times, 3-11:13.

Roger J. Mahony
Roman Catholic Archbishop
of Los Angeles

1

[On TV evangelists]: I have never been terribly impressed with what they call the electronic church. In many cases, the theology is terribly shallow. I think they're misleading in the sense that they're trying for very simplistic solutions to very serious problems. They fail to involve people in the Christian communities. You cannot form a community with a television set, and I think the interaction of people with local churches is important.

Interview/
USA Today, 5-13:(A)11.

Martin E. Marty
Professor of church history,
University of Chicago
Divinity School

2

I have a very glacial view of American religion . . . All the talk we had about the cult explosion, the new religious movements, didn't change the statistics of that at all. I think the 40 per cent who are predisposed to be at worship every week will vary to 42 per cent one year, 39 per cent another and 44 per cent another . . . but it's really glacial.

Los Angeles Times, 5-9:(II)4,5.

3

Take a look at the American [Catholic] Church. It exists in the midst of religious freedom—freedom of choice. People pick and choose on issues like birth control and abortion. They won't come [be won over] by whip cracking. We're a pluralistic society. And he

[the Pope] can only make it by persuasion—not coercion.

The Christian Science Monitor,
9-10:1.

John L. May
Roman Catholic Archbishop
of St. Louis; President,
National Council of
Catholic Bishops

4

There is a certain amount of confusion in the minds of quite a few good, sincere Catholics [in the U.S.] over just what it means to be a Catholic . . . in a wealthy, consumerist, nuclear-armed, secularized country like this one.

News conference, August/
U.S. News & World Report,
9-14:61.

5

There is a clear consensus that the Church must do everything in its power to put an end to unjust discrimination against women in its own structures and practices and also in the structures and practices of society . . . Short of [ordination of women], however, the sense of the synod is that we should examine other roles and functions in the Church and move ahead vigorously—as, in fact, has been happening in recent years—to open up as many of these as is deemed possible to women.

To reporters at world-wide
synod of bishops, Vatican City,
Oct. 9/The Washington Post,
10-10:(A)32.

Patricia McClurg
President-designate,
National Council of
Churches (United States)

6

In order to understand the Christian faith, one must understand the Jewish faith . . . The message of the Bible is [that] the only thing

(PATRICIA McCLURG)

special about a special people is what they do
for the whole world.

Interview, Plainfield, N.J./
The Christian Science Monitor,
12-23:6.

Frank J. McNulty
Vicar for priests,
Roman Catholic
Archdiocese of
Newark, N.J.

1

If priests could open up their hearts and tell
you of their priesthood, they would speak of
worries. There is a real and dramatic shortage
of priests, a situation critical enough to make us
worry about the future. In some areas, each
passing day finds the priest less able to meet
needs and fulfill expectations. Age and ministe-
rial fatigue are harsh realities. Morale suffers
when we see so few young men follow in our
footsteps. Morale suffers when we see parishes
without priests and prayer services taking the
place of Sunday mass. We worry that we might
become only a Church of the word and lose our
sacramental tradition. The suffering intensifies
when we realize that in 10 years we could have
half the present number of priests.

Addressing Pope
John Paul II, Miami,
Sept. 10/The New York Times,
9-11:12.

John Cardinal O'Connor
Roman Catholic Archbishop
of New York City

2

There are those who ask us, as members of
the Catholic Church, what right we have to address the forum of public policy. I ask, "What
right do we *not* have to address it?" We cannot
afford the luxury of silence.

Speech, Albany, N.Y.,
March 9/The New York Times,
3-10:50.

Daniel Ortega
President of Nicaragua

3

I was a practicing Catholic, but it did not
seem to be enough. Man is close to God when
he is close to the people. If we think of God as
something in favor of the betterment of man,
both materially and spiritually, and if we act in
a way that brings about that betterment—if we
do not cling to riches, selfishness or greed—
then I believe we are getting closer to God.

Interview/
World Press Review, April:22.

Joseph Cardinal Ratzinger
Head of Vatican's
Sacred Congregation for
the Doctrine of the Faith

4

The problem of a possible divorce between
the Catholic Church and science is serious. In
fact, it has been a problem since Galileo and
the era of the Enlightenment. In faith, there is
only one truth. In science, there are empirical
truths that sometimes seem to contradict one
another. There can also sometimes be an apparent contradiction between these truths and what
faith says. The Catholic Church has a duty to
maintain relations with scientists and intellectuals who research truth in different domains of
human activity. But, at the same time, it has a
duty to remain faithful to its own truth and
identity. An understanding that opposes prevailing opinion today can be the truth of tomorrow.

Interview/
World Press Review, July:58.

Ronald Reagan
President of
the United States

5

[On which is the better job, that of Pope or
that of President of the United States]: The
Pope's calling is certainly to a higher level than
even this one [the Presidency] is, although I
call upon his superior, I think, maybe as often
as he does for help. I don't know of any Presi-

WHAT THEY SAID IN 1987

(RONALD REAGAN)

dent who's ever failed to do that. Lincoln said that he had been driven to his knees many times, because there was no place else to go. And he also said that he couldn't meet the responsibilities of this position for 15 minutes if he did not feel that he could call upon someone who was stronger and wiser than all others.

Interview,
Washington/USA Today,
9-11:(A)11.

Oral Roberts
Evangelist

1

[Saying that, after his death, he will return to earth to rule with Jesus Christ]: I'm looking to the world-to-come because I'm not going to stay over there. I'm coming back . . . And I'm going to get my rightful place. I'm going to rule and I'm going to reign.

At Oral Roberts University,
June 26/Los Angeles Times,
6-27:(I)33.

Pat Robertson
Evangelist;
Candidate for
the 1988 Republican
Presidential nomination

2

[On the sex and money scandals involving PTL evangelist Jim Bakker]: It is my estimation that . . . the flap is essentially behind us. I think there was one person who was out of line. There is no war going on between these various ministries. I think it was overplayed by the press. I don't think it is going to have a lasting effect. I think it is the prelude to a great spiritual revival in America.

At Northeast Louisiana
University, March 28/
The Christian Science Monitor,
3-30:7.

David Roozen
Associate director,
Center for Social
and Religious Research,
Hartford (Conn.) Seminary

3

Those with a deep spiritual grounding have a sense of security and self-esteem that allows them to risk, and perhaps gives them the ability to accept and move on from non-successes.

U.S. News & World Report,
1-26:62.

Jimmy Swaggart
Evangelist

4

[On the scandal surrounding sex and money in Jim Bakker's PTL ministry]: If you're sincere, you don't drag down millions of dollars a year in salary. Number 2, you don't indulge yourself in all of this activity, this sin, that's going on. I can understand a man that has some kind of a problem, and is fighting it, and trying to overcome it. But I can tell that has not been that way there. If it had been that way, you wouldn't see all this other activity going on at PTL. You wouldn't see the rock and roll, you wouldn't see the dancing, you wouldn't see the social drinking that's advocated . . . The minister of the Gospel is really the yardstick by which the nation measures its morals. That's the reason the whole nation goes up in an uproar, and it's one of the biggest stories of this decade.

Interview/USA Today, 4-23:(A)15.

5

[On the Pope's recent visit to the U.S.]: When it comes to morality, I think that the Pope did an excellent job. When it comes to biblical doctrine, I think that he's wrong. I was pleased to hear him speak forcibly on the moral issues such as divorce, homosexuality. That's our biggest problem. If we self-destruct morally, the country cannot stay together. [But] I'm very opposed to many Catholic traditions. Scripturally, I don't think there's any such thing as a Pope. The basic reason that the Pope is traveling all

(JIMMY SWAGGART)

over the world is because the Catholic Church is in trouble—it's in real trouble. It's literally dying from within.

Interview/USA Today, 9-21:(A)7.

Rembert G. Weakland
Roman Catholic Archbishop
of Milwaukee

1

There are no words to explain so much pain on the part of so many competent women today who feel they are second-class citizens in a Church they love. That pain turns easily to anger and is often shared and transmitted to the younger generation of men and women. Women do not want to be treated as stereotypes of sexual inferiority, but want to be seen as necessary to the full life of a Church that teaches and shows by example the co-discipleship of the sexes as instruments of God's love. They seek a Church where the gifts of women are equally accepted and appreciated.

Addressing Pope John Paul II,
Los Angeles, Sept. 16/
Los Angeles Times, 9-17:(I)6.

Robert J. White
Medical researcher,
Case Western
Reserve University;
Adviser to the Pope
on medical ethics

2

[The Pope] comes to the United States as a reminder of the tradition that is still part of the Church . . . We've had too much emphasis put on the modern-day supermarket Catholic in which you select what aspects of Catholicism appeal to you. I think that with 53 million Catholics in this country, there may be more substance than that.

Interview/Newsweek, 9-21:30.

Science and Technology

Joe Allen
Former American astronaut

1

[On the slowed U.S. space program]: The United States is flirting with becoming to the space age what the Portuguese were to the sea age.

Time, 10-5:72.

George J. Annas
Professor of health law,
School of Public Health,
Boston University

2

The big discussions about genetic engineering took place in the 1970s. Now, most of the discussion in academic centers is about how to do this stuff, the techniques of genetic engineering. There is almost no discussion of the ethics of it . . . It's a slippery slope. Where do we draw the line? I think the next step is the sale and commercialization of human embryos, and that would be just horrible. That's what I would like to see stopped before it starts.

The New York Times,
6-9:18.

Isaac Asimov
Science-fiction writer

3

[On the miniaturization of people, which figures in some of his novels]: You cannot miniaturize anything alive. You can make machines smaller. You can make wires finer. But you can't do that to people. You can probably, by breeding, develop a race of human dwarfs. But there's a limit to how far you can go because, if the brain gets smaller, you have fewer brain cells. If you don't have enough brain cells, I'm afraid you're an idiot.

Interview/USA Today,
10-6:(A)11.

Levon Badalyan
President, Association of
Socialist Countries'
Child Neurologists

4

[Criticizing the setting up of sperm banks to breed people of above-average intelligence]: I hate a veterinarian's approach to man. Man has an intellect. This is what distinguishes him from animals [for which special breeding does occur]. Human nature should not be tampered with. We know too little about it. There is an old saying that "marriages are made in heaven." Let them go on being made there.

Interview/
World Press Review,
August:52.

Malcolm Baldrige
Secretary of Commerce
of the United States

5

The Japanese have run six out of nine companies in the U.S. out of the memory-chip business. If we allow dumping to continue and through those means have them take over our logic-chip business, which is more skilled, more technically advanced, they would without question be able to control the computer industry because all they would have to do is hold back the latest technology for their own computer manufacturers and not sell it to us.

Interview, Washington/
The New York Times,
5-19:10.

Gary L. Bauer
Assistant to President of
the United States
Ronald Reagan for
Domestic Policy

6

. . . our technology sometimes moves much faster than our ability to consider the moral im-

SCIENCE AND TECHNOLOGY

(GARY L. BAUER)

plications of it. Public-policy makers face a real challenge in that regard when it comes to reconciling values and technological advances.

Washington/
The New York Times,
3-12:12.

Mario Bellini
Architect and designer

1

We are overwhelmed by machines. Everything today has a keyboard. We have to learn how to set time on our electronic watches and how to program our electronic washing machines. It's very annoying. It's making us slaves of the very machines that pretend to help us . . . The old tools, like a hammer and scissors, are completely understandable, because when you get them in your hands you immediately know how they work. In electronics, all this physical continuity is broken. You press a keyboard and get a result, but you don't really know how it happened. The human being is completely cut out.

Interview/
The New York Times, 6-25:19.

William J. Bennett
Secretary of Education
of the United States

2

Let's stop fooling around. Let's get three years of science required for every high-school graduate and get it done—not pseudo-science, not quasi-science, not "Science and Wonderment" or "Science and the Threat to the End of Mankind," not "Science Isn't So Hard; Come and See It," but science. Just . . . say to kids: "Some of this is going to be hard, but if you work at it, you'll get it." Stop apologizing for science.

Before National Science
Teachers Association, Washington,
March 27/Los Angeles Times,
3-28:(I)22.

David Black
Chief space-station scientist,
National Aeronautics
and Space Administration
of the United States

3

[On using the planned U.S. space station]: The real benefits come not from what you knew would happen but from the discoveries and capabilities you run into when you open the new horizon. If we do our job well and attract the right people, a Nobel Prize should come from working in this environment.

Newsweek, 1-19:53.

Willian G. Bowen
President,
Princeton University

4

Most people don't appreciate how much more sophisticated science has become. The United States is in a class by itself among major countries for the extent to which the provision of facilities for science has been left in private hands at the same time everyone recognizes the national stake in the quality of what we do. There are many benefits to the partnership between private and public funding, which we would all like to preserve. But it must be noted that there is a limit to what the private sector can do alone to meet the dramatically escalating costs of science.

At symposium sponsored by
"U.S. News & World Report"/
U.S. News & World Report,
4-20:68.

Eugene Cernan
Former American astronaut

5

Low morale and frustration is the description of the U.S. space program. [The Soviet space station] *Mir* is on the high ground, and we are not there.

Time, 10-5:73.

471

WHAT THEY SAID IN 1987

(EUGENE CERNAN)

1

[On his feelings when he landed on the moon]: You stand there, trying to fully understand where you are. You stand there in sunlight, looking at the beauty of our Earth, surrounded by the blackest black a human being can create in his mind. Not darkness, but blackness. You are truly divorced from everything you understand in life, and home, and feeling, and family, civilization, and everything else because you are captured by another planet . . . You know it's a real moment, you know it's not a dream, you know it is truly happening, and you have to accept that it is happening to you. And you come home with that, and you do your best to try to understand the meaning of what you have done and where you have just been.

Interview/
USA Today, 10-22:(A)13.

Charles (Pete) Conrad, Jr.
Staff vice president for
international business development,
McDonnell Douglas Corporation;
Former American astronaut

2

We haven't had a [U.S.] President fire us a good shot on what we ought to do in space since John F. Kennedy . . . I think it is very important to this country to get the lead back and be the one that's providing the services to get into space. People around the world are determined to be in space, and they're going to go there, either with us or without us.

Interview,
Huntington Beach, Calif./
Los Angeles Times,
8-23:(I)3,17.

Richard Cyert
President,
Carnegie-Mellon University

3

In the case of computers in the U.S., we gain a comparative advantage and have a higher standard of living as a result, but it is quickly dissipated as the knowledge spreads [to other countries]. So we have to dip in and find another basis. All comparative advantages are temporary. And the world is ratcheting up its standard of living.

Interview, Boston/
The Christian Science Monitor,
7-16:21.

Thomas M. Donahue
Chairman,
Space Science Board,
National Academy of Sciences
of the United States

4

Our recommendation is that the advancement of science and its applications for human welfare be the key objective of the U.S. space program, and that all other activities . . . be carried out in such a way as to carry out the scientific objectives of the program.

Before American Association
for the Advancement of Science,
Chicago/The Christian Science Monitor,
2-19:5.

5

The stumbling state of the U.S. [space] program, in contrast to this one over here [in the Soviet Union], is shocking to a veteran like me. Not so long ago, meetings like this [a gathering of space scientists] would have occurred in the United States. Now . . . this is where the action is.

Moscow/
The Washington Post,
10-6:(A)28.

Vladimir A. Dzhanibekov
Soviet cosmonaut

6

[On last year's explosion of the U.S. space shuttle *Challenger* which killed seven astronauts]: It shocked us. It was very sad for us . . . It reminded us once again that space is

472

(VLADIMIR A. DZHANIBEKOV)

a very dangerous place, that it is dangerous to be calm in space . . . Every person has inside them some talent. There are some people who are led to test something, to risk, to climb mountains, to fly, to go.

Interview, Cambridge, Mass./
The Christian Science Monitor,
4-16:8.

Jake Garn
United States Senator,
R-Utah

1

[Criticizing scientists who say a U.S. manned space station would do little for science]: I don't care what kind of space station you design . . . You can find a group of scientists to come in and say it's a piece of junk.

U.S. News & World Report,
5-11:7.

2

The appalling thing to me is that there is no real support for space in [the U.S. Congress]. No one calls up . . . and puts any pressure on my colleagues, either in the House or the Senate, to say we need more for space, except those that are directly involved: contractors. We hear from contractors. Well, that is not a wide base of support compared to those who lobby for food stamps . . . I hesitate to say this, but the past two Administrations, including this one, which is mine, and a Republican President [Reagan] I greatly admire, has shown no leadership on space whatsoever.

At space seminar, Washington/
The Washington Post, 12-9:(A)9.

John Glenn
United States Senator,
D-Ohio; Former astronaut

3

[On last year's explosion of the space shuttle *Challenger*, which killed seven astronauts]: Had anyone told the first seven of us [astro-

nauts] back in [the early days of the space program] that we'd go almost 25 years and never have a fatality in space, we'd have thought they were crazy. I think that most of us back then thought that one or maybe even two of us might not be around at the end of Project Mercury. It was brand-new. We were dealing with new speeds and complexities and powers that people hadn't really dealt with before, [and yet we had] triumph after triumph until we were almost complacent. And then we were fallible. And whether the errors [in the *Challenger* disaster] were in personnel or procedures or hardware . . . tragedy paid for triumph.

Interview/
The Washington Post,
2-20:(B)4.

4

Twenty-five years from now, I want America to be first in space. Being first is the only way to design our destiny.

At celebration of 25th anniversary
of Kennedy Space Center,
Cape Canaveral, Fla./
The Christian Science Monitor,3-10:8.

Marvin L. Goldberger
President,
California Institute
of Technology

5

Our [U.S.] space-science program is in very serious trouble—and was even before the *Challenger* [space-shuttle] disaster. Over-emphasis on manned spaceflight, total reliance on the shuttle, the enormous cost of the space station and the absence of a clear commitment to science has threatened our pre-eminent position.

The New York Times, 6-23:17

Ralph Gomory
Senior vice president
for science and technology,
IBM Corporation

6

It is very, very important to make sure that the people in the manufacturing-and-development

WHAT THEY SAID IN 1987

(RALPH GOMORY)

cycle are up to date [on science-and-technology development], because they are often the only conduit for new ideas . . . The focus is on the companies. For instance, the development team and the manufacturing people must have very close ties: You design a printer not only to print clearly but also so it can be put together easily in the factory. We in the U.S. have a great scientific base. We need to exploit it. It's not necessarily the sea of ideas that you live in that matters; it's your ability to put those ideas into the cycle and turn that crank.

Interview/
U.S. News & World Report,
12-14:55.

Theodore Gordon
Aerospace engineer;
Futurist

1

. . . between now and the turn of the century, robotics and further automation will not have the capability, on the whole, of replacing the large percentage of the labor force . . . Beyond the turn of the century, it's much less clear that the over-all impact will be benign. We can talk about machines replacing labor and resulting in large-scale unemployment and catastrophe, or [about] machines replacing labor resulting in much-needed increases in human understanding and leisure and enjoyment.

Interview, Glastonbury, Conn./
The Christian Science Monitor,
4-22:16,17.

Albert Gore, Jr.
United States Senator,
D-Tennessee; Candidate for
the 1988 Democratic
Presidential nomination

2

[On genetic engineering]: People understand at a gut level that there is something wondrous, and perhaps perilous, about a technology that changes the blueprint of life and will force us to make choices that are likely to be more profound than anything we, as a society, have ever faced.

The New York Times, 6-8:10.

William R. Graham
Science Adviser to President
of the United States
Ronald Reagan

3

I'm interested in the national space program, which has a major component in national security and a major component in civil activity. All of us are distressed. Not in our darkest nightmares would any of us have imagined we would have an accident with the shuttle [last year's *Challenger* space-shuttle disaster], two accidents with the *Titan* and one with the *Delta* and *Atlas-Centaur* [rockets] in a period of a year and a half.

The Washington Post, 8-17:(A)3.

Harry Gray
Former chairman,
United Technologies
Corporation

4

A battle for the technological future of the world is being waged—and the U.S. is losing. This country is in legitimate peril of becoming a second-class economic power in the industrial world if technological prowess is allowed to slip away through inferior education.

U.S. News & World Report, 1-19:59.

Paul E. Gray
President,
Massachusetts Institute
of Technology

5

The [U.S.] Reagan Administration is quick to say it has made real advances in funding science since 1981, and that is true. But even with those advances, aggregate funding levels in real terms are only slightly above where they were in 1968, while the whole educational enterprise

(PAUL E. GRAY)

has expanded tremendously in terms of the scope of the scientific frontier, the number of people involved and the expense of equipping laboratories. Funding for facilities has become a major problem. In 1987, Federal support of research facilities in real terms is at 5 per cent of the level it was in 1968. That causes enormous pain for research universities, which cannot expand their facilities to deal with the expanding frontier of science. If you have a biology building that was built in 1960, in 1987 it is an antique, and it means a "strip it back to the frame and start over again" renovation, which will cost four times as much as it did to build it in 1960.

At symposium sponsored by
"U.S. News & World Report"/
U.S. News & World Report, 4-20:68.

David A. Hamburg
President,
Carnegie Corporation

1

Science and science-based technologies have become a pervasive part of human experience in the 20th century and the key to future well-being. Science is not a separate activity, remote from the lives of people—however arcane it may be . . . How to assess and use wisely these technical innovations—that seems to me the proper mandate for the university in the 21st century.

Interview, New York, June 7/
Los Angeles Times, 6-12:(V)1.

2

Universities, scientific academies and research institutes can make a greater contribution than they have in the past if they can organize effectively to share information, ideas and technical abilities widely across traditional barriers and systems . . . To some extent, the scientific community can provide a model for human relations that might transcend the biases and dogmatisms that have torn the species apart

throughout history and have recently become so much more dangerous than ever before.

At California Institute of
Technology commencement, June 12/
Los Angeles Times, 6-13:(I)30.

Carl F. H. Henry
Evangelical theologian

3

Science ought not necessarily do everything that is theoretically possible. It tends to run ahead of moral judgment and it does so at great risk.

The New York Times, 3-12:12.

John Paul II
Pope

4

[Progress has] created new possibilities for evil as well as for good. Technology . . . increases what we can do, but it cannot teach us the right thing to do.

At Mass, Los Angeles, Sept. 15/
The Washington Post, 9-16:(A)8.

George Nelson
American astronaut

5

[On the risk of space flight and the shutdown of the U.S. space program since the *Challenger* space-shuttle disaster in 1986]: For us, the danger has always been real. Before every flight I always got all my affairs in order. [But] it's frustrating not to be flying. That's our job.

News conference, Houston,
Jan. 15/USA Today, 1-16:(A)3.

Roger Nichols
Director,
Boston Museum
of Science

6

[Saying the public doesn't understand science enough]: The pre-eminent cultural traits of

WHAT THEY SAID IN 1987

our time are science and technology. And yet most of our people are disenfranchised from participating in the pre-eminent cultural traits. The echoes of the Reformation—which was really people saying, "We no longer want our major pre-eminent cultural trait to be conducted in a language we can't understand"—are still with us. That was a tremendous disruption in the West . . . Everybody is voting on nuclear power one way or another. If you don't know what radiation is, it's hard to have an informed opinion about it.

Interview, Boston/
The Christian Science Monitor,
3-24:3.

Thomas O. Paine
Former Administrator,
National Aeronautics and
Space Administration of
the United States

1

The way you get [technological leadership] is by adopting broad, very bold programs—like our old *Apollo* program, going to the moon— and stretching American science and technology to do the very best they can, right out on the forefront of what is humanly possible. And when you have those kinds of programs, every graduate school in America is a little sharper. American industry . . . gets an edge and learns how to do things better than anybody else in the world. I think it's no secret that the basic reason why we have such a strong predominance in exports around the world in aerospace is because of the fact that we've had these bold programs in the past. But now we need to take a new look at our civilian space program and ask the question: "Is it really bold enough to maintain that pre-eminence?" And the [answer is]: No. Let's set some new goals. Let's move on out to Mars.

Interview/
The Christian Science Monitor,
8-18:5.

2

[On the 1986 explosion of the space shuttle *Challenger*, which killed seven astronauts]: It was a loss of sense of purpose that caused the *Challenger* disaster, rather than the other way around. *Challenger* was a symptom. NASA's program had withered away, with fewer and fewer goals and challenges to meet, and that's how sloppiness got into the system.

U.S. News & World Report,
12-28:32.

Mike Pride
Editor,
"Concord (N.H.) Monitor"

3

[On the *Challenger* space-shuttle disaster last year that killed seven astronauts, including civilian teacher Christa McAuliffe]: The myth says that we must go on. It says that we've cleaned up the mess at NASA and that McAuliffe and her crewmates would not want their deaths to alter the course of space exploration. The reality is that the investigation of the *Challenger* disaster was too friendly. The reality is that the ideal of space as a destination for ordinary people, for humanists, teachers and poets, died with McAuliffe. That frontier is closed for a long, long time. The reality is that space is now the province of engineers and military men pressed by an urgency to get our weapons up there before the other guy does.

Accepting National Press
Foundation award, February/
The Wall Street Journal, 5-8:20.

Ronald Reagan
President of
the United States

4

Technology is not the enemy of job creation, but its parent—the very source of our economic dynamism and creativity. During the economic expansion of the past 52 months—a time of technological breakthrough after breakthrough—

(RONALD REAGAN)

our nation actually created over 13 million more jobs.

At Purdue University,
April 9/Los Angeles Times,
4-10:(I)27.

Sally K. Ride
American astronaut

1

Because the country should have a strong civilian space program, NASA has been asked by Congress and the American people to do lots of things, but we have not had the budget to do what we've wanted. Part of the fault lies with NASA's own can-do attitude. We've undertaken a lot of complex things on a shoestring budget, and some of the consequences of that were brought home after the *Challenger* [space shuttle] accident. NASA is probably under-funded. We're at a point where we need to recognize that we can do all these things, but not with the money currently allocated.

Interview/
"Ms.," July-Aug.:181.

Nikolai I. Ryzhkov
Premier of
the Soviet Union

2

[On the Soviet Union's offer of bargain rates to launch foreign spacecraft with Soviet launching equipment]: It is against our principles to cash in on others' errors and setbacks. Our program for launches of foreign spacecraft by Soviet carriers has been prompted by a desire to advance space exploration and use Soviet rockets and other space technology . . . efficiently. . . The world has been able to see on more than one occasion that Soviet scientists and designers can develop, and do develop, most advanced equipment which is at least on a par with the best foreign systems.

Interview, Jan. 5/
Los Angeles Times, 1-6:(I)6.

Robert T. Schooley
Specialist in
infectious diseases,
Massachusetts General Hospital

3

In a sense, research is just a microcosm of life. When people think about experiments in science, they think of them as being different from life—but everything you do is an experiment. It's really just the same activity being carried out a little bit more methodically, that's all.

Interview, Boston/
Los Angeles Times, 5-18:(I)1.

Frederick Seitz
Former president,
American Physical Society
and National Academy
of Sciences

4

Personally, I believe that scientific societies and academies serve the fields of science and the nation best when they do all they can to avoid taking political positions on national issues. Scientists in our open countries should treasure the freedoms they have and devote their societies to purely scientific affairs. There are other avenues for expressing political views.

Before House Sciences and
Technology Committee, Washington,
May/The Wall Street Journal, 6-2:26.

Bassam Shakhashiri
Assistant director for
science and engineering education,
National Science Foundation
of the United States

5

We [in the U.S.] are failing to provide an adequate background, an adequate introduction and an adequate level of science literacy for the population as a whole. In a technological world, where we compete with equally sophisticated countries, we cannot afford to focus only on the next generation of Nobel Prize winners . . . The average student receives no real

477

WHAT THEY SAID IN 1987

science until he or she reaches high school, when we pose the question, "Would you like to take physics, chemistry, botany and zoology?" And we know that for years prior to this, without any real exposure to a science course, most students have already decided that science courses are difficult and dull.

Washington, Jan. 29/
The Washington Post,
1-30:(A)17.

Andy Stofan
Associate Administrator
for space stations,
National Aeronautics and
Space Administration of
the United States

1

If we [in the U.S.] want to have manned exploration of space anywhere beyond this planet, the space station is an absolute essential. If this country wants to remain in space and remain in technological leadership . . . that's what we can do with the space station. I cannot imagine this country walking away and turning space over to some other nation.

Los Angeles Times, 12-2:(I)27.

Earl S. Van Inwegen
Brigadier General,
United States Air Force;
Chief of Operations,
Air Force Space Command

2

Operating [space] satellites is kind of like flying. It's hours of boredom, interrupted by moments of sheer terror. We've had a lot of terror lately. It's a tribute to our people that they've been able to do the engineering, to

write the computer programs, in order to prolong the life of the satellites we have in orbit.

Interview/
The New York Times, 7-20:13.

Paul J. Weitz
Deputy Director,
Johnson Space Center;
Former American astronaut

3

[On his now being Deputy Director of the Johnson Space Center]: Just because you put astronauts in management does not mean you do everything the astronaut office wants you to do. We have to be attentive to what comes down from Washington. They are our bosses. All of us have a stake in working together to get the system back in operation . . . But now I'm in a position where I can step in and say, "Wait a minute, I think you're going down the wrong road." Before, [management] may not have listened to me. Rank has its privileges. Rightfully or wrongfully, people listen to you a lot more.

The New York Times, 6-2:21.

Robert M. White
President, American
Academy of Engineering

4

We don't have enough U.S. citizens going into graduate engineering and at the Ph.D. level. About 50 per cent of the students at the Ph.D. level in engineering schools [in the U.S.] are from foreign countries. It's at that level with that kind of training that you're producing the people who can operate at the cutting edge of knowledge. These are the people who are absolutely key to the innovative process. These are the people who are absolutely key to being able to take a scientific discovery and translate it into commercial production.

Interview, Washington/
The Christian Science Monitor, 3-26:5.

Sports

George Allen
Former football coach,
Los Angeles "Rams" and
Washington "Redskins"

1

The name of the game [in football] is defense. There has never been a Super Bowl team, whether they've won or lost, that didn't have a good defense.

At Super Bowl Media Clinic,
Orange, Calif., Jan. 20/
USA Today, 1-21:(C)3.

Sparky Anderson
Baseball manager,
Detroit "Tigers"

2

Every player who comes to [play for a new team in] a new town tells how happy he is. I wish just one guy would stand up and say, "I hate your town, I hate your team, I hate your manager. I'm here for one reason: You shelled out the most."

Interview, Lakeland, Fla./
Time, 3-23:79.

3

Any big-league manager who doesn't have the authority to trade or send any of his players to the minor leagues without having to consult his general manager is operating under a handicap. With today's high salaries and long-term guaranteed contracts, that's one of the few weapons left that a manager can use to keep his players in line. Believe me, that's a necessary power for a manager if he's going to win consistently.

The Christian Science Monitor,
5-20:18.

4

[On why some players today can't keep their minds on baseball]: It's all that outside stuff. You know: endorsements, biographies, commercials, personal appearances and paid autograph sessions. Maybe these guys ought to ask themselves sometime what their main business really is. Is that extra money they earn off the field worth it if it results in them having a bad year? Unfortunately, they never think of that.

The Christian Science Monitor,
7-31:20.

5

I told the team in spring training, "Whatever you want to give me—first place, second place, fifth place—that is okay with me. But give it to me." Sure, we care if we win, but not to the point where we make it a misery. What is a "winning year" anyway? The [Milwaukee] *Brewers* are fourth. I think they had a great year. I don't need aggravation no more. It's how you go about this thing that counts. I'd rather do it this way and finish second than have a bunch of jerks and win.

The Washington Post, 9-11(F)4.

Arthur Ashe
Former tennis player

6

[On tennis stars]: It's difficult to maintain a sense of perspective when you walk on the court wearing $1,000 worth of tennis clothes, and they didn't cost you a dime [because they were given by the manufacturers]. After a while, a player may start thinking that he or she is entitled to all this. The system has coddled the players and made them self-centered.

Interview/
Los Angeles Times, 9-29:(III)3.

Larry Bird
Basketball player,
Boston "Celtics"

7

Some teams don't come to play every night. We do. We win as a team and lose as a team.

WHAT THEY SAID IN 1987

(LARRY BIRD)

Anybody who doesn't get along in the locker room, starts smarting off, we let him know that if he doesn't stop messing up, he's gone. No bitching about minutes, no selfish play. There's four or five of us who'll go to Red [Auerbach, team president] or K.C. [Jones, head coach] and say, "Get him gone. He's not a *Celtic*."

Interview/
Los Angeles Times, 5-28:(III)2.

Jim Boeheim
Basketball coach, Syracuse University

1

I'm a [basketball] coach, and when I'm coaching on that floor, that's my act. That's my stage. A lot of that is emotional acting or whatever, and once the game's over I'm fairly low key, I'm not like [I am during the game] at all. A lot of people don't like me and then they meet me and they say, "Hey, you're not as bad as we thought." Well, that's not really me out there. That's part of the job, part of what we do. [St. John's coach] Lou Carnesecca is one of the nicest, quietest guys you'll ever meet— *away* from the game. [Ohio State's] Gary Williams is the nicest, quietest, calmest guy in the world, one of my best friends, but [while coaching] he's an absolute maniac, 10 times worse than I could ever be. He'll have a complete heart attack some day, right on the court, and die.

Interview, East Rutherford, N.J.,
March 20/Los Angeles Times,
3-21:(III)8.

Hubie Brown
Commentator, CBS Sports;
Former football coach,
New York "Knicks"

2

A commentator should educate the viewer as well as provide entertainment. That's what you strive for. But too many commentators get wrapped up in all the hype, and don't educate. They just repeat what is seen.

Los Angeles Times, 3-13:(III)3.

George Burns
Golfer

3

I know you guys [in the press] who cover other sports don't think golfers are athletes, but the beer and late-night days are over. That's not to say we are all prudes on the tour, but the compensation is too great [for all-night partying].

Interview, San Diego, Calif./
Los Angeles Times, 2-16:(III)3.

Al Campanis
Vice president
of player personnel,
Los Angeles "Dodgers"
baseball club

4

I truly believe that [blacks] may not have some of the necessities to be, let's say, a field manager or perhaps a general manager . . . I don't say that [about] all of them, but they certainly are short. How many quarterbacks do you have, how many pitchers do you have, that are black? Why are black men or black people not good swimmers? Because they don't have the buoyancy.

Broadcast interview/
"Nightline," ABC-TV, 4-6.

Al Campanis
Former vice president
of player personnel,
Los Angeles "Dodgers"
baseball club

5

[On his being fired by the *Dodgers* for having said on a TV interview that blacks don't have the "necessities" to be team managers]: I found myself saying things [during the interview] I didn't mean, explaining things I couldn't. You can understand in that environment where you can hit on a word that does not express exactly what you mean. When I said blacks lacked the "necessities" to be managers or general managers, I meant the necessary experience, not things like inherent intelligence or native ability. You look at the years you have to

(AL CAMPANIS)

have in baseball to be a successful general manager, the situations you have to experience, the contacts you have to make, the mistakes you have to learn by. Look at me. I managed for four years in the minors and the Caribbean. I was a scout for 10 years. I was scouting director for 10 years and then general manager and vice president for 19. That's what I meant. You can't walk in off the street and deal with some of the shrewd characters. You can't build a champion team till you are at the level where you can sit down with crafty, experienced men.

Interview/
Los Angeles Times, 7-2:(III)5.

Harry Carson
Football player,
New York "Giants"

1

[On the current, but soon ending, player strike]: Some [players] are very, very bitter . . . I think [the owners] have played hard ball since the whole process began. It's everyone's opinion that they were out all along to bust the [players] union, humble the players somewhat. It's a little like when you have a person down, you grind on them. I think that's what [the owners] are trying to do.

Los Angeles Times, 10-16:(III)9.

Dennis Conner
America's Cup
boat-race sailor

2

For [boat racing] to become a major sport in America, television will have to be a major part of it. Until the people *en masse*, other than the hard-core sailors, really have the feeling of how exciting it is to be on the boats themselves, I don't think it's going to develop the same sort of support that some of our traditional American sports like football and baseball have. For us to get that type of exposure in America, we're going to have to get the spectator onto the boat and let him feel a part of the drama . . . If

indeed our goal is to [stimulate] this type of support from the people in America, we need to be able to compete on the same basis as some of the other major sports in terms of excitement and letting the fans be part of it.

Los Angeles Times, 1-19:(III)9.

Brian Curran
Hockey player,
New York "Islanders"

3

To me, brawls [between hockey teams during a game] are a joke, and all they do is wreck the game. I don't think they'll ever get rid of the fighting, but I'd rather take a punch than a stick in the face. But brawls are something you had all the time back in juniors, and people can get hurt. Twenty on twenty can be a scary scene.

The New York Times, 10-5:40.

Bill Curry
Football coach,
University of Alabama

4

When I was starting out at [coaching] Georgia Tech in 1980, people told me I couldn't win if I didn't cheat. A team could cheat like a son of a gun for a few years, win the national championship, go on probation for a few years and think [probation] was worth it. You can't do that any more. The specter [for college sports cheating] is not probation now. It's no football. And brother, that's a major change.

Los Angeles Times, 8-30:(III)15.

Ron Darling
Baseball pitcher,
New York "Mets"

5

[On his current losing streak]: I got too cute. I lost some of my—what's the word?—my physicalness. I forgot I could throw it past hitters. You forget what God gave you to get you here. You forget the 6-foot-3 and the 200 pounds . . . You want to raise pitching to an art-form, a profession, but it can defy logic. I

481

(RON DARLING)

asked [pitcher Tom] Seaver to study me in a game last month. He watched me closely, then he said he didn't see anything very wrong. But he warned me not to overreact. We talked about the time he struck out 19 batters, and got 10 in a row; the last 10. That's awesome. That's the perfect mixture of physical and mental strength. That's raising it to an art-form. That's where I got sidetracked. I neglected the purely physical part of it. I was doing more thinking than throwing.

Interview, New York/
The New York Times, 7-3:40.

Anita DeFrantz
United States member,
International Olympic Committee

1

Often in this country [the U.S.], we see sport as being entertainment. The professional leagues are clearly entertainment. But it's more than that. It's a personal experience. It's the one area where you can set a goal and rely on yourself to achieve it. If you want to run a mile in seven minutes, it's up to you to go out and do that. And it's so different from the rest of our society. And the personal development that can come from being involved in sport is just phenomenal. We are just beginning to understand that.

Interview/USA Today, 3-4:(A)9.

Lefty Driesell
Former basketball coach,
University of Maryland

2

I'm a firm believer that, if you know how to use cocaine and use it properly, it can make you play better. I really believe cocaine can be performance enhancing.

June 8/Los Angeles Times,
6-10:(III)3.

3

[On criticism of his recent remark that cocaine can be good for an athlete]: Cocaine, according to the paper that I did [in 1957], will speed up your heart rate and make your reflexes better and make you perform a little bit better for a certain amount of time as an athlete in some cases. But I put in my paper that it was highly toxic and highly habit-forming and should no way be used in athletics, and that's exactly what I said [in his recent statement].

Los Angeles Times, 6-11:(III)13.

Julius Erving
Basketball player,
Philadelphia "76ers"

4

Most of what I do offensively, I do instinctively. It's not like it's planned at all. You see daylight, you go to the basket. You get boxed in, you shoot the jumper. I like to penetrate the lane because the closer you get to the basket, the more the percentage comes over to your side. But mostly I do everything off a reaction, and usually when you do that you catch the defense off balance.

Interview/
The Christian Science Monitor,
2-18:16.

Larry Fleisher
General counsel,
National Basketball Association
Players Association

5

[On the NBA college draft]: It surely does not balance competition as it is meant to be. The lottery makes even more of a joke of the draft when the [Boston] *Celtics* can win the championship last season and wind up with the second draft pick. It is the players' contention that now is the time to let the marketplace work for them as it does for the other professions in society.

The New York Times, 1-16:43.

Ray Floyd
Golfer

6

[Criticizing the practice of toughening up some courses before tournaments to make them

(RAY FLOYD)

seem more demanding]: The [baseball] World Series doesn't throw rocks in the infield to trick it up. Football doesn't narrow the field and make it longer before the Super Bowl. If you take the home runs out of baseball and the bomb out of football, you lose a lot of excitement. We have to watch that in golf. There has to be some discretion.

San Diego, Calif.,
Feb. 12/Los Angeles Times,
2-13:(III)4.

1

Somebody asked me what I want to be remembered [for] most from my career, and I said—and I meant it from the bottom of my heart—that I don't care about my records or anything like that. I would want to be remembered as a person who conducted himself in a proper manner, a person children could look up to, that parents could point to and say, "There's Ray Floyd. Look at him. Watch him conduct himself while he's playing a round of golf." I'm not going to go out there and throw clubs. Golf is a game of integrity. Gentlemen play the game of golf. That's the way it was designed. That's the way I want to be remembered playing it. My records, they don't mean anything. However people want to look at what I accomplished, that's up to them. To ask them to praise you forever, that's just selfish. You know, the more I think about it, I don't want to be remembered for anything.

Interview, San Francisco,
June 16/Los Angeles Times,
6-17:(III)13.

A. Bartlett Giamatti
President, National
(baseball) League

2

[Baseball] has a peculiar hold on the American soul. It was one of the ways you became an American after you got off the boat, whether you were coming from Ulster or from the Ukraine. And you can see the way it still binds the country together—80 million people watched the last game of the World Series this past fall.

Interview/
The Christian Science Monitor,
7-16:36.

3

[On recent cases of hitters tampering with bats to improve their hitting, and pitchers tampering with balls to improve their pitching]: . . . such acts are the result not of impulse, borne of frustration or anger or zeal, as violence is, but are rather acts of a cool, deliberate, premeditated kind. Unlike acts of impulse or violence, intended at the moment to vent frustration or abuse another, acts of cheating are intended to alter the very conditions of play to favor one person. They are secretive, covert acts that strike at and seek to undermine the basic foundation of any contest declaring the winner—that all participants play under indentical rules and conditions. Acts of cheating destroy the necessary foundation and thus strike at the essence of contest. They destroy faith in the game's integrity and fairness; if participants and spectators alike cannot assume integrity and fairness, and proceed from there, the contest cannot in its essence exist.

Opinion on one of
the cheating cases/*
USA Today, 9-11:(C)6.

Bob Golic
Football player,
Cleveland "Browns"

4

[On the current, but soon ending, player strike]: We made a sacrifice for something we believed in. It's not exactly the way we anticipated it ending, so obviously I'm disappointed . . . We're [players] egomaniacs. Professional athletes are egotistical, and they have to be that way. To perform out there, you have to say, "I'm better than he is." Right now, a lot of these guys want to find a way to get their self-respect back. They don't like getting kicked in the tail [by the owners during the strike].

Los Angeles Times, 10-16:(III)9.

WHAT THEY SAID IN 1987

Russ Granik
Executive vice president
and chief negotiator,
National Basketball Association

1

[On why team owners do not want free agency for players]: The owners understand that it isn't a terrific situation for the players to have to stay with a certain team. [But the system] won't work if players can go, without restrictions, wherever they want. There is a genuine concern that some teams won't be able to hold onto their top-quality players if they give up the right of first refusal.

Whittier, Calif./
USA Today, 9-18:(C)7.

Wayne Gretzky
Hockey player,
Edmonton "Oilers"

2

I've always told people that what's scarier about hockey than any other sport is that we athletes have frustrations and we let out our frustrations. But in hockey, we all carry lethal weapons, and sometimes it gets out of hand.

Philadelphia/
Los Angeles Times,
5-25:(III)12.

Bill Gullickson
Baseball pitcher,
New York "Yankees"

3

Baseball is a game of streaks. When you're hot, you're hot; when you're cold, you just try to survive.

Interview, New York, Aug. 28/
The New York Times, 8-29:29.

Ira Michael Heyman
Chancellor,
University of California,
Berkeley

4

[On the increasing importance of athletics at colleges and universities]: We get caught in a spiral. We win in order to cover costs. But we have to spend more in order to win. Then, to cover these added costs, we have to find a way to get an edge over the competition, so we increase the scale and intensity of our programs. We recruit harder, extract more from our athletes, and build bigger and better facilities.

At convention of Presidents
Commission of National Collegiate
Athletics Association, Austin, Texas/
The Christian Science Monitor, 7-2:6.

Kent Hill
Football player,
Houston "Oilers"

5

[Advocating free agency for football players]: Players just want opportunities other workers have. The way it is now, once a team has you, they have you.

U.S. News & World Report,
10-5:30.

Lou Holtz
Football coach,
University of Notre Dame

6

The man who complains about the way the ball bounces is likely the one who dropped it.

Los Angeles Times, 11-4:(III)2.

Benjamin L. Hooks
Executive director,
National Association for
the Advancement of
Colored People

7

We will enter into negotiations with the [baseball] ownership to establish an affirmative-action program that will actively recruit and train blacks for all jobs available in organized baseball. We are dismayed and somewhat embittered by the fact that the ranks of managers, coaches and front-office personnel remain virtually all-white preserves.

News conference, New York, April 15/
The New York Times, 4-16:42.

Tom House
Pitching coach,
Texas "Rangers"
baseball club

1

Most major-league [baseball] players—and most American professional athletes—grow up privileged in a way other people can't really understand. As long as they excel in sports, everything is done for them and handed to them. When their athletic careers end, they have 40 years of life to live and no notion of how to fill them. Most don't fill them very well. We don't do athletes a favor when we idolize them and give them a free ride. As much as I admire [former baseball star] Yogi [Berra], I think he was wrong about one thing: For a lot of jocks, the game is over long before it's over.

Interview, Port Charlotte, Fla./
The Wall Street Journal, 3-13:17.

John Hynes
Football player,
Los Angeles "Raiders"

2

[On the current NFL players strike]: If they [striking players] gotta eat, they can sell their Porsches.

USA Today, 9-25:(A)12.

Jesse L. Jackson
Civil-rights leader;
Candidate for
the 1988 Democratic
Presidential nomination

3

[On the lack of blacks in baseball management]: In 100 years, they've had a total of three black managers [in baseball]. Leaving it in the hands of owners without pressure will perpetuate the problem.

U.S. News & World Report, 7-6:13.

Reggie Jackson
Baseball player,
Oakland "Athletics"

4

[On the pressures of being in a close pennant race late in the season]: The game changes in August and September. The ball seems smaller, the base paths longer, and the bat heavier. Sometimes, when I look, I even think I see an extra infielder!

Interview/
The Christian Science Monitor,
9-4:16.

Tom Jackson
Football player,
Denver "Broncos"

5

The Super Bowl may be the ultimate win, but it's also the ultimate loss.

USA Today, 1-15:(C)11.

Tommy John
Baseball pitcher,
New York "Yankees"

6

Pitching is three things—speed, placement and movement. If you have all three, you're Sandy Koufax, Juan Marichal, Bob Gibson, Steve Carlton and Tom Seaver. And if you have two of the three, like I do, you can be a very successful pitcher. I was never a hard thrower. When I was in my prime, thank God they didn't have the radar [speed] gun. But I still had two of the three.

Interview/
The New York Times, 6-10:53.

7

When you're running a business, and baseball is a business, you have to do everything you can to please the paying customer. By making pitchers throw strikes, you're going to get more extra-base hits, more home runs and more runs scored, which translates into more tickets sold. My only beef is with umpires who aren't consistent. I mean, those who have a different strike zone every inning. But if a guy is consistent with his calls, no matter how bad they are, I can live with that.

Interview/
The Christian Science Monitor,
9-21:20.

WHAT THEY SAID IN 1987

Dave Johnson
Baseball manager,
New York "Mets"

1

[Lamenting all the players on the *Mets'* disabled list this season]: Every time we get a little momentum, someone else goes down. You try to stay optimistic, but we're obviously thin. Can our system provide replacements? Can any system? It can, but to what degree? I mean, how do you replace a Cy Young winner? How do you replace your best reliever? How do you replace four-fifths of your rotation? How do I keep *my* attitude up, let alone the players'? I feel it's a conspiracy.

Interview, San Diego/
Los Angeles Times,
6-1:(III)10.

Earvin "Magic" Johnson
Basketball player,
Los Angeles "Lakers"

2

No matter what you've accomplished, you always have to keep working to improve because the people you play against are out there working hard to beat you. Even though I've been in professional basketball for eight years, I still believe I have to work hard to improve my game and add new tools to my repertoire . . . The point is, I want to be constantly adding new tricks to my game. I want to keep people thinking.

Esquire, December:106.

Jim Killingsworth
Basketball coach,
Texas Christian University

3

[Criticizing basketball's three-point field goal]: It rewards people for not running the offense and working for a shot. It rewards you for being selfish rather than working as a team. It puts so much luck into the game.

USA Today, 1-30:(C)7.

Billy Kilmer
Former football player,
Washington "Redskins"

4

They've taken [football] away from the players. The players are incidental today. They're robots. Numbers. The coaches don't say, "What was Jones doing on that last play?" They say, "What is that Number 39 doing out there?" The coaches send the plays in, and the officials rule on them. That's a game? That's a debate!

Interview, Scottsdale, Ariz./
Los Angeles Times, 5-15:(III)12.

Billie Jean King
Tennis player

5

Tennis is a sport with an unbelievably rich history, and yet it isn't as well-known as it should be. So it's important to make the statement. Each generation does matter. Each builds for the next. But today's kids don't realize that. Let's face it, the frame of reference is "What did I read in the paper this morning?" By the time something's five hours old, it's history. But I think it is important that they see the other side. A lot of time and energy has gone into the game over the years, and it's up to my generation to give youngsters that sense.

Interview/
The Christian Science Monitor,
7-17:18.

Lane Kirkland
President, American
Federation of Labor-Congress
of Industrial Organizations

6

[On the recent NFL players strike]: We are proud of the solidarity [the players] displayed under the most trying circumstances, including all of the pressures, insults, blandishments and inducements to treachery that the cynical club owners, backed by the giant [TV] networks, could think of. The example set by the vast majority of the players who stood fast will speak

486

(LANE KIRKLAND)

eloquently and find its reward long after the weasel words and deeds of the scabs are forgotten.

At AFL-CIO convention,
Miami Beach, Oct. 26/
The New York Times, 10-27:10.

Bob Knight
Basketball coach,
University of Indiana

1

[On whether he would like people to say he was the greatest coach who ever lived]: No, because I know there are guys who were better than I was. What I would like people hopefully to say is: "There goes a guy who got the most out of what he had." You know, I had a guy who told me the greatest compliment in the world for a coach is to be told you're worth a few points just sitting on the bench. That's something I would like to have people think of me . . . As long as I enjoy putting the pieces together, I'll keep coaching. I'm like one of those guys who likes to do puzzles, and when the puzzle is completed, I'm ready to put together another puzzle. It's the puzzle that I enjoy. Victory, winning, has never been a particularly satisfying thing for me. It's how we played. If we lose the national championship, I'm going to look back and wonder what we did wrong. If we win, I'm going to look back and say, "How could I improve things even more?" That's what matters to me.

Interview, March 29/
Los Angeles Times, 3-30:(III)10.

Jack Kramer
Former tennis player

2

The trouble with tennis is that it's ungoverned, and maybe ungovernable. As soon as someone gets to be a star today, he wants to go his own way, and no one has the authority to say he can't. Your top half-dozen players schedule exhibitions that conflict with tournament dates. John McEnroe can walk off a court in the middle of a match for no apparent reason, and get away with it. I'm all for free enterprise, but there ought to be a limit.

Interview, London/
The Wall Street Jounal, 7-1:24.

Tom Lasorda
Baseball manager,
Los Angeles "Dodgers"

3

A relief pitcher is like a safecracker. Not everybody can go in and crack safes. Most people would be scared to death. You get into enough of those situations and it begins to take its toll.

Los Angeles Times, 3-26:(III)8.

Abe Lemons
Basketball coach,
Oklahoma City University:
Former basketball coach,
University of Texas

4

All I do is coach and put my players on the floor. If they win, fine. If they lose, it's their fault.

The Wall Street Journal, 12-4:12.

Chuck Long
Football player,
Detroit "Lions"

5

[On the recent NFL player strike]: Every once in a while, you have to stand up for what you believe in. I believe in the [players'] union. I'm young in my career. I couldn't be a quarterback and cross the [strike picket] line. You have to stick with your teammates. A lot of guys will always remember who crossed the line and hurt our cause. I could never, ever do it. I'll always remember that the owners have a lot of power. They're not negotiable people. If there's ever another strike, I'd go on strike again. Yes, sir, I would.

Oct. 19/USA Today, 10-20(C)5.

WHAT THEY SAID IN 1987

Howie Long
Football player,
Los Angeles "Raiders"

1

[On his team's not making it to the Super Bowl this year, despite his being honored as the NFL's top defensive lineman]: I feel like the guy at the senior prom pressing his nose against the window because he doesn't have a date.

USA Today, 1-23:(C)11.

Mick Luckhurst
Football player,
Atlanta "Falcons"

2

[Saying football players should have free agency]: I'm not comparing players to slaves. What I'm saying is that the mentality of the owners is like the slave owners of the 1840s. They think anything that was changed in the NFL system would be bad. I believe some form of free agency is a Constitutional right. And I say this not as a rebellious union man but as a concerned player.

USA Today, 10-8:(C)4.

John Madden
Commentator, CBS Sports;
Former football player

3

[On boxing]: The scene at a big fight is the greatest thing there is. It's sport where you don't need any experts. Everybody can have an opinion. There aren't any football zone defenses to diagram, no equipment. There are just two guys in their underwear and tennis shoes. You can come from another planet and understand that.

USA Today, 4-3:(A)2.

4

[Criticizing the current NFL players strike]: I have lost some faith in this game. I'm disappointed that the strike had to happen. When they settle, I guarantee you what the players get won't be worth a strike. At no time did I hear

someone say, "How about the good of the game?"

Oct. 8/USA Today, 10-9:(C)3.

Mickey Mantle
Former baseball player,
New York "Yankees"

5

I'm not one of those old-timers who think the young guys playing today aren't as good as we were. The best players are mostly bigger, stronger and faster—people like Eric Davis, Jose Canseco, Mark McGwire. I'm not knocking the quality of the players, but there are just too many people who don't belong in major-league ball. When I played, there were only 16 teams; now there are 26. The talent has been diluted so much that there are fellows in the major leagues that really shouldn't be on that level. And when you have pitchers that aren't very good, that's going to mean more hitting and more home runs.

The New York Times, 6-25:51.

Billy Martin
Former baseball manager

6

[Criticizing civil-rights leader Jesse Jackson for complaining about the lack of blacks in baseball management]: A man or woman should earn a right to be in baseball and not be given the right because of color or creed. Jesse Jackson should stick with religion and keep politics out of baseball.

U.S. News & World Report, 7-6:13.

Don Mattingly
Baseball player,
New York "Yankees"

7

Spring [training] is tough for me. Spring scares me because I don't have that intensity. I wonder if I've lost that teed-off attitude: "Come on, man, get nasty." That's part of my success—I'm nasty. I don't have that here [in spring training] and it scares me. I don't have

488

(DON MATTINGLY)

that intensity. Maybe the older players like the Mike Schmidts and the Dave Winfields know how to handle it and don't worry, but it's scary down here. It's a scary time.

Interview, Tampa, Fla./
The New York Times, 3-16:36.

1

Location is the most important [aspect] of [both] hitting and pitching. If the pitchers could throw where they wanted every time, even if their stuff wasn't that great, you'd [the batter] be just about helpless. What you learn is that none of them can. If you're patient, you can do a lot of things. Everybody can't get you every time.

Los Angeles Times, 8-2:(III)1.

Gene Mauch
Baseball manager,
California "Angels"

2

[On managing in the major leagues]: The first thing you have to realize is that there are 24 people on your ball club who have a preconceived notion of what kind of player they want to be. Now, some are right, actually pretty good at evaluating their own skills. It's the others you have to worry about. Getting them to change their style is tough. If they have some immediate success with what you've suggested, you're all right. Otherwise, they'll go right back to what they were doing wrong before.

The Christian Science Monitor,
4-14:22.

John McEnroe
Tennis player

3

[Saying it is unlikely players would protest as a group about things they consider wrong in the sport]: If you think the football union is weak, you should see our union. We wouldn't be able to stick together. We don't have any strength . . . I don't see it happening. We com-

pete on such an individual basis. There's jealousy. The lower-ranked players are against the higher-ranked players. We are from different parts of the world competing in different parts of the world. They think if they give us more money, they think it's okay, they can do what they want. Maybe it's easy for me to say, but I would take less money if things were run differently.

Los Angeles Times, 10-13:(III)3.

George Miller
Executive director,
United States
Olympic Committee

4

[On the idea that the U.S. should pull out of the 1988 Olympics in South Korea because that country's government violates the rights of its people]: [The] theory is that the human rights of the people of [South] Korea are being violated by the government, and, therefore, the United States should take the initiative to boycott the Games. [This is a] reasonable concern. But that is really not my concern. [The Olympic] movement is not a political movement. This is a movement that tries to avoid political issues where it can. The one goodness of this movement is that it tends to bridge these political problems. It tends to bring people together regardless of political problems. Therefore, it is entirely inappropriate that the movement be used in trying to solve political problems. If the idea of the United States leading a boycott in order to bring attention to what may be perceived as a violation of human rights, we do not think this is the proper thing to do.

Before Olympic Academy,
Indianapolis, June 18/
Los Angeles Times, 6-19:(III)12.

Joe Morgan
Former baseball player,
Cincinnati "Reds" and
San Francisco "Giants"

5

To be a star and to stay a star, I think you have to show the kind of confidence that your

489

(JOE MORGAN)

opponents can read. It's like letting your rival know that I can do this and you can't stop me. It's like when you reach first base, and you're the tying run, and you need to get to second. It doesn't hurt when, through your mannerisms, you're able to show the pitcher that you're going to steal no matter how many times he throws over to take away your lead. Some guys have that kind of cockiness and can make it work, but a lot of really good players don't and you wonder why.

The Christian Science Monitor,
4-20:22.

Edwin Moses
Former world
champion runner

1

[On his recent loss in the hurdles in Madrid]: Instead of thinking about my races technically, I started thinking that if I won I would be successful. And that's dangerous. I think losing that race will force me now to pay more attention to running fast rather than running to win. If you run to win, you accept an inferior performance. I never felt bad about losing, just about not running well. I knew it would take a superior performance to beat me, and it did. So I can't be unhappy about it. It was a good race for me.

Interview, Newport Beach, Calif./
The New York Times, 6-23:52.

Martina Navratilova
Tennis player

2

[On her not winning a tournament yet in 1987]: I know it's psychology. I want to go out on top, but the only way you know you're not on top any more is when you're losing. So then you keep losing. I think I'm beating myself out there, and it's the wrong way to go about it.

Wimbledon, England, June 24/
The New York Times, 6-25:50.

Roger Noll
Professor of economics,
Stanford University

3

Prior to the [current baseball commissioner Peter] Ueberroth era, baseball operated like two leagues. In the [former commissioner] Bowie Kuhn era, the two leagues developed a joint policy about anything. They might have gentlemen's agreements within leagues, but the leagues were pretty competitive against each other. That really helped baseball players have meaningful free agency. Ueberroth's style is more like [football commissioner] Pete Rozelle's: to concentrate decision-making in the owners, rather than in the leagues. The central issue [is], is this really collusion? I don't really know . . . I'm trying to say it in a neutral way. But the end result is that baseball will be more like football because of the way Ueberroth has organized things.

Los Angeles Times, 4-2:(III)12.

Don Ohlmeyer
Television
producer-director

4

As a sports director, I've always believed in what Ring Lardner said, that losers are more interesting than winners. There are a lot more textures to losing than there are to winning. Winning is elation; losing is depression, anxiety, fear. It's a ton of different emotions.

Interview, New York/
Emmy Magazine, Jan.-Feb.:25.

Peter O'Malley
Owner,
Los Angeles "Dodgers"
baseball club

5

We're doing everything possible to put the best team on the field. But we're just not going to go out and buy a championship by buying players who have already turned down millions of dollars from other teams. Ray Kroc tried to buy championships. Steinbrenner tried. Autry

(PETER O'MALLEY)

tried. We tried in Goltz and Stanhouse. Long haul, it doesn't work. Short haul, you can get lucky. You can catch lightning in a jar and you can buy a championship team through free agency, but it does a lot of damage to your program . . . Use it occasionally, but put your money in player development, and there it is well spent.

Interview, Vero Beach, Fla./
Los Angeles Times, 3-24:(III)4.

Rick Pitino
Basketball coach,
Providence (R.I.) College

1

You've got to understand, basketball is not a game; it is a way of life that goes onto a different life and a different game. If you're sound fundamentally in basketball, you'll be sound fundamentally in the other part of your life.

Interview, Providence, R.I./
Los Angeles Times, 3-1:(III)16.

Gary Player
Golfer

2

[Criticizing the U.S. Golf Association for making veteran golfer Arnold Palmer go through qualifying, which he failed, for the U.S. Open]: They don't seem to care a damn about anybody. They don't seem to have any respect for people who have done well in the game. That the USGA makes Arnold Palmer have to qualify is an insult to a man who's done so much for golf. Here they've got some club pros in the tournament who are going to shoot 82s and 83s, and nobody's going to watch; and Arnold Palmer, who helped make that tournament, they ask to pre-qualify. If I were giving a tournament, the first person I'd invite would be Arnold Palmer.

Los Angeles Times, 6-12:(III)2.

3

[Saying new golfers aren't all that great compared with the past, but it's new golf tech-

nology that makes them seem better]: We are eliminating skill. Everybody tells you today, "Oh, all these great young players." Well, they're not the great players everybody makes them out to be. I don't want to sound like I'm knocking the young guys. I just think it's getting out of proportion with the equipment. It's a shame. Let the human being improve in his mind and his body, not in his equipment. It's just a big commercial deal. I just hate to see what's happening in golf. It really bugs me. You see a guy hit a shot out of the rough now [with the new square-grooved club] and the ball hits over the flag and stops within two feet. I can't believe what I'm seeing. And then they say, "What a great shot." Hogwash.

Interview/
Los Angeles Times,
8-30:(III)12.

George Plimpton
Author

4

Baseball . . . is symbolized by . . . three aspects: greed—huge money contracts, stealing second base, charging for a seat behind an iron pillar, etc.; hatred—players despising management, pitchers hating hitters, the *Cubs* detesting the *Mets*, etc.; and delusion—the slider, the pitchout, the hidden-ball trick, and so forth.

Interview/
The Christian Science Monitor,
7-1:24.

Bobby Rahal
Auto-racing driver

5

Driving a [race] car is a "seat-of-the-pants" thing in many cases. The guy who understands and can develop the car will be more competitive. He is the guy who can improve on his performance as well as the performance of the car. I've always said that success in racing is probably more a matter of perseverance in many respects than talent.

Interview/
USA Today, 3-30:(C)6.

WHAT THEY SAID IN 1987

Dennis Rappaport
Manager of boxer
Gerry Cooney

1

When you're a promoter, manager or trainer in the fight game, it's like being a doctor on call 24 hours a day. No—take that one step further. It's like being a chief surgeon who never leaves the operating room. Everything eventually falls on your shoulders. There is no one else past you. You're like president, general manager, coach and publicity department all in one. In that way, boxing is unique.

Atlantic City, N.J./
USA Today, 6-16:(C)3.

Shane Rawley
Baseball pitcher,
Philadelphia "Phillies"

2

Yeah, I guess I'm the "ace" [of the pitching staff], but not because I'm any better at pitching than the other guys. I just have more experience. I'm the veteran. I guess the younger guys can think of me as the experienced one, the guy who can stop a losing streak, tell them about the hitters. That's what "being the ace" is all about.

Interview, Los Angeles/
Los Angeles Times, 6-1(III)6.

Jerry Reuss
Baseball pitcher,
Cincinnati "Reds"

3

[On his losing four out of his last six starts]: If I had a shortstop with a 25-foot wingspan who could leap 25 feet in the air, all my problems would be solved.

USA Today, 6-10:(C)11.

Pat Riley
Basketball coach,
Los Angeles "Lakers"

4

[On his team's winning the 1987 NBA championship]: Because everybody expected us to dominate the playoffs, I always felt like we were in a no-win situation. If we won, almost nobody would be surprised. But if we lost, then summer would never end for any of us. As a coach, I was always concerned with the unexpected, where you know you're the better team and you play well, but lose on a fluke.

Los Angeles/
The Christian Science Monitor,
6-16:22.

Gary Roenicke
Baseball player,
Atlanta "Braves"

5

I hate playing extra innings. I'm one who believes if a game is tied after 10 innings, they ought to just give each team one point or something.

Los Angeles Times, 6-1:(III)2.

Buck Rogers
Baseball manager,
Montreal "Expos"

6

When you first take over [as manager] of a [baseball] club, you want to do it all. I mean, you want to be the pitching coach, you want to be the third-base coach, you want to be the batting instructor. I mean, you want to make sure everything is run right. So to make sure it's run right you want to do it. So now, I've surrounded myself with what I think are some of the best people in baseball, and I sit here on my fanny. I tell them what I want done, and I've got confidence that they can go out and do it. They solve the problems. Major problems—then I talk to people. I bring guys in a lot. Everybody says they've got an open-door policy: "My door is wide open." That's nonsense. Anybody who's been in baseball 15 minutes knows a ballplayer that's going lousy is not going to walk into the manager's office. I've got the hook policy. I reach out and hook 'em, and bring 'em in.

Interview/
The New York Times, 9-15:55.

492

Barry Rona
Executive director,
Major League (baseball)
Player Relations Committee

1

Some [free-agent] players and some agents badly miscalculated the [baseball-player] market. I think by and large the figures of what the clubs offered and the signings that took place demonstrate, in terms of salaries, we are beginning to enter a new era in baseball. I think while the clubs were fair, they're clearly committed to eradicating the financial lunacy [of very high player salaries] that was in existence for a number of years. I think that's a very positive and happy day for baseball.

USA Today, 1-12:(C)8.

Al Rosen
General manager,
San Francisco "Giants"
baseball club

2

[On the effects on a team of disabled star players, such as the *Giants'* Jeff Leonard who was out two months last season]: You can always speculate about it, but these are mind games. The reality was we didn't have Leonard. Everybody knew what it meant when he went down. He's the heart and soul of this club. You can put other people out there, but they're not going to do what he does—the numbers he puts up there, the great defense he plays in left field.

Interview/
The New York Times, 6-8:36.

Pete Rozelle
Commissioner,
National Football League

3

Choosing a head coach is like choosing a wife: It's a very personal thing.

USA Today, 2-20:(A)10.

4

I'm certain we'll have a black head [football] coach when an owner thinks that coach can help him win. Until then, there's nothing I can do about it . . . We have a long way to go on minority hiring. While we can't make black coaches, we can provide the opportunity for them to rise up through the organizations.

At Associated Press sports editors
convention, Lake Buena Vista, Fla.,
June 10/The Washington Post, 6-11:(B)2.

Derek Sanderson
Former hockey player

5

Why is there a drinking problem in the NHL? Canadians. The majority of the sport is Canadian. Most players come from small towns. They start [drinking] in juniors. It's acceptable. It's the macho ethic. Drugs are for low-lifes. Drinking is acceptable.

Los Angeles Times,
6-30:(III)9.

Mike Schmidt
Baseball player,
Philadelphia "Phillies"

6

[On the possibility of his retiring from baseball after this season]: Ego satisfaction is very important to a professional athlete. I climbed up one side of that ego ladder and now am almost halfway down the other side of it. I sat on top of that ladder. I lived for ego satisfaction, material, etc., for the middle years of my career. Now I'm on the backside of it, longing for a chance to be at home more. I'm longing for a chance to drive up to the ball park about 7 o'clock in the evening, go up the back elevator, sit in the press box, watch a ballgame, carry on a nice, casual conversation with somebody, go back down the elevator, get in the car and drive home—and not have a crowd around me.

Interview/
USA Today, 4-24:(C)8.

7

At this stage in my career . . . I don't need to hit 35 home runs to have my ego fulfilled.

WHAT THEY SAID IN 1987

(MIKE SCHMIDT)

When you're young, that's the sort of thing that drives you. Now I'm playing the game at a different level. It's a great feeling. I don't have anything to prove any more, not to myself or anyone else. I can experiment with the game. I could be the team's next anything—manager, general manager, whatever . . . I want to be a manager. Something about it intrigues me. What can I do to encourage a bunch of kids that are teetering on the brink of mediocrity to use their talent and be as good as they can be? Introduce them to Christianity? Throw batting practice at them every day for six months? I love communicating my knowledge about the game. It would be a test of my patience, and that's the kind of test I need.

Interview/
Esquire, May:140,142.

Red Schoendienst
Baseball coach
and former manager,
St. Louis "Cardinals"

1

If I were still managing, there are a lot of talented ballplayers I wouldn't want on my club because they aren't what you call winners. This has nothing to do with working hard, staying in shape, or always giving 100 per cent. These people, for some reason, just never get the job done for you. I remember two pitchers who were on the *Cardinals* roster when I managed them. One was very talented. But he was always losing games 2-1 or 3-2, usually on a fluke hit that was just out of somebody's reach. You were always feeling sorry for him. Well, this other pitcher didn't have anywhere near this first man's ability. In fact, if you brought him in from the bullpen to protect a lead, often he'd let the other team back in the game. Yet when it was all over, he'd be the winning pitcher on scores like 9-7 or 11-10. We had a front office in St. Louis then that was very much into statistics. Evidently they had been looking at this guy's high earned-run average, because they

called me one winter and said they were going to trade him. I fought it, but they made the deal anyway. And you know what? This guy continued to pitch the same way and win the same way!

The Christian Science Monitor,
7-2:24.

Dick Schultz
Athletic director,
University of Virginia;
Executive director-designate,
National Collegiate
Athletic Association

2

We've got the Wall Street scandals and the Federal scandals and everything else. But athletics is so visible. It seems to be the whipping boy for all these other things going on. Athletes are involved in far fewer negative situations than the rest of the population in that same age group. But because they are visible on one side, they're going to be visible on the other side.

Interview/
USA Today, 6-17:(A)13.

John Scolinos
Baseball coach,
California Polytechnic
Institute, Pomona

3

. . . some young coaches are only concerned about winning. At what price? I do have empathy for young coaches in the colleges, or even in the high schools, who are under such pressure to win. I'm over the hill; I can do it my way. But I think they have to realize that we're in the business of education. This isn't a professional deal. You hear about coaches doing anything to get kids and to keep them eligible to win . . . We've got ourselves into a real mess. I'm not saying I've got all the answers, but I just think we have to remember what we're doing. We're teaching.

Interview/
Los Angeles Times,
5-12:(III)10.

James "Bonecrusher" Smith
World Boxing Association
heavyweight champion
of the world

1

A lot of people never stop to think that boxers have fragile feelings, just like anyone else. Well, how would you like to be beaten up by someone, knocked down and cut up, made to look foolish, in front of millions of people? It's humiliating, so you work hard in training, you prepare as best you can. You want the *other* guy to experience that.

Interview,
Lillington, N.C./
Los Angeles Times, 3-3:(III)8.

Michael Spinks
Boxer

2

Even though I'm a heavyweight, I'm probably the smallest heavyweight out there; and I have to admit, boxing all these big guys all the time, it isn't like lying on the beach or a walk in the park. It's work. It's serious work. It leaves me with an attitude of, I mean, really, really wishing, hoping that overnight I just wake up and I'm all that I would ever want to be as a heavyweight, weighing maybe about 250 and punching like a Mack truck.

Interview,
Atlantic City, N.J./
The Washington Post, 6-12:(B)1.

Roger Staubach
Former football player,
Dallas "Cowboys"

3

[On being in the Super Bowl]: There's so much pressure on the players. Guys go into the game so worried about not making mistakes, and the coaches get a little too conservative. I think the players have to play with reckless abandon. Start worrying about mistakes, and you'll lose it.

The Washington Post,
1-20:(D)3.

George Steinbrenner
Owner,
New York "Yankees"
baseball club

4

[Comparing baseball players with race horses]: I prefer horses. They don't talk back to you. They don't talk to sports writers. They don't have a union. They don't have agents and they don't take you to arbitration.

Los Angeles Times,
2-22:(III)12.

5

[Advocating the use of videotape replays to help baseball umpires make close calls]: It's going to come up. I'll bring it up. The traditionalists are going to say it takes away from the grand old game, but I say we've got to stay modern. Pro football has it; why shouldn't baseball stay up to date with football? . . . When [an umpire] blows a call that could mean a pennant, that's when you should be able to go to videotape. The fans have the replay available to them on television. Eight million people can see it's a bad call. In the old days, you didn't have that, and the call became conjecture. But the TV replay has changed a whole facet of the game. Why not make it available to the officials?

Sept. 9/
The New York Times,
9-10:53.

Dennis Swanson
President, ABC Sports

6

[On whether there should be a college-football national championship game]: No . . . I'm a traditionalist. I favor the current bowl structure. What sometimes is forgotten is that bowl games are more than just two teams playing a football game. There are parades and functions that involve the whole community. Oftentimes, money is raised for charity. I don't think the NCAA would be donating much to charity. And under the current setup, we usually end up with a clear-cut national champion, anyway. We certainly did this year with Penn

WHAT THEY SAID IN 1987

State. And we did last year with Oklahoma. No, I say stay with what we've got now.

To reporters, Los Angeles/
Los Angeles Times, 1-9:(III)3.

Jerry Tarkanian
Basketball coach,
University of Nevada,
Las Vegas

1

[Approving of basketball's three-point field goal]: Any rule that forces teams to play man-to-man defense is good. I have a hard time thinking zone defenses are good for the game; it may be good for coaches but not for players and spectators.

USA Today, 1-30:(C)7.

Vinny Testaverde
Football player,
Tampa Bay "Buccaneers"

2

[On whether college players should be paid]: No. First of all, I don't think they deserve it. I know I didn't. You need to work real hard to reach the NFL, where you get paid. Once they start getting paid, they'll want to make all the rules, run the program. Too many kids will get cocky, think they own the world—when they're too young to realize what's going on.

Interview/
Los Angeles Times,
6-30:(III)2.

Tom Trebelhorn
Baseball manager,
Milwaukee "Brewers"

3

Timely hitting makes for winning streaks, and untimely hitting for losing streaks. Those two-out hits with men on base when you're winning regularly—well, you never get them when you're losing. At times like that, it's always the other team that gets them.

The Christian Science Monitor,
7-31:20.

Bryan Trottier
Executive director,
National Hockey League
Players Association

4

I'm 100 per cent behind anything that will stop brawls [between teams during a game]. They make for a terrible headline, no matter what sport you're in. I think it's necessary that any kind of fines be severe enough to keep the player from doing anything stupid. He should have control of himself, and so should the coach.

The New York Times, 10-5:40.

Gene Upshaw
Executive director,
National Football League
Players Association

5

I don't see free agency as a money issue. I don't see pension improvements as a money issue. Or protection for player reps. Or a drug program. Or grievances. Free agency is about a guy being free; let the free market determine if he's worth more, or not.

Washington/
The New York Times,
3-18:47.

6

[On the imminent players strike]: Any [union] player who goes in [and plays despite the strike] is going to cut his career short. He'll never be the same again. His teammates won't like him; the bitterness will be there. You never forget the guy who tried to stab you in the back.

Sept. 21/
Los Angeles Times,
9-22:(I)1.

7

[On the current NFL player strike]: [The owners] tell us we don't have the right to bargain. They tell us, "We push Mayors, Congressmen and cities around." So why would they want to talk to us? Owners have free agency. I see that two owners, Bud Adams in

(GENE UPSHAW)

Houston and Bill Bidwell in St. Louis, are shopping around. That not only affects them, but their team, the fans, the workers, the cities. But they don't care. What really disturbs me is that I know how much the players want to reach an agreement, and you can't get there until the other side wants to.

Interview, Oct. 13/
USA Today, 10-14:(C)6.

1

[On recent labor-management talks which involved an NFL player strike]: When you exchange opening proposals on April 20 and on April 23, they [management] prepare for a scab season; that tells you right away that they are not bargaining in good faith. When I look at the garbage they had on the table, no one—even as badly as every player wanted an agreement—could ever accept what management put on the table. It was takebacks and concessions. Management had one objective in mind and that was to bust the [players] union.

Interview/USA Today,
11-6:(A)11.

Mario Vazquez Rana
President, Pan American
Sports Association;
President, United
Press International

2

We must admit there's a lot of passion in sports events. When it comes to the event everybody wants to win, this passion sometimes blinds the competitors, and this is something we should condemn, but also understand. This passion goes beyond the athletes and also affects the spectators and even the press. That passion, in turn, is sometimes used by high-level politicians who join us, even when not invited, and cause problems with rules and laws which are not always in agreement with our Olympic ideals.

Interview/USA Today,
8-25:(A)11.

Billy Williams
Batting coach, Chicago
"Cubs" baseball club;
Former player

3

We [racial] minorities for the past four decades have demonstrated our talents as players. Now we deserve the chance and consideration to demonstrate similar talents as third-base coaches, as managers on the field, as general managers and executives in the front office, and yes, as owners of major-league ball clubs themselves. Baseball has been considered America's favorite pastime. Now let's make it the sport that reflects the true spirit of our great country— a nation that more than 200 years ago was dedicated to the proposition that all men–*all* men— are created equal.

Upon being inducted
into the Baseball Hall of Fame,
Cooperstown, N.Y., July 26/
The New York Times, 7-27:29.

Maury Wills
Former baseball player

4

[On his former drug-addiction problem]: Someday, I hope and pray the major-league baseball players will consent to drug testing. That is the answer. That's the major answer because there is no way to get around it, no room for denial . . . All the people I let down. The embarrassment. The drugs. Somebody comes along and puts it there for you when you're looking for an escape. As I look back, I had to have an escape, and that was it. It would have been nice if there was someone there with the knowledge I have now to grab me before I got trapped.

Interview, Phoenix/
Los Angeles Times, 2-10:(III)7.

Dave Wolf
Prize-fighter manager

5

The biggest thing [for a potential boxer] is whether the guy can deal with the life of a

(DAVE WOLF)

fighter which, except at its apex, is not a very glamorous life, not a lot of fun. You don't get as much feedback from the public on a regular basis as you do with football and basketball. A lot [of athletes can't deal] with the solitary, painful existence of a fighter. And there's no other sport where you're being hit in the face and around the eyes as a regular occurrence. Simply to endure pain, as a football player does, is not enough. There's something about a hand in your face and blows to the eye that discourages a lot of excellent athletes.

The New York Times, 1-29:21.

Willie Wood
Former football coach,
Philadelphia "Bell"
and Toronto "Argonauts"

1

The NFL teams are like other major corporations. They will give [blacks] a job in a supportive role but not as the Number 1 man, and I suspect racism has something to do with that. The reason there aren't any black head coaches in the NFL is simple—owners don't want them.

Ebony, January: 41.

Dick Young
Sportswriter

2

[On professional athletes who use cocaine and other illegal drugs]: Punish the users . . . There aren't enough jails, you say? Open concentration camps.

Newsweek, 4-13:87.

John Ziegler
President,
National Hockey League

3

If you choose to be involved with illegal drugs, you will not be involved in the NHL. To any who now use, or may want to use, illegal drugs, we say this: We do not want you. Get out and stay out of our business.

Los Angeles Times, 6-30:(III)9.

The Indexes

Index to Speakers

A

Abbott, George, 440
Abdnor, James, 33
Abourezk, James, 329
Abrams, Elliott, 262
Abrams, Floyd, 18
Abshire, David, 57
Abzug, Bella, 18
Achotte, Jan, 461
Adams, F. Gerard, 80
Adelman, Kenneth L., 57, 122, 303
Adler, Allan, 158
Adler, Mortimer, 100
Ahearne, John, 115
Akhromeyev, Sergei F., 57, 287
Aksyonov, Vassily, 449
Alariesto, Andreas, 361
Albert, Stephen, 430
Albertine, John, 237
Alexander, Jane, 416, 440
Alfonsin, Raul, 262-263
Allen, George, 479
Allen, Joe, 470
Allen, Richard, 122
Allen, Woody, 416
Almoayed, Tariq, 329
Amichai, Yehuda, 449
Amis, Martin, 383
Anderson, Robert, 440
Anderson, Sparky, 479
Andrews, Julie, 430
Annas, George J., 470
Annunzio, Frank, 33
Anteweldt, Roger, 33
Aquino, Corazon C., 287-288
Arafat, Yasir, 329
Araskog, Rand V., 33
Arbatov, Georgi A., 58
Archer, Jeffrey, 205
Arens, Moshe, 249
Arias, Oscar, 122, 263-264, 356
Arias Calderon, Ricardo, 264
Armacost, Michael H., 329
Armitage, Richard L., 249, 288
Armstrong, Robert, 100
Ashe, Arthur, 479
Asher, Robert H., 329

Ashmead, Larry, 383
Ashton, Frederick, 440
Asimov, Issac, 470
Aspin, Les, 122, 158, 330
Assad, Hafez al-, 330
Atkins, Chester G., 122
Attenborough, Richard, 417
Auger, Arleen, 430
Augustine, Norman, 58
Avineri, Shlomo, 330
Awad, Louis, 330
Azcona, Jose, 264

B

Babbitt, Bruce, 11, 33, 80, 115, 123, 158, 205, 228, 461
Badalyan, Levon, 470
Baez, Joan, 430
Bagdikian, Ben, 408
Baker, Howard H., Jr., 11, 58, 123, 158, 182, 330, 366
Baker, James A., III, 33-34, 80, 159, 205
Baker, John, 237
Baker, Ross K., 159
Bakker, Jim, 461
Baldrige, Malcolm, 34, 470
Ballinger, Charles E., 100
Baltimore, David, 397
Baram, Amatzia, 331
Baranov, Alexander, 366
Barayi, Elijah, 249
Barber, James David, 124
Barber, Virginia, 383
Barnes, Harry, 264
Barnes, Michael J., 18
Barr, Terry, 34
Barros, Alexandre, 264
Barry, Marion, 159
Barth, John, 383
Bartley, Robert L., 449
Baryshnikov, Mikhail, 441
Bashir, Tahsin, 331
Basil, Robert A., 331
Batenin, Geli, 58
Bator, Paul, 182
Batscha, Robert, 408

C

D

Index to Subjects

A

Abbott, Bud, 458:5
Abortion—*see* Women
Abrams, Elliott, 266:2, 273:1
Abstract, the, 451:5
Acheson, Dean, 450:3
Acquired immune deficiency syndrome (AIDS)—
  see Medicine
Acting/actors, 41:4, 424:5, 454:1
  ambition, 426:2
  awards, 427:3
  character, getting inside of, 425:2
  are children, 420:6, 423:6
  choosing parts, 419:5, 420:4
  comedy/drama aspect, 422:1, 423:5
  crazy people, 418:4
  dedication, 429:1
  directing compared with, 425:3
  dragging one's history with you, 427:5
  jewels of the film, 417:1
  oneself, playing, 422:5
  pay/salary, 410:2, 418:1, 420:4
  rejection, 419:3, 419:4
  stage/theatre aspect, 443:2, 445:4, 446:4,
    447:5, 448:2
    vs. motion pictures, 441:4, 442:4
  stars, 418:1
    instant stardom, 428:4
  starting out, 418:7
  technique, 419:6
  television aspect, 410:2, 414:3, 415:2, 415:5,
    418:7
  typecasting, 429:2
  unpleasant characters, playing, 418:7
  unreality, 420:3
  versatility, 429:2
Adams, Bud, 496:7
Adams, John Quincy, 175:1
Adversity, 452:2
Advertising—*see* Commerce
Affluence, 449:1
Afghanistan:
  Communism, 148:5, 295:4
  human rights, 299:6
  non-aligned/neutralized, 59:5, 291:1, 298:3
  rebels, 287:1, 290:1, 295:4, 298:3, 343:5
  foreign relations with:

Afghanistan *(continued)*
  foreign relations with (continued)
    Iran, 298:3, 352:2
    Pakistan, 287:1, 298:3, 343:5
    Soviet Union, 126:3, 127:6, 133:5, 148:5,
      287:1, 290:1, 290:2, 290:5, 291:1,
      298:3, 299:6, 317:3, 325:3, 343:5
    U.S., 133:5, 287:1, 291:1, 295:4
Africa, pp. 249-261
  economy, 253:4, 254:4, 256:3
  trade, 256:3
  foreign relations with:
    Britain, 316:3
    Europe, 256:3
    Portugal, 318:3
    Soviet Union, 254:3, 258:1
    Third World, 256:3
    U.S., 251:1, 254:3, 256:3, 258:1
  See also specific African countries
Age, 451:3, 455:3, 455:8, 459:1
Agony, 452:3
Agriculture/farming, 15:2
  defense spending, effect of, 64:2
  free market, 49:2
  government aspect, 38:5, 49:2
  importance, 33:1
  prices, 82:7
  risks, taking of, 38:4
  subsidies, 34:3, 42:3, 45:1, 82:7
Alaska, 115:7, 116:5, 118:3, 120:2
Albania, 464:1
Alcoholism—*see* Medicine: drug/substance abuse
Alfonsin, Raul, 269:2
Ambition, 453:2
America/U.S.:
  attraction for foreigners, 12:4
  awful shape, 14:5
  becoming Americans, foreigners, 16:3
  birth rate, 16:4, 17:3
  bland society, 11:2
  classes, social, 12:1
  democracy/freedom, 12:1, 12:2, 15:1, 15:3,
    15:5, 21:1
  dream, American, 13:2, 86:7
  dreams, 14:2
  experience, the American, 12:2
  failures/shortcomings/problems, 14:1, 15:1, 16:5

H

M

Opera—*see* Music
Ortega, Daniel, 157:3, 268:3

P

Pacific—*see* Asia
Pakistan:
    nuclear weapons, 290:3, 301:1, 302:3
    foreign relations with:
        Afghanistan, 287:1, 298:3, 343:5
        China, 301:1
        Middle East, 343:5
        Soviet Union, 343:5
Palestinians, 345:4
    identity, having no, 344:4
    Palestine Liberation Organization (PLO), 336:6,
        345:4, 351:1, 352:6, 353:5, 353:6
        Israel, 336:6, 351:1
        Soviet Union, 352:5
        U.S., 342:5
    self-determination/state/homeland, 329:3, 335:1,
        340:2
    foreign relations with:
        Israel, 329:3, 335:1, 336:6, 337:6, 338:4,
            342:4, 351:1, 353:6
        U.S., 342:5
Paley, William, 409:1
Panama, 264:2, 274:2
Pappas, Ike, 370:3
Paraguay, 273:6, 283:3, 285:1
Parents/adults/children, 452:1, 452:5, 457:2, 460:3
Parks, Rosa, 204:1
Passion, 459:2
Passivity, 456:1
Patriotism—*see* America
Peace—*see* War/peace
Pennsylvania State University, 495:6
Performing arts, pp. 408-448
    See also Acting; Broadcasting; Motion pictures;
        Music; Stage
Persian Gulf—*see* Middle East
Philippines:
    Aquino, Corazon C., 288:3, 295:3, 296:3,
        298:4, 299:5
    Communism, 287:3, 288:3, 288:5, 293:1,
        296:3, 299:5
    democracy, 287:3, 287:4, 288:3, 298:4, 299:5
    economy, 293:1, 296:4
    human resources, 295:2
    insurgency/terrorism, 287:2, 287:3, 288:3,
        288:5, 293:1, 299:5
    military coup attempt, 287:4
    politics, 288:2

Philippines *(continued)*
    Presidency:
        direct rule, 287:5
        weak, 288:1
        See also Aquino, Corazon C. (this section)
    stalemate, state of, 296:3
    work aspect, 288:2
    foreign relations with:
        U.S., 298:4
            Subic Bay/Clark air bases, 295:3
Philosophy, pp. 449-460
Picasso, Pablo, 364:7
Pickens, T. Boone, 43:3
Piedmont Airlines, 241:2
Pinochet, Augusto, 133:1
Poetry—*see* Literature
Poindexter, John M., 130:2, 136:3, 139:2, 139:3,
    144:4, 165:6
Pol Pot, 292:2, 292:4, 294:6
Poland:
    economy, 325:2, 326:2
    human rights, 304:4
    pluralism, 326:2
    reform/openness/change,   312:2,   312:3,
        323:4
    religion, 326:3
    foreign relations with:
        Germany, East, 311:3
        Soviet Union, 312:2
        U.S., 304:4, 312:3, 316:4
Politics, pp. 205-227
    arts aspect, 364:2, 364:3, 364:4, 364:7
    change, people want, 220:1
    consensus/lack of difference, 207:5
    conservatism/right, 180:3, 206:4, 209:3, 211:2,
        214:3, 216:2, 216:3, 219:2, 220:1, 220:2,
        226:6, 227:1, 454:5
    crime aspect, 50:1
    defense/military aspect, 58:5, 62:4, 73:2
    foreign-affairs aspect, 122:4, 124:4, 132:6
    government aspect, 173:1
    judiciary/courts aspect, 175:2
        See also Judiciary: Supreme Court, U.S.:
            liberal/conservative aspect
    Presidency, U.S., aspect, 168:8
    Reagan, Ronald, aspect, 58:4, 226:3
    Republican Party aspect, 216:3, 220:2,
        222:3, 225:6
    Soviets, dealing with, 131:3
    democratic socialism, 213:3
    as dialogue, 293:3
    dream aspect, 451:7
    education/schools aspect, 104:6